D1244169

37653011531681
Main NonFiction: 1st flr
818 IRVING
Astoria ; or, Anecdotes of
an enterprise beyond the
Rocky Mountains

CENTRAL ARKANSAS LIBRARY SYSTEM
LITTLE ROCK PUBLIC LIBRARY
100 ROCK STREET
LITTLE ROCK, ARKANSAS 72201

THE AMERICAN EXPLORATION AND TRAVEL SERIES

(Complete list on page 553)

A S T O R I A

ASTORIA

or Anecdotes of an Enterprise
Beyond the Rocky Mountains

BY WASHINGTON IRVING

Edited and with an Introduction
by EDGELEY W. TODD

UNIVERSITY OF OKLAHOMA PRESS

NORMAN

BY EDGELEY W. TODD

A Listener's Guide to Musical Form (Dubuque, 1949)

The Adventures of Captain Bonneville by Washington Irving (Editor) (Norman, 1961)

Astoria by Washington Irving (Editor) (Norman, 1964)

LIBRARY OF CONGRESS CATALOG CARD NUMBER: 64-20765

New edition copyright 1964 by the University of Oklahoma Press, Publishing Division of the University. Composed and printed at Norman, Oklahoma, U.S.A., by the University of Oklahoma Press. First printing.

917.8
I

Astoria is the second of three books which Washington Irving devoted to separate aspects of the American Far West before it was known to anyone except Indians, explorers, fur traders, and trappers. As an account of John Jacob Astor's effort to control the fur trade of the Pacific Northwest and the Columbia River Basin in the second decade of the nineteenth century, it still provides us with an accurate, authoritative history of that undertaking and of engrossing events related to it.

Although frequently reprinted since its publication in 1836, *Astoria* has unfortunately suffered an unmerited loss in reputation and is now often misunderstood to be unreliable as history. This is a fate the book does not deserve, for in every essential respect *Astoria* remains as reliable as the day it was written. It was based on dependable sources, and Irving used them to good advantage. He made every effort to be faithful to his subject and succeeded in large measure in accomplishing his purpose. Hopefully, this new edition may serve in some measure to reestablish the reputation *Astoria* once had. To that end it seeks to show, wherever possible, the actual sources from which Irving worked. By seeing them in relation to what he wrote and to what is now known, we can assess the value of *Astoria* as history in the only way that is possible.

The value of *Astoria* as an engaging narrative of great charm and interest has never been in doubt. Although some twentieth-century writers have seen it as a piece of hack work produced after the author's creative energy had waned, the fact remains that Irving wrote it with enthusiastic interest and concentration. It was well reviewed in England and America and was received in both countries as something fresh and original. The book has given pleasure to many, and for countless readers it has served as an absorbing introduction to life in the early Far West second only, perhaps, to the unrivaled history of the Lewis and Clark expedition, which preceded the events related in *Astoria* by only a few years. Even today, at a time when we are extending our frontiers

306832
CENTRAL ARKANSAS LIBRARY SYSTEM
LITTLE ROCK PUBLIC LIBRARY
700 LOUISIANA STREET
LITTLE ROCK, ARKANSAS 72201

into limitless outer space, *Astoria* still exerts a fascination from an earlier day when men traveled through uncharted deserts, mountains, and plains and confronted their awesome challenge with singleness of purpose, undaunted will, strength, and perseverance that are now seldom matched. Irving, in recording their efforts and accomplishments, even their failures, succeeded in conveying a part of our heritage that must not be forgotten or lost.

The text of the present work is that of the Author's Revised Edition of 1860–61. This has been collated with the first edition of 1836, and discrepancies between the two have been pointed out in the footnotes. Some errors in the Author's Revised Edition are printer's errors; others are errors of fact. In a few instances, errors which appeared in the first edition were undetected by Irving in revising and were carried over into the later edition. Neither edition, consequently, is completely reliable. The text reproduced here is as accurate in all essential details as careful attention has been able to make it. No effort, however, has been directed toward making punctuation uniform; that which appears is the punctuation of the Author's Revised Edition. Because of its excessive length and because the information contained therein is repeated in the chapter openings, the original table of contents has been omitted. As a feature of special historic interest, the map published in the first edition has been reproduced here.

During the past dozen years, I have worked on various aspects of Irving's writing in relation to the fur trade and the Far West, and in that length of time have incurred so many obligations that to mention them adequately or completely is now impossible. In many respects, indeed, the work on *Astoria* has been inseparable from that directed toward the preparation and publication of Irving's *The Adventures of Captain Bonneville* (Norman, University of Oklahoma Press, 1961). Many persons who contributed in some way to the earlier book have also shared in the preparation of this edition of *Astoria*. To all, I repeat my feeling of obligation and again extend warm thanks. I wish to acknowledge in particular the courtesies of the following individuals and institutions who have responded to my inquiries, have made documents available, or have rendered help of other kinds: Mrs. Jean Brownell, Library Assistant, Oregon Historical Society; Fred. C. Fagergren, Superintendent, Grand Teton National Park; Robert E. Fessenden, Chief Librarian, Oregon Historical Society; W. Neil Franklin, Chief, Diplomatic,

Legal and Fiscal Branch, National Archives and Records Service; Gene M. Gressley, Archivist, Western History Collection, William Robertson Coe Library, University of Wyoming; Earl R. Harris, Park Historian, Scotts Bluff National Monument; Bryan Harry, Assistant Chief Park Naturalist, Yellowstone National Park; the Henry E. Huntington Library and Art Gallery, where, under a series of grants years ago, I did much of my initial research on Irving; Harry E. Lichter, Chief Curator, Oregon Historical Society; Robert W. Lovett, Baker Library, Harvard University Graduate School of Business Administration; the New York Public Library for furnishing microfilms of Irving's several western notebooks in the Seligman Collection of Irvingiana; Miss Irene Payne, Oregon State Highway Department; Daniel J. Reed, Acting Chief, Manuscript Division, The Library of Congress; Miss Francine R. Seders, Librarian, The Washington State Historical Society; Mrs. Marguerite Sellars, Astoria Chamber of Commerce; Mrs. Frances H. Stadler, Archivist, Missouri Historical Society; Merle W. Wells, Historian and Archivist, The Idaho Historical Society; William A. Worf, Forest Supervisor, Bridger National Forest; and the staff of Colorado State University Library. I owe a special debt to my wife, Lois, who has always shared with me her time, enthusiasm, and selfless devotion. Her hand is present on every page of this volume.

Edgeley W. Todd

❧ CONTENTS ❧

MAPS

WHEN Washington Irving returned to New York in May of 1832, he stepped onto the soil of his homeland after seventeen years of unbroken, voluntary exile in the polite centers of European culture, where he had gratified his taste for graceful living and polished manners in age-old surroundings congenial to his romantic sensibility. These years saw him in England, France, Germany, and Spain, and they brought him the admiration and friendship of Sir Walter Scott and other literary lights on the Continent, as well as assignments in the United States diplomatic service in Spain and England. Most important, however, they were years during which he had made his literary reputation, first with the *Sketch Book* (1819–20), with its matchless tales of Rip Van Winkle and Ichabod Crane, and later with *Bracebridge Hall* (1822) and other books which followed.[1]

What had held Irving in Europe so long was that it was there, rather than in America, that he found the cultural climate which he deemed best suited to a man of letters. He had, in fact, rejected the life of his native country, barren and unpromising as it seemed for one who had decided to make his way with the pen. "Europe held forth the charms of storied and poetical association," he had confessed in "The Author's Account of Himself," the introductory essay in the *Sketch Book.* "There were to be seen," he went on,

> the masterpieces of art, the refinements of highly-cultivated society, the quaint peculiarities of ancient and local custom. My native country was full of youthful promise: Europe was rich in the accumulated treasures of age. Her very ruins told the history of times gone by, and every mouldering stone was a chronicle. I longed to wander over the scenes of renowned achievement—to tread, as it were, in the footsteps of antiquity—to loiter about the ruined castle—to meditate on the falling

---

[1] His principal writings were *Tales of a Traveller* (1824), *The Life and Adventures of Christopher Columbus* (3 vols., 1828), *A Chronicle of the Conquest of Granada* (1829), and *The Alhambra* (1832).

tower—to escape, in short, from the commonplace realities of the present, and lose myself among the shadowy grandeurs of the past.

How astonishing it is, then, to find Irving, thirteen years after he wrote these words, suddenly discovering that in America there was, after all, something to write about. By early September, having been welcomed and banqueted in New York by admiring American friends and readers, Irving plunged for a few brief months into an area of life and experience so remarkably different from what he had known in Europe that one finds difficulty in fully sensing the contrast. His departure from Cincinnati on September 3 aboard an Ohio River steamboat that carried him to St. Louis, in company with Henry Leavitt Ellsworth, Indian Commissioner appointed to visit tribes west of the Mississippi, was in a sense a turning point in his literary career. For Irving's acceptance of the invitation from Ellsworth, whom he had met by chance on Lake Erie, meant that not only would he see the western frontier and the Indian country beyond, with its picturesque characters so alien to Irving's past experience, but it would also commit him to the writing of three books about the West, the second of which was devoted to recounting the history of John Jacob Astor's ambitious effort to control the Columbia River as an artery leading into the rich fur country of the Northwest interior.

Irving's journey to St. Louis, to the border town of Independence, to the frontier post of Fort Gibson, and to the rugged country farther west, however strange it may seem to find the suave habitué of European drawing rooms in this rude setting, was really the indulgence of a long-cherished desire on the part of a 51-year-old man, a desire that went back at least to his twentieth year when, on visiting the Canadian frontier, he had seen at first hand the leaders and participants in the Canadian fur trade. They had fired his imagination—these men, as he later wrote in his introduction to *Astoria*, "who had passed years remote from civilized society, among distant and savage tribes, and who had wonders to recount of their wide and wild peregrinations, their hunting exploits, and the perilous adventures and hair-breadth escapes among the Indians. I was at an age," he went on,

> when the imagination lends its coloring to everything, and the stories of these Sinbads of the wilderness made the life of a trapper and fur trader perfect romance to me. I even meditated at one time a visit to

the remote posts of the company in the boats which annually ascended
the lakes and rivers, being thereto invited by one of the partners; and
I have ever since regretted that I was prevented by circumstances from
carrying my intention into effect. . . .

The uncommon experiences of these fur traders and *voyageurs* in the
remote places of the Canadian wilderness, he acknowledged, "have always been themes of charmed interest to me."

The immediate literary result of Irving's journey into the Southwest
with Ellsworth was the publication in the spring of 1835 of *A Tour
on the Prairies.* This little book, along with Irving's *Journals,*[2] which
have since been published, enables the reader to follow Irving day by day
and discover what it meant for him to engage in a way of life completely
foreign to what he had known but which would prove valuable when he
came to write *Astoria* and its sequel, *The Adventures of Captain Bonne-
·ville.* Camping in the wilderness; yearning around the campfire; hunting buffalo and elk; eating strange foods, including skunk meat; seeing
the anomalous types of the frontier, its trappers, hunters, border soldiers,
and Indians—all these aroused his enthusiasm and provided excellent
background for a writer of western books. Personal experience plus
extensive reading made Irving in the 1830's an authority on the West.[3]

A Tour on the Prairies was well received, even better than Irving had
expected. In his own mind he felt the book rather too slight to present
him adequately in the role of interpreter of American life which his
readers expected of him now that he had returned home.[4] But he need
not have feared for the reception of this narrative of a gentleman camper
among the Indians. Edward Everett, writing in the *North American
Review,* lauded the book. "For ourselves," he wrote,

[2] *The Western Journals of Washington Irving* (ed. by John Francis McDermott).
This should be supplemented by Henry Leavitt Ellsworth, *Washington Irving on the
Prairie* (ed. by Stanley T. Williams and Barbara D. Simison), and Charles Joseph
Latrobe, *The Rambler in North America.*

[3] See Edgeley W. Todd, "Washington Irving Discovers the Frontier," *Western Humanities Review,* Vol. XI (1957), 29–39; see also Stanley T. Williams, *The Life of
Washington Irving,* II, 36–42.

[4] He wrote to his brother Peter on November 24, 1834: ". . . I feel reluctant to let
it go before the public. So much has been said in the papers about my tour to the West,
and the work I was preparing on the subject, that I dread the expectations formed,
especially as what I have written is extremely simple, and by no means striking in its
details." Pierre Munro Irving, *The Life and Letters of Washington Irving,* III, 64. Cf.
Williams, *op. cit.,* II, 73.

we wish for nothing so ardently, as that the literature of the country should be the indigenous growth of the soil; indigenous to its topics, associations and spirit,—not for patriotic reasons merely, but on principles of art and taste. For though it is the prerogative of genius to give novelty to the tritest theme . . ., yet the thousand causes, which naturally guide the mind to the choice of subject, . . . point the American writer to his native land. . . . We are proud of Mr. Irving's sketches of English life . . .; but we glow with rapture as we see him coming back from the Prairies, laden with the poetical treasures of the primitive wilderness,—rich with spoil from the uninhabited desert. We thank him for turning these poor barbarous *steppes* into classical land;—and joining his inspiration to that of Cooper, in breathing life and fire into a circle of imagery, which was not known before to exist, for the purpose of the imagination.[5]

No writer could have asked for more. Not until two years had elapsed would Emerson, in 1837, deliver his famous address "The American Scholar" before Phi Beta Kappa at Harvard and declare: "Our day of dependence, our long apprenticeship to the learning of other lands, draws to a close" and "We have listened too long to the courtly muses of Europe."[6]

Even before *A Tour on the Prairies* was published, Irving had committed himself to writing *Astoria* for John Jacob Astor. The friendship between these two men had been of long duration. It is possible that while still a boy Irving may have passed and repassed Astor's store at 149 Broadway, where the future fur magnate sold not only furs but also musical instruments.[7] Not until 1821, however, when Irving was thirty-eight and Astor twenty years his senior, did the two men meet in Paris.[8] From this early meeting developed a friendship that endured until Astor's death twenty-seven years later. Astor regarded the younger man warmly, liked to have him come to his home, and would visit him in turn. He made much of the famous writer and named him in his will as one of the executors of his estate. When Astor died on March

---

[5] *North American Review*, Vol. XLI (1835), 14.

[6] It seems unmistakable that Emerson was pointing to Irving, among others, when he stated in this same address: "Authors we have in numbers, who have written out their vein, and who, moved by a commendable prudence, sail for Greece or Palestine, follow the trapper into the prairie, or ramble round Algiers, to replenish their merchantable stock."

[7] Williams, *op. cit.*, I, 11.   [8] *Ibid.*, II, 74.

29, 1848, the family asked Irving to serve as one of the pallbearers.[9] It was inevitable, perhaps, that Irving's journey to the West, his subsequent writing of *A Tour on the Prairies*, and Astor's ambition to have someone tell the story of his fur-trading venture on the Columbia should have coalesced into a concrete proposal that Irving undertake the task. With some hesitation, he agreed.

The record of what took place from that time until the publication of *Astoria* has been fully related by Irving's nephew, Pierre Munro Irving, in his *Life and Letters of Washington Irving*. Pierre was living in Jacksonville, Illinois, when he received a letter from his famous uncle dated New York, September 15, 1834. "My dear Pierre," the letter begins,

> . . . John Jacob Astor is extremely desirous of having a work written on the subject of his settlement of Astoria, at the mouth of the Columbia River, something that might take with the reading world, and secure to him the reputation of having originated the enterprise and founded the colony that are likely to have such important results in the history of commerce and colonization.
>
> The old gentleman has applied to me repeatedly in the matter, offering to furnish abundance of materials in letters, journals, and verbal narratives, and to pay liberally for time and trouble. I have felt aware that a work might be written on the subject, full of curious and entertaining matter, comprising adventurous expeditions by sea and land, scenes beyond the Rocky Mountains, incidents and scenes illustrative of Indian character, and of that singular and but little known class, the traders and voyageurs of the Fur Companies. Still I am so much engrossed with other plans, that I have not time for the examination of papers, the digesting of the various materials, etc., and have stood aloof from the undertaking, though still keeping the matter open.
>
> Since I have heard of your inclination to return to New York, however, it has occurred to me that you might be disposed to take this subject in hand; to collate the various documents, collect verbal information, and reduce the whole to such form that I might be able to dress it up advantageously, and with little labor, for the press.
>
> In an interview which I had with Mr. Astor, a day or two since, in which he laid before me a variety of documents, I accordingly stated to him my inability at present to give the subject the labor that would

[9] James Parton, "John Jacob Astor," *Harper's Monthly*, Vol. XXV (1865), 319, 322; P. M. Irving, *op. cit.*, IV, 38.

be requisite, but the possibility that you might aid me in the way I have mentioned; in which case I should have no objection to putting the finshing hand to the work. The old gentleman caught at the idea, and begged me to write to you immediately. He said he would be willing to pay you whatever might be deemed proper for your services, and that, if any profit resulted from the sales of the work, it would belong, of course, to the authors.

I lay this matter before you, to be considered in contrast or connection with your other plans. If you take it in hand, I shall take care to secure your being well paid for your current time and labor; the ultimate profits of the work may be a matter of after arrangement between us.

Mr. Astor is a strong-minded man, and one from whose conversation much curious information is to be derived. He feels the want of occupation and amusement, and thinks he may find something of both in the progress of this work. You would find him very kindly disposed, for he was an early friend of your father, for whose memory he entertains great regard; and he has always been on terms of intimacy with your uncle Peter and myself, besides knowing more or less of others of our family. . . .

When you have thought over this matter, and made up your mind, let me hear from you. If you determine in favor of it, the sooner you come on the better. I have entertained the matter thus far for your sake, having no care about it for myself; decide, therefore, as you think fit, or as your inclination prompts.[10]

Pierre replied affirmatively on October 5, saying he would do the work for $2,000 and forego any right to royalties. Irving had this figure raised to $3,000. On October 29, he again wrote to his nephew. The following portion of Irving's letter describes his conception of what he thought the book should be:

My present idea is to call the work by the general name of *Astoria*—the name of the settlement made by Mr. Astor [i.e., by his agents] at the mouth of Columbia River: under this head to give not merely a history of his great colonial and commercial enterprise, and of the fortunes of his colony, but a body of information concerning the whole region beyond the Rocky Mountains, on the borders of Columbia River, comprising the adventures, by sea and land, of traders, trappers, Indian warriors, hunters, &c.; their habits, characters, persons, costume,

[10] *Life and Letters of Washington Irving*, III, 60–62.

&c.; descriptions of natural scenery, animals, plants, &c., &c. I think, in this way, a rich and varied work may be formed, both entertaining and instructive, and laying open scenes in the wild life of that adventurous region which would possess the charm of freshness and novelty. You would be required to look over the various papers, letters, and journals in the possession of Mr. Astor, written by various persons who have been in his employ, to draw anecdotes and descriptions from him, and from Northwest traders who occasionally visit him; to forage among various works in French and English that have been published relative to these regions, and thus to draw together and arrange into some kind of form a great body of facts. In all this I may be able to render you much assistance. When the work is thus crudely prepared, I will take it in hand, and prepare it for the press, as it is a *sine qua non* with Mr. Astor that my name should be to the work. You now have a general idea of what will be your task. I think you may find it a very interesting and agreeable one, and may accomplish it within the space of a year. . . .

Mr. Astor has his papers all arranged, so that you would be able to get to work immediately. Let me hear from you on the receipt of this. If you determine to come, you had better put your portmanteau in the first stage coach, and come on as promptly as possible.[11]

Pierre came on to New York and took up his new assignment. In the meantime, Washington Irving prepared *A Tour on the Prairies* for the press. It was published in London the following March (1835) and in New York in April. Irving had not yet turned his attention to *Astoria*, but Pierre was busily at work.[12] Soon Irving himself would begin writing. By mid-May he could tell Peter Irving: "I am now engaged in the work on the subject of Mr. Astor's great enterprise; and I am much mistaken if I do not make it a very rich, curious, and unique work. Pierre Munro makes an admirable pioneer."[13] He worked throughout the summer on the book, and late in August he again wrote to Peter: "I am working away at the Astor enterprise, and hope to get the narrative in frame in the course of the autumn; after which I shall have nothing to do but enrich it."[14]

About this time, Irving moved to Astor's home, for on September 26 he once more confided to Peter Irving:

[11] *Ibid.*, 63–64. [12] *Ibid.*, 69.
[13] May 16, 1835. *Ibid.*, 70; cf. *ibid.*, 72. [14] August 24. *Ibid.*, 77.

For upward of a month past I have been quartered at Hellgate, with Mr. Astor, and I have not had so quiet and delightful a nest since I have been in America. . . . I cannot tell you how sweet and delightful I have found this retreat; pure air, agreeable scenery, a spacious house, profound quiet, and perfect command of my time and self. The consequence is, that I have written more than a volume, and have got within half a dozen chapters of the end of my work—an achievement which I did not expect to do for months. Of course there will be much to be done afterward in extending some parts, touching up others, enriching and embellishing. It will make two good volumes—probably octavo; and Pierre Munro thinks it will be more liked than anything I have lately written.[15]

Another week's work saw the completion of the first draft after what Irving called "a long and successful fit of writing."[16] He still had some "enriching" to do, which would consist of adding anecdotes obtained from participants in the Astorian venture. As Irving later wrote in his introduction to *The Adventures of Captain Bonneville*,

. . . it was my practice to seek all kinds of oral information connected with the subject. Nowhere did I pick up more interesting particulars than at the table of Mr. John Jacob Astor; who . . . was accustomed to have at his board various persons of adventurous turn, some of whom had been engaged in his own great undertaking; others, on their own account, had made expeditions to the Rocky Mountains and the waters of the Colorado.

Unfortunately, these individuals, with the exception of Bonneville, cannot now be identified. Having to wait for the appearance of some of these Astorians, Irving left Astor's home for a few days and laid the manuscript aside, for on October 8 he wrote: "I have promised old Mr. Astor to return to his rural retreat at Hellgate, and shall go out there today."[17]

That autumn, while Irving was living at Astor's home, he became acquainted with Captain Benjamin Bonneville, recently returned to the East after three years in the Rocky Mountains as a fur trader. Early in September, Bonneville appeared at Astor's estate and there met Irving. They talked at length about Bonneville's recent expedition, for Bonneville knew intimately most of the country that Irving had been writing

[15] September 26. *Ibid.*, 78.   [16] *Ibid.*, 79.   [17] *Ibid.*

about. He had traveled along the Platte River, over and through the Wind River Mountains, into Jackson Hole, along the Snake River as well as Bear River, and had twice been to the Columbia. It was the same country in which many of the scenes of *Astoria* had been enacted. "Being extremely curious, at the time," Irving later recorded, "about every thing connected with the Far West, I addressed numerous questions to him. They drew from him a number of extremely striking details."[18] Both men, it proved, could benefit from the meeting.

Only three or four months later Irving called upon the Captain in his Washington, D. C., quarters and found him writing his memoirs of the expedition, which subsequently formed the basis of Irving's next book. Irving probably discussed further with Bonneville various areas in the mountains about which he needed information. He had already written to the Adjutant General requesting copies of several of Bonneville's maps. Just when he asked Bonneville to write an essay on the western Indians for *Astoria* is not known, but when the book went to press, such an essay made up part of the appendix. It seems likely, besides, that the map published in *Astoria* benefited from Bonneville's information.[19]

Irving resumed work on *Astoria* late in November, and continued through December, January, and February. Pierre informs us that the delay had been caused by Irving's waiting for "a principal actor in the enterprise of Astoria, and from whom he was to get many personal anecdotes for the enriching of his work."[20] The last evidence that Irving was still polishing the manuscript is contained in a letter of February 16, 1836, to Peter Irving. He wrote now: "I am giving my last handling to the Astor work. It is this handling which, like the touching and toning of a picture, gives the richest effects. I am interested [in] and pleased with the work, and feel that the labor I am now bestowing upon it will contribute greatly to its success."[21] In May the manuscript was delivered to the publisher, and by the end of June the book was on press.[22] Three months elapsed before publication. In October it was available simultaneously in London and America. Bentley, Irving's English publisher, paid him £500, and from Carey, Lee, & Blanchard,

---

[18] *The Adventures of Captain Bonneville* (ed. by Edgeley W. Todd), lii.

[19] See *ibid.*, xvii, xix–xxii.

[20] *Life and Letters*, III, 81. There is no way of identifying this individual.

[21] *Ibid.*, 88.   [22] *Ibid.*, 90.

his American publisher, he received $4,000 for the first five thousand copies.[23]

The response of reviewers in both England and America gratified Irving immensely. Early in December he wrote to Pierre Irving:

> Astoria succeeds equal to your anticipations, and far beyond my own. It is highly spoken of in two English reviews which I have read. One pronounces it my *chef d'oeuvre*. I am glad he thinks so, though I don't. Old Mr. Astor appears to be greatly gratified, which is very satisfactory to me. William Astor also expresses himself in the most gratifying terms, and seems surprised that the subject should be made so interesting and entertaining. In fact, I have heard more talk about this work, considering the short time it has been launched, than about any other that I have published for some time past.[24]

One of the reviews to which Irving here alludes appeared in the *London Spectator* in the same month the book was published. "We have been agreeably surprised by these volumes," the reviewer wrote.

> Instead of a novel, which the title, on its first announcement seemed to propose, *Astoria* is the history of as grand and comprehensive a commercial enterprise as ever was planned with any well-grounded prospect of success, and which was prosecuted among scenes as vast and nations as wild, gave rise to incidents as ludicrous, as interesting, as appalling, and developed characters and manners as marked and striking as anything on record respecting the adventurous explorers of the Middle Ages, or the hardy discoverers of more modern days. . . . The result is the production of the most finished narrative of such a series of adventures that ever was written, whether with regard to plan or execution. The arrangement has all the art of fiction, yet without any apparent sacrifice of truth or exactness. The composition we are inclined to rate as the *chef d'oeuvre* of Washington Irving. . . .[25]

---

[23] *Ibid.* The title-page of the first American edition reads: *Astoria, or Anecdotes of an Enterprise / beyond the / Rocky Mountains. / By Washington Irving. / In Two Volumes. / Philadelphia: / Carey, Lea, & Blanchard. / 1836.* A one-volume edition appeared in Paris the same year, and Dutch, German, and Swedish translations soon made their appearance. See William R. Langfeld, *Washington Irving: A Bibliography,* 77.

[24] *Life and Letters,* III, 92.

[25] Quoted in *ibid.,* 93–94. See also *The Athenaeum,* October 22, 1836. The reviewer here concluded that Irving "is the proper person to collect and publish the characteristic legends of America. This work . . . is a valuable addition to Transatlantic literature; and, though it becomes tedious in certain of its details and repetitious, ought to

In the United States, reviewers were equally laudatory. Edward Everett, who wrote a long account in the *North American Review*, declared that he had read the book "with interest and profit," had found many anecdotes of "a soul-stirring character" and "valuable information . . . in a highly attractive form," and judged it to exhibit the "impress of Mr. Irving's taste." And digressing a bit, he added:

> When one contemplates the various scenes of hardship, to which men subject themselves not merely in pursuit of subsistence, but from pure love of adventures and distaste for settled life, we should be almost led to the conclusion, against every thing but inspired authority to the contrary, that a part at least of the human race must have been Rousseau's forest-born wild men, to whom the mountain and the thicket are by nature more congenial than the crowded abodes of civilization.[26]

The Knickerbocker was also commendatory and expressed its "admiration of the exceedingly graphic and picturesque descriptions of exciting expeditions and adventures by land and sea, and the fine sketches of character, with which the work abounds. . . . 'Astoria' is destined to occupy no middle rank in the productions of its author."[27] The *New York Mirror* found *Astoria* "as interesting as any romance."[28] Edgar Allan Poe was particularly impressed with the overland journey of Wilson Price Hunt's party. "No details more intensely exciting," he wrote, "are to be found in any work of travels within our knowledge."[29] Without doubt, *Astoria* must have satisfied the vast majority of its contemporary readers.

What had they read that made such a strong appeal? In *Astoria* they

be welcome in England." In December, Sydney Smith, an English reviewer who once sneeringly asked, "In the four quarters of the globe, who reads an American book?" wrote Sir George Phillips that he had "read *Astoria* with great pleasure; it is a book to put in your library, as an entertaining, well-written—*very* well-written—account of savage life, on a most extensive scale." Quoted in S. Austin Alibone, *A Critical Dictionary of English Literature and British and American Authors*, I, 943. As late as 1841, G. P. R. James, English historical novelist whom Irving had known on the Continent, wrote to Irving to express his "intense delight" in *Astoria*, "every word of which I dwell upon with feelings of excitement and interest, and longings of adventure, which I thought were gone with my boyhood." Quoted in P. M. Irving, *op. cit.*, III, 163.

[26] *North American Review*, Vol. XLIV (1837), 200–237.
[27] *The Knickerbocker*, Vol. IX (1837), 88, 90.
[28] *New York Mirror*, Vol. XIV (1836), 131.
[29] *Southern Literary Messenger*, Vol. III (1837), 64.

found a sweeping panorama of the fur trade in Canada, around the Great Lakes, and in the country bordering the Columbia River and its tributaries. They read of events having a global setting, with aggressive fur companies and rival nations competing for possession of a wilderness promising wealth to those who survived; of ships attempting to supply the trading post at the mouth of the Columbia after tedious and dangerous voyages around Cape Horn and up the Pacific, ventures in which two vessels were lost; of perilous coasting voyages that connected the post on the Columbia with Russian settlements in Alaska, and the extension of these voyages to the rich fur market in China, where proceeds were to be invested in goods shipped back to New York. They must have been impressed by the grasp of imagination which led Astor to envisage an all-embracing scheme linking continents and nations—a well-formed plan that promised success and reward on an investment totaling hundreds of thousands of dollars but a plan defeated, nonetheless, by war, commercial rivalry, possible disloyalty, and bad luck. They could not but sympathize with the men at sea and others on land who suffered excessive toil, pain, hunger, and violent death. Their curiosity was aroused by accounts of little-known Indians living in the interior or on the Columbia River or along the Pacific. Perhaps what held their interest as much as anything else, however, was Irving's deft recital of hazardous adventures—like those of Wilson Price Hunt's arduous journey overland to Astoria and Robert Stuart's strenuous journey from Astoria to St. Louis, whose struggles against a savage country seemed more than human fortitude could bear. But whether they knew it or not, they were responding to sound history concerning events and forces that were enmeshed with America's past, present, and future.

How had Irving managed to turn himself into a historian of actions so out of the ordinary? As already indicated, Astor had placed before him a wealth of documents that Pierre Munro Irving arranged in a manageable order. "Since the days in Rich's library," wrote Stanley T. Williams, Irving's biographer, "he had never examined so extensive a collection of Americana. For Astor held nothing back; Irving saw everything."[30] But much of what Irving had access to in this mass of

[30] *Life of Washington Irving*, II, 84. Obadiah Rich, American consul in Madrid, made his vast Hispano-American bibliographic collection available to Irving in 1826 for the writing of *The Life and Adventures of Christopher Columbus*. See *ibid.*, I, 303–305.

documents, however, will never be known because in the 1870's fifteen large packing cases of Astor's records were intentionally destroyed, and in the next decade many more were burned to save the trouble of moving them to a new location. Kenneth W. Porter, in his biography of Astor, related that

> A few letter books and bundles of paper were marked for preservation, probably as souvenirs, and apparently at random. One bundle of papers consisted of letters, invoices, and accounts relating to the Astoria enterprise, and a couple of others had to do with litigation against the Astor estate. . . . A few journals and small account books of the Pacific Fur Company were saved, but the most important material to escape destruction was three letter books for the years 1813–15, 1831–38, and 1845–48.[31]

In view of the fact that many documents were destroyed, it would appear that we are hopelessly at a loss to reconstruct the sources from which Irving worked. Fortunately, such is not the case. Indeed, for three-fourths of the book and perhaps more, it is possible to show precisely, in some cases down to the very sentence, where Irving's information originated. In some parts of *Astoria,* however, sources cannot be identified, but it is surprising how few in number are such instances in relation to the whole. It will never, of course, be possible to recover sources which originated as conversations with principals in the Pacific Fur Company, discussions which Pierre Munro and Irving elicited from these men and from Astor himself. Astor was at the time the leading authority on the fur trade in the United States. He had in his earlier years annually visited Montreal and the interior of Canada and knew well the financial leaders and the workings of the Canadian companies, in particular the North West Company, his great rival. Much of the information that went into *Astoria* must have come directly from Astor himself.

Of the manuscripts Irving used, the most important was Robert Stuart's revision of his "Journal," the record of the long journey of his party during the summer, fall, and winter of 1812 and the spring of 1813 from Astoria to St. Louis. This draft, which Irving referred to as the "Travelling Memoranda," was subsequently found in a cupboard in Irving's home. It is now at Yale University, where, along with the

---

[31] *John Jacob Astor, Business Man,* II, 1299.

xxviii

Reproduced from the first edition of *Astoria* (1836)

"Journal," it forms part of the William Robertson Coe Collection of Western Americana.[32] Irving also had various letters from Wilson Price Hunt; from Captain Thorn of the *Tonquin*, whose letters to Astor provided Irving with much of his information concerning the voyage from New York to the Columbia; from Captain Sowle of the *Beaver*, the second ship sent to Astoria; and from Captain Northrop of the *Lark*, wrecked in a violent storm near the Hawaiian Islands. There were also documents and letters carried overland from Astoria by Robert Stuart, and across Siberia and Europe by Russel Farnham, plus additional documents relating to Astoria that were preserved by Wilson Price Hunt.[33] These and other manuscript sources are identified, whenever possible, at appropriate points throughout the footnotes in this edition of *Astoria*.

By far the greatest repository of information, however, Irving found in published sources. Of these, the most important was Gabriel Franchère's *Relation d'un Voyage à la Côte du Nord-ouest de l'Amérique Septentrionale, dans les Années 1810, 11, 12, 13, et 14.*[34] Since an English translation did not appear until 1854, Irving worked from the original French version. Franchère's *Relation* was his principal source for the voyage of the *Tonquin* as well as for many of the events which took place at Astoria and along the Columbia. He supplemented Franchère at various points by consulting Ross Cox's *Adventures on the Columbia River*, published in London a few years before *Astoria* was written.[35] A more important source than Cox was a French translation of Wilson P. Hunt's journal of his overland expedition that had appeared in a French publication, *Nouvelles annales des voyages* (Paris,

[32] It has been published in two forms, first in Philip Ashton Rollins (ed.), *The Discovery of the Oregon Trail* (1935), where it appears integrated with the original journal, and also in Kenneth A. Spaulding (ed.), *On the Oregon Trail* (1953).

[33] In the Missouri Historical Society is the Pacific Fur Company Book of 1810–13, which contains the Articles of Agreement of the Pacific Fur Company, as well as letters and other documents written at Astoria. These have been published by T. C. Elliott, "Sale of Astoria, 1813," *Oregon Historical Quarterly*, Vol. XXXIII (1932), 43–50, and by Grace Flandrau, *Astor and the Oregon Country*. See also Stella M. Drumm, "More About Astorians," *Oregon Historical Quarterly*, Vol. XXIV (1923), 335–60.

[34] Montréal, Impr. de C. B. Pasteur, 1820.

[35] Two vols. London, H. Colburn and R. Bentley, 1831. A second edition, entitled *The Columbia River; or, Scenes and Adventures During a Residence of Six Years on the Western Side of the Rocky Mountains*, appeared in London the following year. Which edition Irving used has not been determined.

1821). The French translation in this collection was presumably all that was available to Irving, the original journal having previously been lost.[36] This one source alone provided Irving with the substance of no less than sixteen chapters out of a total of sixty-one. An additional eight chapters came from Stuart's unpublished "Travelling Memoranda," making a total of twenty-four chapters from these two sources alone.

Much valuable information came, in addition, from two books which recorded the voyage of Hunt and his party up the Missouri River to the Arikara Indian villages. The more important of the two was written by John Bradbury, an English botanist, who eagerly accepted Hunt's invitation to travel with him and was thus enabled to collect the flora along the Missouri. His *Travels in the Interior of America, in the Years 1809, 1810, and 1811*[37] provided Irving with an indispensable account of the first stage of Hunt's overland trip. This he supplemented with a parallel account by Henry Marie Brackenridge, who, out of curiosity and a sense of adventure, traveled as far as the Arikara villages in the boats of Hunt's fancied rival, Manuel Lisa of the Missouri Fur Company, who followed Hunt up the Missouri and finally overtook him after a strenuous effort. Brackenridge in 1814 published his *Views of Louisiana; together with a Journal of a Voyage up the Missouri River, in 1811*.[38] Irving used either this or the enlarged second edition, published as *Journal of a Voyage up the River Missouri*.[39] These two writers provided him with an unparalleled record of Hunt's journey up the Missouri, as well as a source for describing the topography of the country and the culture of the Indian tribes, especially the Arikara, that Hunt encountered. Eight chapters, or a total of eighty-nine pages in the first edition of *Astoria*, are based almost entirely on these two sources.

There were other published sources that Irving relied upon. Much important material, for example, came from the *History of the Expedition under the Command of Captains Lewis and Clark*, which had been in print since 1814. From this authoritative source Irving drew chiefly information concerning the Indians, as well as plants and animals along the Columbia River. Other information, notably the story of the Omaha chief, Blackbird, came from Edwin James's account of

[36] An English translation is available today in Rollins (ed.), *op. cit.;* see Appendix A, 281–308.

[37] London, Sherwood, Neely, and Jones, 1817.

[38] Pittsburgh, Cramer, Spear and Eichbaum, 1814.

[39] Baltimore, Coale and Maxwell, 1815.

Long's expedition, published as *Account of an Expedition from Pitts-burgh to the Rocky Mountains.*[40] Irving also resorted to *Nouveaux Voyages de Mr. le Baron de Lahontan, dans l'Amérique Septentrionale* (1703), either in the French version or in the English translation of the same year. He drew from this in connection with his account of the early Canadian fur trade. Some use was also made of Jonathan Carver's *Travels Through the Interior Part of North America* (London, 1778), an immensely popular work in America at the time.

Two notebooks (now in the Seligman Collection of Irvingiana at the New York Public Library) which Irving kept during his preparation for writing *Astoria* reveal additional sources, as well as some already mentioned. One, in spite of an odd discrepancy in dates, was *History of the Indian Tribes of North America* (Philadelphia, 1838–44), by Thomas L. M'Kenney and James Hall. Another was Pierre François Charlevoix's *Historical Journal of a Voyage Made in Northern America* (1744), from which he found a selection in James A. Jones's *Tales of an Indian Camp,*[41] where he also discovered other usable material. The extent to which Irving utilized these printed sources in writing *Astoria* is indicated in the footnotes to the present edition. The above listing is not exhaustive, however, and other sources could probably be identified.

By today's standards, Irving's use of his sources and his scant attention to documentation leave much that is open to criticism. I have made an effort to collate these sources with *Astoria* wherever possible, for only by such means is it possible to gauge the historical accuracy of *Astoria*, to determine how much of the book is allegedly fiction and how much is fact, and in general to assess the degree to which *Astoria* is the work of a creative writer. Irving gave only casual acknowledgment of his authorities in a statement in his introduction, where he wrote:

> As the journals, on which I chiefly depended, had been kept by men of business, intent upon the main object of the enterprise, and but little versed in science, or curious about matters not immediately bearing upon their interests, and as they were written often in moments of fatigue or hurry, amid the inconveniences of wild encampments, they were often meagre in their details, furnishing hints to provoke rather than narratives to satisfy inquiry. I have, therefore, availed myself occa-

[40] Two vols. Baltimore, H. C. Carey and I. Lea, 1822–23.
[41] Three vols. London, Henry Colburn and Richard Bentley, 1829.

sionally of collateral lights supplied by the published journals of other travellers who have visited the scenes described: such as Messrs. Lewis and Clarke, Bradbury, Breckenridge, Long, Franchere, and Ross Cox, and make a general acknowledgment of aid received from these quarters.

As the list of sources previously cited indicates, Irving used more than he here acknowledges, and to say that he availed himself *"occasionally of collateral lights"* is both misleading and inaccurate, for, as stated earlier, most of *Astoria* is actually composed from information derived from these "collateral lights."

When it comes to the actual use made of these sources, Irving again falls far short of what modern scholarship, at least, deems necessary. So closely does he often follow them, frequently changing wording only slightly or sometimes even taking entire clauses and sentences from the originals, that he leaves himself open to the charge of plagiarism. The only mitigation one can offer is that standards of documentation were lax in Irving's time and he probably felt that his acknowledgment in the introduction was sufficient to discharge any obligation he might have to other writers.

There are, to be sure, certain advantages which the modern scholar can derive from Irving's practice. For one thing, if we examine the frequent similarity of phraseology between what he wrote and what appears in other accounts, it becomes possible to identify, with a high degree of accuracy, not only many of the sources themselves, but also the very passages he used therein. Because of this correspondence, the authoritativeness of *Astoria* can be relied upon in all but an exceedingly small number of instances. It is at least as sound as the authorities Irving consulted. What is especially apparent is that, as a result of his proximate adherence to primary source materials, not only is the narrative authentic, but his descriptions of routes of travel and of terrain, vegetation, and animal life are also faithful to the setting in which the events in *Astoria* actually occurred. Anyone familiar with both the book and the country can only remark on the former's fidelity to the latter. Rarely does Irving permit himself to embellish an incident with what might be called fictitious details. The passages in which such embellishment occurs are noted in this edition, and, as the reader will note, they are few. There are, to be sure, a minor number of errors of the sort likely to creep into any book, but a knowledge of sources enables one to correct these.

All of this allows us, besides, to assess the degree to which *Astoria* is the work of a creative writer. The word *creative* is not without its difficulties. If it implies an imaginative invention of something that has not before existed, its application to *Astoria* as a whole is without justification. If, however, it can be taken to mean a re-creation of materials already existing and a presentation of them in a new dress, it can be said to apply in some measure to *Astoria,* and in that sense most historical writing is creative. It must be kept in mind, however, that Irving faithfully presented historical facts as he knew them, and, as already stated, only infrequently did he embellish meager details.

Let us consider a case in point. In relating the return journey of Robert Stuart and his party from Astoria to St. Louis, Irving presents an encounter between Ramsay Crooks and a grizzly bear. He writes:

> On one occasion, Mr. Crooks had wandered about a mile from the camp, and had ascended a small hill commanding a view of the [North Platte] river. He was without his rifle, a rare circumstance, for in these wild regions, where one may put up a wild animal, or a wild Indian, at every turn, it is customary never to stir from the camp-fire unarmed. The hill where he stood overlooked the place where the massacre of the buffalo had taken place. As he was looking around on the prospect, his eye was caught by an object below, moving directly towards him. To his dismay, he discovered it to be a grizzly bear, with two cubs. There was no tree at hand into which he could climb; to run, would only be to provoke pursuit, and he should soon be overtaken. He threw himself on the ground, therefore, and lay motionless, watching the movements of the animal with intense anxiety. It continued to advance until at the foot of the hill, where it turned, and made into the woods, having probably gorged itself with buffalo flesh. Mr. Crooks made all haste back to the camp, rejoicing at his escape, and determining never to stir out again without his rifle. A few days after this circumstance, a grizzly bear was shot in the neighborhood, by Mr. Miller.[42]

Did Irving invent this incident and thus lapse into fiction? No primary source contains any suggestion of Crooks's experience. The "Travelling Memoranda," which Irving was following, makes no mention of it. However, the surrounding circumstances are right. According to Stuart,

[42] Cf. page 413.

he and his companions decided on November 2, 1812, to erect a winter camp, located on the North Platte River. Irving supplies the correct date. On the fourth, says Stuart, five persons killed thirty-two buffalo, thus supplying Irving with his allusion to "the massacre of the buffalo" and the bear's having "gorged itself with buffalo flesh." Fifteen more buffalo were killed on the eighth, and on the ninth and tenth the hunters succeeded in bringing the meat and hides into camp. On the twelfth, Stuart wrote, "we this day procured 20 more [deer], which with a white Bear was the hunt of six persons—[.]"[43] The reference to a white bear, that is, a grizzly, supplied Irving with assurance that such animals were in the vicinity. Was the remaining portion of the incident, then, a fabrication? It might appear to be, yet, for reasons which follow, one cannot state dogmatically that it was.

When Irving was working on *Astoria*, he had occasion, as was pointed out earlier, to visit with and interrogate at Hellgate several participants in the Astorian venture. Ramsay Crooks was still alive and was, in fact, president of the American Fur Company at the time. It is entirely possible—even probable—that Irving had such a recital of a near scrape with a grizzly bear directly from Crooks's own lips. Furthermore, the absence of the incident from Stuart's "Travelling Memoranda" is not evidence that it had not occurred, for it is not likely that Stuart would have recorded that Crooks had lain motionless on the ground to evade detection by a bear. But had Crooks been caught and mangled, that circumstance would certainly have gone in. When a grizzly bear was actually killed, Stuart felt the occasion sufficiently important to record it.

Irving was assiduous in collecting information of this kind. The second of the two extant notebooks he kept in preparation for writing *Astoria* is filled with questions to be answered, questions like the following, for example:

Jones & Carson? Inquire about the circumstances of country with them—

Sickness in the camp on the Big River (5 days after leaving Rickarees. What was the nature of the sickness—How was the weather on the prairies? Did they suffer from flies—musquitoes[?]

Get a description of the two Crows who visited their camp at the foot of the Big Horn mountains.

[43] Spaulding (ed.), *op. cit.*, 130–31; Rollins (ed.), *op. cit.*, 190–91.

These questions, to be sure, relate to Wilson P. Hunt's overland journey rather than to Stuart's, but it is just as likely that Irving asked similar questions of Astor's guests. "It was my practice to seek all kinds of oral information," he wrote in *The Adventures of Captain Bonneville*. The conclusion must be that even where Irving seems to be writing fiction, an element of doubt lingers; there is always the lurking possibility that he had good reason for writing as he did, even though that reason may not appear in the surviving documents.

One practice which Irving occasionally permitted himself cannot so easily be defended. An example appears in his narrative of Hunt's voyage up the Missouri. A large party of well-armed Sioux Indians blocked passage of the boats. To convey the fear of the *voyageurs*, Irving wrote:

> The poor Canadians eyed them [the Sioux] with rueful glances, and now and then a fearful ejaculation escaped them. "Parbleu! this is a sad scrape we are in, brother!" one would mutter to the next oarsman. "Aye, aye," the other would reply, "we are not going to a wedding, my friend!"

Since no dialogue appears in the sources Irving was using at this point, the assumption is that he was here writing fiction.

There are in the entire book, however, only fifteen such examples, of which one is a statement attributed to Astor, which he may actually have made, and another is traceable directly to one of Irving's sources.[44] Three examples consist of only one sentence each, five are of two sentences, four consist of three sentences, and two are made up of five sentences. In all, they make a total of thirty-five sentences, and in the aggregate they would comprise probably less than two of the 547 pages in the first edition. Since they usually occur at a moment of some crucial importance, Irving may have reasoned that they were justified by his desire to heighten such moments and thereby enliven the narrative. Whatever the reasoning, they are usually utterances that might well have been made, and in any case do little violence to the authenticity of the passages in which they appear.

[44] Upon learning of the destruction of the *Tonquin*, Astor went that night to the theater, where a friend commented on his calmness in face of the disaster. " 'What would you have me do?' was his characteristic reply; 'would you have me stay at home and weep for what I cannot help?' "
For the source alluded to, see Chapter LIII, note 18.

Some people have raised questions about the authenticity of what Irving wrote and, in view of his great reputation as a writer of *belles lettres*, have been inclined to think that the creator of literature got the upper hand over the historian. Such challenges have repeatedly arisen almost from the moment *Astoria* was published. What may well be the earliest appeared in 1839 as an editorial in a periodical published in Boston entitled *The Oregonian and Indian's Advocate*, a promotional magazine interested in encouraging colonization in Oregon. It is doubtful that the editor had ever set foot in the territory in question, yet he knew that Irving's descriptions of Oregon could not be trusted. He wrote:

> We find that many persons derive their ideas of the physical character and condition of Oregon from the works of Washington Irving. This gentleman has given to the world, first, "Astoria," which professes to be a narrative of the attempt of John Jacob Astor to establish a fur company in Oregon, and second, "Rocky Mountains, or Adventures in the far West," which is an arrangement of the papers of Capt. Bonneville, a fur trader. As mere literary works these excel. They are among the most finished in our language; but we shall not, therefore, imagine, while we peruse them, that we are reading truth, for both books are, without doubt, highly fictitious. The frame work is fact, but the covering was obtained altogether from the imagination of Mr. Irving. *We put no kind of confidence in the work of Washington Irving respecting Oregon,* and we are fully persuaded that whoever trusts to his "interesting and graphic descriptions," will be most sadly disappointed. Oregon is a land of realities, of stern realities, and fancy must seek its nourishment elsewhere. Let no man, then, go to Oregon, expecting to find it at all as it is described in the romances of the first of American novelists [*sic*], unless he wishes to engage in the pursuit of that which he can never realize.[45]

This charge is especially interesting in view of the fact that Irving's authorities for his account of Oregon were men who had lived there and faithfully reported what they knew and that among these authorities were Lewis and Clark, whose reliability has never been questioned. One can only wonder upon what grounds the editorial writer based his assertions.

[45] "Authority of Irving," *The Oregonian and Indian's Advocate*, I (1839), 220–21. Italics in original. The *Advocate* was published in Lynn, Massachusetts, by the Oregon Provisional Emigration Society, founded in 1838.

One of Irving's most persistent critics was Hubert Howe Bancroft, who in his *History of the Northwest Coast* never overlooked an opportunity to censure Astor, Irving, and *Astoria* (as well as Captain Bonneville) in such severe terms as to suggest personal malice. He wrote of "the current of unqualified sycophancy, trickery, sentimentality, and maudlin praise [for Astor] which runs through *Astoria*." He challenged Irving's "integrity of purpose and faithfulness of execution" and accused him of "unusual warp of judgment" as well as of lending "his brilliant faculties to . . . base purposes." In connection with his narrative of the destruction of the *Tonquin*, Irving is charged with giving "wings to his brilliant imagination, and permit[ting] it to carry him whithersoever it will." Some of the details of the *Tonquin* episode as told by Irving, Bancroft stated, "have not in them . . . a word of truth." He went on to say:

> But it is hardly wise to criticise fiction as though it were fact; I only wish to establish what is fiction, and what is fact. For the elegant and philosophical writer of novels [*sic*] I have the most profound admiration; but as there are many who have all their lives regarded Irving's *Astoria* as true history, it is my duty to inform them that many of its most brilliant passages are pure fiction.

Bancroft also charged him with being "unfair to the Northwest Company" and avowed that in relating the last days of Astoria "Irving lays himself open to the severest criticism and censure." He was particularly severe concerning Irving's alleged unfairness to Duncan McDougall in selling Fort Astoria to the North West Company, and said that Irving, "with strange and effeminate inconsistency with his bold assertion, constantly condemns McDougall while his facts [acts?] exculpate him." This he explained on the grounds that Irving was prejudiced by Astor's wishes: " . . . writing with Astor at his elbow we find flung in from one end of the book to the other, slurs and innuendos upon the character of the Scotch partners, the Northwest Company, and everybody except Mr. Irving and Mr. Astor." And then the final charge: "What shall we say of a writer who so mixed personal feelings with his facts and fiction?"[46]

---

[46] *History of the Northwest Coast*, II, 138n., 145n., 169n., 172n., 221n., 222n., 223n. It would not seem inappropriate, in view of his emotionally toned language, to turn the last statement against Bancroft himself. To whom are we to attribute those portions of *History of the Northwest Coast* that slash at Irving—to Bancroft or to

What can be said against such serious allegations? Hiram Chittenden faced this issue in his *History of the American Fur Trade*. At the time this commendable work was written, Bancroft's denunciation of Irving was still fairly recent. Chittenden excuses the many errors in Bancroft's own books on the grounds that, in a work of such vast scope written in a comparatively short span of time, they were unavoidable. He goes on to say:

> No such indulgence, however, can be extended to Mr. Bancroft's discussion of certain historic questions, for pressure of work can not explain his implacable prejudices and his itching desire to put forth theories which shall subvert popular ideals or overthrow accepted conclusions. Particularly, whenever it is a question of an American view as against a Spanish, British, or Indian view, Mr. Bancroft, if the circumstances will possibly admit it, ranges himself against his own countrymen.
>
> In no instance is this peculiar trait more flagrantly in evidence than in his treatment of Astoria, its founder and its historian. His persistent bias of judgment and his bitter prejudice, which place him in an attitude of constant hostility toward Astor and Irving, and lead him repeatedly into sheer falsifications and downright slander, are wholly without rational explanation. It will be alike idle and wearisome to examine in detail the several pages of close print in which Mr. Bancroft exploits his hatred of these two historic characters; but a few examples illustrate the tenor of the whole.[47]

Chittenden then demonstrates the groundlessness of one statement after another and concludes by asking whether "Irving was so simple as to suppose that he would escape detection at the bar of history if he departed knowingly from the facts?"[48]

Mrs. Frances F. Victor, who became a writer for Bancroft in 1878 and worked for him for eleven years? According to William A. Morris, Mrs. Victor wrote only portions of *History of the Northwest Coast;* see Morris' "Historian of the Northwest," *Oregon Historical Quarterly,* Vol. III (1902), 433. In view of Mrs. Victor's admitted liking for *Astoria,* as well as for *The Adventures of Captain Bonneville* (see her *River of the West,* iii, quoted below on p. xliii), it does not seem likely that she could have been responsible for the hostility concerning *Astoria* and the bitter denunciation of both Bonneville and Irving.

[47] *History of the American Fur Trade of the Far West,* I, 244–45.

[48] *Ibid.,* 246. Another refutation of Bancroft's charges against Astor and Irving appears in P. Koch, "The Story of Astoria, with a Sketch of the Pacific Fur Company," *Magazine of American History,* Vol. XIII (1885), 269–76. In Koch's opinion, Bancroft was "so strongly influenced by personal bias, that not only his judgment but his statements of facts have been warped by it. . . . The chapters devoted to [*Astoria*] . . .

Even more recently, similar charges have been directed against Irving's reliability. For example, Homer C. Hockett, well-known American historian and author of a handbook on research in American history, declared in an essay on "The Literary Motive in Writing History" that

> Like Prescott, Irving was drawn to history as a vehicle of literary expression, and to the end of his career he was the man of letters rather than the historian. . . . It is worthy of remark that the first great success of Irving was the pseudo history of *Diedrich Knickerbocker,* and the interest in this observation lies in the fact that he seems never to have been quite sure where the boundary ran between history and fiction. . . . So much more interested was Irving in form than content that he seldom took adequate pains in the collection of facts.[49]

The *Knickerbocker History,* which was, in fact, a mock history and burlesque of pedantic historians, certainly does not belong in the same class as *Astoria* and *The Adventures of Captain Bonneville,* both of which were motivated by a serious, rather than humorous and satiric, purpose. From what has been presented in this introduction, as well as the evidence assembled in the footnotes of this edition to determine precisely what sources Irving did use and how extensively he used them, the assertion that he was uncertain about the boundary between history and fiction and that he made insufficient effort to collect facts, is patent-

---

appear to be a piece of special pleading, devoted principally to venting the author's spleen against Mr. Irving and Mr. Astor, and the whitewashing of Mr. McDougall." See the first page of Koch's article.

[49] *Mississippi Valley Historical Review,* Vol. XII (1926), 471–72. How strong the feeling became that *Astoria* was largely fictional is evident from the fact that Ernest A. Baker, in his *Guide to Historical Fiction,* 210, includes *Astoria* among the listed books, with the comment: "It is stretching a point to call this fiction; nevertheless, its inclusion here may be justified, as it is a romantic dressing-up of facts vivified by a romantic art, and does not pretend to be historically exact." Irving's introduction is sufficient to disprove this statement about what *Astoria* pretended to be. Going even further than Baker, Bessie Graham, in *The Bookman's Manual: a Guide to Literature* (New York, 1928), 434, lists *Astoria* under the heading "American Fiction—Older Writers." Assuming that such an error might have been corrected in later editions, one turns to *The Reader's Adviser and Bookman's Manual,* revised and enlarged by Hester R. Hoffman (9th ed. New York, 1960), which describes itself (p. 20) as "one of the most widely used book selection tools in the library and book world," and there finds *Astoria* specifically classified as a novel (see p. 934). In contrast, compare Lyle H. Wright, *American Fiction, 1774–1850* (rev. ed. San Marino, 1948), where Irving's fiction is properly listed but *Astoria* is excluded.

Misreading of a statement in the introduction to *Astoria* may have been responsible ly without foundation.[50] We can feel confident that Irving knew his subject, in spite of his paucity of documentation.[51] Working closely with *Astoria* and the hundreds of pages of its sources, the researcher comes in time to respect what Irving says and learns that he should not lightly impugn Irving's accuracy.

This does not mean that *Astoria* is free from error; it is not. But what is impressive is the relative infrequency of such errors, particularly gross errors, when we consider that Irving was not himself a participant in the Astorian enterprise and knew only what had been told him and what he had read.

Not only is *Astoria* generally dependable as history, but it also has literary merit. There is no necessary reason why history should not be well written, and Irving's style has been probably the one quality of his work that has been most persistently praised. It is the chief literary and creative element in *Astoria,* for after mentally digesting the raw material of his sources, Irving presented it in the dress of clear and graceful prose.

Astoria has literary importance in still other ways. By the time it appeared, only one other major American writer had used the American wilderness for creative purposes. Cooper's *Leather-Stocking* Tales were widely read and subsequently imitated, but only one of these romances, *The Prairie* (1827), which presented Natty Bumppo as a western trapper, had its setting in the Trans-Mississippi West, and even it was unreliable as an account of the life it purported to represent. *Astoria,* along with Irving's two other books on the West, must have done much, how-

for the confusion, in part, exhibited by some writers and bibliographers, for there Irving wrote: ". . . the work . . . actually possesses much of that unity so much sought after in *works of fiction,* and considered so important to the interests of *every history.*" Italics supplied.

[50] As respected an authority on the fur trade as Hiram M. Chittenden in 1902 arrived at the same conclusion; see his *History of the American Fur Trade,* I, 240. Chittenden concludes his defense of the historical fidelity of *Astoria* by remarking: "Not in the allurements of style alone but in the essential respect of accuracy and comprehensive treatment, Irving's work stands immeasurably above all others upon the subject." Bernard De Voto also commented on "Irving's usual trustiworthiness" and, in addition, "on the curious decline in reputation which *Astoria* and *Bonneville* have suffered. They are little used by modern writers and yet both are original sources, in some contexts the only sources, and both have remarkable accuracy. Their literary quality is superb." *Across the Wide Missouri,* 426–27. See also J. Neilson Barry, "The Trail of the Astorians," *Oregon Historical Quarterly,* Vol. XIII (1912), 227–39.

[51] There are only six documentary footnotes for the entire book.

ever difficult it is to determine the extent, to awaken an interest in the West as a literary resource and hence to stimulate a gradually emerging frontier literature which attained culmination in Mark Twain thirty years and more later. Frederic L. Paxson recognized the truth of this when he stated: "The literary exploitation of the Far West began at this time, carrying the frontier of letters far beyond the field that James Fenimore Cooper developed in the *Leather Stocking Tales*."[52]

How extensive Irving's influence was in other directions, how much *Astoria* may have drawn attention to Oregon and helped to arouse interest in settlement in that area, is impossible, perhaps, to assess. By coincidence, *Astoria* appeared in the very year that Dr. Marcus Whitman led his wife, Narcissa, and a small group of missionary co-workers across South Pass and into Oregon. Later emigrants followed in increasing numbers. How many of them carried a copy of *Astoria* in their wagons? How many of them, in spite of the *Oregonian and Indian's Advocate*, had formed preconceptions of what they would find along the Platte River, and along the Snake and Columbia, by what they had read in Irving's *Astoria* and *Bonneville*? In the year of the great gold rush to California, Irving's publisher, George P. Putnam, brought out a newly revised edition of *The Works of Washington Irving*. The reviewer in the *North American Review* remarked especially of *A Tour on the Prairies* and *Astoria*:

> These two works, which have all the pleasing characteristics of the author's style, appear very seasonably in a new edition just at the time when the tide of emigration over the prairies of the far West to the shores of the Pacific, after it had slackened for a year or two . . . has just set again with more force than ever, on account of the discovery of the California gold mines.[53]

It would seem most unlikely, whether its effect was small or great, that *Astoria* failed to help American and even European readers to form a conception of that distant and little-known land where a flourishing civilization was to spring up rapidly within the next few decades. One of those readers was the author of another important book on Oregon, the future Mrs. Frances Fuller Victor, who contributed greatly to the

---

[52] *History of the American Frontier, 1763–1893* (Boston, 1924), 333.

[53] Francis Bowen, "Adventures on the Prairies," *North American Review*, Vol. CXLIV (1849), 176.

literary culture of the Northwest. In 1869 she wrote, in her *River of the West*, of the fascination that Irving had held for her:

> When the author of this book has been absorbed in the elegant narratives of Washington Irving, reading and musing over *Astoria* and *Bonneville*, in the cozy quiet of a New York study, no prescient motion of the mind ever gave prophetic indication of that personal acquaintance which has since been formed with the scenes, and even with some of the characters which figure in the works just referred to. Yet so have events shaped themselves that to me Astoria is familiar ground; Fort Vancouver and Walla-Walla pictured forever in my memory. . . .[54]

In depicting one segment of the recession of the frontier, *Astoria* played an important part. After 1836 there gradually emerged a body of literature which displayed that recession in more and more of its numerous facets. Not a single phase of that development has been left untouched by writers, who, with varying degrees of literary and historical merit, have contributed to the preservation of the American heritage. Not the least of these writings, *Astoria* stands, both in time and importance, as one of the first books to depict the early efforts of Americans to turn the western wilderness to their advantage.[55]

[54] *The River of the West*, iii.

[55] For matters concerning Irving, Astor, and *Astoria* not touched on here, three books are especially useful: Chittenden, *History of the American Fur Trade*, I, 163–246, gives a good synopsis of the Astorian undertaking plus an evaluation of *Astoria*; Kenneth W. Porter, *John Jacob Astor, Business Man*, I, 164–290, is indispensable as a well-documented history of the many-sided aspects of the Pacific Fur Company and of the War of 1812 in relation to the fur trade; and Stanley Williams' *Life of Washington Irving*, II, 27–91, carefully examines Irving's return to the United States, his western journey, and his writing of *Astoria*.

IN the course of occasional visits to Canada many years since, I became
intimately acquainted with some of the principal partners of the great
Northwest[1] Fur Company, who at that time lived in genial style at
Montreal, and kept almost open house for the stranger. At their hospitable boards I occasionally met with partners, and clerks, and hardy
fur traders from the interior posts; men who had passed years remote
from civilized society, among distant and savage tribes, and who had
wonders to recount of their wide and wild peregrinations, their hunting exploits, and their perilous adventures and hair-breadth escapes
among the Indians. I was at an age[2] when imagination lends its coloring
to everything, and the stories of these Sinbads of the wilderness made
the life of a trapper and fur trader perfect romance to me. I even meditated at one time a visit to the remote posts of the company in the boats
which annually ascended the lakes and rivers, being thereto invited by
one of the partners; and I have ever since regretted that I was prevented
by circumstances from carrying my intention into effect. From those
early impressions, the grand enterprises[3] of the great fur companies, and
the hazardous errantry of their associates in the wild parts of our vast
continent, have always been themes of charmed interest to me; and I

[1] *North-West* throughout first edition. More properly "North West."

[2] Born in 1783, Washington Irving was twenty years old in 1803 when he visited
Montreal with Josiah O. Hoffmann, his family, and friends; he had become a clerk in
Hoffmann's New York law office the year before. Writing *Astoria* in 1835, Irving was
thus referring here to events in his life that had occurred thirty-two years earlier. As
late as 1851 he alluded, in a letter to H. R. Schoolcraft dated November 10, 1851, to
his meetings with Canadian fur men: "In the course of visits in early life to Canada I
had seen much of the Magnates of the North West Company and of the hearty trappers
and fur traders in their employ, and had been excited by their stories of adventurous
expeditions into the 'Indian Country.' " Quoted in Stanley T. Williams, *The Life of
Washington Irving*, I, 75. Irving's record of that trip, but unfortunately not that part
relating to meetings with the fur traders, has been published as *Journal, 1803* (ed. by
Stanley T. Williams).

[3] Erroneously *enterprise* in Author's Revised Edition.

have felt anxious to get at the details of their adventurous expeditions among the savage tribes that peopled the depths of the wilderness.

About two years ago, not long after my return from a tour upon the prairies of the far West,[4] I had a conversation with my friend, Mr. John Jacob Astor,[5] relative to that portion of our country, and to the adventurous traders to Santa Fé and the Columbia. This led him to advert to a great enterprise set on foot and conducted by him, between twenty and thirty years since, having for its object to carry the fur trade across the Rocky Mountains, and to sweep the shores of the Pacific.

Finding that I took an interest in the subject, he expressed a regret that the true nature and extent of his enterprise and its national character and importance had never been understood, and a wish that I would undertake to give an account of it.[6] The suggestion struck upon the chord of early associations already vibrating in my mind. It occurred to me that a work of this kind might comprise a variety of those curious details, so interesting to me, illustrative of the fur trade; of its remote and adventurous enterprises, and of the various people, and tribes, and castes, and characters, civilized and savage, affected by its operations. The journals, and letters, also, of the adventurers by sea and land employed by Mr. Astor in his comprehensive project, might throw light upon portions of our country quite out of the track of ordinary travel, and as yet but little known. I therefore felt disposed to undertake the

[4] See the Editor's Introduction for Irving's journey into the West. The sources for this important episode in his life are particularly rich. Irving's *A Tour on the Prairies* (1835) is a personal narrative of the journey. See also *The Western Journals of Washington Irving* (ed. by John Francis McDermott). An account of the same trip by Henry Leavitt Ellsworth, at whose invitation Irving made the journey, is in *Washington Irving on the Prairie* (ed. by Stanley T. Williams and Barbara D. Simison). F. A. Sampson (comp.), in "Washington Irving, Travels in Missouri and the South," *Missouri Historical Review*, Vol. V (1910), 27–32, reprints a letter by Irving summarizing his journey. A valuable collateral account by one of Irving's traveling companions is Charles J. Latrobe's *The Rambler in North America*. In addition, see Pierre M. Irving, *The Life and Letters of Washington Irving*, III, 33–43; Stanley T. Williams, *op. cit.*, II, 37–45; and Edgeley W. Todd, "Washington Irving Discovers the Frontier," *Western Humanities Review*, Vol. XI (1957), 29–39.

[5] Irving became acquainted with Astor in Paris, where they met in 1821. Irving was then thirty-eight and Astor fifty-eight. A friendship developed that lasted until Astor's death in 1848, twenty-seven years later.

[6] Astor's proposal must have been made early in September, 1834, for on September 15 of that year Irving wrote to his nephew Pierre Munro Irving to learn whether he would be able to help assemble documents for the projected book. P. M. Irving, *op. cit.*, III, 60–62.

task, provided documents of sufficient extent and minuteness could be furnished to me. All the papers relative to the enterprise were accordingly submitted to my inspection. Among them were journals and letters narrating expeditions by sea, and journeys to and fro across the Rocky Mountains by routes before untravelled, together with documents illustrative of savage and colonial life on the borders of the Pacific. With such materials[7] in hand, I undertook the work. The trouble of rummaging among business papers, and of collecting and collating facts from amidst tedious and commonplace details, was spared me by my nephew, Pierre M. Irving, who acted as my pioneer, and to whom I am greatly indebted for smoothing my path and lightening my labors.[8]

As the journals, on which I chiefly depended, had been kept by men of business, intent upon the main object of the enterprise, and but little versed in science, or curious about matters not immediately bearing upon their interests,[9] and as they were written often in moments of fatigue or hurry, amid the inconveniences of wild encampments, they were often meagre in their details, furnishing hints to provoke rather than narratives to satisfy inquiry.[10] I have, therefore, availed myself occasionally of collateral lights supplied by the published journals of other travellers who have visited the scenes described: such as Messrs. Lewis

[7] Erroneously *material* in Author's Revised Edition.

[8] See Irving's letters of September 15 and October 29, 1834, to Pierre M. Irving in the latter's *Life and Letters of Washington Irving*, III, 60–62, 62–64; quoted in Editor's Introduction, pp. xix–xx, xx–xxi.

[9] Erroneously *interest* in Author's Revised Edition.

[10] For Irving's sources, see Editor's Introduction, pp. xxvi–xxxii. Most of these manuscript sources for *Astoria* have been lost, and in the opinion of Irving's biographer, "collation with Irving's originals is therefore, except in the case of Robert Stuart's journey, impossible." Williams, *op. cit.*, II, 83. Stuart's manuscript journal of 135 pages, still in its original binding, is in the William Robertson Coe Collection of Western Americana at Yale University. It is entitled "Journal of a voyage across the continent of North America from Astoria . . . to the City of New York, kept by Robert Stuart" and runs from June 29, 1812, to May 24, 1813. Stuart later transcribed it, and in a somewhat shortened version it was published in a French translation in *Nouvelles annales des voyages* (Paris, 1821). Irving used Stuart's second version, to which he gave the title "Travelling Memoranda." It was subsequently found in his home at Sunnyside in a cupboard; see Mary C. Withington (comp.), *A Catalogue of Manuscripts in the Collection of Western Americana Founded by William Robertson Coe.* Stuart's journal has been published as *The Discovery of the Oregon Trail: Robert Stuart's Narratives of His Overland Trip Eastward from Astoria in 1812–13* (ed. by Philip Ashton Rollins). The "Travelling Memoranda" also appears in this publication; it has been published separately as *On the Oregon Trail: Robert Stuart's Journey of Discovery* (ed. by Kenneth A. Spaulding).

and Clarke,[11] Bradbury,[12] Breckenridge,[13] Long,[14] Franchere,[15] and Ross Cox,[16] and make a general acknowledgment of aid received from these quarters.[17]

[11] *History of the Expedition under the Command of Captains Lewis and Clark* (ed. by Paul Allen. 2 vols. Philadelphia, Bradford and Inskeep, 1814). The author of this first authentic account of the expedition was Nicholas Biddle, who digested the separate narratives into a single account.

[12] John Bradbury, *Travels in the Interior of America, in the Years 1809, 1810, and 1811* (London, Sherwood, Neely, and Jones, 1817). Irving could have used this edition or the second, published in London in 1819.

[13] Henry Marie Brackenridge, *Journal of a Voyage up the River Missouri; Performed in Eighteen Hundred and Eleven* (2nd ed., revised and enlarged by the author. Baltimore, Coale and Maxwell, 1815). It is possible, but unlikely, that Irving used the shorter first edition, which appeared with the author's *Views of Louisiana; together with a Journal of a Voyage up the Missouri River, in 1811* (Pittsburgh, Cramer, Spear and Eichbaum, 1814).

[14] Edwin James (comp.), *Account of an Expedition from Pittsburgh to the Rocky Mountains, Performed in the Years 1819, 1820 . . . under the Command of Major Stephen H. Long* (2 vols. Philadelphia, H. C. Carey and I. Lea, 1822–23). Also available to Irving was the three-volume London edition of 1823, published by Longman, Hurst, Rees, Orme, and Brown.

[15] Gabriel Franchère, *Relation d'un voyage à la Côte du Nord-ouest de l'Amérique Septentrionale, dans les Années 1810, 11, 12, 13, et 14.* Irving used the original French edition. An English translation did not appear until 1854.

[16] *Adventures on the Columbia River, including the Narrative of a Residence of Six Years on the Western Side of the Rocky Mountains, among Various Tribes of Indians hitherto Unknown; together with a Journey across the American Continent* (2 vols. London, H. Colburn and R. Bentley, 1831). Also available to Irving were an American edition published in New York by J. & J. Harper in 1832 and the third edition, also in two volumes, entitled *The Columbia River; or, Scenes and Adventures during a Residence of Six Years on the Western Side of the Rocky Mountains* (London, H. Colburn and R. Bentley, 1832).

[17] Besides sources alluded to by Irving in his introduction, the following, among other works, were also used. "Wilson Price Hunt's Diary of His Overland Trip Westward to Astoria in 1811–12," in Rollins (ed.), *Discovery of the Oregon Trail*, was available to Irving in a French translation published in *Nouvelles annales des voyages* (Paris, 1821). Three notebooks made by Irving in 1833 contain quotations and paraphrases of western writers which show that he also read Timothy Flint's *History and Geography of the Mississippi Valley* (1828 and after) and Mrs. Mary Austin Holley's *Texas: Observations, Historical, Geographical and Descriptive* (Baltimore, 1833). Obviously this would not have had any value for *Astoria* but possibly would have had for *A Tour on the Prairies*, and therefore added something to Irving's general knowledge of the West. Thomas L. McKenney and James Hall, *History of the Indian Tribes of North America* (3 vols. Philadelphia, 1838–44), was, in spite of the discrepancy in dates, quoted by Irving in the notebook bearing the title "Notes for Astoria, 1835," and he also read James Athearn Jones, *Tales of an Indian Camp* (3 vols. London, 1829). Irving's notebooks cite several passages from Jones, including a quotation from Charlevoix's *A Voyage to North America*. One page lists the names of Pike, Long, and Carver,

The work I here present to the public, is necessarily of a rambling and somewhat disjointed nature, comprising various expeditions and adventures by land and sea. The facts, however, will prove to be linked and banded together by one grand scheme, devised and conducted by a master spirit; one set of characters, also, continues throughout, appearing occasionally, though sometimes at long intervals, and the whole enterprise winds up by a regular catastrophe; so that the work, without any labored attempt at artificial construction, actually possesses much of that unity so much sought after in works of fiction, and considered so important to the interests of every history.

showing that in addition to James's account of Long's expedition, he also read Zebulon Pike's *An Account of Expeditions to the Sources of the Mississippi, and Through the Western Parts of Louisiana* (Philadelphia, 1810). He cites Jonathan Carver's *Travels Through the Interior Parts of North America* (London, 1778) in the third chapter of *Astoria*. Irving's unpublished western notebooks are in the Seligman Collection of Irvingiana at the New York Public Library.

Although Alexander Ross was one of the Astorians, his *Adventures of the First Settlers on the Oregon or Columbia River* (London, 1849) appeared too late for Irving to use. Internal evidence shows that Irving used *Nouveaux Voyages de Mr. le Baron de Lahontan dans l'Amérique Septentrionale* (1703), by Baron Louis Armand de Lahontan. He also had recourse to Astor's correspondence with various government officials, with participants in the Pacific Fur Company, and with the captains of Astor's ships. Finally, he made use of official records kept at Astoria.

ASTORIA

TWO leading objects of commercial gain have given birth to wide and daring enterprise in the early history of the Americas; the precious metals of the South, and the rich peltries of the North. While the fiery and magnificent Spaniard, inflamed with the mania for gold, has extended his discoveries and conquests over those brilliant countries scorched by the ardent sun of the tropics, the adroit and buoyant Frenchman, and the cool and calculating Briton, have pursued the less splendid, but no less lucrative, traffic in furs amidst the hyperborean regions of the Canadas, until they have advanced even within the Arctic Circle.

These two pursuits have thus in a manner been the pioneers and precursors of civilization. Without pausing on the borders, they have penetrated at once, in defiance of difficulties and dangers, to the heart of savage countries: laying open the hidden secrets of the wilderness; leading the way to remote regions of beauty and fertility that might have remained unexplored for ages, and beckoning after them the slow and pausing steps of agriculture and civilization.

It was the fur trade, in fact, which gave early sustenance and vitality to the great Canadian provinces. Being destitute of the precious metals, at that time the leading objects of American enterprise, they were long neglected by the parent country. The French adventurers, however, who had settled on the banks of the St. Lawrence, soon found that in the rich peltries of the interior, they had sources of wealth that might almost rival the mines of Mexico and Peru. The Indians, as yet unacquainted with the artifical value given to some descriptions of furs, in civilized life, brought quantities of the most precious kinds and bartered them away for European trinkets and cheap commodities. Immense profits were thus made by the early traders, and the traffic was pursued with avidity.

As the valuable furs soon became scarce in the neighborhood of the settlements, the Indians of the vicinity were stimulated to take a wider range in their hunting expeditions; they were generally accompanied on these expeditions by some of the traders or their dependents, who shared in the toils and perils of the chase, and at the same time made themselves acquainted with the best hunting and trapping grounds, and with the remote tribes, whom they encouraged to bring their peltries to the settlements. In this way the trade augmented, and was drawn from remote quarters to Montreal.[1] Every now and then a large body of Ottawas, Hurons, and other tribes who hunted the countries bordering on the great lakes, would come down in a squadron of light canoes, laden with beaver skins, and other spoils of their year's hunting. The canoes would be unladen, taken on shore, and their contents disposed in order. A camp of birch bark would be pitched outside of the town, and a kind of primitive fair opened with that grave ceremonial so dear to the Indians. An audience would be demanded of the governor-general, who would hold the conference with becoming state, seated in an elbow-chair, with the Indians ranged in semicircles before him, seated on the ground, and silently smoking their pipes. Speeches would be made, presents exchanged, and the audience would break up in universal good humor.

Now would ensue a brisk traffic with the merchants, and all Montreal would be alive with naked Indians running from shop to shop, bargaining for arms, kettles, knives, axes, blankets, bright-colored cloths, and other articles of use or fancy; upon all which, says an old French writer,[2]

---

[1] Montreal was founded at the base of Mount Royal as a religious colony in 1642 by French missionaries led by Paul de Chomedy, Sieur de Maisonneuve, of the Order of Sulpicians. As the fur trade developed in Canada, Montreal became its financial center.

[2] Baron Louis Armand de Lahontan (1666–1715), who served in Canada in the late seventeenth century. His *Nouveaux voyages . . . dans l'Amérique Septentrionale* was published in 1703; Irving quotes him below. A two-volume English translation, *New Voyages to North-America* (ed. by Reuben Gold Thwaites), was published in 1905.

the merchants were sure to clear at least two hundred per cent. There was no money used in this traffic, and, after a time, all payment in spirituous liquors was prohibited, in consequence of the frantic and frightful excesses and bloody brawls which they were apt to occasion.

Their wants and caprices being supplied, they would take leave of the governor, strike their tents, launch their canoes, and ply their way up the Ottawa to the lakes.

A new and anomalous class of men gradually grew out of this trade. These were called *coureurs des bois*, rangers of the woods; originally men who had accompanied the Indians in their hunting expeditions, and made themselves acquainted with remote tracts and tribes; and who now became, as it were, peddlers of the wilderness. These men would set out from Montreal with canoes well stocked with goods, with arms and ammunition, and would make their way up the mazy and wandering rivers that interlace the vast forests of the Canadas, coasting the most remote lakes, and creating new wants and habitudes among the natives. Sometimes they sojourned for months among them, assimilating to their tastes and habits with the happy facility of Frenchmen, adopting in some degree the Indian dress, and not unfrequently taking to themselves Indian wives.

Twelve, fifteen, eighteen months would often elapse without any tidings of them, when they would come sweeping their way down the Ottawa in full glee, their canoes laden down with packs of beaver skins. Now came their turn for revelry and extravagance. "You would be amazed," says an old writer already quoted, "if you saw how lewd these peddlers are when they return; how they feast and game, and how prodigal they are, not only in their clothes, but upon their sweethearts. Such of them as are married have the wisdom to retire to their own houses; but the bachelors act just as an East Indiaman and pirates are wont to do; for they lavish, eat, drink, and play all away as long as the goods hold out; and when these are gone, they even sell their embroidery, their lace, and their clothes. This done, they are forced upon a new voyage for subsistence."[3]

Many of these *coureurs des bois* became so accustomed to the Indian mode of living, and the perfect freedom of the wilderness, that they lost all relish for civilization, and identified themselves with the sav-

[3] La Hontan, v. i, let. 4. (Irving's note) The reference is to Letter IV in Vol. I. See *New Voyages to North-America*, I, 54.

ages among whom they dwelt, or could only be distinguished from them by superior licentiousness. Their conduct and example gradually corrupted the natives, and impeded the works of the Catholic missionaries, who were at this time prosecuting their pious labors in the wilds of Canada.[4]

To check these abuses, and to protect the fur trade from various irregularities practised by these loose adventurers, an order was issued by the French government prohibiting all persons, on pain of death, from trading into the interior of the country without a license.[5]

These licenses were granted in writing by the governor-general, and at first were given only to persons of respectability; to gentlemen of broken fortunes; to old officers of the army who had families to provide for; or to their widows. Each license permitted the fitting out of two large canoes with merchandise for the lakes, and no more than twenty-five licenses were to be issued in one year. By degrees, however, private licenses were also granted, and the number rapidly increased. Those who did not choose to fit out the expeditions themselves, were permitted to sell them to the merchants; these employed the *coureurs des bois*, or rangers of the woods, to undertake the long voyages on shares, and thus the abuses of the old system were revived and continued.[6]

The pious missionaries, employed by the Roman Catholic Church to convert the Indians, did everything in their power to counteract the

[4] The classic account of the Catholic missionary movement in New France is Francis Parkman's *The Jesuits in North America in the Seventeenth Century* (1867).

[5] Such regulations were imposed as early as 1673. See Harold A. Innis, *The Fur Trade in Canada* (Toronto, 1956), 66–67. The pagination of this revised edition is the same as that of the reprint (New Haven, 1962).

[6] The following are the terms on which these expeditions were commonly undertaken. The merchant holding the license would fit out the two canoes with a thousand crowns' worth of goods, and put them under the conduct of six coureurs des bois, to whom the goods were charged at the rate of fifteen per cent. above the ready money price in the colony. The coureurs des bois, in their turn, dealt so sharply with the savages, that they generally returned, at the end of a year or so, with four canoes well laden, so as to insure a clear profit of seven hundred per cent., insomuch that the thousand crowns invested, produced eight thousand. Of this extravagant profit the merchant had the lion's share. In the first place he would set aside six hundred crowns for the cost of his license, then a thousand crowns for the cost of the original merchandise. This would leave six thousand four hundred crowns, from which he would take forty per cent., for bottomry, amounting to two thousand five hundred and sixty crowns. The residue would be equally divided among the six wood rangers, who would thus receive little more than six hundred crowns for all their toils and perils. (Irving's note) The passage is a close paraphrase of Lahontan; see *New Voyages*, I, 100.

profligacy caused and propagated by these men in the heart of the wilderness. The Catholic chapel might often be seen planted beside the trading house, and its spire surmounted by a cross, towering from the midst of an Indian village, on the banks of a river or a lake. The missions had often a beneficial effect on the simple sons of the forest, but had little power over the renegades from civilization.[7]

At length it was found necessary to establish fortified posts at the confluence of the rivers and the lakes for the protection of the trade, and the restraint of these profligates of the wilderness. The most important of these was at Michilimackinac,[8] situated at the strait of the same name, which connects Lakes Huron and Michigan. It became the great interior mart and place of deposit, and some of the regular merchants who prosecuted the trade in person, under their licenses, formed establishments here. This, too, was a rendezvous for the rangers of the woods, as well those who came up with goods from Montreal as those who returned with peltries from the interior. Here new expeditions were fitted out and took their departure for Lake Michigan and the Mississippi; Lake Superior and the Northwest; and here the peltries brought in return were embarked for Montreal.[9]

The French merchant at his trading post, in these primitive days of Canada, was a kind of commercial patriarch. With the lax habits and easy familiarity of his race, he had a little world of self-indulgence and misrule around him. He had his clerks, canoe men, and retainers of all kinds, who lived with him on terms of perfect sociability, always calling

[7] Writing in 1688, Lahontan gave a different impression of these missionary efforts: "These good Fathers lavish away all their Divinity and Patience to no purpose, in converting such ignorant Infidels: For all the length they can bring 'em to, is, that oftentimes they'll desire Baptism for their dying Children, and some few superannuated Persons consent to receive the Sacrament of Baptism, when they find themselves at the point of Death." *New Voyages*, I, 146.

[8] The French established on what is now Mackinac Island the first white settlement in 1670. The name means "place of the big lame person." Mackinac Island lies in the Straits of Mackinac in Lake Huron and is now in the state of Michigan. United States possession of the island resulted from the Treaty of Paris (1783). Astor's American Fur Company maintained an important post here between 1820 and 1840.

[9] In 1688, Lahontan wrote of Michilimackinac: "The *Coureurs de Bois* have but a small settlement here; though at the same time 'tis not inconsiderable, as being the Staple of all the Goods that they truck with the South and West savages; for they cannot avoid passing this way, when they go to the Seats of the *Illinese,* and the *Oumamis,* or to the Bay *des Puants* [Green Bay], and to the River of Missisipi [*sic*]. The Skins which they import from these different places, must lye here some time before they are transported to the Colony." *New Voyages*, I, 146–47.

him by his Christian name; he had his harem of Indian beauties, and his troop of half-breed children; nor was there ever wanting a louting train of Indians, hanging about the establishment, eating and drinking at his expense in the intervals of their hunting expeditions.

The Canadian traders, for a long time, had troublesome competitors in the British merchants of New York, who inveigled the Indian and hunters the *coureurs de bois* to their posts, and traded with them on more favorable terms. A still more formidable opposition was organized in the Hudson['s] Bay Company, chartered by Charles II., in 1670, with the exclusive privilege of establishing trading houses on the shores of that bay and its tributary rivers; a privilege which they have maintained to the present day. Between this British company and the French merchants of Canada, feuds and contests arose about alleged infringements of territorial limits, and acts of violence and bloodshed occurred between their agents.

In 1762, the French lost possession of Canada,[10] and the trade fell principally into the hands of British subjects. For a time, however, it shrunk within narrow limits. The old *coureurs des bois* were broken up and dispersed, or, where they could be met with, were slow to accustom themselves to the habits and manners of their British employers. They missed the freedom, indulgence, and familiarity of the old French trading houses, and did not relish the sober exactness, reserve, and method of the new-comers. The British traders, too, were ignorant of the country, and distrustful of the natives. They had reason to be so. The treacherous and bloody affairs of Detroit[11] and Michilimackinac showed them

[10] As a result of the Treaty of Paris (1763), which ended the French and Indian War, a phase of the Seven Years' War (1756–63), France lost all her territory in North America.

[11] Founded in 1701 by Antoine de la Mothe Cadillac (1658–1730), Detroit passed into English hands when it was captured by Colonel Robert Rogers in 1760. In 1763, from May 9 to October 12, it was besieged by Indians under Pontiac as part of the Indian uprising against British forts, known as Pontiac's Conspiracy, following the French and Indian Wars. Michilimackinac was attacked early in June, when its commander, Captain George Etherington, was captured, along with Alexander Henry and other traders. Twenty soldiers were killed in the conflict, and subsequently seven prisoners held by Ojibwa Indians were murdered. The uprising was widespread and many posts in addition to the above were attacked, including Fort Niagara, Fort Pitt, Fort Ligonier, Fort Sandusky, Fort St. Joseph, Fort Miami, Fort Ouiatenon, Fort Presque Isle, Fort Le Boeuf, and Fort Venango. Bloodshed occurred at all these places: eleven of the garrison at Fort St. Joseph were massacred; Ensign Holmes, commanding Fort Miami, was killed; Fort Venango went up in flames, its garrison slaughtered and its commander, Lieutenant Gordon, burned alive; a wagon train escorted by twenty-four

the lurking hostility cherished by the savages, who had too long been taught by the French to regard them as enemies.

It was not until the year 1766, that the trade regained its old channels; but it was then pursued with much avidity and emulation by individual merchants, and soon transcended its former bounds. Expeditions were fitted out by various persons from Montreal and Michilimackinac, and rivalships and jealousies of course ensued. The trade was injured by their artifices to outbid and undermine each other; the Indians were debauched by the sale of spirituous liquors, which had been prohibited under the French rule. Scenes of drunkeness, brutality, and brawl were the consequence, in the Indian villages and around the trading houses; while bloody feuds took place between rival trading parties when they happened to encounter each other in the lawless depths of the wilderness.

To put an end to these sordid and ruinous contentions, several of the principal merchants of Montreal entered into a partnership in the winter of 1783,[12] which was augmented by amalgamation with a rival company in 1787.[13] Thus was created the famous "Northwest Company," which for a time held a lordly sway over the wintry lakes and boundless forests of the Canadas, almost equal to that of the East India Company over the voluptuous climes and magnificent realms of the Orient.

The company consisted of twenty-three shareholders, or partners, but held in its employ about two thousand persons as clerks, guides, interpreters, and "voyageurs," or boatmen. These were distributed at various trading posts, established far and wide on the interior lakes and

soldiers was driven over the brink of the Niagara River into Devil's Hole. In all, several hundred lives were lost, and property damage amounted to £100,000. For a brief account, see the article on Pontiac in the *Encyclopaedia Britannica* (11th ed.), XXII, 65–66. See also Francis Parkman, *History of the Conspiracy of Pontiac* (1851). A more recent study is Howard H. Peckham's *Pontiac and the Indian Uprising*.

[12] The earliest combination of rival interests resulting in the formation of the North West Company took place in 1779, although for several years prior to this time there were temporary poolings which were already referred to then as the North West Company. A reorganization in 1783 created a company having sixteen shares, three of which were held by Simon McTavish. The aim of the shareholders was to gain a monopoly over the country west of Lake Superior, but in this they faced strong opposition from the Montreal firm of Gregory, McLeod and Company. See W. Stewart Wallace (ed.), *Documents Relating to the North West Company*, 4–11.

[13] Irving here refers to the union, in 1787, of the North West Company and Gregory, McLeod and Company, whose rivalry had gone so far as to result in the murder of John Ross, a partner in the latter firm. His murder, in fact, precipitated the merger. In this newly organized company, the controlling interest was held by McTavish, Frobisher and Company, in which Simon McTavish was the senior partner. *Ibid.*, 11–14.

rivers, at immense distances from each other, and in the heart of trackless countries and savage tribes.

Several of the partners resided in Montreal and Quebec, to manage the main concerns of the company. These were called agents, and were personages of great weight and importance; the other partners took their stations at the interior posts, where they remained throughout the winter, to superintend the intercourse with the various tribes of Indians. They were thence called wintering partners.

The goods destined for this wide and wandering traffic were put up at the warehouses of the company in Montreal, and conveyed in batteaux, or boats, and canoes, up the river Attawa, or Ottawa, which falls into the St. Lawrence near Montreal, and by other rivers and portages, to Lake Nipising, Lake Huron, Lake Superior, and thence, by several chains of great and small lakes, to Lake Winnipeg, Lake Athabasca, and the Great Slave Lake. This singular and beautiful system of internal seas, which renders an immense region of wilderness so accessible to the frail bark of the Indian or the trader, was studded by the remote posts of the company, where they carried on their traffic with the surrounding tribes.

The company, as we have shown, was at first a spontaneous association of merchants; but, after it had been regularly organized, admission into it became extremely difficult. A candidate had to enter, as it were, "before the mast," to undergo a long probation, and to rise slowly by his merits and services. He began, at an early age, as a clerk, and served an apprenticeship of seven years, for which he received one hundred pounds sterling, was maintained at the expense of the company, and furnished with suitable clothing and equipments. His probation was generally passed at the interior trading posts; removed for years from civilized society, leading a life almost as wild and precarious as the savages around him; exposed to the severities of a northern winter, often suffering from a scarcity of food, and sometimes destitute for a long time of both bread and salt. When his apprenticeship had expired, he received a salary according to his deserts, varying from eighty to one hundred and sixty pounds sterling, and was now eligible to the great object of his ambition, a partnership in the company; though years might yet elapse before he attained to that enviable station.

Most of the clerks were young men of good families, from the Highlands of Scotland, characterized by the perseverance, thrift, and fidelity of their country, and fitted by their native hardihood to encounter the rigorous climate of the North, and to endure the trials and privations of their lot; though it must not be concealed that the constitutions of many of them became impaired by the hardships of the wilderness, and their stomachs injured by occasional famishing, and especially by the want of bread and salt. Now and then, at an interval of years, they were permitted to come down on a visit to the establishment at Montreal, to recruit their health, and to have a taste of civilized life; and these were brilliant spots in their existence.

As to the principal partners, or agents, who resided in Montreal and Quebec, they formed a kind of commercial aristocracy, living in lordly and hospitable style. Their early associations when clerks at the remote trading posts, and the pleasures, dangers, adventures, and mishaps which they had shared together in their wild wood life, had linked them heartily to each other, so that they formed a convivial fraternity. Few travellers that have visited Canada some thirty years since, in the days of the M'Tavishes,[14] the M'Gillivrays,[15] the M'Kenzies,[16] the Frobishers,[17] and the other magnates of the Northwest, when the company was in all its glory, but must remember the round of feasting and revelry kept up among these hyperborean nabobs.

Sometimes one or two partners, recently from the interior posts,

[14] At least four McTavishes were connected at various times with the North West Company. They were Alexander McTavish (1784?–1832), Donald McTavish (d. 1814), John George McTavish (d. 1847), and, the most important of all, Simon McTavish (1750–1804), one of the prime movers in the North West Company. *Ibid.*, 484–86.

[15] No less than eight persons of this name were associated with the North West Company: Archibald McGillivray (*fl.* 1803–1816); Duncan McGillivray (d. 1808); John McGillivray (1777?–1855); Joseph McGillivray (1790–1832); Simon McGillivray (1783–1840); Simon McGillivray, Jr. (d. 1840); William McGillivray (1764?–1825), chief director of the company and for whom Fort William was named; and William McGillivray (1800–1832), a halfblood. *Ibid.*, 469–72.

[16] The Mackenzies included Sir Alexander (1764–1820), famous for his explorations to the Arctic Ocean and the Pacific; Alexander (1767?–1830), a nephew; Alexander (1794–1828), son of John; Andrew (d. 1809), halfblood son of Sir Alexander; Donald (1783–1851), who went into the service of the American Fur Company in 1809 and was one of the overland Astorians with Wilson Price Hunt in 1811–12; Henry (1781?–1832); James (d. 1849); Kenneth (d. 1817); Roderick (d. 1844); Roderick (1772?–1859); Roderick (*fl.* 1804–1821); Roderick (d. 1830); and Roderick (*fl.* 1818–1860). *Ibid.*, 474–79.

[17] The Frobishers were Benjamin (1742?–1787); Benjamin (1782–1818); Joseph (1740–1810), one of the outstanding men in the North West Company; and Thomas (1744–1788). *Ibid.*, 446–47.

would make their appearance in New York, in the course of a tour of pleasure and curiosity. On these occasions there was always a degree of magnificence of the purse about them, and a peculiar propensity to expenditure at the goldsmith's and jewelers' for rings, chain, brooches, necklaces, jeweled watches, and other rich trinkets, partly for their own wear, partly for presents to their female acquaintances; a gorgeous prodigality, such as was often to be noticed in former times in Southern planters and West India creoles, when flush with the profits of their plantations.

To behold the Northwest Company in all its state and grandeur, however, it was necessary to witness an annual gathering at the great interior place of conference established at Fort William, near what is called the Grand Portage, on Lake Superior.[18] Here two or three of the leading partners from Montreal proceeded once a year to meet the partners from the various trading posts of the wilderness, to discuss the affairs of the company during the preceding year, and to arrange plans for the future.

On these occasions might be seen the change since the unceremonious times of the old French traders; now the aristocratic character of the Briton shone forth magnificently, or rather the feudal spirit of the Highlander. Every partner who had charge of an interior post, and a score of retainers at his command, felt like the chieftain of a Highland clan, and was almost as important in the eyes of his dependants as of

[18] In 1802, the post at Grand Portage, established early in the 1780's at the most easterly tip of what is now Minnesota, was moved because it lay within U.S. territory, to a new site farther north, where it was beyond the interference of American officials, and renamed Fort William. Paul Chrisler Phillips states: "In 1798, Roderick Mackenzie rediscovered a long-forgotten French route from the northern shore of Lake Superior, up Dog River to Dog Lake, thence by Mille Lacs to Lac La Croix, where it joined the Grand Portage route." *The Fur Trade*, II, 293. The new post, built about 1803, was situated "where Dog River empties into Lake Superior." *Ibid.*, 294.

Gabriel Franchère, one of the Astorians, returning across Canada to Montreal in 1814, visited Fort William and has left a valuable description. Because Franchère was one of his principal sources, Irving must have been acquainted with this account. See Franchère's *Narrative of a Voyage to the Northwest Coast of America*, in *Early Western Travels* (ed. by Reuben Gold Thwaites), VI, 386–89 (cited hereafter as Franchère, *Narrative*). Irving also read Ross Cox, whose *Adventures on the Columbia River* (1831), Chap. 27, also contains a good description of Fort William; see Ross Cox, *The Columbia River* (ed. by Edgar I. Stewart and Jane R. Stewart), 330–33. Irving apparently drew some details, lacking in the above two narratives, from one or more unidentified sources. For a modern essay on this fort, see "Fort William of the Fur Trade" in W. Stewart Wallace's *The Pedlars from Quebec*, 73–80.

himself. To him a visit to the grand conference at Fort William was a most important event, and he repaired there as to a meeting of parliament.

The partners from Montreal, however, were the lords of the ascendant; coming from the midst of luxurious and ostentatious life, they quite eclipsed their compeers from the woods, whose forms and faces had been battered and hardened by hard living and hard service, and whose garments and equipments were all the worse for wear. Indeed, the partners from below considered the whole dignity of the company as represented in their persons, and conducted themselves in suitable style. They ascended the rivers in great state, like sovereigns making a progress: or rather like Highland chieftains navigating their subject lakes. They were wrapped in rich furs, their huge canoes freighted with every convenience and luxury, and manned by Canadian voyageurs, as obedient as Highland clansmen. They carried up with them cooks and bakers, together with delicacies of every kind, and abundance of choice wines for the banquets which attended this great convocation. Happy were they, too, if they could meet with some distinguished stranger; above all, some titled member of the British nobility, to accompany them on this stately occasion, and grace their high solemnities.

Fort William, the scene of this important annual meeting, was a considerable village on the banks of Lake Superior. Here, in an immense wooden building, was the great council hall, as also the banqueting chamber, decorated with Indian arms and accoutrements, and the trophies of the fur trade. The house swarmed at this time with traders and voyageurs, some from Montreal, bound to the interior posts; some from the interior posts, bound to Montreal. The councils were held in great state, for every member felt as if sitting in parliament, and every retainer and dependant looked up to the assemblage with awe, as to the House of Lords. There was a vast deal of solemn deliberation, and hard Scottish reasoning, with an occasional swell of pompous declamation.

These grave and weighty councils were alternated by huge feasts and revels, like some of the old feasts described in Highland castles. The tables in the great banqueting room groaned under the weight of game of all kinds; of venison from the woods, and fish from the lakes, with hunters' delicacies, such as buffaloes' tongues, and beavers' tails, and various luxuries from Montreal, all served up by experienced cooks brought for the purpose. There was no stint of generous wine, for it was a hard-drinking period, a time of loyal toasts, and bacchanalian songs, and brimming bumpers.

While the chiefs thus revelled in hall, and made the rafters resound with bursts of loyalty and old Scottish songs, chanted in voices cracked and sharpened by the northern blast, their merriment was echoed and prolonged by a mongrel legion of retainers, Canadian voyageurs, half-breeds, Indian hunters, and vagabond hangers-on who feasted sumptuously without on the crumbs that fell from their table, and made the welkin ring with old French ditties, mingled with Indian yelps and yellings.

Such was the Northwest Company in its powerful and prosperous days, when it held a kind of feudal sway over a vast domain of lake and forest. We are dwelling too long, perhaps, upon these individual pictures, endeared to us by the associations of early life, when, as yet a stripling youth, we have sat at the hospitable boards of the "mighty Northwesters," then[19] lords of the ascendant at Montreal and gazed with wondering and inexperienced eye at their[20] baronial wassailing, and listened with astonished ear to their tales of hardships and adventures.[21] It is one object of our task, however, to present scenes of the rough life of the wilderness, and we are tempted to fix these few memorials of a transient state of things fast passing into oblivion;[22]—for the feudal state of Fort William is at an end; its council chamber is silent and deserted; its banquet hall no longer echoes to the burst of loyalty, or the "auld world" ditty; the lords of the lakes and forests have passed away; and the hospitable magnates of Montreal—where are they?

[19] Erroneously *the* in Author's Revised Edition.

[20] Erroneously *the* in Author's Revised Edition.

[21] Irving here recalls his visit to Montreal in 1803. See his introduction.

[22] Here Irving reveals one of his dominant attitudes. As Stanley T. Williams remarked, within Irving "burned one strong response to life, his sadness or romantic melancholy in the presence of the law of change. The underlying idea in all Irving's best essays is that of flux. . . . all declare the terrible brevity of life, the transiency of Man." *Literary History of the United States* (ed. by Robert Spiller *et al.*), I, 247.

*Rise of the Mackinaw Company — Attempt of the American Government
to Counteract Foreign Influence over the Indian Tribes
John Jacob Astor — His Birth-Place — His Arrival in the United States
What First Turned His Attention to the Fur Trade
His Character, Enterprises, and Success
His Communications with the American Government
Origin of the American Fur Company*

THE success of the Northwest Company stimulated further enterprise in this opening and apparently boundless field of profit. The traffic of that company lay principally in the high northern latitudes, while there were immense regions to the south and west, known to abound with valuable peltries; but which, as yet, had been but little explored by the fur trader. A new association of British merchants was therefore formed, to prosecute the trade in this direction. The chief factory was established at the old emporium of Michilimackinac, from which place the association took its name, and was commonly called the Mackinaw Company.[1]

While the Northwesters continued to push their enterprises into the hyperborean regions from their stronghold at Fort William, and to hold almost sovereign sway over the tribes of the upper lakes and rivers, the Mackinaw Company sent forth their light pirogues and barks, by Green Bay, Fox River, and the Wisconsin, to that great artery of the West, the Mississippi; and down that stream to all its tributary rivers.[2] In this way they hoped soon to monopolize the trade with all the tribes on the southern and western waters, and of those vast tracts comprised in ancient Louisiana.

[1] Also known as the Michilimackinac Company. See Innis, *The Fur Trade in Canada*, 187, and Phillips, *The Fur Trade*, II, 131 ff.

[2] Green Bay is a large inlet on the west shore of Lake Michigan in present-day Wisconsin. The Fox River connects it to Lake Winnebago, some twenty miles to the south and west. By a system of rivers, lakes, and portages, *voyageurs* could move southwesterly to the Wisconsin River, which flows into the Mississippi below Prairie du Chien. As a reader of Lahontan, Irving must have seen his account of traveling, in 1689, from Green Bay to the Mississippi by this route. See Letter XVI in *New Voyages to North-America*, I, 167–78.

The government of the United States began to view with a wary eye the growing influence thus acquired by combinations of foreigners, over the aboriginal tribes inhabiting its territories, and endeavored to counteract it. For this purpose, as early as 1796, the government sent out agents to establish rival trading houses on the frontier, so as to supply the wants of the Indians, to link their interests and feelings with those of the people of the United States, and to divert this important branch of trade into national channels.[3]

The expedient,[4] however, was unsuccessful, as most commercial expedients are prone to be, where the dull patronage of government is counted upon to outvie the keen activity of private enterprise. What government failed to effect, however, with all its patronage and all its agents, was at length brought about by the enterprise and perseverance of a single merchant, one of its adopted citizens; and this brings us to speak of the individual whose enterprise is the especial subject of the following pages; a man whose name and character are worthy of being enrolled in the history of commerce, as illustrating its noblest aims and soundest maxims. A few brief anecdotes of his early life, and of the circumstances which first determined him to the branch of commerce of which we are treating, cannot be but interesting.

John Jacob Astor, the individual in question, was born[5] in the honest little German village of Waldorf, near Heidelberg, on the banks of the Rhine. He was brought up in the simplicity of rural life, but, while yet

---

[3] In 1795, the U.S. Congress, finally acting upon a series of recommendations from President Washington, appropriated $50,000 for goods to be utilized in the Indian trade, and in 1796 passed legislation "to establish trading houses at such posts and places on the western frontiers, or in the Indian country, as he [the President] shall judge most convenient for the purpose of carrying on a liberal trade." Quoted in Phillips, *op. cit.*, II, 74. The act which thus created the government factory system was renewed a number of times in later years until legislation abolished the system in May, 1822. *Ibid.*, 67ff. The earliest trading factories were built in the South. President Jefferson established the first trading posts in the Old Northwest at Detroit and Fort Wayne in 1802. Encouraged by successes at these factories, the government built others at Chicago in 1805, at Sandusky, Michigan, in 1806, and at Michilimackinac in 1808. This factory, as Phillips remarks, "began at once to disturb Canadian traders. It also opened the way for private traders, particularly John Jacob Astor, who soon began to plan to obtain control of the Canadian Southwest Company." *Ibid.*, 81.

[4] Erroneously *expedition* in Author's Revised Edition.

[5] On July 17, 1763, in the duchy of Baden. The best biography of Astor is Kenneth W. Porter's *John Jacob Astor, Business Man*.

a mere stripling, left his home, and launched himself amid the busy scenes of London, having had, from his very boyhood, a singular presentiment that he would ultimately arrive at great fortune.[6]

At the close of the American Revolution he was still in London, and scarce on the threshold of active life. An elder brother[7] had been for some few years resident in the United States, and Mr. Astor determined to follow him, and to seek his fortunes in the rising country. Investing a small sum which he had amassed since leaving his native village, in merchandise suited to the American market, he embarked, in the month of November, 1783, in a ship bound to Baltimore, and arrived in Hampton Roads in the month of January. The winter was extremely severe, and the ship, with many others, was detained by the ice in and about Chesapeake Bay for nearly three months.

During this period, the passengers of the various ships used occasionally to go on shore, and mingle sociably together. In this way Mr. Astor became acquainted with a countryman of his,[8] a furrier by trade. Having had a previous impression that this might be a lucrative trade in the New World, he made many inquiries of his new acquaintance on the subject, who cheerfully gave him all the information in his power as to the quality and value of different furs, and the mode of carrying on the traffic. He subsequently accompanied him to New York, and, by his advice, Mr. Astor was induced to invest the proceeds of his merchandise in furs. With these he sailed from New York to London in 1784,[9] disposed of them advantageously, made himself further acquainted with the course of the trade, and returned the same year to New York, with a view to settle in the United States.

He now devoted himself to the branch of commerce with which he

[6] At sixteen, Astor left his father's butcher shop and went to London to join his brother George. Here he may have been employed by—some say he was apprenticed to—his brother, a manufacturer of musical instruments, or he may have worked for Shudi & Broadwood, also instrument makers, famous for their harpsichords and pianofortes.

[7] John Henry Astor.

[8] One of the traditions, about which there may be some doubt, is that while on board ship crossing the Atlantic, Astor met a fellow German returning from London, where he sold furs at higher prices than he could in New York and where he invested his proceeds in goods to be sold, in turn, in America, Porter, *op. cit.*, I, 11.

[9] Porter suggests the possibility that this date may be a year too early, reasoning that Astor's marriage to Sarah Todd in September, 1785, and his desire to open his own shop would have induced him to make the trip to obtain merchandise. *Ibid.*, 26.

had thus casually been made acquainted.[10] He began his career, of course, on the narrowest scale; but he brought to the task a persevering industry, rigid economy, and strict integrity. To these were added an aspiring spirit that always looked upwards; a genius bold, fertile, and expansive; a sagacity quick to grasp and convert every circumstance to its advantage, and a singular and never wavering confidence of signal success.[11]

As yet, trade in peltries was not organized in the United States, and could not be said to form a regular line of business. Furs and skins were casually collected by the country traders in their dealings with the Indians or the white hunters, but the main supply was derived from Canada. As Mr. Astor's means increased, he made annual visits to Montreal, where he purchased furs from the houses at that place engaged in the trade. These he shipped from Canada to London, no direct trade being allowed from that colony to any but the mother country.

In 1794 or '95, a treaty with Great Britain[12] removed the restrictions imposed upon the trade with the colonies, and opened a direct commercial intercourse between Canada and the United States. Mr. Astor was

[10] Astor had started out in New York working for a baker as a peddler of bakery goods. As he became familiar with the city, he developed a knowledge of the fur business by working for Robert Brown, a New York furrier, and for others. He ventured out into the state, going up the Hudson and into other areas to obtain furs from trappers and Indians. At the same time, he sold music, instruments, and musical supplies at his own shop, which he opened in the spring of 1786. Perhaps as early as 1787 he broadened his activities by going to Montreal for furs, and in the next year he advertised pianos and also offered to sell or buy furs. In 1788 he began to import furs from Montreal by way of London, and annually from then on he went to the great Canadian fur mart on business. In this way, he became acquainted with leading Canadian traders; and as his capital grew, his activities as a merchant expanded until by the end of the century, he was one of the leading fur merchants in the United States. See Porter, *op. cit.*, chaps. I and II.

[11] An instance of this buoyant confidence, which no doubt aided to produce the success it anticipated, we have from the lips of Mr. A. himself. While yet almost a stranger in the city, and in very narrow circumstances, he passed by where a row of houses had just been erected in Broadway, and which, from the superior style of their architecture, were the talk and boast of the city. "I'll build, one day or other, a greater house than any of these, in this very street," said he to himself. He has accomplished his prediction. (Irving's note)

[12] Jay's Treaty, which John Jay (1745–1829), sent to England by President Washington, negotiated with Britain's Lord Grenville during the summer and fall of 1794. The treaty was sent to the U.S. Senate in June, 1795, and was ratified in February, 1796. The negotiations and provisions of the treaty are summarized in Phillips, *op. cit.*, II, 33–35.

in London at the time, and immediately made a contract with the agents of the Northwest Company for furs. He was now enabled to import them from Montreal into the United States for the home supply, and to be shipped thence to different parts of Europe, as well as to China, which has ever been the best market for the richest and finest kinds of peltry.

The treaty in question provided, likewise, that the military posts occupied by the British within the territorial limits of the United States, should be surrendered.[13] Accordingly, Oswego, Niagara, Detroit, Michilimackinac, and other posts on the American side of the lakes, were given up. An opening was thus made for the American merchant to trade on the confines of Canada, and within the territories of the United States. After an interval of some years, about 1807, Mr. Astor embarked in this trade on his own account. His capital and resources had by this time greatly augmented, and he had risen from small beginnings to take his place among the first merchants and financiers of the country. His genius had ever been in advance of his circumstances, prompting him to new and wide fields of enterprise beyond the scope of ordinary merchants. With all his enterprise and resources, however, he soon found the power and influence of the Michilimackinac (or Mackinaw) Company too great for him, having engrossed most of the trade within the American borders.[14]

A plan had to be devised to enable him to enter into successful competition. He was aware of the wish of the American government, already stated, that the fur trade within its boundaries should be in the hands of American citizens, and of the ineffectual measures it had taken to accomplish that object. He now offered, if aided and protected by government, to turn the whole of that trade into American channels. He was invited to unfold his plans to government, and they were warmly approved, though the executive could give no direct aid.

Thus countenanced, however, he obtained, in 1809, a charter from

[13] The treaty provided that such posts should be abandoned by June 1, 1796.

[14] Irving seems to be referring here to Astor's offer at one time to purchase the Michilimackinac Company. Had he succeeded in doing so, most of the fur trade south of the Canadian border would have fallen into American hands, whereas this area had been a prime source of Canadian furs. Two Canadian companies, who were partners in the North West Company, offered to Astor the possibility of a joint purchase, but for reasons not disclosed, the proposed transaction was never consummated. See Phillips, *op. cit.*, II, 137–38.

the legislature of the State of New York, incorporating a company under the name of "The American Fur Company,"[15] with a capital of one million of dollars, with the privilege of increasing it to two millions.[16] The capital was furnished by himself—he, in fact, constituted the company; for, though he had a board of directors,[17] they were merely nominal; the whole business was conducted on his plans and with his resources, but he preferred to do so under the imposing and formidable aspect of a corporation, rather than in his individual name, and his policy was sagacious and effective.[18]

As the Mackinaw Company still continued its rivalry, and as the fur trade would not advantageously admit of competition, he made a new arrangement in 1811, by which, in conjunction with certain partners of the Northwest Company, and other persons engaged in the fur trade, he bought out the Mackinaw Company, and merged that and the American Fur Company into a new association, to be called the "Southwest Company."[19] This he likewise did with the privity and approbation of the American government.

By this arrangement Mr. Astor became proprietor of one half of the Indian establishments and goods which the Mackinaw Company had

[15] See below, Chapter III, pp. 32–33 and note 30; see also Porter, *op. cit.*, I, 164ff.

[16] This privilege could be exercised after the expiration of two years. "An Act to incorporate the American fur company," in Porter, *op. cit.*, I, 415.

[17] The board of directors was to consist of nine shareholders. *Ibid.*, 416.

[18] Porter verifies this statement and further characterizes Astor's intention by writing: "It was his purpose to concentrate the western fur trade in the hands of only such American citizens as had been born in Waldorf, Germany, in 1763, and had arrived in the United States from London in the spring of 1784. He had grave doubts whether more than one merchant could be found who would conform to these rather rigid qualifications." *Ibid.*, 169.

[19] Fearful of Astor's competition in the Great Lakes area, the Montreal Michilimackinac Company (composed of McTavish, McGillivrays & Co. and Forsyth, Richardson & Co.) and the North West Company formed an agreement with him—that is, the American Fur Company—in January, 1811, to create the South West Fur Company for the sole purpose of eliminating the financial losses arising from their opposition to each other. The company was to last for five years, each party to share equally in profits and losses. One significant aspect of the agreement was that the North West Company was to withdraw from any trading within U.S. territory and Astor was to do the same with respect to Canada. The imposition of such limitations, however, did not extend to the Missouri River, the Rocky Mountains, or the Pacific Coast. Thus Astor and the North West Company could be allies in one area and competitors in another. See *ibid.*, 253–55; for the "Articles of Agreement for the South West Fur Company, January 28, 1811," see *ibid.*, 461–69. The "Articles of Agreement" are also printed in Wallace (ed.), *Documents*, 239–45.

within the territory of the Indian country in the United States, and it was understood that the whole was to be surrendered into his hands at the expiration of five years, on condition that the American Company would not trade within the British dominions.

Unluckily, the war which broke out in 1812 between Great Britain and the United States suspended the association; and, after the war, it was entirely dissolved; Congress having passed a law prohibiting the British fur traders from prosecuting their enterprises within the territories of the United States.[20]

[20] This law, passed on April 29, 1816, provided that "licenses to trade with the Indians within the territorial limits of the United States shall not be granted to any but citizens of the United States." Quoted in Porter, *op. cit.*, II, 694. Although there is no proof that Astor was the instigator of this law, it was nonetheless one which he had every reason to desire.

Fur Trade in the Pacific — American Coasting Voyages
Russian Enterprises — Discovery of the Columbia River
Carver's Project to Found a Settlement There — Mackenzie's Expedition
Lewis and Clarke's Journey Across the Rocky Mountains
Mr. Astor's Grand Commercial Scheme
His Correspondence on the Subject with Mr. Jefferson
His Negotiations with the Northwest Company
His Steps to Carry His Scheme into Effect

WHILE the various companies we have noticed were pushing their enterprises far and wide in the wilds of Canada, and along the course of the great western waters, other adventurers, intent on the same objects, were traversing the watery wastes of the Pacific and skirting the northwest coast of America. The last voyage of that renowned but unfortunate discoverer, Captain Cook, had made known the vast quantities of the sea-otter[1] to be found along that coast, and the immense prices to be obtained for its fur in China.[2] It was as if a new gold coast had been discovered. Individuals from various countries dashed into this lucrative traffic, so that in the year 1792, there were twenty-one vessels under different flags, plying along the coast and trading with the natives. The greater part of them were American, and owned by Boston merchants.[3] They generally remained on the coast and about the adjacent seas, for two years, carrying on as wandering and adventurous a commerce on the

[1] See Victor B. Scheffer, "The Sea Otter on the Washington Coast," *Pacific Northwest Quarterly*, Vol. XXXI (1940), 371–88.

[2] The fur trade with China resulted from Captain James Cook's voyage to the Northwest Coast in 1778. Bartering with inexpensive trinkets, Cook's men obtained sea-otter pelts from the Indians with which to replace their worn-out clothing. In China they learned that these furs would bring high prices—as much as $120 for a good skin. One crew member sold his pelts for $800. Phillips, *The Fur Trade*, II, 40–41. Rapidly a profitable business in furs began to develop, with net profits in a single year reaching as high as $200,000 or more. Bancroft reported that over one hundred American ships engaged in this trade during the years 1793 to 1818. See *ibid.*, 57, for statistics relating to the number of sea-otter pelts alone shipped to China between 1804 and 1832. In chap. XXXIII, Phillips surveys the sea-otter trade with China.

[3] For reasons why Americans enjoyed an advantage over British traders on the Northwest Coast, see *ibid.*, 53.

water as did the traders and trappers on land. Their trade extended along the whole coast from California to the high northern latitudes. They would run in near shore, anchor, and wait for the natives to come off in their canoes with peltries. The trade exhausted at one place, they would up anchor and off to another. In this way they would consume the summer, and when autumn came on, would run down to the Sandwich Islands[4] and winter in some friendly and plentiful harbor. In the following year they would resume their summer trade, commencing at California and proceeding north; and, having in the course of the two seasons collected a sufficient cargo of peltries, would make the best of their way to China. Here they would sell their furs, take in teas, nankeens, and other merchandise, and return to Boston, after an absence of two or three years.

The people, however, who entered most extensively and effectively in the fur trade of the Pacific, were the Russians.[5] Instead of making casual voyages, in transient ships, they established regular trading houses in the high latitudes, along the northwest coast of America, and upon the chain of the Aleutian Islands between Kamtschatka and the promontory of Alaska.

To promote and protect these enterprises, a company[6] was incorporated by the Russian government with exclusive privileges, and a capital of two hundred and sixty thousand pounds sterling; and the sovereignty of that part of the American continent, along the coast of which the posts had been established, was claimed by the Russian crown, on the plea that the land had been discovered and occupied by its subjects.

As China was the grand mart for the furs collected in these quarters, the Russians had the advantage over their competitors in the trade. The latter had to take their peltries to Canton, which, however, was a mere

[4] The Hawaiian Islands. Captain James Cook (1728–1779), credited with the discovery of the islands in 1778, named them in honor of Edward Montague, Earl of Sandwich (1625–1672).

On the role of the Hawaiian Islands in the fur trade, see Harold Whitman Bradley, "The Hawaiian Islands and the Pacific Fur Trade, 1785–1813," *Pacific Northwest Quarterly*, Vol. XXX (1939), 275–99.

[5] Russian knowledge of the Pacific Northwest and of Alaska dates from 1741, when an expedition headed by Vitus Bering, a Danish navigator in the service of the czar, explored the Alaskan coast southward to Sitka. The Russians gradually moved farther south and in time gained a foothold in California.

[6] The Russian-American Fur Company, founded by Nikolai Petrovich Rezanov (1764–1807) late in the eighteenth century. The monopoly, which ran for twenty years, controlled the Northwest Coast northward from the fifty-fifth degree of latitude.

receiving mart, from whence they had to be distributed over the interior of the empire and sent to the northern parts, where there was the chief consumption. The Russians, on the contrary, carried their furs, by a shorter voyage, directly to the northern parts of the Chinese empire; thus being able to afford them in the market without the additional cost of internal transportation.[7]

We come now[8] to the immediate field of operation of the great enterprise we have undertaken to illustrate.

Among the American ships which traded along the northwest coast in 1792, was the Columbia, Captain Gray,[9] of Boston. In the course of her voyage she discovered the mouth of a large river in lat. 46° 19′ north. Entering it with some difficulty, on account of sand-bars and breakers, she came to anchor in a spacious bay. A boat was well manned,

[7] Russian fur trading in China was prohibited by China in 1791. Thereafter, furs from Russian America could be taken into China only illegally. For a time the Russians chartered American ships for this purpose. See Phillips, *op. cit.*, II, 59–60.

John Jacob Astor's first venture in trading on the Northwest Coast was with the Russians in 1809. An agreement between Astor and the Russian consul general in New York arranged for Astor to exchange supplies for the Russians' sea-otter pelts in Alaska. Late in 1809, Astor sent out the ship *Enterprise* in command of Captain John Ebbets, who conducted a highly profitable business for both parties to the agreement. Further plans for mutual benefit between Astor, the Russian government, and the Russian Fur Company were well advanced when the War of 1812 brought Astor's trading efforts in the Northwest to an end. See *ibid.*, 61–62, 271–72, and Porter, *John Jacob Astor*, I, 171–81, 192–98.

[8] *We now come* in first edition.

[9] Robert Gray (1755–1806) was born in Rhode Island and served in the navy during the American Revolution. In 1787 he and Captain John Kendrick were sent by a number of Boston businessmen to the Pacific Northwest and Nootka Sound to survey the possibilities of the sea-otter trade with China. Gray at first commanded the *Lady Washington* but later transferred to the *Columbia,* which he took to China with furs and then sailed to Boston in the summer of 1790. Here Gray invested some of his own funds, and one month after his arrival he left on the *Columbia* for Nootka Sound, Vancouver Island, which he reached in June, 1791. The following spring he ventured southward along the coast, searching for Indians with furs to trade as well as for the then uncharted and nameless Columbia River, into which he had unsuccessfully tried to sail the year before. He crossed the bar on May 11, 1792, dropped anchor thirty miles above the entrance, and bestowed the name of his ship upon the great river. During this same voyage, he also discovered Gray's Harbor, on the Olympic Peninsula. The later U.S. claim to the country adjoining the Columbia was partly based on Gray's discovery. Astoria was founded eighteen years later on the south shore of the Columbia River estuary. Gray returned to Boston on July 20, 1793, after a second globe-encircling voyage via China. He died of yellow fever in 1806 on the Atlantic and was probably buried at sea. *Encyclopaedia Britannica* (11th ed.), XXVIII; *Dictionary of American Biography*, VII, 522–23; Phillips, *op. cit.*, II, 49–51.

and sent on shore to a village on the beach, but all the inhabitants fled excepting the aged and infirm. The kind manner in which these were treated, and the presents given to them, gradually lured back the others, and a friendly intercourse took place. They had never seen a ship or a white man. When they had first descried the Columbia, they had supposed it a floating island; then some monster of the deep; but when they saw the boat putting for shore with human beings on board, they considered them cannibals sent by the Great Spirit to ravage the country and devour the inhabitants. Captain Gray did not ascend the river farther than the bay in question, which continues to bear his name. After putting to sea, he fell in with the celebrated discoverer, Vancouver,[10] and informed him of his discovery, furnishing him with a chart which he had made of the river. Vancouver visited the river, and his lieutenant, Broughton,[11] explored it by the aid of Captain Gray's chart; ascending it upwards of one hundred miles, until within view of a snowy mountain, to which he gave the name of Mount Hood,[12] which it still retains.

The existence of this river, however, was known long before the visits of Gray and Vancouver, but the information concerning it was vague and indefinite, being gathered from the reports of Indians. It was spoken of by travellers as the Oregon,[13] and as the Great River of the West.[14]

[10] George Vancouver (1758?–1798), English navigator who explored the Northwest Coast between 1792 and 1794. Vancouver Island bears his name. His explorations are recounted in *A Voyage of Discovery to the North Pacific Ocean and around the World* (3 vols., 1798).

[11] Lieutenant William Robert Broughton (1762–1821). See J. Neilson Barry, "Broughton on the Columbia in 1792," *Oregon Historical Quarterly*, Vol. XXVII (1926), 397–411.

[12] Located in the Cascade Range in Clackamas County, Oregon, approximately fifteen miles south of the Columbia River and between forty and fifty miles east of Portland. With an elevation of 11,245 feet above sea level, this extinct volcano is the highest point in Oregon. In 1792, Lieutenant Broughton, attached to Vancouver's exploring expedition, sailed up the Columbia River to the Cascade Range. Mount Hood, whose beautifully symmetrical shape he could see pinnacled in the south, he named in honor of British Rear Admiral Samuel Hood (1724–1816).

[13] The name *Oregon* for the Columbia River originated with Jonathan Carver (see below, notes 16 and 17). The poet William Cullen Bryant, who enjoyed reading Carver's *Travels Through the Interior Parts of North America*, used the name in his poem "Thanatopsis" (1811): "Or lose thyself in the continuous woods / Where rolls the Oregon, and hears no sound / Save his own dashings" (ll. 52–54). And in his poem "The Prairies" (1832) he again wrote of the Oregon: "The beaver builds / . . . among Missouri's springs, / And pools whose issues swell the Oregon / He rears his little Venice" (ll. 92–97). For various theories regarding the origin and meaning of *Oregon*, see George W. Fuller, *A History of the Pacific Northwest*, 348–49, nn. 10–11. See also

A Spanish ship is said to have been wrecked at the[15] mouth, several of the crew of which lived for some time among the natives. The Columbia, however, is believed to be the first ship that made a regular discovery and anchored within its waters, and it has since generally borne the name of that vessel.

As early as 1763, shortly after the acquisition of the Canadas by Great Britain, Captain Jonathan Carver,[16] who had been in the British provincial army, projected a journey across the continent between the forty-third and forty-sixth degrees of northern latitude to the shores of the Pacific Ocean. His objects were to ascertain the breadth of the continent at its broadest part, and to determine on some place on the shores of the Pacific, where government might establish a post to facilitate the discovery of a northwest passage, or a communication between Hudson's Bay and the Pacific Ocean. This place he presumed would be somewhere about the Straits of Annian,[17] at which point he supposed the Oregon

---

T. C. Elliott, "The Origin of the Name Oregon," *Oregon Historical Quarterly*, Vol. XXII (1921), 91–115, and the same author's "Jonathan Carver's Source for the Name Oregon," *ibid.*, Vol. XXIII (1922), 53–69.

[14] Seventeenth-century maps show a mythical river of this name flowing into the Pacific from an equally mythical Western Sea supposedly connected with Hudson Bay. See Bernard De Voto, *The Course of Empire*, 63–74 and map facing p. 57.

[15] *Its* in first edition.

[16] Carver was born in 1710 and died in 1780. In 1766–68 he explored the Great Lakes region and the upper Mississippi River. He kept a journal, but his immensely popular—thirty editions—*Travels Through the Interior Parts of North America* (London, 1778) has been shown to have been in large measure the work of other authorities. See *Encyclopaedia Britannica* (11th ed.), V, 437–38; see also Edward G. Bourne, "The Travels of Jonathan Carver," *American Historical Review*, Vol. XI (1906), 287–302, and Louise P. Kellogg, "The Mission of Jonathan Carver," *Wisconsin Magazine of History*, Vol. XII (1928), 127–45.

[17] Exploration of the Americas was for centuries tied to the search for a northwest passage separating North America from the Asiatic mainland. The mythical Strait of Anian supposedly allowed passage from the Pacific to waters connecting it to the Atlantic. As Bancroft states, "here opened into the broad Pacific the strait of Anian, by which ships, when once the entrance on either side was found, might sail without hindrance from ocean to ocean. Here, on either side the strait, manifold wonders and mysteries had their inaccessible seat for more than two centuries." *History of the Northwest Coast*, I, 3. Chaps. I–VI in this volume survey the concept of what Bancroft calls "the northern mystery." The name was first used on a map of 1574 (see *ibid.*, 53, 54) and thereafter appeared on many maps of North America until careful exploration of the Northwest Coast took place in the late eighteenth century. Many of these early maps are reproduced in Bancroft. The Strait of Anian coincides on some early maps with Bering Strait, and as late as 1821, Lapie's map identified the two; see map in *ibid.*, 98. The strait was also associated with a great river—the River of the West—flowing

disembogued itself. It was his opinion, also, that a settlement on this extremity of America would disclose new sources of trade, promote many useful discoveries, and open a more direct communication with China and the English settlements in the East Indies, than that by the Cape of Good Hope or the Straits of Magellan.[18] This enterprising and intrepid traveller was twice baffled in individual efforts to accomplish this great journey. In 1774, he was joined in the scheme by Richard Whitworth, a member of parliament, and a man of wealth. Their enterprise was projected on a broad and bold plan. They were to take with them fifty or sixty men, artificers and mariners. With these they were to make their way up one of the branches of the Missouri, explore the mountains for the source of the Oregon, or River of the West, and sail down that river to its supposed exit, near the Straits of Annian. Here they were to erect a fort, and build the vessels necessary to carry their discoveries by sea into effect. Their plan had the sanction of the British government, and grants and other requisites were nearly completed, when the breaking out of the American Revolution once more defeated the undertaking.[19]

The expedition of Sir Alexander Mackenzie[20] in 1793, across the con-

from a great inland lake or sea to the ocean. Irving, reading Carver's *Travels* must have examined his map (reproduced in Bancroft, *op. cit.*, I, 132), which shows the River of the West flowing into a body of water, the northern extent of which is labeled "Strait of Anian." In his text, Carver refers to "the River Oregon, or the River of the West, that flows into the Pacific Ocean at the straits of Annian [*sic*; note Irving's same spelling]." Quoted in Bancroft, *op. cit.*, I, 133–34n. It should be mentioned that Carver's claim for such geographical features was based upon rumor and conjecture rather than upon knowledge. See also De Voto, *The Course of Empire*, 62–63, 284–85.

[18] Carver's Travels, Introd. p. iii. Philad. 1796. (Irving's note)

[19] Carver's Travels, p. 360. Philad. 1796. (Irving's note)

[20] Knighted in 1802 for his brilliant success as an explorer, Mackenzie (1764–1820), as a member of the North West Company, made his first great discovery in 1789 by exploring the Mackenzie River to its mouth in the Arctic Sea, hoping thereby to find a river to the Pacific Ocean. Three years later, in October, 1792, he set out from Fort Chipewyan, on Lake Athabasca, on his journey to the Pacific. He had nine men with him, including Alexander McKay, who was later to become one of the Astorians lost in the *Tonquin* disaster. After great difficulty, he crossed the Canadian Rockies and stood at last on what he supposed was the Columbia River but which proved to be the Fraser. Heeding the advice of Indians, he decided not to follow the Fraser. He traveled overland with Indian guides to the Bella Coola River, which he descended. He reached the sea some distance north of Vancouver Island, having on this journey accomplished the first overland crossing to the ocean in the northern part of the continent. For a brief résumé of Mackenzie's journey, see Fuller, *op. cit.*, 59–60. A good synopsis is given in Bancroft, *op. cit.*, I, 666–703. See also Gordon C. Davidson, *The North West*

tinent to the Pacific Ocean, which he reached in lat. 52° 20′ 48″, again suggested the possibility of linking together the trade of both sides of the continent. In lat. 52° 30′ he had descended a river for some distance which flowed towards the south, and was called by the natives Tacoutche Tesse,[21] and which he erroneously supposed to be the Columbia. It was afterwards ascertained that it emptied itself in lat. 49°, whereas the mouth of the Columbia is about three degrees further south.

When Mackenzie some years subsequently published an account of his expeditions,[22] he suggested the policy of opening an intercourse between the Atlantic and Pacific oceans, and forming regular establishments through the interior and at both extremes, as well as along the coasts and islands. By this means, he observed, the entire command of the fur trade of North America might be obtained from lat. 48° north, to the pole, excepting that portion held by the Russians, for as to the American adventurers who had hitherto enjoyed the traffic along the northwest coast, they would instantly disappear, he added, before a well regulated trade.

A scheme of this kind, however, was too vast and hazardous for individual enterprise; it could only be undertaken by a company under the sanction and protection of a government; and as there might be a clashing of claims between the Hudson's Bay and Northwest Company, the one holding by right of charter, the other by right of possession, he proposed that the two companies should coalesce in this great undertaking. The long-cherished jealousies of these two companies, however, were too deep and strong to allow them to listen to such counsel.[23]

In the meantime the attention of the American government was attracted to the subject, and the memorable expedition under Messrs. Lewis and Clarke, fitted out. These gentlemen, in 1804, accomplished

---

Company, 50–68, and De Voto, *The Course of Empire*, 310–12, 348–55. Mackenzie's own account is given in his *Voyages on the River St. Lawrence and through the Continent of North America to the Frozen and Pacific Oceans* (London, 1801). From Irving's reference it would appear that he used Mackenzie's *Voyages* as a source.

Earlier in his career Mackenzie had been a clerk in the firm of Finlay, Gregory and Company (later Gregory, McLeod and Company) and when the merger with the North West Company took place, Mackenzie became a partner. For a summary of his career, see Wallace (ed.), *Documents*, 474–75, and Phillips, *op. cit.*, II, 279–83.

[21] A northern branch of the Fraser River.

[22] See note 20 above.

[23] For Mackenzie's role in seeking a monopolistic merger of the North West Company and the Hudson's Bay Company, see Phillips, *op. cit.*, II, 340ff.

the enterprise which had been projected by Carver and Whitworth, in 1774. They ascended the Missouri, passed through the stupendous gates of the Rocky Mountains, hitherto unknown to white men; discovered and explored the upper waters of the Columbia, and followed that river down to its mouth, where their countryman, Gray, had anchored about twelve years previously. Here they passed the winter, and returned across the mountains in the following spring. The reports published by them of their expedition, demonstrated the practicability of establishing a line of communication across the continent, from the Atlantic to the Pacific Ocean.[24]

[24] The long, unprecedented trek of the Lewis and Clark expedition required nearly three years: from May 13, 1804, to September, 1806, when it returned to St. Louis. Meriwether Lewis was born in Virginia in 1774 and died under mysterious circumstances in 1809. Experience at numerous frontier posts had taught him the ways and languages of Indians. When Thomas Jefferson was elected President of the United States in 1801, he selected Lewis, with whom he had long been acquainted, as his personal secretary, and two years later entrusted him with carrying out his long-cherished dream of exploring the Far West and finding a route to the Pacific, a matter rendered all the more necessary as a consequence of the Louisiana Purchase (1803). Congress sanctioned the proposal with an appropriation of $2,500. Lewis chose William Clark (1770–1838), also seasoned in Indian campaigns, as his second-in-command and assembled some thirty men late in 1803 at their base camp at Rivière du Bois, on the Illinois side of the Mississippi opposite the Missouri River. Starting out in the following spring, they ascended the Missouri in one keelboat and two pirogues as far as the Mandan villages (in what is now North Dakota), wintered here (1804–1805), resumed their journey on the Missouri the next spring, and crossed the Rocky Mountains to the Columbia. Down this river they sailed to its mouth, wintering that year (1805–1806) at Fort Clatsop (erected only a few miles south of where Astoria would be built five years later). They began their return journey on March 23, 1806, and reached St. Louis in the following September. The immediate effect of their return to civilization after an absence of two and one-half years was to stimulate the development of the fur trade on the upper Missouri and in the mountains to the west. Fur-bearing animals, notably the beaver, appeared to be one material advantage which the new country offered for immediate exploitation. Lewis urged government encouragement of merchants and fur hunters to develop trade with the distant Indians, thereby providing a means for controlling them and at the same time excluding the North West Company from these areas. The independent trapper could teach the Indians how to catch beaver with steel traps. "He seems," Lewis wrote, "to form a very necessary link in that chain which is to unite these [Indian] nations and ourselves in a state of commercial enterprise." *History of the Expedition under the Command of Captains Lewis and Clark*, III, 311.

The most nearly complete record of the expedition is in *Original Journals of the Lewis and Clark Expedition, 1804–1806* (ed. by Reuben Gold Thwaites). See also note 11 in Irving's introduction above. A good narrative of the expedition is John E. Bakeless, *Lewis and Clark, Partners in Discovery*. A summary of the principal features of the expedition is in Fuller, *op. cit.*, 61–75.

It was then that the idea presented itself to the mind of Mr. Astor, of grasping with his individual hand this great enterprise, which for years had been dubiously yet desirously contemplated by powerful associations and maternal governments. For some time he revolved the idea in his mind, gradually extending and maturing his plans as his means of executing them augmented. The main feature of his scheme was to establish a line of trading posts along the Missouri and the Columbia, to the mouth of the latter, where was to be founded the chief trading house or mart.[25] Inferior posts would be established in the interior, and on all the tributary streams of the Columbia, to trade with the Indians; these posts would draw their supplies from the main establishment, and bring to it the peltries they collected. Coasting craft would be built and fitted out, also, at the mouth of the Columbia, to trade, at favorable seasons, all along the northwest coast, and return, with the proceeds of their voyages, to this place of deposit. Thus all the Indian trade, both of the interior and the coast, would converge to this point, and thence derive its sustenance.

A ship was to be sent annually from New York to this main establishment with reinforcements and supplies, and with merchandise suited to the trade. It would take on board the furs collected during the preceding year, carry them to Canton, invest the proceeds in the rich merchandise of China, and return thus freighted to New York.

As, in extending the American trade along the coast to the northward, it might be brought into the vicinity of the Russian Fur Company, and produce a hostile rivalry, it was part of the plan of Mr. Astor to conciliate the good-will of that company by the most amicable and beneficial

[25] Early in 1808, while seeking a charter for the American Fur Company, Astor had solicited the support of DeWitt Clinton and on January 25 wrote to him that his plan "would be such as to embrace in the course of 4 or 5 years the whole of the fur trade & to extend it to the western ocean . . . and to have a range of Posts or trading houses on the Rout [sic] made by Captain Lewis to the sea." Astor to Clinton, January 25, 1808, Clinton Papers, Columbia University Library, quoted in Phillips, op. cit., II, 270.

The line of trading posts in the interior was an important part of the plan. As Kenneth Porter points out, "the Americans would thus have a distinct advantage over the Canadians, since their line of communications between the source of supplies and the trading country would be much more direct, and moreover the furs could be sent from New York wherever the owners pleased, whereas the Canadians were restricted to London or the United States as markets for their peltries." Op. cit., I, 165. See also below, pp. 33–34.

The post at the mouth of the Columbia was, of course, Astoria, built in 1811 by men taken out on the Tonquin.

arrangements.[26] The Russian establishment was chiefly dependent for its supplies upon transient trading vessels from the United States. These vessels, however, were often of more harm than advantage. Being owned by private adventurers, or casual voyagers, who cared only for present profit, and had no interest in the permanent prosperity of the trade, they were reckless in their dealings with the natives, and made no scruple of supplying them with fire-arms. In this way several fierce tribes in the vicinity of the Russian posts, or within the range of their trading excursions, were furnished with deadly means of warfare, and rendered troublesome and dangerous neighbors.

The Russian government had made representations to that of the United States of these malpractices on the part of its citizens, and urged to have this traffic in arms prohibited; but, as it did not infringe any municipal law, our government could not interfere. Yet, still it regarded, with solicitude, a traffic which, if persisted in, might give offence to Russia, at that time almost the only friendly power[27] to us. In this dilemma the government had applied to Mr. Astor, as one conversant in this branch of trade, for information that might point out a way to remedy the evil. This circumstance had suggested to him the idea of supplying the Russian establishment[28] regularly by means of the annual ship that should visit the settlement at the mouth of the Columbia (or Oregon); by this means the casual trading vessels would be excluded from those parts of the coast where their malpractices were so injurious to the Russians.[29]

[26] See note 7 above.

[27] *Power friendly* in first edition.

[28] The main post and headquarters for the Russian-American Fur Company was located at Sitka, Alaska, on Baranof Island, six miles from the present community of Sitka. It was established by Aleksandr Andreevich Baranov in May, 1799.

[29] Cf. the following portion of a letter from Astor to President Jefferson: "In June 1809, when Mr. Daschkoff was sent to this country, he was charged by his Government to remonstrate to ours against a trade carried on by citizens of the United States to the North West Coast, supplying the Indians with arms & ammunition, which not only afforded the means of killing one another with greater facility, but also endangered their own settlements.—As the [U.S.] Government could not well prevent this, I proposed a plan to Mr. Daschkoff which it was thought would meet the end required, namely, an agreement between the American Fur Company of this country and the American Fur Company of Russia, that the former should supply the latter with all articles which they needed from this country and from Europe, (thus becoming their carriers &c) and to have an establishment at or near [the] Columbia [River]; but not to trade with natives near the Russian Settlements, and by no means to supply them with arms or ammunition. On the other hand the latter not to deal with any transient traders or ships,

Such is a brief outline of the enterprise projected by Mr. Astor, but which continually expanded in his mind. Indeed it is due to him to say that he was not actuated by mere motives of individual profit. He was already wealthy beyond the ordinary desires of man, but he now aspired to that honorable fame which is awarded to men of similar scope of mind, who by their great commercial enterprises have enriched nations, peopled wildernesses, and extended the bounds of empire. He considered his projected establishment at the mouth of the Columbia as the emporium to an immense commerce; as a colony that would form the germ of a wide civilization; that would, in fact, carry the American population across the Rocky Mountains and spread it along the shores of the Pacific, as it already animated the shores of the Atlantic.

As Mr. Astor, by the magnitude of his commercial and financial relations, and the vigor and scope of his self-taught mind, had elevated himself into the consideration of government and the communion and correspondence with leading statesmen, he, at an early period, communicated his schemes to President Jefferson, soliciting the countenance of government.[30] How highly they were esteemed by that eminent man, we may judge by the following passage, written by him some time afterwards to Mr. Astor.

"I remember well having invited your proposition on this subject,[31] and encouraged it with the assurance of every facility and protection

---

nor with the natives at or near Columbia River. This plan was submitted to the Government of the Russian Settlements on the North West course [sic], who approved it." John Jacob Astor, New York, March 14, 1812, to Thomas Jefferson; the letter in its entirety is printed in Porter, op. cit., I, 508–13.

[30] Before communicating with Jefferson, Astor had approached DeWitt Clinton to gain his support for the granting of a charter by the state legislature of New York. Receiving a favorable answer from Clinton, Astor sought the approval of the U.S. government by presenting his plans to Jefferson, who, on April 13, 1808, gave his approbation. But Astor had not waited for Jefferson's opinion, for the application went before the New York Legislature, which, on April 6, granted the charter for the formation of the American Fur Company. Ibid., 166–67; see ibid., 413–20, for "An Act to incorporate the American fur company."

[31] On this point Mr. Jefferson's memory was in error. The proposition alluded to was the one, already mentioned, for the establishment of an American Fur Company in the Atlantic States. The great enterprise beyond the mountains, that was to sweep the shores of the Pacific, originated in the mind of Mr. Astor, and was proposed by him to the government. (Irving's note)

The letter from which Irving quotes is reproduced in full by Dorothy W. Bridgwater, "John Jacob Astor Relative to His Settlement on Columbia River," Yale University Library Gazette, Vol. XXIV (1949), 55–56.

which the government could properly afford. I considered, as a great public acquisition, the commencement of a settlement on that point of the western coast of America, and looked forward with gratification to the time when its descendants should have spread themselves through the whole length of that coast, covering it with free and independent Americans, unconnected with us but by the ties of blood and interest, and enjoying like us the rights of self-government."[32]

The cabinet joined with Mr. Jefferson in warm approbation of the plan, and held out assurance of every protection that could, consistently with general policy, be afforded.

Mr. Astor now prepared to carry his scheme into prompt execution. He had some competition, however, to apprehend and guard against. The Northwest Company, acting feebly and partially upon the suggestions of its former agent, Sir Alexander Mackenzie, had pushed one or two advanced trading posts[33] across the Rocky Mountains, into a tract of country visited by that enterprising traveller, and since named New Caledonia.[34] This tract lay about two degrees north of the Columbia, and intervened between the territories of the United States and those of Russia. Its length was about five hundred and fifty miles, and its breadth, from the mountains to the Pacific, from three hundred to three hundred and fifty geographical miles.

Should the Northwest Company persist in extending their trade in that quarter, their competition might be of serious detriment to the plans of Mr. Astor. It is true they would contend with him to a vast disadvantage, from the checks and restrictions to which they were sub-

[32] In another letter Jefferson wrote with undiminished enthusiasm: "I view it [the Astorian venture] as the germ of a great, free and independent empire on that side of our continent, and that liberty and self-government spreading from that as well as this side, will ensure their complete establishment over the whole. It must be still more gratifying to yourself to foresee that your name will be handed down with that of Columbus and Raleigh, as the father of the establishment and founder of such an empire. . . . With fervent wishes for a happy issue to this great undertaking, which promises to form a remarkable epoch in the history of mankind, I tender you the assurance of my great esteem and respect." Thomas Jefferson to John Jacob Astor, November 9, 1813, in *Writings of Thomas Jefferson* (ed. by Andrew A. Lipscount and Albert E. Bergh. Washington, 1903–1904), XII, 432–34; also quoted by Frederick Merk in "The Genesis of the Oregon Question," *Mississippi Valley Historical Review*, Vol. XXXVI (1950), 596–97.

[33] Rocky Mountain Fort (c. 1805) on Peace River, McLeod's Fort (1805) on McLeod's Lake, Fort St. James (1806) on Stuart Lake, Fort Fraser (1806) on Fraser Lake, and Fort George (1807). Phillips, *op. cit.*, II, 283.

[34] British Columbia

jected. They were straitened on one side by the rivalry of the Hudson's Bay Company; then they had no good post on the Pacific where they could receive supplies by sea for their establishments beyond the mountains; nor, if they had one, could they ship their furs thence to China, that great mart for peltries; the Chinese trade being comprised in the monopoly of the East India Company. Their posts beyond the mountains had to be supplied in yearly expeditions, like caravans, from Montreal, and the furs conveyed back in the same way, by long, precarious, and expensive routes, across the continent. Mr. Astor, on the contrary, would be able to supply his proposed establishment at the mouth of the Columbia by sea, and to ship the furs collected there directly to China, so as to undersell the Northwest Company in the great Chinese market.

Still, the competition of two rival companies west of the Rocky Mountains could not but prove detrimental to both, and fraught with those evils, both to the trade and to the Indians, that had attended similar rivalries in the Canadas. To prevent any contest of the kind, therefore, he made known his plan to the agents of the Northwest Company, and proposed to interest them, to the extent of one third, in the trade thus to be opened.[35] Some correspondence and negotiation ensued. The company were aware of the advantages which would be possessed by Mr. Astor should he be able to carry his scheme into effect; but they anticipated a monopoly of the trade beyond the mountains by their establishments in New Caledonia, and were loath to share it with an individual who had already proved a formidable competitor in the Atlantic trade. They hoped, too, by a timely move, to secure the mouth of the Columbia before Mr. Astor would be able to put his plans into operation; and, that key to the internal trade once in their possession, the whole country would be at their command. After some negotiation and delay, therefore, they declined the proposition that had been made to them, but subsequently despatched a party for the mouth of the Columbia, to establish a post there before any expedition sent out by Mr. Astor might arrive.[36]

[35] Irving is apparently the only authority for Astor's proposal. Porter is uncertain as to just what Astor was doing in Montreal in the autumn of 1808 and says only that it was "likely that he was engaged in negotiating with the two great Canadian companies in an attempt to forestall any too great opposition to his program. . . . He doubtless presented some offer for cooperation or the delimitation of sphere of influence." *Op. cit.*, I, 171.

[36] This party was led by David Thompson, who reached the mouth of the Columbia on July 15, 1811, four months after the first Astorians arrived on the *Tonquin.* How

In the meantime Mr. Astor, finding his overtures rejected,[37] proceeded fearlessly to execute his enterprise in face of the whole power of the Northwest Company. His main establishment once planted at the mouth of the Columbia, he looked with confidence to ultimate success. Being able to reinforce and supply it amply by sea, he would push his interior posts in every direction up the rivers and along the coast; supplying the natives at a lower rate, and thus gradually obliging the Northwest Company to give up the competition, relinquish New Caledonia, and retire to the other side of the mountains. He would then have possession of the trade, not merely of the Columbia and its tributaries, but of the regions farther north, quite to the Russian possessions. Such was a part of his brilliant and comprehensive plan.

He now proceeded, with all diligence, to procure proper agents and

thoroughly accurate Irving was in reviewing the competition between Astor and the North West Company is evident from an examination of a memorial of that company, dated June 30, 1812, to the British government seeking a monopoly over the country west of the Rocky Mountains as a way of forestalling Astor's rivalry. See "Petition of the North West Company for a Charter," in Davidson, op. cit., Appendix L, 285–92. This petition is especially interesting as indicating that more than rivalry in trade was at stake. The writers of the petition stated: "Your Memorialists . . . humbly conceive that the Territorial Possession of the extensive Country bordering on the North West Coast of America, and on the Columbia River will ultimately accompany the Trade now about to be established." Ibid., 291.

[37] It appears, however, that the matter was still unsettled even as late as David Thompson's arrival at Astoria. A covering letter addressed to Astor by Duncan McDougall, David Stuart, and Robert Stuart and dated Fort Astoria, Columbia River, July 22, 1811, reads in part: "Inclosed you will please receive Copy of our correspondence with Mr. Thompson of the North West Company and of extract of a letter addressed to Wm. McGillivray Esqr. Montreal, by the Wintering Partners [of the North West Company], impowering him to accept of your offer of one third of our Concern[.]

"We are happy to learn their decision, as their experience and local knowledge of the Country this side of the Rocky Mountains will enable us the sooner to derive every possible advantage the Country affords." Bridgwater, loc. cit., 52. The letters were carried to Montreal by Thompson.

Thompson's letter to McDougall, D. Stuart, and R. Stuart, dated Columbia River, July 15, 1811, the day of his arrival, reads in part: "With pleasure I acquaint you that the Wintering Partners have acceded to the offer of Mr. Astor, accepting one third share of the business you are engaged in, their share of Capital not to exceed £10.000 without further permission—[.]" Ibid. See also the letter from McDougall, D. Stuart and R. Stuart to Thompson, July 16, 1811, in ibid., 53. The letter to McGillivray from the partners of the North West Company reads in part: "We perfectly coincide with you in opinion that Mr. Astor's expedition to the North West Coast of America, if successful, without the influence of the British Government, or any other check may prove injurious to our Concern & we are willing . . . that you accept the third proposed." Ibid., 53.

coadjutors, habituated to the Indian trade and to the life of the wilderness. Among the clerks of the Northwest Company were several of great capacity and experience, who had served out their probationary terms, but who, either through lack of interest and influence, or a want of vacancies, had not been promoted. They were consequently much dissatisfied, and ready for any employment in which their talents and acquirements might be turned to better account.

Mr. Astor made his overtures to several of these persons, and three of them entered into his views. One of these, Mr. Alexander M'Kay,[38] had accompanied Sir Alexander Mackenzie in both of his expeditions to the northwest coast of America in 1789 and 1793. The other two were Duncan M'Dougal[39] and Donald M'Kenzie.[40] To these were subsequently added Mr. Wilson Price Hunt,[41] of New Jersey. As this gentle-

[38] McKay, who entered the North West Company sometime before 1791, became a partner in 1799. He was with Alexander Mackenzie in 1793 when the latter made his celebrated crossing of the continent to the Pacific, but that he accompanied him to the Arctic is no longer accepted. He retired from the North West Company in 1808, two years before he joined Astor. He lost his life at the hands of Indians in 1811 at the time of the *Tonquin* disaster. He had a halfblood son, Thomas, whose mother eventually married Dr. John McLaughlin, subsequently factor at Fort Vancouver. See Wallace (ed.), *Documents*, 473.

[39] Nothing positive is known about McDougall prior to his becoming a partner with Astor in 1810, but that he was a British subject is evident. Neither his date of birth nor the time of his death is available. That he was before 1810 a clerk in the North West Company is uncertain, but he did enter its service with the transfer of Astoria and remained there until 1817 (see below, Chapter LIV). In 1813 he married the daughter of Chief Comcomly of the Chinooks (for details of this marriage as related by Irving, see pp. 461–63). According to Franchère, *Narrative*, Appendix, he "died a miserable death at Bas de la Rivière, Winipeg." Wallace (ed.), *Documents*, 466.

[40] McKenzie (1783–1851) was a native of Scotland. He went to Canada in 1800 and became a clerk in the North West Company. When Astor formed the American Fur Company in 1809, McKenzie entered Astor's services. Later he returned to the North West Company upon its acquisition of Astoria, became a partner, and went into the Hudson's Bay Company as chief factor in 1821 when it absorbed the former company. In 1833 he retired to Mayville, New York. Wallace (ed.), *Documents*, 477.

[41] Born in Asbury, New Jersey, Hunt (1783?–1842) moved to St. Louis in 1804 and went into partnership with John Hankinson as a merchant. He gave this up in 1810 to go into partnership with Astor. Not only was he, as Irving says, Astor's "chief agent," but, without any experience in the fur trade or beyond the frontier, he became head of the Overland Astorians from St. Louis to Astoria. When Astoria was acquired by the North West Company, Hunt returned to the United States and in 1817 took up farming in Missouri near St. Louis, where, between 1822 and 1840 he served as postmaster. In 1837 he advertised himself as a dealer in furs. See Rollins (ed.), *Discovery of the Oregon Trail*, 17; see also T. C. Elliott, "Wilson Price Hunt, 1783–1842," *Oregon Historical Quarterly*, Vol. XXXII (1931), 130–34.

man was a native born citizen of the United States, a person of great probity and worth, he was selected by Mr. Astor to be his chief agent, and to represent him in the contemplated establishment.

On the 23d of June, 1810, articles of agreement were entered into between Mr. Astor and those four gentlemen, acting for themselves and for the several persons who had already agreed to become, or should thereafter become, associated under the firm of "The Pacific Fur Company."[42]

According to these articles, Mr. Astor was to be at the head of the company, and to manage its affairs in New York. He was to furnish vessels, goods, provisions, arms, ammunition, and all other requisites for the enterprise at first cost and charges, provided that they did not, at any time, involve an advance of more than four hundred thousand dollars.

The stock of the company was to be divided into a hundred equal shares, with the profits accruing thereon. Fifty shares were to be at the disposition of Mr. Astor, and the other fifty to be divided among the partners and their associates.[43]

Mr. Astor was to have the privilege of introducing other persons into the connection, as partners, two of whom, at least, should be conversant with the Indian trade, and none of them entitled to more than three shares.

A general meeting of the company was to be held annually at Columbia River, for the investigation and regulation of its affairs; at which absent members might be represented, and might vote by proxy under certain specified conditions.

The association, if successful, was to continue for twenty years; but the parties had full power to abandon and dissolve it within the first five years, should it be found unprofitable. For this term Mr. Astor covenanted to bear all the loss that might be incurred; after which it was to be borne by all the partners, in proportion to their respective shares.

The parties of the second part were to execute faithfully such duties

[42] The Articles of Agreement of the Pacific Fur Company are in W. P. Hunt MS Book, Missouri Historical Society. They have been published in Flandrau, *Astoria and the Oregon Country*, 24–35. Irving accurately summarizes the main points of the thirty provisions of the agreement.

[43] After Astor's fifty shares, the remaining shares were distributed as follows: five shares each to McKay, McKenzie, McDougall, D. Stuart, Hunt, and Crooks. Later, when Robert McClellan and Joseph Miller entered, two and one-half shares were assigned to each. The remaining fifteen shares were kept in reserve.

as might be assigned to them by a majority of the company on the northwest coast, and to repair to such place or places as the majority might direct.

An agent, appointed for the term of five years, was to reside at the principal establishment on the northwest coast, and Wilson Price Hunt was the one chosen for the first term. Should the interests of the concern at any time require his absence, a person was to be appointed, in general meeting, to take his place.[44]

Such were the leading conditions of this association; we shall now proceed to relate the various hardy and eventful expeditions, by sea and land, to which it gave rise.

[44] Until Hunt reached Astoria and later during his absences, Duncan McDougall served in this capacity.

IN prosecuting his great scheme of commerce and colonization, two expeditions were devised by Mr. Astor, one by sea, the other by land. The former was to carry out the people, stores, ammunition, and merchandise, requisite for establishing a fortified trading post at the mouth of Columbia River. The latter, conducted by Mr. Hunt, was to proceed up the Missouri, and across the Rocky Mountains, to the same point; exploring a line of communication across the continent, and noting the places where interior trading posts might be established. The expedition by sea is the one which comes first under consideration.

A fine ship was provided called the Tonquin, of two hundred and ninety tons burden, mounting ten guns, with a crew of twenty men. She carried an assortment of merchandise for trading with the natives of the seaboard and of the interior, together with the frame of a schooner, to be employed in the coasting trade. Seeds also were provided for the cultivation of the soil, and nothing was neglected for the necessary supply of the establishment. The command of the ship was intrusted to Jonathan Thorn, of New York, a lieutenant in the United States navy, on leave of absence.[1] He was a man of courage and firmness, who had

---

[1] Gabriel Franchère wrote: "The vessel on which we were to sail was called the *Tonquin*, of about 300 tons burden, commanded by Captain Thorn (a first-lieutenant of the American navy, on furlough for this purpose), with a crew of twenty-one men." *Narrative*, 193. Thorn had enlisted in the U.S. Navy as a midshipman in 1800. He saw service in the Mediterranean and in 1803 served under Stephen Decatur on the *Enterprise;* he was cited by Decatur for gallantry at Tripoli. Thorn received a promotion to lieutenant in 1807 and was furloughed in 1810 in order to command the *Tonquin*. *Ibid.*, 193n.

Irving refers to him in the next sentence euphemistically as "a man of courage and firmness." The evidence shows that Thorn was a martinet of the worst sort, ill disposed distinguished himself in our Tripolitan war,[2] and, from being accustomed to naval discipline, was considered by Mr. Astor as well fitted to take charge of an expedition of the kind. Four of the partners were to embark in the ship, namely, Messrs. M'Kay, M'Dougal, David Stuart,[3] and his nephew, Robert Stuart.[4] Mr. M'Dougal was empowered by

to accommodate himself to the civilians on his ship, and heedless to the point of sadism concerning the safety of his men, eight of whom lost their lives because of his despotic sense of duty at the mouth of the Columbia. The loss of his entire crew resulted later from his lack of judgment in handling Indians and his refusal to heed the advice of his officers. Captain Thorn stands in maritime history as an extreme example of naval authority, and in spite of Irving's efforts to temper his behavior, the Captain's harsh and unfeeling discipline cannot be concealed. Franchère minces no words in describing him as "a strict disciplinarian, of a quick and passionate temper, accustomed to exact obedience, considering nothing but duty, and giving himself no trouble about the murmurs of his crew, taking counsel of nobody, and following Mr. Astor's instructions to the letter. Such was the man who had been selected to command our ship. His haughty manners, his rough and overbearing disposition, had lost him the affection of most of the crew and of all the passengers; he knew it, and in consequence sought every opportunity to mortify us." *Narrative*, 207.

Alexander Ross, who also sailed on the *Tonquin*, summed up his opinion of Thorn at the end of the voyage in the following words: "Captain Thorn was an able and expert seaman; but, unfortunately, his treatment of the people under his command was strongly tinctured with cruelty and despotism. He delighted in ruling with a rod of iron; his officers were treated with harshness, his sailors with cruelty, and every one else was regarded by him with contempt. With a jealous and peevish temper, he was easily excited; and the moment he heard the Scotch Highlanders speak to each other in the Scottish dialect, or the Canadians in the French language, he was on his high horse, making every one on board as unhappy as himself." *Adventures of the First Settlers on the Oregon or Columbia River*, in *Early Western Travels* (ed. by Reuben Gold Thwaites), VII, 87 (cited hereafter as Ross, *Adventures*). Cf. Cox, *Columbia River*, 51.

In the drama of the Astorians, the character of Captain Thorn, like that of some protagonist in an ancient Greek tragedy, played a decisive role. Not only did a flaw of character dictate his own destruction but that of many innocent men besides.

[2] American naval action against Tripoli and the Barbary States (1801–1805) brought an end to piracy when the United States resorted to war in preference to paying annual tribute and ransoming captives.

[3] David Stuart (1765–1853) emigrated to Canada from his native Scotland, but his activities before he joined Astor are obscure. He may have been in the service of the North West Company, but this is uncertain. As a partner in the Pacific Fur Company, he built Fort Okanogan, the most important of the interior posts, the construction of which is related in Chapter X. He remained with the American Fur Company after the North West Company acquired Astoria. He retired in 1833 and lived with his nephew, Robert Stuart, in Detroit. See Wallace (ed.), *Documents*, 500.

[4] Born in Scotland, Robert Stuart (1785–1848) went to Canada in 1807 and found employment as a clerk in the North West Company before he joined Astor. As one of the founders of Astoria, he is best known for his heroic journey overland from the Columbia to St. Louis and New York in 1812–13, carrying dispatches to Astor. Later,

Mr. Astor to act as his proxy in the absence of Mr. Hunt, to vote for him and in his name, on any question that might come before any meeting of the persons interested in the voyage.

Beside the partners, there were twelve clerks[5] to go out in the ship, several of them natives of Canada, who had some experience in the Indian trade.[6] They were bound to the service of the company for five years, at the rate of one hundred dollars a year, payable at the expiration

as a partner in the American Fur Company, he served as its agent at Michilimackinac until 1834. See *ibid.*, 500; Rollins (ed.), *Discovery of the Oregon Trail*, which prints Stuart's journal and gives a biographical sketch on pp. xxxv–liii; and Spaulding (ed.), *On the Oregon Trail*, which reprints the "Travelling Memoranda."

[5] Franchère lists the names of all the passengers and all but five or six of the crew. The clerks—eleven in number instead of twelve—were Russel Farnham from Massachusetts and James Lewis and William W. Matthews from New York. The remaining clerks were from Canada: Alexander Ross, Donald McGillis, Ovide de Montigny, Francis B. Pillot (Pillet), Donald McLennon, William Wallace, Thomas McKay, and Franchère himself. *Narrative*, 194. Of these several clerks, only Franchère and Ross kept a written record of the journey of the *Tonquin* and of affairs at Astoria.

Franchère was born in Montreal in 1786. He remained at Astoria until 1814 and then temporarily joined the North West Company while he returned to Montreal through Canada. He became Astor's Montreal agent the following year and subsequently served at Sault Ste Marie and in St. Louis. He finally moved to New York and went into the fur business for himself. He died in St. Paul, Minnesota, in 1863. *Ibid.*, 13–18.

Alexander Ross (1783–1856), a native of Scotland, moved to Canada in 1805 and taught school. With the transfer of Astoria to the North West Company, he continued to serve as a clerk and remained in the Northwest until after 1821, retiring from the fur trade four years later. He was the author of three books: *Adventures*, to which reference has already been made; *The Fur Hunters of the Far West* (2 vols. London, 1855); and *The Red River Settlement* (London, 1856). See Wallace (ed.), *Documents*, 495.

[6] Franchère relates how he himself was engaged as a clerk: "It was in the course of that winter [1810] that one of my friends made me acquainted in confidence with the plan of these gentlemen [the partners], under the injunction of strictest secrecy. The desire of seeing strange countries, joined to that of acquiring a fortune, determined me to solicit employment of the new association; on the 20th of May I had an interview with Mr. A[lexander] M'Kay, with whom the preliminaries were arranged; and on the 24th of the same month I signed an agreement as an apprentice clerk for the term of five years." *Narrative*, 187.

Alexander Ross also tells of how he was invited by McKay to join. He went to Montreal in May "and there, for the first time, I saw the gilded prospectus of the new Company, and, accepting the proposals made to me by Mr. Astor, was the first to join the expedition;—and who at the time would not have joined it, for, although the North-Westerns [North West Company] tried to throw all the cold water of the St. Lawrence on the project, yet they could not extinguish the flame it had spread abroad. The flattering hopes and golden prospects held out to adventurers, so influenced the public mind, that the wonder-stricken believers flocked in from all quarters to share in the wonderful riches of the far west." *Adventures*, 40.

of the term, and an annual equipment of clothing to the amount of forty dollars. In case of ill conduct they were liable to forfeit their wages and be dismissed; but, should they acquit themselves well, the confident expectation was held out to them of promotion, and partnership. Their interests were thus, to some extent, identified with those of the company.

Several artisans[7] were likewise to sail in the ship, for the supply of the colony; but the most peculiar and characteristic part of this motley embarkation consisted of thirteen Canadian "voyageurs," who had enlisted for five years.[8] As this class of functionaries will continually recur in the course of the following narrations, and as they form one of those distinct and strongly marked castes or orders of people, springing up in this vast continent out of geographical circumstances, or the varied pursuits, habitudes, and origins of its population, we shall sketch a few of their characteristics for the information of the reader.

The "voyageurs" form a kind of confraternity in the Canadas, like the arrieros, or carriers of Spain,[9] and, like them, are employed in long internal expeditions of travel and traffic: with this difference, that the arrieros travel by land, the voyageurs by water; the former with mules and horses, the latter with batteaux and canoes. The voyageurs may be said to have sprung up out of the fur trade, having originally been employed by the early French merchants in their trading expeditions through the labyrinth of rivers and lakes of the boundless interior. They were coeval with the *coureurs des bois*, or rangers of the woods, already noticed, and, like them, in the intervals of their long, arduous, and laborious expeditions, were prone to pass their time in idleness and revelry about the trading posts or settlements; squandering their hard earnings

[7] These were Johann Koaster, a Russian, who was ship's carpenter; George Bell, a cooper from New York; Job Aitken, from Scotland, as rigger and calker; and Augustus Roussil, blacksmith from Canada. Franchère. *Narrative*, 194.

[8] They were all French Canadians: Antoine Belleau, J. Baptiste Belleau, Louis Bruslé, P. D. Jeremie, Jacques Lafantaisie, Michel Laframboise, Basile Lapensée, Ignace Lapensée, Oliver Roy Lapensée, Joseph Lapierre, Giles Leclerc, Joseph Nadeau, and Benjamin Roussel. *Ibid*.

Concerning men of this class, Alexander Ross remarked that "the Canadian voyageurs are among the most expert and venturesome canoe men in the world." *Adventures*, 43. Such men would be of invaluable service on the Columbia and other rivers of the Northwest.

[9] A characteristic remark of Irving. Having lived many years in European countries, including Spain, and well versed in their literature, history, and general way of life, Irving frequently tapped his fund of European lore to suggest a comparison to American life and manners. His three Western books often display this inclination.

in heedless conviviality, and rivaling their neighbors, the Indians, in indolent indulgence and an imprudent disregard of the morrow.[10]

When Canada passed under British domination,[11] and the old French trading houses were broken up, the voyageurs, like the *coureurs des bois,* were for a time disheartened and disconsolate, and with difficulty could reconcile themselves to the service of the new-comers, so different in habits, manners, and language from their former employers. By degrees, however, they became accustomed to the change, and at length came to consider the British fur traders, and especially the members of the Northwest Company, as the legitimate lords of creation.

The dress of these people is generally half civilized, half savage. They wear a capot or surcoat, made of a blanket, a striped cotton shirt, cloth trowsers, or leathern leggins, moccasins of deer-skin, and a belt of variegated worsted, from which are suspended the knife, tobacco-pouch, and other implements.[12] Their language is of the same piebald character, being a French patois, embroidered with Indian and English words and phrases.

The lives of the voyageurs are passed in wild and extensive rovings, in the service of individuals, but more especially of the fur traders. They are generally of French descent, and inherit much of the gayety and lightness of heart of their ancestors, being full of anecdote and song, and ever ready for the dance. They inherit, too, a fund of civility and complaisance; and, instead of that hardness and grossness

[10] Nearly 150 years had little changed the character of the Canadian *voyageurs* and *coureurs de bois* since Lahontan described them in 1684: "You would be amaz'd if you saw how lewd these Pedlers are when they return [after a year or more in the wilderness]; how they Feast and Game, and how prodigal they are, not only in their Cloaths, but upon Women. Such of 'em as are married, have the wisdom to retire to their own Houses; but the Batchelors act just as our *East-India-Men,* and Pirates are wont to do; for they Lavish, Eat, Drink, and Play all away as long as the Goods hold out; and when these are gone, they e'en sell their Embroidery, their Lace, and their Cloaths. This done, they are forc'd to go upon a new Voyage for Subsistence."*New Voyages to North-America,* I, 54.

Ross Cox provides an excellent description of *voyageurs,* saying: "There is not perhaps in the world a more thoughtless or improvident race of people." See his *Columbia River,* 354-58.

[11] In 1763.

[12] Irving paraphrases the following passage from Cox: "The dress of a *voyageur* generally consists of a capot made out of a blanket, with leather or cloth trowsers, mocassins, a striped cotton shirt, and a hat or fur cap. . . . They all wear belts of variegated worsted, from which their knives, smoking-bags, &c., are suspended." *Ibid.,* 356-57.

which men in laborious life are apt to indulge towards each other, they are mutually obliging and accommodating; interchanging kind offices, yielding each other assistance and comfort in every emergency, and using the familiar appellations of "cousin" and "brother" when there is in fact no relationship.[13] Their natural good-will is probably heightened by a community of adventure and hardship in their precarious and wandering life.

No men are more submissive to their leaders and employers, more capable of enduring hardship, or more good-humored under privations. Never are they so happy as when on long and rough expeditions, toiling up rivers or coasting lakes; encamping at night on the borders, gossiping round their fires, and bivouacking in the open air. They are dextrous boatmen, vigorous and adroit with the oar and paddle, and will row from morning until night without a murmur. The steersman often sings an old traditionary French song, with some regular burden in which they all join, keeping time with their oars; if at any time they flag in spirits or relax in exertion, it is but necessary to strike up a song of the kind to put them all in fresh spirits and activity. The Canadian waters are vocal with these little French chansons, that have been echoed from mouth to mouth and transmitted from father to son, from the earliest days of the colony; and it has a pleasing effect, in a still golden summer evening, to see a batteau gliding across the bosom of a lake and dipping its oars to the cadence of these quaint old ditties, or sweeping along in full chorus on a bright sunny morning, down the transparent current of one of the Canada rivers.[14]

But we are talking of things that are fast fading away! The march of mechanical invention is driving everything poetical before it. The steamboats, which are fast dispelling the wildness and romance of our lakes and rivers, and aiding to subdue the world into commonplace, are proving as fatal to the race of the Canadian voyageurs as they have been to that of the boatmen of the Mississippi. Their glory is departed. They are no longer the lords of our internal seas, and the great navigators of

[13] Here again Irving paraphrases Cox: "They are remarkably good-natured and affectionate to each other, and it is no uncommon thing to hear one man address his comrade as 'mon frère,' or 'mon cousin,' without any degree of consanguinity existing between them." *Ibid.*, 355. Other passages are also traceable to Cox.

[14] See Marius Barbeau, "The Ermatinger Collection of Voyageur Songs (ca. 1830)," *Journal of American Folklore*, Vol. LXVII (1954), 147–61. This article provides music, texts, and analyses.

the wilderness. Some of them may still occasionally be seen coasting the lower lakes with their frail barks, and pitching their camps and lighting their fires upon the shores; but their range is fast contracting to those remote waters and shallow and obstructed rivers unvisited by the steamboat. In the course of years they will gradually disappear; their songs will die away like the echoes they once awakened, and the Canadian voyageurs will become a forgotten race, or remembered, like their associates, the Indians, among the poetical images of past times, and as themes for local and romantic associations.[15]

An instance of the buoyant temperament and the professional pride of these people was furnished in the gay and braggart style in which they arrived at New York to join the enterprise. They were determined to regale and astonish the people of the "States" with the sight of a Canadian boat and a Canadian crew. They accordingly fitted up a large but light bark canoe, such as is used in the fur trade; transported it in a wagon from the banks of the St. Lawrence to the shores of Lake Champlain; traversed the lake in it, from end to end; hoisted it again in a wagon and wheeled it off to Lansingburgh, and there launched it upon the waters of the Hudson. Down this river they plied their course merrily on a fine summer's day, making its banks resound for the first time with their old French boat-songs; passing by the villages with whoop and halloo, so as to make the honest Dutch farmers mistake them for a crew of savages. In this way they swept, in full song and with regular flourish of the paddle, round New York, in a still summer evening, to the wonder and admiration of its inhabitants, who had never before witnessed on their waters, a nautical apparition of the kind.[16]

[15] A typically Irvingesque attitude, echoing the phrase "a transient state of things fast passing into oblivion." See Chapter I, note 22.

[16] Irving here draws upon a passage in Franchère; see *Narrative*, 189–90. Most of the journey was by water in a birchbark canoe "manned by nine Canadians." At the Hudson, writes Franchère, "we got our canoe once more afloat, passed by Troy, and by Albany, everywhere hospitably received, our Canadian boatmen, having their hats decorated with parti-colored ribands and feathers, being taken by the Americans for so many wild Indians, and arrived at New York on the 3d [of August], at eleven o'clock in the evening." The next day they sailed around the city to Long Island, where their quarters were located. "We sang as we rowed," Franchère writes, "which, joined to the unusual sight of a birch bark canoe impelled by nine stout Canadians, dark as Indians, and as gayly adorned, attracted a crowd upon the wharves to gaze at us as we glided along."

The remaining Canadians, of whom one was Alexander Ross, had already proceeded to New York by some other means which Ross does not specify, and there awaited

Such was the variegated band of adventurers about to embark in the Tonquin on this arduous and doubtful enterprise. While yet in port and on dry land, in the bustle of preparation and the excitement of novelty, all was sunshine and promise. The Canadians, especially, who, with their constitutional vivacity, have a considerable dash of the gascon, were buoyant and boastful, and great braggarts as to the future; while all those who had been in the service of the Northwest Company, and engaged in the Indian trade, plumed themselves upon their hardihood and their capacity to endure privations. If Mr. Astor ventured to hint at the difficulties they might have to encounter, they treated them with scorn. They were "northwesters;" men seasoned to hardships, who cared for neither wind nor weather. They could live hard, lie hard, sleep hard, eat dogs!—in a word they were ready to do and suffer anything for the good of the enterprise. With all this profession of zeal and devotion, Mr. Astor was not over-confident of the stability and firm faith of these mercurial beings. He had received information, also, that an armed brig from Halifax, probably at the instigation of the Northwest Company, was hovering on the coast, watching for the Tonquin, with the purpose of impressing the Canadians on board of her, as British subjects, and thus interrupting the voyage. It was a time of doubt and anxiety, when the relations between the United States and Great Britain were daily assuming a more precarious aspect and verging towards that war[17] which shortly ensued. As a precautionary measure, therefore, he required that the voyageurs, as they were about to enter into the service of an American association, and to reside within the limits of the United States, should take the oaths of naturalization as American citizens. To this they readily agreed, and shortly afterward assured him that they had actually done so. It was not until after they had sailed that he discovered that they had entirely deceived him in the matter.

———

the arrival of the boatmen. His account confirms Franchère's description, but he adds some additional details: "What was the astonishment [of the spectators], when, in the twinkling of an eye, two of the crew were seen to shoulder their craft, capable of containing two tons weight, and to convey it to a place of safety on terra firma. Mr. Astor, who happened to be present, was so delighted with the vivacity and dexterity of the two men, that he gave them an eagle to drink his health; then turning around, observed to some gentlemen who were standing by, that 'six Americans could not do what these two brawny fellows had done.'" *Adventures*, 42. McKay offered to race the swiftest boat in New York, but the challenge was not accepted.

[17] War of 1812.

Washington Irving at the time he wrote *Astoria*. This lithograph of a
bust by Ball Hughes is from Pierre M. Irving, *Life and Letters of
Washington Irving* (1863), Volume III.

John Jacob Astor about the time of the Astorian venture. From a portrait by Alonzo Chappel.

The confidence of Mr. Astor was abused in another quarter. Two of the partners,[18] both of them Scotchmen, and recently in the service of the Northwest Company, had misgivings as to an enterprise which might clash with the interests and establishments protected by the British flag. They privately waited upon the British minister, Mr. Jackson, then in New York, laid open to him the whole scheme of Mr. Astor, though intrusted to them in confidence, and dependent, in a great measure, upon secrecy at the outset for its success, and inquired whether they, as British subjects, could lawfully engage in it. The reply satisfied their scruples, while the information they imparted excited the surprise and admiration of Mr. Jackson, that a private individual should have conceived and set on foot at his own risk and expense so great an enterprise.[19]

This step on the part of those gentlemen was not known to Mr. Astor until some time afterwards, or it might have modified the trust and confidence reposed in them.

To guard against any interruption to the voyage by the armed brig, said to be off the harbor, Mr. Astor applied to Commodore Rodgers,[20] at that time commanding at New York, to give the Tonquin safe convoy off the coast. The commodore having received from a high official source assurance of the deep interest which the government took in the enterprise, sent directions to Captain Hull,[21] at that time cruising off the

[18] One was Alexander McKay; the other may have been Duncan McDougall.

[19] Irving's source was Franchère's *Narrative*, 193. Astor had, in fact, counted on his Canadian partners to help smooth the way should any difficulty arise between the two countries. Ross writes: "Some . . . of the more sagacious and influential among the Americans themselves observed to Mr. Astor at the time, that his plan would be likely to give umbrage to the British, and arouse them to assert more speedily their claims of prior discovery to the Oregon quarter, and that such a step would operate against him. To these suggestions Mr. Astor simply observed, 'that he had thought of that, but intended chiefly to employ in his undertaking British subjects, and that he should on that account give less offence; besides,' added he, 'the claims of prior discovery and territorial right are claims to be settled by Government only, and not by an individual.' " *Adventures*, 37.

[20] John Rodgers (1773–1838), commodore of the U.S. frigate *President* in 1811. His attack upon the British sloop *Little Belt* on May 16, 1811, helped precipitate the War of 1812, which dealt a mortal blow to the Astorian enterprise. Astor's appeal to him to give safe convoy to the *Tonquin* is, consequently, not lacking in a certain unintentional irony.

[21] Isaac Hull (1773–1843), who was made commodore of the *Constitution* in 1810. Hull's greatest victory was his capture, on August 19, 1812, of the British frigate *Guerrière* in one of the decisive sea battles of the War of 1812. Oliver Wendell Holmes's "Old Ironsides" (1830), as every schoolboy used to know, aroused public support to save the ship when she was threatened with dismantling in 1828. It is of special interest

harbor, in the frigate Constitution, to afford the Tonquin the required protection when she should put to sea.

Before the day of embarkation, Mr. Astor addressed a letter of instruction to the four partners who were to sail in the ship. In this he enjoined them, in the most earnest manner, to cultivate harmony and unanimity, and recommended that all differences of opinions on points connected with the objects and interests of the voyage should be discussed by the whole, and decided by a majority of votes. He, moreover, gave them especial caution as to their conduct on arriving at their destined port; exhorting them to be careful to make a favorable impression upon the wild people among whom their lot and the fortunes of the enterprise would be cast. "If you find them kind," said he, "as I hope you will, be so to them. If otherwise, act with caution and forbearance, and convince them that you come as friends."

With the same anxious forethought he wrote a letter of instructions to Captain Thorn, in which he urged the strictest attention to the health of himself and his crew, and to the promotion of good-humor and harmony on board his ship.[22] "To prevent any misunderstanding," added he, "will require your particular good management." His letter closed with an injunction of wariness in his intercourse with the natives, a subject on which Mr. Astor was justly sensible he could not be too earnest. "I must recommend you," said he, "to be particularly careful on the coast, and not to rely too much on the friendly disposition of the natives. All accidents which have as yet happened there arose from too much confidence in the Indians."

The reader will bear these instructions in mind, as events will prove their wisdom and importance, and the disasters which ensued in consequence of the neglect of them.[23]

---

that the very start of Astor's undertaking should have been so closely associated with two naval officers and a ship that were soon to become involved in the clash between Great Britain and the United States that led inevitably to the loss of Astoria.

[22] That Captain Thorn failed to maintain harmony has already been pointed out; but Franchère testifies "that though a stern commander and an irritable man, he paid the strictest attention to the health of his crew." *Narrative*, 408.

[23] The allusion, of course, is to the destruction of the *Tonquin* after it left Astoria to cruise along the Northwest Coast to trade with Indians. Captain Thorn, failing to heed Astor's admonition, permitted natives carrying concealed weapons to come aboard after he had aroused their antagonism. In the fight which resulted, everyone on ship (except an Indian translator) lost his life, and the ship itself was destroyed when its magazine exploded.

ON the eighth of September, 1810,[1] the Tonquin put to sea, where she was soon joined by the frigate Constitution.[2] The wind was fresh and fair from the southwest, and the ship was soon out of sight of land and free from the apprehended danger of interruption. The frigate, therefore, gave her "God speed," and left her to her course.

The harmony so earnestly enjoined by Mr. Astor on this heterogeneous crew, and which had been so confidently promised in the buoyant moments of preparation, was doomed to meet with a check at the very outset.[3]

Captain Thorn was an honest, straightforward, but somewhat dry

[1] Both Franchère and Ross mention September 6 as the date of departure. The discrepancy in dates is explained by what Franchère states: "The wind soon fell off, and the first day was spent in drifting down to Staten Island, where we came to anchor for the night. The next day we weighed anchor again; but there came on another dead calm, and we were were forced to cast anchor near the lighthouse at Sandy Hook. On the 8th we weighed anchor for the third time, and by the help of a fresh breeze from the southwest, we succeeded in passing the bar; the pilot quitted us at about eleven o'clock, and soon after we lost sight of the coast." *Narrative*, 196.

[2] "We perceived very soon in the S.W., which was our weather side, a vessel that bore directly toward us; she made a signal that was understood by our captain; we hove to, and stood on her bow. It turned out to be the American frigate *Constitution*. We sent our boat on board of her, and sailed in company till toward five o'clock, when, our papers having been sent back, we separated." *Ibid.*, 197. Ross says the *Constitution* met them on the sixth and rejoined them on the eighth.

[3] Franchère was apprehensive from the start, noting that "the hopeless confusion and incumberment of the vessel's deck, the great number of strangers among whom I found myself, the brutal style which the captain and his subalterns used toward our Canadians; all, in a word, conspired to make me augur a vexatious and disagreeable voyage. The sequel will show that I did not deceive myself in that." *Narrative*, 197.

and dictatorial commander, who, having been nurtured in the system and discipline of a ship of war, and in a sacred opinion of the supremacy of the quarter-deck, was disposed to be absolute lord and master on board of his ship. He appears, moreover, to have had no great opinion, from the first, of the persons embarked with him. He had stood by with surly contempt while they vaunted so bravely to Mr. Astor of all they could do and all they could undergo; how they could face all weathers, put up with all kinds of fare, and even eat dogs with a relish, when no better food was to be had. He had set them down as a set of landlubbers and braggadocios, and was disposed to treat them accordingly. Mr. Astor was, in his eyes, his only real employer, being the father of the enterprise, who furnished all funds and bore all losses. The others were mere agents and subordinates, who lived at his expense. He evidently had but a narrow idea of the scope and nature of the enterprise, limiting his views merely to his part of it; everything beyond the concerns of his ship was out of his sphere; and anything that interfered with the routine of his nautical duties put him in a passion.

The partners, on the other hand, had been brought up in the service of the Northwest Company, and in a profound idea of the importance, dignity, and authority of a partner. They already began to consider themselves on a par with the M'Tavishes, the M'Gillivrays, the Frobishers, and the other magnates of the Northwest, whom they had been accustomed to look up to as the great ones of the earth; and they were a little disposed, perhaps, to wear their suddenly-acquired honors with some air of pretension. Mr. Astor, too, had put them on their mettle with respect to the captain, describing him as a gunpowder fellow who would command his ship in fine style, and, if there was any fighting to do, would "blow all out of the water."

Thus prepared to regard each other with no very cordial eye, it is not to be wondered at that the parties soon came into collision. On the very first night Captain Thorn began his man-of-war discipline by ordering the lights in the cabin to be extinguished at eight o'clock.

The pride of the partners was immediately in arms. This was an invasion of their rights and dignities not to be borne. They were on board of their own ship, and entitled to consult their ease and enjoyment. M'Dougal was the champion of their cause. He was an active, irritable, fuming, vainglorious little man, and elevated in his own opinion, by being the proxy of Mr. Astor. A violent altercation ensued, in the course of which Thorn threatened to put the partners in irons should they prove refractory; upon which M'Dougal seized a pistol and swore to be the death of the captain should he ever offer such an indignity. It was some time before the irritated parties could be pacified by the more temperate bystanders.[4]

Such was the captain's outset with the partners. Nor did the clerks stand much higher in his good graces; indeed, he seems to have regarded all the landsmen on board his ship as a kind of live lumber, continually in the way. The poor voyageurs, too, continually irritated his spleen by their "lubberly" and unseemly habits, so abhorrent to one accustomed to the cleanliness of a man-of-war. These poor fresh-water sailors, so vainglorious on shore, and almost amphibious when on lakes and rivers, lost all heart and stomach the moment they were at sea. For days they suffered the doleful rigors and retchings of sea-sickness, lurking below in their berths in squalid state, or emerging now and then like spectres from the hatchways, in capotes and blankets, with dirty nightcaps, grizzly beard, lantern visage and unhappy eye, shivering about the deck, and ever and anon crawling to the sides of the vessel, and offering up their tributes to the windward, to the infinite annoyance of the captain.

His letters to Mr. Astor, wherein he pours forth the bitterness of his soul, and his seamanlike impatience of what he considers the "*lubberly*" character and conduct of those around him, are before us, and are amusingly characteristic. The honest captain is full of vexation on his own account, and solicitude on account of Mr. Astor, whose property he considers at the mercy of a most heterogeneous and wasteful crew.

As to the clerks, he pronounced[5] them mere pretenders, not one of

---

[4] Neither Franchère nor Ross mentions this first dispute, and Franchère is silent until they reached the Falkland Islands. Ross, however, relates in detail a dispute arising early in the voyage out of Captain Thorn's assigning "the mechanics" (i.e., Job Aitken, George Bell, Johann Koaster, Guilleaume Perreault, and Augustus Roussil) to take their places with the common sailors before the mast and "to perform the duties of common seamen both by day and night." Appeals to the partners led only to an intensification of the dispute. "Both parties then getting into a violent passion, Mr. M'Kay said, 'That his people would defend themselves rather than suffer such treatment.' On hearing this, the captain, suddenly turning round on his heel, defied Mr. M'Kay and his people, adding 'that he would blow out the brains of the first man who dared to disobey his order on board his own ship.' In the midst of this scene, Mr. David Stuart, a good old soul, stept up, and by his gentle and timely interference put an end to the threatening altercation." *Adventures*, 44–45.

[5] *Pronounces* in first edition.

whom had ever been among the Indians, nor farther to the northwest than Montreal, nor of higher rank than barkeeper of a tavern or marker of a billiard-table, excepting one, who had been a school-master,[6] and whom he emphatically sets down for "as foolish a pedant as ever lived."[7]

Then as to the artisans and laborers who had been brought from Canada and shipped at such expense, the three most respectable, according to the captain's account, were culprits, who had fled from Canada on account of their misdeeds; the rest had figured in Montreal as draymen, barbers, waiters, and carriole drivers, and were the most helpless, worthless beings "that ever broke sea-biscuit."

It may easily be imagined what a series of misunderstandings and cross-purposes would be likely to take place between such a crew and such a commander. The captain, in his zeal for the health and cleanliness of his ship, would make sweeping visitations to the "lubber nests" of the unlucky "voyageurs" and their companions in misery, ferret them out of their berths, make them air and wash themselves and their accoutrements, and oblige them to stir about briskly and take exercise.[8]

---

[6] Alexander Ross.

[7] In the appendix written for the English translation of his *Narrative*, which appeared after *Astoria*, Franchère expressly commented on this paragraph: "Notwithstanding the illiberal remarks made by Captain Thorn on the persons who were on board the ill-fated Tonquin, and reproduced by Mr. Irving in his 'Astoria'—these young men who were represented as 'Bar keepers or Billiard markers, most of whom had fled from Justice [see Irving's next paragraph], &c.'—I feel it a duty to say that they were for the most part, of good parentage, liberal education and every way were qualified to discharge the duties of their respective stations. The remarks on the general character of the voyageurs employed as boat-men and Mechanics, and the attempt to cast ridicule on their 'Braggart and swaggering manners' came with a bad grace from the author of 'Astoria,' when we consider that in that very work Mr. Irving is compelled to admit their indomitable energy, their fidelity to their employers, and their cheerfulness under the most trying circumstances in which men can be placed." *Narrative*, 407–408.

Franchère's feelings are understandable, since he was one of those unjustly criticized by Captain Thorn, but in defense of Irving it must be stated that his remarks were less a reflection upon the Canadians than upon the character of the Captain. His inclusion of these passages is clearly intended to show how Thorn's poor judgment and prickly attitude contributed to the disharmony that prevailed on the ship.

[8] The following remarks of Franchère, who acknowledges Captain Thorn's concern for the health of his crew, present the condition of the *voyageurs* in relation to the Captain in a different light: "His complaints of the squalid appearance of the Canadians and mechanics . . . can be abated of their force by giving a description of the accommodation of these people. The Tonquin was a small ship; its forecastle was destined for the crew performing duty before the mast. The room allotted for the accommodation of the twenty men destined for the establishment, was abaft the fore-

Nor did his disgust and vexation cease when all hands had recovered from seasickness, and become accustomed to the ship, for now broke out an alarming keenness of appetite that threatened havoc to the provisions. What especially irritated the captain was the daintiness of some of his cabin passengers. They were loud in their complaints of the ship's fare, though their table was served with fresh pork, hams, tongues, smoked beef, and puddings. "When thwarted in their cravings for delicacies," said he, "they would exclaim it was d—d hard they could not live as they pleased upon their own property, being on board their own ship, freighted with their own merchandise. And these," added he, "are the fine fellows who made such boast that they could 'eat dogs.'"

In his indignation at what he termed their effeminacy, he would swear that he would never take them to sea again "without having Fly-market on the forecastle, Covent-garden on the poop, and a cool spring from Canada in the maintop."

As they proceeded on their voyage and got into the smooth seas and pleasant weather of the tropics, other annoyances occurred to vex the spirit of the captain. He had been crossed by the irritable mood of one of the partners; he was now excessively annoyed by the good-humor of another. This was the elder Stuart,[9] who was an easy soul, and of a social disposition. He had seen life in Canada, and on the coast of Labrador; had been a fur trader in the former, and a fisherman on the latter; and, in the course of his experience, had made various expeditions with voyageurs. He was accustomed, therefore, to the familiarity which prevails between that class and their superiors, and the gossipings which take place among them when seated round a fire at their encampments. Stuart was never so happy as when he could seat himself on the deck with a number of these men round him, in camping style, smoke together, passing the pipe from mouth to mouth, after the manner of the Indians, sing old Canadian boat-songs, and tell stories about their hardships and

castle; a bulk-head had been let across, and a door led from the forecastle into a dark, unventilated, unwholesome place, where they were all heaped together, without means of locomotion, and consequently deprived of that exercise of the body so necessary to health. Add to that, we had no physician on board. In view of these facts, can the complaints of the gallant Captain be sustained? Of course, Mr. Irving was ignorant of these circumstances, as well as of many others which he might have known, had some one suggested to him to ask a few questions of persons who were within his reach at the time of his publication." *Narrative*, 408.

[9] David Stuart.

adventures, in the course of which he rivaled Sinbad in his long tales of the sea, about his fishing exploits on the coast of Labrador.

This gossiping familiarity shocked the captain's notions of rank and subordination, and nothing was so abhorrent to him as the community of pipe between master and man, and their mingling in chorus in the outlandish boat-songs.

Then there was another whimsical source of annoyance to him. Some of the young clerks, who were making their first voyage, and to whom everything was new and strange, were, very rationally, in the habit of taking notes and keeping journals.[10] This was a sore abomination to the honest captain, who held their literary pretensions in great contempt. "The collecting of materials for long histories of their voyages[11] and travels," said he, in his letter to Mr. Astor, "appears to engross most of their attention." We can conceive what must have been the crusty impatience of the worthy navigator, when, on any trifling occurrence in the course of the voyage, quite commonplace in his eyes, he saw these young landsmen running to record it in their journals; and what indignant glances he must have cast to right and left, as he worried about the deck, giving out his orders for the management of the ship, surrounded by singing, smoking, gossiping, scribbling groups, all, as he thought, intent upon the amusement of the passing hour, instead of the great purposes[12] and interests of the voyage.

It is possible the captain was in some degree right in his notions. Though some of the passengers had much to gain by the voyage, none of them had anything positively to lose. They were mostly young men, in the heyday of life; and having got into fine latitudes, upon smooth seas, with a well-stored ship under them, and a fair wind in the shoulder of the sail, they seemed to have got into a holiday world, and were disposed to enjoy it. That craving desire, natural to untravelled men of fresh and lively minds, to see strange lands, and to visit scenes famous in history or fable, was expressed by some of the partners and clerks, with respect to some of the storied coasts and islands that lay within their route. The captain, however, who regarded every coast and island with a matter-of-fact eye, and had no more associations connected with

[10] Franchère's *Narrative*, which he wrote in French, and Ross's *Adventures* are the only two known accounts of the voyage of the *Tonquin* kept by passengers. It is possible that some journals were never published or that some were lost when the *Tonquin* exploded.

[11] *Voyage* in first edition.   [12] *Purpose* in first edition.

them than those laid down in his sea-chart, considered all this curiosity as exceedingly idle and childish. "In the first part of the voyage," says he in his letter, "they were determined to have it said they had been in Africa, and therefore insisted on my stopping at the Cape de Verds.[13] Next they said the ship should stop on the coast of Patagonia, for they must see the large and uncommon inhabitants of that place. Then they must go to the island where Robinson Crusoe had so long lived. And lastly, they were determined to see the handsome inhabitants of Easter Island."

To all these resolves the captain opposed his peremptory veto, as "contrary to instructions." Then would break forth an unavailing explosion of wrath on the part of certain of the partners, in the course of which they did not even spare Mr. Astor for his act of supererogation in furnishing orders for the control of the ship while they were on board, instead of leaving them to be the judges where it would be best for her to touch, and how long to remain. The choleric M'Dougal took the lead in these railings, being, as has been observed, a little puffed up with the idea of being Mr. Astor's proxy.[14]

The captain, however, became only so much the more crusty and dogged in his adherence to his orders, and touchy and harsh in his dealings with his passengers, and frequent altercations ensued. He may in some measure have been influenced by his seamanlike impatience of the interference of landsmen, and his high notions of naval etiquette and quarter-deck authority; but he evidently had an honest, trusty concern for the interests of his employer. He pictured to himself the anxious projector of the enterprise, who had disbursed so munificently in its outfit, calculating on the zeal, fidelity, and singleness of purpose of his associates and agents; while they, on the other hand, having a good ship at their disposal, and a deep pocket at home to bear them out, seemed ready to loiter on every coast, and amuse themselves in every port.

[13] Franchère explains why they did not stop at Cape Verde: "We should have been very glad to touch at these islands to take on water; but as our vessel was an American bottom, and had on board a number of British subjects, our captain did not think fit to expose himself to meet the English ships-of-war cruising on these coasts, who certainly would not have failed to make a strict search, and to take from us the best part of our crew." *Narrative*, 198. English impressment on the high seas was still in force, and the impressment of American sailors on the allegation that they were English was one of the causes of the impending War of 1812.

[14] See above, pp. 40–41.

On the fourth of December they came in sight of the Falkland Islands.[15] Having been for some time on an allowance of water, it was resolved to anchor here and obtain a supply.[16] A boat was sent into a small bay to take soundings. Mr. M'Dougal and Mr. M'Kay took this occasion to go on shore, but with a request from the captain that they would not detain the ship. Once on shore, however, they were in no haste to obey his orders, but rambled about in search of curiosities. The anchorage proving unsafe, and water difficult to be procured, the captain stood out to sea, and made repeated signals for those on shore to rejoin the ship, but it was not until nine at night that they came on board.[17]

The wind being adverse, the boat was again sent on shore the following morning, and the same gentlemen again landed, but promised to come off at a moment's warning; they again forgot their promise in their eager pursuit of wild geese and sea-wolves. After a time the wind hauled fair, and signals were made for the boat. Half and hour elapsed but no boat put off. The captain reconnoitred the shore with his glass, and, to his infinite vexation, saw the loiters in the full enjoyment of their "wild-goose-chase." Nettled to the quick, he immediately made sail. When those on shore saw the ship actually under way, they embarked with all speed, but had a hard pull of eight miles before they got on board, and

[15] Discovered in 1592 by John Davis, the Falkland Islands lie about 250 miles east of the tip of South America. Collateral accounts of the events that occurred when the *Tonquin* reached this point are Franchère's *Narrative*, 202–204, and Ross's *Adventures*, 49–53. Irving used Franchère plus a letter to Astor from Captain Thorn. According to Franchère, they sighted land on the evening of December 3; Ross gives December 5.

[16] Franchère states that the daily allowance of water had been steadily reduced since they crossed the Tropic of Capricorn, "till we were reduced to three gills a day, a slender modicum considering that we had only salt provisions." *Narrative*, 201. Ross adds: "On the 20th [of November] our allowance of water, already short by one-half, was lessened to a pint and a half per man, and on the 2nd of December to a pint each man per day—then a gallon of brandy was offered for a pint of fresh water! but on the 5th, when the joyful sight of land was announced, a hogshead of water was offered in return for a pint of brandy." *Adventures*, 49.

[17] Of this first landing Franchère writes matter-of-factly: "The first mate [Ebenezer D. Fox] being sent ashore to look for water, several of our gentlemen accompanied him. They returned in the evening with the disappointing intelligence that they had not been able to find fresh water. They brought us, to compensate for this, a number of wild geese and two seals." *Narrative*, 202.

Ross goes into more detail, and relates that a sailor named Johnston (Joseph Johnson, according to Franchère's roster) wandered off by himself and had lain down to sleep. When he failed to show up, Thorn was only with difficulty prevailed upon not to sail off without him. *Adventures*, 49–50.

then experienced a grim reception, notwithstanding that they came well laden with the spoils of the chase.[18]

Two days afterwards, on the seventh of December, they anchored at Port Egmont,[19] in the same island, where they remained four days taking in water and making repairs. This was a joyous time for the landsmen. They pitched a tent[20] on shore, had a boat at their command, and passed their time merrily in rambling about the island, and coasting along the shores, shooting sea-lions, seals, foxes, geese, ducks, and penguins. None were keener in pursuit of this kind of game than M'Dougal and David Stuart; the latter was reminded of aquatic sports on the coast of Labrador, and his hunting exploits in the Northwest.

In the meantime the captain addressed himself steadily to the business of his ship,[21] scorning the holiday spirit and useless pursuits of his emancipated messmates, and warning them, from time to time, not to wander away nor be out of hail. They promised, as usual, that the ship should never experience a moment's detention on their account, but, as usual, forgot their promise.

On the morning of the 11th, the repairs being all finished, and the water casks replenished, the signal was given to embark, and the ship began to weigh anchor. At this time several of the passengers were dispersed about the island, amusing themselves in various ways.[22] Some of

[18] No mention appears in either Franchère or Ross of this second episode. Both are in agreement that there were but two landings, not three as in Irving's account.

[19] Erroneously *Fort Egmont* in Author's Revised Edition. Port Egmont is on Saunders Island, one of the smaller islands of the Falklands, of which West Falkland and East Falkland are the largest. Nearly two hundred islands comprise the whole group.

[20] Franchère and Ross both mention the tent, which was placed near the springs where the water casks were being filled. The birds and animals enumerated by Irving appear in Franchère.

[21] Not entirely, for Ross relates that one of the party had tied a goose to a stone between the tent and the place of landing. "Soon afterwards the captain, happening to come on shore, and seeing the goose, he up with his gun to shoot at it. Thinking, however, that he had missed it, he instantly loaded and fired again, and seeing the goose flutter he ran up to catch it, when he discovered his mistake, on which we all burst out a laughing. Nettled at this, he immediately turned round and went on board again." *Adventures*, 51.

[22] If there is no discrepancy in dates—and there seems to be none—then the fact that some men were still on shore was reasonable enough; for, according to Ross, the water casks had been filled on the tenth, "and the captain on going on board that evening said to Mr. M'Dougall, that the ship would probably sail the next day [the eleventh]. Soon after, however, Messrs. M'Kay and M'Dougall also went on board, where they passed the night; but coming ashore the next morning [the eleventh], they told us that

the young men had found two inscriptions, in English, over a place where two unfortunate mariners had been buried in this desert island. As the inscriptions were nearly worn out by time and weather, they were playing the part of "Old Mortality," and piously renewing them.[23] The signal from the ship summoned them from their labors; they saw the sails unfurled, and that she[24] was getting under way. The two sporting partners, however, Mr. M'Dougal and David Stuart, had strolled away to the south of the island in pursuit of penguins. It would never do to put off without them, as there was but one boat to convey the whole.

While this delay took place on shore, the captain was storming on board. This was the third time his orders had been treated with contempt, and the ship wantonly detained, and it should be the last; so he spread all sail and put to sea, swearing he would leave the laggards to shift for themselves. It was in vain that those on board made remonstrances and entreaties, and represented the horrors of abandoning men upon a sterile and uninhabited island; the sturdy captain was inflexible.

In the meantime the penguin hunters had joined the engravers of tombstones, but not before the ship was already out at sea. They all, to the number of eight, threw themselves into their boat, which was about twenty feet in length, and rowed with might and main.[25] For three

---

the ship would not sail till the 12th, and that all hands were ordered on board that night." *Ibid.* Two explanations of what happened might be suggested: either McKay and McDougall were mistaken, which seems unlikely, or Captain Thorn deliberately changed his mind when he saw a good chance to throw a scare into those ashore or, worse, even to abandon them. From what Irving writes below and from his quotation from Thorn's letter to Astor, that he actually intended to leave them stranded seems unmistakable.

[23] The incident of the graves appears in both Franchère and Ross. Ross's account is the more detailed: "Mr. M'Kay, myself, and some others [including Franchère], went up the bay a little to repair two old graves which we had discovered in a dilapidated state the day before. On one of the graves was the following rudely-cut inscription on a board:—'William Stevens, aged twenty-two years, killed by a fall from a rock, on the 21st of September, 1794;' on the other, 'Benjamin Peak died of the smallpox on the 5th of January, 1803, ship *Eleonora*, Captain Edmund Cole, Providence, Rhode Island.'" *Ibid.*, 52. Franchère writes: "This pious attention to two dead men nearly proved fatal to a greater number of the living; for . . . the captain gave orders to re-embark, and without troubling himself to inquire if this order had been executed or not, caused the anchor to be weighed on the morning of the 11th, while I and some of my companions were engaged in erecting the inscription . . . others were cutting grass for the hogs, and Messrs. M'Dougall and D. Stuart had gone to the south side of the isle to look for game." *Narrative*, 204.

[24] *It* in first edition.

[25] Irving paraphrases Franchère: "We then lost no time, but pushed off, being eight

---

hours and a half did they tug anxiously and severely at the oar, swashed occasionally by the surging waves of the open sea, while the ship inexorably kept on her course, and seemed determined to leave them behind.

On board of the ship was the nephew of David Stuart, a young man of spirit and resolution. Seeing, as he thought, the captain obstinately bent upon abandoning his uncle and the others, he seized a pistol, and in a paroxysm of wrath swore he would blow out the captain's brains, unless he put about or shortened sail.

Fortunately for all parties, the wind just then came ahead, and the boat was enabled to reach the ship; otherwise, disastrous circumstances

in number, with our little boat, only twenty feet keel. We rowed with all our might, but gained nothing upon the vessel." *Narrative*, 204. Ross's account is longer and deserves quotation: "In half an hour we were all at the water's edge; the ship by this time was three miles out at sea. We were now nine persons [cf. Franchère's eight] on shore, and we had to stow, squat, and squeeze ourselves into a trumpery little boat, scarcely capable of holding half our number. In this dreadful dilemma, we launched on a rough and tempestuous sea, and, against wind and tide, followed the ship. The wind blowing still fresher and fresher, every succeeding wave threatened our immediate destruction. Our boat already half full of water, and ourselves, as may be supposed, drenched with the surges passing over her, we gave up all hope of succeeding in the unequal struggle, and a momentary pause ensued, when we deliberated whether we should proceed . . . or return to land. The ship was now at least two leagues [between five and ten miles] ahead of us, and just at this time the man who was bailing . . . let go and lost the pail, and one of our oars being broken in the struggle to recover it, our destiny seemed sealed beyond a doubt. A second deliberation ended in the resolve to reach the ship or perish in the attempt. The weather now grew more violent; the wind increased; and, what was worst of all, the sun had just sunk under the horizon. . . . Every ray of hope now vanished: but so short-sighted is man, that the moment when he least expects it, relief comes from an unseen hand; and such was our case; for in an instant our hopeless anxiety was turned into joy by the ship making down to our assistance. . . . At length, after many ineffectual attempts and much manoeuvring, we succeeded in getting on board; having been in the boat upwards of six hours. That the captain's determination was to leave us to our fate, there is not the least doubt; for he declared so afterwards, in a letter to Mr. Astor from the Sandwich Islands, and he was only prevented from carrying his purpose into effect by the determined conduct of Mr. Robert Stuart, who, seizing a brace of pistols, peremptorily told the captain to order about ship and save the boat; or, he added, 'You are a dead man this instant.' " *Adventures*, 53.

There are two discrepancies between Ross's and Franchère's accounts. Franchère says they were in the boat only three and a half hours, as opposed to Ross's six, and were taken on board about three o'clock in the afternoon rather than in the dark of night. Irving's knowledge of Robert Stuart's action comes directly from Franchère (*Narrative*, 207). Both he and Ross learned of this episode, of course, only from what was told them after they boarded ship. Ross adds revealingly: "All the former feuds and squabbles between the captain and passengers sink into insignificance compared to the recent one." *Adventures*, 54.

might have ensued. We can hardly believe that the captain really intended to carry his threat into full effect, and rather think he meant to
let the laggards off for a long pull and a hearty fright. He declared,
however, in his letter to Mr. Astor, that he was serious in his threats,
and there is no knowing how far such an iron man may push his notions
of authority.

"Had the wind," writes he, "(unfortunately) not hauled ahead soon
after leaving the harbor's mouth, I sould positively have left them;
and, indeed, I cannot but think it an unfortunate circumstance for you
that it so happened, for the first loss in this instance would, in my opinion,
have proved the best, as they seem to have no idea of the value of property, nor any apparent regard for your interest, although interwoven
with their own."

This, it must be confessed, was acting with a high hand, and carrying a regard to the owner's property to a dangerous length. Various
petty feuds occurred also between him and the partners in respect to
the goods on board the ship, some articles of which they wished to dis-
tribute for clothing among the men, or other purposes which they
deemed essential. The captain, however, kept a mastiff watch upon the
cargo, and growled and snapped if they but offered to touch box or bale.
"It was contrary to orders; it would forfeit his insurance; it was out of
all rule." It was in vain they insisted upon their right to do so, as part
owners, and as acting for the good of the enterprise; the captain only
stuck to his point the more stanuchly. They consoled themselves, therefore, by declaring, that as soon as they made land, they would assert
their rights, and do with ship and cargo as they pleased.

Beside[s] these feuds between the captain and the partners, there were
feuds between the partners themselves, occasioned, in some measure, by
jealousy of rank. M'Dougal and M'Kay began to draw plans for the
fort, and other buildings of the intended establishment. They agreed
very well as to the outline and dimensions, which were on a sufficiently
grand scale; but when they came to arrange the details, fierce disputes
arose, and they would quarrel by the hour about the distribution of the
doors and windows. Many were the hard words and hard names bandied
between them on these occasions, according to the captain's account.
Each accused the other of endeavoring to assume unwarrantable power,
and take the lead; upon which Mr. M'Dougal would vauntingly lay

down Mr. Astor's letter, constituting him his representative and proxy, a document not to be disputed.

These wordy contests, though violent, were brief; "and within fifteen minutes," says the captain, "they would be caressing each other like children."[26]

While all this petty anarchy was agitating the little world within the Tonquin, the good ship prosperously pursued her course, doubled Cape Horn on the 25th of December, careered across the bosom of the Pacific, until, on the 11th of February, the snowy peaks of Owyhee were seen brightening above the horizon.[27]

---

[26] Nothing supporting Thorn's description of such quarrels between the partners appears in either Franchère or Ross.

[27] For the passage to Hawaii, see Franchère, *Narrative*, 207–209, and Ross, *Adventures*, 54–56. The voyage passed free of incident except for the near drowning of one of the Canadians, whom Franchère identifies as Guilleaume Perreault and Ross as Joseph La Pierre. The dates as given by Irving in this paragraph agree with those in Franchère.

Owyhee — Sandwich Islanders — Their Nautical Talents
Tamaahmaah — His Navy — His Negotiations
Views of Mr. Astor with Respect to the Sandwich Islands
Karakakooa — Royal Monopoly of Pork
Description of the Islanders — Gayeties on Shore
Chronicler of the Island — Place Where Captain Cook Was Killed
John Young, A Nautical Governor — His Story — Waititi
A Royal Residence — a Royal Visit — Grand Ceremonials
Close Dealing — A Royal Pork Merchant
Grievances of a Matter-of-Fact Man

OWYHEE, or Hawaii, as it is written by more exact orthographers, is the largest of the cluster, ten in number, of the Sandwich Islands. It is about ninety-seven miles in length, and seventy-eight in breadth, rising gradually into three pyramidal summits or cones; the highest, Mouna Roa, being eighteen thousand feet above the level of the sea, so as to domineer over the whole archipelago, and to be a landmark over a wide extent of ocean.[1] It remains a lasting monument of the enterprising and unfortunate Captain Cook, who was murdered by the natives of this island.

The Sandwich Islanders, when first discovered, evinced a character superior to most of the savages of the Pacific isles. They were frank and open in their deportment, friendly and liberal in their dealings, with an apt ingenuity apparent in all of their rude inventions.

The tragical fate of the discoverer, which, for a time, brought them

[1] The highest of the three volcanoes on Hawaii is Mauna Kea (13,796 feet). Mauna Loa (Irving's Mouna Roa) is 13,680 feet in elevation and the largest in actual volume. The lowest of the three, Hualalai, rises to only 8,269 feet.

Franchère related his impression of the approach to the island: "On the 11th [February] we saw the peak of a mountain covered with snow, which the first mate, who was familiar with these seas, told me was the summit of *Mona-Roah*, a high mountain on the island of *Ohehy* [Hawaii], one of those which the circumnavigator Cook named the Sandwich Isles, and where he met his death in 1779. We headed to the land all day, and although we made eight or nine knots an hour, it was not till evening that we were near enough to distinguish the huts of the islanders; which is sufficient to prove the prodigious elevation of *Mona Roah* above the level of the sea." *Narrative*, 209.

under the charge of ferocity, was, in fact, the result of sudden exaspera-
tion, caused by the seizure of their chief.[2]

At the time of the visit of the Tonquin, the islanders had profited, in
many respects, by occasional intercourse with white men; and had shown
a quickness to observe and cultivate those arts important to their mode
of living. Originally they had no means of navigating the seas by which
they were surrounded, superior to light pirogues, which were little competent to contend with the storms of the broad ocean. As the islanders[3]
are not in sight of each other, there could, therefore, be but casual intercourse between them. The traffic with white men had put them in possession of vessels of superior description; they had made themselves
acquainted with their management, and had even made rude advances
in the art of ship-building.

These improvements had been promoted, in a great measure, by
the energy and sagacity of one man, the famous Tamaahmaah.[4] He
had originally been a petty eri, or chief; but, being of an intrepid and
aspiring nature, he had risen in rank, and, availing himself of the superior advantages now afforded in navigation, had brought the whole
archipelago in subjection to his arms. At the time of the arrival of the
Tonquin he had about forty schooners, of from twenty to thirty tons
burden, and one old American ship. With these he held[5] undisputed
sway over his insular domains, and carried on intercourse with the chiefs
or governors whom he had placed in command of the several islands.

The situation of this group of islands, far in the bosom of the vast
Pacific, and their abundant fertility, render them important stopping-
places on the highway to China, or to the northwest coast of America.
Here the vessels engaged in the fur trade touched to make repairs and
procure provisions; and here they often sheltered themselves during
the winters that occurred in their long coasting expeditions.

The British navigators were, from the first, aware of the value of
these islands to the purposes of commerce; and Tamaahmaah, not long
after he had attained the sovereign sway, was persuaded by Vancouver,
the celebrated discoverer, to acknowledge, on behalf of himself and sub-

[2] Cook died on February 14, 1779, in a skirmish with islanders while he was attempting to recover a boat stolen from his ship, the *Discovery*.

[3] *Islands* in first edition.

[4] Kamehameha I (1737?–1819). He became king of Hawaii in 1782 and by 1795
had gained control of all but two of the islands.

[5] *Maintained* in first edition.

jects, allegiance to the king of Great Britain.[6] The reader cannot but call to mind the visit which the royal family and court of the Sandwich Islands was, in late years, induced to make to the court of St. James; and the serio-comic ceremonials and mock parade which attended that singular travesty of monarchal style.[7]

It was a part of the wide and comprehensive plan of Mr. Astor to establish a friendly intercourse between these islands and his intended colony, which might, for a time, have occasion to draw supplies thence; and he even had a vague idea of, some time or other, getting possession of one of their islands as a rendezvous for his ships, and a link in the chain of his commercial establishments.

On the evening of the 12th of February,[8] the Tonquin anchored in the bay of Karakakooa, in the island of Owyhee. The surrounding shores were wild and broken, with overhanging cliffs and precipices of black volcanic rock. Beyond these, however, the country was fertile and well cultivated, with inclosures of yams, plantains, sweet potatoes, sugarcanes, and other productions of warm climates and teeming soils; and the numerous habitations of the natives were pleasantly sheltered beneath clumps of cocoanut and bread-fruit trees, which afforded both food and shade. This mingled variety of garden and grove swept gradually up the sides of the mountains, until succeeded by dense forests, which in turn gave place to naked and craggy rocks, until the summits rose into the regions of perpetual snow.

The royal residence of Tamaahmaah was at this time at another island named Woahoo. The island of Owyhee was under the command of one of his eris, or chiefs, who resided at the village of Tocaigh, situated on a different part of the coast from the bay of Karakakooa.

On the morning after her arrival, the ship was surrounded by canoes and pirogues, filled with the islanders of both sexes, bringing off supplies of fruits and vegetables, bananas, plantains, watermelons, yams, cabbages, and taro. The captain was desirous, however, of purchasing a number of hogs, but there were none to be had.[9] The trade in pork was

---

[6] Vancouver visited the islands in 1792.

[7] Kamehameha II, who succeeded his father in 1819, visited England with his queen in 1824. While there they contracted measles and died. It is possible that Irving recalled their visit, for he, too, was in London that year.

[8] The date agrees with Franchère.

[9] The list of fruits and vegetables comes from Franchère, who adds, however: "The next day the islanders visited the vessel in great numbers all day long, bringing, as on

a royal monopoly, and no subject of the great Tamaahmaah dared to meddle with it. Such provisions as they could furnish, however, were brought by the natives in abundance, and a lively intercourse was kept up during the day, in which the women mingled in the kindest manner.

The islanders are a comely race, of a copper complexion. The men are tall and well made, with forms indicating strength and activity; the women with regular and occasionally handsome features, and a lascivious expression, characteristic of their temperament. Their style of dress was nearly the same as in the days of Captain Cook. The men wore the maro, a band one foot in width and several feet in length, swathed round the loins, and formed of tappa, or cloth of bark; the kihei, or mantle, about six feet square, tied in a knot over one shoulder, passed under the opposite arm, so as to leave it bare, and falling in graceful folds before and behind, to the knee, so as to bear some resemblance to a Roman toga.

The female dress consisted of the pau, a garment formed of a piece of tappa, several yards in length and one in width, wrapped round the waist, and reaching like a petticoat, to the knees. Over this [was] a kihei, or mantle, larger than that of the men, sometimes worn over both shoulders, like a shawl, sometimes over one only. These mantles were seldom worn by either sex during the heat of the day, when the exposure of their persons was at first very revolting to a civilized eye.[10]

Towards evening several of the partners and clerks went on shore, where they were well received and hospitably entertained. A dance was performed for their amusement, in which nineteen young women and one man figured very gracefully, singing in concert, and moving to the cadence of their song.

All this, however, was nothing to the purpose in the eyes of Captain Thorn, who, being disappointed in his hope of obtaining a supply of pork, or finding good water, was anxious to be off. This it was not so easy to effect. The passengers, once on shore, were disposed, as usual,

the day before, fruits, vegetables, and some pigs, in exchange for which we gave them glass beads, iron rings, needles, cotton cloth, &c." *Ibid.*, 211. He appears to have been in error concerning the pigs, for Ross's account agrees with Irving: "We . . . were desirous of purchasing hogs and goats, but were told that the sale of pork had been prohibited by royal proclamation, and that, without the permission of the king, who resided in the island of Woahoo, no subject could dispose of any." *Adventures*, 60. Irving probably had his information from Captain Thorn's letter to Astor.

[10] This and the preceding paragraph are drawn largely from Franchère's *Narrative*, 223.

to profit by the occasion. The partners had many inquiries to make relative to the island, with a view to business; while the young clerks were delighted with the charms and graces of the dancing damsels.

To add to their gratifications, an old man offered to conduct them to the spot where Captain Cook was massacred. The proposition was eagerly accepted, and all hands set out on a pilgrimage to the place. The veteran islander performed his promise faithfully, and pointed out the very spot where the unfortunate discoverer fell. The rocks and cocoatrees around bore record of the fact, in the marks of the balls fired from the boats upon the savages. The pilgrims gathered round the old man, and drew from him all the particulars he had to relate respecting this memorable event; while the honest captain stood by and bit his nails with impatience. To add to his vexation, they employed themselves in knocking off pieces of the rocks, and cutting off the bark of the trees marked by the balls, which they conveyed back to the ship as precious relics.[11]

Right glad, therefore, was he to get them and their treasures fairly on board, when he made sail from this unprofitable place, and steered for the bay of Tocaigh,[12] the residence of the chief or governor of the is-

[11] Franchère recalls this incident but omits the Captain's biting his nails: "An old man showed us the spot [at Kealakekua] where Captain Cook was killed, on the 14th of February, 1779, with the cocoa-nut trees pierced by the balls from the boats which the unfortunate navigator commanded. This old man . . . seemed extremely affected and even shed tears, in showing us these objects. As for me, I could not help feeling it a little singular to be thus, by mere chance, upon this spot, on the 14th of February, 1811; that is to say, thirty-two years after, on the anniversary of the catastrophe which has rendered it ever celebrated." *Ibid.*, 212–13.

[12] They left on February 16. *Ibid.*, 213. Tocaigh Bay is now known as Kihola or Kailua Bay. Ross relates that several men had deserted before the ship left Hawaii: "The Captain's conduct . . . had fostered a spirit of desertion among the sailors: Jack Tar, slipping off in the night was seen no more. This new feature . . . brought about a sweeping change, for the captain had now no resource but to place his chief confidence in those whom he had all along maltreated and affected to despise. In this state of things, the natives were employed to bring back the deserters. One Roberts [Charles Roberts from New York], a yankee, was confined below; Ems [Edward Aymes], a Welshman, was tied up and flogged; Johnston [Joseph Johnson], an Englishman, was put in irons; and Anderson [John Anderson], the boatswain, could not be found. Storming and stamping on deck, the captain called up all hands; he swore, he threatened, and abused the whole ships company, making, if possible, things worse. I really pitied the poor man, although he had brought all this trouble upon himself: with all his faults he had some good qualities, and in his present trying situation we forgot our wrongs, and cheerfully exerted ourselves to help him out of his difficulties." *Adventures*, 58.

land, where he hoped to be more successful in obtaining supplies. On coming to anchor the captain went on shore, accompanied by Mr. M'Dougal and Mr. M'Kay, and paid a visit to the governor. This dignitary proved to be an old sailor, by the name of John Young; who, after being tossed about the seas like another Sinbad, had, by one of the whimsical freaks of fortune, been elevated to the government of a savage island. He received his visitors with more hearty familiarity than personages in his high station are apt to indulge, but soon gave them to understand that provisions were scanty at Tocaigh, and that there was no good water, no rain having fallen in the neighborhood in three years.[13]

The captain was immediately for breaking up the conference and departing, but the partners were not so willing to part with the nautical governor, who seemed disposed to be extremely communicative, and from whom they might be able to procure some useful information. A long conversation accordingly ensued, in the course of which they made many inquiries about the affairs of the islands, their natural productions, and the possibility of turning them to advantage in the way of trade; nor did they fail to inquire into the individual history of John Young, and how he came to be governor. This he gave with great condescension, running through the whole course of his fortunes "even from his boyish days."[14]

He was a native of Liverpool, in England, and had followed the sea from boyhood, until, by dint of good conduct, he had risen so far in his profession as to be boatswain of an American ship called the Eleanor, commanded by Captain Metcalf. In this vessel he had sailed in 1789, on one of those casual expeditions to the northwest coast, in quest of furs. In the course of the voyage, the captain left a small schooner, named the Fair American, at Nootka,[15] with a crew of five men, commanded by his son, a youth of eighteen. She was to follow on in the track of the Eleanor.

In February, 1790, Captain Metcalf touched at the island of Mowee, one of the Sandwich group. While anchored here, a boat which was astern of the Eleanor was stolen, and a seaman who was in it was killed.

[13] Irving's information is from Franchère, *Narrative*, 213–14. Cf. Ross, *Adventures*, 59–60.

[14] Shakespeare's *Othello*, I, iii, 132.

[15] Nootka Sound, Vancouver Island, British Columbia.

The natives, generally, disclaimed the outrage, and brought the shattered remains of the boat and the dead body of the seaman to the ship. Supposing that they had thus appeased the anger of the captain, they thronged, as usual, in great numbers about the vessel, to trade. Captain Metcalf, however, determined on a bloody revenge. The Eleanor mounted ten guns. All these he ordered to be loaded with musket-balls, nails, and pieces of old iron, and then fired them, and the small arms of the ship, among the natives. The havoc was dreadful; more than a hundred, according to Young's account, were slain.

After this signal act of vengeance, Captain Metcalf sailed from Mowee, and made for the island of Owyhee, where he was well received by Tamaahmaah. The fortunes of this warlike chief were at that time on the rise. He had originally been of inferior rank, ruling over only one or two districts of[16] Owyhee, but had gradually made himself sovereign of his native island.

The Eleanor remained some few days at anchor here, and an apparently friendly intercourse was kept up with the inhabitants. On the 17th [of] March, John Young obtained permission to pass the night on shore. On the following morning a signal-gun summoned him to return on board.

He went to the shore to embark, but found all the canoes hauled up on the beach and rigorously tabooed, or interdicted. He would have launched one himself, but was informed by Tamaahmaah that if he presumed to do so he would be put to death.

Young was obliged to submit, and remained all day in great perplexity to account for this mysterious taboo, and fearful that some hostility was intended. In the evening he learned the cause of it, and his uneasiness was increased. It appeared that the vindictive act of Captain Metcalf had recoiled upon his own head. The schooner Fair American, commanded by his son, following in his track, had fallen into the hands of the natives to the southward of Tocaigh Bay, and young Metcalf and four of the crew had been massacred.

On receiving intelligence of this event, Tamaahmaah had immediately tabooed all the canoes, and interdicted all intercourse with the ship, lest the captain should learn the fate of the schooner, and take his revenge upon the island. For the same reason he prevented Young from rejoining his countrymen. The Eleanor continued to fire signals from

[16] *In* in first edition.

time to time for two days, and then sailed; concluding, no doubt, that the boatswain had deserted.

John Young was in despair when he saw the ship make sail, and found himself abandoned among savages;—and savages, too, sanguinary in their character, and inflamed by acts of hostility. He was agreeably disappointed, however, in experiencing nothing but kind treatment from Tamaahmaah and his people. It is true, he was narrowly watched whenever a vessel came in sight, lest he should escape and relate what had passed; but at other times he was treated with entire confidence and great distinction. He became a prime favorite, cabinet counsellor, and active coadjutor of Tamaahmaah, attending him in all his excursions, whether of business or pleasure, and aiding in his warlike and ambitious enterprises. By degrees he rose to the rank of a chief, espoused one of the beauties of the island, and became habituated and reconciled to his new way of life; thinking it better, perhaps, to rule among savages than serve among white men; to be a feathered chief than a tarpaulin[17] boatswain. His favor with Tamaahmaah never declined; and when that sagacious, intrepid, and aspiring chieftain had made himself sovereign over the whole group of islands, and removed his residence to Woahoo, he left his faithful adherent John Young in command of Owyhee.

Such is an outline of the history of Governor Young, as furnished by himself; and we regret that we are not able to give any account of the state maintained by this seafaring worthy, and the manner in which he discharged his high functions; though it is evident he had more of the hearty familiarity of the forecastle than the dignity of the gubernatorial office.[18]

These long conferences were bitter trials to the patience of the captain, who had no respect either for the governor or his island, and was anxious to push on in quest of provisions and water. As soon as he could get his inquisitive partners once more on board, he weighed anchor,[19] and

---

[17] *Tarpawling* in first edition.

[18] Irving's information about Young does not appear in Franchère. Ross states: "He is about 60 years of age, shrewd, and healthy; but, from his long residence among the natives, he has imbibed so much of their habits and peculiarities, that he is now more Indian [*sic*] than white man." *Adventures*, 59. Franchère adds: "The governor dismissed our gentlemen with a present of four fine fat hogs; and we, in return, sent him some tea, coffee, and chocolate, and a keg of Madeira wine." *Narrative*, 214.

[19] But not until the passengers had gone mountain climbing: "On the 17th [of February] we found ourselves abreast of *Mona-Wororayea* a snow-capped mountain,

made sail for the island of Woahoo,[20] the royal residence of Tamaah-maah.

This is the most beautiful island of the Sandwich group. It is forty-six miles in length and twenty-three in breadth. A ridge of volcanic mountains extends through the centre, rising into lofty peaks, and skirted by undulating hills and rich plains, where the cabins of the natives peep out from beneath groves of cocoanut and other luxuriant trees.

On the 21st of February the Tonquin cast anchor in the beautiful bay before the village of Waititi,[21] (pronounced Whyteetee,) the abode of Tamaahmaah. This village contained about two hundred habitations, composed of poles set in the ground, tied together at the ends, and thatched with grass, and was situated in an open grove of cocoanuts. The royal palace of Tamaahmaah was a large house of two stories; the lower of stone, the upper of wood. Round this his body-guard kept watch, composed of twenty-four men in long blue cassocks turned up with yellow, and each armed with a musket.[22]

While at anchor at this place, much ceremonious visiting and long conferences took place between the potentate of the islands and the partners of the company. Tamaahmaah came on board of the ship in royal style, in his double pirogue. He was between fifty and sixty years of age, above the middle size, large and well made, though somewhat corpulent. He was dressed in an old suit of regimentals, with a sword by his side, and seemed somewhat embarrassed by his magnificent attire. Three of his wives accompanied him. They were almost as tall, and quite as corpulent as himself; but by no means to be compared with him in grandeur of habiliments, wearing no other garb than the pau. With him, also, came his great favorite and confidential counsellor, Kraimaker; who, from holding a post equivalent to that of prime minister, had been familiarly named Billy Pitt by the British visitors to the islands.

The sovereign was received with befitting ceremonial. The American flag was displayed, four guns were fired, and the partners appeared in scarlet coats, and conducted their illustrious guests to the cabin, where

like *Mona-Roah*, but which appeared to me less lofty than the latter." Franchère, *Narrative*, 214. They left on the eighteenth.

[20] Oahu.

[21] Now Honolulu. Both Franchère and Ross confirm the date.

[22]This paragraph is adapted from Franchère, *Narrative*, 219. Ross gives 740 houses and states that the population numbered 2,025 persons.

they were regaled with wine.[23] In this interview the partners endeavored to impress the monarch with a sense of their importance, and of the importance of the association to which they belonged. They let him know that they were eris, or chiefs, of a great company about to be established on the northwest coast, and talked of the probability of opening a trade with his islands, and of sending ships there occasionally. All this was gratifying and interesting to him, for he was aware of the advantages of trade, and desirous of promoting frequent intercourse with white men. He encouraged Europeans and Americans to settle in his islands and intermarry with his subjects. There were between twenty and thirty white men at that time resident in the island, but many of them were mere vagabonds, who remained there in hopes of leading a lazy and an easy life. For such Tamaahmaah had a great contempt; those only had his esteem and countenance who knew some trade or mechanic art, and were sober and industrious.[24]

On the day subsequent to the monarch's visit, the partners landed and waited upon him in return. Knowing the effect of show and dress upon men in savage life and wishing to make a favorable impression as the eris, or chiefs, of the great American Fur Company, some of them appeared in Highland plaids and kilts,[25] to the great admiration of the natives.

While visits of ceremony and grand diplomatic conferences were going on between the partners and the king, the captain, in his plain, matter-of-fact way, was pushing what he considered a far more important negotiation; the purchase of a supply of hogs. He found that the king had profited in more ways than one by his intercourse with white men. Above all other arts he had learned the art of driving a bargain. He was a magnanimous monarch, but a shrewd pork merchant; and perhaps thought he could not do better with his future allies, the American Fur Company, than to begin by close dealing. Several interviews

[23] Ross adds: "The king was conducted to the cabin followed by his valet, who held a spitting-box in his hand, but the queens preferred remaining on deck. While here, they very unceremoniously disrobed themselves, plunged overboard, and after swimming and sporting for some time in the water, came on board again and dressed themselves, after which they joined Tammeatameah in the cabin, where they did ample justice to a good collation, drank two bottles of wine, and left us apparently well pleased with their reception. The chiefs remained all the time in the royal yacht alongside." *Adventures*, 61.

[24] Cf. Franchère, *Narrative*, 221–22.

[25] Uniformly spelled *kelts* in first edition.

were requisite, and much bargaining, before he could be brought to part with a bristle of his bacon, and then he insisted upon being paid in hard Spanish dollars; giving as a reason that he wanted money to purchase a frigate from his brother George, as he affectionately termed the king of England.[26]

At length the royal bargain was concluded; the necessary supply of hogs obtained, beside several goats, two sheep, a quantity of poultry, and vegetables in abundance. The partners now urged to recruit their forces from the natives of this island. They declared they had never seen watermen equal to them, even among the voyageurs of the Northwest; and, indeed, they are remarkable for their skill in managing their light craft, and can swim and dive like waterfowl. The partners were inclined, therefore, to take thirty or forty with them to the Columbia, to be employed in the service of the company. The captain, however, objected that there was not room in his vessel for the accommodation of such a number. Twelve, only, were therefore enlisted for the company, and as many more for the service of the ship. The former engaged to serve for the term of three years, during which they were to be fed and clothed; and at the expiration of the time were to receive one hundred dollars in merchandise.[27]

And now, having embarked his live-stock, fruits, vegetables, and water, the captain made ready to set sail. How much the honest man

[26] Irving paraphrases Franchère, *Narrative*, 218.

It appears, from the accounts of subsequent voyageurs, that Tamaahmaah afterwards succeeded in his wish of purchasing a large ship. In this he sent a cargo of sandal-wood to Canton, having discovered that the foreign merchants trading with him made large profits on this wood, shipped by them from the islands to the Chinese markets. The ship was manned by natives, but the officers were Englishmen. She accomplished her voyage, and returned in safety to the islands, with the Hawaiian flag floating gloriously in the breeze. The king hastened on board, expecting to find his sandal-wood converted into crapes and damasks, and other rich stuffs of China, but found, to his astonishment, by the legerdemain of traffic, the cargo had all disappeared, and, in place of it, remained a bill of charges amounting to *three thousand dollars*. It was some time before he could be made to comprehend certain of the most important items of the bill, such as pilotage, anchorage, and custom-house fees; but when he discovered that maritime states in other countries derived large revenues in this manner, to the great cost of the merchant, "Well," cried he, "then I will have harbor fees also." He established them accordingly. Pilotage a dollar a foot on the draft of each vessel. Anchorage from sixty to seventy dollars. In this way he greatly increased the royal revenue, and turned his China speculation to account. (Irving's note)

[27] The details concerning the employment of the islanders are from Franchère, *Narrative*, 229.

had suffered in spirit by what he considered the freaks and vagaries of his passengers, and how little he had understood their humors and intentions, is amusingly shown in a letter written to Mr. Astor from Woahoo, which contains his comments on the scenes we have described.

"It would be difficult," he writes, "to imagine the frantic gambols that are daily played off here; sometimes dressing in red coats, and otherwise very fantastically, and collecting a number of ignorant natives around them, telling them that they are the great *eares* of the Northwest, and making arrangements for sending three or four vessels yearly to them from the coast with spars, &c.; while those very natives cannot even furnish a hog to the ship. Then dressing in Highland plaids and kilts, and making similar arrangements, with presents of rum, wine, or anything that is at hand. Then taking a number of clerks and men on shore to the very spot on which Captain Cook was killed, and each fetching off a piece of the rock or tree that was touched by the shot. Then sitting down with some white man or some native who can be a little understood, and collecting the history of those islands, of Tamaahmaah's wars, the curiosities of the islands, &c., preparatory to the histories of their voyages; and the collection is indeed ridiculously contemptible. To enumerate the thousand instances of ignorance, filth, &c., or to particularize all the frantic gambols that are daily practiced, would require volumes."

Before embarking, the great eris of the American Fur Company took leave of their illustrious ally in due style, with many professions of lasting friendship and promises of future intercourse; while the matter-of-fact captain anathematized him in his heart for a grasping, trafficking savage; as shrewd and sordid in his dealings as a white man. As one of the vessels of the company will, in the course of events, have to appeal to the justice and magnanimity of this island potentate, we shall see how far the honest captain was right in his opinion.[28]

[28] See Chapter LVIII.

IT was on the 28th of February[1] that the Tonquin set sail from the Sandwich Islands.[2] For two days the wind was contrary, and the vessel was detained in their neighborhood; at length a favorable breeze sprang up, and in a little while the rich groves, green hills, and snowy peaks of those happy islands one after another sank from sight, or melted into the blue distance, and the Tonquin ploughed her course towards the sterner regions of the Pacific.

The misunderstandings between the captain and his passengers still

[1] The date agrees with Franchère.

[2] An instance of Captain Thorn's tyrannical brutality is absent from Irving's account of the departure. Franchère relates: "We left another man (Edward Aymes) at Wahoo. He belonged to a boat's crew . . . sent ashore for a load of sugar-canes. By the time the boat was loaded . . . the ebb of the tide had left her aground, and Aymes asked leave of the coxswain to take a stroll, engaging to be back for the flood. Leave was granted him, but during his absence, the tide having come in sufficiently to float the boat, James Thorn, the coxswain, did not wait for the young sailor, who was thus left behind. The captain immediately missed the man, and, on being informed that he had strolled away from the boat on leave, flew into a violent passion. Aymes soon made his appearance alongside, having hired some natives to take him on board; on perceiving him, the captain ordered him to stay in the long-boat, then lashed to the side of its load of sugar-cane. The captain then himself got into the boat, and, taking one of the canes, beat the poor fellow most unmercifully with it; after which, not satisfied with his act of brutality, he seized the victim and threw him overboard! Aymes . . . being an excellent swimmer, made for the nearest native canoe. . . . The islanders . . . took in the poor fellow, who, in spite of his entreaties to be received on board, could only succeed in getting his clothes, which were thrown into the canoe." *Narrative*, 227–28. Ross relates the incident in more detail; see *Adventures*, 66–67. He also adds that two other men reached the *Tonquin* in native canoes fifteen minutes late; "they were tied up, flogged, and then put in irons." Ross is led to remark that Thorn "was capable of going any lengths, and would rather have destroyed the expedition, the ship, and every one on board, than be thwarted in what he considered as ship discipline, or his nautical duties."

continued; or rather, increased in gravity. By his altercations and his moody humors, he had cut himself off from all community of thought, or freedom of conversation with them. He disdained to ask any questions as to their proceedings, and could only guess at the meaning of their movements, and in so doing indulged in conjectures and suspicions, which produced the most whimsical self-torment.

Thus, in one of his disputes with them, relative to the goods on board, some of the packages of which they wished to open, to take out articles of clothing for the men or presents for the natives, he was so harsh and peremptory that they lost all patience, and hinted that they were the strongest party, and might reduce him to a very ridiculous dilemma, by taking from him the command.

A thought now flashed across the captain's mind that they really had a design to depose him, and that, having picked up some information at Owyhee, possibly of war between the United States and England, they meant to alter the destination of the voyage; perhaps to seize upon ship and cargo for their own use.

Once having conceived this suspicion, everything went to foster it. They had distributed fire-arms among some of their men, a common precaution among the fur traders when mingling with the natives. This, however, looked like preparation. Then several of the partners and clerks and some of the men, being Scotsmen, were acquainted with the Gaelic, and held long conversations together in that language. These conversations were considered by the captain of a "mysterious and un-warrantable nature," and related, no doubt, to some foul conspiracy that was brewing among them. He frankly avows such suspicions, in his letter to Mr. Astor, but intimates that he stood ready to resist any treasonous outbreak; and seems to think that the evidence of preparation on his part had an effect in overawing the conspirators.

The fact is, as we have since been informed by one of the parties,[3] it was a mischievous pleasure with some of the partners and clerks, who were young men, to play upon the suspicious temper and splenetic humors of the captain. To this we may ascribe many of their whimsical pranks and absurd propositions, and, above all, their mysterious colloquies in Gaelic.[4]

[3] As this statement indicates, some of Irving's information for *Astoria* came from participants in the venture.

[4] Ross confirms this resort to strange tongues; see *Adventures*, 54.

In this sore and irritable mood did the captain pursue his course, keeping a wary eye on every movement, and bristling up whenever the detested sound of the Gaelic language grated upon his ear. Nothing occurred, however, materially to disturb the residue of the voyage excepting a violent storm; and on the twenty-second of March, the Tonquin arrived at the mouth of the Oregon, or Columbia River.[5]

The aspect of the river and the adjacent coast was wild and dangerous. The mouth of the Columbia is upwards of four miles wide with a peninsula and promontory on one side, and a long low spit of land on the other; between which a sand bar and chain of breakers almost block up the entrance. The interior of the country rises into successive ranges of mountains, which, at the time of the arrival of the Tonquin, were covered with snow.

A fresh wind from the northwest sent a rough tumbling sea upon the coast, which broke upon the bar in furious surges, and extended a sheet of foam almost across the mouth of the river. Under these circumstances the captain did not think it prudent to approach within three leagues, until the bar should be sounded and the channel ascertained. Mr. Fox, the chief mate, was ordered to this service in the whaleboat, accompanied by John Martin, an old seaman, who had formerly visited the river, and by three Canadians. Fox requested to have regular sailors to man the boat, but the captain would not spare them from the service of the ship, and supposed the Canadians, being expert boatmen on lakes and rivers, were competent to the service, especially when directed and aided by Fox and Martin. Fox seems to have lost all firmness of spirit on the occasion, and to have regarded the service with a misgiving heart. He came to the partners for sympathy, knowing their differences with the captain, and the tears were in his eyes as he represented his case. "I am sent off," said he, "without seamen to man my boat, in boisterous weather, and on the most dangerous part of the northwest coast. My uncle was lost a few years ago on this same bar, and I am now going to

---

[5] Franchère, *Narrative*, 228, describes the storm, as does Ross, *Adventures*, 75. Ross relates that "almost everything on deck was carried off or dashed to pieces; all our live stock were either killed or washed overboard; and so bad was the weather, first with rain, and then with sleet, hail, frost, and snow which froze in the rigging as it fell, that there was no bending either ropes or sails, and the poor sailors were harassed to death." Both Franchère and Ross confirm the date of arrival at the Columbia as being March 22.

lay my bones alongside of his." The partners sympathized in his apprehensions, and remonstrated with the captain. The latter, however, was not to be moved. He had been displeased with Mr. Fox in the earlier part of the voyage, considering him indolent and inactive; and probably thought his present repugnance arose from a want of true nautical spirit. The interference of the partners in the business of the ship, also, was not calculated to have a favorable effect on a stickler for authority like himself, especially in his actual state of feeling towards them.

At one o'clock, P.M., therefore, Fox and his comrades set off in the whaleboat, which is represented as small in size, and crazy in condition. All eyes were strained after the little bark as it pulled for shore, rising and sinking with the huge rolling waves, until it entered, a mere speck, among the foaming breakers, and was soon lost to view. Evening set in, night succeeded and passed away, and morning returned, but without the return of the boat.[6]

As the wind had moderated, the ship stood near to the land, so as to command a view of the river's mouth. Nothing was to be seen but a wild chaos of tumbling waves breaking upon the bar, and apparently forming a foaming barrier from shore to shore. Towards night the ship again stood out to gain sea-room, and a gloom was visible in every countenance. The captain himself shared in the general anxiety, and prob-

---

[6] The loss of the sounding boat is related in Franchère and Ross. Ross's account is the fuller of the two and closely parallels Irving's while giving additional details: "Mr. Fox . . . represented the impossibility of performing the business in such weather, and in such a rough sea, even with the best seamen, adding, that the waves were too high for any boat to live in. The captain, turning sharply round, said—'Mr. Fox, if you are afraid of water, you should have remained in Boston.' On this, Mr. Fox immediately ordered the boat to be lowered, and the men to embark." *Adventures*, 76. The boat was small and hardly seaworthy, and when the partners attempted to intervene, Thorn "was deaf to entreaties, stamped, and swore that a combination was formed to frustrate all his designs." Fox, "seeing that the captain was immoveable, turned to the partners with tears in his eyes and said—'My uncle was drowned here not many years ago, and now I am going to lay my bones with his.' He then shook hands with all around him, and bade them adieu. Stepping into the boat—'Farewell, my friends!' said he; 'we will perhaps meet again in the next world.' And his words were prophetic." When it was evident the boat was in real danger and a distress signal had been hoisted, "all the people crowded round the captain, and implored him to try and save the boat; but in an angry tone he ordered about ship, and we saw the ill-fated boat no more." *Ibid.*, 77. The men lost with Fox were Basile Lapensée, Ignace Lapensée, Joseph Nadeau, and John Martin. Franchère, *Narrative*, 230.

ably repented of his peremptory orders. Another weary and watchful night succeeded, during which the wind subsided, and the weather became serene.

On the following day, the ship having drifted near the land, anchored in fourteen fathoms water, to the northward of the long peninsula or promontory which forms the north side of the entrance, and is called Cape Disappointment.[7] The pinnace was then manned, and two of the partners, Mr. David Stuart and Mr. M'Kay, set off in the hope of learning something of the fate of the whaleboat.[8] The surf, however, broke with such violence along the shore that they could find no landing place. Several of the natives appeared on the beach and made signs to them to row round the cape, but they thought it most prudent to return to the ship.

The wind now springing up, the Tonquin got under way, and stood in to seek the channel; but was again deterred by the frightful aspect of the breakers, from venturing within a league. Here she hove to; and Mr. Mumford, the second mate, was despatched with four hands, in the pinnace, to sound across the channel until he should find four fathoms depth. The pinnace entered among the breakers, but was near being lost, and with difficulty got back to the ship. The captain insisted that Mr. Mumford had steered too much to the southward. He now turned to Mr. Aiken, an able mariner, destined to command the schooner intended for the coasting trade, and ordered him, together with John

[7] Named by Captain John Meares in 1788. Ross's description of the area follows: "The river at its mouth is 4½ miles broad, confined by Cape Disappointment on the north, and Point Adams on the south; the former is a rocky cliff or promontory, rising about 500 feet above the level of the water, and covered on the top with a few scattered trees of stinted growth; the latter a low sandy point, jutting out about 300 yards into the river, directly opposite to Cape Disappointment: the deepest water is near the Cape, but the channel is both narrow and intricate. The country is low, and the impervious forests give to the surrounding coast a wild and gloomy aspect." *Adventures*, 78. Ross Cox, who came to Astoria on the *Beaver* the next year, stated that from Cape Disappointment "to the opposite point on the southern side . . . extends a chain or reef of rocks and sand-banks, over which the dreadful roaring of the mighty waters of the Columbia, in forcing their passage to the ocean, is heard for miles distant." *Columbia River*, 47.

Lewis and Clark visited Cape Disappointment, which Clark described as "an elevated, circular knob, rising with a steep ascent one hundred and fifty or one hundred feet above the water . . . and covered with thick timber on the inner side, but open and grassy in the exposure next the sea." *History of the Expedition*, II, 263.

[8] Besides Stuart and McKay, there were also Ross and a number of others, including John Mumford, second mate, who was at the helm. Ross, *Adventures*, 79.

Salmon fishing at Chinook Point. From a drawing in James G. Swan,
The Northwest Coast (1857).

Courtesy Oregon Historical Society

Modern Indians fishing in the ancient manner for steelhead trout and salmon on the Deschutes River.

Courtesy Oregon State Highway Commission

Coles, sail-maker, Stephen Weekes, armorer, and two Sandwich Islanders, to proceed ahead and take soundings, while the ship should follow
under easy sail. In this way they proceeded until Aiken had ascertained
the channel, when signal was given from the ship for him to return on
board. He was then within pistol shot, but so furious was the current,
and tumultuous the breakers, that the boat became unmanageable, and
was hurried away, the crew crying out piteously for assistance.[9] In a
few moments she could not be seen from the ship's deck. Some of the
passengers climbed to the mizzen top, and beheld her still struggling to
reach the ship; but shortly after she broached broadside to the waves,
and her case seemed desperate. The attention of those on board of the
ship was now called to their own safety. They were in shallow water;
the vessel struck repeatedly, the waves broke over her, and there was
danger of her foundering.[10] At length she got into seven fathoms water,
and the wind lulling, and the night coming on, cast anchor. With the
darkness their anxieties increased. The wind whistled, the sea roared,
the gloom was only broken by the ghastly glare of the foaming breakers, the minds of the seamen were full of dreary apprehensions, and
some of them fancied they heard the cries of their lost comrades mingling with the uproar of the elements. For a time, too, the rapidly ebb-
ing tide threatened to sweep them from their precarious anchorage. At
length the reflux of the tide, and the springing up of the wind, enabled
them to quit their dangerous situation and take shelter in a small bay
within Cape Disappointment, where they rode in safety during the

[9] Ross relates in detail what happened: "As the ship and boat drew near to each
other, the latter steered a little aside to be out of the ship's way, then lay upon her
oars in smooth water, waiting to be taken on board." The ship passed in silence and
no effort was made to secure the boat on board; "every one appeared thunderstruck,
and Mr. M'Kay was the first that spoke,—'Who,' said he, 'is going to throw a rope to
the boat?' No one answered; but by this time she had fallen astern, and began to pull
after the ship. Every one now called out, 'The boat, the boat!' The partners, in astonishment, entreated the captain to take the boat on board, but he coolly replied, 'I can
give them no assistance.' Mr. Mumford said it would not be the work of a minute.
'Back a sail, throw a rope overboard,' cried the partners; the answer was, 'No, I will
not endanger the ship.' We now felt convinced that the boat and crew were devoted
to destruction—no advice was given them, no assistance offered, no reasons assigned for
risking so cruel a sacrifice of human life—for the place where the boat met us was
free from the influence of the breakers, and a long way from the bar." *Adventures*,
80–81.

[10] Ross says the water decreased to two and one-half fathoms and that as the waves
swept across the deck, sometimes ten feet deep, the men clambered up the rigging to
save their lives.

residue of a stormy night, and enjoyed a brief interval of refreshing sleep.

With the light of day returned their cares and anxieties. They looked out from the mast-head over a wild coast, and wilder sea, but could discover no trace of the two boats and their crews that were missing. Several of the natives came on board with peltries, but there was no disposition to trade. They were interrogated by signs after the lost boats, but could not understand the inquiries.

Parties now went on shore and scoured the neighborhood. One of these was headed by the captain.[11] They had not proceeded far when they beheld a person at a distance in civilized garb. As he drew near he proved to be Weekes, the armorer. There was a burst of joy, for it was hoped his comrades were near at hand. His story, however, was one of disaster. He and his companions had found it impossible to govern their boat, having no rudder, and being beset by rapid and whirling currents and boisterous surges. After long struggling they had let her go at the mercy of the waves, tossing about, sometimes with her bow, sometimes with her broadside to the surges, threatened each instant with destruction, yet repeatedly escaping, until a huge sea broke over and swamped her. Weekes was overwhelmed by the boiling waves, but emerging above the surface, looked round for his companions. Aiken and Coles were not to be seen; near him were the two Sandwich Islanders, stripping themselves of their clothing that they might swim more freely. He did the same, and the boat floating near to him he seized hold of it. The two islanders joined him, and, uniting their forces, they succeeded in turning the boat upon her keel; then bearing down her stern and rocking her, they forced out so much water that she was able to bear the weight of a man without sinking. One of the islanders now got in, and in a little while bailed out the water with his hands. The other swam about and collected the oars, and they all three got once more on board.

By this time the tide had swept them beyond the breakers, and Weekes called on his companions to row for land. They were so chilled and benumbed by the cold, however, that they lost all heart, and absolutely refused. Weekes was equally chilled, but had superior sagacity and self-command. He counteracted the tendency to drowsiness and

[11] With Captain Thorn were McKay and Ross besides a few others. Their object was to go to the top of Cape Disappointment to look for the two boats. They met Weekes: " 'You did it purposely,' said he, in great agitation." Ross, *Adventures*, 83.

stupor which cold produces by keeping himself in constant exercise; and seeing that the vessel was advancing, and that everything depended upon himself, he set to work to scull the boat clear of the bar, and into quiet water.

Towards midnight one of the poor islanders expired: his companion threw himself on his corpse and could not be persuaded to leave him. The dismal night wore away amidst these horrors: as the day dawned, Weekes found himself near the land. He steered directly for it, and at length, with the aid of the surf, ran his boat high upon a sandy beach.

Finding that one of the Sandwich Islanders yet gave signs of life, he aided him to leave the boat, and set out with him towards the adjacent woods. The poor fellow, however, was too feeble to follow him, and Weekes was soon obliged to abandon him to his fate and provide for his own safety. Falling upon a beaten path, he pursued it, and after a few hours came to a part of the coast, where, to his surprise and joy, he beheld the ship at anchor and was met by the captain and his party.

After Weekes had related his adventures, three parties were despatched to beat up the coast in search of the unfortunate islander. They returned at night without success, though they had used the utmost diligence. On the following day the search was resumed, and the poor fellow was at length discovered lying beneath a group of rocks, his legs swollen, his feet torn and bloody from walking through bushes and briers, and himself half-dead with cold, hunger, and fatigue. Weekes and this islander were the only survivors of the crew of the jolly-boat, and no trace was ever discovered of Fox and his party. Thus eight men were lost on the first approach to the coast; a commencement that cast a gloom over the spirits of the whole party, and was regarded by some of the superstitious as an omen that boded no good to the enterprise.

Towards night the Sandwich Islanders went on shore, to bury the body of their unfortunate countryman who had perished in the boat. On arriving at the place where it had been left, they dug a grave in the sand, in which they deposited the corpse, with a biscuit under one of the arms, some lard under the chin, and a small quantity of tobacco, as provisions for its journey in the land of spirits. Having covered the body with sand and flints, they kneeled along the grave in a double row, with their faces turned to the east, while one who officiated as a priest sprinkled them with water from a hat. In so doing he recited a kind of prayer or invocation, to which, at intervals, the others made responses. Such were the simple rites performed by these poor savages at the grave of their comrade on the shores of a strange land; and when these were done, they rose and returned in silence to the ship, without once casting a look behind.[12]

[12] The previous eleven paragraphs are a close paraphrase of Franchère, *Narrative*, 230–38. See also Ross, *Adventures*, 78–85. Ross Cox, in his *Columbia River*, 52–54, also relates the efforts of the *Tonquin* to enter the Columbia, but at second hand.

CHAPTER VIII

Mouth of the Columbia — The Native Tribes — Their Fishing
Their Canoes — Bold Navigators — Equestrian Indians and
Piscatory Indians, Difference in Their Physical Organization
Search for a Trading Site — Expedition of M'Dougal and David Stuart
Comcomly, the One-Eyed Chieftain — Influence of Wealth in Savage Life
Slavery Among the Natives — An Aristocracy of Flatheads
Hospitality Among the Chinooks — Comcomly's Daughter
Her Conquest

THE Columbia, or Oregon, for the distance of thirty or forty miles from its entrance into the sea, is, properly speaking, a mere estuary, indented by deep bays so as to vary from three to seven miles in width; and is rendered extremely intricate and dangerous by shoals reaching nearly from shore to shore, on which, at times, the winds and currents produce foaming and tumultuous breakers. The mouth of the river proper is but about half a mile wide, formed by the contracting shores of the estuary. The entrance from the sea, as we have already observed, is bounded on the south side by a flat sandy spit of land, stretching into the ocean. This is commonly called Point Adams. The opposite, or northern side, is Cape Disappointment; a kind of peninsula, terminating in a steep knoll or promontory crowned with a forest of pine-trees, and connected with the mainland by a low and narrow neck. Immediately within this cape is a wide, open bay, terminating at Chinook Point, so called from a neighboring tribe of Indians. This was called Baker's Bay, and here the Tonquin was anchored.

The natives inhabiting the lower part of the river, and with whom the company was likely to have the most frequent intercourse, were divided at this time into four tribes, the Chinooks,[1] Clatsops,[2] Wahkia-

---

[1] The Chinooks occupied the north side of the Columbia near its mouth and had been known to coastal traders for many years. Lewis and Clark described them in 1805. "From their proximity to Astoria and their intimate relation with the early traders, they soon became well known, and their language formed the chief Indian basis for the Chinook jargon, first employed as a trade jargon," writes John R. Swanton in *The Indian Tribes of North America*, 418 (cited hereafter as Swanton, *Indian Tribes*). Lewis and Clark estimated that there were four hundred of these Indians on the

cums,[3] and Cathlamahs.[4] They resembled each other in person, dress, language, and manner; and were probably from the same stock, but broken into tribes, or rather hordes, by those feuds and schisms frequent among Indians.

These people generally live by fishing. It is true they occasionally hunt the elk and deer, and ensnare the waterfowl of their ponds and rivers, but these are casual luxuries. Their chief subsistence is derived from the salmon and other fish which abound in the Columbia and its tributary streams, aided by roots and herbs, especially the wappatoo,[5] which is found on the islands of the river.

As the Indians of the plains who depend upon the chase are bold and expert riders, and pride themselves upon their horses, so these piscatory tribes of the coast excel in the management of canoes, and are never more at home than when riding upon the waves. Their canoes vary in form and size. Some are upwards of fifty feet long, cut out of a single

Columbia at the time of their visit. They are now extinct or nearly so. *Ibid.*, 418–19. As did other tribes in the area, the Chinooks flattened the heads of their children in infancy. On the "Chinook jargon," see Chester Anders Fee, "Oregon's Historical Esperanto—the Chinook Jargon," *Oregon Historical Quarterly*, Vol. XLII (1941), 176–85.

[2] Linguistically, the Clatsops, of whom Lewis and Clark estimated there were three hundred, were related to the Chinooks. They lived on the south side of the Columbia and along the coast to the south. Lewis and Clark named their winter camp in 1805–1806 Fort Clatsop. The name means "dried salmon." See Swanton, *Indian Tribes*, 458.

[3] This tribe was first named and described by Lewis and Clark. Frederick Webb Hodge says of them: "A Chinookan tribe formerly living on the N. bank of Columbia r. near its mouth. Their territory adjoined that of the Chinook and extended upstream toward Oak point. According to Stuart (1821) they were an offshoot of the Chinook who had separated from the main body about two generations before under chief Wahkiacum and were afterward known by his name. . . . Their principal village seems to have been near Pillar rock, a short distance above Grays bay." *Handbook of American Indians*, II, 890.

[4] Of Chinookan stock, the Cathlamahs (or Cathlamets) lived on both sides of the Columbia near its mouth. There were about three hundred of them during the visit of Lewis and Clark. Swanton, *Indian Tribes*, 414.

[5] A potato-like tuber of either of two species, *Sagittaria latifolia* or *Sagittaria cuneata*; the word belongs to Chinook jargon. Wappatoo Island (now Sauvie Island) was named for the abundance of these plants growing on it. Lewis and Clark left a carefully detailed description of the plant (see *History of the Expedition*, II 351–52), both the bulb and the fruit of which were eaten. The plant was used for trading purposes by the Indians. Cox says: "In size they resemble a small potatoe, for which it is a good substitute when roasted or boiled; it has a very slight tinge of bitterness, but not unpleasantly so, and is highly esteemed by the natives, who collect vast quantities of it for their own use and for barter." *Columbia River*, 79.

tree, either fir or white cedar, and capable of carrying thirty persons. They have thwart pieces from side to side about three inches thick, and their gunwales flare outwards, so as to cast off the surges of the waves. The bow and stern are decorated with grotesque figures of men and animals, sometimes five feet in height.[6]

In managing their canoes they kneel two and two along the bottom, sitting on their heels, and wielding paddles from four to five feet long, while one sits on the stern and steers with a paddle of the same kind. The women are equally expert with the men in managing the canoe, and generally take the helm.

It is surprising to see with what fearless unconcern these savages venture in their light barks upon the roughest and most tempestuous seas. They seem to ride upon the waves like sea-fowl. Should a surge throw the canoe upon its side and endanger its overturn, those to windward lean over the upper gunwale, thrust their paddles deep into the wave, apparently catch the water and force it under the canoe, and by this action not merely regain an equilibrium, but give their bark a vigorous impulse forward.[7]

The effect of different modes of life upon the human frame and human character is strikingly instanced in the contrast between the hunting Indians of the prairies, and the piscatory Indians of the sea-coast. The former, continually on horseback scouring the plains, gaining their food by hardy exercise, and subsisting chiefly on flesh, are generally tall, sinewy, meagre, but well formed, and of bold and fierce deportment: the

[6] Cf. the following description by Alexander Henry of a war canoe belonging to the eldest son of Comcomly: "She was about six fathoms long and wide in proportion, the stem rising upright about six feet, on top of which was a figure of some imaginary monster of uncouth sculpture, having the head of a carnivorous animal with large erect ears, but no body, clinging by arms and legs to the upper end of the canoe, and grinning horribly. The ears were painted green, the other parts red and black. The stern also rose about five feet in height, but had no figure carved on it. On each side of both stem and stern broad strips of wood rose about four feet, having holes cut in them to shoot arrows through. She had a high spritsail made of handkerchiefs and gunahs [pieces of gunny cloth or jute], forming irregular strips. I am told these Indians commonly have pieces of squared timber, not unlike three-inch plank, high and broad, perforated to shoot arrows through, fixed on the bow of the war canoes to serve as bulwarks in battle." Elliott Coues (ed.), *New Light on the Early History of the Greater Northwest: The Manuscript Journals of Alexander Henry . . . and of David Thompson*, II, 835 (cited hereafter as *Henry-Thompson Journals*).

[7] The description of the canoes is from Lewis and Clark, a long paragraph on this subject being quoted in Cox's *Columbia River*, 175. Irving, who also used Cox elsewhere in this chapter, obviously drew his information from the quotation.

latter, lounging about the river banks, or squatting and curved up in their canoes, are generally low in stature, ill-shaped, with crooked legs, thick ankles, and broad flat feet.[8] They are inferior also in muscular power and activity, and in *game* qualities and appearance, to their hard-riding brethren of the prairies.

Having premised these few particulars concerning the neighboring Indians, we will return to the immediate concerns of the Tonquin and her crew.

Further search was made for Mr. Fox and his party, but with no better success, and they were at length given up as lost. In the meantime, the captain and some of the partners explored the river for some distance in a large boat, to select a suitable place for the trading post. Their old jealousies and differences continued; they never could coincide in their choice, and the captain objected altogether to any site so high up the river. They all returned therefore, to Baker's Bay in no very good humor. The partners proposed to examine the opposite shore, but the captain was impatient of any further delay. His eagerness to "get on" had increased upon him. He thought all these excursions a sheer loss of time, and was resolved to land at once, build a shelter for the reception of that part of his cargo destined for the use of the settlement, and having cleared his ship of it and of his irksome shipmates, to depart upon the prosecution of his coasting voyage, according to orders.

On the following day, therefore, without troubling himself to consult the partners, he landed in Baker's Bay, and proceeded to erect a shed for the reception of the rigging, equipments, and stores of the schooner that was to be built for the use of the settlement.[9]

This dogged determination on the part of the sturdy captain gave high offense to Mr. M'Dougal, who now considered himself at the head of the concern, as Mr. Astor's representative and proxy. He set off the same day, (April 5th,)[10] accompanied by Mr. David Stuart, for the southern shore, intending to be back by the seventh. Not having the

---

[8] Irving read in Cox: "The limbs of the men are in general well-shaped; but the women, owing to tight ligatures which they wear on the lower part of the legs, are quite bandy, with thick ankles, and broad flat feet." *Ibid.*, 165.

[9] In his *Narrative*, 239, Franchère states: "The next day, the 27th [of March, 1811], desirous of clearing the gangways of the live stock, we sent some men on shore to construct a pen, and soon after landed about fifty hogs, committing them to the care of the hands."

[10] The date agrees with Franchère.

captain to contend with, they soon pitched upon a spot which appeared to them favorable for the intended establishment. It was on a point of land called Point George, having a very good harbor, where vessels, not exceeding two hundred tons burden might anchor within fifty yards of the shore.

After a day thus profitably spent, they recrossed the river, but landed on the northern shore several miles above the anchoring ground of the Tonquin, in the neighborhood of Chinook, and visited the village of that tribe. Here they were received with great hospitality by the chief, who was named Comcomly,[11] a shrewd old savage, with but one eye, who will occasionally figure in this narrative. Each village forms a petty sovereignty, governed by its own chief, who, however, possesses but little authority, unless he be a man of wealth and substance; that is to say, possessed of canoes, slaves, and wives. The greater the number of these, the greater is the chief.[12] How many wives this one-eyed potentate maintained we are not told, but he certainly possessed great sway, not merely over his own tribe, but over the neighborhood.

Having mentioned slaves, we would observe that slavery exists among several of the tribes beyond the Rocky Mountains. The slaves are well treated while in good health, but occupied in all kinds of drudgery. Should they become useless, however, by sickness or old age, they are totally neglected, and left to perish; nor is any respect paid to their bodies after death.[13]

A singular custom prevails, not merely among the Chinooks, but among most of the tribes about this part of the coast, which is the flattening of the forehead. The process by which this deformity is effected commences immediately after birth. The infant is laid in a wooden trough, by way of cradle. The end on which the head reposes is higher than the rest. A padding is placed on the forehead of the infant, with a piece of bark above it, and is pressed down by cords, which pass through

[11] Lewis and Clark had become acquainted with Comcomly in 1805 and presented him with a medal. He appears frequently in early narratives concerning the Columbia River. See J. F. Santee, "Comcomly and the Chinooks," *Oregon Historical Quarterly*, Vol. XXXIII (1932), 271–78. His skull is preserved in an English museum. See A. G. Harvey, "Chief Comcomly's Skull," *ibid.*, Vol. XL (1939), 161–67.

[12] How closely Irving sometimes followed his sources is evident from the following passage from Cox: "Each village is governed by its own chief. He possesses little authority, and is respected in proportion to the number of wives, slaves, &c., which he may keep. The greater the number of these, the greater the chief." *Op. cit.*, 173.

[13] Irving's information is derived from *ibid.*, 166. Cf. Franchère, *Narrative*, 324.

holes on each side of the trough. As the tightening of the padding and the pressing of the head to the board is gradual, the process is said not to be attended with much pain. The appearance of the infant, however, while in this state of compression, is whimsically hideous, and "its little black eyes," we are told,[14] "being forced out by the tightness of the bandages, resemble those of a mouse choked in a trap."

About a year's pressure is sufficient to produce the desired effect, at the end of which time the child emerges from its bandages a complete flathead, and continues so through life. It must be noted, however, that this flattening of the head has something in it of aristocratical significancy, like the crippling of the feet among the Chinese ladies of quality. At any rate, it is a sign of freedom. No slave is permitted to bestow this enviable deformity upon his child; all the slaves, therefore, are roundheads.

With this worthy tribe of Chinooks the two partners passed a part of the day[15] very agreeably. M'Dougal, who was somewhat vain of his official rank, had given it to be understood that they were two chiefs of a great trading company, about to be established here, and the quicksighted, though one-eyed chief, who was somewhat practiced in traffic with white men, immediately perceived the policy of cultivating the friendship of two such important visitors. He regaled them, therefore, to the best of his ability, with abundance of salmon and wappatoo. The next morning, April 7th, they prepared to return to the vessel, according to promise. They had eleven miles of open bay to traverse; the wind was fresh, the waves ran high. Comcomly remonstrated with them on the hazard to which they would be exposed. They were resolute, however, and launched their boat, while the wary chieftain followed at some short distance in his canoe. Scarce had they rowed a mile, when a wave broke over their boat and upset it. They were in imminent peril of drowning, especially Mr. M'Dougal, who could not swim. Comcomly, however, came bounding over the waves in his light canoe, and snatched them from a watery grave.

They were taken on shore and a fire made, at which they dried their clothes, after which Comcomly conducted them back to his village. Here everything was done that could be devised for their entertainment during three days that they were detained by bad weather. Comcomly

---

[14] By Ross Cox. Irving's description of the process paraphrases Cox; see *op. cit.*, 164–65.

[15] *A day* in first edition.

made his people perform antics before them; and his wives and daughters endeavored, by all the soothing and endearing arts of women, to find favor in their eyes. Some even painted their bodies with red clay, and anointed themselves with fish oil, to give additional lustre to their charms. Mr. M'Dougal seems to have had a heart susceptible to the influence of the gentler sex. Whether or no it was first touched on this occasion we do not learn; but it will be found, in the course of this work, that one of the daughters of the hospitable Comcomly eventually made a conquest of the great eri of the American Fur Company.

When the weather had moderated and the sea become tranquil, the one-eyed chief of the Chinooks manned his state canoe, and conducted his guests in safety to the ship, where they were welcomed with joy, for apprehensions had been felt for their safety. Comcomly and his people were then entertained on board of the Tonquin, and liberally rewarded for their hospitality and services. They returned home highly satisfied, promising to remain faithful friends and allies of the white men.[16]

[16] The last three paragraphs are drawn from Franchère, *Narrative*, 239–41.

Point George — Founding of Astoria — Indian Visitors
Their Reception — The Captain Taboos the Ship
Departure of the Tonquin — Comments on the Conduct of Captain Thorn

FROM the report made by the two exploring partners, it was determined that Point George should be the site of the trading house. These
gentlemen, it is true, were not perfectly satisfied with the place, and
were desirous of continuing their search; but Captain Thorn was impatient to land his cargo and continue his voyage, and protested against
any more of what he termed "sporting excursions."

Accordingly, on the 12th of April the launch was freighted with all
things necessary for the purpose, and sixteen persons departed in her to
commence the establishment, leaving the Tonquin to follow as soon as
the harbor could be sounded.[1]

Crossing the wide mouth of the river, the party landed, and encamped
at the bottom of a small bay within Point George.[2] The situation chosen
for the fortified post was on an elevation facing to the north, with the
wide estuary, its sand bars and tumultuous breakers spread out before it,
and the promontory of Cape Disappointment, fifteen miles distant, closing the prospect to the left. The surrounding country was in all the freshness of spring; the trees were in the young leaf, the weather was superb,
and everything looked delightful to men just emancipated from a long
confinement on shipboard.[3] The Tonquin shortly afterwards made her
way through the intricate channel, and came to anchor in the little bay,

[1] Franchère relates that there were but twelve persons "furnished with tools, and
with provisions for a week." *Narrative*, 241. But Ross, referring to this same date, declares that "the whole party, consisting of thirty-three persons . . . left the ship and encamped on shore." *Adventures*, 88.

[2] So named by Vancouver in 1792; now called Smith Point. Today the city of
Astoria occupies this site.

[3] Details and tone are from Franchère, who declared, "We imagined ourselves
in a garden of Eden." *Narrative*, 241. Not everyone shared his enthusiasm. Ross, though
glad to be off the ship, said: "The day was not one of pleasure, but of labor. . . . Silent
and with heavy hearts we began the toil of the day, in clearing away brush and rotten
wood for a spot to encamp on." *Adventures*, 89.

and was saluted from the encampment with three volleys of musketry and three cheers. She returned the salute with three cheers and three guns.

All hands now set to work cutting down trees, clearing away thickets, and marking out the place for the residence, store-house, and powder magazine, which were to be built of logs and covered with bark.[4] Others landed the timbers intended for the frame of the coasting vessel,[5] and

[4] Though using Franchère for his information, Irving neglects to mention that a warehouse measuring sixty feet by twenty feet was constructed for storage of goods from the *Tonquin*. Fifteen days, from May 16 to the thirtieth were occupied "in stowing away the goods and other effects intended for the establishment." The buildings were constructed of hewn logs, and roofs were made of cedar bark. *Narrative*, 250, 251. As June wore on, other buildings were begun and defenses were constructed. "The dwelling house was raised parallel to the warehouse; we cut a great quantity of pickets [a foot and a half in diameter] in the forest, and formed a square, with palisades in front and rear, of about 90 feet by 120; the warehouse, built on the edge of a ravine, formed one flank, the dwelling house and shops the other; with a little bastion at each angle north and south, on which were mounted four small cannon. The whole was finished in six days, and had a sufficiently formidable aspect to deter the Indians from attacking us; and for greater surety, we organized a guard for day and night." *Ibid.*, 255. Living quarters were not actually completed until September 26, when they were first occupied. Large enough to accommodate everyone, the building had "a sitting, a dining room, some lodging or sleeping rooms, and an apartment for the men and artificers, all under the same roof. We also completed a shop for the blacksmith, who till that time had worked in the open air." *Ibid.*, 259. At the same time, during August and September, a building measuring forty-five by thirty-five feet was built as a hospital and as a lodging for mechanics. *Ibid.*, 278. See also Cox, *Columbia River*, 70.

In front of the fort, on a sloping piece of ground, garden seeds carried from New York were planted in May, but only potatoes, turnips, and radishes matured. Twelve potatoes survived the sea voyage, but these produced 190 potatoes the first season; using some for seed, the Astorians raised five bushels the second year and fifty the third. Franchère, *Narrative*, 319.

Ross gives the impression that "this pioneer corps, composed of traders, shopkeepers, voyageurs, and Owhyhees, all ignorant alike in this new walk of life, and the most ignorant of all, the leader" (*Adventures*, 90), were sadly lacking in the qualities needed to construct a post such as Astoria on a wild, uncivilized coast. For many, the handling of an ax and a gun was something strangely new. Ross, in fact, gives a far less optimistic account of the building of Astoria than does Franchère. He says, for example, that their hard labor and toil cleared less than an acre of land in two months; that two men were injured by the felling of trees; that three were killed by Indians; and that one lost a hand from exploding gunpowder being used to blast out stumps. The weather, with sleet, rain, and fog, was bad, as was the food; and many men became sick and had no physician to help them. Conditions became bad enough that some men deserted. Ross blames Astor for all this in failing to send a physician with the expedition and "in his choice of the great pasha, M'Dougall, whom he placed at the head of his affairs." *Ibid.*, 92–93.

[5] These timbers had been prefabricated in New York. The vessel was to be thirty

proceeded to put them together, while others prepared a garden spot, and sowed the seeds of various vegetables.

The next thought was to give a name to the embryo metropolis: the one that naturally presented itself was that of the projector and supporter of the whole enterprise. It was accordingly named ASTORIA.

The neighboring Indians now swarmed about the place. Some brought a few land-otter and sea-otter skins to barter, but in very scanty parcels; the greater number came prying about to gratify their curiosity, for they are said to be impertinently inquisitive; while not a few came with no other design than to pilfer; the laws of *meum* and *tuum* being but slightly respected among them. Some of them beset the ship in their canoes, among whom was the Chinook chief Comcomly, and his liege subjects. These were well received by Mr. M'Dougal, who was delighted with an opportunity of entering upon his functions, and acquiring importance in the eyes of his future neighbors. The confusion thus produced on board, and the derangement of the cargo caused by this petty trade, stirred the spleen of the captain, who had a sovereign contempt for the one-eyed chieftain and all his crew. He complained loudly of having his ship lumbered by a host of "Indian ragamuffins," who had not a skin to dispose of, and at length put his positive interdict upon all trafficking on board. Upon this Mr. M'Dougal was fain to land, and establish his quarters at the encampment, where he could exercise his rights and enjoy his dignities without control.[6]

The feud, however, between these rival powers still continued, but was chiefly carried on by letter. Day after day and week after week elapsed, yet the store-house requisite for the reception of the cargo was not completed, and the ship was detained in port; while the captain was teased by frequent requisitions for various articles for the use of the establishment, or the trade with the natives. An angry correspondence took place, in which he complained bitterly of the time wasted in "smoking and sporting parties," as he termed the reconnoitring expeditions, and in clearing and preparing meadow ground and turnip patches, in-

---

tons, and was built by John Weekes and Johann Koaster, ship's carpenter, with the help of others. It was not until October 2 that the schooner, which was named *Dolly*, was finally launched. See Franchère, *Narrative*, 242, 259. Ross points out that the *Dolly* was too small for any use except river navigation. *Adventures*, 90.

[6] Irving hints at McDougall's self-importance. Ross is forthright in saying that "he was a man of but ordinary capacity, with an irritable, peevish temper; the most unfit man in the world to head an expedition or command men." *Adventures*, 89.

stead of despatching his ship. At length all these jarring matters were adjusted, if not to the satisfaction, at least to the acquiescence of all parties. The part of the cargo destined for the use of Astoria was landed, and the ship left free to proceed on her voyage.

As the Tonquin was to coast to the north, to trade for peltries at the different harbors, and to touch at Astoria on her return in the autumn, it was unanimously determined that Mr. M'Kay should go in her as supercargo, taking with him Mr. Lewis as ship's clerk.[7] On the first of June[8] the ship got under way, and dropped down to Baker's Bay, where she was detained for a few days by a head wind; but early in the morning of the fifth stood out to sea with a fine beeze and swelling canvas, and swept off gaily on her fatal voyage, from which she was never to return!

On reviewing the conduct of Captain Thorn, and examining his peevish and somewhat whimsical correspondence, the impression left upon our mind is, upon the whole, decidedly in his favor. While we smile at the simplicity of his heart and the narrowness of his views, which made him regard everything out of the direct path of his daily duty, and the rigid exigencies of the service, as trivial and impertinent, which inspired him with contempt for the swelling vanity of some of his coadjutors, and the literary exercises and curious researches of others, we cannot but applaud that strict and conscientious devotion to the interests of his employer, and to what he considered the true objects of the enterprise in which he was engaged. He certainly was to blame occasionally for the asperity of his manners, and the arbitrary nature of his measures, yet much that is exceptionable in this part of his conduct may be traced to rigid notions of duty acquired in that tyrannical school, a ship of war, and to the construction given by his companions to the orders of Mr. Astor, so little in conformity with his own. His mind, too, appears to have become almost diseased by the suspicions he had formed as to the loyalty of his associates, and the nature of their ultimate designs; yet

[7] Ovide de Montigny, one of the clerks, was also selected, but he was released because he easily became seasick. Louis Bruslé, a Canadian boatman, was chosen to take his place. Because of his incompatibility with Jonathan Thorn, John Mumford, the second mate, was also allowed to remain behind. He was replaced by Job Aitken. Franchère says of himself: "I had the good fortune not to be chosen for this disastrous voyage, thanks to my having made myself useful at the establishment." By such choices were the fates of these men determined. See Franchère, Narrative, 250–51.

[8] The date is confirmed by Franchère.

on this point there were circumstances to, in some measure, justify him. The relations between the United States and Great Britain were at that time in a critical state; in fact, the two countries were on the eve of a war. Several of the partners were British subjects, and might be ready to desert the flag under which they acted, should a war take place. Their application to the British minister at New York shows the dubious feeling with which they had embarked in the present enterprise. They had been in the employ of the Northwest Company, and might be disposed to rally again under that association, should events threaten the prosperity of this embryo establishment of Mr. Astor. Besides, we have the fact, averred to us by one of the partners,[9] that some of them, who were young and heedless, took a mischievous and unwarrantable pleasure in playing upon the jealous temper of the captain, and affecting mysterious consultations and sinister movements.

These circumstances are cited in palliation of the doubts and surmises of Captain Thorn, which might otherwise appear strange and unreasonable. That most of the partners were perfectly upright and faithful in the discharge of the trust reposed in them we are fully satisfied; still the honest captain was not invariably wrong in his suspicions; and that he formed a pretty just opinion of the integrity of that aspiring personage, Mr. M'Dougal, will be substantially proved[10] in the sequel.[11]

[9] This is another indication that some of Irving's information came orally from various members of the expedition. A likely person in this case is Robert Stuart, who had made the voyage in the *Tonquin* and who, in 1835, was living in Detroit. Another possible candidate is David Stuart, his uncle, who lived with Robert. He died in 1853.

[10] *Proven* in first edition.

[11] Granted that there were positive things to be said in Jonathan Thorn's favor, still Irving's attempts to justify his actions are not entirely convincing in light of the circumstances related by Franchère and Ross. Irving read Thorn's letters to Astor, and these would have presented the Captain in a favorable light while casting an unfavorable one over the passengers. On the other side, Irving had only Franchère's narrative to counter Thorn's complaints. What might have been his opinion of Thorn had he been able to read Ross's *Adventures*, not published until thirteen years after *Astoria*, one can not say, but that it would have been different is likely. Thorn's brutality and arrogance, his willingness to abandon men on an uninhabited island, and his actions leading to the deaths of eight men at the entrance of the Columbia—actions that were little short of murder—can hardly be mitigated.

◄{ C H A P T E R   X }►

WHILE the Astorians were busily occupied in completing their factory and fort, a report was brought to them by an Indian from the upper part of the river, that a party of thirty white men had appeared on the banks of the Columbia, and were actually building houses at the second rapids. This information caused much disquiet. We have already mentioned that the Northwest Company had established posts to the west of the Rocky Mountains, in a district called by them New Caledonia, which extended from lat. 52° to 55° north, being within the British territories.[1]

[1] See above, p. 33.

For the push of the North West Company west of the Continental Divide, see Phillips, *The Fur Trade*, II, 279–91. The posts of this company on the Columbia and its tributaries were six in number. Kootenay House was erected near the source of the main Columbia in British Columbia near Toby Creek. This, the first trading post on the Columbia, was built by David Thompson in 1807–1808. A log trading house was built by Finan McDonald on the Kootenai (spelled *Kootenay* in Canada) River near today's Libby, Montana, in 1808. Fort Kootenay was built on Kootenai River near present-day Jennings, Montana, about 1811. Kullyspell House was built in 1809 by David Thompson near modern Hope, Idaho, on Pend Oreille Lake; Finan McDonald was left in charge. It was used only two winters. Salish (or Saleesh) House was built on the Clark Fork River two miles below Thompson River on Thompson Prairie about 1809–10. It was moved several times to other near-by points. Spokane House, probably constructed by Jaco Finley (Jacques Raphael Finlay), perhaps with the help of Finan McDonald, was located at the junction of Spokane and Little Spokane rivers in the summer of 1810. See T. C. Elliott, "The Fur Trade in the Columbia River Basin Prior to 1811," *Oregon Historical Quarterly*, Vol. XV (1914), 241–51. On the building of Kullyspell House, see *idem*, "David Thompson and Beginnings in Idaho," *ibid.*, Vol. XXI (1920), 49–61. See also M. Catherine White (ed.), *David Thompson's Journals Relating to Montana and Adjacent Regions, 1808–1812*; "Saleesh House: The First

It was now apprehended that they were advancing within the American limits, and were endeavoring to seize upon the upper part of the river and forestall the American Fur Company in the surrounding trade; in which case bloody feuds might be anticipated, such as had prevailed between the rival fur companies in former days.

A reconnoitring party was sent up the river to ascertain the truth of the report. They ascended to the foot of the first rapid, about two hundred miles, but could hear nothing of any white men being in the neighborhood.[2]

Not long after their return, however, further accounts were received, by two wandering Indians, which established the fact, that the Northwest Company had actually erected a trading-house on the Spokan River, which falls into the north branch of the Columbia.[3]

What rendered this intelligence the more disquieting, was the inability of the Astorians, in their present reduced state as to numbers, and the exigencies of their new establishment, to furnish detachments to penetrate the country in different directions, and fix the posts necessary to secure the interior trade.

It was resolved, however, at any rate, to advance a counter-check to this post on the Spokan, and one of the partners, Mr. David Stuart, prepared to set out for the purpose with eight men and a small assortment of goods. He was to be guided by the two Indians, who knew the country, and promised to take him to a place not far from the Spokan River, and in a neighborhood abounding with beaver. Here he was to establish himself and to remain for a time, provided he found the situation advantageous and the natives friendly.

On the 15th of July, when Mr. Stuart was nearly ready to embark,

---

Trading Post Among the Flatheads," *Pacific Northwest Quarterly*, Vol. XXXIII (1942), 251–63.

David Thompson, descending the Columbia River, reached the mouth of the Snake River on July 9, 1811. Here, he wrote, "I erected a small Pole, with a half Sheet of Paper well tied about it, with these words on it—Know hereby that this country is claimed by Great Britain as part of its Territories, & that the N W Company of Merchants from Canada, finding the Factory for this People inconvenient for them, do hereby intend to erect a Factory in this Place for the Commerce of the Country around. D. Thompson." *Henry-Thompson Journals*, II, 748n.; also quoted in Phillips, *op. cit.*, II, 290. When Thompson reached the mouth of the Columbia on July 15, 1811, he found Astoria already established.

[2] The journey of this party is recounted in Franchère *Narrative*, 242–49.

[3] See *ibid.*, 251.

a canoe made its appearance, standing for the harbor, and manned by nine white men. Much speculation took place who these strangers could be, for it was too soon to expect their own people, under Mr. Hunt, who were to cross the continent. As the canoe drew near, the British standard was distinguished: on coming to land, one of the crew stepped on shore, and announced himself as Mr. David Thompson,[4] astronomer, and partner of the Northwest Company. According to his account, he had set out in the preceding year with a tolerably strong party, and a supply of Indian goods, to cross the Rocky Mountains. A part of his people, however, had deserted him on the eastern side, and returned with the goods to the nearest Northwest post. He had persisted in crossing the mountains with eight men, who remained true to him. They had traversed the higher regions, and ventured near the source of the Columbia,[5] where, in the spring, they had constructed a cedar canoe, the same in which they had reached Astoria.

This, in fact, was the party despatched by the Northwest Company to anticipate Mr. Astor in his intention of effecting a settlement at the mouth of the Columbia River. It appears, from information subsequently derived from other sources, that Mr. Thompson had pushed on his course with great haste, calling at all the Indian villages in his march, presenting them with British flags, and even planting them at the forks of the rivers, proclaiming formally that he took possession of the country in the name of the king of Great Britain for the Northwest Company. As his original plan was defeated by the desertion of his people, it is

[4] Born in England, Thompson (1770–1857) came to the New World, where he was apprenticed in 1784 to the Hudson's Bay Company, remaining with it until 1794. In that year he became associated with the North West Company as a clerk and later, in 1804, as a partner. Thompson is especially notable for his geographical explorations in Canada and the Pacific Northwest. In arriving at Astoria, he became the first white man to descend the entire length of the Columbia River. Much of his geographical knowledge was applied to the making of an important map of the fur-trading country. He devoted ten years (1816–26) to surveying the boundary between the United States and Canada. See Wallace (ed.), *Documents*, 502; Phillips, *op. cit.*, II, *passim*; T. C. Elliott (ed.), "Journal of David Thompson," *Oregon Historical Quarterly*, Vol. XV (1914), 39–63 and 104–25.

Thompson's journal confirms Irving's date, which fell on a Monday. "At 1 P.M.," he wrote, "thank God for our safe arrival, we came to the House of Mr. Astor's Company, Messrs. McDougal, Stuart & Stuart, who received me in the most polite manner, and here we hope to stay a few days to refresh ourselves." Elliott (ed.), "Journal of David Thompson," *loc. cit.*, 63.

[5] See T. C. Elliott, "Discovery of the Source of the Columbia River," *Oregon Historical Quarterly*, Vol. XXVI (1925), 23–49.

probable that he descended the river simply to reconnoitre, and ascertain whether an American settlement had been commenced.

Mr. Thompson was, no doubt, the first white man who descended the northern branch of the Columbia from so near its source. Lewis and Clarke struck the main body of the river at the forks,[6] about four hundred miles from its mouth. They entered it from Lewis River,[7] its southern branch, and thence descended.

Though Mr. Thompson could be considered as little better than a spy in the camp, he was received with great cordiality by Mr. M'Dougal, who had a lurking feeling of companionship and good-will for all of the Northwest Company. He invited him to head-quarters, where he and his people were hospitably entertained. Nay, further, being somewhat in extremity, he was furnished by Mr. M'Dougal with goods and provisions for his journey back, across the mountains, much against the wishes of Mr. David Stuart, who did not think the object of his visit entitled him to any favor.[8]

On the 23d of July, Mr. Stuart set out upon his expedition to the interior. His party consisted of four of the clerks, Messrs. Pillet, Ross, M'Lennon, and Montigny, two Canadian voyageurs, and two natives of the Sandwich Islands.[9] They had three canoes well laden with provisions, and with goods and necessaries for a trading establishment.

Mr. Thompson and his party set out in company with them, it being

[6] The confluence of the Snake and Columbia rivers.

[7] Snake River.

[8] Ross's version of Thompson's appearance at Astoria follows: "M'Dougall received him like a brother; nothing was too good for Mr. Thompson; he had access everywhere; saw and examined everything; and whatever he asked for he got, as if he had been one of ourselves. . . . His . . . visit had evidently no other object but to discourage us—a manoeuvre of the Northwest policy to extend their own trade at the expense of ours; but he failed." *Adventures*, 101.

Franchère said he was "more like a geographer than a fur-trader," and in this Franchère judged correctly. "He was provided with a sextant, chronometer and barometer, and during a week's sojourn [with us] had an opportunity to make several astronomical observations." *Narrative*, 254.

[9] Irving follows Franchère here except for changing Franchère's "M'Clellan" to "M'Lennon," but Franchère mentions four *voyageurs* instead of three and omits any mention of the two Sandwich Islanders. Ross, however, includes them but says there were three *voyageurs*. He adds that twenty-one persons left in two, not three, canoes at eleven o'clock on the morning of July 22, 1811. Each canoe was laden "with fifteen or twenty packages of goods, of ninety pounds weight." *Adventures*, 115–16. For Franchère, see *Narrative*, 254–55.

his intention to proceed direct to Montreal.[10] The partners at Astoria forwarded by him a short letter to Mr. Astor,[11] informing him of their safe arrival at the mouth of the Columbia, and that they had not yet heard of Mr. Hunt. The little squadron of canoes set sail with a favorable breeze, and soon passed Tongue Point,[12] a long, high, and rocky promontory, covered with trees, and stretching far into the river. Opposite to this, on the northern shore, is a deep bay, where the Columbia anchored at the time of the discovery, and which is still called Gray's Bay, from the name of her commander.

From hence, the general course of the river for about seventy miles, was nearly southeast; varying in breadth according to its bays and indentations, and navigable for vessels of three hundred tons. The shores were in some places high and rocky, with low marshy islands at their feet, subject to inundation, and covered with willows, poplars, and other trees that love an alluvial soil. Sometimes the mountains receded, and gave place to beautiful plains and noble forests. While the river margin was richly fringed with trees of deciduous foliage, the rough uplands were crowned by majestic pines, and firs of gigantic size, some towering to the height of between two and three hundred feet, with proportionate circumference. Out of these the Indians wrought their great canoes and pirogues.

At one part of the river, they passed, on the northern side, an isolated rock, about one hundred and fifty feet high, rising from a low marshy soil, and totally disconnected with the adjacent mountains. This was held in great reverence by the neighboring Indians, being one of their principal places of sepulture. The same provident care for the deceased that prevails among the hunting tribes of the prairies is observable among the piscatory tribes of the rivers and sea-coast. Among the former, the favorite horse of the hunter is buried with him in the same funereal mound, and his bow and arrows are laid by his side, that he may be perfectly equipped for the "happy hunting grounds" of the land of spirits. Among the latter, the Indian is wrapped in his mantle of

[10] Thompson's journal gives Monday, July 22, as the date of departure. He wrote: "A fine day. Arranged for setting off for the Interior in company with Mr. David Stuart and 8 of his men in 3 canoes. I pray Kind Providence to send us a good journey to my family and friends. At 1-24 P.M. set off." Elliott (ed.), "Journal of David Thompson," *loc. cit.*, 106.

[11] See Chapter III, note 37.

[12] Three miles east of Astoria, according to both Ross and Cox.

skins, laid in his canoe, with his paddle, his fishing spear, and other implements beside him, and placed aloft on some rock or other[13] eminence overlooking the river, or bay, or lake, that he has frequented He is thus fitted out to launch away upon those placid streams and sunny lakes stocked with all kinds of fish and waterfowl, which are prepared in the next world for those who have acquitted themselves as good sons, good fathers, good husbands, and, above all, good fishermen, during their mortal sojourn.

The isolated rock in question presented a spectacle of the kind, numerous dead bodies being deposited in canoes on its summit; while on poles around were trophies, or, rather, funereal offerings of trinkets, garments, baskets of roots, and other articles for the use of the deceased. A reverential feeling protects these sacred spots from robbery or insult. The friends of the deceased, especially the women, repair here at sunrise and sunset for some time after his death, singing his funeral dirge, and uttering loud wailings and lamentations.[14]

From the number of dead bodies in canoes observed upon this rock by the first explorers of the river, it received the name of Mount Coffin, which it continues to bear.[15]

Beyond this rock they passed the mouth of a river on the right bank of the Columbia, which appeared to take its rise in a distant mountain, covered with snow. The Indian name of this river was the Cowleskee.[16] Some miles further on they came to the great Columbian Valley, so called by Lewis and Clarke. It is sixty miles in width, and extends far to the southeast between parallel ridges of mountains,[17] which bound it on the east and west. Through the centre of this valley flowed a large and beautiful stream, called the Wallamot,[18] which came wandering for

[13] *Other* is lacking in first edition.

[14] Irving pieced together his information on Indian burial customs from Franchère, *Narrative*, 333, 334; from Cox's *Columbia River*, 77, 179; and possibly from Lewis and Clark, *History of the Expedition*, II, 314.

[15] Derived from Franchère, *Narrative*, 244. Mount Coffin was named by Lieutenant Broughton.

[16] The Cowlitz River, which flows southwest out of the Cascade Range into the Columbia a few miles south of modern Kelso, Washington.

[17] The Cascade Range.

[18] Pronounced Wallámot, the accent being upon the second syllable. (Irving's note) The Willamette River flows north through Oregon west of the Cascade Range and empties into the Columbia near Portland. Lewis and Clark referred to it as the Multnomah River. It appears correctly on the map published in the first edition of *Astoria*.

several hundred miles, through a yet unexplored wilderness. The sheltered situation of this immense valley had an obvious effect upon the climate. It was a region of great beauty and luxuriance, with lakes and pools, and green meadows shaded by noble groves. Various tribes were said to reside in this valley, and along the banks of the Wallamot.

About eight miles above the mouth of the Wallamot the little squadron arrived at Vancouver's Point, so called in honor of that celebrated voyager by his lieutenant (Broughton) when he explored the river. This point is said to present one of the most beautiful scenes on the Columbia; a lovely meadow, with a silver sheet of limpid water in the centre, enlivened by wild-fowl, a range of hills crowned by forests, while the prospect is closed by Mount Hood, a magnificent mountain rising into a lofty peak, and covered with snow; the ultimate landmark of the first explorers of the river.

Point Vancouver is about one hundred miles from Astoria. Here the reflux of the tide ceases to be perceptible. To this place vessels of two and three hundred tons burden may ascend. The party under the command of Mr. Stuart had been three or four days in reaching it, though we have forborne to notice their daily progress and nightly encampments.[19]

From Point Vancouver the river turned towards the northeast, and became more contracted and rapid, with occasional islands and frequent sand-banks. These islands are furnished with a number of ponds, and at certain seasons abound with swans, geese, brants, cranes, gulls, plover, and other wild-fowl. The shores, too, are low and closely wooded, and[20] such an undergrowth of vines and rushes as to be almost impassable.

[19] Irving left their journey undescribed because he had no record of this trip. Instead, he contented himself with descriptions of scenery along the river and adjacent areas, much of his information coming from Franchère's account of an earlier journey which the Astorians made up the Columbia. See *Narrative*, 242–49. And some details appear to have been derived from Cox, *op. cit.*, chap. 6. But Irving had by now also turned to Robert Stuart's journal (or, more properly, to the redaction that Irving named the "Travelling Memoranda"), as evidenced by the following passage in Stuart, which supplied Irving with his description of Vancouver's Point. Stuart wrote: "Vancouver's Point, as beautiful a piece of scenery as any the Columbia affords, it is composed of an enchanting meadow near the river bank, while the rear is a ridge of considerable elevation, moderately wooded . . .; in the middle of the meadow stands a pond of pure limpid water, well stocked with Fish . . . and in Spring and Autumn, the surface is covered with wild fowl." Spaulding (ed.), *On the Oregon Trail*, 49; see also Rollins (ed.), *Discovery of the Oregon Trail*, 33.

[20] *With* in first edition.

About thirty miles above Point Vancouver the mountains again approach on both sides of the river, which is bordered by stupendous precipices, covered with the fir and the white cedar, and enlivened occasionally by beautiful cascades leaping from a great height, and sending up wreaths of vapor. One of these precipices, or cliffs, is curiously worn by time and weather so as to have the appearance of a ruined fortress, with towers and battlements, beetling high above the river, while two small cascades, one hundred and fifty feet in height, pitch down from the fissures of the rocks.

The turbulence and rapidity of the current continually augmenting as they advanced, gave the voyagers intimation that they were approaching the great obstructions of the river, and at length they arrived at Strawberry Island,[21] so called by Lewis and Clarke, which lies at the foot of the first rapid. As this part of the Columbia will be repeatedly mentioned in the course of this work, being the scene of some of its incidents, we shall give a general description of it in this place.

The falls[22] or rapids of the Columbia are situated about [23] one hundred and eighty miles above the mouth of the river. The first is a perpendicular cascade of twenty feet, after which there is a swift descent for a mile, between islands of hard black rock, to another pitch of eight feet divided by two rocks. About two and a half miles below this the river expands into a wide basin, seemingly dammed up by a perpendicular ridge of black rock. A current, however, sets diagonally to the left of this rocky barrier, where there is a chasm forty-five yards in width. Through this the whole body of the river roars along, swelling and whirling and boiling for some distance in the wildest confusion. Through this tremendous channel the intrepid explorers of the river, Lewis and Clarke, passed safely in their boats; the danger being, not from the rocks, but from the great surges and whirlpools.[24]

At the distance of a mile and a half from the foot of this narrow

[21] Lewis and Clark, under the date of November 2, 1805, described Strawberry Island in the following words: "This island . . . is three miles in length and about one in width; its situation is high and open, the land rich, and at this time covered with grass and a great number of strawberry vines, from which we gave it the name of Strawberry island." *History of the Expedition*, II, 243–44.

[22] Celilo Falls.

[23] Erroneously *above* in Author's Revised Edition. *About* appears in the first edition.

[24] Irving's information came from Lewis and Clark under date of October 24, 1805. *History of the Expedition*, II, 217.

channel is a rapid, formed by two rocky islands; and two miles beyond is a second great fall, over a ledge of rocks twenty feet high, extending nearly from shore to shore. The river is again compressed into a channel from fifty to a hundred feet wide, worn through a rough bed of hard black rock, along which it boils and roars with great fury for the distance of three miles. This is called "the Long Narrows."[25]

Here is the great fishing place of the Columbia. In the spring of the year, when the water is high, the salmon ascend the river in incredible numbers. As they pass through this narrow strait, the Indians, standing on the rocks, or on the end of wooden stages projecting from the banks, scoop them up with small nets distended on hoops and attached to long handles, and cast them on the shore.[26]

They are then cured and packed in a peculiar manner. After having been opened and disemboweled, they are exposed to the sun on scaffolds erected on the river banks. When sufficiently dry, they are pounded fine between two stones, pressed into the smallest compass, and packed in baskets or bales of grass matting, about two feet long and one in diameter, lined with the cured skin of a salmon. The top is likewise covered with fish skins, secured by cords passing through holes in the edge of the basket. Packages are then made, each containing twelve of these bales, seven at bottom, five at top, pressed close to each other, with the corded side upward, wrapped in mats and corded. These are placed in dry situations, and again covered with matting. Each of these packages contains from ninety to a hundred pounds of dried fish, which in this state will keep sound for several years.[27]

We have given this process at some length, as furnished by the first explorers, because it marks a practiced ingenuity in preparing articles of traffic for a market, seldom seen among our aboriginals. For like reason we would make especial mention of the village of Wish-ram,[28]

[25] Irving paraphrases Lewis and Clark, October 25, 1805, who had described this place as follows: "The channel for three miles is worn through a hard rough black rock from fifty to one hundred yards wide, in which the water swells and boils in a tremendous manner." *Ibid.*, 221–22. Note that Irving carelessly copied *feet* for *yards*. The Long Narrows, also known as the Dalles and as the Great Dalles, is now referred to as Five Mile Rapids. Cf. below, Chapter XXXVII, note 46.

[26] Irving seems here to condense a passage in Stuart's "Travelling Memoranda"; see Spaulding (ed.), *op cit.*, 54, and Rollins (ed.), *op. cit.*, 52.

[27] Lewis and Clarke, vol. ii, p. 32. (Irving's note) This description is given in Lewis and Clark under date of October 22, 1805. *History of the Expedition*, II, 212.

[28] Irving is apparently the first to record the name *Wishram*. The village has been

at the head of the Long Narrows, as being a solitary instance of an aboriginal trading mart, or emporium. Here the salmon caught in the neighboring rapids were "warehoused," to await customers. Hither the tribes from the mouth of the Columbia repaired with the fish of the sea-coast, the roots, berries, and especially the wappatoo, gathered in the lower parts of the river, together with goods and trinkets obtained from the ships which casually visit the coast. Hither also the tribes from the Rocky Mountains brought down horses, bear-grass, quamash, and other commodities of the interior. The merchant fishermen at the falls acted as middlemen or factors, and passed the objects of traffic, as it were, cross-handed; trading away part of the wares received from the mountain tribes to those of the rivers and plains, and *vice versa*: their packages of pounded salmon entered largely into the system of barter, and being carried off in opposite directions, found their way to the savage hunting camps far in the interior, and to the casual white traders who touched upon the coast.

We have already noticed certain contrarieties of character between the Indian tribes, produced by their diet and mode of life; and nowhere are they more apparent than about the falls of the Columbia. The Indians of this great fishing mart are represented by the earliest explorers as sleeker and fatter, but less hardy and active, than the tribes of the mountains and prairies, who live by hunting, or of the upper parts of the river, where fish is scanty, and the inhabitants must eke out their subsistence by digging roots or chasing the deer. Indeed, whenever an Indian of the upper country is too lazy to hunt, yet is fond of good living, he repairs to the falls, to live in abundance without labor.

"By such worthless dogs as these," says an honest trader[29] in his journal, which now lies before us, "by such worthless dogs as these are these noted fishing-places peopled, which, like our great cities, may with propriety be called the headquarters of vitiated principles."

The habits of trade and the avidity of gain have their corrupting

---

shown to have been located on the north, or Washington, side of the Columbia River at the east end of the Long Narrows. Lewis and Clark referred to it as the village of the Echelutes. Today the Indian village of Spedis is located at this site. See Henry J. Biddle, "Wishram," *Oregon Historical Quarterly*, Vol. XXVII (1926), 113–30.

[29] Robert Stuart, whose manuscript Irving slightly misquotes. Stuart wrote: "By such worthless dogs are these noted fishing places peopled, which like our great cities may with propriety be called the head quarters of vitiated principles." Spaulding (ed.), *op. cit.*, 66, and Rollins (ed.), *op. cit.*, 62.

effects even in the wilderness, as may be instanced in the members of this aboriginal emporium; for the same journalist denounces them as "saucy, impudent rascals, who will steal when they can, and pillage whenever a weak party falls in their power."[30]

That he does not belie them will be evidenced hereafter, when we have occasion again to touch at Wish-ram and navigate the rapids.[31] In the present instance the travellers effected the laborious ascent of this part of the river, with all its various portages, without molestation, and once more launched away in smooth water above the high falls.

The two parties continued together, without material impediment, for three or four hundred miles further up the Columbia; Mr. Thompson appearing to take great interest in the success of Mr. Stuart, and pointing out places favorable, as he said, to the establishment of his contemplated trading post.

Mr. Stuart, who distrusted his sincerity, at length pretended to adopt his advice, and, taking leave of him, remained as if to establish himself, while the other proceeded on his course towards the mountains. No sooner, however, had he fairly departed than Mr. Stuart again pushed forward, under guidance of the two Indians, nor did he stop until he had arrived within about one hundred and forty miles of the Spokan River, which he considered near enough to keep the rival establishment in check.

The place which he pitched upon for his trading post was a point of land about three miles in length and two in breadth, formed by the junction of the Oakinagan with the Columbia.[32] The former is a river which has its source in a considerable lake about one hundred and fifty miles west of the point of junction. The two rivers, about the place of their confluence, are bordered by immense prairies covered with herbage,

[30] Robert Stuart actually wrote: "The Indians at these rapids [below Strawberry Island] are composed of the Cath-lak-a-keckits & Cath-lath-la-las, each mustering about 150 warriors, are saucy impudent rascals, will steal when they can, and pillage whenever a weak party falls into their clutches." Spaulding (ed.), *op. cit.*, 53–54, and Rollins (ed.), *op. cit.*, 51–52.

[31] See Chapter XXXVIII, p. 318.

[32] The Okanogan (spelled *Okanagan* in Canada) River flows south into the Columbia east of modern Brewster, Washington, in Okanogan County. Its source is Okanagan Lake in British Columbia, north, not west, of the junction of the two rivers. Irving's description of the area and the selection of the site for a trading post is from Cox, *op. cit.*, 231–33. See Judge William C. Brown, "Old Fort Okanogan and the Okanogan Trail," *Oregon Historical Quarterly*, Vol. XV (1914), 1–38.

but destitute of trees. The point itself was ornamented with wild flowers of every hue, in which innumerable humming-birds were "banqueting nearly the livelong day."[33]

The situation of this point appeared to be well adapted for a trading post. The climate was salubrious, the soil fertile, the rivers well stocked with fish, the natives peaceable and friendly. There were easy communications with the interior by the upper waters of the Columbia and the lateral stream of the Oakinagan, while the downward current of the Columbia furnished a highway to Astoria.

Availing himself, therefore, of the driftwood which had collected in quantities in the neighboring bends of the river, Mr. Stuart and his men set to work to erect a house, which in a little while was sufficiently completed for their residence; and thus was established the first interior post of the company. We will now return to notice the progress of affairs at the mouth of the Columbia.

[33] Cox, *op. cit.*, 232.

THE sailing of the Tonquin, and the departure of Mr. David Stuart and his detachment, had produced a striking effect on affairs at Astoria. The natives who had swarmed about the place began immediately to drop off, until at length not an Indian was to be seen. This, at first, was attributed to the want of peltries with which to trade; but in a little while the mystery was explained in a more alarming manner. A conspiracy was said to be on foot among the neighboring tribes to make a combined attack upon the white men, now that they were so reduced in number. For this purpose there had been a gathering of warriors in a neighboring bay, under pretext of fishing for sturgeon; and fleets of canoes were expected to join them from the north and south. Even Comcomly, the one-eyed chief, notwithstanding his professed friendship for Mr. M'Dougal, was strongly suspected of being concerned in this general combination.

Alarmed at rumors of this impending danger, the Astorians suspended their regular labor, and set to work, with all haste, to throw up temporary works for refuge and defense. In the course of a few days they surrounded their dwelling-house and magazines with a picket fence ninety feet square, flanked by two bastions, on which were mounted four four-pounders. Every day they exercised themselves in the use of their weapons, so as to qualify themselves for military duty, and at night ensconced[1] themselves in their fortress and posted sentinels, to guard against surprise. In this way they hoped, even in case of attack, to be able to hold out until arrival of the party to be conducted by Mr. Hunt across the Rocky Mountains, or until the return of the Tonquin. The latter dependence, however, was doomed soon to be destroyed. Early in August, a wandering band of savages from the Strait of Juan

[1] First edition reads *they ensconced.*

de Fuca,[2] made their appearance at the mouth of the Columbia, where they came to fish for sturgeon. They brought disastrous accounts of the Tonquin, which were at first treated as mere fables, but which were too sadly confirmed by a different tribe that arrived a few days subsequently.[3] We shall relate the circumstances of this melancholy affair as correctly as the casual discrepancies in the statements that have reached us will permit.[4]

We have already stated that the Tonquin set sail from the mouth of the river on the fifth of June. The whole number of persons on board amounted to twenty-three.[5] In one of the outer bays they picked up, from a fishing canoe, an Indian named Lamazee,[6] who had already made two voyages along the coast, and knew something of the language of the various tribes. He agreed to accompany them as interpreter.

Steering to the north, Captain Thorn arrived in a few days at Vancouver's Island, and anchored in the harbor of Neweetee,[7] very much against the advice of his Indian interpreter, who warned him against the perfidious character of the natives of this part of the coast. Numbers of canoes soon came off, bringing sea-otter skins to sell. It was too

[2] Between Vancouver Island and the Olympic Peninsula of Washington.

[3] In relating the threat to Astoria, the Astorians' military preparations, and the rumors concerning the Tonquin, Irving follows Franchère, Narrative, 255, 256.

[4] There are several early narratives of the Tonquin disaster. All rest finally on the story of what happened as related by the Indian interpreter, whom Irving names "Lamazee," and all differ from each other in detail. The accounts by Franchère, Narrative, 288–93, and Ross, Adventures, 162–72, allegedly report the words of the Indian as each writer heard them. Another version by an Astorian is recorded in Cox, Columbia River, 63–67. For another version as told by the Indian, see Samuel Hancock, The Narrative of Samuel Hancock, 172–75. The earliest published account appears in the Missouri Gazette, May 15, 1813, reprinted in Hiram M. Chittenden, History of the American Fur Trade of the Far West, II, 909–11. See also Chittenden's redaction, ibid., I, 176–81, and Nouvelles annales des voyages, translated as "An Account of the Tonquin's Voyage," in Rollins (ed.), Discovery of the Oregon Trail, 271–72.

[5] Franchère says there were twenty-nine men on the Tonquin, of whom twelve were Sandwich Islanders. Narrative, 293.

[6] Franchère and Cox leave the Indian unnamed. Ross quotes the Indian as saying, "'My name is Kasiascall, but the Chinooks and other Indians hereabouts call me Lamazue.'" Adventures, 165. Irving's authority for the name Lamazee is unknown.

[7] Bancroft challenges Irving here; see History of the Northwest Coast, II, 155–56n. Franchère, Narrative, 289, names the village "Newity," but Ross reports that the Indian interpreter said, "We cast anchor in Eyuck Whoola, Newcetu [Nootka?] Bay." Adventures, 165. Cox says the ship "anchored opposite a large village, named 'New Whitty,' in the vicinity of Nootka." op. cit., 63. The account in Nouvelles annales refers to the "Nionetians"; see Rollins (ed.), op. cit., 271. The Missouri Gazette names "Woody Point"; see Chittenden, op. cit., II, 909.

late in the day to commence a traffic, but Mr. M'Kay, accompanied by a few of the men, went on shore to a large village to visit Wicananish,[8] the chief of the surrounding territory, six of the natives remaining on board as hostages. He was received with great professions of friendship, entertained hospitably, and a couch of sea-otter skins was prepared for him in the dwelling of the chieftain, where he was prevailed upon to pass the night.

In the morning, before Mr. M'Kay had returned to the ship, great numbers of the natives came off in their canoes to trade, headed by two sons of Wicananish. As they brought abundance of sea-otter skins, and there was every appearance of a brisk trade, Captain Thorn did not wait for the return of Mr. M'Kay, but spread his wares upon deck,[9] making a tempting display of blankets, cloths, knives, beads, and fish-hooks, expecting a prompt and profitable sale. The Indians, however, were not so eager and simple as he had supposed, having learned the art of bargaining and the value of merchandise from the casual traders along the coast. They were guided, too, by a shrewd old chief named Nookamis,[10] who had grown gray in traffic with New England skippers, and prided himself upon his acuteness. His opinion seemed to regulate the market. When Captain Thorn made what he considered a liberal offer for an otter-skin, the wily old Indian treated it with scorn, and asked more than double. His comrades all took their cue from him, and not an otter-skin was to be had at a reasonable rate.

The old fellow, however, overshot his mark, and mistook the character of the man he was treating with. Thorn was a plain, straightforward sailor, who never had two minds nor two prices in his dealings, was deficient in patience and pliancy, and totally wanting in the chicanery of traffic. He had a vast deal of stern, but honest pride in his nature, and, moreover, held the whole savage race in sovereign contempt. Abandoning all further attempts, therefore, to bargain with his shuf-

[8] The closest that any of the early accounts come to this name is that in the *Missouri Gazette*, which refers to "a powerful nation called Wake-a-ninishes." Chittenden, *op. cit.*, II, 909. The Indian interpreter also stated that he belonged "to the Wick-a-nook tribe of Indians near Nootka Sound." Ross, *Adventures*, 165. It is fairly obvious that some of Irving's information comes from sources in Astor's papers or from conversation with members of the Astorian undertaking. Almost anything could happen to the rendition of unfamiliar Indian names through oral transmission, which probably accounts for the discrepancies.

[9] The first edition reads *but spread out his wares upon the deck.*

[10] This name is absent from all other known accounts, as is the name *Shewish* below.

fling customers, he thrust his hands into his pockets, and paced up and down the deck in sullen silence. The cunning old Indian followed him to and fro, holding out a sea-otter skin to him at every turn, and pestering him to trade. Finding other means unavailing, he suddenly changed his tone, and began to jeer and banter him upon the mean prices he offered. This was too much for the patience of the captain, who was never remarkable for relishing a joke, especially when at his own expense. Turning suddenly upon his persecutor, he snatched the proffered otter-skin from his hands, rubbed it in his face, and dismissed him over the side of the ship with no very complimentary application to accelerate his exit. He then kicked the peltries to the right and left about the deck, and broke up the market in the most ignominious manner. Old Nookamis made for shore in a furious passion, in which he was joined by Shewish, one of the sons of Wicananish, who went off breathing vengeance, and the ship was soon abandoned by the natives.

When Mr. M'Kay returned on board, the interpreter related what had passed, and begged him to prevail upon the captain to make sail, as from his knowledge of the temper and pride of the people of the place, he was sure they would resent the indignity offered to one of their chiefs. Mr. M'Kay, who himself possessed some experience of Indian character, went to the captain, who was still pacing the deck in moody humor, represented the danger to which his hasty act had exposed the vessel, and urged him to weigh anchor. The captain made light of his counsels, and pointed to his cannon and fire-arms as sufficient safeguard against naked savages. Further remonstrances only provoked taunting replies and sharp altercations. The day passed away without any signs of hostility, and at night the captain retired as usual to his cabin, taking no more than the usual precautions.

On the following morning, at daybreak, while the captain and Mr. M'Kay were yet asleep, a canoe came alongside in which were twenty Indians, commanded by young Shewish. They were unarmed, their aspect and demeanor friendly, and they held up otter-skins, and made signs indicative of a wish to trade. The caution enjoined by Mr. Astor, in respect to the admission of Indians on board of the ship,[11] had been

[11] The American custom had long been to permit Indians to come on deck to trade. This practice, in fact, was one of the advantages American traders had over the British, who never permitted the natives to board their vessels. See Phillips, *The Fur Trade*, II, 53, 55. Captain Thorn's trouble with the Indians was not, however, unprecedented; see *ibid.*, 56, for instances of assaults on trading vessels.

The *Tonquin* entering the Columbia River, March 25, 1811. From
Gabriel Franchère, *Narrative of a Voyage to the Northwest Coast of
America* (1854).

Fort Astoria. From Gabriel Franchère, *Narrative of a Voyage to the Northwest Coast of America* (1854).

neglected for some time past, and the officer of the watch, perceiving those in the canoe to be without weapons, and having received no orders to the contrary, readily permitted them to mount the deck. Another canoe soon succeeded, the crew of which was likewise admitted. In a little while other canoes came off, and Indians were soon clambering into the vessel on all sides.

The officer of the watch now felt alarmed, and called to Captain Thorn and Mr. M'Kay. By the time they came on deck, it was thronged with Indians. The interpreter noticed to Mr. M'Kay that many of the natives wore short mantles of skins, and intimated a suspicion that they were secretly armed. Mr. M'Kay urged the captain to clear the ship and get under way. He again made light of the advice; but the augmented swarm of canoes about the ship, and the numbers still putting off from shore, at length awakened his distrust, and he ordered some of the crew to weigh anchor, while some were sent aloft to make sail.

The Indians now offered to trade with the captain on his own terms, prompted, apparently, by the approaching departure of the ship. Accordingly, a hurried trade was commenced. The main articles sought by the savages in barter were knives; as fast as some were supplied they moved off ond others succeeded. By degrees they were thus distributed about the deck, and all with weapons.

The anchor was now nearly up, the sails were loose, and the captain, in a loud and peremptory tone, ordered the ship to be cleared. In an instant, a signal yell was given; it was echoed on every side, knives and war-clubs were brandished in every direction, and the savages rushed upon their marked victims.

The first that fell was Mr. Lewis,[12] the ship's clerk. He was leaning, with folded arms, over a bale of blankets, engaged in bargaining, when he received a deadly stab in the back, and fell down the companion-way.

Mr. M'Kay, who was seated on the taffrail, sprang on his feet, but was instantly knocked down with a war-club and flung backwards into the sea, where he was despatched by the women in the canoes.

In the meantime Captain Thorn made desperate fight against fearful odds. He was a powerful as well as a resolute man, but he had come upon deck without weapons. Shewish, the young chief, singled him out as his peculiar prey, and rushed upon him at the first outbreak. The

---

[12] James Lewis, one of the clerks. He is the subject of a novel entitled *I, James Lewis*, by Gilbert W. Gabriel.

captain had barely time to draw a clasp-knife, with one blow of which he laid the young savage dead at his feet. Several of the stoutest followers of Shewish now set upon him. He defended himself vigorously, dealing crippling blows to right and left, and strewing the quarter-deck with the slain and wounded. His object was to fight his way to the cabin, where there were fire-arms; but he was hemmed in with foes, covered with wounds, and faint with loss of blood. For an instant he leaned upon the tiller wheel, when a blow from behind, with a war-club, felled him to the deck, where he was despatched with knives and thrown overboard.

While this was transacting upon the quarter-deck, a chance-medley fight was going on throughout the ship. The crew fought desperately with knives, handspikes, and whatever weapon they could seize upon in the moment of surprise. They were soon, however, overpowered by numbers, and mercilessly butchered.

As to the seven who had been sent aloft to make sail, they contemplated with horror the carnage that was going on below. Being destitute of weapons, they let themselves down by the running rigging, in hopes of getting between decks. One fell in the attempt, and was instantly despatched; another received a death-blow in the back as he was descending; a third, Stephen Weekes, the armorer, was mortally wounded as he was getting down the hatchway.

The remaining four made good their retreat into the cabin, where they found Mr. Lewis, still alive, though mortally wounded. Barricading the cabin door, they broke holes through the companion-way, and, with the muskets and ammunition which were at hand, opened a brisk fire that soon cleared the deck.

Thus far the Indian interpreter, from whom these particulars are derived, had been an eye-witness to[13] the deadly conflict.[14] He had taken no part in it, and had been spared by the natives as being of their race. In the confusion of the moment he took refuge with the rest, in the canoes. The survivors of the crew now sallied forth, and discharged some of the deck guns, which did great execution among the canoes, and drove all the savages to shore.

For the remainder of the day no one ventured to put off to the ship, deterred by the effects of the fire-arms. The night passed away without

[13] *Of* in first edition.

[14] From what Ross relates, the interpreter was not on board the *Tonquin* during the fighting; he was, in fact, "privy to the whole plot." *Adventures,* 171.

any further attempt on the part of the natives. When the day dawned, the Tonquin still lay at anchor in the bay, her sails all loose and flapping in the wind, and no one apparently on board of her. After a time, some of the canoes ventured forth to reconnoitre, taking with them the interpreter. They paddled about her, keeping cautiously at a distance, but growing more and more emboldened at seeing her quiet and lifeless. One man at length made his appearance on the deck, and was recognized by the interpreter as Mr. Lewis. He made friendly signs, and invited them on board. It was long before they ventured to comply. Those who mounted the deck met with no opposition; no one was to be seen on board; for Mr. Lewis, after inviting them, had disappeared. Other canoes now pressed forward to board the prize; the decks were soon crowded, and the sides covered with clambering savages, all intent on plunder. In the midst of their eagerness and exultation, the ship blew up with a tremendous explosion. Arms, legs, and mutilated bodies were blown into the air, and dreadful havoc was made in the surrounding canoes. The interpreter was in the main-chains at the time of the explosion, and was thrown unhurt into the water, where he succeeded in getting into one of the canoes. According to his statement, the bay presented an awful spectacle after the catastrophe. The ship had disappeared, but the bay was covered with fragments of the wreck, with shattered canoes, and Indians swimming for their lives, or struggling in the agonies of death; while those who had escaped the danger remained aghast and stupefied, or made with frantic panic for the shore. Upwards of a hundred savages were destroyed by the explosion, many more were shockingly mutilated, and for days afterwards the limbs and bodies of the slain were thrown upon the beach.

The inhabitants of Neweetee were overwhelmed with consternation at this astounding calamity, which had burst upon them in the very moment of triumph. The warriors sat mute and mournful, while the women filled the air with loud lamentations. Their weeping and wailing, however, was suddenly changed into yells of fury at the sight of four unfortunate white men, brought captive into the village. They had been driven on shore in one of the ship's boats, and taken at some distance along the coast.

The interpreter was permitted to converse with them. They proved to be the four brave fellows who had made such desperate defense from the cabin. The interpreter gathered from them some of the particulars already related. They told him further, that after they had beaten off the enemy and cleared the ship, Lewis advised that they should slip the cable and endeavor to get to sea. They declined to take his advice, alleging that the wind set too strongly into the bay and would drive them on shore. They resolved, as soon as it was dark, to put off quietly in the ship's boat, which they would be able to do unperceived, and to coast along back to Astoria. They put their resolution into effect; but Lewis refused to accompany them, being disabled by his wound, hopeless of escape, and determined on a terrible revenge. On the voyage out, he had repeatedly expressed a presentiment that he should die by his own hands; thinking it highly probable that he should be engaged in some contest with the natives, and being resolved, in case of extremity, to commit suicide rather than be made a prisoner. He now declared his intention to remain on board of the ship until daylight, to decoy as many of the savages on board as possible, then to set fire to the powder magazine, and terminate his life by a signal act of vengeance.[15] How well he succeeded has been shown. His companions bade him a melancholy adieu, and set off on their precarious expedition. They strove with might and main to get out of the bay, but found it impossible to weather a point of land, and were at length compelled to take shelter in a small cove, where they hoped to remain concealed until the wind should be more favorable. Exhausted by fatigue and watching, they fell into a sound sleep, and in that state were surprised by the savages. Better had it been for those unfortunate men had they remained with Lewis, and shared his heroic death: as it was, they perished in a more painful and protracted manner, being sacrificed by the natives to the manes of their friends with all the lingering tortures of savage cruelty.[16] Some time after their death, the interpreter, who had remained a kind of prisoner at large, effected his escape, and brought the tragical tidings to Astoria.

Such is the melancholy story of the Tonquin, and such was the fate of

[15] Franchère, supposedly quoting the interpreter, tells of the explosion without accounting for its cause. Ross, also reproducing the interpreter's story, has the Indian say that Weekes caused the explosion (*Adventures*, 170). In Cox's version, the explosion was the work of John Anderson, John Weekes, and Stephen Weekes, who, after igniting a fuse, escaped through a cabin window into a boat and got away (*op. cit.*, 65–66). In Gabriel's novel, *I, James Lewis*, the author follows Irving as Lewis relates his story from the grave.

[16] Franchère says that four men escaped but says nothing about their fate. Ross says nothing about anyone's escaping except the Indian interpreter. Cox, however, related essentially what Irving records; indeed, Cox is Irving's source at this point.

her brave, but headstrong commander, and her adventurous crew.[17] It is a catastrophe that shows the importance, in all enterprises of moment, to keep in mind the general instructions of the sagacious heads which devise them. Mr. Astor was well aware of the perils to which ships were exposed on this coast from quarrels with the natives, and from perfidious attempts of the latter to surprise and capture them in unguarded moments. He had repeatedly enjoined it upon Captain Thorn, in conversation, and at parting, in his letter of instructions, to be courteous and kind in his dealings with the savages, but by no means to confide in their apparent friendship, *nor to admit more than a few on board of his ship at a time.*

Had the deportment of Captain Thorn been properly regulated, the insult so wounding to savage pride would never have been given. Had he enforced the rule to admit but a few at a time, the savages would not have been able to get the mastery. He was too irritable, however, to practice the necessary self-command, and, having been nurtured in a proud contempt of danger, thought it beneath him to manifest any fear of a crew of unarmed savages.

With all his faults and foibles, we cannot but speak of him with esteem, and deplore his untimely fate; for we remember him well in early life,[18] as a companion in pleasant scenes and joyous hours. When on shore, among his friends, he was a frank, manly, sound-hearted sailor. On board ship he evidently assumed the hardness of deportment and sternness of demeanor which many deem essential to naval service. Throughout the whole of the expedition, however, he showed himself loyal, single-minded, straightforward, and fearless; and if the fate of his vessel may be charged to his harshness and imprudence, we should recollect that he paid for his error with his life.

The loss of the Tonquin was a grievous blow to the infant establishment of Astoria, and one that threatened to bring after it a train of dis-

[17] A comparison of Irving's narrative of the *Tonquin* disaster with those of Franchère and Cox indicates that some of his information was derived from their works. However, it is also evident that he relied on other sources of information, perhaps materials in Astor's library or others that are not now identifiable. Concerning the destruction of the *Tonquin*, see F. W. Howay, "The Loss of the Tonquin," *Washington Historical Quarterly*, Vol. XIII (1922), 83–92.

[18] This is the only evidence that Irving and Jonathan Thorn had once been acquainted. Irving's biographer, Stanley Williams, does not touch upon their previous friendship. The fact that they had once been companions may help to explain Irving's efforts here and earlier in *Astoria* to exonerate Thorn's behavior.

asters. The intelligence of it did not reach Mr. Astor until many months afterwards.[19] He felt it in all its force, and was aware that it must cripple, if not entirely defeat, the great scheme of his ambition. In his letters, written at the time, he speaks of it as "a calamity, the length of which he could not foresee." He indulged, however, in no weak and vain lamentation, but sought to devise a prompt and efficient remedy. The very same evening he appeared at the theatre with his usual serenity of countenance. A friend, who knew the disastrous intelligence he had received, expressed his astonishment that he could have calmness of spirit sufficient for such a scene of light amusement. "What would you have me do?" was his characteristic reply; "would you have me stay at home and weep for what I cannot help?"

[19] He had the information at least by May 10, 1812, for on that day he wrote to Charles Gratiot in St. Louis and told him what had happened. Gratiot replied: "I am realy sorry of the information you give me respecting the first ship you sent at the Colombia River, with some Canadians & that the Ship and Cargo was lost from having been attacked by the indians, I hope & I wish Such information may not be confirmed." Gratiot to Astor, May 31, 1812, Gratiot Letter Book, Missouri Historical Society.

CHAPTER XII

Gloom at Astoria — An Ingenious Stratagem — The Small-pox Chief
Launching of the Dolly — An Arrival — A Canadian Trapper
A Freeman of the Forest — An Iroquois Hunter
Winter on the Columbia — Festivities of New Year

THE tidings of the loss of the Tonquin, and the massacre of her crew, struck dismay into the hearts of the Astorians. They found themselves a mere handful of men, on a savage coast, surrounded by hostile tribes, who would doubtless be incited and encouraged to deeds of violence by the late fearful catastrophe. In this juncture Mr. M'Dougal, we are told, had recourse to a stratagem by which to avail himself of the ignorance and credulity of the savages, and which certainly does credit to his ingenuity.

The natives of the coast, and, indeed, of all the regions west of the mountains, had an extreme dread of the small-pox; that terrific scourge having, a few years previously, appeared among them, and almost swept off entire tribes. Its origin and nature were wrapped in mystery, and they conceived it an evil inflicted upon them by the Great Spirit, or brought among them by the white men. The last idea was seized upon by Mr. M'Dougal. He assembled several of the chieftains whom he believed to be in the conspiracy. When they were all seated around, he informed them that he had heard of the treachery of some of their northern brethren towards the Tonquin, and was determined on vengeance. "The white men among you," said he, "are few in number, it is true, but they are mighty in medicine. See here," continued he, drawing forth a small bottle and holding it before their eyes, "in this bottle I hold the small-pox, safely corked up; I have but to draw the cork, and let loose the pestilence, to sweep man, woman, and child from the face of the earth."

The chiefs were struck with horror and alarm. They implored him not to uncork the bottle, since they and all their people were firm friends of the white men, and would always remain so; but, should the small-

117

pox be once let out, it would run like wildfire throughout the country, sweeping off the good as well as the bad; and surely he would not be so unjust as to punish his friends for crimes committed by his enemies.

Mr. M'Dougal pretended to be convinced by their reasoning, and assured them that, so long as the white people should be unmolested, and the conduct of their Indian neighbors friendly and hospitable, the phial of wrath should remain sealed up; but, on the least hostility,[1] the fatal cork should be drawn.

From this time, it is added, he was much dreaded by the natives, as one who held their fate in his hands, and was called, by way of preëminence, "the Great Small-pox Chief."[2]

All this while, the labors at the infant settlement went on with unremitting assiduity, and, by the 26th of September, a commodious mansion, spacious enough to accommodate all hands, was completed. It was built of stone and clay, there being no calcareous stone in the neighborhood from which lime for mortar could be procured. The schooner was also finished, and launched, with the accustomed ceremony, on the second of October, and took her station below the fort. She was named the Dolly, and was the first American vessel launched on this coast.[3]

On the 5th of October, in the evening, the little community at Astoria was enlivened by the unexpected arrival of a detachment from Mr. David Stuart's post on the Oakinagan. It consisted of two of the clerks and two of the privates.[4] They brought favorable accounts of the new establishment, but reported that, as Mr. Stuart was apprehensive there might be a difficulty of subsisting his whole party throughout the winter, he had sent one half back to Astoria, retaining with him only Ross,[5] Montigny,[6] and two others. Such is the hardihood of the Indian trader. In the heart of a savage and unknown country, seven hundred miles from the main body of his fellow-adventurers, Stuart had dismissed half

---

[1] The first edition reads *on the least act of hostility.*

[2] Irving relies for information upon Franchère, who, however, says nothing about McDougall's smallpox threat.

[3] The date is confirmed by Franchère, who is Irving's source for this paragraph. See *Narrative*, 259.

[4] The date agrees with Franchère, who names the arrivals as Francis B. Pillet (or Pillot) and Donald M'Lellan (or M'Lennan). *Ibid.* Cf. Cox, *Columbia River*, 56.

[5] Alexander Ross.

[6] Ovide de Montigny, who had been, luckily, one of those excused from going to Vancouver Island on the *Tonquin.*

of his little number, and was prepared with the residue to brave all the perils of the wilderness, and the rigors of a long and dreary winter.

With the return party came a Canadian creole named Regis Brugiere[7] and an Iroquis hunter, with his wife and two children. As these two personages belong to certain classes which have derived their peculiar characteristics from the fur trade, we deem some few particulars concerning them pertinent to the nature of this work.

Brugiere was of a class of beaver trappers and hunters technically called "Freemen,"[8] in the language of the traders. They are generally Canadians by birth, and of French descent, who have been employed for a term of years by some fur company, but, their term being expired, continue to hunt and trap on their own account, trading with the company like the Indians. Hence they derive their appellation of Freemen, to distinguish them from the trappers who are bound for a number of years, and receive wages, or hunt on shares.

Having passed their early youth in the wilderness, separated almost entirely from civilized man, and in frequent intercourse with the Indians, they relapse,[9] with a facility common to human nature, into the habitudes of savage life. Though no longer bound by engagements to continue in the interior, they have become so accustomed to the freedom of the forest and the prairie, that they look back with repugnance upon the restraints of civilization. Most of them intermarry with the natives, and, like the latter, have often a plurality of wives. Wanderers of the wilderness, according to the vicissitudes of the seasons, the migrations of animals, and the plenty or scarcity of game, they lead a precarious and unsettled existence; exposed to sun and storm, and all kinds of hardships, until they resemble Indians[10] in complexion as well as in tastes and habits. From time to time, they bring the peltries they have collected to the trading houses of the company in whose employ they have been brought up. Here they traffic them away for such articles of merchandise or ammunition as they may stand in need of. At the time when Montreal was the great emporium of the fur trader, one of these freemen of the wilderness would suddenly return, after an absence of many

---

[7] Franchère, whom Irving is using, spells his name *Régis Bruguier* and states that "I had known [him] in Canada as a respectable country merchant." *Narrative*, 260. Cf. Cox, *op. cit.*, 56.

[8] No capitals or quotation marks here and below in the first edition.

[9] *Lapse* in first edition.   [10] The first edition reads *resemble the Indians*.

years, among his old friends and comrades. He would be greeted as one risen from the dead; and with the greater welcome, as he returned flush of money. A short time, however, spent in revelry, would be sufficient to drain his purse and sate him with civilized life, and he would return with new relish to the unshackled freedom of the forest.

Numbers of men of this class were scattered throughout the northwest territories. Some of them retained a little of the thrift and forethought of the civilized man, and became wealthy among their improvident neighbors; their wealth being chiefly displayed in large bands of horses, which covered the prairies in the vicinity of their abodes. Most of them, however, were prone to assimilate to the red man in their heedlessness of the future.[11]

Such was Regis Brugiere, a freeman and rover of the wilderness. Having been brought up in the service of the Northwest Company, he had followed in the train of one of its expeditions across the Rocky Mountains, and undertaken to trap for the trading post established on the Spokan River. In the course of his hunting excursions he had either accidentally, or designedly, found his way to the post of Mr. Stuart, and had been prevailed upon[12] to descend the Columbia, and "try his luck" at Astoria.

Ignace Shonowane,[13] the Iroquois hunter, was a specimen of a different class. He was one of those aboriginals of Canada who had partially conformed to the habits of civilization and the doctrines of Christianity, under the influence of the French colonists and the Catholic priests; who seem generally to have been more successful in conciliating, taming, and converting the savages, than their English and Protestant rivals. These half-civilized Indians retained some of the good, and many of the evil qualities of their original stock. They were first-rate hunters, and dexterous in the management of the canoe. They could undergo great privations, and were admirable for the service of the rivers, lakes, and forests, provided they could be kept sober, and in proper subordi-

[11] Irving's description of the freemen is an elaboration of two paragraphs in Cox, *op. cit.*, 358.

[12] The first edition reads *and been prevailed upon.*

[13] Franchère mentions the arrival of "an Iroquoy family" but says nothing about this individual. See *Narrative*, 260. Cox refers to "two Iroquois hunters." *Op. cit.*, 56. Irving's information for his description of the aboriginal type of hunter is from Cox, *op. cit.*, 364; Cox puts this type into a third class, distinct from the halfbloods and the freemen. Cf. *ibid.*, 354–64, for these types.

nation; but once inflamed with liquor, to which they were madly addicted, all the dormant passions inherent in their nature were prone to break forth, and to hurry them into the most vindictive and bloody acts of violence.

Though they generally professed the Roman Catholic religion, yet it was mixed, occasionally, with some of their ancient superstitions; and they retained much of the Indian belief in charms and omens. Numbers of these men were employed by the Northwest Company as trappers, hunters, and canoe men, but on lower terms than were allowed to white men. Ignace Shonowane had, in this way, followed the enterprise of the company to the banks of the Spokan,[14] being, probably, one of the first of his tribe that had traversed the Rocky Mountains.

Such were some of the motley populace of the wilderness, incident to the fur trade, who were gradually attracted to the new settlement of Astoria.

The month of October now began to give indications of approaching winter. Hitherto, the colonists had been well pleased with the climate. The summer had been temperate, the mercury never rising above eighty degrees. Westerly winds had prevailed during the spring and the early part of the summer, and been succeeded by fresh breezes from the northwest. In the month of October the southerly winds set in, bringing with them frequent rain.

The Indians now began to quit the borders of the ocean, and to retire to their winter quarters in the sheltered bosom of the forests, or along the small rivers and brooks. The rainy season, which commences in October, continues, with little intermission, until April; and though the winters are generally mild, the mercury seldom sinking below the freezing point, yet the tempests of wind and rain are terrible. The sun is sometimes obscured for weeks, the brooks swell into roaring torrents, and the country is threatened with a deluge.

The departure of the Indians to their winter quarters gradually rendered provisions scanty, and obliged the colonists to send out foraging expeditions in the Dolly.[15] Still the little handful of adventurers kept up their spirits in their lonely fort at Astoria, looking forward to the

[14] Probably to Spokane House, which the North West Company had built not long before.

[15] Here and in the previous paragraph Irving's source is Franchère, *Narrative*, 260–61.

time when they should be animated and reinforced by the party under Mr. Hunt, that was to come to them across the Rocky Mountains.

The year gradually wore way. The rain, which had poured down almost incessantly since the first of October, cleared up towards the evening of the 31st of December, and the morning of the first of January ushered in a day of sunshine.[16]

The hereditary French holiday[17] spirit of the French voyageurs is hardly to be depressed by any adversities; and they can manage to get up a *fête* in the most squalid situations, and under the most untoward circumstances. An extra allowance of rum, and a little flour to make cakes and puddings, constitute a "regale;" and they forget all their toils and troubles in the song and dance.[18]

On the present occasion, the partners endeavored to celebrate the new year with some effect. At sunrise the drums beat to arms, the colors were hoisted, with three rounds of small arms and three discharges of cannon.[19] The day was devoted to games of agility and strength, and other amusements; and grog was temperately distributed, together with bread, butter, and cheese. The best dinner their circumstances could afford was served up at midday. At sunset the colors were lowered, with another discharge of artillery. The night was spent in dancing; and, though there was a lack of female partners to excite their gallantry, the voyageurs kept up the ball with true French spirit, until three o'clock in the morning. So passed the new year festival of 1812 at the infant colony of Astoria.

[16] From *ibid.*, 267.
[17] *Holyday* in first edition.
[18] The first edition reads *and the dance.*
[19] Franchère, *Narrative*, 267.

WE have followed up the fortunes of the maritime part of this enterprise to the shores of the Pacific, and have conducted the affairs of the embryo establishment to the opening of the new year; let us now turn back to the adventurous band to whom was intrusted the land expedition, and who were to make their way to the mouth of the Columbia, up vast rivers, across trackless plains, and over the rugged barriers of the Rocky Mountains.

The conduct of this expedition, as has been already mentioned, was assigned to Mr. Wilson Price Hunt, of Trenton, New Jersey, one of the partners of the company, who was ultimately to be at the head of the establishment at the mouth of the Columbia. He is represented as a man scrupulously upright and faithful in his dealings, amicable[1] in his disposition, and of most accommodating manners; and his whole conduct will be found in unison with such a character. He was not practically experienced in the Indian trade; that is to say, he had never made any expeditions of traffic into the heart of the wilderness, but he had been engaged in commerce at St. Louis, then a frontier settlement on the Mississippi, where the chief branch of his business had consisted in furnishing Indian traders with goods and equipments. In this way, he had acquired much knowledge of the trade at second hand, and of the various tribes, and the interior country over which it extended.

[1] *Amiable* in first edition.

123

Another of the partners, Mr. Donald M'Kenzie,[2] was associated with Mr. Hunt in the expedition, and excelled on those points in which the other was deficient; for he had been ten years in the interior, in the service of the Northwest Company, and valued himself on his knowledge of "woodcraft," and the strategy of Indian trade and Indian warfare. He had a frame seasoned to toils and hardships; a spirit not to be intimidated, and was reputed to be a "remarkable shot;" which of itself was sufficient to give him renown upon the frontier.

Mr. Hunt and his coadjutor repaired, about the latter part of July, 1810, to Montreal, the ancient emporium of the fur trade, where everything requisite for the expedition could be procured.[3] One of the first objects was to recruit a complement of Canadian voyageurs from the disbanded herd usually to be found loitering about the place. A degree of jockeyship, however, is required for this service, for a Canadian voyageur is as full of latent tricks and vice as a horse; and when he makes the greatest external promise, is prone to prove the greatest "take in." Besides, the Northwest Company, who maintained a long established control at Montreal, and knew the qualities of every voyageur, secretly interdicted the prime hands from engaging in this new service; so that, although liberal terms were offered, few presented themselves but such as were not worth having.

From these Mr. Hunt engaged a number sufficient, as he supposed,

[2] Born in Scotland, McKenzie (1783–1851) had ventured to America in 1800, at which time he became a clerk for the North West Company, to whose services he later returned after the acquisition of Astoria in 1813. He then became a partner in the North West Company, remaining in the Columbia area until the merger with the Hudson's Bay Company in 1821. He became a chief factor in that company as well as a member of the Council of the North West Territories. For eight years, until 1833, he was governor of Assiniboia, when he retired and moved to the state of New York, where he died in 1851. See Wallace (ed.), *Documents*, 477, and Frederick Merk (ed.), *Fur Trade and Empire: George Simpson's Journal, 1824–1825* (Cambridge, 1931), 358–59. Of him Ross wrote: "This gentleman had already acquired great experience in the Indian countries, was bold, robust, and peculiarly qualified to lead Canadian voyageurs through thick and thin. Mr. Astor placed great confidence in his abilities, perseverance, and prudence. Under . . . two such leaders as Hunt and M'Kenzie, he had, in fact, everything to hope and little to fear." *Adventures*, 174.

[3] Two manuscript journals in the form of account books, probably kept by John Reed, clerk for Hunt's expedition, record the business transactions of the party all the way to Astoria. The first volume begins with entries made on July 6, 1810, at Lachine, located on the outskirts of Montreal. These two journals are among the Astor Papers, Harvard Graduate School of Business Administration.

for present purposes;[4] and, having laid in a supply of ammunition, provisions, and Indian goods, embarked all on board one of those great canoes at that time universally used by the fur traders for navigating the intricate and often-obstructed rivers. The canoe was between thirty and forty feet long, and several feet in width; constructed of birch bark, sewed with fibres of the roots of the spruce tree, and daubed with resin of the pine, instead of tar. The cargo was made up in packages, weighing from ninety to one hundred pounds each, for the facility of loading and unloading, and of transportation at portages. The canoe itself, though capable of sustaining a freight of upwards of four tons, could readily be carried on men's shoulders. Canoes of this size are generally managed by eight or ten men, two of whom are picked veterans, who receive double wages, and are stationed, one at the bow and the other at the stern, to keep a look-out and to steer. They are termed the foreman and the steersman. The rest, who ply the paddles, are called middle men. When there is a favorable breeze, the canoe is occasionally navigated with a sail.[5]

The expedition took its regular departure, as usual, from St. Anne's, near the extremity of the island of Montreal, the great starting-place of the traders to the interior. Here stood the ancient chapel of St. Anne, the patroness of the Canadian voyageurs; where they made confession, and offered up their vows, previous to departing on any hazardous expedition. The shrine of the saint was decorated with relics and votive offerings hung up by these superstitious beings, either to propitiate her favor, or in gratitude for some signal deliverance in the wilderness. It was the custom, too, of these devout vagabonds, after leaving the chapel,

---

[4] Franchère states: "When the associates [of Astor] had engaged a sufficient number of Canadian boatmen, they equipped a bark canoe under charge of Messrs. Hunt and M'Kenzie, with a Mr. Perrault as clerk, and a crew of fourteen men. These gentlemen were to proceed to Mackinaw, and thence to St. Louis, hiring on the way as many men as they could to man the canoes, in which . . . they were to ascend the Missouri to its source." *Narrative*, 187. Ross adds further details: "The land party at its outset consisted of only seventeen persons, but Mr. Hunt's object was to augment that number to about eighty as he passed along, by means of American trappers and hunters from the south [i.e., of Canada]. Here M'Kenzie strongly recommended Mr. Hunt to take all his men from Canada, as too much time might probably be lost in collecting them from the south; and besides, Canadians, as he thought, would answer much better; but Mr. Hunt adhered to his first plan." *Adventures*, 41; cf. 176.

[5] Irving could have drawn a few details concerning the canoe and its handling from Cox, *Columbia River*, 354, but he appears to have had an additional source.

Route of Overland Astorians, July 1810–July 1811

to have a grand carouse, in honor of the saint and for the prosperity of the voyage. In this part of their devotions, the crew of Mr. Hunt proved themselves by no means deficient. Indeed, he soon discovered that his recruits, enlisted at Montreal, were fit to vie with the ragged regiment of Falstaff.[6] Some were able-bodied, but inexpert; others were expert, but lazy; while a third class were expert and willing, but totally worn out, being broken-down veterans, incapable of toil.

With this inefficient crew he made his way up the Ottawa River, and by the ancient route of the fur traders, along a succession of small lakes and rivers, to Michilimackinac. Their progress was slow and tedious. Mr. Hunt was not accustomed to the management of "voyageurs," and he had a crew admirably disposed to play the old soldier, and balk their work; and ever ready to come to a halt, land, make a fire, put on the great pot, and smoke, and gossip, and sing by the hour.

It was not until the 22d of July that they arrived at Mackinaw,[7] situ-

[6] See Shakespeare's *Henry IV, Part I*, IV, ii.

Ross gives a different picture of the quality of men chosen: "Crowds of blustering voyageurs, of all grades and qualities, flocked thither to enroll themselves under the banner of this grand undertaking . . . [but McKenzie] drew a line of distinction and selected those only who had already given proofs of capacity." *Adventures*, 175.

[7] The first entry in Hunt's account book at Mackinac is dated July 28, but this does not necessarily mean that he arrived on that date. The last entry here is dated August 12.

126

ated on the island of the same name, at the confluence of Lakes Huron and Michigan. This famous old French trading post continued to be a rallying point for a multifarious and motley population. The inhabitants were amphibious in their habits, most of them being, or having been voyageurs or canoe men. It was the great place of arrival and departure of the southwest fur trade. Here the Mackinaw Company had established its principal post, from whence it communicated with the interior and with Montreal. Hence its various traders and trappers set out for their respective destinations about Lake Superior and its tributary waters, or for the Mississippi, the Arkansas, the Missouri, and the other regions of the west. Here, after the absence of a year, or more, they returned with their peltries, and settled their accounts; the furs rendered in by them being transmitted in canoes from hence to Montreal. Mackinaw was, therefore, for a great part of the year, very scantily peopled; but at certain seasons the traders arrived from all points, with their crews of voyageurs, and the place swarmed like a hive.

Mackinaw, at that time, was a mere village, stretching along a small bay, with a fine broad beach in front of its principal row of houses, and dominated by the old fort, which crowned an impending height. The beach was a kind of public promenade, where were displayed all the vagaries of a seaport on the arrival of a fleet from a long cruise. Here voyageurs frolicked away their wages, fiddling and dancing in the booths and cabins, buying all kinds of knick-knacks, dressing themselves out finely, and parading up and down, like arrant braggarts and coxcombs. Sometimes they met with rival coxcombs in the young Indians from the opposite shore, who would appear on the beach painted and decorated in fantastic style, and would saunter up and down, to be gazed at and admired, perfectly satisfied that they eclipsed their pale-faced competitors.

Now and then a chance party of "Northwesters" appeared at Mackinaw from the rendezvous at Fort William. These held themselves up as the chivalry of the fur trade. They were men of iron; proof against cold weather, hard fare, and perils of all kinds. Some would wear the Northwest button, and a formidable dirk, and assume something of a military air. They generally wore feathers in their hats, and affected the "brave." "Je suis un homme du nord!"—"I am a man of the north," —one of these swelling fellows would exclaim, sticking his arms akimbo and ruffling by the Southwesters, whom he regarded with great contempt, as men softened by mild climates and the luxurious fare of bread and bacon, and whom he stigmatized with the inglorious name of pork-eaters. The superiority assumed by these vainglorious swaggerers was, in general, tacitly admitted. Indeed, some of them had accquired great notoriety for deeds of hardihood and courage; for the fur trade had its heroes, whose names resounded throughout the wilderness.

Such was Mackinaw at the time of which we are treating.[8] It now, doubtless, presents a totally different aspect. The fur companies no longer assemble there; the navigation of the lakes is carried on by steamboats and various shipping, and the race of traders, and trappers, and voyageurs, and Indian dandies, have vapored out their brief hour and disappeared. Such changes does the lapse of a handful of years make in this ever-changing country.

At this place Mr. Hunt remained for some time, to complete his assortment of Indian goods, and to increase his number of voyageurs, as well as to engage some of a more efficient character than those enlisted at Montreal.

And now commenced another game of jockeyship. There were able and efficient men in abundance at Mackinaw, but for several days not one presented himself. If offers were made to any, they were listened to with a shake of the head. Should any one seem inclined to enlist, there were officious idlers and busybodies, of that class who are ever ready to dissuade others from any enterprise in which they themselves have no concern. These would pull him by the sleeve, take him on one side, and murmur in his ear, or would suggest difficulties outright.

It was objected that the expedition would have to navigate unknown rivers, and pass through howling wildernesses infested by savage tribes, who had already cut off the unfortunate voyageurs that had ventured among them; that it was to climb the Rocky Mountains and descend into desolate and famished regions, where the traveller was often obliged to subsist on grasshoppers and crickets, or to kill his own horse for food.

[8] See Ross, *Adventures*, 176–78, for a parallel description of Mackinac. Irving's source has not been determined.

Ross describes the *voyageurs* here by saying: "That Canadians in general drink, and sometimes even to excess, must be admitted; but to see drunkenness and debauchery, with all their concomitant vices, carried on systematically, it is necessary to see Mackina . . . [which] at this time resembled a great bedlam, the frantic inmates running to and fro in wild forgetfulness." *Ibid.*, 176.

At length one man was hardy enough to engage, and he was used like a "stool-pigeon," to decoy others; but several days elapsed before any more could be prevailed upon to join him. A few then came to terms. It was desirable to engage them for five years, but some refused to engage for more than three. Then they must have part of their pay in advance, which was readily granted. When they had pocketed the amount, and squandered it in regales or in outfits, they began to talk of pecuniary obligations at Mackinaw, which must be discharged before they would be free to depart; or engagements with other persons, which were only to be canceled by a "reasonable consideration."

It was in vain to argue or remonstrate. The money advanced had already been sacked and spent, and must be lost and the recruits left behind, unless they could be freed from their debts and engagements. Accordingly, a fine was paid for one; a judgment for another; a tavern bill for a third, and almost all had to be bought off from some prior engagement, either real or pretended.

Mr. Hunt groaned in spirit at the incessant and unreasonable demands of these worthies upon his purse; yet with all this outlay of funds, the number recruited was but scanty, and many of the most desirable still held themselves aloof, and were not to be caught by a golden bait. With these he tried another temptation. Among the recruits who had enlisted he distributed feathers and ostrich plumes. These they put in their hats, and thus figured about Mackinaw, assuming airs of vast importance, as "voyageurs" in a new company, that was to eclipse the Northwest.[9] The effect was complete. A French Canadian is too vain and mercurial a being to withstand the finery and ostentation of the feather. Numbers immediately pressed into the service. One must have an ostrich plume; another, a white feather with a red end; a third, a bunch of cocks' tails. Thus all paraded about, in vainglorious style, more delighted with the feathers in their hats than with the money in their pockets; and considering themselves fully equal to the boastful "men of the north."

While thus recruiting the number of rank and file, Mr. Hunt was joined by a person whom he had invited, by letter, to engage as a partner in the expedition. This was Mr. Ramsay Crooks,[10] a young man, a native

---

[9] In the first edition, *voyageurs in a new company, that was to eclipse the Northwest* is all in quotation marks.

[10] Before entering the Pacific Fur Company, Ramsay Crooks (1787–1859) had

of Scotland, who had served under the Northwest Company, and been engaged in trading expeditions upon his individual account, among the tribes of the Missouri. Mr. Hunt knew him personally, and had conceived a high and merited opinion of his judgment, enterprise, and integrity; he was rejoiced, therefore, when the latter consented to accompany him. Mr. Crooks, however, drew from experience a picture of the dangers to which they would be subjected, and urged the importance of going with a considerable force. In ascending the upper Missouri they would have to pass through the country of the Sioux Indians, who had manifested repeated hostility to the white traders, and rendered their expeditions extremely perilous; firing upon them from the river banks as they passed beneath in their boats, and attacking them in their encampments. Mr. Crooks himself, when voyaging in company with another trader of the name of M'Lellan,[11] had been interrupted by these marauders, and had considered himself fortunate in escaping down the river without loss of life or property, but with a total abandonment of his trading voyage.[12]

Should they be fortunate enough to pass through the country of the Sioux without molestation, they would have another tribe still more savage and warlike beyond, and deadly foes of the white men.

These were the Blackfeet Indians, who ranged over a wide extent of country which they would have to traverse. Under all these circumstances, it was thought advisable to augment the party considerably. It already exceeded the number of thirty, to which it had originally been limited; but it was determined, on arriving at St. Louis, to increase it to the number of sixty.

These matters being arranged, they prepared to embark; but the

been in the fur trade in Canada, emigrating there from Scotland, his birthplace, when he was sixteen. In 1807 he went to St. Louis and engaged in the fur trade on the upper Missouri with Robert McClellan until both joined Astor in the Pacific Fur Company, from which Crooks resigned in May, 1812. He returned to St. Louis with Robert Stuart in 1812–13. He then re-engaged with Astor in 1813, and, subsequently, as a member of the American Fur Company, he was in charge of its business at Mackinac. Later, in 1822, he was shifted to the Western Department of this company. Upon Astor's retirement, Crooks became president of the American Fur Company. See Chittenden, *History of the American Fur Trade*, I, 381–82; Rollins (ed.), *Discovery of the Oregon Trail*, lxxxii–xci; Reuben Gold Thwaites (ed.), *Early Western Travels*, V, 36–37n. and 228–34, where Thwaites gives "Mr. Crooks' narrative of Mr. Hunt's expedition from the Aricaras to the Pacific."

[11] See note 10 above.

[12] See Rollins (ed.), *op. cit.*, lxxxiii.

embarkation of a crew of Canadian voyageurs, on a distant expedition, is not so easy a matter as might be imagined; especially of such a set of vainglorious fellows with money in both pockets, and cocks' tails in their hats. Like sailors, the Canadian voyageurs generally preface a long cruise with a carouse. They have their cronies, their brothers, their cousins, their wives, their sweethearts, all to be entertained at their expense. They feast, they fiddle, they drink, they sing, they dance, they frolic and fight, until they are all as mad as so many drunken Indians. The publicans are all obedience to their commands, never hesitating to let them run up scores without limit, knowing that, when their own money is expended, the purses of their employers must answer for the bill, or the voyage must be delayed. Neither was it possible, at that time, to remedy the matter at Mackinaw. In that amphibious community there was always a propensity to wrest the laws in favor of riotous or mutinous boatmen. It was necessary, also, to keep the recruits in good humor, seeing the novelty and danger of the service into which they were entering, and the ease with which they might at any time escape it, by jumping into a canoe and going down the stream.

Such were the scenes that beset Mr. Hunt, and gave him a foretaste of the difficulties of his command. The little cabarets and sutlers' shops along the bay resounded with the scraping of fiddles, with snatches of old French songs, with Indian whoops and yells, while every plumed and feathered vagabond had his troop of loving cousins and comrades at his heels. It was with the utmost difficulty they could be extricated from the clutches of the publicans and the embraces of their pot companions, who followed them to the water's edge with many a hug, a kiss on each cheek, and a maudlin benediction in Canadian French.

It was about the 12th of August[13] that they left Mackinaw, and pursued the usual route by Green Bay, Fox and Wisconsin rivers, to Prairie du Chien,[14] and thence down the Mississippi to St. Louis, where they landed on the 3d of September.[15]

[13] As noted above, the last entry in Hunt's account book at Mackinac is dated August 12.

[14] Prairie du Chien is at the Wisconsin River's junction with the Mississippi. As Hunt's account book shows, they were here at least by August 24.

[15] The date agrees with the first entry in Hunt's account book at St. Louis. Irving undoubtedly made slight use of this account book since it contains only business entries without any narrative details. Very likely his main source for this chapter was information acquired orally from Hunt, McKenzie, or Crooks.

CHAPTER XIV

St. Louis — Its Situation — Motley Population
French Creole Traders and Their Dependants — Missouri Fur Company
Mr. Manuel Lisa — Mississippi Boatmen — Vagrant Indians
Kentucky Hunters — Old French Mansions — Fiddling
Billiards — Mr. Joseph Miller — His Character — Recruits
Voyage up the Missouri — Difficulties of the River
Merits of Canadian Voyageurs — Arrival at the Nodowa
Mr. Robert M'Lellan Joins the Party — John Day, a Virginia Hunter
Description of Him — Mr. Hunt Returns to St. Louis

ST. LOUIS, which is situated on the right bank of the Mississippi River, a few miles below the mouth of the Missouri, was, at that time, a frontier settlement, and the last fitting-out place for the Indian trade of the Southwest. It possessed a motley population, composed of the creole descendants of the original French colonists; the keen traders from the Atlantic States; the backwoodsmen of Kentucky and Tennessee; the Indians and half-breeds of the prairies; together with a singular aquatic race that had grown up from the navigation of the rivers—the "boatmen of the Mississippi;"[1] who possessed habits, manners, and almost a language, peculiarly their own, and strongly technical. They, at that time, were extremely numerous, and conducted the chief navigation and commerce of the Ohio and the Mississippi, as the voyageurs did of the Canadian waters; but, like them, their consequence and characteristics are rapidly vanishing before the all-pervading intrusion of steamboats.

The old French houses engaged in the Indian trade had gathered round them a train of dependants, mongrel Indians, and mongrel Frenchmen, who had intermarried with Indians. These they employed in their various expeditions by land and water. Various individuals of other countries had, of late years, pushed the trade further into the interior, to the upper waters of the Missouri, and had swelled the number

---

[1] Mike Fink has come to stand as the representative of this class and around him a considerable body of folklore and literature has developed. See Walter Blair and Franklin J. Meine (eds.), *Half Horse Half Alligator: The Growth of the Mike Fink Legend*. See also Mark Twain's *Life on the Mississippi*, chap. III, for his account of Mississippi boatmen of the Mike Fink type.

of these hangers-on. Several of these traders had, two or three years previously, formed themselves into a company, composed of twelve partners, with a capital of about forty thousand dollars, called the Missouri Fur Company;[2] the object of which was, to establish posts along the upper part of that river, and monopolize the trade. The leading partner of this company was Mr. Manuel Lisa,[3] a Spaniard by birth, and a man of bold and enterprising character, who had ascended the Missouri almost to its source, and made himself well acquainted and popular with several of its tribes. By his exertions, trading posts had been established, in 1808, in the Sioux country, and among the Arickara and Mandan tribes; and a principal one, under Mr. Henry,[4] one of the partners, at the forks of the Missouri. This company had in its employ about two hundred and fifty men, partly American hunters, and partly creoles and Canadian voyageurs.

All these circumstances combined to produce a population at St. Louis even still more motley than that at Mackinaw. Here were to be seen,

[2] See Chittenden, *History of the American Fur Trade*, I, 137–57, and Phillips, *The Fur Trade*, II, *passim*.

[3] Manuel Lisa was born in New Orleans in 1772 and died in St. Louis in 1820. He went to St. Louis about 1798 and soon engaged in the fur trade on the Missouri River. By 1807 he had pushed up the Missouri as far as the Big Horn River, where he built Manuel's Fort, at that time the most distant American post in the Indian country. He helped organize the St. Louis Missouri Fur Company the next year (1808–1809), and some years later became its president. He exerted wide influence over the Indians, and during the War of 1812 helped persuade those on the upper Missouri to maintain their loyalty to the U.S. as opposed to the British fur trade. He ascended the Missouri River many times and by pursuing his interests with unflagging energy and perseverance, he proved himself one of the ablest traders of his time. See Chittenden, *op. cit.*, I, 125–36; Phillips, *op. cit.*, II, *passim*; W. B. Douglas, "Manuel Lisa," Missouri Historical Society *Collections*, Vol. III (1911), 233–68 and 367–406. Lisa's life is the subject of an excellent novel by Shirley Seifert entitled *Those Who Go Against the Current*. A recent biography is *Manual Lisa and the Opening of the Missouri Fur Trade*, by Richard E. Oglesby. Lisa figures prominently in John Bradbury's *Travels in the Interior of America* (cited hereafter as Bradbury, *Travels*) and H. M. Brackenridge's *Journal of a Voyage up the River Missouri* (cited hereafter as Brackenridge, *Journal*). As will be seen, Lisa clashed with Hunt on the Missouri.

[4] Andrew Henry, one of Lisa's close associates, helped organize the Missouri Fur Company in 1808–1809. In 1810, with Pierre Menard, John Colter, and others, he built a stockade at Three Forks, in what is now Montana, but was shortly driven out by the Blackfeet. In 1822 he became a partner of General William Ashley in the fur trade. See Chittenden, *op. cit.*, I, 141–45, 251–52, and *passim*; Harrison C. Dale (ed.), *The Ashley-Smith Explorations*; Donald McKay Frost, *Notes on General Ashley, the Overland Trail, and South Pass*; Dale L. Morgan, *Jedediah Smith*; Phillips, *op. cit.*, II; Washington Irving, *The Adventures of Captain Bonneville*, 4–5n.

about the river banks, the hectoring, extravagant, bragging boatmen of the Mississippi, with the gay, grimacing, singing, good-humored Canadian voyageurs. Vagrant Indians, of various tribes, loitered about the streets. Now and then a stark Kentucky hunter, in leathern hunting-dress, with rifle on shoulder and knife in belt, strode along. Here and there were new brick houses and shops, just set up by bustling, driving, and eager men of traffic from the Atlantic States; while, on the other hand, the old French mansions, with open casements, still retained the easy, indolent air of the original colonists; and now and then the scraping of a fiddle, a strain of an ancient French song, or the sound of billiard balls, showed that the happy Gallic turn for gayety and amusement still lingered about the place.[5]

Such was St. Louis at the time of Mr. Hunt's arrival there, and the appearance of a new fur company, with ample funds at its command, produced a strong sensation among the Indian traders of the place, and awakened keen jealousy and opposition on the part of the Missouri Company. Mr. Hunt proceeded to strengthen himself against all competition. For this purpose, he secured to the interests of the association another of those enterprising men, who had been engaged in individual traffic with the tribes of the Missouri. This was a Mr. Joseph Miller,[6]

---

[5] Shortly after *Astoria* was published, Hunt took exception to what he considered to be Irving's one-sided sketch of St. Louis at this time. His comment deserves to be quoted in full: "I have had a glimpse today [November 16, 1836] of 'Astoria,' but have had time only to see some things that would have been well to have been otherwise expressed, what particularly struck me was a description of St. Louis in 1810 . . . which so varies from the situation of the place according to my views, it places me in rather an awkward position. St. Louis was always remarkable since I have known it for a degree of gentility among the better sort of its inhabitants and the correctness with which they spoke French. One would suppose that on reading this Book that it never contained such men as Charles Gratiot, Auguste Chouteau, and many others who were gentlemen in any country. I am sorry my name is blended with a description of merely the Boatmen, Motlies, etc. A review of the proof sheets by some one who knew and could appreciate the character of the place in all things would have been well for the writer and the fame of those concerned." Quoted by John Francis McDermott in "The Confines of a Wilderness," *Missouri Historical Review*, Vol. XXIX (1934), 9, from Missouri Historical Society *Collections*, Vol. VI (1931), 324–25.

Franchère, who subsequently lived in St. Louis, also took exception to Irving's description; see *Narrative*, 403. There is little question, however, about the authenticity of what Irving wrote.

[6] Not a great deal more is known of Miller than what Irving writes. His birthplace was Pennsylvania. He saw military service from 1799 to 1805, and upon his resignation he became a trapper and trader. He threw in his lot with the Pacific Fur Company and aided Hunt in recruiting men, but being somewhat irascible, he went with Hunt

a gentleman well educated and well informed, and of a respectable family of Baltimore. He had been an officer in the army of the United States, but had resigned in disgust, on being refused a furlough, and had taken to trapping beaver and trading among the Indians. He was easily induced by Mr. Hunt to join as a partner, and was considered by him, on account of his education and acquirements, and his experience in Indian trade, a valuable addition to the company.

Several additional men were likewise enlisted at St. Louis, some as boatmen, and others as hunters. These last were engaged, not merely to kill game for provisions, but also, and indeed chiefly, to trap beaver and other animals of rich furs, valuable in the trade. They enlisted on different terms. Some were to have a fixed salary of three hundred dollars; others were to be fitted out and maintained at the expense of the company, and were to hunt and trap on shares.[7]

As Mr. Hunt met with much opposition on the part of rival traders, especially the Missouri Fur Company, it took him some weeks to complete his preparations.[8] The delays which he had previously experienced at Montreal, Mackinaw, and on the way, added to those at St. Louis, had thrown him much behind his original calculations, so that it would be impossible to effect his voyage up the Missouri in the present year. This river, flowing from high and cold latitudes, and through wide and

only as far as Henry's Fork of the Snake River and then resigned from the expedition and joined several trappers (Hoback, Reznor, Robinson, Cass) whom Hunt sent out. Miller subsequently met Robert Stuart along the Snake and with him returned to St. Louis in 1813, after which he drops from sight. See Rollins (ed.), *Discovery of the Oregon Trail*, c–ci; Thwaites (ed.), *Early Western Travels*, V, 106n.; Chittenden, *op. cit.*, II, 907–908.

[7] For those who enlisted with Hunt, see Kenneth W. Porter, "Roll of Overland Astorians, 1810–12," *Oregon Historical Quarterly*, Vol. XXXIV (1933), 103–12. On the basis of Porter's evidence, there were forty-six Canadians, not including two deserters at Mackinac; twenty-six Americans, including all classes—hunters, leaders, etc.; five halfbloods; and a few others not classified.

[8] Hunt's account book shows that the following equipment was purchased at St. Louis; although the list is probably incomplete, it gives a good idea of the kind of equipment and goods required to outfit an expedition of this kind: one large keelboat, oars, etc., for $250; oilcloth, sail, a Schenectady barge, a sail for the barge, an anchor, two large awls, two handsaws, two padlocks, two large copper kettles, one medium-size kettle, one hammer, one drawknife, one gimlet, nails, calking iron, auger, cable, nineteen bearskins, nine linen bags, hulled corn, one teakettle, four canisters, two tin pans, knives and forks, tin cups, coffee, tea, pepper, beaver traps, bacon, medicine chest, bar salt, flannel, buttons, socks, blankets, linen cloth, tobacco, trading tobacco, trousers, "capeaus," combs, shoes, hunters' knives, thread. Account Book, Vol. I, 69–71.

open plains, exposed to chilling blasts, freezes early. The winter may be dated from the first of November; there was every prospect, therefore, that it would be closed with ice long before Mr. Hunt could reach its upper waters. To avoid, however, the expense of wintering at St. Louis, he determined to push up the river as far as possible, to some point above the settlements,[9] where game was plenty, and where his whole party could be subsisted by hunting, until the breaking up of the ice in the spring should permit them to resume their voyage.

Accordingly on the twenty-first of October he took his departure from St. Louis. His party was distributed in three boats. One was the barge which he had brought from Mackinaw; another was of a larger size, such as was formerly used in navigating the Mohawk River, and known by the generic name of the Schenectady barge; the other was a large keel boat, at that time the grand conveyance on the Mississippi.

In this way they set out from St. Louis, in buoyant spirits, and soon arrived at the mouth of the Missouri. This vast river, three thousand miles in length, and which, with its tributary streams, drains such an immense extent of country, was as yet but casually and imperfectly navigated by the adventurous bark of the fur trader. A steamboat had never yet stemmed its turbulent current.[10] Sails were but of casual assistance, for it required a strong wind to conquer the force of the stream. The main dependence was on bodily strength and manual dexterity. The boats, in general, had to be propelled by oars and setting poles, or drawn by the hand and by grappling hooks from one root or overhanging tree to another; or towed by the long cordelle, or towing line, where the shores were sufficiently clear of woods and thickets to permit the men to pass along the banks.

[9] As Irving explains later, this place was on the Nodaway River, which, flowing south out of Iowa, enters the Missouri a few miles above present-day St. Joseph, Missouri.

[10] The first attempt to navigate the Missouri with a steamboat took place in 1819. The American Fur Company introduced the steamboat in the fur trade in 1831, when the *Yellowstone*, built especially for the purpose, went as far as Fort Tecumseh. The next year, it traveled all the way to the Yellowstone River, and thereafter steamboats remained a regular feature of western navigation. Chittenden, *op. cit.*, I, 338–41; II, 106.

By coincidence, when Irving went to St. Louis in 1832, the steamer on which he was a passenger collided with the *Yellowstone* as the latter was returning to St. Louis after its first historic run to the upper Missouri. His journal records the event; see *Western Journals of Washington Irving*, 80.

During this slow and tedious progress the boat would be exposed to frequent danger from floating trees and great masses of drift-wood, or to be impaled upon snags and sawyers; that is to say, sunken trees, presenting a jagged or pointed end above the surface of the water. As the channel of the river frequently shifted from side to side according to the bends and sand-banks, the boat had, in the same way, to advance in a zigzag course. Often a part of the crew would have to leap into the water at the shallows, and wade along with the towing line, while their comrades on board toilfully assisted with oar and setting pole. Sometimes the boat would seem to be retained motionless, as if spell-bound, opposite some point round which the current set with violence, and where the utmost labor scarce effected any visible progress.

On these occasions it was that the merits of the Canadian voyageurs came into full action. Patient of toil, not to be disheartened by impediments and disappointments, fertile in expedients, and versed in every mode of humoring and conquering the wayward current, they would ply every exertion, sometimes in the boat, sometimes on shore, sometimes in the water, however cold; always alert, always in good humor; and, should they at any time flag or grow weary, one of their popular boat-songs, chanted by a veteran oarsman, and responded to in chorus, acted as a never-failing restorative.[11]

By such assiduous and persevering labor they made their way about four hundred and fifty miles up the Missouri, by the 16th of November, to the mouth of the Nodowa.[12] As this was a good hunting country, and as the season was rapidly advancing, they determined to establish their winter quarters at this place; and, in fact, two days after they had come to a halt, the river closed just above their encampment.

The party had not been long at this place when they were joined by Mr. Robert M'Lellan,[13] another trader of the Missouri; the same who

[11] Irving's information for this detailed and accurate description of the method of ascending the Missouri could well have come from scattered passages in Brackenridge, *Journal*, although another source is possible. Bradbury, *Travels*, 39–40n., records one of the *voyageur* songs.

[12] The first entry in Hunt's account book here is dated November 18, 1810. All the following entries until April 19 are made at Nodaway.

[13] Robert McClellan (c. 1770–1815) was born near Mercersburg, Pennsylvania. He saw military service from 1790 to 1794 or 1795 under "Mad Anthony" Wayne as a spy in campaigns against Indians. Following his resignation he went to New Orleans, where he contracted yellow fever. A long illness followed. In 1810 he was employed by the government in the Commissary Department, his duties taking him to St. Louis in

had been associated with Mr. Crooks in the unfortunate expedition in which they had been intercepted by the Sioux Indians, and obliged to make a rapid retreat down the river.

M'Lellan was a remarkable man. He had been a partisan under General Wayne, in his Indian wars, where he had distinguished himself by his fiery spirit and reckless daring, and marvelous stories were told of his exploits. His appearance answered to his character. His frame was meagre, but muscular; showing strength, activity, and iron firmness. His eyes were dark, deep-set, and piercing. He was restless, fearless, but of impetuous and sometimes ungovernable temper. He had been invited by Mr. Hunt to enroll himself as a partner, and gladly consented; being pleased with the thoughts of passing with a powerful force through the country of the Sioux, and perhaps having an opportunity of revenging himself upon that lawless tribe for their past offenses.

Another recruit that joined the camp at Nodowa deserves equal mention. This was John Day,[14] a hunter from the backwoods of Virginia,

---

the same year. In 1802 he began to trade with the Indians on the Missouri, and in 1807 he formed a partnership with Ramsay Crooks. In that year they went up the Missouri, but upon meeting Ensign Nathaniel Prior, from whom they learned of the hostility of the Arikara Indians, they withdrew downstream and erected a post near Council Bluffs, where they stayed until 1809. Another attempt to move up the river with the Missouri Fur Company was stopped by the Sioux, who forced them to erect a post. McClellan charged this against Manuel Lisa, and thus arose his threat to shoot Lisa on sight. McClellan and Crooks dissolved their partnership in 1810, the former continuing to trade alone. He built a post on the Missouri about two hundred miles above the Nodaway River but again had trouble with the Sioux, who plundered him of $3,000 worth of goods, of which he was able to recover about $500 worth by bold intervention. He then started downstream and met Hunt's party at the Nodaway, where he joined as a partner with two and one-half shares. He continued as far as Astoria but resigned in the spring of 1812, when he started overland for St. Louis with Robert Stuart and the Returning Astorians. Once more in Missouri, he engaged in business, farming, and horse racing. When he died on November 22, 1815, he was buried on the farm of General William Clark. See Stella M. Drumm, "More About Astorians," *Oregon Historical Quarterly*, Vol. XXIV (1923), 345–52; Rollins (ed.), *op. cit.*, xci–xcv; Chittenden, *op. cit.*, I, 159–62.

[14] Born in Virginia, John Day (1770?–1820) had by 1798 gone to Missouri, where securing a grant of land from the Spanish, he engaged in farming, trapping, and, later, salt mining near Franklin. He was also employed by Ramsay Crooks as a trader or trapper. He found Hunt's winter camp on the Nodaway late in 1810 or early in 1811 and thereupon signed on as a member of the expedition. He reached Astoria and started back to Missouri with Robert Stuart, but was returned to Astoria after becoming deranged. He eventually recovered and entered the North West Company when Astoria

who[15] had been several years on the Missouri in the service of Mr. Crooks, and of other traders. He was about forty years of age, six feet two inches high, straight as an Indian; with an elastic step as if he trod on springs, and a handsome, open, manly countenance. It was his boast that, in his younger days, nothing could hurt or daunt him; but he had "lived too fast," and injured his constitution by his excesses. Still he was strong of hand, bold of heart, a prime woodman, and an almost unerring shot. He had the frank spirit of a Virginian, and the rough heroism of a pioneer of the west.

The party were now brought to a halt for several months. They were in a country abounding with deer and wild turkeys, so that there was no stint of provisions, and everyone appeared cheerful and contented. Mr. Hunt determined to avail himself of this interval to return to St. Louis and obtain a reinforcement. He wished to procure an interpreter, acquainted with the language of the Sioux, as, from all accounts, he apprehended difficulties in passing through the country of that nation. He felt the necessity, also, of having a greater number of hunters, not merely to keep up a supply of provisions throughout their long and arduous expedition, but also as a protection and defense, in case of Indian hostilities. For such service the Canadian voyageurs were little to be depended upon, fighting not being a part of their profession. The proper kind of men were American hunters, experienced in savage life and savage warfare, and possessed of the true game spirit of the west.

Leaving, therefore, the encampment in charge of the other partners, Mr. Hunt set off on foot on the first of January (1811),[16] for St. Louis. He was accompanied by eight men as far as Fort Osage, about one hundred and fifty miles below Nodowa. Here he procured a couple of horses, and proceeded on the remainder of his journey with two men, sending the other six back to the encampment. He arrived at St. Louis on the 20th of January.

was sold. He remained in the Snake River country and died in the Salmon River Mountains of Idaho on February 16, 1820. The John Day River in Oregon is named for him. See Rollins (ed.), *op. cit.*, xcvii–c; Chittenden, *op. cit.*, II, 905–906; Thwaites (ed.), *Early Western Travels*, V, 181n. See also T. C. Elliott (ed.), "Last Will and Testament of John Day," *Oregon Historical Quarterly*, Vol. XVII (1916), 373–79, and Drumm, "More About Astorians," *ibid.*, Vol. XXIV (1923), 356.

[15] The first edition reads *but who*.

[16] Both the first edition and the Author's Revised Edition erroneously have 1810.

CHAPTER XV

Opposition of the Missouri Fur Company — Blackfeet Indians
Pierre Dorion, a Half-Breed Interpreter — Old Dorion and His Hybrid Progeny
Family Quarrels — Cross-Purposes Between Dorion and Lisa
Renegadoes from Nodowa — Perplexities of a Commander
Messrs. Bradbury and Nuttall Join the Expedition
Legal Embarrassments of Pierre Dorion — Departure from St. Louis
Conjugal Discipline of a Half-Breed — Annual Swelling of the Rivers
Daniel Boone, the Patriarch of Kentucky — John Colter
His Adventures Among the Indians — Rumors of Danger Ahead
Fort Osage — An Indian War-Feast — Troubles in the Dorion Family
Buffaloes and Turkey-Buzzards

ON this his second visit to St. Louis, Mr. Hunt was again impeded in his plans by the opposition of the Missouri Fur Company. The affairs of that company were, at this time, in a very dubious state. During the preceding year, their principal establishment at the forks of the Missouri had been so much harassed by the Blackfeet Indians, that its commander, Mr. Henry, one of the partners, had been compelled to abandon the post and cross the Rocky Mountains, with the intention of fixing himself upon one of the upper branches of the Columbia. What had become of him and his party was unknown.[1] The most intense anxiety was felt concerning them, and apprehensions that they might have been cut off

[1] Phillips, *The Fur Trade*, II, 262–66, summarizes most of what is known about Andrew Henry's abandonment of the fort at Three Forks and his journey west of the Continental Divide. The fullest account of what occurred at Three Forks that year is found in chap. II of Thomas James, *Three Years among the Indians and Mexicans* (Waterloo, Ill., 1846; various reprints). When Henry left this location, owing to the hostility of the Blackfeet, he moved to the region west of the Teton Range onto tributaries of the Snake River, he and his men becoming the first to explore that area. On Henry's Fork, which bears his name, he built a fortification. There is also evidence of another encampment near present-day Drummond, Idaho, where a series of unusual stones have been discovered, one inscribed with the words "Camp Henry Sept 1810." On another stone are found the names of A. Henry, J. Hoback, P. McBride, B. Jackson, and L. Cather, plus a cross and a face in profile. Having visited this spot and photographed the stones, I am convinced of their genuineness. See Margaret Hawkes Lindsley, "Major Andrew Henry," *Scenic Idaho*, Vol. X (1955), 6ff. This area figures in Hunt's overland journey, and one of the men whom Hunt picked up on the Missouri was J. Hoback.

by the savages. At the time of Mr. Hunt's arrival St. Louis, the Missouri Company were fitting out an expedition to go in quest of Mr. Henry. It was to be conducted by Mr. Manuel Lisa, the enterprising partner already mentioned.[2]

There being thus two expeditions on foot at the same moment, an unusual demand was occasioned for hunters and voyageurs, who accordingly profited by the circumstance, and stipulated for high terms. Mr. Hunt found a keen and subtle competitor in Lisa, and was obliged to secure his recruits by liberal advances of pay, and by other pecuniary indulgences.

The greatest difficulty was to procure the Sioux interpreter. There was but one man to be met with at St. Louis who was fitted for the purpose, but to secure him would require much management. The individual in question was a half-breed, named Pierre Dorion;[3] and, as he figures hereafter in this narrative, and is, withal, a striking specimen of the hybrid race on the frontier, we shall give a few particulars concerning him. Pierre was the son of Dorion, the French interpreter, who accompanied Messrs. Lewis and Clarke in their famous exploring expedition across the Rocky Mountains. Old Dorion was one of those French creoles, descendants of the ancient Canadian stock, who abound on the western frontier, and amalgamate or cohabit with the savages. He had sojourned among various tribes, and perhaps left progeny among them all; but his regular, or habitual wife, was a Sioux squaw. By her he had a hopeful brood of half-breed sons, of whom Pierre was one. The domestic affairs of old Dorion were conducted on the true Indian plan. Father and sons would occasionally get drunk together, and then the cabin was a scene of ruffian brawl and fighting, in the course of which the old Frenchman was apt to get soundly belabored by his mongrel offspring. In a furious scuffle of the kind, one of the sons got the old man upon the ground, and was upon the point of scalping him. "Hold! my son," cried the old fellow, in imploring accents, "you are too brave, too *honorable* to scalp your father!" This last appeal touched the French side of the half-breed's heart, so he suffered the old man to wear his scalp unharmed.

Of this hopeful stock was Pierre Dorion, the man whom it was now the desire of Mr. Hunt to engage as an interpreter. He had been em-

[2] Irving here draws upon Brackenridge, *Journal*, 27–30.
[3] Little is known about Dorion beyond what appears here and later in *Astoria*.

ployed in that capacity by the Missouri Fur Company during the preceding year, and conducted[4] their traders in safety through the different tribes of the Sioux. He had proved himself faithful and serviceable while sober; but the love of liquor, in which he had been nurtured and brought up, would occasionally break out, and with it the savage side of his character.

It was his[5] love of liquor which had embroiled him with the Missouri Company. While in their service at Fort Mandan, on the frontier, he had been seized with a whiskey mania; and, as the beverage was only to be procured at the company's store, it had been charged in his account at the rate of ten dollars a quart. This item had ever remained unsettled, and a matter of furious dispute, the mere mention of which was sufficient to put him in a passion.

The moment it was discovered by Mr. Lisa that Pierre Dorion was in treaty with the new and rival association, he endeavored, by threats as well as promises, to prevent his engaging in their service. His promises might, perhaps, have prevailed; but his threats, which related to the whiskey debt, only served to drive Pierre into the opposite ranks. Still he took advantage of this competition for his services to stand out with Mr. Hunt on the most advantageous terms, and, after a negotiation of nearly two weeks, capitulated to serve in the expedition, as hunter and interpreter, at the rate of three hundred dollars a year, two hundred of which were to be paid in advance.

When Mr. Hunt had got everything ready for leaving St. Louis, new difficulties arose. Five of the American hunters from the encampment at Nodowa, suddenly made their appearance. They alleged that they had been ill treated by the partners at the encampment, and had come off clandestinely, in consequence of a dispute. It was useless at the present moment, and under present circumstances, to attempt any compulsory measures with these deserters. Two of them Mr. Hunt prevailed upon, by mild means, to return with him. The rest refused; nay, what was worse, they spread such reports of the hardships and dangers to be apprehended in the course of the expedition, that they struck a panic into those hunters who had recently engaged at St. Louis, and when the hour of departure arrived, all but one refused to embark. It was in vain to plead or remonstrate; they shouldered their rifles and turned their backs upon the expedition, and Mr. Hunt was fain to put off from shore with

[4] The first edition reads *had conducted*.   [5] *This* in first edition.

Fort Okanogan as it appeared in the 1850's, by John Mix Stanley. From Isaac I. Stevens, *Narrative and Final Report . . . Reports of Explorations and Surveys to Ascertain the Most Practicable and Economical Route for a Railroad from the Mississippi River to the Pacific Ocean* (1860).

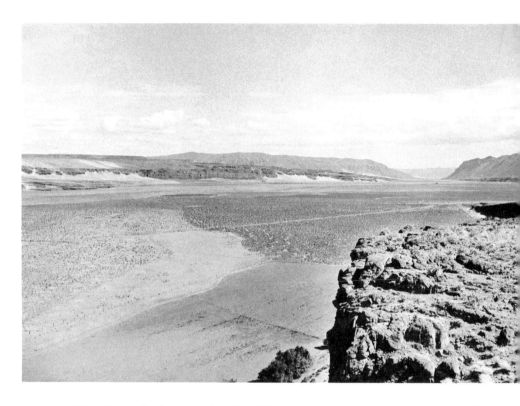

The channel of the Columbia River, now covered by the waters of Wanapum Dam, in central Washington. Up this valley (toward the viewer) traveled the Astorians on their way to Fort Okanogan.

Photograph by Edgeley W. Todd

the single hunter and a number of voyageurs whom he had engaged. Even Pierre Dorion, at the last moment, refused to enter the boat until Mr. Hunt consented to take his squaw[6] and two children on board also. But the tissue of perplexities, on account of this worthy individual, did not end here.

Among the various persons who were about to proceed up the Missouri with Mr. Hunt, were two scientific gentlemen: one Mr. John Bradbury,[7] a man of mature age, but great enterprise and personal activity, who had been sent out by the Linnæan Society of Liverpool to make a collection of American plants; the other, a Mr. Nuttall,[8] likewise an Englishman, younger in years, who has since made himself

[6] See J. Neilson Barry, "Madame Dorion of the Astorians," *Oregon Historical Quarterly*, Vol. XXX (1929), 272–78. See also below, Chapter LXI, pp. 498–500. She lived until September 3, 1850.

[7] Born a Scotsman, Bradbury came to the United States in 1809 and was received by President Jefferson, who recommended him to Meriwether Lewis, then governor of Louisiana Territory. Bradbury arrived at St. Louis on December 31, 1809, and in the following spring and summer made numerous field trips to collect plants. His meeting with Hunt enabled him to travel up the Missouri for more extensive collecting as far as the Mandan Indian villages. He descended the river, when Hunt set out west of the Arikara villages, and returned to St. Louis within two weeks on a boat sent down by Manuel Lisa. Later, after a period of illness, Bradbury went to New Orleans and to New York. The War of 1812 detained him in the United States. He later returned to England but subsequently came back to St. Louis. See Thwaites (ed.), *Early Western Travels*, V, 9–15; R. H. True, "A Sketch of the Life of John Bradbury, Including His Unpublished Correspondence with Thomas Jefferson," *Proceedings of the American Philosophical Society*, Vol. LXVIII (1929), 133–50. In 1817, Bradbury published his *Travels in the Interior of America, in the Years 1809, 1810, and 1811* in London. The importance of this volume, which Irving, in his introduction, acknowledges as one of his sources, is that for Irving, at least, it offered an indispensable record of Hunt's voyage up the Missouri as far as the Arikara villages. Very fortunately for Irving, moreover, with Manuel Lisa was another traveler, Hugh M. Brackenridge, whose *Journal of a Voyage up the River Missouri* provided him with a useful record of the competition between Hunt and Lisa and of their relationship at the Arikara villages. Irving was thus able to relate the voyage up the river with complete accuracy as well as being able to see events from the standpoint of Hunt and Lisa simultaneously. See Bradbury's *Travels*, 35–36, for his account of joining Hunt's party.

[8] Thomas Nuttall (1786–1859). Born in Yorkshire, England, he came to the United States in 1808 and became interested in collecting native plants. Eventually he became curator of the botanical collection at Harvard University (1822–32). Unfortunately, he left no record of his voyage up the Missouri with Hunt. In 1818 he published his *Genera of North American Plants, and a Catalogue of the Species to the Year 1817* (2 vols.) and in 1821 *Journal of Travels into the Arkansas Territory during the year 1819*, to both of which Irving refers. Other publications on botany and ornithology appeared in later years.

known as the author of "Travels in Arkansas," and a work on the "Genera of American Plants." Mr. Hunt had offered them the protection and facilities of his party, in their scientific researches up the Missouri. As they were not ready to depart at the moment of embarkation,[9] they put their trunks on board of the boat, but remained at St. Louis until the next day, for the arrival of the post, intending to join the expedition at St. Charles,[10] a short distance above the mouth of the Missouri.

The same evening, however, they learned that a writ had been issued against Pierre Dorion for his whiskey debt, by Mr. Lisa, as agent of the Missouri Company, and that it was the intention to entrap the mongrel linguist on his arrival at St. Charles. Upon hearing this, Mr. Bradbury and Mr. Nuttall set off a little after midnight, by land, got ahead of the boat as it was ascending the Missouri, before its arrival at St. Charles, and gave Pierre Dorion warning of the legal toil prepared to ensnare him. The knowing Pierre immediately landed and took to the woods, followed by his squaw laden with their papooses, and a large bundle containing their most precious effects, promising to rejoin the party some distance above St. Charles. There seemed little dependence to be placed upon the promises of a loose adventurer of the kind, who was at the very time playing an evasive game with his former employers; who had already received two-thirds of his year's pay, and his rifle[11] on his shoulder, his family and worldly fortune at his heels, and the wild woods before him. There was no alternative, however, and it was hoped his

[9] Bradbury states that Hunt left St. Louis on the morning of March 12. On March 14, the *Louisiana Gazette* published the following notice of his departure:

"Mr. Wilson P. Hunt, left this place [St. Louis] last Monday, with a well equipped barge, to join his associates, at the Otto village, to proceed on his expedition to the Columbia river. His party amounted to about seventy able bodied men, nerved to hardship.

"We understand, the New York Fur Company, to whom Mr. Hunt is attached, have dispatched a well-furnished ship, to meet the party on the shore of the Pacific.

"Mr. Hunt is accompanied by Mr. Bradbury and a Mr. Nuttall. . . ."
Less than two weeks before Hunt's departure from St. Louis, the *Tonquin* had sailed from the Hawaiian Islands for the Columbia.

[10] On the north side of the Missouri, some twenty miles from its mouth. Manuel Lisa, who began his up-river journey later than Hunt, started from St. Charles on the following April 2. Brackenridge, *Journal*, 31.

Lewis and Clark described St. Charles as having one street, a mile long, parallel to the river, about 100 small houses, a chapel, and a population at that time (1804) of about 450, most of French-Canadian descent, who also called the town Petite Côte. *History of the Expedition*, I, 38–39.

[11] The first edition reads *and had his rifle*.

pique against his old employers would render him faithful to his new ones.

The party reached St. Charles in the afternoon, but the harpies of the law looked in vain for their expected prey. The boats resumed their course on the following morning,[12] and had not proceeded far when Pierre Dorion made his appearance on the shore. He was gladly taken on board, but he came without his squaw. They had quarreled in the night; Pierre had administered the Indian discipline of the cudgel, whereupon she had taken to the woods, with their children and all their worldly goods. Pierre evidently was deeply grieved and disconcerted at the loss of his wife and his knapsack, whereupon[13] Mr. Hunt despatched one of the Canadian voyageurs in search of the fugitive; and the whole party, after proceeding a few miles further, encamped on an island to wait his return. The Canadian rejoined the party, but without the squaw; and Pierre Dorion passed a solitary and anxious night, bitterly regretting his indiscretion in having exercised his conjugal authority so near home. Before daybreak, however, a well-known voice reached his ears from the opposite shore. It was his repentant spouse, who had been wandering the woods all night in quest of the party, and had at length descried it by its fires. A boat was despatched for her, the interesting family was once more united, and Mr. Hunt now flattered himself that his perplexities with Pierre Dorion were at an end.[14]

Bad weather, very heavy rains, and an unusually early rise in the Missouri, rendered the ascent of the river toilsome, slow, and dangerous. The rise of the Missouri does not generally take place until the month of May or June: the present swelling of the river must have been caused by a freshet in some of its more southern branches. It could not have been the great annual flood, as the higher branches must still have been ice-bound.

And here we cannot but pause, to notice the admirable arrangement of nature, by which the annual swellings of the various great rivers which empty themselves into the Mississippi, have been made to precede each other at considerable intervals. Thus, the flood of the Red River precedes that of the Arkansas by a month. The Arkansas, also, rising in a much more southern latitude than the Missouri, takes the lead of it in its

---

[12] March 14.
[13] *Wherefore* in first edition.
[14] Irving's information is from Bradbury, *Travels*, 38–41.

annual excess, and its superabundant waters are disgorged and disposed of long before the breaking up of the icy barriers of the north; otherwise, did all these mighty streams rise simultaneously, and discharge their vernal floods into the Mississippi, an inundation would be the consequence, that would submerge and devastate all the lower country.

On the afternoon of the third day, March 17th,[15] the boats touched at Charette,[16] one of the old villages founded by the original French colonists. Here they met with Daniel Boone,[17] the renowned patriarch of Kentucky, who had kept in the advance of civilization, and on the borders of the wilderness, still leading a hunter's life, though now in his eighty-fifth year.[18] He had but recently returned from a hunting and trapping expedition, and had brought nearly sixty beaver skins as trophies of his skill. The old man was still erect in form, strong in limb, and unflinching in spirit, and as he stood on the river bank, watching the departure of an expedition destined to traverse the wilderness to the very shores of the Pacific, very probably felt a throb of his old pioneer spirit, impelling him to shoulder his rifle and join the adventurous band. Boone flourished several years after this meeting, in a vigorous old age, the Nestor of hunters and backwoodsmen; and died, full of sylvan honor and renown, in 1818, in his ninety-second year.[19]

The next morning early, as the party were yet encamped at the mouth of a small stream, they were visited by another of these heroes of the wilderness, one John Colter,[20] who had accompanied Lewis and

[15] Both the first edition and the Author's Revised Edition erroneously have January 17. The date of March 17 is confirmed by Bradbury. If Hunt had left St. Louis on March 12, as Bradbury says, they reached Charette on the sixth day of travel.

[16] Charette (or La Charette) was founded about 1766. Eventually it was lost to the erosion of the river. Thwaites (ed.), *Early Western Travels*, V, 42–43n.

[17] Irving follows Bradbury, *Travels*, 43–44, in writing about Boone (1734–1820), who had moved to Missouri, where he secured a land grant about 1799. The Boone legend was already in process of formation, probably sparked by John Filson (c. 1747–1788), who in 1784 published *The Adventures of Col. Daniel Boon*. The best recent biography is John Bakeless, *Daniel Boone* (New York, 1939). Bradbury had come up the river prepared to meet the famous old Kentuckian, for he carried with him a letter of introduction from Boone's nephew, and, while Hunt went ahead with the boat, Bradbury stopped and visited with him.

[18] Actually his seventy-seventh year. Irving follows Bradbury's error.

[19] Boone died in 1820; thus he would have been eighty-six.

[20] As Irving indicates below, his information concerning John Colter (c. 1770–1813) is derived from Bradbury's *Travels*, where it appears as a long footnote (see *ibid.*, 44–47n.). Bradbury's account is one of the principal sources for the experience in Colter's life that it details. Another important source for Colter is Thomas James,

Clarke in their memorable expedition. He had recently made one of those vast internal voyages so characteristic of this fearless class of men, and of the immense regions over which they hold their lonely wanderings; having come from the head waters of the Missouri to St. Louis in a small canoe. This distance of three thousand miles he had accomplished in thirty days. Colter kept with the party all the morning. He had many particulars to give them concerning the Blackfeet Indians, a restless and predatory tribe, who had conceived an implacable hostility to the white men, in consequence of one of their warriors having been killed by Captain Lewis, while attempting to steal horses.[21] Through the country infested by these savages the expedition would have to proceed, and Colter was urgent in reiterating the precautions that ought to be observed respecting them. He had himself experienced their vindictive cruelty, and his story deserves particular citation, as showing the hair-breadth adventures to which these solitary rovers of the wilderness are exposed.

Colter, with the hardihood of a regular trapper, had cast himself loose from the party of Lewis and Clarke[22] in the very heart of the wilderness, and had remained to trap beaver alone on the head waters of the Missouri. Here he fell in with another lonely trapper, like himself, named Potts,[23] and they agreed to keep together. They were in the very region of the terrible Blackfeet, at that time thirsting to revenge the death of their companion, and knew that they had to expect no mercy at their hands. They were obliged to keep concealed all day in the woody margins of the rivers, setting their traps after nightfall and taking them up before daybreak. It was running a fearful risk for the sake of a few beaver skins; but such is the life of the trapper.

Three Years among the Indians and Mexicans. For biographies of Colter, see Stallo Vinton, *John Colter, Discoverer of Yellowstone Park,* and Burton Harris, *John Colter: His Years in the Rockies.* See also Edgeley W. Todd, "John Colter, Mountain Man," *Colorado Quarterly,* Vol. II (1953), 79–91. Colter has been since his lifetime the subject of much legendizing, and his remarkable experiences have appeared in many narratives. If Irving read Lewis and Clark thoroughly, he would have learned of Colter and his separation from the expedition to trap. See *History of the Expedition,* III, 252–53, under date of August 14, 1806.

[21] This unfortunate incident took place on the Marias River in 1806 on the return journey to St. Louis. See *History of the Expedition,* III, 191–93, and *Original Journals of the Lewis and Clark Expedition,* V, 223–25.

[22] On August 17, 1806.

[23] John Potts, also a former member of the Lewis and Clark expedition.

They were on a branch of the Missouri called Jefferson[24] Fork, and had set their traps at night, about six miles up a small river that emptied into the fork. Early in the morning they ascended the river in a canoe, to examine the traps. The banks on each side were high and perpendicular, and cast a shade over the stream. As they were softly paddling along, they heard the trampling of many feet upon the banks. Colter immediately gave the alarm of "Indians!" and was for instant retreat. Potts scoffed at him for being frightened by the trampling of a herd of buffaloes. Colter checked his uneasiness and paddled forward. They had not gone much further when frightful whoops and yells burst forth from each side of the river, and several hundred Indians appeared on either bank. Signs were made to the unfortunate trappers to come on shore. They were obliged to comply. Before they could get out of their canoe, a savage seized the rifle belonging to Potts. Colter sprang on shore, wrested the weapon from the hands of the Indian, and restored it to his companion, who was still in the canoe, and immediately pushed into the stream. There was the sharp twang of a bow, and Potts cried out that he was wounded. Colter urged him to come on shore and submit, as his only chance for life; but the other knew there was no prospect of mercy, and determined to die game. Leveling his rifle, he shot one of the savages dead on the spot. The next moment he fell himself, pierced with innumerable arrows.[25]

The vengeance of the savages now turned upon Colter. He was stripped naked, and, having some knowledge of the Blackfoot language, overheard a consultation as to the mode of despatching him, so as to derive the greatest amusement from his death. Some were for setting him up as a mark, and having a trial of skill at his expense. The chief, however, was for nobler sport. He seized Colter by the shoulder, and demanded if he could run fast. The unfortunate trapper was too well acquainted with Indian customs not to comprehend the drift of the question. He knew he was to run for his life, to furnish a kind of human hunt to his persecutors. Though in reality he was noted among his brother hunters for swiftness of foot, he assured the chief that he was a very bad runner. His stratagem gained him some vantage ground. He was led by the chief into the prairie, about four hundred yards from the main body of savages, and then turned loose to save himself if he could.

[24] *Jefferson's* in first edition.
[25] Or, as Colter quaintly expressed it, "he was made a riddle of."

A tremendous yell let him know that the whole pack of bloodhounds were off in full cry. Colter flew rather than ran; he was astonished at his own speed; but he had six miles of prairie to traverse before he should reach the Jefferson Fork of the Missouri; how could he hope to hold out such a distance with the fearful odds of several hundred to one against him! The plain, too, abounded with the prickly pear, which wounded his naked feet. Still he fled on, dreading each moment to hear the twang of a bow, and to feel an arrow quivering at his heart. He did not even dare to look round, lest he should lose an inch of that distance on which his life depended. He had run nearly half way across the plain when the sound of pursuit grew somewhat fainter, and he ventured to turn his head. The main body of his pursuers were a considerable distance behind; several of the fastest[26] runners were scattered in the advance; while a swift-footed warrior, armed with a spear, was not more than a hundred yards behind him.

Inspired with new hope, Colter redoubled his exertions, but strained himself to such a degree, that the blood gushed from his mouth and nostrils, and streamed down his breast. He arrived within a mile of the river. The sound of footsteps gathered upon him. A glance behind showed his pursuer within twenty yards, and preparing to launch his spear. Stopping short he turned round and spread out his arms. The savage, confounded by this sudden action, attempted to stop and hurl[27] his spear, but fell in the very act. His spear stuck in the ground, and the shaft broke in his hand. Colter plucked up the pointed part, pinned the savage to the earth, and continued his flight. The Indians, as they arrived at their slaughtered companion, stopped to howl over him. Colter made the most of this precious delay, gained the skirt of cottonwood bordering the river, dashed through it, and plunged into the stream. He swam to a neighboring island, against the upper end of which the drift-wood had lodged in such quantities as to form a natural raft; under this he dived, and swam below water until he succeeded in getting a breathing place between the floating trunks of trees, whose branches and bushes formed a covert several feet above the level of the water.[28] He had scarcely drawn breath after all his toils, when he heard

[26] *Faster* in first edition.

[27] *To hurl* in first edition.

[28] According to Thomas James, to whom Colter also told his story, he took refuge in a beaver lodge. *Three Years among the Indians and Mexicans* (Philadelphia, 1962), 62.

his pursuers on the river bank, whooping and yelling like so many fiends. They plunged in the river, and swam to the raft. The heart of Colter almost died within him as he saw them, through the chinks of his concealment, passing and repassing, and seeking for him in all directions. They at length gave up the search, and he began to rejoice in his escape, when the idea presented itself that they might set the raft on fire. Here was a new source of horrible apprehension, in which he remained until nightfall. Fortunately the idea did not suggest itself to the Indians. As soon as it was dark, finding by the silence around that his pursuers had departed, Colter dived again and came up beyond the raft. He then swam silently down the river for a considerable distance, when he landed, and kept on all night, to get as far as possible from this dangerous neighborhood.

By daybreak he had gained sufficient distance to relieve him from the terrors of his savage foes; but now new sources of inquietude presented themselves. He was naked and alone, in the midst of an unbounded wilderness; his only chance was to reach a trading post of the Missouri Company, situated on a branch of the Yellowstone River.[29] Even should he elude his pursuers, days must elapse before he could reach his post, during which he must traverse immense prairies destitute of shade, his naked body exposed to the burning heat of the sun by day, and the dews and chills of the night season, and his feet lacerated by the thorns of the prickly pear. Though he might see game in abundance around him, he had no means of killing any for his sustenance, and must depend for food upon the roots of the earth. In defiance of these difficulties he pushed resolutely forward, guiding himself in his trackless course by those signs and indications known only to Indians and backwoodsmen; and after braving dangers and hardships enough to break down any spirit but that of a western pioneer, arrived safe at the solitary post in question.[30]

Such is a sample of the rugged experience which Colter had to relate of savage life; yet, with all these perils and terrors fresh in his recollection, he could not see the present band on their way to those regions of danger and adventure, without feeling a vehememt impulse to join them. A western trapper is like a sailor; past hazards only stimulate him

[29] Lisa's fort at the junction of the Big Horn River and the Yellowstone, about two hundred miles away on an air line.
[30] Bradbury, *Travels in America*, p. 17. (Irving's note)

to further risks. The vast prairie is to the one what the ocean is to the other, a boundless field of enterprise and exploit. However he may have suffered in his last cruise, he is always ready to join a new expedition; and the more adventurous its nature, the more attractive is it to his vagrant spirit.

Nothing seems to have kept Colter from continuing with the party to the shores of the Pacific but the circumstance of his having recently married. All the morning he kept with them, balancing in his mind the charms of his bride against those of the Rocky Mountains; the former, however, prevailed, and after a march of several miles, he took a reluctant leave of the travellers, and turned his face homeward.[31]

Continuing their progress up the Missouri, the party encamped on the evening of the 21st of March, in the neighborhood of a little frontier village[32] of French creoles. Here Pierre Dorion met with some of his old comrades, with whom he had a long gossip, and returned to the camp with rumors of bloody feuds between the Osages and the Ioways, or Ayaways, Potowatomies, Sioux, and Sawkees. Blood had already been shed, and scalps been taken. A war party, three hundred strong, were prowling in the neighborhood; others might be met with higher up the river; it behooved the travellers, therefore, to be upon their guard against robbery or surprise, for an Indian war party on the march is prone to acts of outrage.[33]

In consequence of this report, which was subsequently confirmed by further intelligence, a guard was kept up at night round the encampment, and they all slept on their arms. As they were sixteen in number, and well supplied with weapons and ammunition, they trusted to be able to give any marauding party a warm reception. Nothing occurred, however, to molest them on their voyage, and on the 8th of April they came in sight of Fort Osage.[34] On their approach the flag was hoisted on the

[31] According to Bradbury, Colter "seemed to have a great inclination to accompany the expedition; but having been lately married, he reluctantly took leave of us." *Travels*, 45–46.

[32] Côte sans Dessein, which Bradbury places "about two miles below the mouth of the Osage River." *Ibid.*, 48. In 1811 it was only three years old. It was roughly eight miles east of today's Jefferson City, Missouri.

[33] *Ibid.*, 48–49. The "travellers," Bradbury states, "were sixteen men, well armed . . . determined to resist any act of aggression."

[34] Fort Osage had been built only three years before, in 1808, by General William Clark. It served until 1822 as a frontier garrison and government trading post, when the U.S. factory system of Indian trading was discontinued. It was beautifully located

fort, and they saluted it by a discharge of fire-arms. Within a short distance of the fort was an Osage village, the inhabitants of which, men, women, and children, thronged down to the water side to witness their landing. One of the first persons they met on the river bank was Mr. Crooks, who had come down in a boat, with nine men, from the winter encampment at Nodowa, to meet them.

They remained at Fort Osage a part of three days, during which they were hospitably entertained at the garrison by Lieutenant Brownson,[35] who held a temporary command. They were regaled also with a war-feast at the village; the Osage warriors having returned from a successful foray against the Ioways, in which they had taken seven scalps. They[36] were paraded on poles about the village, followed by the warriors decked out in all their savage ornaments, and hideously painted as if for battle.

By the Osage warriors, Mr. Hunt and his companions were again warned to be on their guard in ascending the river, as the Sioux tribe meant to lay [sic] in wait and attack them.

On the 10th of April they again embarked, their party being now augmented to twenty-six, by the addition of Mr. Crooks and his boat's crew. They had not proceeded far, however, when there was a great outcry from one of the boats; it was occasioned by a little domestic discipline in the Dorion family. The squaw of the worthy interpreter, it appeared, had been so delighted with the scalp-dance, and other festivities of the Osage village, that she had taken a strong inclination to remain there.

on the south, or right, bank of the Missouri River on a high bluff, where today an excellent replica, built in solid oak, stands on the old site. In 1836, Alphonso Wetmore wrote: "It was a point where the Osages and Kanzas resorted to trade, when the United States bartered powder, traps, and scalping-knives for furs and peltries." *Gazetteer of the State of Missouri* (St. Louis, 1837), 97.

Irving's information here and in the next two paragraphs is from Bradbury, *Travels*, 60–66. According to Bradbury, the Osage village, numbering about two hundred Indians, was located within three hundred yards of the fort.

Brackenridge also left an interesting description of Fort Osage, which he says was "about one hundred feet above the level of the river, which makes an elbow at this place, giving an extensive view up and down the river. Its form is triangular, its size but small, not calculated for more than a company of men." *Journal*, 59. He located it over three hundred miles from the mouth of the Missouri. From this point, Captain Bonneville, the subject of Irving's next book, started in 1832 on a trapping and exploring expedition to the Rocky Mountains.

[35] Lieutenant John Brownson. Serving as factor at Fort Osage was George C. Sibley, for whom the town of Sibley, at this site, was later named.

[36] *These* in first edition.

This had been as strongly opposed by her liege lord, who had compelled her to embark. The good dame had remained sulky ever since, whereupon Pierre, seeing no other mode of exorcising the evil spirit out of her, and being, perhaps, a little inspired by whiskey, had resorted to the Indian remedy of the cudgel, and before his neighbors could interfere, had belabored her so soundly, that there is no record of her having shown any refractory symptoms throughout the remainder of the expedition.[37]

For a week they continued their voyage, exposed to almost incessant rains. The bodies of drowned buffaloes floated past them in vast numbers; many had drifted upon the shore, or against the upper ends of the rafts and islands. These had attracted great flights of turkey-buzzards; some were banqueting on the carcasses, others were soaring far aloft in the sky, and others were perched on the trees, with their backs to the sun, and their wings stretched out to dry, like so many vessels in harbor, spreading their sails after a shower.[38]

The turkey-buzzard (*vultur aura*, or golden vulture), when on the wing, is one of the most specious and imposing of birds. Its flight in the upper regions of the air is really sublime, extending its immense wings, and wheeling slowly and majestically to and fro, seemingly without exerting a muscle or fluttering a feather, but moving by mere volition, and sailing on the bosom of the air, as a ship upon the ocean. Usurping the empyreal realm of the eagle, he assumes for a time the port and dignity of that majestic bird, and often is mistaken for him by ignorant crawlers upon earth. It is only when he descends from the clouds to pounce upon carrion that he betrays his low propensities, and reveals his caitiff character. Near at hand he is a disgusting bird, ragged in plumage, base in aspect, and of loathsome odor.

On the 17th of April[39] Mr. Hunt arrived with his party at the station near the Nodowa River, where the main body had been quartered during the winter.

[37] Irving builds this paragraph from nine lines in Bradbury, *Travels*, 67, who says "it rained very hard" when they left.

[38] *Ibid.,* 69.

[39] Bradbury confirms the date.

Return of Spring — Appearance of Snakes — Great Flights of Wild Pigeons
Renewal of the Voyage — Night Encampments — Platte River
Ceremonials on Passing It — Signs of Indian War Parties
Magnificent Prospect at Papillion Creek — Desertion of Two Hunters
An Irruption into the Camp of Indian Desperadoes
Village of the Omahas — Anecdotes of the Tribe
Feudal Wars of the Indians
Story of Blackbird, the Famous Omaha Chief

THE weather continued rainy and ungenial for some days after Mr. Hunt's return to Nodowa; yet spring was rapidly advancing and vegetation was putting forth with all its early freshness and beauty. The snakes began to recover from their torpor and crawl forth into day; and the neighborhood of the wintering house seems to have been much infested with them. Mr. Bradbury, in the course of his botanical researches, found a surprising number in a half torpid state, under flat stones upon the banks which overhung the cantonment, and narrowly escaped being struck by a rattlesnake, which darted at him from a cleft in the rock, but fortunately gave him warning by his rattle.[1]

The pigeons, too, were filling the woods in vast migratory flocks. It is almost incredible to describe the prodigious flights of these birds in the western wildernesses. They appear absolutely in clouds, and move with astonishing velocity, their wings making a whistling sound as they fly. The rapid evolutions of these flocks, wheeling and shifting suddenly as if with one mind and one impulse; the flashing changes of color they present, as their backs, their breasts, or the under part of their wings are turned to the spectator, are singularly pleasing. When they alight, if on the ground, they cover whole acres at a time; if upon trees, the branches often break beneath their weight. If suddenly startled while feeding in the midst of a forest, the noise they make in getting on the wing is like the roar of a cataract or the sound of distant thunder.

A flight of this kind, like an Egyptian flight of locusts, devours every-

[1] Bradbury relates this under date of April 11. *Travels,* 70.

thing that serves for its food as it passes along. So great were the numbers in the vicinity of the camp that Mr. Bradbury, in the course of a morning's excursion, shot nearly three hundred with a fowling-piece. He gives a curious, though apparently a faithful, account of the kind of discipline observed in these immense flocks, so that each may have a chance of picking up food. As the front ranks must meet with the greatest abundance, and the rear ranks must have scanty pickings, the instant a rank finds itself the hindmost, it rises in the air, flies over the whole flock and takes its place in the advance. The next rank follows in its course, and thus the last is continually becoming first and all by turns have a front place at the banquet.[2]

The rains having at length subsided, Mr. Hunt broke up the encampment and resumed his course up the Missouri.[3]

The party now consisted of nearly sixty persons; of whom five were partners, one, John Reed,[4] was a clerk; forty were Canadian "voyageurs," or "*engagés,*" and there were several hunters. They embarked in four boats, one of which was of a large size, mounting a swivel and two howitzers. All were furnished with masts and sails, to be used when the wind was sufficiently favorable and strong to overpower the current of the river. Such was the case for the first four or five days, when they were wafted steadily up the stream by a strong southeaster.[5]

Their encampments at night were often pleasant and picturesque: on some beautiful bank, beneath spreading trees, which afforded them shelter and fuel. The tents were pitched, the fires made, and the meals prepared by the voyageurs, and many a story was told, and joke passed, and song sung round the evening fire. All, however, were asleep at an early hour. Some under the tents, others wrapped in blankets before the fire, or beneath the trees; and some few in the boats and canoes.[6]

---

[2] *Ibid.,* 68–69. Irving's previous paragraph describing the vast numbers of these wild passenger pigeons is undoubtedly based on personal observation in 1832.

[3] They left the encampment at Nodaway River on April 21. *Ibid.,* 70.

[4] Reed figures in dramatic incidents later in *Astoria.* See Rollins (ed.), *Discovery of the Oregon Trail, passim;* see also Porter, "Roll of Overland Astorians," *Oregon Historical Quarterly,* Vol. XXXIV (1933), 110–11. Cox referred to him as "a rough, warm-hearted, brave, old Irishman." *Columbia River,* 154. His name appears as a witness on the Articles of Agreement of the Pacific Fur Company.

[5] From Bradbury, *Travels,* 70.

[6] The scene is reminiscent of encampments described in Irving's *Western Journals,* and he may have drawn on personal experience for certain details.

On the 28th, they breakfasted on one of the islands which lie at the mouth of the Nebraska or Platte River[7]—the largest tributary of the Missouri, and about six hundred miles above its confluence with the Mississippi. This broad but shallow stream flows for an immense distance through a wide and verdant valley scooped out of boundless prairies. It draws its main supplies, by several forks or branches, from the Rocky Mountains. The mouth of this river is established as the dividing point between the upper and lower Missouri; and the earlier voyagers, in their toilsome ascent, before the introduction of steamboats, considered one-half of their labors accomplished when they reached this place. The passing of the mouth of the Nebraska, therefore, was equivalent among boatmen to the crossing of the line among sailors, and was celebrated with like ceremonials of a rough and waggish nature, practiced upon the uninitiated; among which was the old nautical joke of shaving. The river deities, however, like those of the sea, were to be propitiated by a bribe, and the infliction of these rude honors to be parried by a treat to the adepts.

At the mouth of the Nebraska new signs were met with of war parties which had recently been in the vicinity. There was the frame of a skin canoe, in which the warriors had traversed the river. At night, also, the lurid reflection of immense fires hung in the sky, showing the conflagration of great tracts of the prairies. Such fires not being made by hunters so late in the season, it was supposed they were caused by some wandering war parties. These often take the precaution to set the prairies on fire behind them to conceal their traces from their enemies. This is chiefly done when the party has been unsuccessful, and is on the retreat and apprehensive of pursuit. At such time it is not safe even for friends to fall in with them, as they are apt to be in savage humor, and disposed to vent their spleen in capricious outrage. These signs, therefore, of a band of marauders on the prowl, called for some degree of vigilance on the part of the travellers.[8]

After passing the Nebraska, the party halted for part of two days on the bank of the river, a little above Papillion Creek,[9] to supply them-

[7] The map in the first edition of *Astoria* correctly shows the drainage of the Platte River.

[8] From Bradbury, *Travels*, 71–72.

[9] Papillion Creek flows from the northwest into the Missouri about four miles above the mouth of the Platte. Lewis and Clark camped above this point in 1804 and described it as being nearly eighteen yards in width. *History of the Expedition*, I, 71.

selves with a stock of oars and poles from the tough wood of the ash, which is not met with higher up the Missouri. While the voyagers[10] were thus occupied, the naturalists rambled over the adjacent country to collect plants. From the summit of a range of bluffs on the opposite side of the river, about two hundred and fifty feet high, they had one of those vast and magnificent prospects which sometimes unfold themselves in those[11] boundless regions. Below them was the valley of the Missouri, about seven miles in breadth, clad in the fresh verdure of spring, enameled with flowers and interspersed with clumps and groves of noble trees, between which the mighty river poured its turbulent and turbid stream. The interior of the country presented a singular scene; the immense waste being broken up by innumerable green hills, not above eighty[12] feet in height, but extremely steep, and actually pointed at their summits. A long line of bluffs extended for upwards of thirty miles parallel to the Missouri, with a shallow lake stretching along their base, which had evidently once formed a bed of the river. The surface of this lake was covered with aquatic plants, on the broad leaves of which numbers of water-snakes, drawn forth by the genial warmth of spring, were basking in the sunshine.[13]

On the 2d day of May,[14] at the usual hour of embarking, the camp was thrown into some confusion by two of the hunters, named Harrington,[15] expressing their intention to abandon the expedition and return home. One of these had joined the party in the preceding autumn, having been hunting for two years on the Missouri; the other had engaged at St. Louis, in the following March, and had come up from thence with Mr. Hunt. He now declared that he had enlisted merely for the purpose of following his brother, and persuading him to return; having been enjoined to do so by his mother, whose anxiety had been awakened by the idea of his going on such a wild and distant expedition.

The loss of two stark hunters and prime riflemen was a serious affair to the party, for they were approaching the region where they might expect hostilities from the Sioux; indeed, throughout the whole of their

---

[10] *Voyageurs* in first edition.   [11] *These* in first edition.
[12] Erroneously *eight* in Author's Revised Edition. The first edition reads *eighty*.
[13] From Bradbury, *Travels*, 72–73.
[14] The first edition reads *On the 2d of May.*
[15] Samuel and William Harrington. Irving follows Bradbury, *Travels*, 75, in what he says about them and Hunt's treatment of them. Brackenridge, *Journal*, 73, reports meeting these men on their way downstream "in a bark canoe."

perilous journey, the services of such men would be all important, for little reliance was to be placed upon the valor of the Canadians in case of attack. Mr. Hunt endeavored by arguments, expostulations, and entreaties, to shake the determination of the two brothers. He represented to them that they were between six and seven hundred miles above the mouth of the Missouri; that they would have four hundred miles to go before they could reach the habitation of a white man, throughout which they would be exposed to all kinds of risks; since, he declared, if they persisted in abandoning him and breaking their faith, he would not furnish them with a single round of ammunition. All was in vain; they obstinately persisted in their resolution; whereupon, Mr. Hunt, partly incited by indignation, partly by the policy of deterring others from desertion, put his threat into execution, and left them to find their way back to the settlement without, as he supposed, a single bullet or charge of powder.

The boats now continued their slow and toilsome course for several days, against the current of the river. The late signs of roaming war parties caused a vigilant watch to be kept up at night when the crews encamped on shore; nor was this vigilance superfluous; for on the night of the seventh instant, there was a wild and fearful yell, and eleven Sioux warriors, stark naked, with tomahawks in their hands, rushed into the camp. They were instantly surrounded and seized, whereupon their leader called out to his followers to desist from any violence, and pretended to be perfectly pacific in his intentions. It proved, however, that they were a part of the war party, the skeleton of whose canoe had been seen at the mouth of the river Platte, and the reflection of whose fires had been descried in the air. They had been disappointed or defeated in the foray, and in their rage and mortification these eleven warriors had "devoted their clothes to the medicine." This is a desperate act of Indian braves when foiled in war, and in dread of scoffs and sneers. In such case they sometimes throw off their clothes and ornaments, devote themselves to the Great Spirit, and attempt some reckless exploit with which to cover their disgrace. Woe to any defenseless party of white men that may then fall in their way!

Such was the explanation given by Pierre Dorion, the half-breed interpreter, of this wild intrusion into the camp; and the party were so exasperated when apprised of the sanguinary intentions of the prisoners, that they were for shooting them on the spot. Mr. Hunt, however, exerted his usual moderation and humanity, and ordered that they should be conveyed across the river in one of the boats, threatening them, however, with certain death, if again caught in any hostile act.[16]

On the 10th of May the party arrived at the Omaha[17] (pronounced Omawhaw) village, about eight hundred and thirty miles above the mouth of the Missouri, and encamped in its neighborhood. The village was situated under a hill on the bank of the river, and consisted of about eighty lodges. These were of a circular and conical form, and about sixteen feet in diameter; being mere tents of dressed buffalo skins, sewed together and stretched on long poles, inclined towards each other so as to cross at about half their height. Thus the naked tops of the poles diverge in such a manner that, if they were covered with skins like the lower ends, the tent would be shaped like an hour-glass, and present the appearance of one cone inverted on the apex of another.

The forms of Indian lodges are worthy of attention, each tribe having a different mode of shaping and arranging them, so that it is easy to tell, on seeing a lodge or an encampment at a distance, to what tribe the inhabitants belong. The exterior of the Omaha lodges have often a gay and fanciful appearance, being painted with undulating bands of red or yellow, or decorated with rude figures of horses, deer, and buffaloes, and with human faces, painted like full moons, four and five feet broad.[18]

The Omahas were once one of the numerous and powerful tribes of the prairies, vying in warlike might and prowess with the Sioux,[19] the Pawnees,[20] the Sauks,[21] the Kanzas,[22] and the Iatans.[23] Their wars with

[16] Although Bradbury, with Crooks, was absent on the night of May 8, he later learned from McKenzie what had happened, and this became Irving's source of information. See *Travels*, 91–92.

[17] Linguistically of Siouan stock, the Omahas are believed to have lived at one time in Ohio and on migrating west settled finally in South Dakota. Their name means "those who go against the current." Swanton, *Indian Tribes*, 286.

[18] The details for Irving's description of the Omaha village are from Bradbury, *Travels*, 88–89.

[19] The Sioux are properly the Dakota Indians. They were a numerous tribe with many subdivisions and bands. They occupied a large area in the north-central part of the country in Minnesota, Wisconsin, and parts of Iowa, and are believed to have crossed west of the Missouri sometime in the mid–eighteenth century. Swanton, *Indian Tribes*, 280–84.

[20] The Pawnees occupied a region between the Platte and Republican Rivers. They were seen by Coronado in 1541. Linguistically they belong to the Caddoan stock. Their name means either "horn" or "hunter." *Ibid.*, 289–90.

[21] The original home of the Sauks was Michigan, but they later settled in Wisconsin along Green Bay. They also extended into Illinois, and one band separated from the

the Sioux, however, had thinned their ranks, and the small-pox[24] in 1802 had swept off two-thirds of their number. At the time of Mr. Hunt's visit they still boasted about two hundred warriors and hunters, but they are now fast melting away, and before long, will be numbered among those extinguished nations of the west that exist but in tradition.

In his correspondence with Mr. Astor,[25] from this point of his journey, Mr. Hunt gives a sad account of the Indian tribes bordering on the river. They were in continual war with each other, and their wars were of the most harassing kind; consisting, not merely of main conflicts and expeditions of moment, involving the sackings, burnings, and massacres of towns and villages, but of individual acts of treachery, murder, and cold-blooded cruelty; or of vaunting and foolhardy exploits of single warriors, either to avenge some personal wrong, or gain the vainglorious trophy of a scalp. The lonely hunter, the wandering wayfarer, the poor squaw cutting wood or gathering corn, was liable to be surprised and slaughtered. In this way tribes were either swept away at once, or gradually thinned out, and savage life was surrounded with constant horrors and alarms. That the race of red men should diminish from year to year, and so few should survive of the numerous nations which evidently once peopled the vast regions of the west, is nothing surprising; it is rather matter of surprise that so many should survive; for the existence

main tribe and settled in Missouri. In 1832 they conducted the Black Hawk War against the whites. *Ibid.*, 256–57.

[22] The Kansa or Kaw Indians belonged to the Siouan linguistic stock. Their principal location was along the Kansas River. *Ibid.*, 293–94.

[23] Or Tetan, "a term," says Hodge, "which, with 'Tetau' and other forms of the name [Ayutan, Ietan, L'Iatan, Aliatan, Jatan, Jetan], was applied by writers of the early part of the 19th century to several western tribes. . . . As the early traders and explorers knew but little of the mountain tribes, they frequently confounded those of the same generic stock, so that almost any of these forms may mean Shoshoni, Ute, or Comanche, according to the general context of the description." *Handbook of American Indians*, I, 594. The term is derived from the word *Yuta*.

[24] This epidemic reduced their number to about three hundred. Swanton, *Indian Tribes*, 286. Irving's source is Bradbury, *Travels*, 90.

[25] Hunt's correspondence to Astor was carried down river by James Aird. Since his name appears on the Articles of Agreement of the Pacific Fur Company (see Flandrau, *Astor and the Oregon Country*, 34), it would appear that he had been with Hunt from the beginning of the expedition. His name first appears on the account books of the expedition at St. Louis, May 12, 1811; see Porter, "Roll of Overland Astorians," *loc. cit.*, 105. Bradbury, who refers to him as "an old and respectable trader, with whom I had become acquainted at St. Louis," says further: "He informed me that he should go to the United States in a few days; I therefore availed myself of this opportunity to forward letters, and was employed in writing until the 12th at noon." *Travels*, 87.

of a savage in these parts seems little better than a prolonged and all-besetting death. It is, in fact, a caricature of the boasted romance of feudal times; chivalry in its native and uncultured state, and knight-errantry run wild.

In their most prosperous days, the Omahas looked upon themselves as the most powerful and perfect of human beings, and considered all created things as made for their peculiar use and benefit. It is this tribe of whose chief, the famous Wash-ing-guh-sah-ba, or Blackbird, such savage and romantic stories are told. He had died about ten years previous to the arrival of Mr. Hunt's party, but his name was still mentioned with awe by his people. He was one of the first among the Indian chiefs on the Missouri to deal with the white traders, and showed great sagacity in levying his royal dues. When a trader arrived in his village, he caused all his goods to be brought into his lodge and opened. From these he selected whatever suited his sovereign pleasure; blankets, tobacco, whiskey, powder, balls, beads, and red paint; and laid the articles on one side, without deigning to give any compensation. Then calling to him his herald or crier, he would order him to mount on top of the lodge and summon all the tribe to bring in their peltries, and trade with the white man. The lodge would soon be crowded with Indians bringing bear, beaver, otter, and other skins. No one was allowed to dispute the prices fixed by the white trader upon his articles; who took care to indemnify himself five times over for the goods set apart by the chief. In this way the Blackbird enriched himself, and enriched the white men, and became exceedingly popular among the traders of the Missouri. His people, however, were not equally satisfied by a regulation of trade which worked so manifestly against them, and began to show signs of discontent. Upon this a crafty and unprincipled trader revealed a secret to the Blackbird, by which he might acquire unbounded sway over his ignorant and superstitious subjects. He instructed him in the poisonous qualities of arsenic, and furnished him with an ample supply of that baneful drug. From this time the Blackbird seemed endowed with supernatural powers, to possess the gift of prophecy, and to hold the disposal of life and death within his hands. Woe to any one who questioned his authority or dared to dispute his commands! The Blackbird prophesied his death within a certain time, and he had the secret means of verifying his prophecy. Within the fated period the offender was smitten with strange and sudden disease, and perished from the face of the earth.

Every one stood aghast at these multiplied examples of his superhuman might, and dreaded to displease so omnipotent and vindictive a being; and the Blackbird enjoyed a wide and undisputed sway.[26]

It was not, however, by terror alone that he ruled his people; he was a warrior of the first order, and his exploits in arms were the theme of young and old. His career had begun by hardships, having been taken prisoner by the Sioux, in early youth. Under his command, the Omahas obtained great character for military prowess, nor did he permit an insult or an injury to one of his tribe to pass unrevenged. The Pawnee republicans had inflicted a gross indignity on a favorite and distinguished Omaha brave. The Blackbird assembled his warriors, led them against the Pawnee town, attacked it with irresistible fury, slaughtered a great number of its inhabitants, and burnt it to the ground. He waged fierce and bloody war against the Ottoes for many years, until peace was effected between them by the mediation of the whites. Fearless in battle, and fond of signalizing himself, he dazzled his followers by daring acts.[27] In attacking a Kanza village, he rode singly round it, loading and discharging his rifle at the inhabitants as he galloped past them. He kept up in war the same idea of mysterious and supernatural power. At one time, when pursuing a war party by their tracks across the prairies, he repeatedly discharged his rifle into the prints made by their feet and by the hoofs of their horses, assuring his followers that he would thereby cripple the fugitives, so that they would easily be overtaken. He in fact did overtake them, and destroyed them almost to a man; and his victory was considered miraculous, both by friend and foe. By these and similar exploits, he made himself the pride and boast of his people, and became popular among them, notwithstanding his death-denouncing fiat.

With all his savage and terrific qualities, he was sensible of the power of female beauty, and capable of love. A war party of the Poncas[28] had made a foray into the lands of the Omahas, and carried off a number of

---

[26] Irving's information for this paragraph comes from Bradbury, *Travels*, 85n. He was also acquainted with what Brackenridge wrote about Blackbird. See *Journal*, 81–82. Blackbird's Indian name, Wash-ing-guh-sah-ba, Irving found in Edwin James, *Account of an Expedition from Pittsburgh to the Rocky Mountains*, in Thwaites (ed.), *Early Western Travels*, XIV, 317.

[27] The first edition reads *by his daring acts*.

[28] The Poncas were related linguistically to the Omahas, the Kansas, the Osages, and the Quapaws. See Swanton, *Indian Tribes*, 291.

women and horses. The Blackbird was roused to fury, and took the
field with all his braves, swearing to "eat up the Ponca nation"—the
Indian threat of exterminating war. The Poncas, sorely pressed, took
refuge behind a rude bulwark of earth; but the Blackbird kept up so
galling a fire, that he seemed likely to execute his menace. In their extremity they sent forth a herald, bearing the calumet or pipe of peace,
but he was shot down by order of the Blackbird. Another herald was
sent forth in similar guise, but he shared a like fate. The Ponca chief
then, as a last hope, arrayed his beautiful daughter in her finest ornaments, and sent her forth with a calumet to sue for peace. The charms of
the Indian maid touched the stern heart of the Blackbird; he accepted
the pipe at her hand, smoked it, and from that time a peace took place
between the Poncas and the Omahas.

This beautiful damsel, in all probability, was the favorite wife whose
fate makes so tragic an incident in the story of the Blackbird. Her youth
and beauty had gained an absolute sway over his rugged heart, so that
he distinguished her above all of his other wives.[29] The habitual gratification of his vindictive impulses, however, had taken away from him
all mastery over his passions, and rendered him liable to the most furious
transports of rage. In one of these his beautiful wife had the misfortune
to offend him, when suddenly drawing his knife, he laid her dead at his
feet with a single blow.

In an instant his frenzy was at an end. He gazed for a time in mute
bewilderment upon his victim; then drawing his buffalo robe over his
head, he sat down beside the corpse, and remained brooding over his
crime and his loss. Three days elapsed, yet the chief continued silent
and motionless; tasting no food, and apparently sleepless. It was apprehended that he intended to starve himself to death; his people approached him in trembling awe, and entreated him once more to un-
cover his face and be comforted; but he remained unmoved. At length
one of his warriors brought in a small child, and laying it on the ground,
placed the foot of the Blackbird upon its neck. The heart of the gloomy
savage was touched by this appeal; he threw aside his robe; made a
harangue upon what he had done; and from that time forward seemed
to have thrown the load of grief and remorse from his mind.[30]

[29] The first edition reads *above all his other wives*.

[30] Irving's account of the death of Blackbird's wife and of his remorse is from
Edwin James. See Thwaites (ed.), *Early Western Travels*, XIV, 319–20.

He still retained his fatal and mysterious secret, and with it his terrific power; but, though able to deal death to his enemies, he could not avert it from himself or his friends. In 1802 the small-pox, that dreadful pestilence, which swept over the land like a fire over the prairie, made its appearance in the village of the Omahas. The poor savages saw with dismay the ravages of a malady, loathsome and agonizing in its details, and which set the skill and experience of their conjurers and medicine men at defiance. In a little while, two thirds of the population were swept from the face of the earth, and the doom of the rest seemed sealed. The stoicism of the warriors was at an end; they became wild and desperate; some set fire to the village as a last means of checking the pestilence; others, in a frenzy of despair, put their wives and children to death, that they might be spared the agonies of an inevitable disease, and that they might all go to some better country.

When the general horror and dismay was at its height, the Blackbird himself was struck down with the malady. The poor savages, when they saw their chief in danger, forgot their own miseries, and surrounded his dying bed. His dominant spirit, and his love for the white men, were evinced in his latest breath, with which he designated his place of sepulture. It was to be on a hill or promontory, upwards of four hundred feet in height, overlooking a great extent of the Missouri, from whence he had been accustomed to watch for the barks of the white men. The Missouri washes the base of the promontory, and after winding and doubling in many links and mazes in the plain below, returns to within nine hundred yards of its starting-place; so that for thirty miles navigating with sail and oar, the voyager finds himself continually near to this singular promontory as if spell-bound.

It was the dying command of the Blackbird that his tomb should be on the summit of this hill, in which he should be interred, seated on his favorite horse, that he might overlook his ancient domain, and behold the barks of the white men as they came up the river to trade with his people.

His dying orders were faithfully obeyed. His corpse was placed astride of his war-steed and a mound raised over them on the summit of the hill. On top of the mound was erected a staff, from which fluttered the banner of the chieftain, and the scalps that he had taken in battle. When the expedition under Mr. Hunt visited that part of the country, the staff still remained, with the fragments of the banner; and the superstitious rite of placing food from time to time on the mound, for the use of the deceased, was still observed by the Omahas.[31] That rite has since fallen into disuse, for the tribe itself is almost extinct. Yet the hill of the Blackbird continues an object of veneration to the wandering savage, and a landmark to the voyager of the Missouri; and as the civilized traveller comes within sight of its spell-bound crest, the mound is pointed out to him from afar, which still incloses the grim skeletons of the Indian warrior and his horse.

[31] Irving's knowledge of Blackbird's interment came from *ibid.*, 317–18. While Irving was preparing to write his three western books, he made a series of notebooks, one of which, entitled "No 3. Notes Concerning the Far West, 1833," contains (on p. 9) a quotation from James which Irving used in writing this passage. He cites his source as "Long, v. 1, 226." The notebook is in the Seligman Collection of Irvingiana at the New York Public Library.

Rumors of Danger from the Sioux Tetons
Ruthless Character of Those Savages — Pirates of the Missouri
Their Affair with Crooks and M'Lellan — A Trading Expedition Broken Up
M'Lellan's Vow of Vengeance — Uneasiness in the Camp
Desertions — Departure from the Omaha Village
Meeting with Jones and Carson, Two Adventurous Trappers
Scientific Pursuits of Messrs. Bradbury and Nuttall
Zeal of a Botanist — Adventure of Mr. Bradbury with a Ponca Indian
Expedient of the Pocket Compass and Microscope
A Messenger from Lisa — Motives for Pressing Forward

WHILE Mr. Hunt and his party were sojourning at the village of the Omahas, three Sioux Indians of the Yankton Ahna tribe arrived, bringing unpleasant intelligence. They reported that certain bands of the Sioux Tetons, who inhabited a region many leagues further up the Missouri, were near at hand, awaiting the approach of the party, with the avowed intention of opposing their progress.[1]

The Sioux Tetons were at that time a sort of pirates of the Missouri, who considered the well-freighted bark of the American trader fair game. They had their own traffic with the British merchants of the Northwest, who brought them regular supplies of merchandise by the way of the river St. Peter. Being thus independent of the Missouri traders for their supplies, they kept no terms with them, but plundered them whenever they had an opportunity. It has been insinuated that they were prompted to these outrages by the British merchants, who wished to keep off all rivals in the Indian trade; but others allege another motive, and one savoring of a deeper policy. The Sioux, by their intercourse with the British traders, had acquired the use of fire-arms, which had given them vast superiority over other tribes higher up the Missouri. They had made themselves also, in a manner, factors for the upper tribes, supplying them at second hand, and at greatly advanced prices, with goods derived from the white men. The Sioux, therefore, saw with jealousy the American traders pushing their way up the Mis-

[1] Bradbury, *Travels*, 90–91, gives this information under date of May 14.

souri; foreseeing that the upper tribes would thus be relieved from all dependence on them for supplies; nay, what was worse, would be furnished with fire-arms, and elevated into formidable rivals.[2]

We have already alluded to a case in which Mr. Crooks and Mr. M'Lellan had been interrupted in a trading voyage by these ruffians of the river, and, as it is in some degree connected with circumstances hereafter to be related, we shall specify it more particularly.[3]

About two years before the time of which we are treating, Crooks and M'Lellan were ascending the river in boats with a party of about forty men, bound on one of their trading expeditions to the upper tribes. In one of the bends of the river, where the channel made a deep curve under impending banks, they suddenly heard yells and shouts above them, and beheld the cliffs overhead covered with armed savages. It was a band of Sioux warriors, upwards of six hundred strong. They brandished their weapons in a menacing manner, and ordered the boats to turn back and land lower down the river. There was no disputing these commands, for they had the power to shower destruction upon the white men, without risk to themselves. Crooks and M'Lellan, therefore, turned back with feigned alacrity, and, landing, had an interview with the Sioux. The latter forbade them, under pain of exterminating hostility, from attempting to proceed up the river, but offered to trade peacefully with them if they would halt where they were. The party, being principally composed of voyageurs, was too weak to contend with so superior a force, and one so easily augmented; they pretended, therefore, to comply cheerfully with their arbitrary dictation, and immediately proceeded to cut down trees and erect a trading house. The warrior band departed for their village, which was about twenty miles distant, to collect objects of traffic; they left six or eight of their number, however, to keep watch upon the white men, and scouts were continually passing to and fro with intelligence.

Mr. Crooks saw that it would be impossible to prosecute his voyage without the danger of having his boats plundered, and a great part of his

---

[2] Irving's source for this paragraph is an address made by Meriwether Lewis before Congress in February of 1806 which Bradbury quotes in a footnote; *ibid.*, 103–104n.

[3] A memorandum in one of Irving's notebooks, "Astoria, 1835," reads as follows: "Qu[ery]. About the affair of Crooks and M'Lellan with the Sioux Tetons. Was it one or two years previous to the expedition of Mr. Hunt—Was Mr. Miller with them—. What were the particulars." Seligman Collection of Irvingiana, New York Public Library.

men massacred; he determined, however, not to be entirely frustrated in the objects of his expedition. While he continued, therefore, with great apparent earnestness and assiduity, the construction of the trading house, he despatched the hunters and trappers of his party in a canoe, to make their way up the river to the original place of destination, there to busy themselves in trapping and collecting peltries, and to await his arrival at some future period.

As soon as the detachment had had sufficient time to ascend beyond the hostile country of the Sioux, Mr. Crooks suddenly broke up his feigned trading establishment, embarked his men and effects, and, after giving the astonished rear-guard of savages a galling and indignant message to take to their countrymen, pushed down the river with all speed, sparing neither oar nor paddle, day and night, until fairly beyond the swoop of these river hawks.

What increased the irritation of Messrs. Crooks and M'Lellan, at this mortifying check to their gainful enterprise, was the information that a rival trader was at the bottom of it; the Sioux, it is said, having been instigated to this outrage by Mr. Manuel Lisa, the leading partner and agent of the Missouri Fur Company, already mentioned. This intelligence, whether true or false, so roused the fiery temper of M'Lellan, that he swore, if ever he fell in with Lisa in the Indian country, he would shoot him on the spot; a mode of redress perfectly in unison with the character of the man, and the code of honor prevalent beyond the frontier.[4]

If Crooks and M'Lellan had been exasperated by the insolent conduct of the Sioux Tetons, and the loss which it had occasioned, those free-booters had been no less indignant at being outwitted by the white men, and disappointed of their anticipated gains, and it was apprehended they would be particulary hostile against the present expedition, when they should learn that these gentlemen were engaged in it.

All these causes of uneasiness were concealed as much as possible from the Canadian voyageurs, lest they should become intimidated;[5] it was impossible, however, to prevent the rumors brought by the Indians from leaking out, and they became subjects of gossiping and exaggeration.

[4] Irving's source of information concerning Crooks's difficulties with the Sioux has not been determined, although he read a brief account of it in Brackenridge's *Journal*, 83. It is very likely that he got the information orally from Crooks.

[5] Bradbury wrote: "This news was concealed as much as possible from the voyageurs." *Travels*, 91.

The chief of the Omahas, too, on returning from a hunting excursion, reported that two men had been killed some distance above, by a band of Sioux. This added to the fears that already began to be excited. The voyageurs pictured to themselves bands of fierce warriors stationed along each bank of the river, by whom they would be exposed to be shot down in their boats: or lurking hordes, who would set on them at night, and massacre them in their encampments. Some lost heart, and proposed to return, rather than fight their way, and, in a manner, run the gauntlet through the country of these piratical marauders. In fact, three men deserted while at this village. Luckily, their place was supplied by three others who happened to be there, and who were prevailed on to join the expedition by promises of liberal pay, and by being fitted out and equipped in complete style.

The irresolution and discontent visible among some of his people, arising at times almost to mutiny, and the occasional desertions which took place while thus among friendly tribes, and within reach of the frontiers, added greatly to the anxieties of Mr. Hunt, and rendered him eager to press forward and leave a hostile tract behind him, so that it would be as perilous to return as to keep on, and no one would dare to desert.

Accordingly, on the 15th of May he departed from the village of the Omahas, and set forward towards the country of the formidable Sioux Tetons.[6] For the first five days they had a fair and fresh breeze, and the boats made good progress. The wind then came ahead, and the river beginning to rise, and to increase in rapidity, betokened the commencement of the annual flood, caused by the melting of the snow on the Rocky Mountains, and the vernal rains of the upper prairies.

As they were now entering a region where foes might be lying in wait on either bank, it was determined, in hunting for game, to confine themselves principally to the islands, which sometimes extend to considerable length, and are beautifully wooded, affording abundant pasturage and shade. On one of these they killed three buffaloes and two elks, and halting on the edge of a beautiful prairie, made a sump-

[6] Irving does not mention that early that day they passed Floyd's Bluff, where the only man lost by Lewis and Clark, namely, Sergeant John Floyd (who died of natural causes), was buried on the east bank of the Missouri south of what is today Sioux City, Iowa. A tall shaft now commemorates his death. See Bradbury, *Travels*, 91; cf. Brackenridge, *Journal*, 85.

tuous hunter's repast.[7] They had not long resumed their boats and pulled along the river banks when they descried a canoe approaching, navigated by two men, whom, to their surprise, they ascertained to be white men. They proved to be two of those strange and fearless wanderers of the wilderness, the trappers. Their names were Benjamin Jones[8] and Alexander Carson.[9] They had been for two years past hunting and trapping near the head of the Missouri, and were thus floating for thousands of miles in a cockleshell, down a turbulent stream, through regions infested by savage tribes, yet apparently as easy and unconcerned as if navigating securely in the midst of civilization.

The acquisition of two such hardy, experienced, and dauntless hunters was peculiarly desirable at the present moment. They needed but little persuasion. The wilderness is the home of the trapper; like the sailor, he cares but little to which point of the compass he steers; and Jones and Carson readily abandoned their voyage to St. Louis, and turned their faces towards the Rocky Mountains and the Pacific.[10]

The two naturalists, Mr. Bradbury and Mr. Nuttall, who had joined the expedition at St. Louis, still accompanied it, and pursued their researches on all occasions. Mr. Nuttall seems to have been exclusively devoted to his scientific pursuits. He was a zealous botantist, and all his enthusiasm was awakened at beholding a new world, as it were, opening upon him in the boundless prairies, clad in the vernal and variegated robe of unknown flowers. Whenever the boats landed at meal times, or for any temporary purpose, he would spring on shore, and set out on a hunt for new specimens. Every plant or flower of a rare or unknown species was eagerly seized as a prize. Delighted with the treasures spreading themselves out before him, he went groping and stumbling along among the wilderness of sweets, forgetful of everything but his immediate pursuit, and had often to be sought after when the boats were

---

[7] From Bradbury, *Travels*, 93.

[8] Jones and Carson joined Hunt on May 22. They had lived among the Arikara Indians during the preceding winter. See Bradbury, *Travels*, 93, 178. See also Drumm, "More About Astorians," *Oregon Historical Quarterly*, Vol. XXIV (1923), 357–59, and Porter, "Roll of Overland Astorians," *ibid.*, Vol. XXXIV (1933), 103–12. From Astoria, Jones returned with Robert Stuart to Missouri in 1812–13 and there died of cholera in June, 1835, leaving a widow and five children.

[9] See Alice B. Maloney, "Alexander Carson, Wilhamot Freeman," *Oregon Historical Quarterly*, Vol. XXXIX (1938), 16–21; also Porter, "Roll of Overland Astorians," *ibid.*, Vol. XXXIV (1933), 105.

[10] From Bradbury, *Travels*, 93.

about to resume their course. At such times he would be found far off in the prairies, or up the course of some petty stream, laden with plants of all kinds.

The Canadian voyageurs, who are a class of people that know nothing out of their immediate line, and with constitutional levity make a jest of anything they cannot understand, were extremely puzzled by this passion for collecting what they considered mere useless weeds. When they saw the worthy botantist coming back heavy laden with his specimens, and treasuring them up as carefully as a miser would his hoard, they used to make merry among themselves at his expense, regarding him as some whimsical kind of madman.

Mr. Bradbury was less exclusive in his tastes and habits, and combined the hunter and sportsman with the naturalist. He took his rifle or his fowling-piece with him in his geological researches, conformed to the hardy and rugged habits of the men around him, and of course gained favor in their eyes. He had a strong relish for incident and adventure, was curious in observing savage manners, and savage life, and ready to join any hunting or other excursion. Even now, that the expedition was proceeding through a dangerous neighborhood, he could not check his propensity to ramble. Having observed, on the evening of the 22d of May, that the river ahead made a great bend which would take up the navigation of the following day, he determined to profit by the circumstance. On the morning of the 23d, therefore, instead of embarking, he filled his shot-pouch with parched corn, for provisions, and set off to cross the neck on foot and meet the boats in the afternoon at the opposite side of the bend. Mr. Hunt felt uneasy at his venturing thus alone, and reminded him that he was in an enemy's country; but Mr. Bradbury made light of the danger, and started off cheerily upon his ramble. His day was passed pleasantly in traversing a beautiful tract, making botanical and geological researches, and observing the habits of an extensive village of prairie dogs, at which he made several ineffectual shots, without considering the risk he ran of attracting the attention of any savages that might be lurking in the neighborhood. In fact he had totally forgotten the Sioux Tetons, and all the other perils of the country, when, about the middle of the afternoon, as he stood near the river bank, and was looking out for the boat, he suddenly felt a hand laid on his shoulder. Starting and turning round, he beheld a naked savage with a bow bent, and the arrow pointed at his breast. In an instant his gun was leveled and his hand upon the lock. The Indian drew his bow still further, but forebore to launch the shaft. Mr. Bradbury, with admirable presence of mind, reflected that the savage, if hostile in his intents, would have shot him without giving him a chance of defense; he paused, therefore, and held out his hand. The other took it in sign of friendship, and demanded in the Osage language whether he was a Big Knife, or American. He answered in the affirmative, and inquired whether the other were a Sioux. To his great relief he found that he was a Ponca. By this time two other Indians came running up, and all three laid hold of Mr. Bradbury and seemed disposed to compel him to go off with them among the hills. He resisted, and sitting down on a sand hill contrived to amuse them with a pocket compass. When the novelty of this was exhausted they again seized him, but he now produced a small microscope. This new wonder again fixed the attention of the savages, who have more curiosity[11] than it has been the custom to allow them. While thus engaged, one of them suddenly leaped up and gave a warwhoop. The hand of the hardy naturalist was again on his gun, and he was prepared to make battle, when the Indian pointed down the river and revealed the true cause of his yell. It was the mast of one of the boats appearing above the low willows which bordered the stream. Mr. Bradbury felt infinitely relieved by the sight. The Indians on their part now showed signs of apprehension, and were disposed to run away; but he assured them of good treatment and something to drink if they would accompany him on board of the boats. They lingered for a time, but disappeared before the boats came to land.[12]

On the following morning they appeared at camp[13] accompanied by several of their tribe. With them came also a white man, who announced himself as a messenger bearing missives for Mr. Hunt. In fact he brought a letter from Mr. Manuel Lisa, partner and agent of the Missouri Fur Company.[14] As has already been mentioned, this gentleman was going in search of Mr. Henry and his party, who had been dislodged from the forks of the Missouri by the Blackfeet Indians, and had shifted his post somewhere beyond the Rocky Mountains. Mr. Lisa had left St. Louis three weeks after Mr. Hunt,[15] and having heard of the hostile

[11] The first edition reads *who have far more curiosity.*

[12] Bradbury relates this adventure in some detail, including conversation that Irving omitted. *Travels,* 93–96.

[13] The first edition reads *at the camp.*   [14] Bradbury, *Travels,* 96–97.

[15] Lisa probably went overland from St. Louis to St. Charles and left in his boats

intentions of the Sioux, had made the greatest exertions to overtake him, that they might pass through the dangerous part of the river together. He had twenty stout oarsmen in his service and they plied their oars so vigorously, that he had reached the Omaha village just four days after the departure of Mr. Hunt. From this place he despatched the messenger[16] in question, trusting to his overtaking the barges as they toiled up against the stream, and were delayed by the windings of the river. The purport of his letter was to entreat Mr. Hunt to wait until he could come up with him, that they might unite their forces and be a protection to each other in their perilous course through the country of the Sioux. In fact, as it was afterwards ascertained, Lisa was apprehensive that Mr. Hunt would do him some ill office with the Sioux band, securing his own passage through their country by pretending that he, with whom they were accustomed to trade, was on his way to them with a plentiful supply of goods. He feared, too, that Crooks and M'Lellan would take this opportunity to retort upon him the perfidy which they accused him of having used, two years previously, among these very Sioux. In this respect, however, he did them signal injustice. There was no such thing as covert design or treachery in their thought; but M'Lellan, when he heard that Lisa was on his way up the river, renewed his open threat of shooting him the moment he met him on Indian land.

The representations made by Crooks and M'Lellan of the treachery they had experienced, or fancied, on the part of Lisa, had great weight with Mr. Hunt, especially when he recollected the obstacles that had

from there, for Brackenridge writes: "We sat [sic] off from the village of St. Charles, on Tuesday, the 2d of April, 1811." *Journal*, 31. The *Louisiana Gazette*, April 11, 1811, reported Lisa's departure in the following notice:

"A few days ago, Mr. Manual Lisa sailed from here [St. Louis], on a voyage to Fort Mandan. Should Mr. Lisa join Mr. Hunt's party, on the head waters of the Missouri, they will form an army able to oppose any number of Blackfeet which may attack them. It is thought there will be upwards of 300 Americans on the Columbia River next year."

That Irving was now reading Brackenridge as a parallel record is evident from his use of Brackenridge's phrase "twenty stout oars-men." Compare also Irving's wording with Brackenridge's: "We anxiously hoped to overtake him [Hunt] before he entered the Sioux nation; for this purpose it was resolved to strain every nerve, as upon it, in a great measure depended the safety of our voyage." *Journal*, 32.

[16] Brackenridge writes: "It was . . . deemed adviseable to despatch a messenger by land. . . . For this purpose a half Indian was hired, and set off immediately in company with Charboneau." *Journal*, 84. Charboneau was Toussaint Charbonneau, a Frenchman. His wife, the Shoshoni Indian Sacagawea, famed for her services on the Lewis and Clark expedition, was aboard Lisa's boat.

been thrown in his own way by that gentleman at St. Louis. He doubted, therefore, the fair dealing of Lisa, and feared that, should they enter the Sioux country together, the latter might make use of his influence with that tribe, as he had in the case of Crooks and M'Lellan, and instigate them to oppose his progress up the river.

He sent back, therefore, an answer calculated to beguile Lisa, assuring him that he would wait for him at the Poncas village, which was but a little distance in advance; but, no sooner had the messenger departed, than he pushed forward with all diligence, barely stopping at the village to procure a supply of dried buffalo meat,[17] and hastening to leave the other party as far behind as possible, thinking there was less to be apprehended from the open hostility of Indian foes than from the quiet strategy of an Indian trader.

[17] Bradbury reports that for tobacco costing only two dollars, they bought one thousand pounds of jerked buffalo meat. *Travels*, 97. As Hunt's account book shows, they were at the Ponca village for only one day, May 24.

IT was about noon when the party left the Poncas village, about a league beyond which they passed the mouth of the Quicourt, or Rapid River (called, in the original French, *l' Eau Qui Court*).[1] After having proceeded some distance further, they landed, and encamped for the night. In the evening camp, the voyageurs gossiped, as usual, over the events of the day; and especially over intelligence picked up among the Poncas. These Indians had confirmed the previous reports of the hostile intentions of the Sioux, and had assured them that five tribes, or bands, of that fierce nation were actually assembled higher up the river, and waiting to cut them off. This evening gossip, and the terrific stories of Indian warfare to which it gave rise, produced a strong effect upon the imaginations of the irresolute; and in the morning it was discovered that the two men, who had joined the party at the Omaha[2] village, and been so bounteously fitted out, had deserted in the course of the night, carrying with them all their equipments. As it was known that one of them could not swim, it was hoped that the banks of the Quicourt River would bring them to a halt. A general pursuit was therefore instituted, but without success.[3]

On the following morning (May 26th),[4] as they were all on shore, breakfasting on one of the beautiful banks of the river, they observed

[1] The Niobrara River, which enters the Missouri from the west near Niobrara, Nebraska. They passed it on May 24.

[2] *Maha* in first edition.

[3] From Bradbury's *Travels*, 97. The two deserters were Joseph La Gemonier and Louis Rivard. Porter, "Roll of Overland Astorians," *Oregon Historical Quarterly*, Vol. XXXIV (1933), 108, 111.

[4] The date is confirmed by Bradbury.

two canoes descending along the opposite side. By the aid of spy-glasses, they ascertained that there were two white men in one of the canoes, and one in the other. A gun was discharged, which called the attention of the voyagers, who crossed over. They proved to be three Kentucky hunters, of the true "dreadnought" stamp. Their names were Edward Robinson, John Hoback, and Jacob Rezner. Robinson was a veteran backwoodsman, sixty-six years of age. He had been one of the first set-tlers of Kentucky, and engaged in many of the conflicts of the Indians on "the Bloody Ground." In one of these battles he had been scalped, and he still wore a handkerchief bound round his head to protect the part.[5] These men had passed several years in the upper wilderness. They had been in the service of the Missouri Company under Mr. Henry,[6] and had crossed the Rocky Mountains with him in the preceding year, when driven from his post on the Missouri by the hostilities of the Blackfeet. After crossing the mountains, Mr. Henry had established himself on one of the head branches of the Columbia River.[7] There they had re-mained with him some months,[8] hunting and trapping, until, having satisfied their wandering propensities, they felt disposed to return to the families and comfortable homes which they had left in Kentucky. They had accordingly made their way back across the mountains, and down the rivers, and were in full career for St. Louis, when thus suddenly interrupted. The sight of a powerful party of traders, trappers, hunters, and voyageurs, well armed and equipped, furnished at all points, in high

[5] Survival after being scalped was not unknown. For example, John Long reported that "where scalping only is inflicted, it puts the person to excruciating pain, though death does not always ensue. There are instances of persons of both sexes, now living in America . . . who, after having been scalped, by wearing a plate of silver or tin on the crown of the head, to keep it from cold, enjoy a good state of health, and are seldom afflicted with pain." *Voyages and Travels of an Indian Interpreter and Trader* (1791), in Thwaites (ed.), *Early Western Travels*, II, 58–59.

[6] See Chapter XV, note 1. Hoback's name is chiseled on one of the rocks marking the site of Camp Henry west of the Tetons.

Hoback, Robinson, and Reznor, upon leaving the Henry's Fork area, had crossed the Teton Range into Jackson Hole and had then probably left the valley by crossing Togwotee Pass, rather than Union Pass, into the valley of the Wind River. See Rollins (ed.), *Discovery of the Oregon Trail*, cxxx–cxxxi. In so doing, they were traveling country little known to white men, with the possible exception of John Colter. Irving makes clear what consequences this knowledge was to have for the overland Astorians. For these three men, see Porter, "Roll of Overland Astorians," *loc. cit.*, 107, 111.

[7] On Henry's Fork, a tributary of the Snake River, which in turn flows into the Columbia.

[8] The first edition reads *For some months*.

health and spirits, and banqueting lustily on the green margin of the
river, was a spectacle equally stimulating to these veteran backwoodsmen with the glorious array of a campaigning army to an old soldier;
but when they learned the grand scope and extent of the enterprise in
hand it was irresistible; homes and families and all the charms of green
Kentucky vanished from their thoughts; they cast loose their canoes to
drift down the stream, and joyfully enlisted in the band of adventurers.
They engaged on similar terms with some of the other hunters. The
company was to fit them out, and keep them supplied with the requisite
equipments and munitions, and they were to yield one half of the produce of their hunting and trapping.[9]

The addition of three such staunch recruits was extremely acceptable
at this dangerous part of the river. The knowledge of the country which
they had acquired, also, in their journeys and hunting excursions along
the rivers and among the Rocky Mountains was all important; in fact,
the information derived from them induced Mr. Hunt to alter his
future course.[10] He had hitherto intended to proceed by the route taken
by Lewis and Clarke in their famous exploring expedition, ascending
the Missouri to its forks, and thence going, by land, across the mountains. These men informed him, however, that, on taking that course
he would have to pass through the country infested by the savage tribe
of the Blackfeet, and would be exposed to their hostilities; they being,
as has already been observed, exasperated to deadly animosity against
the whites, on account of the death of one of their tribe by the hand of
Captain Lewis.[11] They advised him rather to pursue a route more to the
southward, being the same by which they had returned. This would
carry them over the mountains about where the head waters of the Platte
and the Yellowstone take their rise,[12] at a place much more easy and practicable than that where Lewis and Clarke had crossed. In pursuing this

[9] Irving builds upon Bradbury, *Travels*, 98.
[10] By making this decision, which was based on sound reason, Hunt, unable to see
the future, led his expedition to disaster.
[11] See Chapter XV, note 21. The first edition reads *the hands of Captain Lewis.*
[12] One of the tributaries of the North Platte is the Sweetwater, which flows east
out of the southern extremity of the Wind River Mountains near South Pass. To the
north and east is the Popo Agie, which meets Wind River to form the Big Horn, which
in turn flows into the Yellowstone, whose source is Yellowstone Lake. The route of
Hoback, Robinson, and Reznor would not take them near the Sweetwater but, rather,
up Wind River, which they would leave near present-day Bubois, Wyoming, crossing
the Continental Divide at Union Pass.

course, also, he would pass through a country abounding with game, where he would have a better chance of procuring a constant supply of provisions than by the other route, and would run less risk of molestation from the Blackfeet. Should he adopt this advice, it would be better for him to abandon the river at the Arickara town, at which he would arrive in the course of a few days. As the Indians at that town possessed horses in abundance, he might purchase a sufficient number of them for his great journey overland, which would commence at that place.[13]

After reflecting on this advice, and consulting with his associates, Mr. Hunt came to the determination to follow the route thus pointed out, to which[14] the hunters engaged to pilot him.

The party continued their voyage with delightful May weather. The prairies bordering on the river were gayly painted with innumerable flowers, exhibiting the motley confusion of colors of a Turkey carpet. The beautiful islands, also, on which they occasionally halted, presented the appearance of mingled grove and garden. The trees were often covered with clambering grapevines in blossom, which perfumed the air. Between the stately masses of the groves were grassy lawns and glades, studded with flowers, or interspersed with rose-bushes in full bloom. These islands were often the resort of the buffalo, the elk, and the antelope, who had made innumerable paths among the trees and thickets, which had the effect of the mazy walks and alleys of parks and shrubberies. Sometimes, where the river passed between high banks and bluffs, the roads, made by the tramp of buffaloes for many ages along the face of the heights, looked like so many well-travelled highways. At other places the banks were banded with great veins of iron ore, laid bare by the abrasion of the river. At one place the course of the river was nearly in a straight line for about fifteen miles. The banks sloped gently to its margin, without a single tree, but bordered with grass and herbage of a vivid green. Along each bank, for the whole fifteen miles, extended a stripe, one hundred yards in breath, of a deep rusty brown, indicating an inexhaustible bed of iron, through the centre of which the Missouri had worn its way. Indications of the continuance of this bed were afterwards observed higher up the river. It is, in fact, one of the mineral magazines which nature has provided in the heart of this vast realm of fertility, and which, in connection with the immense beds of

13 This paragraph is based upon Bradbury, *Travels,* 99–100.
14 The first edition reads *in which.*

coal on the same river, seem garnered up as the elements of the future wealth and power of the mighty West.[15]

The sight of these mineral treasures greatly excited the curiosity of Mr. Bradbury, and it was tantalizing to him to be checked in his scientific researches, and obliged to forego his usual rambles on shore; but they were now entering the fated country of the Sioux Tetons, in which it was dangerous to wander about unguarded.

This country extends for some days' journey along the river, and consists of vast prairies, here and there diversified by swelling hills, and cut up by ravines, the channels of turbid streams in the rainy seasons, but almost destitute of water during the heats of summer. Here and there on the sides of the hills, or along the alluvial borders and bottoms of the ravines, are groves and skirts of forest; but for the most part the country presented to the eye a boundless waste, covered with herbage, but without trees.

The soil of this immense region is strongly impregnated with sulphur, copperas, alum, and glauber salts; its various earths impart a deep tinge to the streams which drain it, and these, with the crumbling of the banks along the Missouri, give to the waters of that river much of the coloring matter with which they are clouded.

Over this vast tract the roving bands of the Sioux Tetons hold their vagrant sway, subsisting by the chase of the buffalo, the elk, the deer, and the antelope, and waging ruthless warfare with other wandering tribes.

As the boats made their way up the stream bordered by this land of danger, many of the Canadian voyageurs, whose fears had been awakened, would regard with a distrustful eye the boundless waste extending on each side. All, however, was silent, and apparently untenanted by a human being. Now and then a herd of deer would be seen feeding tranquilly among the flowery herbage, or a line of buffaloes, like a caravan on its march, moving across the distant profile of the prairie. The Canadians, however, began to apprehend an ambush in every thicket, and to regard the broad, tranquil plain as a sailor eyes some shallow and perfidious sea, which, though smooth and safe to the eye, conceals the lurking rock or treacherous shoal. The very name of a Sioux became a watchword of terror. Not an elk, a wolf, or any other animal, could appear on the hills, but the boats resounded with exclama-

[15] From Bradbury, *Travels*, 100–102.

179

tions from stem to stern, *"voila les Sioux! voila les Sioux!"* (there are the Sioux! there are the Sioux!)[.] Whenever it was practicable, the night encampment was on some island in the centre of the stream.

On the morning of the 31st of May,[16] as the travellers were break-fasting on the right bank of the river, the usual alarm was given, but with more reason, as two Indians actually made their appearance on a bluff on the opposite or northeast side, and harangued them in a loud voice. As it was impossible at that distance to distinguish what they said, Mr. Hunt, after breakfast, crossed the river with Pierre Dorion, the interpreter, and advanced boldly to converse with them, while the rest remained watching in mute suspense the movements of the parties. As soon as Mr. Hunt landed, one of the Indians disappeared behind the hill, but shortly reappeared on horseback, and went scouring off across the heights. Mr. Hunt held some conference with the remaining savage, and then recrossed the river to his party.

These two Indians proved to be spies or scouts of a large war party encamped about a league off, and numbering two hundred and eighty lodges, or about six hundred warriors, of three different tribes of Sioux; the Yanktons Ahna, the Tetons Bois-brulé, and the Tetons Min-na-kine-azzo. They expected daily to be reinforced by two other tribes, and had been waiting eleven days for the arrival of Mr. Hunt's party, with a determination to oppose their progress up the river; being resolved to prevent all trade of the white men with their enemies the Arickaras, Mandans, and Minatarees. The Indian who had galloped off on horse-back had gone to give notice of the approach of the party, so that they might now look out for some fierce scenes with those piratical savages, of whom they had received so many formidable accounts.

The party braced up their spirits to the encounter, and reëmbarking, pulled resolutely up the stream. An island for some time intervened between them and the opposite side of the river; but on clearing the upper end, they came in full view of the hostile shore. There was a ridge of hills down which the savages were pouring in great numbers, some on horseback, and some on foot. Reconnoitring them with the aid of glasses, they perceived that they were all in warlike array, painted and decorated for battle. Their weapons were bows and arrows, and a few short car-bines, and most of them had round shields. Altogether they had a wild and gallant appearance, and, taking possession of a point which com-

---

[16] The date is confirmed by Bradbury.

manded the river, ranged themselves along the bank as if prepared to dispute their[17] passage.

At sight of this formidable front of war, Mr. Hunt and his companions held counsel together. It was plain that the rumors they had heard were correct, and the Sioux were determined to oppose their progress by force of arms. To attempt to elude them and continue along the river was out of the question. The strength of the mid-current was too violent to be withstood, and the boats were obliged to ascend along the river banks. These banks were often high and perpendicular, affording the savages frequent stations, from whence, safe themselves, and almost unseen, they might shower down their missiles upon the boats below, and retreat at will, without danger from pursuit. Nothing apparently remained, therefore, but to fight or turn back. The Sioux far outnumbered them, it is true, but their own party was about sixty strong, well armed and supplied with ammunition; and, beside[s] their guns and rifles, they had a swivel and two howitzers mounted in the boats. Should they succeed in breaking this Indian force by one vigorous assault, it was likely they would be deterred from making any future attack of consequence. The fighting alternative was, therefore, instantly adopted, and the boats pulled to shore nearly opposite to the hostile force. Here the arms were all examined and put in order. The swivel and howitzers were then loaded with powder and discharged, to let the savages know by the report how formidably they were provided. The noise echoed along the shores of the river, and must have startled the warriors who were only accustomed to sharp reports[18] of rifles. The same pieces were then loaded with as many bullets as they would probably bear; after which the whole party embarked, and pulled across the river. The Indians remained watching them in silence, their painted forms and visages glaring in the sun, and their feathers fluttering in the breeze. The poor Canadians eyed them with rueful glances, and now and then a fearful ejaculation escaped[19] them. "Parbleu! this is a sad scrape we are in, brother!" one would mutter to the next oarsman. "Aye, aye!" the other would reply, "we are not going to a wedding, my friend!"

When the boats arrived within rifle shot, the hunters and other fight-

[17] *The* in first edition.
[18] The first edition reads *to the sharp report*.
[19] *Would escape* in first edition.

ing personages on board seized their weapons, and prepared for action. As they rose to fire, a confusion took place among the savages. They displayed their buffalo robes, raised them with both hands above their heads, and then spread them before them on the ground. At sight of this, Pierre Dorion eagerly cried out to the party not to fire, as this movement was a peaceful signal, and an invitation to a parley. Immediately about a dozen of the principal warriors, separating from the rest, descended to the edge of the river, lighted a fire, seated themselves in a semicircle round it, and, displaying the calumet, invited the party to land. Mr. Hunt now called a council of the partners on board of his boat. The question was, whether to trust to the amicable overtures of these ferocious people? It was determined in the affirmative; for, otherwise, there was no alternative but to fight them. The main body of the party were ordered to remain on board of the boats, keeping within shot and prepared to fire in case of any signs of treachery; while Mr. Hunt and the other partners (M'Kenzie, Crooks, Miller, and M'Lellan) proceeded to land, accompanied by the interpreter and Mr. Bradbury. The chiefs, who awaited them on the margin of the river, remained seated in their semicircle, without stirring a limb or moving a muscle, motionless as so many statues. Mr. Hunt and his companions advanced without hesitation, and took their seats on the sand so as to complete the circle. The band of warriors who lined the banks above stood looking down in silent groups and clusters, some ostentatiously equipped and decorated, others entirely naked but fantastically painted, and all variously armed.

The pipe of peace was now brought forward with due ceremony. The bowl was of a species of red stone resembling porphyry; the stem was six feet in length, decorated with tufts of horse-hair dyed red. The pipe-bearer stepped within the circle, lighted the pipe, held it towards the sun, then towards the different points of the compass, after which he handed it to the principal chief. The latter smoked a few whiffs, then, holding the head of the pipe in his hand, offered the other end to Mr. Hunt, and to each one successively in the circle. When all had smoked, it was considered that an assurance of good faith and amity had been interchanged. Mr. Hunt now made a speech in French, which was interpreted as he proceeded by Pierre Dorion. He informed the Sioux of the the real object of the expedition of himself and his companions, which was, not to trade with any of the tribes up the river, but to cross the mountains to the great salt lake in the west, in search of some of their brothers, whom they had not seen for eleven months. That he had heard of the intention of the Sioux to oppose his passage, and was prepared, as they might see, to effect it at all hazards; nevertheless, his feelings toward the Sioux were friendly, in proof of which he had brought them a present of tobacco and corn. So saying, he ordered about fifteen carottes[20] of tobacco, and as many bags of corn, to be brought from the boat and laid in a heap near the council fire.

The sight of these presents mollified the chieftain, who had, doubtless, been previously rendered considerate by the resolute conduct of the white men, the judicious disposition of their little armament, the completeness of their equipments, and the compact array of battle which they presented. He made a speech in reply, in which he stated the object of their hostile assemblage, which had been merely to prevent supplies of arms and ammunition from going to the Arickaras, Mandans, and Minatarees, with whom they were at war; but being now convinced that the party were carrying no supplies of the kind, but merely proceeding in quest of their brothers beyond the mountains, they would not impede them in their voyage. He concluded by thanking them for their present, and advising them to encamp on the opposite side of the river, as he had some young men among his warriors for whose discretion he could not be answerable, and who might be troublesome.

Here ended the conference: they all arose, shook hands, and parted. Mr. Hunt and his companions reëmbarked, and the boats proceeded on their course unmolested.[21]

[20] Twisted bundles.
[21] Irving's account of the meeting with the Sioux follows Bradbury, *Travels*, 104–109, very closely, sometimes to the point of reproducing phrases verbatim. The exclamations of the Canadian *voyageurs* are Irving's invention.

183

The Great Bend of the Missouri
Crooks and M'Lellan Meet with Two of Their Indian Opponents
Wanton Outrage of a White Man the Cause of Indian Hostility
Dangers and Precautions — An Indian War Party
Dangerous Situation of Mr. Hunt — A Friendly Encampment
Feasting and Dancing — Approach of Manuel Lisa and His Party
A Grim Meeting Between Old Rivals — Pierre Dorion in a Fury
A Burst of Chivalry

ON the afternoon of the following day (June 1st) they arrived at the great bend,[1] where the river winds for thirty miles round a circular peninsula, the neck of which is not above two thousand yards across. On the succeeding morning, at an early hour, they descried two Indians standing on a high bank of the river, waving and spreading their buffalo robes in signs of amity. They immediately pulled to shore and landed. On approaching the savages, however, the latter showed evident symptoms of alarm, spreading out their arms horizontally, according to their mode of supplicating clemency. The reason was soon explained. They proved to be two chiefs of the very war party that had brought Messrs. Crooks and M'Lellan to a stand two years before, and obliged them to escape down the river. They ran to embrace these gentlemen, as if delighted to meet with them; yet they evidently feared some retaliation of their past misconduct, nor were they quite at ease until the pipe of peace had been smoked.

Mr. Hunt having been informed that the tribe to which these men belonged had killed three white men during the preceding summer, reproached them with the crime, and demanded their reasons for such

[1] Located in South Dakota, the Great Bend (or "Grand Detour," as it was referred to by the French) is a large loop in the Missouri, "said to be twenty-one miles in circuit by the course of the river, and only nineteen hundred yards across the neck." Bradbury, *Travels*, 110. Irving, however, followed Lewis and Clark, who wrote: "A man, whom we had despatched to step off the distance across the bend, made it two thousand yards: the circuit is thirty miles." *History of the Expedition*, I, 126. Great Bend Dam is now located on the western side of the loop. The date is confirmed by Bradbury.

savage hostility. "We kill white men," replied one of the chiefs, "because white men kill us. That very man," added he, pointing to Carson, one of the new recruits, "killed one of our brothers last summer. The three white men were slain to avenge his death."

Their chief[2] was correct in his reply. Carson admitted that, being with a party of Arickaras on the banks of the Missouri, and seeing a war party of Sioux on the opposite side, he had fired with his rifle across. It was a random shot, made without much expectation of effect, for the river was full half a mile in breadth. Unluckily it brought down a Sioux warrior, for whose wanton destruction threefold vengeance had been taken, as has been stated.[3] In this way outrages are frequently committed on the natives by thoughtless or mischievous white men; the Indians retaliate according to a law of their code, which requires blood for blood; their act, of what with them is pious vengeance, resounds throughout the land, and is represented as wanton and unprovoked; the neighborhood is roused to arms; a war ensues, which ends in the destruction of half the tribe, the ruin of the rest, and their expulsion from their hereditary homes. Such is too often the real history of Indian warfare, which in general is traced up only to some vindictive act of a savage; while the outrage of the scoundrel white man that provoked it is sunk in silence.

The two chiefs, having smoked their pipe of peace and received a few presents, departed well satisfied. In a little while two others appeared on horseback, and rode up abreast of the boats. They had seen the presents given to their comrades, but were dissatisfied with them, and came after the boats to ask for more. Being somewhat peremptory and insolent in their demands, Mr. Hunt gave them a flat refusal, and threatened, if they or any of their tribe followed him with similar demands, to treat them as enemies. They turned and rode off in a furious passion. As he was ignorant what force these chiefs might have behind the hills, and as it was very possible that they might take advantage of some pass of the river to attack the boats, Mr. Hunt called all stragglers on board and prepared for such emergency. It was agreed that the large boat commanded by Mr. Hunt should ascend along the northeast side of the river, and the three smaller boats along the south side. By this arrangement each party would command a view of the opposite heights

[2] *The chief* in first edition
[3] The meeting with the two Indians follows Bradbury, *Travels*, 110–11. The remainder of the paragraph is Irving's interpolation.

above the heads and out of sight[4] of their companions, and could give the alarm should they perceive any Indians lurking there. The signal of alarm was to be two shots fired in quick succession.

The boats proceeded for the greater part of the day without seeing any signs of an enemy. About four o'clock in the afternoon the large boat, commanded by Mr. Hunt, came to where the river was divided by a long sand-bar, which apparently, however, left a sufficient channel between it and the shore along which they were advancing. He kept up this channel, therefore, for some distance, until the water proved too shallow for the boat. It was necessary, therefore, to put about, return down the channel, and pull round the lower end of the sand-bar into the main stream. Just as he had given orders to this effect to his men, two signal-guns were fired from the boats on the opposite side of the river. At the same moment, a file of savage warriors was observed pouring down from the impending bank, and gathering on the shore at the lower end of the bar. They were evidently a war party, being armed with bows and arrows, battle clubs and carbines, and round bucklers of buffalo hide, and their naked bodies were painted with black and white stripes. The natural inference was, that they belonged to the two tribes of Sioux which had been expected by the great war party, and that they had been incited[5] to hostility by the two chiefs who had been enraged by the refusal and the menace of Mr. Hunt. Here then was a fearful predicament. Mr. Hunt and his crew seemed caught, as it were, in a trap. The Indians, to the number of about a hundred, had already taken possession of a point near which the boat would have to pass: others kept pouring down the bank, and it was probable that some would remain posted on the top of the height.

The hazardous situation of Mr. Hunt was perceived by those in the other boats, and they hastened to his assistance. They were at some distance above the sand-bar, however, and on the opposite side of the river, and saw, with intense anxiety, the number of savages continually augmenting, at the lower end of the channel, so that the boat would be exposed to a fearful attack before they could render it any assistance. Their anxiety increased as they saw Mr. Hunt and his party descending the channel and dauntlessly approaching the point of danger; but it suddenly changed into surprise on beholding the boat pass close by the savage horde unmolested, and steer out safely into the broad river.

[4] *The sight* in first edition.

The next moment the whole band of warriors was in motion. They ran along the bank until they were opposite to the boats, then throwing by their weapons and buffalo robes, plunged into the river, waded and swam off to the boats and surrounded them in crowds, seeking to shake hands with every individual on board; for the Indians have long since found this to be the white man's token of amity, and they carry it to an extreme.

All uneasiness was now at an end. The Indians proved to be a war party of Arickaras, Mandans, and Minatarees, consisting of three hundred warriors, and bound on a foray against the Sioux. Their war plans were abandoned for the present, and they determined to return to the Arickara town, where they hoped to obtain from the white men arms and ammunition that would enable them to take the field with advantage over their enemies.

The boats now sought the first convenient place for encamping. The tents were pitched; the warriors fixed their camp at about a hundred yards distant; provisions were furnished from the boats sufficient for all parties; there was hearty though rude feasting in both camps, and in the evening the red warriors entertained their white friends with dances and songs, that lasted until after midnight.

On the following morning (June 3)[6] the travellers reëmbarked and took temporary leave of their Indian friends, who intended to proceed immediately for the Arickara town, where they expected to arrive in three days, long before the boats could reach there. Mr. Hunt had not proceeded far before the chief came galloping along the shore and made signs for a parley. He said, his people could not go home satisfied unless they had something to take with them to prove that they had met with the white men. Mr. Hunt understood the drift of the speech, and made the chief a present of a cask of powder, a bag of balls, and three dozen knives, with which he was highly pleased. While the chief was receiving these presents an Indian came running along the shore, and announced that a boat, filled with white men, was coming up the river.[7] This was by no means agreeable tidings to Mr. Hunt, who correctly concluded it to be the boat of Mr. Manuel Lisa; and he was vexed to find that alert

[5] Erroneously *invited* in first edition.

[6] *July 3* appears erroneously in both the first edition and the Author's Revised Edition. June 3 is confirmed by Bradbury.

[7] This paragraph down to this point plus the preceding six paragraphs closely follow Bradbury's *Travels*, 111–17.

and adventurous trader upon his heels, whom he hoped[8] to have out-maneuvered, and left far behind. Lisa, however, was too much experienced in the wiles of Indian trade to be lulled by the promise of waiting for him at the Poncas village; on the contrary, he had allowed himself no repose, and had strained every nerve to overtake the rival party, and availing himself of the moonlight, had even sailed during a considerable part of the night.[9] In this he was partly prompted by his apprehensions of the Sioux, having met a boat which had probably passed Mr. Hunt's party in the night, and which had been fired into by these savages.

On hearing that Lisa was so near at hand, Mr. Hunt perceived that it was useless to attempt any longer to evade him; after proceeding a few miles further, therefore, he came to a halt and waited for him to come up. In a little while the barge of Lisa made its appearance. It came sweeping gently up the river, manned by its twenty stout oarsmen, and armed by a swivel mounted at the bow. The whole number on board amounted to twenty-six men; among whom was Mr. Henry Breckenridge,[10] then a young, enterprising man; who was a mere passenger, tempted by notions of curiosity to accompany Mr. Lisa. He has since made himself known by various writings, among which may be noted a narrative of this very voyage.

The approach of Lisa, while it was regarded with uneasiness by Mr. Hunt, roused the ire of M'Lellan; who, calling to mind old grievances, began to look round for his rifle, as if he really intended to carry his threat into execution and shoot him on the spot;[11] and it was with some difficulty that Mr. Hunt was enabled to restrain his ire, and prevent a scene of outrage and confusion.

The meeting between the two leaders, thus mutually distrustful, could not be very cordial: and as to Messrs. Crooks and M'Lellan, though they refrained from any outbreak, yet they regarded in grim de-

[8] The first edition reads *he had hoped*.

[9] Irving turns briefly to Brackenridge, who, for May 28, writes: "We continued under sail the rest of the day, and determining to strain every nerve, in order to overtake Hunt, we resolved to run the risk of sailing after night, and fortunately it happened to be moonlight. We continued under way until eleven o'clock." *Journal*, 94–95. For the next sentence, Irving shifts back to Bradbury, *Travels*, 117.

[10] Irving consistently spells the name this way instead of *Brackenridge*.

[11] This threat does not appear in Bradbury. Irving probably had it from a footnote in Brackenridge, which reads: "That if ever he fell in with Lisa, in the Indian country, he would shoot him." *Journal*, 107n.

fiance their old rival and underplotter. In truth a general distrust prevailed throughout the party concerning Lisa and his intentions. They considered him artful and slippery, and secretly anxious for the failure of their expedition. There being now nothing more to be apprehended from the Sioux, they suspected that Lisa would take advantage of his twenty-oared barge to leave them and get first among the Arickaras. As he had traded with those people and possessed great influence over them, it was feared he might make use of it to impede the business of Mr. Hunt and his party. It was resolved, therefore, to keep a sharp look-out upon his movements; and M'Lellan swore that if he saw the least sign of treachery on his part, he would instantly put his old threat into execution.

Notwithstanding these secret jealousies and heart-burnings, the two parties maintained an outward appearance of civility, and for two days continued forward in company with some degree of harmony. On the third day,[12] however, an explosion took place, and it was produced by no less a personage than Pierre Dorion, the half-breed interpreter. It will be recollected that this worthy had been obliged to steal a march from St. Louis, to avoid being arrested for an old whiskey debt which he owed to the Missouri Fur Company, and by which Mr. Lisa had hoped to prevent his enlisting in Mr. Hunt's expedition. Dorion, since the arrival of Lisa, had kept aloof and regarded him with a sullen and dogged aspect. On the fifth of June[13] the two parties were brought to a halt by a heavy rain, and remained encamped about a hundred yards apart. In the course of the day Lisa undertook to tamper with the faith of Pierre Dorion, and, inviting him on board of his boat, regaled him with his favorite whiskey. When he thought him sufficiently mellowed, he proposed to him to quit the service of his new employers and return to his old allegiance. Finding him not to be moved by soft words, he called to mind his old debt to the company, and threatened to carry him off by force, in payment of it. The mention of this debt always stirred up the gall of Pierre Dorion, bringing with it the remembrance of the whiskey extortion. A violent quarrel arose between him and Lisa, and he left the boat in high dudgeon. His first step was to repair to the tent of Mr. Hunt and reveal the attempt that had been made to shake his faith.

12 June 5.
13 Both the first edition and the Author's Revised Edition erroneously have *July 5*. June 5 is confirmed by Bradbury and Brackenridge.

While he was yet talking Lisa entered the tent, under the pretext of coming to borrow a towing line. High words instantly ensued between him and Dorion, which ended by the half-breed's dealing him a blow. A quarrel in the "Indian country," however, is not to be settled with fisticuffs. Lisa immediately rushed to his boat for a weapon.[14] Dorion snatched up a pair of pistols belonging to Mr. Hunt, and placed himself in battle array. The noise had roused the camp, and every one pressed to know the cause. Lisa now reappeared upon the field with a knife stuck in his girdle. Mr. Breckenridge, who had tried in vain to mollify his ire, accompanied him to the scene of action.[15] Pierre Dorion's pistols gave him the advantage, and he maintained a most warlike attitude. In the meantime, Crooks and M'Lellan had learnt the cause of the affray, and were each eager to take the quarrel into their own hands. A scene of uproar and hubbub ensued that defies description. M'Lellan would have brought his rifle into play and settled all old and new grudges by a pull of the trigger, had he not been restrained by Mr. Hunt. That gentleman acted as moderator, endeavoring to prevent a general mêlée; in the midst of the brawl, however, an expression was made use of by Lisa derogatory to his own honor. In an instant the tranquil spirit of Mr. Hunt was in a flame. He now became as eager for the fight[16] as any one on the ground, and challenged Lisa to settle the dispute on the spot with pistols. Lisa repaired to his boat to arm himself for the deadly feud. He was followed by Messrs. Bradbury and Breckenridge, who, novices in Indian life and the "chivalry" of the frontier, had no relish for scenes of blood and brawl. By their earnest mediation the quarrel was brought to a close[17] without bloodshed; but the leaders of the camp separated in anger, and all personal intercourse ceased between them.[18]

[14] Bradbury reports that Lisa fled to his boat, exclaiming, "O mon Dieu, ou est mon couteau [O my God, where is my knife]!" *Travels*, 122.

[15] Irving here went to Brackenridge, where he read: "On my return to our camp, I found Mr. Lisa furious with rage, buckling on his knife, and preparing to return: finding that I could not dissuade, I resolved to accompany him." *Journal*, 107.

[16] The first edition reads *for fight*.

[17] The first edition reads *the quarrel was with great difficulty brought to a close*.

[18] Bradbury, *Travels*, 121–22, is Irving's main source for this fracas, but he also read Brackenridge, who records the affair in *Journal*, 106–107.

THE rival parties now coasted along the opposite sides of the river, within sight of each other; the barges of Mr. Hunt always keeping some distance in the advance, lest Lisa should push on and get first to the Arickara village. The scenery and objects, as they proceeded, gave evidence that they were advancing deeper and deeper into the domains of savage nature. Boundless wastes kept extending to the eye, more and more animated by herds of buffalo. Sometimes these unwieldly animals were seen moving in long procession across the silent landscape; at other times they were scattered about, singly or in groups, on the broad, enameled prairies and green acclivities, some cropping the rich pasturage, others reclining amidst the flowery herbage; the whole scene realizing in a manner the old Scriptural descriptions of the vast pastoral countries of the Orient, with "cattle upon a thousand hills."[1]

At one place the shores seemed absolutely lined with buffaloes; many were making their way across the stream, snorting, and blowing, and floundering. Numbers, in spite of every effort, were borne by the rapid current within shot of the boats, and several were killed. At another place a number were descried on the beach of a small island, under the shade of the trees, or standing in the water, like cattle, to avoid the flies and the heat of the day.

Several of the best marksmen stationed themselves in the bow of a barge which advanced slowly and silently, stemming the current with

[1] "For every beast of the forest is mine, and the cattle on a thousand hills." Psalm 50:10.

the aid of a broad sail and a fair breeze. The buffaloes stood gazing quietly at the barge as it approached, perfectly unconscious of their danger. The fattest of the herd was selected by the hunters, who all fired together and brought down their victim.

Beside[s] the buffaloes they saw abundance of deer, and frequent gangs of stately elks together with light troops of sprightly antelopes, the fleetest and most beautiful inhabitants of the prairies.[2]

There are two kinds of antelopes in these regions, one nearly the size of the common deer, the other not much larger than a goat. Their color is a light gray, or rather dun, slightly spotted with white; and they have small horns like those of the deer, which they never shed. Nothing can surpass the delicate and elegant finish of their limbs, in which lightness, elasticity, and strength are wonderfully combined. All the attitudes and movements of this beautiful animal are graceful and picturesque; and it is altogether as fit a subject for the fanciful uses of the poet as the oft-sung gazelle of the East.

Their habits are shy and capricious; they keep on the open plains, are quick to take the alarm, and bound away with a fleetness that defies pursuit. When thus skimming across a prairie in the autumn, their light gray or dun color blends with the hue of the withered herbage, the swiftness of their motion baffles the eye, and they almost seem unsubstantial forms, driven like gossamer before the wind.

While they thus keep to the open plain and trust to their speed, they are safe; but they have a prurient curiosity that sometimes betrays them to their ruin. When they have scud[ded] for some distance and left their pursuer behind, they will suddenly stop and turn to gaze at the object of their alarm. If the pursuit is not followed up they will, after a time, yield to their inquisitive hankering, and return to the place from whence they have been frightened.

John Day, the veteran hunter already mentioned, displayed his experience and skill in entrapping one of these beautiful animals. Taking advantage of its well-known curiosity, he laid [sic] down flat among the grass, and putting his handkerchief on the end of his ramrod, waved it gently in the air. This had the effect of the fabled fascination of the rattlesnake. The antelope approached[3] timidly, pausing and reconnoitring

---

[2] Irving appears to have worked up the preceding passage from various passages in both Bradbury, *Travels*, 124–26, 148–49, and Brackenridge, *Journal*, 109–10, 133–34.

with increased curiosity; moving round the point of attraction in a circle, but still drawing nearer and nearer, until being within range[4] of the deadly rifle, he fell a victim to his curiosity.[5]

On the 10th of June,[6] as the party were making brisk progress with a fine breeze, they met a canoe with three Indians descending the river. They came to a parley, and brought news from the Arickara village. The war party, which had caused such alarm at the sand-bar, had reached the village some days previously, announced the approach of the party of traders, and displayed with great ostentation the presents they had received from them. On further conversation with these three Indians, Mr. Hunt learnt the real danger which he had run, when hemmed up within the sand-bar. The Mandans who were of the war party, when they saw the boat so completely entrapped and apparently within their power, had been eager for attacking it, and securing so rich a prize. The Minatarees, also, were nothing loth, feeling in some measure committed in hostility to the whites, in consequence of their tribe having killed two white men above the fort of the Missouri Fur Company. Fortunately, the Arickaras, who formed the majority of the war party, proved true in their friendship to the whites, and prevented any hostile act, otherwise a bloody affray, and perhaps a horrible massacre might have ensued.[7]

On the 11th of June, Mr. Hunt and his companions encamped near an island about six miles below the Arickara village. Mr. Lisa encamped, as usual, at no great distance; but the same sullen and jealous reserve, and non-intercourse continued between them. Shortly after pitching the tents, Mr. Breckenridge made his appearance as an ambassador from the rival camp. He came on behalf of his companions, to arrange the manner of making their entrance into the village and of receiving the chiefs; for everything of the kind is a matter of grave ceremonial among the Indians.[8]

[3] The first edition reads *The antelope gazed at the mysterious object for some time at a distance, then approached.*

[4] *The range* in first edition.

[5] In his account of the antelope, Irving makes use of Bradbury, *Travels*, 123, and Brackenridge, *Journal*, 103, 106.

[6] The date is confirmed by Bradbury and Brackenridge.

[7] This paragraph is based on Bradbury, *Travels*, 126–27.

[8] For this paragraph Irving drew upon both Bradbury, *Travels*, 127, and Brackenridge, *Journal*, 111. Both confirm the date.

The partners now expressed frankly their deep distrust of the intentions of Mr. Lisa, and their apprehensions, that, out of the jealousy of trade, and resentment of recent disputes, he might seek to instigate the Arickaras against them. Mr. Breckenridge assured them that their suspicions were entirely groundless, and pledged himself that nothing of the kind should take place. He found it difficult, however, to remove their distrust; the conference, therefore, ended without producing any cordial understanding; and M'Lellan recurred to his old threat of shooting Lisa the instant he discovered anything like treachery in his proceedings.[9]

That night the rain fell in torrents, accompanied by thunder and lightning.[10] The camp was deluged, and the bedding and baggage drenched. All hands embarked at an early hour, and set forward for the village. About nine o'clock, when half way, they met a canoe, on board of which were two Arickara dignitaries. One, a fine-looking man, much above the common size, was hereditary chief of the village; he was called the Left-handed, on account of a personal peculiarity. The other, a ferocious-looking savage, was the war chief, or generalissimo; he was known by the name of the Big Man, an appellation he well deserved from his size, for he was of a gigantic frame. Both were of fairer complexion than is usual with savages.

They were accompanied by an interpreter;[11] a French creole, one of those haphazard wights of Gallic origin who abound upon our frontier, living among the Indians like one of their own race. He had been twenty years among the Arickaras, had a squaw and troop[12] of piebald children, and officiated as interpreter to the chiefs. Through this worthy organ the two dignitaries signified to Mr. Hunt their sovereign intention to oppose

[9] Irving's method was to move back and forth from Bradbury and Brackenridge. Here he read in Brackenridge, for example: "The leaders of the party of Hunt were still suspicious that Lisa intended to betray them.—M'Clelland declared that he would shoot him the moment he discovered any thing like it." *Journal*, 111.

[10] Even a simple sentence like this illustrates how Irving sometimes produced an amalgam of Bradbury and Brackenridge. Bradbury had written, for example: "During this night we had a severe thunderstorm, accompanied by torrents of rain, so that our beds were completely wet." *Travels*, 127. Brackenridge, in turn, had recorded: "Heavy rains accompanied by thunder and lightning last night." *Journal*, 111.

[11] This may have been Joseph Gravelines, referred to by Lewis and Clark as "a Mr. Gravelines, a man who has acquired the language [of the Arikaras]." *History of the Expedition*, I, 152. See also Annie Heloise Abel (ed.), *Tabeau's Narrative of Loisel's Expedition to the Upper Missouri*, *passim*.

[12] The first edition reads *a troop*.

194

the further progress of the expedition up the river unless a boat were left to trade with them. Mr. Hunt in reply, explained the object of his voyage, and his intention of debarking at their village and proceeding thence by land; and that he would willingly trade with them for a supply of horses for his journey. With this explanation they were perfectly satisfied, and putting about, steered for their village to make preparations for the reception of the strangers.[13]

The village of the Rikaras, Arickaras, or Ricarees,[14] for the name is thus variously written, is between the 46th and 47th parallels of north latitude, and fourteen hundred and thirty miles above the mouth of the Missouri. The party reached it about ten o'clock in the morning,[15] but landed on the opposite side of the river, where they spread out their baggage and effects to dry. From hence they commanded an excellent view of the village. It was divided into two portions, about eighty yards apart, being inhabited by two distinct bands. The whole extended about three-quarters of a mile along the river bank, and was composed of conical lodges, that looked like so many small hillocks, being wooden frames intertwined with osier, and covered with earth. The plain beyond the village swept up into hills of considerable height, but the whole country was nearly destitute of trees. While they were regarding the village, they beheld a singular fleet coming down the river. It consisted of a number of canoes, each made of a single buffalo hide stretched on sticks, so as to form a kind of circular trough. Each one was navigated by a single squaw, who knelt in the bottom and paddled; towing after her frail bark a bundle of floating wood intended for firing. This kind of canoe is in frequent use among the Indians; the buffalo hide being readily made up into a bundle and transported on horseback; it is very serviceable in conveying baggage across the rivers.

The great numbers of horses grazing around the village, and scattered over the neighboring hills and valleys, bespoke the equestrian habit of the Arickaras, who are admirable horsemen. Indeed, in the number of his horses consists the wealth of an Indian of the prairies; who resembles

[13] The meeting with the Arikaras is from Bradbury, *Travels*, 127–28.
[14] The Arikaras, or Rees, as they are often called, occupied an area extending along the Missouri River in South and North Dakota. A peculiarity of the Arikaras is that they were agriculturists and, consequently, not nomadic. They lived in villages consisting of houses of the kind Irving describes. Linguistically they belonged to the Caddoan stock. Swanton, *Indian Tribes*, 273–75.
[15] June 12.

an Arab in his passion for this noble animal, and in his adroitness in the management of it.[16]

After a time, the voice of the sovereign chief, "the Left-handed," was heard across the river, announcing that the council lodge was preparing, and inviting the white men to come over. The river was half a mile in width, yet every word uttered by the chieftain was heard; this may be partly attributed to the distinct manner in which every syllable of the compound words in the Indian languages is articulated and accented; but in truth, a savage warrior might often rival Achilles himself for force of lungs.[17]

Now came the delicate point of management—how the two rival parties were to conduct their visit to the village with proper circumspection and due decorum. Neither of the leaders had spoken to each other since their quarrel. All communication had been by ambassadors. Seeing the jealousy entertained of Lisa, Mr. Beckenridge, in his negotiation, had arranged that a deputation from each party should cross the river at the same time, so that neither would have the first access to the ear of the Arickaras.

The distrust of Lisa, however, had increased in proportion as they approached the sphere of action; and M'Lellan, in particular, kept a vigilant eye upon his motions, swearing to shoot him if he attempted to cross the river first.

About two o'clock the large boat of Mr. Hunt was manned, and he stepped on board, accompanied by Messrs. M'Kenzie and M'Lellan; Lisa at the same time embarked in his barge; the two deputations amounted in all to fourteen persons, and never was any movement of rival potentates conducted with more wary exactness.

They landed amidst a rabble crowd, and were received on the bank by the left-handed chief, who conducted them into the village with grave courtesy; driving to the right and left the swarms of old squaws, imp-like boys, and vagabond dogs, with which the place abounded. They wound their way between the cabins, which looked like dirt-heaps huddled together without any plan, and surrounded by old palisades; all filthy in the extreme, and redolent of villainous smells.

[16] The preceding two paragraphs are taken chiefly from Brackenridge, *Journal*, 112, with a few details from Bradbury, *Travels*, 128.

[17] Bradbury, p. 110. (Irving's note) It is unaccountable why Irving, who has depended so heavily upon Bradbury for his narrative of Hunt's voyage, should suddenly feel an obligation to document a paragraph. See *Travels*, 128.

196

At length they arrived at the council lodge. It was somewhat spacious, and formed of four forked trunks of trees placed upright, supporting cross-beams and a frame of poles interwoven with osiers, and the whole covered with earth. A hole sunken in the centre formed the fireplace, and immediately above was a circular hole in the apex of the lodge, to let out the smoke and let in the daylight. Around the lodge were recesses for sleeping, like the berths on board ships, screened from view by curtains of dressed skins. At the upper end of the lodge was a kind of hunting and warlike trophy, consisting of two buffalo heads garishly painted, surmounted by shields, bows, quivers of arrows, and other weapons.[18]

On entering the lodge the chief pointed to mats or cushions which had been placed around for the strangers, and on which they seated themselves, while he placed himself on a kind of stool. An old man then came forward with the pipe of peace or good-fellowship, lighted and handed it to the chief, and then falling back, squatted himself near the door. The pipe was passed from mouth to mouth, each one taking a whiff, which is equivalent to the inviolable pledge of faith, of taking salt together among the ancient Britons. The chief then made a sign to the old pipe-bearer, who seemed to fill, likewise, the station of herald, seneschal, and public crier, for he ascended to the top of the lodge to make proclamation. Here he took his post beside the aperture for the emission of smoke and the admission of light; the chief dictated from within what he was to proclaim, and he bawled it forth with a force of lungs that resounded over all the village. In this way he summoned the warriors and great men to council; every now and then reporting progress to his chief through the hole in the roof.

In a little while the braves and sages began to enter one by one, as their names were called or announced, emerging from under the buffalo robe suspended over the entrance instead of a door, stalking across the lodge to the skins placed on the floor, and crouching down on them in silence. In this way twenty entered and took their seats, forming an assemblage worthy of the pencil: for the Arickaras are a noble race of men, large and well formed, and maintain a savage grandeur and gravity of demeanor in their solemn ceremonials.

All being seated, the old seneschal prepared the pipe of ceremony or council, and having lit it, handed it to the chief. He inhaled the sacred smoke, gave a puff upward to the heaven, then downward to the earth,

[18] In the two previous paragraphs, Irving relies on Brackenridge, *Journal*, 114–15.

then towards the east; after this it was as usual passed from mouth to mouth, each holding it respectfully until his neighbor had taken several whiffs; and now the grand council was considered as opened in due form.

The chief made an harangue welcoming the white men to his village, and expressing his happiness in taking them by the hand as friends; but at the same time complaining of the poverty of himself and his people; the usual prelude among Indians to begging or hard bargaining.

Lisa rose to reply, and the eyes of Hunt and his companions were eagerly turned upon him, those of M'Lellan glaring like a basilisk's. He began by the usual expressions of friendship, and then proceeded to explain the object of his own party. Those persons, however, said he, pointing to Mr. Hunt and his companions, are of a different party, and are quite distinct in their views; but, added he, though we are separate parties, we make but one common cause when the safety of either is concerned. Any injury or insult offered to them I shall consider as done to myself, and will resent it accordingly. I trust, therefore, that you will treat them with the same friendship that you have always manifested for me, doing everything in your power to serve them and to help them on their way. The speech of Lisa, delivered with an air of frankness and sincerity, agreeably surprised and disappointed the rival party.

Mr. Hunt then spoke, declaring the object of his journey to the great salt lake[19] beyond the mountains, and that he should want horses for the purpose, for which he was ready to trade, having brought with him plenty of goods. Both he and Lisa concluded their speeches by making presents of tobacco.

The left-handed chieftain in reply promised his friendship and aid to the new-comers, and welcomed them to his village. He added that they had not the number of horses to spare that Mr. Hunt required, and expressed a doubt whether they should be able to part with any. Upon this, another chieftain, called Gray Eyes, made a speech, and declared that they could readily supply Mr. Hunt with all the horses he might want, since, if they had not enough in the village, they could easily steal more. This honest expedient immediately removed the main difficulty; but the chief deferred all trading for a day or two; until he should have time to consult with his subordinate chiefs as to market rates; for the

[19] The first edition reads *to be the great Salt Lake*. The reference, of course, is to the Pacific Ocean.

principal chief of a village, in conjunction with his council, usually fixes the prices at which articles shall be bought and sold, and to them the village must conform.

The council now broke up. Mr. Hunt transferred his camp across the river at a little distance below the village, and the left-handed chief placed some of his warriors as a guard to prevent the intrusion of any of his people. The camp was pitched on the river bank just above the boats. The tents, and the men wrapped in their blankets and bivouaking on skins in the open air, surrounded the baggage at night. Four sentinels also kept watch within sight of each other outside of the camp until midnight, when they were relieved by four others who mounted guard until daylight. Mr. Lisa encamped near to Mr. Hunt, between him and the village.

The speech of Mr. Lisa in the council had produced a pacific effect in the encampment. Though the sincerity of his friendship and good-will towards the new company still remained matter of doubt, he was no longer suspected of an intention to play false. The intercourse between the two leaders was therefore resumed, and the affairs of both parties went on harmoniously.[20]

[20] In his account of the meeting in the council lodge, Irving weaves together details from both Bradbury, *Travels*, 129–31, and Brackenridge, *Journal*, 111–13.

A TRADE now commenced with the Arickaras under the regulation and supervision of their two chieftains. Lisa sent a part of his goods to the lodge of the left-handed dignitary, and Mr. Hunt established his mart in the lodge of the Big Man. The village soon presented the appearance of a busy fair; and as horses were in demand, the purlieus and the adjacent plain were like the vicinity of a Tartar encampment; horses were put through all their paces, and horsemen were careering about with that dexterity and grace for which the Arickaras are noted. As soon as a horse was purchased, his tail was cropped, a sure mode of distinguishing him from the horses of the tribe; for the Indians disdain to practice this absurd, barbarous, and indecent mutilation, invented by some mean and vulgar mind, insensible to the merit and perfections of the animal. On the contrary, the Indian horses are suffered to remain in every respect the superb and beautiful animals which nature formed them.[1]

The wealth of an Indian of the far west consists principally in his horses, of which each chief and warrior possesses a great number, so that the plains about an Indian village or encampment are covered with them. These form objects of traffic, or objects of depredation, and in

[1] Worth noting is Irving's embellishment of Bradbury's statement, which reads: "The instant a horse was bought, his tail was cropped, to render him more easily distinguished from those belonging to the Indians, which are in all respects as nature found them." *Travels,* 134.

this way pass from tribe to tribe over great tracts of country. The horses owned by the Arickaras are, for the most part, of the wild stock of the prairies; some, however, had been obtained from the Poncas, Pawnees, and other tribes to the southwest, who had stolen them from the Spaniards in the course of horse-stealing expeditions into the Mexican territories. These were to be known by being branded; a Spanish mode of marking horses not practiced by the Indians.[2]

As the Arickaras were meditating another expedition against their enemies the Sioux, the articles of traffic most in demand were guns, tomahawks, scalping-knives, powder, ball, and other munitions of war.[3] The price of a horse, as regulated by the chiefs, was commonly ten dollars' worth of goods at first cost.[4] To supply the demand thus suddenly created, parties of young men and braves had sallied forth on expeditions to steal horses; a species of service among the Indians which takes precedence of hunting, and is considered a department of honorable warfare.

While the leaders of the expedition were actively engaged in preparing for the approaching journey, those who had accompanied it for curiosity or amusement,[5] found ample matter for observation in the village and its inhabitants. Wherever they went they were kindly entertained. If they entered a lodge, the buffalo robe was spread before the fire for them to sit down; the pipe was brought, and while the master of the lodge conversed with his guests, the squaw put the earthen vessel over the fire, well filled with dried buffalo meat and pounded corn; for the Indian in his native state, before he has mingled much with white men, and acquired their sordid habits, has the hospitality of the Arab: never does a stranger enter his door without having food placed before

[2] This paragraph is an elaboration of the following two sentences in Bradbury: "The chief part of their riches consists in horses, many of which are obtained from the nations southwest of them, as the Chayennes, Poncars [Poncas], Panies [Pawnees], &c. who make predatory excursions into Mexico, and steal horses from the Spaniards. A considerable number of those bought from the Aricaras were branded, and were doubtless brought from Mexico, as the Indians do not practice branding." *Ibid.*, 176-77.

[3] "The species of goods most in demand were carbines, powder, ball, tomahawks, knives, &c. as another expedition against the Sioux was meditated." *Ibid.*, 132.

[4] "The price of a horse was commonly ten dollars worth of goods at first cost." Brackenridge, *Journal*, 116.

[5] John Bradbury, Thomas Nuttall, and H. M. Brackenridge. The first two had serious scientific objects in mind. Brackenridge admits his motive was only "idle curiosity," as he phrased it.

him; and never is the food thus furnished made a matter of traffic.[6]

The life of an Indian when at home in his village is a life of indolence and amusement. To the woman is [*sic*] consigned the labors of the household and the field; she arranges the lodge; brings wood for the fire; cooks; jerks venison and buffalo meat; dresses the skins of the animals killed in the chase; cultivates the little patch of maize, pumpkins, and pulse, which furnishes a great part of their provisions. Their time for repose and recreation is at sunset, when the labors of the day being ended, they gather together to amuse themselves with petty games, or to hold gossiping convocations on the tops of their lodges.

As to the Indian, he is a game animal, not to be degraded by useful or menial toil. It is enough that he exposes himself to the hardships of the chase and the perils of war; that he brings home food for his family, and watches and fights for its protection. Everything else is beneath his attention. When at home, he attends only to his weapons and his horses, preparing the means of future exploit. Or he engages with his comrades in games of dexterity, agility and strength; or in gambling games in which everything is put at hazard with a recklessness seldom witnessed in civilized life.

A great part of the idle leisure of the Indians when at home, is passed in groups, squatted together on the bank of a river, on the top of a mound on the prairie, or on the roof of one of their earth-covered lodges, talking over the news of the day, the affairs of the tribe, the events and exploits of their last hunting or fighting expedition; or listening to the stories of old times told by some veteran chronicler; resembling a group of our village quidnuncs and politicians, listening to the prosings of some superannuated oracle, or discussing the contents of an ancient newspaper.

As to the Indian women, they are far from complaining of their lot. On the contrary, they would despise their husbands could they stoop to any menial office, and would think it conveyed an imputation upon their own conduct. It is the worst insult one virago can cast upon another in a moment of altercation. "Infamous woman!" will she cry, "I have seen your husband carrying wood into his lodge to make the fire. Where was his squaw, that he should be obliged to make a woman of himself!"

Mr. Hunt and his fellow-travellers had not been many days at the Arickara village, when rumors began to circulate that the Sioux had followed them up, and that a war party, four or five hundred in num-

[6] Cf. Bradbury, *Travels*, 133, 178, and Brackenridge, *Journal*, 116–17.

ber, were lurking somewhere in the neighborhood. These rumors produced much embarrassment in the camp. The white hunters were deterred from venturing forth in quest of game, neither did the leaders think it proper to expose them to such a risk. The Arickaras, too, who had suffered greatly in their wars with this cruel and ferocious tribe, were roused to increased vigilance, and stationed mounted scouts upon the neighboring hills. This, however, is a general precaution among the tribes of the prairies. Those immense plains present a horizon like the ocean, so that any object of importance can be descried afar, and information communicated to a great distance. The scouts are stationed on the hills, therefore, to look out both for game and for enemies, and are, in a manner, living telegraphs conveying their intelligence by concerted signs. If they wish to give notice of a herd of buffalo in the plain beyond, they gallop backwards and forwards abreast, on the summit of the hill. If they perceive an enemy at hand, they gallop to and fro, crossing each other; at sight of which the whole village flies to arms.

Such an alarm was given in the afternoon of the 15th.[7] Four scouts were seen crossing and recrossing each other at full gallop, on the summit of a hill about two miles distant down the river. The cry was up that the Sioux were coming. In an instant the village was in an uproar. Men, women, and children were all brawling and shouting; dogs barking, yelping and howling. Some of the warriors ran for the horses to gather and drive them in from the prairie, some for their weapons. As fast as they could arm and equip they sallied forth; some on horseback, some on foot. Some hastily arrayed in their war dress, with coronets of fluttering feathers, and their bodies smeared with paint; others naked and only furnished with the weapons they had snatched up. The women and children gathered on the tops of the lodges and heightened the confusion of the scene by their vociferation. Old men who could no longer bear arms took similar stations, and harangued the warriors as they passed, exhorting them to valorous deeds. Some of the veterans took arms themselves, and sallied forth with tottering steps. In this way, the savage chivalry of the village to the number of five hundred, poured forth, helter-skelter, riding and running, with hideous yells and warwhoops, like so many bedlamites or demoniacs let loose.

After a while the tide of war rolled back, but with far less uproar. Either it had been a false alarm, or the enemy had retreated on finding

[7] June 15. The date is confirmed by Bradbury and Brackenridge.

themselves discovered, and quiet was restored to the village.[8] The white hunters continuing to be fearful of ranging this dangerous neighborhood, fresh provisions began to be scarce in the camp. As a substitute, therefore, for venison and buffalo meat, the travellers had to purchase a number of dogs to be shot and cooked for the supply of the camp. Fortunately, however chary the Indians might be of their horses, they were liberal of their dogs. In fact, these animals swarm about an Indian village as they do about a Turkish town. Not a family but has two or three dozen belonging to it, of all sizes and colors; some of a superior breed are used for hunting; others, to draw the sledge, while others, of a mongrel breed, and idle vagabond nature, are fattened for food. They are supposed to be descended from the wolf, and retain something of his savage but cowardly temper, howling rather than barking; showing their teeth and snarling on the slightest provocation, but sneaking away on the least attack.[9]

The excitement of the village continued from day to day. On the day following the alarm just mentioned, several parties arrived from different directions, and were met and conducted by some of the braves to the council lodge, where they reported the events and success of their expeditions, whether of war or hunting; which news was afterwards promulgated throughout the village, by certain old men who acted as heralds or town criers. Among the parties which arrived was one that had been among the Snake nation stealing horses, and returned crowned with success. As they passed in triumph through the village they were cheered by the men, women, and children, collected as usual on the tops of the lodges, and were exhorted by the Nestors of the village to be generous in their dealings with the white men.[10]

The evening was spent in feasting and rejoicing among the relations of the successful warriors; but the sounds of grief and wailing were heard from the hills adjacent to the village—the lamentations of women who had lost some relative in the foray.

An Indian village is subject to continual agitations and excitements. The next day arrived a deputation of braves from the Cheyenne or Shienne nation; a broken tribe, cut up, like the Arickaras, by wars with the

[8] For his account of the Sioux alarm, Irving combined details from Bradbury, *Travels*, 135–36, and Brackenridge, *Journal*, 117–18.

[9] Information about Indian dogs and the purchase of dogs for food is derived from Bradbury, *Travels*, 135, and Brackenridge, *Journal*, 114–15.

[10] From Brackenridge, *Journal*, 118–19.

Sioux, and driven to take refuge among the Black Hills, near the sources of the Cheyenne River, from which they derive their name. One of these deputies was magnificently arrayed in a buffalo robe, on which various figures were fancifully embroidered with split quills dyed red and yellow; and the whole was fringed with the slender hoofs of young fawns, that rattled as he walked.[11]

The arrival of this deputation was the signal for another of those ceremonials which occupy so much of Indian life; for no being is more courtly and punctilious, and more observing[12] of etiquette and formality than an American savage.

The object of the deputation was to give notice of an intended visit of the Shienne (or Cheyenne) tribe to the Arikara village in the course of fifteen days.[13] To this visit Mr. Hunt looked forward to procure additional horses for his journey; all his bargaining being ineffectual in obtaining a sufficient supply from the Arickaras. Indeed, nothing could prevail upon the latter to part with their prime horses, which had been trained to buffalo hunting.

As Mr. Hunt would have to abandon his boats at this place, Mr. Lisa now offered to purchase them, and such of his merchandise as was superfluous, and to pay him in horses to be obtained at a fort belonging to the Missouri Fur Company, situated at the Mandan villages, about a hundred and fifty miles further up the river. A bargain was promptly made, and Mr. Lisa and Mr. Crooks, with several companions, set out for the fort to procure the horses. They returned, after upwards of a fortnight's absence, bringing with them the stipulated number of horses.[14] Still the

---

[11] Bradbury describes this robe in these words: "One of these Indians was covered with a buffalo robe, curiously ornamented with figures worked with much taste, and the border of the robe entirely hung round with the hoofs of young fawns, which at every movement made a noise much resembling that of the rattlesnake when that animal is irritated." *Travels*, 139. He attempted unsuccessfully to buy it. The next day, however, McClellan bought it and then sold it to Bradbury "for silver ornaments and other articles, which amount to about ten dollars."

[12] Less correctly, *observant* in first edition.   [13] Brackenridge, *Journal*, 119.

[14] The trip to the Missouri Fur Company fort Irving condenses from Bradbury, *Travels*, 138–68; see also Brackenridge, *Journal*, 132–42. Lisa left with a party by boat on June 19. On the same day, Hunt sent a group headed by Ramsay Crooks. Their guide, says Bradbury, who was a member of this group, was "a person of the name of Jones, who was acquainted with the whole of the country betwixt the Mandans and Aricaras." (Jones was Benjamin Jones, who had spent two years on the upper Missouri before joining Hunt; see Porter, "Roll of Overland Astorians," *Oregon Historical Quarterly*, Vol. XXXIV [1933], 108.) They reached the fort on June 22 and were

cavalry was not sufficiently numerous to convey the party and baggage[15] and merchandise, and a few days more were required to complete the arrangements for the journey.

On the 9th of July,[16] just before daybreak, a great noise and vocifera-tion was [sic] heard in the village. This being the usual Indian hour of attack and surprise, and the Sioux being known to be in the neighbor-hood, the camp was instantly on the alert. As the day broke Indians were descried in considerable number on the bluffs, three or four miles down the river. The noise and agitation in the village continued. The tops of the lodges were crowded with the inhabitants, all earnestly looking towards the hills, and keeping up a vehement chattering. Presently an Indian warrior galloped past the camp towards the village, and in a little while the legions began to pour forth.

The truth of the matter was now ascertained. The Indians upon the distant hills were three hundred Arickara braves, returning home from a foray. They had met the war party of Sioux who had been so long hovering about the neighborhood, had fought them[17] the day before, killed several, and defeated the rest with the loss of but two or three of their own men and about a dozen wounded; and they were now halting at a distance until their comrades in the village should come forth to meet them, and swell the parade of their triumphal entry. The warrior who had galloped past the camp was the leader of the party hastening home to give tidings of his victory.

Preparations were now made for this great martial ceremony. All the finery and equipments of the warriors were sent forth to them, that they might appear to the greatest advantage. Those, too, who had re-mained at home, tasked their wardrobes and toilets to do honor to the procession.

The Arickaras generally go naked, but like all savages, they have their gala dress, of which they are not a little vain. This usually consists of a gray surcoat and leggins of the dressed skin of the antelope, re-sembling chamois leather, and embroidered with porcupine quills bril-

greeted by Reuben Lewis, brother of Meriwether Lewis. After five days, Crooks left, June 27, on the return journey with the extra horses. On July 6, Lisa set out by boat for the Arikara camp, which he reached the next day. According to Bradbury, Hunt had by now acquired about eighty horses, but he still hoped to obtain additional animals from the Cheyennes. Brackenridge, *Journal*, 142.

[15] *The baggage* in first edition. [16] According to Bradbury, the date was July 10.
[17] *Fought with them* in first edition.

liantly dyed. A buffalo robe is thrown over the right shoulder, and across the left is slung a quiver of arrows. They wear gay coronets of plumes, particularly those of the swan; but the feathers of the black eagle are considered the most worthy, being a sacred bird among the Indian warriors. He who has killed an enemy in his own land, is entitled to drag at his heels a fox-skin attached to each moccasin; and he who has slain a grizzly bear, wears a necklace of his claws, the most glorious trophy that a hunter can exhibit.[18]

An Indian toilet is an operation of some toil and trouble; the warrior often has to paint himself from head to foot, and is extremely capricious and difficult to please, as to the hideous distribution of streaks and colors. A great part of the morning, therefore, passed away before there were any signs of the distant pageant. In the meantime a profound stillness reigned over the village. Most of the inhabitants had gone forth; others remained in mute expectation. All sports and occupations were suspended, excepting that in the lodges the painstaking squaws were silently busied in preparing[19] the repasts for the warriors.

It was near noon that a mingled sound of voices and rude music, faintly heard from a distance, gave notice that the procession was on the march. The old men and such of the squaws as could leave their employments hastened forth to meet it. In a little while it emerged from behind a hill, and had a wild and picturesque appearance as it came moving over the summit in measured step, and to the cadence of songs and savage instruments; the warlike standards and trophies flaunting aloft, and the feathers, and paint, and silver ornaments of the warriors glaring and glittering in the sunshine.

The pageant had really something chivalrous in its arrangement. The Arickaras are divided into several bands, each bearing the name of some animal or bird, as the buffalo, the bear, the dog, the pheasant. The present party consisted of four of these bands, one of which was the dog, the most esteemed in war, being composed of young men under thirty, and noted for prowess. It is engaged on the most desperate occasions. The bands marched in separate bodies under their several leaders. The warriors on foot came first, in platoons of ten or twelve abreast; then the horsemen. Each band bore as an ensign a spear or bow

---

[18] This paragraph Irving paraphrases from an account by Brackenridge, *Journal*, 120–21, of the customs of the Arikaras.

[19] *Busied preparing* in first edition.

decorated with beads, porcupine quills, and painted feathers. Each bore its trophies of scalps, elevated on poles, their long black locks streaming in the wind. Each was accompanied by its rude music and minstrelsy. In this way the procession extended nearly a quarter of a mile. The warriors were variously armed, some few with guns, others with bows and arrows, and war-clubs; all had shields of buffalo hide, a kind of defense generally used by the Indians of the open prairies, who have not the covert of trees and forests to protect them. They were painted in the most savage style. Some had the stamp of a red hand across their mouths, a sign that they had drunk the life-blood of a foe!

As they drew near to the village the old men and the women began to meet them, and now a scene ensued that proved the fallacy of the old fable of Indian apathy and stoicism. Parents and children, husbands and wives, brothers and sisters met with the most rapturous expressions of joy; while wailings and lamentations were heard from the relatives of the killed and wounded. The procession, however, continued on with slow and measured step, in cadence to the solemn chant, and the warriors maintained their fixed and stern demeanor.

Between two of the principal chiefs rode a young warrior who had distinguished himself in the battle. He was severely wounded, so as with difficulty to keep on his horse; but he preserved a serene and steadfast countenance, as if perfectly unharmed. His mother had heard of his condition. She broke through the throng, and rushing up, threw her arms around him and wept aloud. He kept up the spirit and demeanor of a warrior to the last, but expired shortly after he had reached his home.

The village was now a scene of the utmost festivity and triumph. The banners, and trophies, and scalps, and painted shields were elevated on poles near the lodges. There were war-feasts, and scalp-dances, with warlike songs and savage music; all the inhabitants were arrayed in their festal dresses; while the old heralds went round from lodge to lodge, promulgating with loud voices the events of the battle and the exploits of the various warriors.[20]

Such was the boisterous revelry of the village; but sounds of another kind were heard on the surrounding hills; piteous wailings of the women, who had retired thither to mourn in darkness and solitude for those

[20] Both Bradbury, *Travels*, 168–71, and Brackenridge, *Journal*, 142–45, narrate the return of the Arikara warriors. Irving draws details from both.

who had fallen in battle. There the poor mother of the youthful warrior who had returned home in triumph but to die, gave full vent to the anguish of a mother's heart. How much does this custom among the Indian women of repairing to the hilltops in the night, and pouring forth their wailings for the dead, call to mind the beautiful and affecting passage of Scripture, "In Rama was there a voice heard, lamentation, and weeping, and great mourning, Rachel weeping for her children, and would not be comforted, because they are not."[21]

[21] Jeremiah 31:15.

Wilderness of the Far West — Great American Desert
Parched Seasons — Black Hills — Rocky Mountains
Wandering and Predatory Hordes
Speculations on What May Be the Future Population
Apprehended Dangers — A Plot to Desert — Rose the Interpreter
His Sinister Character — Departure from the Arickara Village

WHILE Mr. Hunt was diligently preparing for his arduous journey, some of his men began to lose heart at the perilous prospect before them; but before we accuse them of want of spirit, it is proper to consider the nature of the wilderness into which they were about to adventure.[1] It was a region almost as vast and trackless as the ocean, and, at the time of which we treat, but little known, excepting through the vague accounts of Indian hunters. A part of their route would lay [*sic*] across an immense tract, stretching north and south for hundreds of miles along the foot of the Rocky Mountains, and drained by the tributary streams of the Missouri and the Mississippi. This region, which resembles one of the immeasurable steppes of Asia, has not inaptly been termed "the great American desert."[2] It spreads forth into undulating and treeless plains, and desolate sandy wastes wearisome to the eye from their extent and monotony, and which are supposed by geologists to have formed the ancient floor of the ocean, countless ages since, when its primeval waves beat against the granite bases of the Rocky Mountains.

It is a land where no man permanently abides; for, in certain seasons

---

[1] Irving's sources for the following discussion of the western wilderness have not been determined; but he read Edwin James's account of Long's expedition, which contains an abundance of information on the same subject, and he also must have read an extract from Brackenridge's *Views of Louisiana*, which was added to the *Journal* as an appendix; see Thwaites (ed.), *Early Western Travels*, VI, 153–63. Echoes from this appear in the present chapter.

[2] The idea that the area up to the Rocky Mountains was a vast desert was firmly embeddel in the writings of explorers such as Pike and Long, as well as in the attitudes that people held regarding the West. See Henry Nash Smith, *Virgin Land*, chap. XVI, for a survey of the garden *versus* desert concept. See also Walter Prescott Webb, *The Great Plains*, chap. V, sec. 2.

of the year there is no food either for the hunter or his steed. The herbage is parched and withered; the brooks and streams are dried up; the buffalo, the elk and the deer have wandered to distant parts keeping within the verge of expiring verdure, and leaving behind them a vast uninhabited solitude, seamed by ravines, the beds of former torrents, but now serving only to tantalize and increase the thirst of the traveller.

Occasionally the monotony of this vast wilderness is interrupted by mountainous belts of sand and limestone, broken into confused masses; with precipitous cliffs and yawning ravines, looking like the ruins of a world; or is traversed by lofty and barren ridges of rock, almost impassable, like those denominated the Black Hills. Beyond these rise the stern barriers of the Rocky Mountains, the limits, as it were, of the Atlantic world. The rugged defiles and deep valleys of this vast chain form sheltering places for restless and ferocious bands of savages, many of them the remnants of tribes, once inhabitants of the praires, but broken up by war and violence, and who carry into their mountain haunts the fierce passions and reckless habits of desperadoes.

Such is the nature of this immense wilderness of the far West; which apparently defies cultivation, and the habitation of civilized life. Some portions of it along the rivers may partially be subdued by agriculture, others may form vast pastoral tracts, like those of the East; but it is to be feared that a great part of it will form a lawless interval between the abodes of civilized man, like the wastes of the ocean or the deserts of Arabia; and, like them, be subject to the depredations of the marauder. Here may spring up new and mongrel races, like new formations in geology, the amalgamation of the "debris" and "abrasions" of former races, civilized and savage; the remains of broken and almost extinguished tribes; the descendants of wandering hunters and trappers; of fugitives from the Spanish and American frontiers; of adventurers and desperadoes of every class and country, yearly ejected from the bosom of society into the wilderness. We are contributing incessantly to swell this singular and heterogeneous cloud of wild population that is to hang about our frontier, by the transfer of whole tribes from[3] the east of the Mississippi to the great wastes of the far West.[4] Many of these

[3] The first edition reads *whole tribes of savages from.*

[4] This sentence reflects Irving's own journey beyond the frontier in 1832. Two years earlier, Congress had passed the Indian Removal Bill, which required tribes to move from the eastern to the western side of the Mississippi River. Clashes between the Cherokees and Creeks and white squatters led in 1832 to the appointment of three

bear with them the smart of real or fancied injuries; many consider themselves expatriated beings, wrongfully exiled from their hereditary homes, and the sepulchres of their fathers, and cherish a deep and abiding animosity against the race that has dispossessed them. Some may gradually become pastoral hordes, like those rude and migratory people, half shepherd, half warrior, who, with their flocks and herds, roam the plains of upper Asia; but others, it is to be apprehended, will become predatory bands, mounted on the fleet steeds of the prairies, with the open plains for their marauding grounds, and the mountains for their retreats and lurking-places. Here they may resemble those great hordes of the North, "Gog and Magog with their bands," that haunted the gloomy imaginations of the prophets. "A great company and a mighty host, all riding upon horses, and warring upon those nations which were at rest, and dwelt peaceably, and had gotten cattle and goods."[5]

The Spaniards changed the whole character and habits of the Indians when they brought the horse among them. In Chili, Tucuman, and other parts, it has converted them, we are told, into Tartar-like tribes, and enabled them to keep the Spaniards out of their country, and even to make it dangerous for them to venture far from their towns and settlements. Are we not in danger of producing some such state of things in the boundless regions of the far West? That these are not mere fanciful and extravagant suggestions we have sufficient proofs in the dangers already experienced by the traders to the Spanish mart of Santa Fé, and to the distant posts of the fur companies. These are obliged to proceed in armed caravans, and are subject to murderous attacks from bands of Pawnees, Camanches, and Blackfeet, that come scouring upon them in their weary march across the plains, or lie in wait for them among the passes of the mountains.[6]

---

commissioners who were to try to adjust the problems involved. One of these men was Henry L. Ellsworth, whom Irving accompanied on his mission. See Ellsworth's *Washington Irving on the Prairie*, x–xi.

[5] See Ezekiel 38 and 39.

[6] Irving's "Notes Concerning the Far West, 1833" shows that in preparing to write about the West he read, among other books, Mrs. Mary Austin Holley's *Texas: Observations, Historical, Geographical and Descriptive*. One of his notes is a quotation about Comanche Indians from page 89 of Mrs. Holley's book. Another reads: "This inland trader now passes in large caravans, from St. Louis, in Missouri, to S'Fe, in N Mexico, a wilderness infested with Indians." *Ibid.*, 85. Irving abbreviates *Santa Fe* and *New Mexico* and omits *through* before "a wilderness." Seligman Collection of Irvingiana, New York Public Library.

We are wandering, however, into excursive speculations, when our intention was merely to give an idea of the nature of the wilderness which Mr. Hunt was about to traverse; and which at that time was far less known than at present; though it still remains in a great measure an unknown land.[7] We cannot be surprised, therefore, that some of the least resolute of his party should feel dismay at the thoughts of adventuring into this perilous wilderness under the uncertain guidance of three hunters,[8] who had merely passed once through the country and might have forgotten the landmarks. Their apprehensions were aggravated by some of Lisa's followers, who, not being engaged in the expedition, took a mischievous pleasure in exaggerating its dangers. They painted in strong colors, to the poor Canadian voyageurs, the risk they would run of perishing with hunger and thirst; of being cut off by war parties of the Sioux who scoured the plains; of having their horses stolen by the Upsarokas[9] or Crows, who infested the skirts of the Rocky Mountains; or of being butchered by the Blackfeet, who lurked among the defiles. In a word, there was little chance of their getting alive across the mountains; and even if they did, those three guides knew nothing of the howling wilderness that lay beyond.

The apprehensions thus awakened in the minds of some of the men came well-nigh proving detrimental to the expedition. Some of them determined to desert, and to make their way back to St. Louis. They accordingly purloined several weapons and a barrel of gunpowder, as ammunition for their enterprise, and buried them in the river bank, intending to seize one of the boats, and make off in the night. Fortunately their plot was overheard by John Day, the Kentuckian, and com-

---

[7] The Overland Astorians were the first organized expedition to move into this wilderness area across South Dakota and Wyoming.

[8] Hoback, Robinson, and Reznor.

[9] Absaroka was the name by which the Crows designated themselves. The name means "crow or bird-people," which the French trappers rendered *gens des corbeaux*. The Absaroka Range, forming the eastern boundary of the Yellowstone National Park, commemorates this name. Although the Crows wandered east of the Continental Divide from as far south as the Laramie River in southern Wyoming to as far north as the Musselshell River in Montana, they centered on the area east of the Wind River Mountains and on the borders of the Wind River, the Big Horn, the Powder, and the Yellowstone. Linguistically they are of Siouan stock. Today they are on a reservation on the Big Horn River. Hunt would encounter these people as he moved west. See Swanton, *Indian Tribes*, 390–91.

municated to the partners, who took quiet and effectual means to frustrate it.[10]

The dangers to be apprehened from the Crow Indians had not been overrated by the camp gossips. These savages, through whose mountain haunts the party would have to pass, were noted for daring and excursive habits, and great dexterity in horse stealing. Mr. Hunt, therefore, considered himself fortunate in having met with a man who might be of great use to him in any intercourse he might have with the tribe. This was a wandering individual named Edward Rose,[11] whom he had picked

[10] Irving had this from Bradbury, *Travels*, 180–81. The powder cask belonged to Bradbury. As a sequel to this theft, Lisa later, in St. Louis, delivered to Bradbury a letter from Hunt, which informed him "that after my departure from the Aricaras, whilst the men were still assembled to watch our boats descend [cf. *ibid.*, 183], he addressed them on the subject of my cask of powder, which was stolen, and with such effect, that one of the Canadians came privately to his tent the night following, and informed him where it was buried in the bank of the river. Mr. Hunt caused a search to be made the day after, and found it. As Mr. Lisa was in want of powder, he bought it, and paid me for it on his return." *Ibid.*, 199.

[11] Exactly when Rose joined the expedition cannot be determined. He may have joined at St. Louis or anywhere between there and the Arikara villages. His name first appears in the expedition's account books, however, on June 13, 1811, at the villages, but this does not mean that he had not joined earlier.

Rose was of mixed blood; his mother was half-Cherokee and half-Negro, and his father a white man. A good deal of what we know of Rose appears in *Astoria* and in Irving's *Adventures of Captain Bonneville*. He may have ascended the Missouri as early as 1807 or 1809, and not long thereafter went to live among the Crows, with whom he remained in all likelihood until shortly before he joined Hunt. The bad light in which he appears in *Astoria* may be unjustified, and, although Rose had a doubtful reputation, "the singular thing is," remarks Chittenden, "that everything definite that is known of him is entirely to his credit." *History of the American Fur Trade*, II, 685.

Rose's purchases at the Arikara villages may be given as an example of the goods obtained from the commissary by men in the expedition. On July 8 he bought one yard of green cloth, $5.00; one-half yard of blue cloth, $2.00; one yard of blue flannel, $2.00; three and one-third pounds of balls, $1.75; one and one-half pounds of powder, $2.25; four scalping knives, $2.00; one-half pound of white beads, $2.00; one ax, $5.00; a coffee kettle, $6.00; a handkerchief, $2.00; six pipes, $1.50; two-thirds of a pound of beads, $0.34; one-half pound of powder, $0.50; total, $32.34. On July 15 he bought one carrot of tobacco for $3.00. On July 16 further purchases were two dozen brass rings, $1.00; one handkerchief, $2.00; a quarter-pound of blue beads, $1.00; three fathoms of gartering, $1.50. The next day he also bought one "cartouch" knife, $0.75; a bridle, $2.00. Later, after leaving the Arikara Indians, he bought a cotton shirt on August 29 for $4.00, and on September 1 a half-yard of blue cloth, $2.00; four dozen buttons, $3.00; four "green carvers" (Green River knives?), $6.00; three horse bells, $3.00; and three pounds of beads, $12.00. See Hunt's account book. Some of these items were intended to procure for him the favors of Indian women.

For Rose's career after he left Hunt, see Chittenden, *op. cit.*, II, 684–88; Captain up somewhere on the Missouri—one of those anomalous beings found on the frontier, who seem to have neither kin nor country. He had lived some time among the Crows, so as to become acquainted with their language and customs; and was, withal, a dogged, sullen, silent fellow, with a sinister aspect, and more of the savage than the civilized man in his appearance. He was engaged to serve in general as a hunter, but as guide and interpreter when they should reach the country of the Crows.

On the 18th of July,[12] Mr. Hunt took up his line of march by land from the Arickara village, leaving Mr. Lisa and Mr. Nuttall there, where they intended to await the expected arrival of Mr. Henry from the Rocky Mountains. As to Messrs. Bradbury and Breckenridge they had departed some days previously, on a voyage down the river to St. Louis, with a detachment from Mr. Lisa's party. With all his exertions, Mr. Hunt had been unable to obtain a sufficient number of horses for the accommodation of all his people. His cavalcade consisted of eighty-two horses,[13] most of them heavily laden with Indian goods, beaver traps,

Reuben Holmes, "The Five Scalps," St. Louis *Reveille*, July 8–20, 1848, reprinted in Missouri Historical Society, *Glimpses of the Past* (ed. by Stella M. Drumm), V (1938), 3–54; "Edward Rose, the First White Renegade of the Crows," *Contributions to the Historical Society of Montana*, Vol. VIII (1917), 156–61; *Dictionary of American Biography*, XVI, 157–58; Irving, *The Adventures of Captain Bonneville*, 166–68, 167n., 168n.

[12] On the previous day, Hunt took time on the eve of his cross-country journey to write to Astor. Apparently, all that is known of what Hunt wrote is contained in a letter from Astor to President Jefferson, where what Hunt had written is presumably summarized. Astor wrote: "The last account which I had of the party which ascended the Missouri was by letter of 17 July last, about 180 miles below the Mandan Village, where they left the Missouri, and took the Big River in a southern course, this being recommended as nearer and easier to the south branch of the Columbia [i.e., the Snake River] than the route taken by Mr. Lewis: they were well provided, and had procured near a hundred horses to transport their baggage.—The accounts as to ultimate success were fair and encouraging, and they had no doubt of meeting their friends who went by sea." John Jacob Astor, New York, March 14, 1812, to Thomas Jefferson, in Library of Congress, Thomas Jefferson Papers, Vol. CXCV, January 27–April 30, 1812, reprinted in Porter, *John Jacob Astor*, I, 509.

With Hunt's departure from the Arikara Indians, Irving turned from the accounts of the expedition by Bradbury and Brackenridge, who returned down the river to St. Louis, to Hunt's "Journal," available to him in a French translation published in Paris (1821). A translation appears in Rollins (ed.), *Discovery of the Oregon Trail*, Appendix A, 281–308, where it appears under the title "Journey of Mr. Hunt and His Companions from Saint Louis to the Mouth of the Columbia" (cited hereafter as Hunt's "Journal"). The date of July 18 is confirmed by this source.

[13] Astor's statement above that Hunt had "near a hundred horses" is an overestimate.

ammunition, Indian corn, corn meal and other necessaries. Each of the partners was mounted, and a horse was allotted to the interpreter, Pierre Dorion, for the transportation of his luggage and his two children. His squaw, for the most part of the time, trudged on foot, like the residue of the party; nor did any of the men show more patience and fortitude than this resolute woman in enduring fatigue and hardship.[14]

The veteran trappers and voyageurs of Lisa's party shook their heads as their comrades set out, and took leave of them as of doomed men; and even Lisa himself gave it as his opinion, after the travellers had departed, they would never reach the shores of the Pacific, but would either perish with hunger in the wilderness, or be cut off by the savages.

Hunt's "Journal" gives, as does Irving, eighty-two horses. Rollins (ed.), *op. cit.*, 291. Later, Hunt acquired thirty-six more animals from the Cheyenne Indians.

[14] "All travelled on foot except the company's partners and the woman or squaw." *Ibid.*, 281. This meant that six horses were ridden. Assuming an equal number of unmounted spare riding horses, which may not have been the case, at least seventy horses, and perhaps more, were loaded, which gives a good idea of the large amount of supplies being transported, but understandable in view of the fact that sixty-four or sixty-five people made up the cavalcade and that trading goods had to be carried also. The addition of thirty-six horses from the Cheyennes later on alleviated some of the walking.

Summer Weather of the Prairies — Purity of the Atmosphere
Canadians on the March — Sickness in the Camp — Big River
Vulgar Nomenclature — Suggestions About the Original Indian Names
Camp of Cheyennes — Trade for Horses
Character of the Cheyennes — Their Horsemanship
Historical Anecdotes of the Tribe

THE course taken by Mr. Hunt was at first to the northwest, but soon turned and kept generally to the southwest, to avoid the country infested by the Blackfeet. His route took him across some of the tributary streams of the Missouri, and over immense prairies, bounded only by the horizon, and destitute of trees. It was now the height of summer, and these naked plains would be intolerable to the traveller were it not for the breezes which sweep over them during the fervor of the day, bringing with them tempering airs from the distant mountains. To the prevalence of these breezes, and to the want of all leafy covert, may we also attribute the freedom from those flies and other insects so tormenting to man and beast during the summer months, in the lower plains, which are bordered and interspersed with woodland.

The monotony of these immense landscapes, also, would be as wearisome as that of the ocean, were it not relieved in some degree by the purity and elasticity of the atmosphere, and the beauty of the heavens. The sky has that delicious blue for which the sky of Italy is renowned; the sun shines with a splendor unobscured by any cloud or vapor, and a starlight night on the prairies is glorious.[1] This purity and elasticity of atmosphere increases as the traveller approaches the mountains and gradually rises into more elevated prairies.[2]

On the second day[3] of the journey, Mr. Hunt arranged the party into small and convenient messes, distributing among them the camp-kettles. The encampments at night were as before; some sleeping under tents, and others bivouacking in the open air. The Canadians proved

---

[1] Another reflection of Irving's personal experience on the prairie.
[2] The first edition reads *into the more elevated prairies.*   [3] July 19.

Route of Overland Astorians, July 18, 1811–February 15, 1812

as patient of toil and hardship on the land as on the water; indeed, nothing could surpass the patience and good-humor of these men upon the march. They were the cheerful drudges of the party, loading and unloading the horses, pitching the tents, making the fires, cooking; in short, performing all those household and menial offices which the Indians usually assign to the squaws; and, like the squaws, they left all the hunting and fighting to others. A Canadian has but little affection for the exercise of the rifle.

The progress of the party was but slow for the first few days. Some of the men were indisposed;[4] Mr. Crooks, especially, was so unwell that he could not keep on his horse. A rude kind of litter was, therefore, prepared for him, consisting of two long poles, fixed, one on each side of two horses, with a matting between them, on which he reclined at full length, and was protected from the sun by a canopy of boughs.

On the evening of the 23d (July) they encamped on the banks of what they term Big River;[5] and here we cannot but pause to lament the

[4] Hunt's "Journal," 281, states: "Several members of the party being indisposed, a halt was made until August 5." Information about Crooks's illness comes from an unidentified source, perhaps from Crooks himself.

[5] This river appears on the map (reproduced herein) accompanying the first edition of *Astoria*. Its modern name is Grand River, located in northern South Dakota. Above it a few miles, on the west bank of the Missouri, were located the Arikara villages. The

218

stupid, commonplace, and often ribald names entailed upon the rivers and other features of the great West, by traders and settlers. As the aboriginal tribes of these magnificent regions are yet in existence, the Indian names might easily be recovered; which, beside[s] being in general more sonorous and musical, would remain mementoes of the primitive lords of the soil, of whom in a little while scarce any traces will be left. Indeed, it is to be wished that the whole of our country could be rescued, as much as possible, from the wretched nomenclature inflicted upon it, by ignorant and vulgar minds; and this might be done, in a great degree, by restoring the Indian names, wherever significant and euphonious. As there appears to be a spirit of research abroad in respect to our aboriginal antiquities, we would suggest, as a worthy object of enterprise, a map, or maps, of every part of our country, giving the Indian names wherever they could be ascertained. Whoever achieves such an object worthily, will leave a monument to his own reputation.

To return from this digression. As the travellers were now in a country abounding with buffalo, they remained for several days encamped upon the banks of Big River, to obtain a supply of provisions, and to give the invalids time to recruit.[6]

On the second day of their sojourn, as Ben Jones, John Day, and others of the hunters were in pursuit of game, they came upon an Indian camp on the open prairie, near to a small stream which ran through a ravine. The tents or lodges were of dressed buffalo skins, sewn together and stretched on tapering pine poles, joined at top, but radiating

Astoria map shows Hunt's route starting from below Big River, which is obviously an error. The direction of the indicated route is correct, however, for Irving states at the beginning of this chapter that the course was at first northwest but then turned southwest, and with this latter direction Hunt's "Journal" agrees. The "Journal" also states that before coming to Big River they reached the Ramparée (i.e., Rampart or Owl Creek, Bradbury's "Ma-ra-pa"; see his *Travels*, 127 and 127n.), "a small watercourse which empties into the Missouri below the Aricaras' village." *Travels*, 281. "On the 18th," the "Journal" continues, "camp was made near a small stream a short distance from its junction with the Big River . . . which was crossed on the 21st." In Hunt's account book, entries appear for July 18 at the Ramparée and for July 20 at Big River.

[6] An entry in one of two notebooks Irving made in 1835 while preparing *Astoria* shows that he wanted more information about the illness of Hunt's men. This notation reads: "Sickness in the camp at Big River (5 days after leaving Rickarees) What was the nature of the sickness—How was the weather on the prairies? Did they suffer from flies—musquitoes[?] No." Seligman Collection of Irvingiana, New York Public Library. Note that in the first paragraph of this chapter, Irving comments on the absence of flies.

at bottom, so as to form a circle capable of admitting fifty persons.[7] Numbers of horses were grazing in the neighborhood of the camp, or straying at large in the prairie; a sight most acceptable to the hunters. After reconnoitring the camp for some time, they ascertained it to belong to a band of Cheyenne Indians,[8] the same that had sent a deputation to the Arickaras. They received the hunters in the most friendly manner; invited them to their lodges, which were more cleanly than Indian lodges are prone to be, and set food before them with true uncivilized hospitality. Several of them accompanied the hunters back to the camp, when a trade was immediately opened. The Cheyennes were astonished and delighted to find a convoy of goods and trinkets thus brought into the very heart of the prairie; while Mr. Hunt and his companions were overjoyed to have an opportunity of obtaining a further supply of horses from these equestrain savages.[9]

During a fortnight that the travellers lingered at this place, their encampment was continually thronged by the Cheyennes. They were a civil, well-behaved people, cleanly in their persons and decorous in their habits. The men were tall, straight and vigorous, with aquiline noses, and high cheek bones. Some were almost as naked as ancient statues, and might have stood as models for a statuary; others had leggins and moccasins of deer-skin, and buffalo robes, which they threw gracefully over their shoulders. In a little while, however, they began to appear in more gorgeous array, tricked out in the finery obtained from the white men; bright cloths, brass rings, beads of various colors; and happy was he who could render himself hideous with vermilion.

[7] That Irving is following Hunt's "Journal" is evident from a comparison with Hunt's statement: "Their tents are made of the skins of this animal [buffalo] well-prepared, carefully sewn together and supported by poles which are joined at the top; they can hold fifty people." See "Journal," 281. But much more concerning the Cheyennes is in *Astoria* than Irving could have found in Hunt.

[8] The Cheyennes occupied many different areas in the West, from Minnesota before the eighteenth century to as far as southern Colorado. After moving west of the Missouri, they lived along the Cheyenne River and near the Black Hills of South Dakota. Linguistically they were remotely connected with the Algonquin family. Their name is from the Dakota and means "people of alien speech." See Swanton, *Indian Tribes*, 278–80.

[9] "I there bought thirty-six horses . . . at a much better price than at the Aricaras' village. The camp was in the middle of the prairie near a little stream." Hunt, "Journal," 281. Rollins tentatively identifies the stream as a branch of Firesteel Creek or some other tributary of the Grand River. *Discovery of the Oregon Trail*, 313n.

The travellers had frequent occasion to admire the skill and grace with which these Indians managed their horses. Some of them made a striking display when mounted; themselves and their steeds decorated in gala style; for the Indians often bestow more finery upon their horses than upon themselves. Some would hang around the necks, or rather on the breasts of their horses, the most precious ornaments they had obtained from the white men; others interwove feathers in their manes and tails. The Indian horses, too, appear to have an attachment to their wild riders, and indeed it is said that the horses of the prairies readily distinguish an Indian from a white man by the smell, and give a preference to the former. Yet the Indians, in general, are hard riders, and, however they may value their horses, treat them with great roughness and neglect. Occasionally the Cheyennes joined the white hunters in pursuit of the elk and buffalo; and when in the ardor of the chase, spared neither themselves nor their steeds, scouring the prairies at full speed, and plunging down precipices and frightful ravines that threatened the necks of both horse and horseman. The Indian steed, well trained to the chase, seems as mad as the rider,[10] and pursues the game as eagerly as if it were his natural prey, on the flesh of which he was to banquet.

The history of the Cheyennes is that of many of those wandering tribes of the prairies. They were the remnant of a once powerful people called the Shaways, inhabiting a branch of the Red River which flows into Lake Winnipeg. Every Indian tribe has some rival tribe with which it wages implacable hostility. The deadly enemies of the Shaways were the Sioux, who, after a long course of warfare, proved too powerful for them, and drove them across the Missouri. They again took root near the Warricanne Creek, and established themselves there in a fortified village.

The Sioux still followed them with deadly animosity; dislodged them from their village, and compelled them to take refuge in the Black Hills, near the upper waters of the Sheyenne or Cheyenne River. Here they lost even their name, and became known among the French colonists by that of the river they frequented.

The heart of the tribe was now broken; its numbers were greatly thinned by their harassing wars. They no longer attempted to establish themselves in any permanent abode that might be an object of attack to

10 *His rider* in first edition.

their cruel foes. They gave up the cultivation of the fruits of the earth, and became a wandering tribe, subsisting by the chase, and following the buffalo in its migrations.

Their only possessions were horses, which they caught on the prairies, or reared, or captured on predatory incursions into the Mexican territories, as has already been mentioned. With some of these they repaired once a year to the Arickara villages, exchanged them for corn, beans, pumpkins, and articles of European merchandise, and then returned into the heart of the prairies.[11]

Such are the fluctuating fortunes of these savage nations. War, famine, pestilence, together or singly, bring down their strength and thin their numbers. Whole tribes are rooted up from their native places, wander for a time about these immense regions, become amalgamated with other tribes, or disappear from the face of the earth. There appears to be a tendency to extinction among all the savage nations; and this tendency would seem to have been in operation among the aboriginals of this country long before the advent of the white men, if we may judge from the traces and traditions of ancient populousness in regions which were silent and deserted at the time of the discovery; and from the mysterious and perplexing vestiges of unknown races, predecessors of those found in actual possession, and who must long since have become gradually extinguished or been destroyed. The whole history of the aboriginal population of this country, however, is an enigma, and a grand one—will it ever be solved?

[11] The origin of Irving's knowledge of the Cheyennes has not been determined. The source of European merchandise was fur traders from Missouri and traders from Canada. See A. P. Nasatir (ed.), *Before Lewis and Clark: Documents Illustrating the History of the Missouri, 1785–1804.*

*New Distribution of Horses — Secret Information of Treason in the Camp
Rose the Interpreter — His Perfidious Character — His Plots
Anecdotes of the Crow Indians — Notorious Horse Stealers
Some Account of Rose — A Desperado of the Frontier*

ON the sixth of August[1] the travellers bade farewell to the friendly band of Cheyennes, and resumed their journey. As they had obtained thirty-six additional horses by their recent traffic, Mr. Hunt made a new arrangement. The baggage was made up in smaller loads. A horse was allotted to each of the six prime hunters, and others were distributed among the voyageurs, a horse for every two, so that they could ride and walk alternately.[2] Mr. Crooks being still too feeble to mount the saddle, was carried on a litter.

Their march this day lay among singular hills and knolls of an in-durated red earth, resembling brick, about the bases of which were scattered pumice stones and cinders, the whole bearing traces of the action of fire.[3] In the evening they encamped on a branch of Big River.

They were now out of the tract of country infested by the Sioux, and had advanced such a distance into the interior that Mr. Hunt no longer felt apprehensive of the desertion of any of his men. He was doomed, however, to experience new cause of anxiety. As he was seated in his tent after nightfall, one of the men came to him privately, and informed him that there was mischief brewing in the camp. Edward Rose, the inter-preter, whose sinister looks we have already mentioned, was denounced by this secret informer as a designing, treacherous scoundrel, who was tampering with the fidelity of certain of the men, and instigating them to a flagrant piece of treason.[4] In the course of a few days they would arrive at the mountainous district infested by the Upsarokas or Crows,

---

[1] The date is confirmed by Hunt's "Journal."

[2] From *ibid.*, 281–82.   [3] *Ibid.*, 282.

[4] In his "Journal," Hunt wrote: "We had in our party a hunter of the name of *Rose;* he was a very bad fellow full of daring. We had been warned that he had planned to desert us as soon as we should be near the Absarokas, take with him as many of our men as he could seduce, and steal our horses." *Ibid.*, 284.

the tribe among which Rose was to officiate as interpreter. His plan was that several of the men should join with him, when in that neighborhood, in carrying off a number of the horses with their packages of goods, and deserting to those savages. He assured them of good treatment among the Crows, the principal chiefs and warriors of whom he knew; they would soon become great men among them, and have the finest women, and the daughters of the chiefs for wives; and the horses and goods they carried off would make them rich for life.

The intelligence of this treachery on the part of Rose gave much disquiet to Mr. Hunt, for he knew not how far it might be effective among his men. He had already had proofs that several of them were disaffected to the enterprise, and loath to cross the mountains. He knew also that savage life had charms for many of them, especially the Canadians, who were prone to intermarry and domesticate themselves among the Indians.

And here a word or two concerning the Crows may be of service to the reader, as they will figure occasionally in the succeeding narration.

The tribe consists of four bands, which have their nestling-places in fertile, well-wooded valleys, lying among the Rocky Mountains, and watered by the Big Horse River[5] and its tributary streams; but, though these are properly their homes, where they shelter their old people, their wives, and their children, the men of the tribe are almost continually on the foray and the scamper. They are, in fact, notorious marauders and horse-stealers; crossing and recrossing the mountains, robbing on the one side, and conveying their spoils to the other. Hence, we are told, is derived their name, given to them on account of their unsettled and predatory habits; winging their flight, like the crows, from one side of the mountains to the other, and making free booty of everything that lies in their way. Horses, however, the the especial objects of their depredations, and their skill and audacity in stealing them are said to be astonishing. This is their glory and delight; an accomplished horse-stealer fills up their idea of a hero. Many horses are obtained by them, also, in barter from tribes in and beyond the mountains. They have an absolute passion for this noble animal; beside[s] which he is with them an important object of traffic. Once a year they make a visit to the Mandans, Minatarees, and other tribes of the Missouri, taking with them

[5] This name appears also in the first edition. It is obviously an error for Big Horn River.

droves of horses which they exchange for guns, ammunition, trinkets, vermilion, cloths of bright colors, and various other articles of European manufacture. With these they supply their own wants and caprices, and carry on the internal trade for horses already mentioned.

The plot of Rose to rob and abandon his countrymen when in the heart of the wilderness, and to throw himself into the hands of a horde of savages, may appear strange and improbable to those unacquainted with the singular and anomalous characters that are to be found about the borders. This fellow, it appears, was one of those desperadoes of the frontiers, outlawed by their crimes, who combine the vices of civilized and savage life, and are ten times more barbarous than the Indians with whom they consort. Rose had formerly belonged to one of the gangs of pirates who infested the islands of the Mississippi, plundering boats as they went up and down the river, and who sometimes shifted the scene of their robberies to the shore, waylaying travellers as they returned by land from New Orleans with the proceeds of their downward voyage, plundering them of their money and effects, and often perpetrating the most atrocious murders.

These hordes of villians being broken up and dispersed, Rose had betaken himself to the wilderness, and associated himself with the Crows, whose predatory habits were congenial with his own, had married a woman of the tribe, and, in short, had identified himself with those vagrant savages.

Such was the worthy guide and interpreter, Edward Rose. We give his story, however, not as it was known to Mr. Hunt and his companions at the time, but as it has been subsequently ascertained.[6] Enough was known of the fellow and his dark and perfidious character to put Mr. Hunt upon his guard: still, as there was no knowing how far his plans might have succeeded, and as any rash act might blow the mere smouldering sparks of treason into a sudden blaze, it was thought advisable by those with whom Mr. Hunt consulted, to conceal all knowledge or suspicion of the meditated treachery, but to keep up a vigilant watch upon the movements of Rose, and a strict guard upon the horses at night.

[6] By whom has not come to light.

CHAPTER XXV

Substitute for Fuel on the Prairies — Fossil Trees
Fierceness of the Buffaloes When in Heat — Three Hunters Missing
Signal Fires and Smokes — Uneasiness Concerning the Lost Men
A Plan to Forestall a Rogue — New Arrangement with Rose
Return of the Wanderers

THE plains over which the travellers were journeying continued to be destitute of trees or even shrubs; insomuch that they had to use the dung of the buffalo for fuel, as the Arabs of the desert use that of the camel. This substitute for fuel is universal among the Indians of these upper prairies, and is said to make a fire equal to that of turf. If a few chips are added, it throws out a cheerful and kindly blaze.

These plains, however, had not always been equally destitute of wood, as was evident from the trunks of the trees[1] which the travellers repeatedly met with, some still standing, others lying about in broken fragments, but all in a fossil state, having flourished in times long past. In these singular remains, the original grain of the wood was still so distinct that they could be ascertained to be the ruins of oak trees. Several pieces of the fossil wood were selected by the men to serve as whetstones.[2]

In this part of the journey there was no lack of provisions, for the prairies were covered with immense herds of buffalo. These, in general, are animals of peaceful[3] demeanor, grazing quietly like domestic cattle; but this was the season when they are in heat, and when the bulls are usually[4] fierce and pugnacious. There was accordingly a universal restlessness and commotion throughout the plain; and the amorous herds gave utterance to their feelings in low bellowings that resounded like distant thunder. Here and there fierce duellos took place between rival enamorados; butting their huge shagged fronts together, goring each

[1] The first edition reads *trunks of trees.*
[2] Hunt's "Journal," 282, states: "Many petrifactions were seen; several persons gathered them to use as whetstones."
[3] *Peaceable* in first edition. [4] *Unusually* in first edition.

other with their short black horns, and tearing up the earth with their feet in perfect fury.[5]

In one of the evening halts, Pierre Dorion, the interpreter, together with Carson and Gardpie,[6] two of the hunters, were missing, nor had they returned by morning. As it was supposed they had wandered away in pursuit of buffalo, and would readily find the track of the party, no solicitude was felt on their account. A fire was left burning, to guide them by its column of smoke, and the travellers proceeded on their march. In the evening a signal-fire was made on a hill adjacent to the camp, and in the morning it was replenished with fuel so as to last throughout the day.[7] These signals are usual among the Indians, to give warnings to each other, or to call home straggling hunters; and such is the transparency of the atmosphere in those elevated plains, that a slight column of smoke can be discerned from a great distance, particularly in the evenings. Two or three days elapsed, however, without the reappearance of the three hunters; and Mr. Hunt slackened his march to give them time to overtake him.

A vigilant watch continued to be kept upon the movements of Rose, and of such of the men as were considered doubtful in their loyalty; but nothing occurred to excite immediate apprehensions. Rose evidently was not a favorite among his comrades, and it was hoped that he had not been able to make any real partisans.

On the 10th of August[8] they encamped among hills, on the highest peak of which Mr. Hunt caused a huge pyre of pine wood to be made, which soon sent up a great column of flame that might be seen far and wide over the prairies. This fire blazed all night, and was amply replenished at daybreak; so that the towering pillar of smoke could not but be descried by the wanderers if within the distance of a day's journey.

[5] "They were all around us. As it was the rutting season, they made a frightful noise like the sound of distant thunder; the males tearing the ground with their hoofs and horns." Hunt, "Journal," 282.

[6] Jean Baptiste Gardpie. See Porter, "Roll of Overland Astorians," *Oregon Historical Quarterly,* Vol. XXXIV (1933), 107.

[7] All Hunt says is that "we made fires on the summits to guide our hunters. At first we used buffalo chips, afterward we could use pine wood." See "Journal," 282. Hunt does not identify the hunters.

[8] Irving had to infer the date from Hunt's "Journal" since it is not specifically stated.

It is a common occurrence in these regions, where the features of the country so much resemble each other, for hunters to lose themselves and wander for many days, before they can find their way back to the main body of their party. In the present instance, however, a more than common solicitude was felt, in consequence of the distrust awakened by the sinister designs of Rose.

The route now became excessively toilsome, over a ridge of steep rocky hills, covered with loose stones.[9] These were intersected by deep valleys, formed by two branches of Big River, coming from the south of west, both of which they crossed. These streams were bordered by meadows, well stocked with buffaloes. Loads of meat were brought in by the hunters; but the travellers were rendered dainty by profusion, and would cook only the choice pieces.

They had now travelled for several days at a very slow rate, and had made signal-fires and left traces of their route at every stage, yet nothing was heard or seen of the lost men. It began to be feared that they might have fallen into the hands of some lurking band of savages. A party numerous as that of Mr. Hunt, with a long train of pack-horses, moving across open plains or naked hills, is discoverable at a great distance by Indian scouts, who spread the intelligence rapidly to various points, and assemble their friends to hang about the skirts of the travellers, steal their horses, or cut off any stragglers from the main body.

Mr. Hunt and his companions were more and more sensible how much it would be in the power of this sullen and daring vagabond Rose, to do them mischief, when they should become entangled in the defiles of the mountains, with the passes of which they were wholly unacquainted, and which were infested by his freebooting friends, the Crows. There, should he succeed in seducing some of the party into his plans, he might carry off the best horses and effects, throw himself among his savage allies, and set all pursuit at defiance. Mr. Hunt resolved, therefore, to frustrate the knave, divert him, by management, from his plans, and make it sufficiently advantageous for him to remain honest. He took occasion, accordingly, in the course of conversation, to inform Rose

---

[9] "On the 11th, there was crossed a range of mountains like the preceding ones. The road was irksome because of steepness and the great numbers of stones." Hunt, "Journal," 282. Rollins identifies the mountains as being Slim Buttes, as they are now named, in Harding County, South Dakota. *Discovery of the Oregon Trail*, 313n. This would mean that the Overland Astorians had left or were about to leave the South Fork of Grand River (Big River).

that, having engaged him chiefly as a guide and interpreter through the country of the Crows, they would not stand in need of his services beyond. Knowing, therefore, his connection by marriage with that tribe, and his predilection for a residence among them, they would put no restraint[10] upon his will, but, whenever they met with a party of that people, would leave him at liberty to remain among his adopted brethren. Furthermore, that, in thus parting with him, they would pay him half a year's wages in consideration of his past services, and would give him a horse, three beaver traps, and sundry other articles calculated to set him up in the world.

This unexpected liberality, which made it nearly as profitable and infinitely less hazardous for Rose to remain honest than to play the rogue, completely disarmed him. From that time his whole deportment underwent a change. His brow cleared up and appeared more cheerful; he left off his sullen, skulking habits, and made no further attempts to tamper with the faith of his comrades.[11]

On the 13th of August Mr. Hunt varied his course, and inclined westward, in hopes of falling in with the three lost hunters; who, it was now thought, might have kept to the right hand of Big River.[12] This course soon brought him to a fork of the Little Missouri, about a hundred yards wide, and resembling the great river of the same name in the strength of its current, its turbid water, and the frequency of drift-wood and sunken trees.[13]

Rugged mountains appeared ahead, crowding down to the water

---

[10] *Constraint* in first edition.

[11] Hunt wrote about Rose: "We kept close watch during the night. Fearing moreover that, if despite our vigilance, he should succeed in fulfilling his evil designs, he would seriously cripple our expedition and that his schemes might be more extensive than we had supposed, we resolved to forestall him. On September 2nd, we had received a visit from some Absarokas of a band which was different from the one we had recently left and which was camped in the mountain. Consequently, I suggested to Rose that he remain with these indians, offering him half of his year's wages, a horse, three beaver-traps, and some other things. He accepted these terms and immediately quitted his confederates, who, no longer having a leader, continued the journey." See "Journal," 284–85. As the date given by Hunt shows, Irving took liberties with chronology.

[12] Hunt wrote: "On the 13th [of August], we marched in a more westerly direction, as we thought that our hunters were still to our right." *Ibid.*, 282.

[13] "We crossed a confluent of the Little Missouri, 300 feet wide, swift, muddy and filled with eddies." *Ibid.* The Little Missouri rises in northeastern Wyoming, flows across the southeastern corner of Montana, the northwestern corner of South Dakota, and generally northeast through North Dakota until it joins the Missouri proper.

edge, and offering a barrier to further progress on the side they were ascending. Crossing the river, therefore, they encamped on its northwest bank, where they found good pasturage and buffalo in abundance. The weather was overcast and rainy, and a general gloom pervaded the camp; the voyageurs sat moping[14] in groups with their shoulders as high as their heads, croaking their foreboding[s], when suddenly towards evening a shout of joy gave notice that the lost men were found.[15] They came slowly lagging into the camp, with weary looks, and horses jaded and wayworn. They had, in fact, been for several days incessantly on the move. In their hunting excursion on the prairies they had pushed so far in pursuit of buffalo, as to find it impossible to retrace their steps over plains trampled by innumerable herds; and were baffled by the monotony of the landscape in their attempts to recall landmarks. They had ridden to and fro until they had almost lost the points of the compass, and become totally bewildered; nor did they ever perceive any of the signal-fires and columns of smoke made by their comrades. At length, about two days previously, when almost spent by anxiety and hard riding, they came, to their great joy, upon the "trail" of the party, which they had since followed up steadily.

Those only, who have experienced the warm cordiality that grows up between comrades in wild and adventurous expeditions of the kind, can picture to themselves the hearty cheering with which the stragglers were welcomed to the camp. Every one crowded round them to ask questions, and to hear the story of their mishaps; and even the squaw of the moody half-breed, Pierre Dorion, forgot the sternness of his domestic rule, and the conjugal discipline of the cudgel, in her joy at his safe return.

[14] The Author's Revised Edition erroneously has *smoking*. *Moping* appears in the first edition.

[15] Under date of August 13, which agrees with Irving, Hunt wrote: "Three of our hunters returned at sunset." See "Journal," 282. On the basis of his "Journal" these men had been separated from the main party since August 7 or 8. There are but three brief and casual references to them, and there appears none of the anxiety that Irving interjects into his narrative.

MR. HUNT and his party were now on the skirts of the Black Hills, or Black Mountains, as they are sometimes called; an extensive chain, lying about a hundred miles east of the Rocky Mountains, and stretching in a northeast direction from the south fork of the Nebraska, or Platte River, to the great north bend of the Missouri. The Sierra or ridge of the Black Hills, in fact, forms the dividing line between the waters of the Missouri and those of the Arkansas and the Mississippi, and gives rise to the Cheyenne, the Little Missouri, and several tributary streams of the Yellowstone.[1]

The wild recesses of these hills, like those of the Rocky Mountains, are retreats and lurking-places for broken and predatory tribes, and it was among them that the remnant of the Cheyenne tribe took refuge, as has been stated, from their conquering enemies, the Sioux.

The Black Hills are chiefly composed of sandstone, and in many places are broken into savage cliffs and precipices, and present the most singular and fantastic forms; sometimes resembling towns and castellated fortresses. The ignorant inhabitants of plains are prone to clothe the mountains that bound their horizon with fanciful and superstitious attributes. Thus the wandering tribes of the prairies, who often behold

[1] The Black Hills lie in western South Dakota and partly in Wyoming but are not as extensive as Irving states. North and south they extend for about one hundred miles, their width being approximately fifty miles. Irving's geography here is quite mistaken. It is possible that he confused what now bears the name *Black Hills* with the Front Range of the Rocky Mountains, which was often referred to by early travelers and explorers as the Black Hills.

clouds gathering round the summits of these hills, and lightning flashing, and thunder pealing from them, when all the neighboring plains are serene and sunny, consider them the abode of the genii or thunder-spirits who fabricate storms and tempests. On entering their defiles, therefore, they often hang offerings on the trees, or place them on the rocks, to propitiate the invisible "lords of the mountains," and procure good weather and successful hunting; and they attach unusual significance to the echoes which haunt the precipices. This superstition may also have arisen, in part, from a natural phenomenon of a singular nature. In the most calm and serene weather, and at all times of the day or night, successive reports are now and then heard among these mountains, resembling the discharge of several pieces of artillery. Similar reports were heard by Messrs. Lewis and Clarke in the Rocky Mountains, which they say were attributed by the Indians to the bursting of the rich mines of silver contained in the bosom of the mountains.[2]

In fact, these singular explosions have received fanciful explanations from learned men, and have not been satisfactorily accounted for even by philosophers. They are said to occur frequently in Brazil. Vasconcelles, a Jesuit father, describes one which he heard in the Sierra, or mountain region of Piratininga, and which he compares to the discharges of a park of artillery. The Indians told him that it was an explosion of stones. The worthy father had soon a satisfactory proof of the truth of their information, for the very place was found where a rock had burst and exploded from its entrails a stony mass, like a bomb-shell, and of the size of a bull's heart. This mass was broken either in its ejection or

[2] In one of Irving's memoranda books, "Notes for Astoria, 1835," he copied the following passage from Lewis and Clark: "Since our arrival at the falls [Great Falls] we have repeatedly heard a strange noise coming from the mountains in a direction a little to the north of west. It is heard at different periods of the day & night, sometimes when the air is perfectly still & without a cloud & consists of one stroke only, or of five or six in quick succession. It is loud & resembles precisely the sound of a 6 pound piece of ordnance at the distance of three miles. The Minnetarees frequently mentioned they were like thunder, which they said the mountains made; but we paid no attention to it, believing it to have been some superstition or perhaps a falsehood. The watermen also of the party say that the Pawnees & Ricarees give the same account of a noise heard in the Black mountains to the westward of them. The solution of the mystery given by the philosophy of the watermen is that it is occasioned by the bursting of the rich mines of silver contained in the bosom of the mountains. Lewis & Clark, V.i. P 292[.]" Seligman Collection of Irvingiana, New York Public Library. The passage is given here as Irving quoted it. In *History of the Expedition* it is entered under date of July 4, 1805.

its fall, and wonderful was the internal organization revealed. It had a shell harder even than iron; within which were arranged, like the seeds of a pomegranate, jewels of various colors; some transparent as crystal; others of a fine red, and others of mixed hues. The same phenomenon is said to occur occasionally in the adjacent province of Guayra, where stones of the bigness of a man's hand are exploded, with a loud noise, from the bosom of the earth, and scatter about glittering and beautiful fragments that look like precious gems, but are of no value.

The Indians of the Orellanna,[3] also, tell of horrible noises heard occasionally in the Paraguaxo, which they consider the throes and groans of the mountain, endeavoring to cast forth the precious stones hidden within its entrails. Others have endeavored to account for these discharges of "mountain artillery" on humbler principles; attributing them to the loud reports made by the disruption and fall of great masses of rock, reverberated and prolonged by the echoes; others, to the disengagement of hydrogen, produced by subterraneous beds of coal in a state of ignition. In whatever way this singular phenomenon may be accounted for, the existence of it appears to be well established. It remains one of the lingering mysteries of nature which throw something of a supernatural charm over her wild mountain solitudes; and we doubt whether the imaginative reader will not rather join with the poor Indian in attributing it to the thunder-spirits, or the guardian genii of unseen treasures, than to any commonplace physical cause.

Whatever might be the supernatural influences among these mountains, the travellers found their physical difficulties hard to cope with. They made repeated attempts to find a passage through or over the chain, but were as often turned back by impassible barriers. Sometimes a defile seemed to open a practicable path, but it would terminate in some wild chaos of rocks and cliffs, which it was impossible to climb.[4] The animals of these solitary regions were different from those they had been accustomed to. The black-tailed deer would bound up the ravines on their approach, and the bighorn would gaze fearlessly down upon them from some impending precipice, or skip playfully from rock to rock. These animals are only to be met with in mountainous regions. The former is larger than the common deer, but its flesh is not equally

---

[3] The Amazon River, discovered by Francisco de Orellana (c. 1490–c. 1546).

[4] Hunt's "Journal," 282, states: "The country was extremely rugged; it became more so on the 17th, and a way out of these mountains could not be found."

esteemed by hunters. It has very large ears, and the tip of the tail is black, from which it derives its name.[5]

The bighorn is so named from its horns; which are of a great size, and twisted like those of a ram. It is called by some the argali, by others the ibex, though differing from both of these animals. The Mandans call it the ahsahta, a name much better than the clumsy appellation which it generally bears. It is of the size of a small elk, or large deer, and of a dun color, excepting the belly and round the tail, where it is white. In its habits it resembles the goat, frequenting the rudest percipices; cropping the herbage from their edges; and like the chamois, bounding lightly and securely among dizzy heights, where the hunter dares not venture. It is difficult, therefore, to get within shot of it. Ben Jones the hunter, however, in one of the passes of the Black Hills, succeeded in bringing down a bighorn from the verge of a precipice, the flesh of which was pronounced by the gormands[6] of the camp to have the flavor of excellent mutton.[7]

Baffled in his attempts to traverse this mountain chain, Mr. Hunt skirted along it to the southwest, keeping it on the right; and still in hopes of finding an opening.[8] At an early hour one day, he encamped in a narrow valley on the banks of a beautifully clear but rushy pool; surrounded by thickets bearing abundance of wild cherries, currants, and yellow and purple gooseberries.[9]

While the afternoon's meal was in preparation, Mr. Hunt and Mr. M'Kenzie ascended to the summit of the nearest hill, from whence, aided by the purity and transparency of the evening atmosphere, they commanded a vast prospect on all sides. Below them extended a plain, dotted with innumerable herds of buffalo. Some were lying down among the herbage, others roaming in their unbounded pastures, while

---

[5] Irving's source for the black-tailed deer (the mule deer) is solely Hunt's "Journal," 283. See also *ibid.*, 313, n. 66.

[6] *Gourmands* in first edition.

[7] All that Hunt says about the bighorn is: "A big-horn was killed; the flesh is good and much resembles mutton. These animals are usually found in the mountains where no other can go. Several were espied running and jumping on the edge of the precipice." See "Journal," 282–83. The fact that Hunt does not mention Ben Jones shows that Irving had a supplementary source.

[8] "On the 18th, it was necessary to leave the mountains and return to the broken country ... [where] camp was made to the left of pine-covered mountains." *Ibid.*, 283.

[9] Hunt mentions all these fruits and states that the camp was "near a pond of limpid water," which Irving makes into "a beautifully clear but rushy pool."

many were engaged in fierce contests like those already described, their low bellowings reaching the ear like the hoarse murmurs of the surf on a distant shore.

Far off in the west they descried a range of lofty mountains printing the clear horizon, some of them evidently capped with snow. These they supposed to be the Bighorn Mountains, so called from the animal of that name, with which they abound. They are a spur of the great Rocky chain. The hill from whence Mr. Hunt had this prospect was, according to his computation, about two hundred and fifty miles from the Arickara village.[10]

On returning to the camp, Mr. Hunt found some uneasiness prevailing among the Canadian voyageurs. In straying among the thickets they beheld tracks of grizzly bears in every direction, doubtless attracted thither by the fruit. To their dismay, they now found that they had encamped in one of the favorite resorts of this dreaded animal. The idea marred all the comfort of the encampment. As night closed, the surrounding thickets were peopled with terrors; insomuch that, according to Mr. Hunt, they could not help starting at every little breeze that stirred the bushes.[11]

The grizzly bear is the only really formidable quadruped of our continent. He is the favorite theme of the hunters of the far West, who describe him as equal in size to a common cow and of prodigious strength. He makes battle if assailed, and often, if pressed by hunger, is the assailant. If wounded, he becomes furious and will pursue the hunter. His speed exceeds that of a man but is inferior to that of a horse. In attacking he rears himself on his hind legs, and springs the length of his body. Woe to horse or rider that comes within the sweep of his terrific

[10] The "Journal," 283, reads: "Mr. Hunt and Mr. Mackenzie climbed the nearest ones [i.e., mountains]. Their view extended in all directions. They saw far off in the west mountains which appeared white in several places; they assumed that this was Mount Big Horn covered with snow. Below them numerous bands of bison wandered on the plain." Comparison of this passage with what Irving wrote illustrates his elaboration of raw material.

A memorandum in one of Irving's 1835 *Astoria* notebooks reads: "In the course of the march after first seeing the Big Horn mountains, they must be kept in sight." Seligman Collection of Irvingiana, New York Public Library.

[11] Irving elaborates the following statement: "The clumps of cherry trees showed signs of the paths used by black bear; so that, with the slightest breeze moving in the bushes, one felt in spite of oneself a shiver of dread. However, only three of these animals, had been seen as yet." Hunt, "Journal," 283. Note that Irving changes "black bear" to "grizzly," a much more ferocious animal sincerely to be dreaded.

claws, which are sometimes nine inches in length, and tear everything before them.

At the time we are treating of, the grizzly bear was still frequent on the Missouri and in the lower country, but, like some of the broken tribes of the prairie,[12] he has gradually fallen back before his enemies, and is now chiefly to be found in the upland regions, in rugged fastnesses like those of the Black Hills and the Rocky Mountains. Here he lurks in caverns, or holes which he has digged in the sides of hills, or under the roots and trunks of fallen trees. Like the common bear, he is fond of fruits, and mast, and roots, the latter of which he will dig up with his foreclaws. He is carnivorous also, and will even attack and conquer the lordly buffalo, dragging his huge carcass to the neighborhood of his den, that he may prey upon it at his leisure.

The hunters, both white and red men, consider this the most heroic game. They prefer to hunt him on horseback, and will venture so near as sometimes to singe his hair with the flash of the rifle. The hunter of the grizzly bear, however, must be an experienced hand, and know where to aim at a vital part; for of all quadrupeds, he is the most difficult to be killed. He will receive repeated wounds without flinching, and rarely is a shot mortal unless through the head or heart.[13]

That the dangers apprehended from the grizzly bear, at this night encampment, were not imaginary, was proved on the following morning. Among the hired men of the party was one William Cannon,[14] who had been a soldier at one of the frontier posts, and entered into the employ of Mr. Hunt at Mackinaw. He was an inexperienced hunter and a poor shot, for which he was much bantered by his more adroit comrades. Piqued at their raillery, he had been practicing ever since he had joined the expedition, but without success. In the course of the present

[12] *Prairies* in first edition.

[13] Accounts of grizzly bears are common in early western narratives. Numerous passages appear in Lewis and Clark. A good description is in Edwin James, *Account of an Expedition from Pittsburgh to the Rocky Mountains*, in Thwaites (ed.), *Early Western Travels*, XVI, 45–51. Irving may have compiled data from several such sources. It is noteworthy that he devoted several pages in *A Tour on the Prairies* to a discussion of the grizzly bear; parts of his discussion here resemble the above passage. See *Tour*, chap. XXVII.

[14] He had been with the expedition since August 7, 1810, having joined, as Irving says, at Mackinac. See Porter, "Roll of Overland Astorians," *Oregon Historical Quarterly*, Vol. XXXIV (1933), 105.

afternoon, he went forth by himself to take a lesson in venerie, and, to his great delight, had the good fortune to kill a buffalo. As he was a considerable distance from the camp, he cut out the tongue and some of the choice bits, made them into a parcel, and slinging them on his shoulders by a strap passed round his forehead, as the voyageurs carry packages of goods, set out all glorious for the camp, anticipating a triumph over his brother hunters. In passing through a narrow ravine, he heard a noise behind him, and looking round beheld, to his dismay, a grizzly bear in full pursuit, apparently attracted by the scent of the meat. Cannon had heard so much of the invulnerability of this tremendous animal, that he never attempted to fire, but, slipping the strap from his forehead, let go the buffalo meat and ran for his life. The bear did not stop to regale himself with the game, but kept on after the hunter. He had nearly overtaken him when Cannon reached a tree, and, throwing down his rifle, scrambled up it. The next instant Bruin was at the foot of the tree; but, as this species of bear does not climb, he contented himself with turning the chase into a blockade. Night came on. In the darkness Cannon could not perceive whether or not the enemy maintained his station; but his fears pictured him rigorously mounting guard. He passed the night, therefore, in the tree, a prey to dismal fancies. In the morning the bear was gone. Cannon warily descended the tree, gathered up his gun, and made the best of his way back to the camp, without venturing to look after his buffalo meat.[15]

While on this theme we will add another anecdote of an adventure with a grizzly bear, told of John Day, the Kentucky hunter, but which happened at a different period of the expedition. Day was hunting in company with one of the clerks of the Company, a lively youngster, who was a great favorite with the veteran, but whose vivacity he had continually to keep in check. They were in search of deer, when suddenly a huge grizzly bear emerged from a thicket about thirty yards distant, rearing himself upon his hind legs with a terrific growl, and displaying a hideous array of teeth and claws. The rifle of the young man was leveled in an instant, but John Day's iron hand was as quickly upon his arm. "Be quiet, boy! be quiet!" exclaimed the hunter between his clenched teeth, and without turning his eyes from the bear. They remained motionless. The monster regarded them for a time, then, lowering himself on his forepaws, slowly withdrew. He had not gone many paces before

---

[15] This episode does not appear in Hunt's "Journal."

he again returned,[16] reared himself on his hind legs, and repeated his menace. Day's hand was still on the arm of his young companion; he again pressed it hard, and kept repeating between his teeth, "Quiet, boy! —keep quiet!—keep quiet!"—though the latter had not made a move since his first prohibition. The bear again lowered himself on all fours, retreated some twenty yards further, and again turned, reared, showed his teeth, and growled. This third menace was too much for the game spirit of John Day. "By Jove!" exclaimed he, "I can stand this no longer," and in an instant a ball from his rifle whizzed into the foe. The wound was not mortal; but, luckily, it dismayed instead of enraging the animal, and he retreated into the thicket.

Day's young companion reproached him for not practicing the caution which he enjoined upon others. "Why, boy," replied the veteran, "caution is caution, but one must not put up with too much, even from a bear. Would you have me suffer myself to be bullied all day by a varmint?"[17]

[16] *Turned* in first edition.
[17] Irving's source for this story is also unknown.

FOR the two following days, the travellers pursued a westerly course for thirty-four miles along a ridge of country dividing the tributary waters of the Missouri and the Yellowstone. As landmarks they guided themselves by the summits of the far distant mountains, which they supposed to belong to the Bighorn chain. They were gradually rising into a higher temperature, for the weather was cold for the season, with a sharp frost in the night, and ice of an eighth of an inch in thickness.[1]

On the twenty-second of August,[2] early in the day, they came upon the trail of a numerous band. Rose and the other hunters examined the foot-prints with great attention, and determined it to be the trail of a party of Crows, returning from an annual trading visit to the Mandans. As this trail afforded more commodious travelling, they immediately struck into it, and followed it for two days. It led them over rough hills, and through broken gullies, during which time they suffered great fatigue from the ruggedness of the country. The weather, too, which had recently been frosty, was now opresively warm, and there was a great scarcity of water, insomuch that a valuable dog belonging to Mr. M'Kenzie died of thirst.

At one time they had twenty-five miles of painful travel, without

[1] See Hunt, "Journal," 283. Hunt says they were "on a branch of the Little Missouri" at a "spot which divides the water flowing into the Missouri from those which discharge into the Yellowstone." Their location was probably between the Little Missouri and the Little Powder River in northeast Wyoming.

[2] The date is confirmed by Hunt.

a drop of water, until they arrived at a small running stream. Here they eagerly slaked their thirst; but, this being allayed, the calls of hunger became equally importunate. Ever since they had got among these barren and arid hills, where there was a deficiency of grass, they had met with no buffaloes; those animals keeping in the grassy meadows near the streams. They were obliged, therefore, to have recourse to their corn meal, which they reserved for such emergencies. Some, however, were lucky enough to kill a wolf, which they cooked for supper, and pronounced excellent food.[3]

The next morning they resumed their wayfaring, hungry and jaded, and had a dogged march of eighteen miles among the same kind of hills. At length they emerged upon a stream of clear water, one of the forks of Powder River,[4] and to their great joy beheld once more wide grassy meadows, stocked with herds of buffalo. For several days they kept along[5] the banks of the river, ascending it about eighteen miles. It was a hunter's paradise; the buffaloes were in such abundance that they were enabled to kill as many as they pleased, and to jerk a sufficient supply of meat for several day's journeying.[6] Here, then, they revelled and reposed after their hungry and weary travel, hunting and feasting, and reclining upon the grass. Their quiet, however, was a little marred by coming upon traces of Indians, who, they concluded, must be Crows: they were therefore obliged to keep a more vigilant watch than ever upon their horses. For several days they had been directing their march towards the lofty mountain[7] descried by Mr. Hunt and Mr. M'Kenzie on the 17th of August,[8] the height of which rendered it a landmark over a vast extent of country. At first it had appeared to them solitary and detached; but as they advanced towards it, it proved to be the principal

[3] The above two paragraphs follow Hunt closely; see "Journal," 283.

[4] Both Hunt's "Journal" and his account book show that they reached this tributary of the Powder on August 22. The Powder drains the eastern slopes of the Big Horn Mountains and flows north into the Yellowstone in eastern Montana.

[5] *About* in first edition.

[6] Hunt says they followed the fork of the river for two days. "Because many buffalo were killed, a halt was made on the 28th and 29th in order to dry their flesh at a fire." See "Journal," 283–84.

[7] The highest elevation of the Big Horn Mountains is Cloud Peak (13,165 feet), which is undoubtedly what they saw. In his "Journal," Hunt refers to it as Mount Big Horn.

[8] An error for August 18, which appears in Hunt's "Journal."

summit of a chain of mountains.[9] Day by day it varied in form, or rather its lower peaks, and the summits of others of the chain emerged above the clear horizon, and finally the inferior line of hills which connected most of them rose to view. So far, however, are objects discernible in the pure atmosphere of these elevated plains, that, from the place where they first descried the main mountain, they had to travel a hundred and fifty miles before they reached its base. Here they encamped on the 30th of August, having come nearly four hundred miles since leaving the Arickara village.[10]

The mountain which now towered above them was one of the Bighorn chain, bordered by a river, of the same name, and extending for a long distance rather east of north and west of south. It was a part of the great system of granite mountains which forms one of the most important and striking features of North America, stretching parallel to the coast of the Pacific from the Isthmus of Panama almost to the Arctic Ocean; and presenting a corresponding chain to that of the Andes in the southern hemisphere. This vast range has acquired, from its rugged and broken character and its summits of naked granite, the appellation of the Rocky Mountains, a name by no means distinctive, as all elevated ranges are rocky. Among the early explorers it was known as the range of Chippewyan Mountains, and this Indian name is the one it is likely to retain in poetic usage. Rising from the midst of vast plains and prairies, traversing several degrees of latitude, dividing the waters of the Atlantic and the Pacific, and seeming to bind with diverging ridges the level regions on its flanks, it has been figuratively termed the backbone of the northern continent.

The Rocky Mountains do not present a range of uniform elevation, but rather groups and occasionally detached peaks. Though some of these rise to the region of perpetual snows, and are upwards of eleven

[9] The Big Horn Mountains, the general contour of which is shown on the *Astoria* map.

[10] Their daily average would therefore have been nine miles, for they consumed forty-four days in traveling this distance.

"On the 30th, the river was quitted and the camp pitched near Mount Big Horn, which had been before us for so long a time." Hunt, "Journal," 284. Mount Big Horn may here designate Cloud Peak, as Irving's next sentence would suggest; but possibly it denotes the range as a whole, for early on August 18 Hunt states: "They saw far off in the west mountains which appeared white in several places; they assumed that this was Mount Big Horn covered with snow." *Ibid.*, 283. Hunt confirms the date.

thousand feet in real altitude, yet their height from their immediate basis[11] is not so great as might be imagined, as they swell up from elevated plains, several thousand feet above the level of the ocean. These plains are often of a desolate sterility; mere sandy wastes, formed of the detritus of the granite heights, destitute of trees and herbage, scorched by the ardent and reflected rays of the summer's sun, and in winter swept by chilling blasts from the snow-clad mountains. Such is a great part of that vast region extending north and south along the mountains, several hundred miles in width, which has not improperly been termed the Great American Desert. It is a region that almost discourages all hope of cultivation, and can only be traversed with safety by keeping near the streams which intersect it. Extensive plains likewise occur among the higher regions of the mountains, of considerable fertility. Indeed, these lofty plats of table-land seem to form a peculiar feature in the American continents. Some occur among the Cordilleras of the Andes, where cities, and towns, and cultivated farms are to be seen eight thousand feet above the level of the sea.

The Rocky Mountains, as we have already observed, occur sometimes singly or in groups, and occasionally in collateral ridges. Between these are deep valleys, with small streams winding through them, which find their way into the lower plains, augmenting as they proceed, and ultimately discharging themselves into those vast rivers, which traverse the prairies like great arteries, and drain the continent.

While the granite summits of the Rocky Mountains are bleak and bare, many of the inferior ridges are scantily clothed with scrubbed pines, oaks, cedar, and furze. Various parts of the mountains also bear traces af volcanic action. Some of the interior valleys are strewed with scoria and broken stones, evidently of volcanic origin; the surrounding rocks bear the like character, and vestiges of extinguished craters are to be seen on the elevated heights.

We have already noticed the superstitious feelings with which the Indians regard the Black Hills; but this immense range of mountains, which divides all that they know of the world, and gives birth to such mighty rivers, is still more an object of awe and veneration. They call it "the crest of the world,"[12] and think that Wacondah, or the master

[11] The first edition correctly reads *bases*.
[12] In his "Notes for Astoria, 1835," Irving made the following brief memorandum:

of life, as they designate the Supreme Being, has his residence among these aerial heights.[13] The tribes on the eastern prairies call them the mountains of the setting sun.[14] Some of them place the "happy hunting-grounds," their ideal paradise, among the recesses of these mountains;[15] but say that they are invisible to living men. Here also is the "Land of Souls," in which are the "towns of the free and generous spirits," where those who have pleased the master of life while living, enjoy after death all manner of delights.[16]

Wonders are told of these mountains by the distant tribes, whose warriors or hunters have ever wandered in their neighborhood. It is thought by some that, after death, they will have to travel to these mountains and ascend one of their highest and most rugged peaks, among rocks and snows and tumbling torrents. After many moons of painful toil they will reach the summit, from whence they will have a view over the land of souls. There they will see the happy hunting-grounds, with the souls of the brave and good living in tents in green meadows, by bright running streams, or hunting the herds of buffalo, and elk, and deer, which have been slain on earth. There, too, they will see the villages or towns of the free and generous spirits brightening in the midst of delicious prairies. If they have acquitted themselves well while living, they will be permitted to descend and enjoy this happy country; if otherwise they will but be tantalized with this prospect of it,

"The crest of the world (i.e. The Rocky Mount)[.]" Seligman Collection of Irvingiana, New York Public Library.

[13] The same notebook (see note 12 above) contains the following quotation from Pierre François de Charlevoix (1682–1761): "Very many of the Western Indians believe that the Supreme being has his residence in the Rocky mountains; & some of them make him the sun." This sentence from Charlevoix's *Voyage Made in Northern America* (1744) Irving found in James A. Jones, *Tales of an Indian Camp* (see I, 40n. and 167n.).

[14] *Mountains of the setting sun* also appears in the 1835 *Astoria* notebook.

[15] This probably was suggested by the following quotation in the 1835 *Astoria* notebook: "while the nations of the Ottoes had their hunting grounds in the shade [?] of the mountains of the great being." Irving gives no source; possibly it is Jones, *op. cit.*

[16] Irving's notebook contains the following quotation attributed to "Long, vol. 1, p.17": "That imaginary region of happiness & contentment, which, like the 'town of the brave and generous spirits,' the expected heaven of the aboriginal American, lies always 'beyond the place where the sun goes down.' " See Edwin James, *Account of an Expedition*, in Thwaites (ed.), *Early Western Travels*, XIV, 59. Curiously, here James is writing about the Allegheny and Ohio rivers.

and then hurled back from the mountain to wander about the sandy plains, and endure the eternal pangs of unsatisfied thirst and hunger.[17]

[17] This paragraph comes from the following quotation as copied into the 1835 *Astoria* notebook: "The Blackfoot believes that the people of his tribe when released from the load of flesh come to a steep mountain, up whose huge projecting sides they have to scramble. After many moons of unwearied labor, tired & exhausted they reach the top, from which they behold the land of the dead. They see stretched out before them an extensive plain, interspread with new tents, pitched by the sides of beautiful streams, the banks of which resound with the humming of bees & the music of birds, & are shaded from the summer sun by the ever-blooming tree with great white flowers. Some of the tents are pitched upon hills, some in valleys; some to meet the whispering breezes of the month of Buds and from the strengthening winds of the Harvest Moon." Jones, *op. cit.*, I, 245.

Region of the Crow Indians — Scouts on the Look-Out
Visit from a Crew of Hard Riders — A Crow Camp
Presents to the Crow Chief — Bargaining — Crow Bullies
Rose Among His Indian Friends — Parting with the Crows
Perplexities Among the Mountains — More of the Crows
Equestrian Children — Search After Stragglers

THE travellers had now arrived in the vicinity of the mountain regions infested by the Crow Indians. These restless marauders, as has already been observed, are apt to be continually on the prowl about the skirts of the mountains, and even when encamped in some deep and secluded glen, they keep scouts upon the cliffs and promontories, who, unseen themselves, can discern every living thing that moves over the subjacent plains and valleys. It was not to be expected that our travellers could pass unseen through a region thus vigilantly sentineled; accordingly, in the edge of the evening, not long after they had encamped at the foot of the Bighorn Sierra, a couple of wild-looking beings, scantily clad in skins, but well armed, and mounted on horses as wild-looking as themselves, were seen approaching with great caution from among the rocks. They might have been mistaken for two of the evil spirits of the mountains so formidable in Indian fable.

Rose was immediately sent out to hold a parley with them, and invite them to the camp. They proved to be two scouts from the same band that had been tracked for some days past, and which was now encamped at some distance in the folds of the mountain. They were easily prevailed upon to come to the camp, where they were well received, and, after remaining there until late in the evening, departed to make a report of all they had seen and experienced to their companions.[1]

The following day[2] had scarce dawned, when a troop of these wild mountain scamperers came galloping with whoops and yells into the

---

[1] Hunt's "Journal," 284, says only: "For several days we had been on the heights; our hunters had seen, the previous day, traces of Indians; they discovered us first. On the evening of the 30th, two Absarokas came to our camp."

[2] August 31.

camp, bringing an invitation from their chief for the white men to visit him. The tents were accordingly struck, the horses laden, and the party were soon on the march. The Crow horsemen, as they escorted them, appeared to take pride in showing off their equestrain skill and hardihood; careering at full speed on their half-savage steeds, and dashing among rocks and crags, and up and down the most rugged and dangerous places with perfect ease and unconcern.[3]

A ride of sixteen miles brought them, in the afternoon, in sight of the Crow camp. It was composed of leathern tents, pitched in a meadow on the border of a small clear stream at the foot of the mountain. A great number of horses were grazing in the vicinity, many of them doubtless captured in marauding excursions.[4]

The Crow chieftain came forth to meet his guests with great professions of friendship, and conducted them to his tents, pointing out, by the way, a convenient place where they might fix their camp. No sooner had they done so, than Mr. Hunt opened some of the packages and made the chief a present of a scarlet blanket and a quantity of powder and ball; he gave him also some knives, trinkets, and tobacco to be distributed among his warriors,[5] with all which the grim potentate seemed, for the time, well pleased. As the Crows, however, were reputed to be perfidious in the extreme, and as errant freebooters as the bird after which they were so worthily named; and as their general feelings towards the whites were known to be by no means friendly, the intercourse with them was conducted with great circumspection.

The following day was passed in trading with the Crows for buffalo robes and skins, and in bartering galled and jaded horses for others that were in good condition. Some of the men, also, purchased horses on their own account, so that the number now amounted to one hundred and twenty-one, most of them sound and active, and fit for mountain service.[6]

[3] Hunt continues: "The next morning, more of them arrived. They were all on horseback. Even the children do not go afoot. These indians are such good horsemen that they climb and descend the mountains and rocks as though they were galloping in a riding school." *Ibid.*, 284.

[4] "We followed them to their camp," Hunt goes on, "which was near a clear stream on the side of the mountain." *Ibid.* For the possible location, see Rollins (ed.), *Discovery of the Oregon Trail*, 314, n. 88.

[5] This follows Hunt closely, except that instead of "scarlet blanket" he had "a piece of scarlet cloth." See "Journal," 284.

[6] *Ibid.*

Their wants being supplied, they ceased all further traffic, much to the dissatisfaction of the Crows, who became extremely urgent to continue the trade, and, finding their importunities of no avail, assumed an insolent and menacing tone. All this was attributed by Mr. Hunt and his associates to the perfidious instigations of Rose the interpreter, whom they suspected of the desire to foment ill-will between them and the savages, for the promotion of his nefarious plans. M'Lellan, with his usual *tranchant* mode of dealing out justice, resolved to shoot the desperado on the spot in case of any outbreak. Nothing of the kind, however, occurred. The Crows were probably daunted by the resolute, though quiet demeanor of the white men, and the constant vigilance and armed preparations which they maintained; and Rose, if he really still harbored his knavish designs, must have perceived that they were suspected, and, if attempted to be carried into effect, might bring ruin on his own head.[7]

The next morning,[8] bright and early, Mr. Hunt proposed to resume his journeying. He took a ceremonious leave of the Crow chieftain, and his vagabond warriors, and according to previous arrangements, consigned to their cherishing friendship and fraternal adoption, their worthy confederate Rose;[9] who, having figured among the water pirates of the Mississippi, was well fitted to rise to distinction among the land pirates of the Rocky Mountains.

It is proper to add, that the ruffian was well received among the tribe, and appeared to be perfectly satisfied with the compromise he had made; feeling much more at his ease among savages than among white men. It is outcasts from civilization, fugitives from justice, and heartless desperadoes of this kind who sow the seeds of enmity and bitterness among the unfortunate tribes of the frontier. There is no enemy so implacable against a country or a community as one of its own people who has rendered himself an alien by his crimes.

Right glad to be delivered from this treacherous companion, Mr. Hunt pursued his course along the skirts of the mountain, in a southern direction, seeking for some practicable defile by which he might pass

[7] None of this paragraph is traceable to Hunt.

[8] September 2. For this date the "Journal," 284, says only: "On the 2nd the journey was continued along the mountains, and a halt was made near a small stream which is said to be a tributary of Powder River."

[9] See *ibid.*, 284–85; see also Chapter XXIV, note 4, and Chapter XXV, note 11, above.

through it; none such presented, however, in the course of fifteen miles, and he encamped on a small stream, still on the outskirts. The green meadows which border these mountain streams are generally well stocked with game, and the hunters killed[10] several fat elks, which supplied the camp with fresh meat. In the evening the travellers were surprised by an unwelcome visit from several Crows belonging to a different band from that which they recently left,[11] and who said their camp was among the mountains. The consciousness of being environed by such dangerous neighbors, and of being still within the range of Rose[12] and his fellow ruffians, obliged the party to be continually on the alert, and to maintain weary vigils throughout the night, lest they should be robbed of their horses.

On the third of September,[13] finding that the mountain still stretched onwards, presenting a continued barrier, they endeavored to force a passage to the westward, but soon became entangled among rocks and precipices which set all their efforts at defiance. The mountain seemed, for the most part, rugged, bare, and sterile; yet here and there it was clothed with pines, and with shrubs and flowering plants, some of which were in bloom. In toiling among these weary places, their thirst became excessive, for no water was to be met with. Numbers of the men wandered off into rocky dells and ravines in hopes of finding some brook or fountain; some of whom lost their way and did not rejoin the main party.

After a day[14] of painful and fruitless scrambling, Mr. Hunt gave up the attempt to penetrate in this direction, and, returning to the little stream on the skirts of the mountain, pitched his tents within six miles of his encampment of the preceding night. He now ordered that signals

---

10 The first edition reads *hunters soon killed.*

11 The first edition reads *which they had recently left.*

12 According to what Irving says here and what he says above, Rose had already left Hunt. But what Hunt tells us is that Rose's separation coincided with the arrival of this new band of Crows. The "Journal" reads: "On September 2nd, we had received a visit from some Absarokas of a band which was different from the one we had recently left. . . . Consequently, I suggested to Rose that he remain with these indians. . . . He accepted. . . . Accordingly, Rose went to join the first Absarokas that we had met." *Ibid.*, 284–85.

13 The date is confirmed by Hunt.

14 The text should read *After half a day*, which appears in the first edition. Hunt's "Journal" confirms this reading: "An effort was made, for half of the day on the 3rd, to get out of the precipices and the arid mountains." *Ibid.*, 284.

should be made for the stragglers in quest of water; but the night passed away without their return.

The next morning, to their surprise, Rose made his appearance at the camp, accompanied by some of his Crow associates. His unwelcome visit revived their suspicions; but he announced himself as a messenger of good-will from the chief, who, finding they had taken the wrong road, had sent Rose and his companions to guide them to a nearer and better one across the mountain.[15]

Having no choice, being themselves utterly at fault, they set out under this questionable escort. They had not gone far before they fell in with the whole party of Crows, who, they now found, were going the same road with themselves. The two cavalcades of white and red men, therefore, pushed on together, and presented a wild and picturesque spectacle, as, equipped with various weapons and in various garbs, with trains of pack-horses, they wound in long lines through the rugged defiles, and up and down the crags and steeps of the mountain.

The travellers had again an opportunity to see and admire the equestrian habitudes and address of this hard-riding tribe. They were all mounted, man, woman, and child, for the Crows have horses in abundance, so that no one goes on foot. The children are perfect imps on horseback. Among them was one so young that he could not yet speak. He was tied on a colt of two years old, but managed the reins as if by instinct, and plied the whip with true Indian prodigality. Mr. Hunt inquired the age of this infant jockey, and was answered that "he had seen two winters."[16]

This is almost realizing the fable of the centaurs; nor can we wonder at the equestrian adroitness of these savages, who are thus in a manner cradled in the saddle, and become in infancy almost identified with the animal they bestride.

The mountain defiles were exceedingly rough and broken, and the travelling painful to the burdened horses. The party, therefore, proceeded but slowly, and were gradually left behind by the band of Crows, who had taken the lead. It is more than probable that Mr. Hunt loitered in his course, to get rid of such doubtful fellow-travellers. Certain it is

---

[15] Hunt is silent about the many difficulties Irving refers to, stating only that "their chief, knowing that we had taken a wrong road, sent Rose on the 4th [of September] to tell us this and to place us on the right road which crossed the mountains and which was shorter and better." *Ibid.*, 285. Rollins gives the route in detail; see *op. cit.*, 315n.

[16] Hunt's "Journal," 285.

that he felt a sensation of relief as he saw the whole crew, the renegade Rose and all, disappear among the windings of the mountain, and heard the last yelp of the savages die away in the distance.

When they were fairly out of sight, and out of hearing, he encamped on the head waters of the little stream of the preceding day, having come about sixteen miles.[17] Here he remained all the succeeding day, as well to give time for the Crows to get in the advance, as for the stragglers, who had wandered away in quest of water two days previously, to rejoin the camp. Indeed, considerable uneasiness began to be felt concerning these men, lest they should become utterly bewildered in the defiles of the mountains, or should fall into the hands of some marauding band of savages. Some of the most experienced hunters were sent in search of them; others, in the meantime, employed themselves in hunting. The narrow valley in which they encamped being watered by a running stream, yielded fresh pasturage, and though in the heart of the Bighorn Mountains, was well stocked with buffalo. Several of these were killed, as also a grizzly bear. In the evening, to the satisfaction of all parties, the stragglers made their appearance, and provisions being in abundance, there was hearty good cheer in the camp.[18]

[17] They made camp on September 4. The stream was probably either the north or middle fork of Crazy Woman Creek.
[18] *Ibid.*, 285.

Mountain Glens — Wandering Band of Savages
Anecdotes of Shoshonies and Flatheads — Root Diggers
Their Solitary Lurking Habits — Gnomes of the Mountains
Wind River — Scarcity of Food — Alteration of Route
The Pilot Knobs or Tetons — Branch of the Colorado — Hunting Camp

RESUMING their course on the following morning,[1] Mr. Hunt and his companions continued on westward through a rugged region of hills and rocks, but diversified in many places by grassy little glens, with springs of water, bright sparkling brooks, clumps of pine trees, and a profusion of flowering plants, which were in bloom,[2] although the weather was frosty. These beautiful and verdant recesses, running through and softening the rugged mountains, were cheering and refreshing to the wayworn travellers.

In the course of the morning, as they were entangled in a defile, they beheld a small band of savages,[3] as wild-looking as the surrounding scenery, who reconnoitred them warily from the rocks before they ventured to advance. Some of them were mounted on horses rudely caparisoned with bridles or halters of buffalo hide, one end trailing after them on the ground. They proved to be a mixed party of Flatheads and Shoshonies, or Snakes;[4] and as these tribes will be frequently mentioned in the course of this work, we shall give a few introductory particulars concerning them.

The Flatheads in question are not to be confounded with those of the name who dwell about the lower waters of the Columbia; neither do

---

[1] September 6. Hunt supplies the nature description: "We encountered many beautiful bits of country, abundant springs, stretches of green grass, groves of pine, innumerable quantities of blooming plants; and yet it froze continually." See "Journal," 285.

[2] The first edition reads *in full bloom.*

[3] Hunt says "eight indians and three families who were of the nation of Flatheads and of that of the Snakes." See "Journal," 285.

[4] Swanton, *Indian Tribes*, 403–10, distinguishes between the Northern Shoshonis (occupying western Wyoming, eastern Idaho, and northeastern Utah) and the Western Shoshonis (located in the central and western parts of Idaho, Utah in the northwest and over into Nevada, and parts of California).

they flatten their heads, as the others do. They inhabit the banks of a river on the west side of the mountains, and are described as simple, honest, and hospitable. Like all people of similar character, whether civilized or savage, they are prone to be imposed upon; and are especially maltreated by the ruthless Blackfeet,[5] who harass them in their villages, steal their horses by night, or openly carry them off in the face of day, without provoking pursuit or retaliation.

The Shoshonies are a branch of the once powerful and prosperous tribe of the Snakes, who possessed a glorious hunting country about the upper forks of the Missouri, abounding in beaver and buffalo. Their hunting ground was occasionally invaded by the Blackfeet, but the Snakes battled bravely for their domains, and a long and bloody feud existed, with variable success. At length the Hudson's Bay Company, extending their trade into the interior, had dealings with the Blackfeet, who were nearest to them, and supplied them with fire-arms. The Snakes, who occasionally traded with the Spaniards, endeavored, but in vain, to obtain similar weapons; the Spanish traders wisely refused to arm them so formidably. The Blackfeet had now a vast advantage, and soon dispossessed the poor Snakes of their favorite hunting grounds, their land of plenty, and drove them from place to place, until they were fain to take refuge in the wildest and most desolate recesses of the Rocky Mountains. Even here they are subject[6] to occasional visits from their implacable foes, as long as they have horses, or any other property to tempt the plunderer. Thus by degrees the Snakes have become a scattered, broken-spirited, impoverished people; keeping about lonely rivers and mountain streams, and subsisting chiefly upon fish. Such of them as still possess horses, and occasionally figure as hunters, are called Shoshonies; but there is another class, the most abject and forlorn, who are called Shuckers, or more commonly Diggers and Root Eaters. These are a shy, secret, solitary race, who keep in the most retired parts of the mountains, lurking like gnomes in caverns and clefts of the rocks, and subsisting in a great measure on the roots of the earth. Sometimes, in passing through a solitary mountain valley, the traveller comes perchance upon the bleeding carcass of a deer or buffalo that has just been slain. He looks round in vain for the hunter; the whole landscape is life-

[5] More properly the Siksikas, the native word denoting Blackfeet. Their territory extended from Montana into Canada. *Ibid.*, 395–98.

[6] *Subjected* in first edition.

less and deserted: at length he perceives a thread of smoke, curling up from among the crags and cliffs, and scrambling to the place, finds some forlorn and skulking brood of Diggers, terrified at being discovered.

The Shoshonies, however, who, as has been observed, have still "horse to ride and weapon to wear," are somewhat bolder in their spirit, and more open and wide in their wanderings. In the autumn, when salmon disappear from the rivers, and hunger begins to pinch, they even venture down into their ancient hunting grounds, to make a foray among the buffaloes. In this perilous enterprise they are occasionally joined by the Flatheads, the persecutions of the Blackfeet having produced a close alliance and coöperation between these luckless and maltreated tribes. Still, notwithstanding their united force, every step they take within the debatable ground is taken in fear and trembling, and with the utmost precaution: and an Indian trader assures us that he has seen at least five hundred of them, armed and equipped for action, and keeping watch upon the hill tops, while about fifty were hunting in the prairie. Their excursions are brief and hurried; as soon as they have collected and jerked sufficient buffalo meat for winter provisions, they pack their horses, abandon the dangerous hunting grounds, and hasten back to the mountains, happy if they have not the terrible Blackfeet rattling after them.[7]

Such a confederate band of Shoshonies and Flatheads was the one met by our travellers. It was bound on a visit to the Arapahoes, a tribe inhabiting the banks of the Nebraska. They were armed to the best of their scanty means, and some of the Shoshonies had bucklers of buffalo hide, adorned with feathers and leathern fringes, and which have a charmed virtue in their eyes, from having been prepared, with mystic ceremonies, by their conjurers.

In company with this wandering band our travellers proceeded all day. In the evening they encamped near to each other in a defile of the mountains, on the borders of a stream running north, and falling into Bighorn River. In the vicinity of the camp, they found gooseberries, strawberries, and currants, in great abundance. The defile bore traces of having been a thoroughfare for countless herds of buffaloes, though not

[7] Most of Irving's information on the Shoshonis comes from Lewis and Clark (see *History of the Expedition*, II, 115–17), with some details perhaps furnished by Captain Bonneville, who may be the Indian trader to whom Irving refers. Bonneville had spent a good deal of time among the Shoshonis and was able to observe them closely; see *The Adventures of Captain Bonneville*, passim.

one was to be seen. The hunters succeeded in killing an elk and several black-tailed deer.[8]

They were now in the bosom of the second Bighorn ridge,[9] with another lofty and snow-crowned mountain full in view to the west. Fifteen miles of western course brought them, on the following day, down into an intervening plain,[10] well stocked with buffalo. Here the Snakes and Flatheads joined with the white hunters in a successful hunt, that soon filled the camp with provisions.

On the morning of the 9th of September, the travellers parted company with their Indian friends, and continued on their course to the west.[11] A march of thirty miles brought them, in the evening, to the banks of a rapid and beautifully clear stream about a hundred yards wide. It is the north fork or branch of the Bighorn River, but bears its peculiar name of the Wind River, from being subject in the winter season to a continued blast which sweeps its banks and prevents the snow from lying on them. This blast is said to be caused by a narrow gap or funnel in the mountains, through which the river forces its way between perpendicular precipices, resembling cut rocks.[12]

This river[13] gives its name to a whole range of mountains consisting of three parallel chains,[14] eighty miles in length, and about twenty or

[8] In this paragraph, Irving returns to Hunt's "Journal," 285.

[9] The description is puzzling. The Big Horns and the mountains to the west form a gigantic horseshoe-shaped formation, with a large basin between.

[10] Big Horn Basin.

[11] The Shoshonis, as Hunt clearly states, left on the previous day: "On the morning of the 8th, the indians, having received the price for a horse which they had offered us, left us to go to the home of the Arrôpolous [Arapahos], a tribe of the Panis [Pawnees] who live along the Platte River. One of our party left a gun at camp; the indians made off with it before he could return there." See "Journal," 286.

[12] The Big Horn River is formed by the Wind River, which flows southeast out of the Wind River Mountains, and its confluence (near Riverton, Wyoming) with the Popo Agie, flowing northeast. At their junction the combined river flows north through Wind River Canyon, which cuts through the Owl Creek Mountains, and emerges from the canyon near modern Thermopolis, Wyoming, and continues north through the basin and finally joins the Yellowstone River in Montana. The *Astoria* map incorrectly shows Wind River flowing from the southwest before joining the Popo Agie. Hunt wrote: "The Big Horn in the place where we were camped is swift, clear and 300 feet wide. We could see below us the opening in the mountains by which it escapes. It is a very narrow pass bordered on both sides by precipices." See "Journal," 286.

[13] Wind River.

[14] The Wind River Mountains, consisting of one range, not "three parallel chains."

Overland Astorians through western Wyoming,
September 10–October 5, 1811

twenty-five broad. One of its peaks[15] is probably fifteen thousand feet
above the level of the sea, being one of the highest of the Rocky Sierra.
These mountains give rise, not merely to the Wind or Bighorn River,
but to several branches of the Yellowstone and the Missouri on the
east,[16] and of the Columbia and Colorado on the west;[17] thus dividing
the sources of these mighty streams.

For five succeeding days, Mr. Hunt and his party continued up the
course of the Wind River, to the distance of about eighty miles, crossing
and recrossing it, according to its windings, and the nature of its banks;
sometimes passing through valleys, at other times scrambling over rocks

[15] Gannett Peak, with an elevation of 13,785 feet, is the highest peak in the Wind
River Mountains.

[16] The Popo Agie, Wind River, Big Horn, and their tributaries, plus the Sweetwater,
an affluent of the North Platte.

[17] The principal river flowing from the western watershed of the Wind River Mountains is Green River, which, after joining several other rivers to become the Colorado,
flows into the Gulf of California. Northwest of the headwaters of Wind River is the
Snake River, which drains the southern part of present-day Yellowstone National Park
and Jackson Hole. After flowing west and north through Idaho, it joins the Columbia
River in Washington. The Continental Divide runs along the crest of the Wind River
Mountains, thus separating the Atlantic from the Pacific drainage.

and hills. The country in general was destitute of trees, but they passed through groves of wormwood,[18] eight and ten feet in height, which they used occasionally for fuel, and they met with large quantities of wild flax.

The mountains were destitute of game; they came in sight of two grizzly bears, but could not get near enough for a shot; provisions, therefore, began to be scanty. They saw large flights of the kind of thrush commonly called the robin, and many smaller birds of migratory species; but the hills in general appeared lonely and with few signs of animal life. On the evening of the 14th September,[19] they encamped on the forks of the Wind or Bighorn River.[20] The largest of these forks came from the range of Wind River Mountains.

The hunters[21] who served as guides to the party in this part of their route, had assured Mr. Hunt that, by following up Wind River, and crossing a single mountain ridge, he would come upon the head waters of the Columbia.[22] This scarcity of game, however, which already had been felt to a pinching degree, and which threatened them with famine among the sterile heights which lay before them, admonished them to change their course. It was determined, therefore, to make for a stream,[23] which they were informed passed the neighboring moun-

[18] Sagebrush. Cf. Hunt, "Journal," 286: "For fire-making . . . we often used sagebrush, which here attains a considerable size. I crossed a clump of it that was as high as I when on horseback and was extremely thick-spread."

[19] Hunt's "Journal" confirms the date.

[20] A misleading statement because it would seem to designate the main fork where the Popo Agie and Wind River meet. But Irving means a point higher up on Wind River, near present-day Dubois, Wyoming. This paragraph and the preceding one follow Hunt's "Journal," September 10–14, 286.

[21] Hoback, Robinson, and Reznor, who had come through this area after leaving Andrew Henry on Henry's Fork in 1810–11. It will be remembered that Hunt had left the Missouri and had come cross country at their suggestion because they knew from personal experience the hostility of the Blackfeet on the upper Missouri River.

[22] That is, the Snake, which was sometimes referred to as the Columbia and also as Lewis River.

[23] Green River, also called the Seeds-ke-dee as well as Spanish River. Hunt's "Journal" at this point reads: "On the 15th [of September], Wind River was quitted and an Indian trail was followed southwesterly into the mountains. . . . On the 16th, snow was frequently encountered; there were large patches of it on the summit and on the slopes of the mountains exposed to the north. Halt was made beside Spanish River." *Ibid.*, 286. Later he stated that a "lack of provisions forced us to make for the banks of Spanish River." *Ibid.*, 288.

By following the Indian trail, Hunt had crossed the Wind River Mountains at Union Pass. Had he followed Wind River, he would have crossed the Divide at Togwotee tains,[24] to the south of west, on the grassy banks of which it was probable they would meet with buffalo. Accordingly, about three o'clock on the following day, meeting with a beaten Indian road which led in the proper direction, they struck into it, turning their backs upon Wind River.

In the course of the day, they came to a height[25] that commanded an almost boundless prospect. Here one of the guides paused, and, after considering the vast landscape attentively, pointed to three mountain peaks[26] glistening with snow, which rose, he said, above a fork of Columbia River. They were hailed by the travellers with that joy with which a beacon on a sea-shore is hailed by mariners after a long and dangerous voyage. It is true there was many a weary league to be traversed before they should reach these landmarks, for, allowing for their evident height and the extreme transparency of the atmosphere, they could not be much less than a hundred miles distant.[27] Even after reaching them, there would yet remain hundreds of miles of their journey to be accomplished. All these matters were forgotten in the joy at seeing the first landmarks of the Columbia, that river which formed the bourne of the expedition. These remarkable peaks were known as the Tetons; as guiding points for many days, to Mr. Hunt, he gave them the names of the Pilot Knobs.[28]

The travellers continued their course to the south of west for about forty miles, through a region so elevated that patches of snow lay on the highest summits and on the northern declivities. At length they came to the desired stream, the object of their search, the waters of

Pass, but his reference to Spanish, or Green, River confirms the direction of his march. Union Pass led him to Green River where, after flowing north out of the Green River Lakes, it gradually turns west and then abruptly south. This is a beautiful, open valley, where his chances of finding game would have been good.

[24] The first edition reads *passed through the neighboring mountains.*

[25] Union Pass. "One of our hunters, who had been on the shores of the Columbia [i.e., the Snake] showed us three immensely high and snow-covered peaks which, he said, were situated on the banks of a tributary [Snake River] of that river." Hunt, "Journal," 286.

[26] The Three Tetons—Grand Teton, Middle Teton, and South Teton. The highest of these, Grand Teton, rises to 13,766 feet. They do not appear on the *Astoria* map (1836), but they do for the first time on Bonneville's map of 1837; see *The Adventures of Captain Bonneville*, facing p. 154.

[27] On an air line, closer to seventy-five miles.

[28] This sentence, following the first edition (I, 280), should read: "These remarkable peaks are known to some travellers as the Tetons; as they had been guiding points for many days, to Mr. Hunt, he gave them the name of the Pilot Knobs."

which flowed to the west. It was, in fact, a branch of the Colorado, which falls into the Gulf of California, and had received from the hunters the name of Spanish River, from information given by the Indians that Spaniards resided upon its lower waters.

The aspect of this river and its vicinity was cheering to the wayworn and hungry travellers. Its banks were green, and there were grassy valleys running from it in various directions, into the heart of the rugged mountains, with herds of buffalo quietly grazing. The hunters sallied forth with keen alacrity, and soon returned laden with provisions.

In this part of the mountains Mr. Hunt met with three different kinds of gooseberries. The common purple, on a low and very thorny bush; a yellow kind, of an excellent flavor, growing on a stock free from thorns; and a deep purple, of the size and taste of our winter grape, with a thorny stalk. There were also three kinds of currants, one very large and well tasted, of a purple color, and growing on a bush eight or nine feet high. Another of a yellow color, and of the size and taste of the large red currant, the bush four or five feet high; and the third a beautiful scarlet, resembling the strawberry in sweetness, though rather insipid, and growing on a low bush.[29]

On the 17th[30] they continued down the course of the river, making fifteen miles to the southwest. The river abounded with geese and ducks, and there were signs of its being inhabited by beaver and otters: indeed they were now approaching regions where these animals, the great objects of the fur trade, are said to abound.[31] They encamped for the night opposite the end of a mountain in the west,[32] which was probably the last chain of the Rocky Mountains. On the following morning they abandoned the main course of the Spanish River,[33] and taking a northwest direction for eight miles, came upon one of its little tributaries,[34]

[29] Hunt is very specific in enumerating the flora of the Green River Valley, and Irving paraphrases him closely. Here, Hunt also says, "numerous herds of bison graze." See "Journal," 287.

[30] The date is confirmed by Hunt's "Journal."

[31] It was in the valley of Green River that Ashley's trappers in 1824 found rich fur-bearing waters. Had Hunt left a party of trappers here, they would have been abundantly rewarded and conceivably could have changed the course of the mountain fur trade.

[32] Gros Ventre Range. Their obvious purpose was to cross the southern extremity of this range and move over to the Hoback River, now named for one of the party. This river would take them northwest directly to the Snake, of which it is a tributary.

[33] The first edition reads *of Spanish River*.

[34] Middle Beaver Creek.

issuing out of the bosom of the mountains,[35] and running through green meadows, yielding pasturage to herds of buffalo. As these were probably the last of that animal they would meet with, they encamped on the grassy banks of the river, determined to spend several days in hunting, so as to be able to jerk sufficient meat to supply them until they should reach the waters of the Columbia, where they trusted to find fish enough for their support. A little repose, too, was necessary for both men and horses, after their rugged and incessant marching; having in the course of the last seventeen days traversed two hundred and sixty miles of rough, and in many parts sterile, mountain country.

[35] Southeast of present-day Bondurant, Wyoming.

CHAPTER XXX

*A Plentiful Hunting Camp — Shoshonie Hunters — Hoback's River
Mad River — Encampment Near the Pilot Knobs — A Consultation
Preparations for a Perilous Voyage*

FIVE days were passed by Mr. Hunt and his companions in the fresh
meadows watered by the bright little mountain stream. The hunters
made great havoc among the buffaloes, and brought in quantities of
meat; the voyageurs busied themselves about the fires, roasting and
stewing for present purposes, or drying provisions for the journey; the
pack-horses, eased of their burdens, rolled on the grass, or grazed at
large about the ample pastures; those of the party who had no call upon
their services, indulged in the luxury of perfect relaxation, and the camp
presented a picture of rude feasting and revelry, of mingled bustle and
repose, characteristic of a halt in a fine hunting country.[1] In the course
of one of their excursions, some of the men came in sight of a small party
of Indians, who instantly fled in great apparent consternation. They immediately returned to camp with the intelligence: upon which Mr.
Hunt and four others[2] flung themselves upon their horses, and sallied
forth to reconnoitre. After riding for about eight miles, they came upon
a wild mountain scene. A lonely green valley stretched before them, surrounded by rugged heights. A herd of buffalo were careering madly
through it, with a troop of savage horsemen in full chase, plying them
with their bows and arrows. The appearance of Mr. Hunt and his companions put an abrupt end to the hunt; the buffalo scuttled off in one
direction, while the Indians plied their lashes and galloped off in another,
as fast as their steeds could carry them. Mr. Hunt gave chase; there was
a sharp scamper, though of short continuance. Two young Indians, who
were indifferently mounted, were soon overtaken. They were terribly

[1] Irving built up this scene from imagination and from what he remembered of his
own trip to the Indian country in 1832. The only suggestions from Hunt were in the
following sentence: "Halt was made there to dry bison enough to last as far as the
shores of the Columbia [Snake] and of rivers where we hoped to procure some fish."
See "Journal," 287.

[2] McKenzie and McClellan plus two left unnamed.

frightened, and evidently gave themselves up for lost. By degrees their fears were allayed by kind treatment; but they continued to regard the strangers with a mixture of awe and wonder, for it was the first time in their lives they had ever seen a white man.

They belonged to a party of Snakes who had come across the mountains on their autumnal hunting excursion to provide buffalo meat for the winter. Being persuaded of the peaceable intentions of Mr. Hunt and his companions, they willingly conducted them to their camp. It was pitched in a narrow valley on the margin of a stream. The tents were of dressed skins, some of them fantastically painted; with horses grazing about them. The approach of the party caused a transient alarm in the camp, for these poor Indians were ever on the look-out for cruel foes. No sooner, however, did they recognize the garb and complexion of their visitors, than their apprehensions were changed into joy; for some of them had dealt with white men, and knew them to be friendly, and to abound with articles of singular value. They welcomed them, therefore, to their tents, set food before them; and entertained them to the best of their power.

They had been successful in their hunt, and their camp was full of jerked buffalo meat, all of the choicest kind, and extremely fat. Mr. Hunt purchased[3] enough of them, in addition to what had been killed and cured by his own hunters, to load all the horses excepting those reserved for the partners and the wife of Pierre Dorion. He found, also, a few beaver skins in their camp, for which he paid liberally, as an inducement to them to hunt for more; informing them that some of his party intended to live among the mountains, and trade with the native hunters for their peltries. The poor Snakes soon comprehended the advantages thus held out to them, and promised to exert themselves to procure a quantity of beaver skins for future traffic.

Being now well supplied with provisions, Mr. Hunt broke up his encampment on the 24th of September,[4] and continued on to the west. A march of fifteen miles, over a mountain ridge, brought them to a stream[5] about fifty feet in width, which Hoback, one of their guides,

[3] Irving's description paraphrases Hunt's longer-than-usual entry for September 18; *ibid.*, 287. From the Snakes, Hunt bought about two thousand pounds of dried meat.

[4] Irving arrived at the date by inference, there being no dates indicated by Hunt between the eighteenth and the twenty-fifth.

[5] Hoback River, which flows northwest into the Snake River below present-day Jackson, Wyoming.

who had trapped[6] about the neighborhood when in the service of Mr. Henry, recognized for one of the head waters of the Columbia. The travellers hailed it with delight, as the first stream they had encountered tending toward their point of destination. They kept along it for two days, during which, from the contribution of many rills and brooks, it gradually swelled into a small river. As it meandered among rocks and precipices, they were frequently obliged to ford it, and such was its rapidity, that the men were often in danger of being swept away. Sometimes the banks advanced so close upon the river, that they were obliged to scramble up and down their rugged promontories, or to skirt along their bases where there was scarce a foothold. Their horses had dangerous falls in some of these passes. One of them rolled, with his load, nearly two hundred feet down hill into the river, but without receiving any injury. At length they emerged from these stupendous defiles, and continued for several miles along the bank of Hoback's River, through one of the stern mountain valleys. Here it was joined by a river of greater magnitude and swifter current,[7] and their united waters swept off through the valley in one impetuous stream, which, from its rapidity and turbulence, had received the name of the Mad River.[8] At the confluence of these streams the travellers encamped. An important point in their arduous journey had been attained, a few miles from their camp rose the three vast snowy peaks called the Tetons, or the Pilot Knobs, the great landmarks of the Columbia, by which they had shaped their course through this mountain wilderness.[9] By their feet flowed the rapid current of Mad River, a stream ample enough to admit of the navigation of canoes, and down which they might possibly be able to steer their course to the main body of the Columbia.[10] The Canadian voyageurs rejoiced at the idea of once more launching themselves upon their favorite element; of exchanging their horses for canoes, and of gliding down the bosoms of rivers, instead of scrambling over the backs of mountains. Others of the party, also, inexperienced in this kind of travelling, considered their toils and troubles as drawing to a close. They had conquered the chief difficulties of this great rocky barrier, and now flattered

[6] They were the first white men who had trapped here and in Jackson Hole.

[7] The Snake, which Hunt referred to as Mad River, as it emerges from Jackson Hole and is about to enter the Grand Canyon of the Snake Range.

[8] The first edition reads *of Mad River*.

[9] Irving has carefully followed Hunt for September 25–27. "Journal," 288.

[10] This delusion was to lead Hunt's party to disaster.

themselves with the hope of an easy downward course for the rest of their journey. Little did they dream of the hardships and perils by land and water, which were yet to be encountered in the frightful wilderness that intervened between them and the shores of the Pacific![11]

[11] This marks the end of Volume I of the first edition.

ON the banks of Mad River Mr. Hunt held a consultation with the other partners as to their future movements. The wild and impetuous current of the river rendered him doubtful whether it might not abound with impediments lower down, sufficient to render the navigation of it slow and perilous, if not impracticable. The hunters who had acted as guides, knew nothing of the character of the river below; what rocks, and shoals, and rapids might obstruct it, or through what mountains and deserts it might pass. Should they then abandon their horses, cast themselves loose in fragile barks upon this wild, doubtful, and unknown river; or should they continue their more toilsome and tedious, but perhaps more certain wayfaring by land?

The vote, as might have been expected, was almost unanimous for embarkation; for when men are in difficulties every change seems to be for the better. The difficulty now was to find timber of sufficient size for the construction of canoes, the trees in these high mountain regions being chiefly a scrubbed growth of pines and cedars, aspens, haws, and serviceberries, and a small kind of cotton-tree, with a leaf resembling that of the willow. There was a species of large fir, but so full of knots as to endanger the axe in hewing it. After searching for some time, a growth of timber, of sufficient size, was found lower down the river, whereupon the encampment was moved to the vicinity.

The men were now set to work to fell trees, and the mountains echoed to the unwonted sound of their axes. While preparations were thus going on for a voyage down the river, Mr. Hunt, who still entertained doubts of its practicability, despatched an exploring party, consisting of John Reed, the clerk, John Day, the hunter, and Pierre Dorion, the interpreter, with orders to proceed several days' march along the stream, and notice its course and character.[1]

After their departure, Mr. Hunt turned his thoughts to another object of importance. He had now arrived at the head waters of the Columbia, which were among the main points embraced by the enterprise of Mr. Astor. These upper streams were reputed to abound in beaver, and had as yet been unmolested by the white trapper.[2] The numerous signs of beaver met with during the recent search for timber, gave evidence that the neighborhood was a good "trapping ground."[3] Here, then, it was proper to begin to cast loose those leashes of hardy trappers that are detached from trading parties in the very heart of the wilderness. The men detached in the present instance were Alexander Carson, Louis St. Michel, Pierre Detayé, and Pierre Delaunay. Trappers generally go in pairs, that they may assist, protect, and comfort each other in their lonely and perilous occupations. Thus Carson and St. Michel formed one couple, and Detayé and Delaunay another. They were fitted out with traps, arms, ammunition, horses, and every other requisite, and were to trap upon the upper part of Mad River, and upon the neighboring streams of the mountains. This would probably occupy them for some months; and, when they should have collected a sufficient quantity of peltries, they were to pack them upon their horses and make the best of their way to the mouth of Columbia River, or to any intermediate post which might be established by the company. They took leave of their comrades and started off on their several courses with stout

[1] Hunt provides all of Irving's details for the above paragraphs but names only John Reed as one of the three men sent out to explore. The men remaining with Hunt cut trees for canoes. "On the 30th, we set to work, and felled many trees that were not suitable. Nevertheless, as I feared that the river would not be navigable below the point where it enters the mountains [Snake Range], Mr. Reed, attended by two men, set out downstream to explore it for a distance of four day's march." See "Journal," 288.

[2] It is possible that Hoback, Robinson, and Reznor had trapped in the Jackson Hole area during the winter and spring of 1810-11; see Merrill J. Mattes, "Jackson Hole, Crossroads of the Western Fur Trade, 1807-1829," *Pacific Northwest Quarterly*, Vol. XXXVII (1946), 93. Nothing in Hunt's "Journal" substantiates Irving's statement.

[3] Hunt stated: "Having ascended with a man some twelve miles on the other [i.e., west] side of the river, I saw many indications of beaver, some signs of gray bear and a band of elk." See "Journal," 288.

hearts and cheerful countenances; though these lonely cruisings into a wild and hostile wilderness seem to the uninitiated equivalent to being cast adrift in the ship's yawl in the midst of the ocean.[4]

Of the perils that attend the lonely trapper, the reader will have sufficient proof, when he comes, in the after part of this work, to learn the hard fortunes of these poor fellows in the course of their wild peregrinations.[5]

The trappers had not long departed, when two Snake Indians wandered into the camp. When they perceived that the strangers were fabricating canoes, they shook their heads and gave them to understand that the river was not navigable. Their information, however, was scoffed at by some of the party, who were obstinately bent on embarkation, but was confirmed by the exploring party, who returned after several days' absence. They had kept along the river with great difficulty for two days, and found it a narrow, crooked, turbulent stream, confined in a rocky channel, with many rapids, and occasionally overhung with precipices. From the summit of one of these they had caught a bird's-eye view of its boisterous career for a great distance through the heart of the mountain, with impending rocks and cliffs. Satisfied from this view that it was useless to follow its course, either by land or water, they had given up all further investigation.[6]

These concurring reports determined Mr. Hunt to abandon Mad River, and seek some more navigable stream. This determination was concurred in by all his associates excepting Mr. Miller, who had become impatient of the fatigue of land travel, and was for immediate embarkation at all hazards. This gentleman had been in a gloomy and irritated state of mind for some time past, being troubled with a bodily malady that rendered travelling on horseback extremely irksome to him, and being, moreover, discontented with having a smaller share in the expedition than his comrades. His unreasonable objections to a further march by land were overruled, and the party prepared to decamp.[7]

Robinson, Hoback, and Rezner, the three hunters who had hitherto

---

[4] Hunt says only: "Several of our men departed to catch beaver." *Ibid.*, 289. They left on October 1.

[5] See below, p. 439.

[6] This paragraph faithfully paraphrases Hunt's "Journal," 289.

[7] Hunt says nothing about Miller's objections.

served as guides among the mountains, now stepped forward, and advised Mr. Hunt to make for the post established during the preceding year by Mr. Henry, of the Missouri Fur Company. They had been with Mr. Henry, and, as far as they could judge by the neighboring landmarks, his post could not be very far off. They presumed there could be but one intervening ridge[8] of mountains, which might be passed without any great difficulty. Henry's post, or fort,[9] was on an upper branch of the Columbia, down which they made no doubt it would be easy to navigate in canoes.

The two Snake Indians being questioned in the matter, showed a perfect knowledge of the situation of the post, and offered, with great alacrity, to guide them to the place. Their offer was accepted, greatly to the displeasure of Mr. Miller, who seemed obstinately bent upon braving the perils of Mad River.

The weather for a few days past had been stormy, with rain and sleet. The Rocky Mountains are subject to tempestuous winds from the west; these sometimes come in flaws or currents, making a path through the forests many yards in width, and whirling off trunks and branches to a great distance. The present storm subsided on the third of October,[10] leaving all the surrounding heights covered with snow; for while rain had fallen in the valley, it had snowed on the hill tops.

On the 4th, they broke up their encampment, and crossed the river, the water coming up to the girths of their horses. After travelling four miles, they encamped at the foot of the mountain, the last, as they hoped, which they should have to traverse. Four days more took them across it,[11] and over several plains, watered by beautiful little streams, tributaries of Mad River. Near one of their encampments there was a hot

[8] The Teton Range, forming the western wall of Jackson Hole.

[9] On Henry's Fork, near modern St. Anthony, Idaho.

[10] Hunt shows the date to be October 4: "All day long on the 3rd, rain and sleet fell. Everything was in readiness for crossing the mountain which was regarded as the last. The storm ceased on the 4th, but all the mountains were covered with snow." See "Journal," 289.

[11] They crossed at Teton Pass, west of today's Jackson, Wyoming. Hunt recorded: "We crossed Mad River—the water being up to the horses' bellies—and camped at the foot of the mountain [near present-day Wilson, Wyoming]. On the 5th, the mountain was crossed by an easy and well-broken trail. . . . The Snakes served us as guides, although last year two [three] of our hunters had come into this region." *Ibid.*, 289. The hunters were Hoback, Robinson, and Reznor.

spring continually emitting a cloud of vapor. These elevated plains, which give a peculiar character to the mountains, are frequented by large gangs of antelopes, fleet as the wind.

On the evening of the 8th of October,[12] after a cold wintery day, with gusts of westerly wind and flurries of snow, they arrived at the sought-for post of Mr. Henry.[13] Here he had fixed himself, after being compelled by the hostilities of the Blackfeet, to abandon the upper waters of the Missouri. The post, however, was deserted, for Mr. Henry had left it in the course of the preceding spring, and, as it afterwards appeared, had fallen in with Mr. Lisa, at the Arickara village on the Missouri, some time after the separation of Mr. Hunt and his party.

The weary travellers gladly took possession of the deserted log huts which had formed the post, and which stood on the bank of a stream upwards of a hundred yards wide, on which they intended to embark. There being plenty of suitable timber in the neighborhood, Mr. Hunt immediately proceeded to construct canoes.[14] As he would have to leave his horses and their accoutrements here, he determined to make this a trading post, where the trappers and hunters, to be distributed about the country, might repair; and where the traders might touch on their way through the mountains to and from the establishment at the mouth of the Columbia. He informed the two Snake Indians of this determination, and engaged them to remain in that neighborhood and take care of the horses until the white men should return, promising them ample rewards for their fidelity. It may seem a desperate chance to trust to the faith and honesty of two such vagabonds; but, as the horses would have, at all events, to be abandoned, and would otherwise become the property of the first vagrant horde that should encounter them, it was one chance in favor of their being regained.

At this place another detachment of hunters prepared to separate from the party for the purpose of trapping beaver. Three of these had already been in this neighborhood, being the veteran Robinson and his companions, Hoback and Rezner, who had accompanied Mr. Henry across the mountains, and who had been picked up by Mr. Hunt on the Missouri, on their way home to Kentucky. According to agreement they

[12] The date is confirmed by Hunt.

[13] See M. D. Beal, *A History of Southeastern Idaho*, for an account of an excavation of a cabin at this site.

[14] "On the 9th, we had already begun eight, all of cottonwood." Hunt, "Journal," 289–91.

were fitted out with horses, traps, ammunition, and everything requisite for their undertaking, and were to bring in all the peltries they should collect, either to this trading post, or to the establishment at the mouth of Columbia River. Another hunter, of the name of Cass, was associated with them in their enterprise. It is in this way that small knots of trappers and hunters are distributed about the wilderness by the fur companies, and like cranes and bitterns, haunt its solitary streams. Robinson, the Kentuckian, the veteran of the "Bloody Ground," who, as has already been noted, had been scalped by the Indians in his younger days, was the leader of this little band. When they were about to depart, Mr. Miller called the partners together and threw up his share in the company, declaring his intention of joining the party of trappers.[15]

This resolution struck every one with astonishment, Mr. Miller being a man of education and of cultivated habits, and little fitted for the rude life of a hunter. Besides, the precarious and slender profits arising from such a life were beneath the prospects of one who held a share in the general enterprise. Mr. Hunt was especially concerned and mortified at his determination, as it was through his advice and influence he had entered into the concern. He endeavored, therefore, to dissuade him from this sudden resolution; representing its rashness, and the hardships and perils to which it would expose him. He earnestly advised him, however he might feel dissatisfied with the enterprise, still to continue on in company until they should reach the mouth of Columbia River. There they would meet the expedition that was to come by sea; when, should he still feel disposed to relinquish the undertaking, Mr. Hunt pledged himself to furnish him a passage home in one of the vessels belonging to the company.

To all this Miller replied abruptly, that it was useless to argue with him, as his mind was made up. They might furnish him, or not, as they pleased, with the necessary supplies, but he was determined to part company here, and set off with the trappers. So saying, he flung out of their presence without vouchsafing any further conversation.[16]

---

[15] Later at Astoria the partners took the following action: "Resolved that Joseph Miller having been permitted to retire from the concern on the 9th day of October last, be considered from that date to have no interest whatever in the Pacific Fur Company, and that he is no longer entitled to any right, privilege, or emolument arising from his having been a Partner thereof." Missouri Historical Society, printed in Flandrau, *Astor and the Oregon Country*, 36.

[16] Hunt says only that "on the 10th Mr. Miller, with four hunters and four horses,

Much as this wayward conduct gave them anxiety, the partners saw it was in vain to remonstrate. Every attention was paid to fit him out for his headstrong undertaking. He was provided with four horses, and all the articles he required. The two Snakes undertook to conduct him and his companions to an encampment of their tribe, lower down among the mountains, from whom they would receive information as to the best trapping grounds. After thus guiding them, the Snakes were to return to Fort Henry, as the new trading post was called, and take charge of the horses which the party would leave there, of which, after all the hunters were supplied, there remained seventy-seven.[17] These matters being all arranged, Mr. Miller set out with his companions, under guidance of the two Snakes, on the 10th of October;[18] and much did it grieve the friends of that gentleman to see him thus wantonly casting himself loose upon savage life. How he and his comrades fared in the wilderness, and how the Snakes acquitted themselves of their trust respecting the horses, will hereafter appear in the course of these rambling anecdotes.

----

left to go beaver-trapping. They took with them the two Snakes, and descended along the mountains in the hope of finding a band of indians from whom they trusted to obtain information useful for their hunt." See "Journal," 290.

[17] The number of horses agrees with Hunt's statement.

[18] The statement and date are confirmed by Hunt's "Journal."

CHAPTER XXXII

Scanty Fare — A Mendicant Snake — Embarkation on Henry River
Joy of the Voyageurs — Arrival at Snake River
Rapids and Breakers — Beginning of Misfortunes
Snake Encampment — Parley with a Savage — A Second Disaster
Loss of a Boatman — The Caldron Linn

WHILE the canoes were in preparation, the hunters ranged about the neighborhood, but with little success. Tracks of buffaloes were to be seen in all directions, but none of a fresh date. There were some elk, but extremely wild; two only were killed. Antelopes were likewise seen, but too shy and fleet to be approached. A few beavers were taken every night, and salmon trout of a small size, so that the camp had principally to subsist upon dried buffalo meat.

On the 14th,[1] a poor, half-naked Snake Indian, one of that forlorn caste called the Shuckers, or Diggers, made his appearance at the camp. He came from some lurking-place among the rocks and cliffs, and presented a picture of that famishing wretchedness to which these lonely fugitives among the mountains are sometimes reduced. Having received wherewithal to allay his hunger, he disappeared, but in the course of a day or two returned to the camp, bringing with him his son, a miserable boy, still more naked and forlorn than himself. Food was given to both; they skulked about the camp like hungry hounds, seeking what they might devour, and having gathered up the feet and entrails of some beavers that were lying about, slunk off with them to their den among the rocks.

By the 18th of October,[2] fifteen canoes were completed, and on the following day the party embarked with their effects; leaving their horses grazing about the banks, and trusting to the honesty of the two Snakes, and some special turn of good luck for their future recovery.[3]

[1] The date is confirmed by Hunt's "Journal."
[2] The date is given by Hunt.
[3] The above two paragraphs incorporate Hunt's entries, October 14 through the

271

The current bore them along at a rapid rate; the light spirits of the Canadian voyageurs, which had occasionally flagged upon land, rose to their accustomed buoyancy on finding themselves again upon the water. They wielded their paddles with their wonted dexterity, and for the first time made the mountains echo with their favorite boat-songs.

In the course of the day the little squadron arrived at the confluence of Henry and Mad rivers,[4] which, thus united, swelled into a beautiful stream of a light pea-green color, navigable for boats of any size, and which from the place of junction, took the name of Snake River,[5] a stream doomed to be the scene of much disaster to the travellers. The banks were here and there fringed with willow thickets and small cottonwood trees. The weather was cold, and it snowed all day, and great flocks of ducks and geese, sporting in the water or streaming through the air, gave token that winter was at hand; yet the hearts of the travellers were light, and, as they glided down the little river, they flattered themselves with the hope of soon reaching the Columbia. After making thirty miles in a southerly direction, they encamped for the night in a neighborhood which required some little vigilance, as there were recent traces of grizzly bears among the thickets.

On the following day the river increased in width and beauty; flowing parallel to a range of mountains on the left, which at times were finely reflected in its light green waters. The three snowy summits of the Pilot Knobs[6] or Tetons were still seen towering in the distance. After pursuing a swift but placid course for twenty miles, the current began to foam and brawl, and assume the wild and broken character common to the streams west of the Rocky Mountains. In fact the rivers which flow from these mountains to the Pacific, are essentially different from those which traverse the great prairies on their eastern declivities. The latter, though sometimes boisterous, are generally free from obstructions, and easily

---

nineteenth. Abandoning their horses and setting forth in canoes, the party committed the most serious mistake of the journey. Here was the turning point, and after traveling approximately three hundred miles on the Snake River, they realized, too late, what a costly mistake it was. Had they continued on land, their going would not always have been easy, but they would have been able to travel faster and without loss of human life or the need to cache most of their goods. The horses would also have provided a supply of food in an emergency.

[4] Henry's Fork meets the Snake near today's Menan, Idaho.

[5] Hunt refers to the Snake below its confluence with Henry's Fork as Canoe River.

[6] Hunt refers only to "the Pilot Knob."

272

navigated; but the rivers to the west of the mountains descend more steeply and impetuously, and are continually liable to cascades and rapids. The latter abounded in the part of the river which the travellers were now descending. Two of the canoes filled among the breakers; the crews were saved, but much of the lading was lost or damaged, and one of the canoes drifted down the stream and was broken among the rocks.[7]

On the following day, October 21st,[8] they made but a short distance when they came to a dangerous strait, where the river was compressed for nearly half a mile between perpendicular rocks, reducing it to the width of twenty yards, and increasing its violence. Here they were obliged to pass the canoes down cautiously by a line from the impending banks.[9] This consumed a great part of a day; and after they had re-ëmbarked they were soon again impeded by rapids, when they had to unload their canoes and carry them and their cargoes for some distance by land. It is at these places, called "portages," that the Canadian voyageur exhibits his most valuable qualities; carrying heavy burdens, and toiling to and fro, on land and in the water, over rocks and precipices, among brakes and brambles, not only without a murmur, but with the greatest cheerfulness and alacrity, joking and laughing and singing scraps of old French ditties.

The spirits of the party, however, which had been elated on first varying their journeying from land to water, had now lost some of their buoyancy. Everything ahead was wrapped in uncertainty. They knew nothing of the river on which they were floating. It had never been navigated by a white man,[10] nor could they meet with an Indian to give them any information concerning it. It kept on its course through a vast wilderness of silent and apparently uninhabited mountains, without a savage wigwam upon its banks, or bark upon its waters. The difficulties and perils they had already passed, made them apprehend others before them, that might effectually bar their progress. As they glided onward, however, they regained heart and hope. The current continued to be strong; but it was steady, and though they met with frequent

[7] This occurred on October 20. For the above two paragraphs, into which Irving interjected additional material, see "Journal," 290–291.

[8] The date is confirmed by Hunt.

[9] They portaged a mile and a quarter. *Ibid.*, 291.

[10] Irving is correct in pointing out that the Astorians were the first to attempt to navigate the river.

rapids, none of them were bad. Mountains were constantly to be seen in different directions, but sometimes the swift river glided through prairies,[11] and was bordered by small cotton-wood trees and willows. These prairies at certain seasons are ranged by migratory herds of the wide-wandering buffalo, the tracks of which, though not of recent date, were frequently to be seen. Here, too, were to be found the prickly pear or Indian fig, a plant which loves a more southern climate. On the land were large flights of magpies and American robins; whole fleets of ducks and geese navigated the river, or flew off in long streaming files at the approach of the canoes; while the frequent establishments of the painstaking and quiet-loving beaver, showed that the solitude of these waters was rarely disturbed, even by the all-pervading savage.

They had now come near two hundred and eighty miles since leaving Fort Henry, yet without seeing a human being, or a human habitation; a wild and desert solitude extended on either side of the river, apparently almost destitute of animal life. At length, on the 24th of October,[12] they were gladdened by the sight of some savage tents, and hastened to land and visit them, for they were anxious to procure information to guide them on their route. On their approach, however, the savages fled in consternation. They proved to be a wandering band of Shoshonies. In their tents were great quantities of small fish about two inches long,[13] together with roots and seeds, or grain, which they were drying for winter provisions. They appeared to be destitute of tools of any kind, yet there were bows and arrows very well made; the former were formed of pine, cedar, or bone, strengthened by sinews, and the latter of the wood of rose-bushes, and other crooked plants, but carefully straightened, and tipped with stone of a bottle-green color.

There were also vessels of willow and grass, so closely wrought as to hold water, and a seine neatly made with meshes, in the ordinary manner, of the fibres of wild flax or nettle. The humble effects of the poor savages remained unmolested by their visitors, and a few small articles, with a knife or two, were left in the camp, and were no doubt regarded as invaluable prizes.

[11] The Snake River Plain.

[12] Irving arrived at the date, which is not given in Hunt's "Journal," by inference. Entries appear for October 23 and 25.

[13] Hunt says "not more than an inch long." See "Journal," 291.

Shortly after leaving this deserted camp, and reëmbarking in the canoes, the travellers met with three of the Snakes on a triangular raft made of flags or reeds; such was their rude mode of navigating the river. They were entirely naked excepting small mantles of hare skins over their shoulders. The canoes approached near enough to gain a full view of them, but they were not to be brought to a parley.[14]

All further progress for the day was barred by a fall[15] in the river of about thirty feet perpendicular; at the head of which the party encamped for the night.

The next day was one of excessive toil and but little progress: the river winding through a wild rocky country, and being interrupted by frequent rapids, among which the canoes were in great peril.[16] On the succeeding day they again visited a camp of wandering Snakes, but the inhabitants fled with terror at the sight of a fleet of canoes, filled with white men, coming down their solitary river.

As Mr. Hunt was extremely anxious to gain information concerning his route, he endeavored by all kinds of friendly signs to entice back the fugitives. At length one, who was on horseback, ventured back with fear and trembling. He was better clad, and in better condition, than most of his vagrant tribe that Mr. Hunt had yet seen. The chief object of his return appeared to be to intercede for a quantity of dried meat and salmon trout, which he had left behind; on which, probably, he depended for his winter's subsistence. The poor wretch approached with hesitation, the alternate dread of famine and of white men operating upon his mind. He made the most abject signs, imploring Mr. Hunt not to carry off his food. The latter tried in every way to reassure him, and offered him knives in exchange for his provisions; great as was the temptation, the poor Snake could only prevail upon himself to spare a part; keeping a feverish watch over the rest, lest it should be taken away. It was in vain Mr. Hunt made inquiries of him concerning his route, and the course of the river. The Indian was too much frightened and bewildered to comprehend him or to reply; he did nothing but alternately commend himself to the protection of the Good Spirit, and supplicate

[14] The above three paragraphs are derived from *ibid.*

[15] American Falls. Rollins (ed.), *Discovery of the Oregon Trail,* 319n.

[16] Hunt says that on October 25 they crossed to the south side of the river in order to avoid some falls and continued for six miles on land. At an obstruction in the river, they lost more goods while letting a canoe down on a towline.

Mr. Hunt not to take away his fish and buffalo meat; and in this state they left him, trembling about his treasures.[17]

In the course of that and the next day they made nearly eighty miles; the river inclining to the south of west, and being clear and beautiful, nearly half a mile in width, with many populous communities of the beaver along its banks.[18] The 28th of October,[19] however, was a day of disaster. The river again became rough and impetuous, and was chafed and broken by numerous rapids. These grew more and more dangerous, and the utmost skill was required to steer among them. Mr. Crooks was seated in the second canoe of the squadron, and had an old experienced Canadian for steersman, named Antoine Clappine, one of the most valuable of the voyageurs. The leading canoe had glided safely among the turbulent and roaring surges, but in following it, Mr. Crooks perceived that his canoe was bearing towards a rock. He called out to the steersman, but his warning voice was either unheard or unheeded. In the next moment they struck upon the rock. The canoe was split and overturned. There were five persons on board. Mr. Crooks and one of his companions were thrown amidst roaring breakers and a whirling current, but succeeded, by strong swimming, to reach the shore. Clappine and two others clung to the shattered bark, and drifted with it to a rock. The wreck struck the rock with one end, and swinging round, flung poor Clappine off into the raging stream, which swept him away, and he perished. His comrades succeeded in getting upon the rock, from whence they were afterwards taken off.[20]

This disastrous event brought the whole squadron to a halt, and struck a chill into every bosom. Indeed they had arrived at a terrific strait, that forbade all further progress in the canoes, and dismayed the most experienced voyageur. The whole body of the river was compressed into a space of less than thirty feet in width, between two ledges of rocks, upwards of two hundred feet high, and formed a whirling and tumul-

[17] From Hunt's "Journal," October 26.

[18] They were now probably in the vicinity of present-day Burley, Idaho.

[19] The date agrees with the "Journal."

[20] Hunt records laconically: "After passing several rapids, we came to the entrance of a canyon. Mr. Crooks's canoe upset, one of his men was drowned, many goods were lost." *Ibid.*, 292. Clappine's name is not given in the "Journal," and Irving must have learned it orally or from reading Hunt's account books. Clappine is listed in Porter's "Roll of Overland Astorians," *Oregon Historical Quarterly*, Vol. XXXIV (1933), 106.

tuous vortex, so frightfully agitated, as to receive the name of "The Caldron Linn."[21] Beyond this fearful abyss, the river kept raging and roaring on, until lost to sight among impending precipices.

[21] Robert Stuart, returning this way the next summer (August 29, 1812), left a vivid description of Caldron Linn: "The whole body of the River is confined between 2 ledges of Rock somewhat less than 40 feet apart & Here indeed its terrific appearance beggars all description—Hecate's caldron was never half so agitated when vomiting even the most diabolical spells, as is this Linn in a low state of [*the*] water." Rollins (ed.), *op. cit.*, 112; Spaulding (ed.), *On the Oregon Trail*, 88. Regarding the location of Caldron Linn, see Rollins (ed.), *op. cit.*, 321n. On the basis of evidence in Robert Stuart's "Journal," Rollins argues that the whirlpool was located at today's Murtaugh, Idaho. This site has been questioned, however, by the Idaho Historical Society in correspondence with me, and until further evidence is available, Rollins' location must be regarded as conjectural.

Gloomy Council — Exploring Parties — Discouraging Reports
Disastrous Experiment — Detachments in Quest of Succor
Caches, How Made — Return of One of the Detachments
Unsuccessful — Further Disappointments — The Devil's Scuttle Hole

MR. HUNT and his companions encamped upon the borders of the Caldron Linn, and held gloomy counsel as to their future course. The recent wreck had dismayed even the voyageurs, and the fate of their popular comrade, Clappine, one of the most adroit and experienced of their fraternity, had struck sorrow to their hearts, for with all their levity, these thoughtless beings have great kindness towards each other.

The whole distance they had navigated since leaving Henry's Fort, was computed to be about three hundred and forty miles; strong apprehensions were now entertained that the tremendous impediments before them would oblige them to abandon their canoes. It was determined to send exploring parties on each side of the river to ascertain whether it was possible to navigate it further. Accordingly, on the following morning, three men were despatched along the south bank, while Mr. Hunt and three others proceeded along the north. The two parties returned after a weary scramble among swamps, rocks, and precipices, and with very disheartening accounts. For nearly forty miles that they had explored, the river foamed and roared along through a deep and narrow channel, from twenty to thirty yards wide, which it had worn, in the course of ages, through the heart of a barren, rocky country. The precipices on each side were often two and three hundred feet high, sometimes perpendicular, and sometimes overhanging, so that it was impossible, excepting in one or two places, to get down to the margin of the stream. This dreary strait was rendered the more dangerous by frequent rapids, and occasionally perpendicular falls from ten to forty feet in height; so that it seemed almost hopeless to attempt to pass the canoes down it.[1] The party, however, who had explored the south side

---

[1] Irving follows Hunt's "Journal" for October 29, but Hunt gives thirty-five miles

of the river had found a place, about six miles from the camp, where they thought it possible the canoes might be carried down the bank and launched upon the stream, and from whence they might make their way with the aid of occasional portages. Four of the best canoes were accordingly selected for the experiment, and were transported to the place on the shoulders of sixteen of the men. At the same time Mr. Reed the clerk, and three men, were detached to explore the river still further down than the previous scouting parties had been, and at the same time to look out for Indians, from whom provisions might be obtained, and a supply of horses, should it be found necessary to proceed by land.

The party who had been sent with the canoes returned on the following day, weary and dejected. One of the canoes had been swept away with all the weapons and effects of four of the voyageurs, in attempting to pass it down a rapid by means of a line. The other three had stuck fast among the rocks, so that it was impossible to move them; the men returned, therefore, in despair, and declared the river unnavigable.[2]

The situation of the unfortunate travellers was now gloomy in the extreme. They were in the heart of an unknown wilderness, untraversed as yet by a white man. They were at a loss what route to take, and how far they were from the ultimate place of their destination, nor could they meet in these uninhabited wilds with any human being to give them information. The repeated accidents to their canoes had reduced their stock of provisions to five days' allowance, and there was now every appearance of soon having famine added to their other sufferings.

This last circumstance rendered it more perilous to keep together than to separate. Accordingly, after a little anxious but bewildered counsel, it was determined that several small detachments should start off in different directions, headed by the several partners. Should any of them succeed in falling in with friendly Indians, within a reasonable distance, and obtaining a supply of provisions and horses, they were to return to the aid of the main body: otherwise they were to shift for themselves, and shape their course according to circumstances; keeping the mouth of the Columbia River as the ultimate point of their wayfaring. According-

instead of "nearly forty" for the distance he explored downstream. Also the state of their provisions is indicated by Hunt's saying that "for supper we had only some fruits of the rose bushes." *Ibid.*, 292. He had passed two high falls, Shoshone (212 feet) and Twin Falls (182 feet). Rollins (ed.), *Discovery of the Oregon Trail*, 319–20n.

[2] See Hunt's entries for October 29 through November 1.

ly, three several parties set off from the camp at Caldron Linn, in opposite directions. Mr. M'Lellan, with three men, kept down along the bank of the river. Mr. Crooks, with five others, turned their steps up it; retracing by land the weary course they had made by water, intending, should they not find relief nearer at hand, to keep on until they should reach Henry's Fort, where they hoped to find the horses they had left there, and to return with them to the main body.

The third party, composed of five men, was headed by Mr. M'Kenzie, who struck to the northward, across the desert plains, in hopes of coming upon the main stream of the Columbia.

Having seen these three adventurous bands depart upon their forlorn expeditions, Mr. Hunt turned his thoughts to provide for the subsistence of the main body left to his charge, and to prepare for their future march. There remained with him thirty-one men, beside[s] the squaw and two children of Pierre Dorion. There was no game to be met with in the neighborhood; but beavers were occasionally trapped about the river banks, which afforded a scanty supply of food; in the meantime they comforted themselves that some one or other of the foraging detachments would be successful, and return with relief.

Mr. Hunt now set to work with all diligence, to prepare *caches*, in which to deposit the baggage and merchandise, of which it would be necessary to disburden themselves, preparatory to their weary march by land; and here we shall give a brief description of those contrivances, so noted in the wilderness.

A cache is a term common among traders and hunters, to designate a hiding-place for provisions and effects. It is derived from the French word *cacher*, to conceal, and originated among the early colonists of Canada and Louisiana; but the secret depository which it designates was in use among the aboriginals long before the intrusion of the white men. It is, in fact, the only mode that migatory hordes have of preserving their valuables from robbery, during their long absences from their villages or accustomed haunts, on hunting expeditions, or during the vicissitudes of war. The utmost skill and caution are required to render these places of concealment invisible to the lynx eye of an Indian. The first care is to seek out a proper situation, which is generally some dry, low, bank of clay, on the margin of a water-course. As soon as the precise spot is pitched upon, blankets, saddle-cloths, and other coverings, are spread over the surrounding grass and bushes, to prevent foot-tracks, or any other derangement; and as few hands as possible are employed. A circle of about two feet in diameter is then nicely cut in the sod, which is carefully removed, with the loose soil immediately beneath it, and laid aside in a place where it will be safe from anything that may change its appearance. The uncovered area is then digged perpendicularly to the depth of about three feet, and is then gradually widened so as to form a conical chamber six or seven feet deep. The whole of the earth displaced by this process, being of a different color from that on the surface, is handed up in a vessel, and heaped into a skin or cloth, in which it is conveyed to the stream and thrown into the midst of the current, that it may be entirely carried off. Should the cache not be formed in the vicinity of a stream, the earth thus thrown up is carried to a distance, and scattered in such manner as not to leave the minutest trace. The cave being formed, is well lined with dry grass, bark, sticks, and poles, and occasionally a dried hide. The property intended to be hidden is then laid in, after having been well aired: a hide is spread over it, and dried grass, brush, and stones thrown in, and trampled down until the pit is filled to the neck. The loose soil which had been put aside is then brought and rammed down firmly, to prevent its caving in, and is frequently sprinkled with water, to destroy the scent, lest the wolves and bears should be attracted to the place, and root up the concealed treasure. When the neck of the cache is nearly level with the surrounding surface, the sod is again fitted in with the utmost exactness, and any bushes, stocks, or stones, that may have originally been about the spot, are restored to their former places. The blankets and other coverings are then removed from the surrounding herbage; all tracks are obliterated; the grass is gently raised by the hand to its natural position, and the minutest chip or straw is scrupulously gleaned up and thrown into the stream. After all this is done, the place is abandoned for the night, and, if all be right next morning, is not visited again, until there be a necessity for reopening the cache. Four men are sufficient, in this way, to conceal the amount of three tons weight of merchandise[3] in the course of two days. Nine caches were required to contain the goods and baggage which Mr. Hunt found it necessary to leave at this place.[4]

[3] The first edition reads *weight of provisions or merchandize*.

[4] They started digging the caches on October 31 but were unable to proceed because of heavy rain, which continued the next day. On November 2 they were able to complete them. Hunt's "Journal" notes six caches, but Robert Stuart, returning here on August 29 and 30, 1812, mentions nine. Six of them he found had been opened and

Three days had been thus employed since the departure of the several detachments, when that of Mr. Crooks unexpectedly made its appearance. A momentary joy was diffused through the camp, for they supposed succor to be at hand. It was soon dispelled. Mr. Crooks and his companions had been[5] completely disheartened by this retrograde march through a bleak and barren country; and had found, computing from their progress and the accumulating difficulties besetting every step, that it would be impossible to reach Henry's Fort, and return to the main body in the course of the winter. They had determined, therefore, to rejoin their comrades, and share their lot.

One avenue of hope was thus closed upon the anxious sojourners at the Caldron Linn; their main expectation of relief was now from the two parties under Reed and M'Lellan, which had proceeded down the river; for, as to Mr. M'Kenzie's detachment, which had struck across the plains, they thought it would have sufficient difficulty in struggling forward through the trackless wilderness. For five days they continued to support themselves by trapping and fishing. Some fish of tolerable size were speared at night by the light of cedar torches; others that were very small were caught in nets with fine meshes. The product of their fishing, however, was very scanty. Their trapping was also precarious; and the tails and bellies of the beavers were dried and put by for the journey.[6]

At length two of the companions of Mr. Reed returned, and were hailed with the most anxious eagerness. Their report served but to increase the general despondency. They had followed Mr. Reed for some distance below the point to which Mr. Hunt had explored, but had met with no Indians from whom to obtain information and relief. The river still presented the same furious aspect, brawling and boiling along a narrow and rugged channel, between rocks that rose like walls.

A lingering hope, which had been indulged by some of the party, of proceeding by water, was now finally given up: the long and terrific

---

all the goods taken, except for books scattered around flapping in the wind. He opened the three remaining caches and removed "a few Dry Goods Traps & Ammunition." Rollins (ed.), *op. cit.*, 112–13; Spaulding (ed.), *On the Oregon Trail*, 87, 89.

[5] The first edition reads *had become*.

[6] They had caught twelve beaver by November 5. Two days later they caught eight more. Some jerked buffalo meat still remained, for Hunt states that "I had the dried meat inspected and exposed to the air." See "Journal," 293. They soon ate this meat, preferring it to beaver.

strait of the river set all further progress at defiance, and in their disgust at the place, and their vexation at the disasters sustained there, they gave it the indignant, though not very decorous, appellation of the Devil's Scuttle Hole.[7]

[7] The name does not appear in Hunt's "Journal." Irving obtained it from Robert Stuart's "Travelling Memoranda" for August 29, 1812. For this chapter Irving used Hunt's "Journal," October 29 to November 7, 292–93.

THE resolution of Mr. Hunt and his companions was now taken to set out immediately on foot. As to the other detachments that had in a manner gone forth to seek their fortunes, there was little chance of their return; they would probably make their own way through the wilderness. At any rate, to linger in the vague hope of relief from them, would be to run the risk of perishing with hunger. Besides, the winter was rapidly advancing, and they had a long journey to make through an unknown country, where all kinds of perils might await them. They were yet, in fact, a thousand miles from Astoria, but the distance was unknown to them at the time: everything before and around them was vague and conjectural, and wore an aspect calculated to inspire despondency.

In abandoning the river, they would have to launch forth upon vast trackless plains destitute of all means of subsistence, where they might perish of hunger and thirst. A dreary desert of sand and gravel extends from Snake River almost to the Columbia. Here and there is a thin and scanty herbage, insufficient for the pasturage of horse or buffalo. Indeed, these treeless wastes between the Rocky Mountains and the Pacific, are even more desolate and barren than the naked, upper prairies on the Atlantic side; they present vast desert tracts that must ever defy cultivation, and interpose dreary and thirsty wilds between the habitations of man, in traversing which, the wanderer will often be in danger of perishing.[1]

Seeing the hopeless character of these wastes, Mr. Hunt and his companions determined to keep along the course of the river, where they would always have water at hand, and would be able occasionally to procure fish and beaver, and might perchance meet with Indians, from whom they could obtain provisions.

They now made their final preparations for the march. All their remaining stock of provisions consisted of forty pounds of Indian corn, twenty pounds of grease, about five pounds of portable soup, and a sufficient quantity of dried meat to allow each man a pittance of five pounds and a quarter, to be reserved for emergencies.[2] This being properly distributed, they deposited all their goods and superfluous articles in the caches, taking nothing with them but what was indispensable to the journey. With all their management, each man had to carry twenty pounds' weight beside[s] his own articles and equipments.

That they might have the better chance of procuring subsistence in the scanty region they were to traverse, they divided their party into two bands, Mr. Hunt, with eighteen men, beside[s] Pierre Dorion and his family, was to proceed down the north side of the river, while Mr. Crooks, with eighteen men,[3] kept along the south side.

---

[1] Some of Irving's knowledge of the Snake River country was acquired from Captain B. L. E. Bonneville, whom he met in late August or early September, 1835, at Astor's home. Not only must Irving have questioned Bonneville, who was thoroughly acquainted with the country, having just returned from there, but he also soon communicated with the War Department in Washington in order to obtain copies of Bonneville's maps. On September 20, 1835, he wrote to Major General Alexander Macomb from New York: "Capt Bonneville, who has recently returned from the Rocky Mountains has had the kindness to show me his journals in which are a few small maps of various parts of the mountains. As these maps throw a light on the topography of certain portions of the country about which I feel some curiosity I am desirous of getting copies of two or three of them. . . . I should take it as a great favor if you would have copied for me the maps of Wind River mountains, and another containing Henry[']s Fort and the upper branches of Snake river. There are two other maps illustrating the course of Snake river which I should likewise have." National Archives, "Appointment, Commission and Personal Branch File relating to Benjamin L. E. Bonneville." See also *The Adventures of Captain Bonneville*, xx–xxii.

[2] The soup was in the form of bouillon tablets. After enumerating the amount of meat, corn, grease, and soup, Hunt remarked tersely: "That was what must serve for the subsistence of more than twenty people." See "Journal," October 8, 293.

[3] Irving's figure should be nineteen. *Ibid.*, 293.

On the morning of the 9th of October,[4] the two parties separated and set forth on their several courses. Mr. Hunt and his companions followed along the right bank of the river, which made its way far below them, brawling at the foot of perpendicular precipices of solid rock, two and three hundred feet high. For twenty-eight miles that they travelled this day, they found it impossible to get down to the margin of the stream. At the end of this distance they encamped for the night at a place which admitted a scrambling descent. It was with the greatest difficulty, however, that they succeeded in getting up a kettle of water from the river for the use of the camp. As some rain had fallen in the afternoon, they passed the night under the shelter of the rocks.[5]

The next day they continued thirty-two miles to the northwest, keeping along the river, which still ran in its deep-cut channel.[6] Here and there a shady beach or a narrow strip of soil, fringed with dwarf willows, would extend for a little distance along the foot of the cliffs, and sometimes a reach of still water would intervene like a smooth mirror between the foaming rapids.

As through the preceding day, they journeyed on without finding, except in one instance, any place where they could get down to the river's edge, and they were fain to allay the thirst caused by hard travelling, with the water collected in the hollow of the rocks.

In the course of their march on the following morning,[7] they fell into a beaten horse path leading along the river, which showed that they were in the neighborhood of some Indian village or encampment. They had not proceeded far along it, when they met with two Shoshonies, or Snakes. They approached with some appearance of uneasiness, and accosting Mr. Hunt, held up a knife, which by signs they let him know they had received from some of the white men of the advance parties. It was with some difficulty that Mr. Hunt prevailed upon one of the savages to conduct him to the lodges of his people. Striking into a trail or path which led up from the river, he guided them for some distance in the prairie, until they came in sight of a number of lodges made of straw, and shaped like hay-stacks. Their approach, as on former occasions, caused the wildest affright among the inhabitants. The women hid

---

[4] The date is given by Hunt.

[5] The date and other details of this paragraph are faithful to Hunt's "Journal."

[6] Hunt states that it was two hundred to three hundred feet deep.

[7] November 11.

such of their children as were too large to be carried, and too small to take care of themselves, under straw, and, clasping their infants to their breasts, fled across the prairies.[8] The men awaited the approach of the strangers, but evidently in great alarm.

Mr. Hunt entered the lodges, and, as he was looking about, observed where the children were concealed; their black eyes glistening like those of snakes, from beneath the straw.[9] He lifted up the covering to look at them; the poor little beings were horribly frightened, and their fathers stood trembling, as if a beast of prey were about to pounce upon their[10] brood.

The friendly manner of Mr. Hunt soon dispelled these apprehensions; he succeeded in purchasing some excellent dried salmon, and a dog, an animal much esteemed as food by the natives; and when he returned to the river one of the Indians accompanied him. He now came to where the lodges were frequent along the banks, and, after a day's journey of twenty-six miles to the northwest, encamped in a populous neighborhood. Forty or fifty of the natives soon visited the camp, conducting themselves in a very amicable manner. They were well clad, and all had buffalo robes, which they procured from some of the hunting tribes in exchange for salmon. Their habitations were very comfortable; each had its pile of wormwood at the door for fuel, and within was abundance of salmon, some fresh, but the greater part cured. When the white men visited the lodges, however, the women and children hid themselves through fear. Among the supplies obtained here were two dogs, on which our travellers breakfasted, and found them to be very excellent, well-flavored, and hearty food.

In the course of the three following days[11] they made about sixty-three miles, generally in a northwest direction. They met with many of the natives in their straw-built cabins, who received them without alarm. About their dwellings were immense quantities of the heads and skins of salmon, the best part of which had been cured, and hidden in the ground. The women were badly clad; the children worse; their garments were buffalo robes, or the skins of foxes, hares, and badgers, and

---

[8] This sentence is an example of Irving's imaginatively building on the facts without misrepresenting what happened. Compare Hunt: "The women fled so precipately that they had not time to take with them such of their children as could not walk. They had covered them with straw." *Ibid.*, 294.

[9] The image of glistening, snakelike eyes is Irving's.

[10] *The* in first edition.   [11] November 13, 14, 15.

sometimes the skins of ducks, sewed together, with the plumage on. Most of the skins must have been procured by traffic with other tribes, or in distant hunting excursions, for the naked prairies in the neighborhood afforded few animals, excepting horses, which were abundant. There were signs of buffaloes having been there, but a long time before.

On the 15th of November[12] they made twenty-eight miles along the river, which was entirely free from rapids. The shores were lined with dead salmon, which tainted the whole atmosphere. The natives whom they met spoke of Mr. Reed's party having passed through that neighborhood. In the course of the day Mr. Hunt saw a few horses, but the owners of them took care to hurry them out of the way. All the provisions they were able to procure, were two dogs and a salmon. On the following day they were still worse off, having to subsist on parched corn, and the remains of their dried meat. The river this day had resumed its turbulent character, forcing its way through a narrow channel between steep rocks, and down violent rapids. They made twenty miles over a rugged road, gradually approaching a mountain in the northwest, covered with snow, which had been in sight for three days past.

On the 17th they met with several Indians, one of whom had a horse. Mr. Hunt was extremely desirous of obtaining it as a pack-horse; for the men, worn down by fatigue and hunger, found the loads of twenty pounds weight which they had to carry, daily growing heavier and more galling. The Indians, however, along this river, were never willing to part with their horses, having none to spare. The owner of the steed in question seemed proof against all temptation; article after article of great value in Indian eyes was offered and refused. The charms of an old tin kettle, however, were irresistible, and a bargain was concluded.[13]

A great part of the following morning was consumed in lightening the packages of the men and arranging the load for the horse. At this encampment there was no wood for fuel, even the wormwood on which they had frequently depended, having disappeared. For the two last days they had made thirty miles to the northwest.[14]

On the 19th of November, Mr. Hunt was lucky enough to purchase

---

[12] The date is confirmed by Hunt.

[13] The entire paragraph is based on the following statement by Hunt: "On the 17th, I happily obtained a horse in exchange for an old kettle; the indians not wishing any other of my goods." Ibid., 295.

[14] Their food had been almost consumed, for about a quart of corn plus a small amount of grease remained for each person.

another horse for his own use, giving in exchange a tomahawk, a knife, a fire steel, and some beads and gartering.[15] In an evil hour, however, he took the advice of the Indians to abandon the river, and follow a road or trail, leading into the prairies. He soon had cause to regret[16] the change. The road[17] led across a dreary waste, without verdure; and where there was neither fountain, nor pool, nor running stream. The men now began to experience the torments of thirst, aggravated by their usual diet of dried fish. The thirst of the Canadian voyageurs became so insupportable as to drive them to the most revolting means of allaying it.[18] For twenty-five miles did they toil on across this dismal desert, and laid themselves down at night, parched and disconsolate, beside their wormwood fires; looking forward to still greater sufferings on the following day. Fortunately it began to rain in the night, to their infinite relief; the water soon collected in puddles and afforded them delicious draughts.

Refreshed in this manner, they resumed their wayfaring as soon as the first streaks of dawn gave light enough for them to see their path. The rain continued all day,[19] so that they no longer suffered from thirst, but hunger took its place, for, after travelling thirty-three miles they had nothing to sup on but a little parched corn.

The next day brought them to the banks of a beautiful little stream,[20] running to the west, and fringed with groves of cotton-wood and willow. On its borders was an Indian camp, with a great many horses grazing around it. The inhabitants, too, appeared to be better clad than usual. The scene was altogether a cheering one to the poor half-famished wanderers. They hastened to their lodges, but on arriving at them met with a check that at first dampened their cheerfulness. An Indian immediately laid claim to the horse of Mr. Hunt, saying that it had been stolen

---

[15] Hunt says only that they bought a horse but does not mention the items traded for it. Irving's date, however, follows the "Journal."

[16] *Repent* in first edition.

[17] Since the Snake flowed northwest, Hunt would have been traveling almost due north toward Boise River. His party found no water and anticipated finding none the next day. "What vexation for men whose food consisted principally of dried fish!" he could not help exclaiming in his "Journal."

[18] Under date of November 20, after recording that rain had fallen the night before, Hunt remarked: "This alleviation was timely, as several Canadians had begun to drink their urine." *Ibid.*, 295.

[19] And all night, according to Hunt.

[20] Boise River, flowing out of the Sawtooth Range of central Idaho.

from him. There was no disproving a fact supported by numerous by-standers, and which the horse-stealing habits of the Indians rendered but too probable; so Mr. Hunt relinquished his steed to the claimant; not being able to retain him by a second purchase.

At this place they encamped for the night, and made a sumptuous repast upon fish and a couple of dogs, procured from their Indian neighbors. The next day[21] they kept along the river, but came to a halt after ten miles' march, on account of the rain. Here they again got a supply of fish and dogs from the natives; and two of the men were fortunate enough each to get a horse in exchange for a buffalo robe.[22] One of these men was Pierre Dorion, the half-breed interpreter, to whose suffering family the horse was a timely acquisition. And here we cannot but notice the wonderful patience, perseverance, and hardihood of the Indian women, as exemplified in the conduct of the poor squaw of the interpreter. She was now far advanced in her pregnancy, and had two children to take care of; one four, and the other two years of age. The latter of course she had frequently to carry on her back, in addition to the burden usually imposed upon the squaw, yet she had borne all her hardships without a murmur, and throughout this weary and painful journey had kept pace with the best of the pedestrians. Indeed on various occasions in the course of this enterprise, she displayed a force of character that won the respect and applause of the white men.[23]

Mr. Hunt endeavored to gather some information from these Indians concerning the country and the course of the rivers. His communications with them had to be by signs, and a few words which he had learnt, and of course were extremely vague. All that he could learn from them was, that the great river, the Columbia, was still far distant, but he could ascertain nothing as to the route he ought to take to arrive at it. For the two following days[24] they continued westward upwards of forty miles along the little stream, until they crossed it just before its junction with Snake River, which they found still running to the north.

[21] November 21.

[22] "We obtained some fish, seven dogs and two horses." *Ibid.*, 296. No mention is made in the "Journal" of Pierre Dorion, whom Irving names in the next sentence.

[23] Irving's eulogy of Dorion's wife is not suggested by anything at this point in Hunt's "Journal."

[24] November 23, 24. They crossed Boise River from its south to its north bank and continued along the right, or east, side of the Snake.

Before them was a wintry-looking mountain covered with snow on all sides.

In three days more they made about seventy miles; fording two small rivers,[25] the waters of which were very cold. Provisions were extremely scarce; their chief sustenance was portable soup; a meagre diet for weary pedestrians.

On the 27th of November[26] the river led them into the mountains through a rocky defile where there was scarcely room to pass. They were frequently obliged to unload the horses to get them by the narrow places; and sometimes to wade through the water in getting round rocks and butting cliffs. All their food this day was a beaver which they had caught the night before; by evening, the cravings of hunger were so sharp, and the prospect of any supply among the mountains so faint, that they had to kill one of the horses. "The men," says Mr. Hunt in his journal, "find the meat very good, and, indeed, so should I, were it not for the attachment I have to the animal."[27]

Early in the following day, after proceeding ten miles to the north, they came to two lodges of Shoshonies, who seemed in nearly as great extremity as themselves, having just killed two horses for food. They had no other provisions excepting the seed of a weed[28] which they gather in great quantities, and pound fine. It resembles hemp-seed. Mr. Hunt purchased a bag of it, and also some small pieces of horse flesh, which he began to relish, pronouncing them "fat and tender."

From these Indians he received information that several white men had gone down the river, some one side, and a good many on the other; these last he concluded to be Mr. Crooks and his party. He was thus released from much anxiety about their safety, especially as the Indians spoke about[29] Mr. Crooks['s] having one of his dogs yet, which showed that he and his men had not been reduced to extremity of hunger.

As Mr. Hunt feared that he might be several days in passing through this mountain defile, and run the risk of famine, he encamped in the neighborhood of the Indians, for the purpose of bartering with them for

[25] First Payette River, which they waded waist deep, and then Weiser River.
[26] The date is given by Hunt.
[27] What Hunt actually wrote was: "My men found the flesh very good. I ate it reluctantly because of my fondness for the poor beast." Ibid., 296.
[28] Rollins (ed.), Discovery of the Oregon Trail, 317n., identifies it as flax.
[29] Of in first edition.

a horse. The evening was expended in ineffectual trials. He offered a gun, a buffalo robe, and various other articles.[30] The poor fellows had, probably, like himself, the fear of starvation before their eyes. At length the women, learning the object of his pressing solicitations, and tempting offers, set up such a terrible hue and cry, that he was fairly howled and scolded from the ground.

The next morning early, the Indians seemed very desirous to get rid of their visitors, fearing, probably, for the safety of their horses. In reply to Mr. Hunt's inquiries about the mountains, they told him that he would have to sleep but three nights more among them; and that six days' travelling would take him to the falls of the Columbia; information in which he put no faith, believing it was only given to induce him to set forward.[31] These, he was told, were the last Snakes he would meet with, and that he would soon come to a nation called Sciatogas.

Forward then did he proceed on his tedious journey, which, at every step, grew more painful. The road continued for two days, through narrow defiles, where they were repeatedly obliged to unload the horses. Sometimes the river passed through such rocky chasms and under such steep precipices that they had to leave it, and make their way, with excessive labor, over immense hills, almost impassable for horses. On some of these hills were a few pine-trees, and their summits were covered with snow. On the second day of this scramble one of the hunters killed a black-tailed deer, which afforded the half-starved travellers a sumptuous repast. Their progress these two days was twenty-eight miles, a little to the northward of east.

The month of December set in drearily, with rain in the valleys, and snow upon the hills. They had to climb a mountain with snow to the midleg, which increased their painful toil. A small beaver supplied them with a scanty meal, which they eked out with frozen blackberries, haws, and choke-cherries, which they found in the course of their scramble. Their journey this day, though excessively fatiguing, was but thirteen miles; and all the next day they had to remain encamped, not being able to see half a mile ahead, on account of a snow-storm. Having nothing else to eat, they were compelled to kill another of their horses. The next day they resumed their march in snow and rain, but with all their efforts could only get forward nine miles, having for a part of the dis-

[30] Hunt does not mention these, only that he tried to buy a horse "for some goods."
[31] If they could average twenty-five miles a day, this estimate was not far wrong.

tance to unload the horses and carry the packs themselves. On the succeeding morning they were obliged to leave the river, and scramble up
the hills. From the summit of these, they got a wide view of the surrounding country, and it was a prospect almost sufficient to make them
despair. In every direction they beheld snowy mountains, partially
sprinkled with pines and other evergreens, and spreading a desert and
toilsome world around them. The wind howled over the bleak and
wintry landscape, and seemed to penetrate to the marrow of their
bones. They waded on through the snow, which at every step was more
than knee deep.

After toiling in this way all day, they had the mortification to find
that they were but four miles distant from the encampment of the preceding night, such was the meandering of the river among these dismal
hills. Pinched with famine, exhausted with fatigue, with evening approaching, and a wintry wild still lengthening as they advanced; they
began to look forward with sad forebodings to the night's exposure upon
this frightful waste. Fortunately they succeeded in reaching a cluster of
pines about sunset. Their axes were immediately at work; they cut down
trees, piled them in great heaps, and soon had huge fires "to cheer their
cold and hungry hearts."

About three o'clock in the morning it again began to snow, and at
daybreak they found themselves, as it were, in a cloud; scarcely being
able to distinguish objects at the distance of a hundred yards. Guiding
themselves by the sound of running water, they set out for the river,
and by slipping and sliding contrived to get down to its bank. One of
the horses, missing his footing, rolled down several hundred yards with
his load, but sustained no injury. The weather in the valley was less
rigorous than on the hills. The snow lay but ankle deep, and there was
a quiet rain now falling. After creeping along for six miles, they encamped on the border of the river. Being utterly destitute of provisions,
they were again compelled to kill one of their horses to appease their
famishing hunger.[32]

[32] This chapter relies entirely on Hunt's "Journal," which it follows faithfully,
October 9 to December 5, 293–97.

CHAPTER XXXV

An Unexpected Meeting — Navigation in a Skin Canoe
Strange Fears of Suffering Men — Hardships of Mr. Crooks and His Comrades
Tidings of M'Lellan — A Retrograde March — A Willow Raft
Extreme Suffering of Some of the Party
Illness of Mr. Crooks — Impatience of Some of the Men
Necessity of Leaving the Laggards Behind

THE wanderers had now accomplished four hundred and seventy-two miles of their dreary journey since leaving the Caldron Linn; how much further they had yet to travel, and what hardships to encounter, no one knew.

On the morning of the 6th of December,[1] they left their dismal encampment, but had scarcely begun their march, when, to their surprise, they beheld a party of white men coming up along the opposite bank of the river. As they drew nearer, they were recognized for Mr. Crooks and his companions. When they came opposite, and could make themselves heard across the murmuring of the river, their first cry was for food; in fact, they were almost starved. Mr. Hunt immediately returned to the camp, and had a kind of canoe made out of the skin of the horse, killed on the preceding night. This was done after the Indian fashion, by drawing up the edges of the skin with thongs, and keeping them distended by sticks or thwart pieces. In this frail bark, Sardepie,[2] one of the Canadians, carried over a portion of the flesh of the horse to the famishing party on the opposite side of the river, and brought back with him Mr. Crooks, and the Canadian, Le Clerc. The forlorn and wasted looks, and starving condition of these two men, struck dismay to the hearts of Mr. Hunt's followers. They had been accustomed to each other's appearance, and to the gradual operation of hunger and hardship upon their frames, but the change in the looks of these men, since last they parted, was a type of the famine and desolation of the land; and they now began to indulge the horrible presentiment that they

---

[1] The date is confirmed by Hunt's "Journal."

[2] An error for Gardpie. The error appears also in the first edition. See Porter, "Roll of Overland Astorians," *Oregon Historical Quarterly*, Vol. XXXIV (1933), 107.

would all starve together, or be reduced to the direful alternative of casting lots!

When Mr. Crooks had appeased his hunger, he gave Mr. Hunt some account of his wayfaring. On the side of the river, along which he had kept, he had met with but few Indians, and those were too miserably poor to yield much assistance. For the first eighteen days after leaving the Caldron Linn, he and his men had been confined to half a meal in twenty-four hours; for three days following, they had subsisted on a single beaver, a few wild cherries, and the soles of old moccasins; and for the last six days their only animal food had been the carcass of a dog.[3] They had been three days' journey further down the river than Mr. Hunt, always keeping as near to its banks as possible, and frequently climbing over sharp and rocky ridges that projected into the stream. At length they had arrived to where the mountains increased in height, and came closer to the river, with perpendicular precipices, which rendered it impossible to keep along the stream. The river here rushed with incredible velocity through a defile not more than thirty yards wide, where cascades and rapids succeeded each other almost without intermission. Even had the opposite banks, therefore, been such as to permit a continuance of their journey, it would have been madness to attempt to pass the tumultuous current either on rafts or otherwise. Still bent, however, on pushing forward, they attempted to climb the opposing mountains; and struggled on through the snow for half a day until, coming to where they could command a prospect, they found that they were not half way to the summit, and that mountain upon mountain lay piled beyond them, in wintry desolation. Famished and emaciated as they were, to continue forward would be to perish; their only chance seemed to be to regain the river, and retrace their steps up its banks. It was in this forlorn and retrograde march that they had met Mr. Hunt[4] and his party.

Mr. Crooks also gave information of some others of their fellow-adventurers. He had spoken several days previously with Mr. Reed and Mr. M'Kenzie, who with their men were on the opposite side of the river, where it was impossible to get over to them. They informed him

---

[3] A summary of Crooks's experiences since leaving Caldron Linn does not appear in Hunt's "Journal." The frequency with which Irving includes information about Crooks that does not appear in Hunt is presumptive evidence that he learned such information directly from Crooks, perhaps orally.

[4] The first edition reads *met with Mr. Hunt.*

that Mr. M'Lellan had struck across from the little river above the mountains, in the hope of falling in with some of the tribe of Flatheads, who inhabit the western skirts of the Rocky range. As the companions of Reed and M'Kenzie were picked men, and had found provisions more abundant on their side of the river, they were in better condition, and more fitted to contend with the difficulties of the country, than those of Mr. Crooks, and when he lost sight of them, were pushing onward, down the course of the river.

Mr. Hunt took a night to revolve over his critical situation, and to determine what was to be done. No time was to be lost; he had twenty men and more, in his own party, to provide for, and Mr. Crooks and his men to relieve. To linger would be to starve. The idea of retracing his steps was intolerable, and, notwithstanding all the discouraging accounts of the ruggedness of the mountains lower down the river, he would have been disposed to attempt them, but the depth of the snow with which they were covered deterred him; having already experienced the impossibility of forcing his way against such an impediment.

The only alternative, therefore, appeared to be, to return and seek the Indian bands scattered along the small rivers[5] above the mountains. Perhaps, from some of these he might procure horses enough to support him until he could reach the Columbia; for he still cherished the hope of arriving at that river in the course of the winter, though he was apprehensive that few of Mr. Crooks's party would be sufficiently strong to follow him. Even in adopting this course, he had to make up his mind to the certainty of several days of famine at the outset, for it would take that time to reach the last Indian lodges from which he had parted, and until they should arrive there, his people would have nothing to subsist upon but haws and wild berries, excepting one miserable horse, which was little better than skin and bone.

After a night of sleepless cogitation, Mr. Hunt announced to his men the dreary alternative he had adopted, and preparations were made to take Mr. Crooks and Le Clerc across the river, with the remainder of the meat, as the other party were to keep up along the opposite bank. The skin canoe had unfortunately been lost in the night; a raft was constructed therefore, after the manner of the natives, of bundles of willows, but it could not be floated across the impetuous current. The men were directed, in consequence, to keep on along the river by themselves,

[5] Boise, Payette, and Weiser rivers.

while Mr. Crooks and Le Clerc would proceed with Mr. Hunt. They all, then, took up their retrograde march with drooping spirits.

In a little while, it was found that Mr. Crooks and Le Clerc were so feeble as to walk with difficulty, so that Mr. Hunt was obliged to retard his pace, that they might keep up with him.[6] His men grew impatient at the delay. They murmured that they had a long and desolate region to traverse, before they could arrive at the point where they might expect to find horses; that it was impossible for Crooks and Le Clerc, in their feeble condition, to get over it; that to remain with them would only be to starve in their company. They importuned Mr. Hunt, therefore, to leave these unfortunate men to their fate, and think only of the safety of himself and his party. Finding him not to be moved either by entreaties or their clamors, they began to proceed without him, singly and in parties. Among those who thus went off was Pierre Dorion, the interpreter. Pierre owned the only remaining horse; which was now a mere skeleton. Mr. Hunt had suggested, in their present extremity, that it should be killed for food; to which the half-breed flatly refused his assent, and cudgeling the miserable animal forward, pushed on sullenly, with the air of a man doggedly determined to quarrel for his right. In this way Mr. Hunt saw his men, one after another, break away, until but five remained to bear him company.[7]

On the following morning, another raft was made, on which Mr. Crooks and Le Clerc again attempted to ferry themselves across the river, but after repeated trials had to give up in despair. This caused additional delay; after which they continued to crawl forward at a snail's pace. Some of the men who had remained with Mr. Hunt now became impatient of these incumbrances, and urged him clamorously to push forward, crying out that they should all starve. The night which succeeded was intensely cold, so that one of the men was severely frost-bitten. In the course of the night,[8] Mr. Crooks was taken ill, and in the morning was still more incompetent to travel. Their situation was now desperate, for their stock of provisions was reduced to three beaver skins. Mr. Hunt, therefore, resolved to push on,[9] overtake his people, and in-

---

[6] The date was now December 7.

[7] The demoralization of the expedition, as marked by its persistent disintegration since the disaster at Caldron Linn, here reaches its extreme point.

[8] December 8.

[9] Hunt wrote: "Seeing that this mishap [Crooks's illness] would delay for two days

sist upon having the horse of Pierre Dorion sacrificed for the relief of all hands. Accordingly, he left two of his men to help Crooks and Le Clerc on their way, giving them two of the beaver skins for their support; the remaining skin he retained, as provision for himself and the three other men who struck forward with him.[10]

my arrival among the indians, I left three men with him; and departed on the 9th with two others to rejoin my party." See "Journal," 299.

[10] For this chapter, Irving relates chiefly what he read in Hunt's "Journal" for December 6 to 9. *Ibid.*, 297–99.

Mr. Hunt Overtakes the Advance Party
Pierre Dorion, and His Skeleton Horse — A Shoshonie Camp
A Justifiable Outrage — Feasting on Horse Flesh
Mr. Crooks Brought to the Camp — Undertakes to Relieve His Men
The Skin Ferry-Boat — Frenzy of Prevost — His Melancholy Fate
Enfeebled State of John Day — Mr. Crooks Again Left Behind
The Party Emerge from Among the Mountains — Interview with Shoshonies
A Guide Procured to Conduct the Party Across a Mountain
Ferriage Across Snake River — Reunion with Mr. Crooks's Men
Final Departure from the River

ALL that day, Mr. Hunt and his three comrades travelled without eating. At night they made a tantalizing supper on their beaver skin, and were nearly exhausted[1] by hunger and cold. The next day, December 10th,[2] they overtook the advance party, who were all as much famished as themselves, some of them not having eaten since the morning of the seventh. Mr. Hunt now proposed the sacrifice of Pierre Dorion's skeleton horse. Here he again met with positive and vehement opposition from the half-breed, who was too sullen and vindictive a fellow to be easily dealt with. What was singular, the men, though suffering such pinching hunger, interfered in favor of the horse. They represented, that it was better to keep on as long as possible without resorting to this last resource. Possibly the Indians, of whom they were in quest, might have shifted their encampment, in which case it would be time enough to kill the horse to escape starvation. Mr. Hunt, therefore, was prevailed upon to grant Pierre Dorion's horse a reprieve.[3]

Fortunately, they had not proceeded much further, when, towards evening, they came in sight of a lodge of Shoshonies, with a number of horses grazing around it. The sight was as unexpected at is was joyous. Having seen no Indians in this neighborhood as they passed down the river, they must have subsequently come out from among the moun-

---

[1] Less accurately *starved* in first edition.

[2] The date is confirmed by Hunt's "Journal."

[3] "I the more willingly approved this plan," Hunt wrote, "since the poor beast was only skin and bones." *Ibid.,* 299.

tains. Mr. Hunt, who first descried them, checked the eagerness of his companions, knowing the unwillingness of these Indians to part with their horses, and their aptness to hurry off and conceal them, in case of an alarm. This was no time to risk such a disappointment. Approaching, therefore, stealthily and silently, they came upon the savages by surprise, who fled in terror. Five of their horses were eagerly seized, and one was despatched upon the spot.[4] The carcass was immediately cut up, and a part of it hastily cooked and ravenously devoured. A man was now sent on horseback with a supply of the flesh to Mr. Crooks and his companions. He reached them in the night; they were so famished that the supply sent them seemed but to aggravate their hunger, and they were almost tempted to kill and eat the horse that had brought the messenger. Availing themselves of the assistance of the animal, they reached the camp early in the morning.

On arriving there, Mr. Crooks was shocked to find that, while the people on this side of the river were amply supplied with provisions, none had been sent to his own forlorn and famishing men on the opposite bank. He immediately caused a skin canoe to be constructed, and called out to his men to fill their camp-kettles with water and hang them over the fire, that no time might be lost in cooking the meat the moment it should be received. The river was so narrow, though deep, that everything could be distinctly heard and seen across it. The kettles were placed on the fire, and the water was boiling by the time the canoe was completed. When all was ready, however, no one would undertake to ferry the meat across. A vague and almost superstitious terror had infected the minds of Mr. Hunt's followers, enfeebled and rendered imaginative of horrors by the dismal scenes and sufferings through which they had passed. They regarded the haggard crew, hovering like spectres of famine on the opposite bank, with indefinite feelings of awe and apprehension: as if something desperate and dangerous was to be feared from them.

Mr. Crooks tried in vain to reason or shame them out of this singular state of mind. He then attempted to navigate the canoe himself, but found his strength incompetent to brave the impetuous current. The good feelings of Ben Jones, the Kentuckian, at length overcame his

[4] Irving makes it appear to be a case of theft. What Hunt wrote, however, was: "They sold us five." *Ibid.*

fears, and he ventured over. The supply he brought was received with trembling avidity. A poor Canadian, however, named Jean Baptiste Prevost,[5] whom famine had rendered wild and desperate, ran frantically about the bank, after Jones had returned, crying out to Mr. Hunt to send the canoe for him, and take him from that horrible region of famine, declaring that otherwise he would never march another step, but would lie down there and die.

The canoe was shortly sent over again, under the management of Joseph Delaunay,[6] with further supplies. Prevost immediately pressed forward to embark. Delaunay refused to admit him, telling him that there was now a sufficient supply of meat on his side of the river. He replied that it was not cooked, and he should starve before it was ready; he implored, therefore, to be taken where he could get something to appease his hunger immediately. Finding the canoe putting off without him, he forced himself aboard. As he drew near the opposite shore, and beheld meat roasting before the fire, he jumped up, shouted, clapped his hands, and danced in a delirium of joy, until he upset the canoe. The poor wretch was swept away by the current and drowned, and it was with extreme difficulty that Delaunay reached the shore.[7]

Mr. Hunt now sent all his men forward excepting two or three. In the evening he caused another horse to be killed, and a canoe to be made out of the skin, in which he sent over a further supply of meat to the opposite party. The canoe brought back John Day, the Kentucky hunter, who came to join his former employer and commander, Mr. Crooks. Poor Day, once so active and vigorous, was now reduced to a condition even more feeble and emaciated than his companions. Mr. Crooks had such a value for the man, on account of his past services and faithful character, that he determined not to quit him; he exhorted Mr. Hunt, however, to proceed forward, and join the party, as his presence was all

[5] Also spelled *Provost*. He had been engaged by Hunt at Mackinac or perhaps at Lachine. See Porter, "Roll of Overland Astorians," *Oregon Historical Quarterly*, Vol. XXXIV (1933), 110.

[6] He had probably been engaged by Hunt at St. Louis early in the preceding March. See *ibid.*, 106.

[7] Except for Hunt's reference to the drowning, the details of the preceding three paragraphs do not appear in his "Journal"; they may be another instance of Irving's use of information obtained orally from Crooks. Concerning the drowning, Hunt says only: "One of Mr. Crooks's men was drowned while crossing the river in a canoe which capsized with many goods." See "Journal," 299.

important to the conduct of the expedition. One of the Canadians, Jean Baptiste Dubreuil,[8] likewise remained with Mr. Crooks.

Mr. Hunt left two horses with them, and a part of the carcass of the last that had been killed. This, he hoped, would be sufficient to sustain them until they should reach the Indian encampment.

One of the chief dangers attending the enfeebled condition of Mr. Crooks and his companions, was their being overtaken by the Indians whose horses had been seized: though Mr. Hunt hoped that he had guarded against any resentment on the part of the savages, by leaving various articles in their lodge, more than sufficient to compensate for the outrage he had been compelled to commit.[9]

Resuming his onward course, Mr. Hunt came up with his people in the evening. The next day, December 13th,[10] he beheld several Indians, with three horses, on the opposite side of the river, and after a time came to the two lodges which he had seen on going down. Here he endeavored in vain to barter a rifle for a horse, but again succeeded in effecting the purchase with an old tin kettle, aided by a few beads.

The two succeeding days were cold and stormy; the snow was augmenting, and there was a good deal of ice running in the river. Their road, however, was becoming easier; they were getting out of the hills, and finally emerged into the open country, after twenty days of fatigue, famine, and hardship of every kind, in the ineffectual attempt to find a passage down the river.

They now encamped on a little willowed stream,[11] running from the east, which they had crossed on the 26th of November. Here they found a dozen lodges of Shoshonies, recently arrived, who informed them that had they persevered along the river, they would have found their difficulties augment until they became absolutely insurmountable. This intelligence added to the anxiety of Mr. Hunt for the fate of Mr. M'Kenzie and his people, who had kept on.

Mr. Hunt now followed up the little river,[12] and encamped at some

---

[8] The earliest record of Dubreuil is in Hunt's account books for September 15, 1810, at St. Louis. Porter, "Roll of Overland Astorians," *loc. cit.*, 107.

[9] None of the details of the three preceding paragraphs appears in Hunt's "Journal."

[10] Hunt's "Journal" confirms the date as well as the details of this paragraph.

[11] Weiser River. Irving's date is confirmed by Hunt.

[12] That is, he traveled up the Weiser to the east. If he followed it far enough, he began to turn north after ten or eleven miles.

The Three Tetons—or the "Pilot Knobs," as they were named by
Wilson P. Hunt in 1811.

Photograph by Edgeley W. Todd

Jackson Hole from the summit of Teton Pass, traversed by both the Overland and the Returning Astorians, 1811 and 1812.

Photograph by Edgeley W. Todd

lodges of Shoshonies, from whom he procured a couple of horses, a dog, a few dried fish, and some roots and dried cherries. Two or three days[13] were exhausted in obtaining information about the route, and what time it would take to get to the Sciatogas, a hospitable tribe, on the west of the mountains,[14] represented as having many horses. The replies were various, but concurred in saying that the distance was great, and would occupy from seventeen to twenty-one nights. Mr. Hunt then tried to procure a guide; but though he sent to various lodges up and down the river, offering articles of great value in Indian estimation, no one would venture. The snow, they said, was waist deep in the mountains; and to all his offers they shook their heads, gave a shiver, and replied, "we shall freeze! we shall freeze!" at the same time they urged him to remain and pass the winter among them.

Mr. Hunt was in a dismal dilemma. To attempt the mountains without a guide, would be certain death to him and his people; to remain there, after having already been so long on the journey, and at such great expense, was worse to him, he said, than two "deaths."[15] He now changed his tone with the Indians, charged them with deceiving him in respect to the mountains, and talking with a "forked tongue," or, in other words, with lying. He upbraided them with their want of courage, and told them they were women, to shrink from the perils of such a journey. At length one of them, piqued by his taunts, or tempted by his offers, agreed to be his guide; for which he was to receive a gun, a pistol, three knives, two horses, and a little of every article in possession of the party;[16] a reward sufficient to make him one of the wealthiest of his vagabond nation.

Once more, then, on the 21st of December,[17] they set out upon their wayfaring, with newly excited spirits. Two other Indians accompanied their guide, who led them immediately back to Snake River, which they followed down for a short distance, in search of some Indian rafts made of reeds, on which they might cross. Finding none, Mr. Hunt caused a

[13] Hunt's "Journal" shows that he was gone four days from the Snake, from December 17 through 20.

[14] The first edition reads *the west side of the mountains*.

[15] *Two deaths* is enclosed in quotation marks in the first edition. If Irving is quoting Hunt's exact words, his source is not the "Journal."

[16] The "Journal" mentions only "a gun, some pistols, a horse, etc." *Ibid.*, 300.

[17] The date appears in Hunt.

horse to be killed, and a canoe to be made out of its skin.[18] Here, on the opposite bank, they saw the thirteen men of Mr. Crooks's party, who had continued up along the river. They told Mr. Hunt, across the stream, that they had not seen Mr. Crooks, and the two men who had remained with him, since the day that he had separated from them.

The canoe proving too small, another horse was killed, and the skin of it joined to that of the first. Night came on before the little bark had made more than two voyages. Being badly made it was taken apart and put together again, by the light of the fire. The night was cold; the men were weary and disheartened with such varied and incessant toil and hardship. They crouched, dull and drooping, around their fires; many of them began to express a wish to remain where they were for the winter. The very necessity of crossing the river dismayed some of them in their present enfeebled and dejected state. It was rapid and turbulent, and filled with floating ice, and they remembered that two of their comrades had already perished in its waters. Others looked forward with misgivings to the long and dismal journey through lonesome regions that awaited them, when they should have passed this dreary flood.[19]

At an early hour of the morning, December 23d,[20] they began to cross the river. Much ice had formed during the night, and they were obliged to break it for some distance on each shore. At length they all got over in safety to the west side; and their spirits rose on having achieved this perilous passage. Here they were rejoined by the people of Mr. Crooks, who had with them a horse and a dog,[21] which they had recently procured. The poor fellows were in the most squalid and emaciated state. Three of them[22] were so completely prostrated in strength and spirits, that they expressed a wish to remain among the Snakes. Mr. Hunt, therefore, gave them the canoe, that they might cross the river, and a few articles, with which to procure necessaries, until they should meet with Mr. Crooks. There was another man, named Michael Car-

---

[18] Irving says in the next paragraph that a second horse was killed later. But when the reed raft was not found, Hunt says, "two horses were slain, a canoe was made from their hide, and we crossed." *Ibid.*, 300.

[19] The details of this paragraph do not appear in the "Journal."

[20] The date is confirmed by Hunt.

[21] The "Journal" lists a horse and some goods but no dog.

[22] Their names were Turcotte, La Chapelle, and Francis Landry. See below, p. 438.

riere,[23] who was almost equally reduced, but he determined to proceed with his comrades, who were now incorporated with the party of Mr. Hunt. After the day's exertions they encamped together on the banks of the river. This was the last night they were to spend upon its borders. More than eight hundred miles of hard travelling, and many weary days, had it cost them; and the sufferings connected with it rendered it hateful in their remembrance, so that the Canadian voyageurs always spoke of it as "La maudite riviere enragée"[24]—the accursed mad river—thus coupling a malediction with its name.[25]

[23] Carriere is not mentioned at this point in the "Journal." He first appears in Hunt's account books on September 10, 1810, at St. Louis. See Porter, "Roll of Overland Astorians," *loc. cit.*, 105. He disappears from the record on the following January 8, 1812; see below, p. 311.

[24] This appellation does not appear in Hunt's "Journal."

[25] Chapter XXXVI narrates what appears chiefly in Hunt's "Journal," December 10 to 23, 299–301.

ON the 24th of December,[1] all things being arranged, Mr. Hunt turned his back upon the disastrous banks of Snake River, and struck his course westward for the mountains.[2] His party being augmented by the late followers of Mr. Crooks, amounted now to thirty-two white men, three Indians, and the squaw[3] and two children of Pierre Dorion. Five jaded, half-starved horses were laden with their luggage, and, in case of need, were to furnish them with provisions. They travelled painfully about fourteen miles a day, over plains and among hills, rendered dreary by occasional falls of snow and rain. Their only sustenance was a scanty meal of horse flesh once in four-and-twenty hours.

On the third day the poor Canadian, Carriere, one of the famished party of Mr. Crooks, gave up in despair, and lying down upon the ground declared he could go no further. Efforts were made to cheer him up, but it was found that the poor fellow was absolutely exhausted

---

[1] The date is confirmed by Hunt's "Journal."

[2] Upon leaving the Snake, they went west along a route that closely approximated the course of what later became the Oregon Trail, now followed by U.S. 30. The area in which they spent December 23 was later known to travelers on the Oregon Trail as Farewell Bend. In his restrained manner, Hunt recorded in his "Journal": "On the 24th, I quitted the Canoe River [Snake], of which we all shall keep a very sad recollection." *Ibid.*, 300. Twenty-two years later, John C. Frémont here left the Snake River, "which," he wrote, "is said henceforth to pursue its course through cañons, amidst rocky and impracticable mountains, where there is no possibility of travelling with animals." *Report of the Exploring Expedition to the Rocky Mountains*, 176.

[3] Hunt mentions that she was over eight months pregnant.

and could not keep on his legs. He was mounted, therefore, upon one of the horses, though the forlorn animal was in little better plight than himself.[4]

On the 28th, they came upon a small stream[5] winding to the north, through a fine level valley; the mountains receding on each side. Here their Indian friends pointed out a chain of woody mountains[6] to the left, running north and south, and covered with snow; over which they would have to pass. They kept along the valley for twenty-one miles on the 29th,[7] suffering much from a continued fall of snow and rain, and being twice obliged to ford the icy stream. Early in the following morning the squaw of Pierre Dorion, who had hitherto kept on without murmuring or flinching, was suddenly taken in labor, and enriched her husband with another child. As the fortitude and good conduct of the poor woman had gained for her the good-will of the party, her situation caused concern and perplexity. Pierre, however, treated the matter as an occurrence that could soon be arranged and need cause no delay. He remained by his wife in the camp, with his other children and his horse, and promised soon to rejoin the main body, who proceeded on their march.

Finding that the little river entered the mountains, they abandoned it, and turned off for a few miles among hills. Here another Canadian, named La Bonté,[8] gave out, and had to be helped on horseback. As the horse was too weak to bear both him and his pack, Mr. Hunt took the latter upon his own shoulders. Thus, with difficulties augmenting at every step, they urged their toilsome way among the hills, half famished and faint at heart, when they came to where a fair valley[9] spread out before them, of great extent and several leagues in width, with a beautiful stream[10] meandering through it. A genial climate seemed to prevail here, for though the snow lay upon all the mountains within

---

[4] No word of Carriere's collapse appears in the "Journal."

[5] Powder River, which here flows north before making a sudden turn to flow southeast into the Snake. Irving's date is confirmed by Hunt.

[6] The Blue Mountains of Oregon.

[7] The date is given by Hunt.

[8] He is not named in the "Journal." For La Bonté see Porter, "Roll of Overland Astorians," *Oregon Historical Quarterly*, Vol. XXXIV (1933), 108; see also H. S. Lyman, "Reminiscences of Louis Labonte," *ibid.*, Vol. I (1900), 169–88.

[9] Grande Ronde Valley. They arrived here on December 30.

[10] Grande Ronde River, which flows northeast, emptying into the Snake a short distance above the present Oregon-Washington state line.

sight, there was none to be seen in the valley. The travellers gazed with delight upon this serene, sunny landscape, but their joy was complete on beholding six lodges of Shoshonies pitched upon the borders of the stream, with a number of horses and dogs about them. They all pressed forward with eagerness and soon reached the camp. Here their first attention was to obtain provisions. A rifle, an old musket, a tomahawk, a tin kettle, and a small quantity of ammunition, soon procured them four horses, three dogs, and some roots. Part of the live-stock was immediately killed, cooked with all expedition, and as promptly devoured. A hearty meal restored every one to good spirits. In the course of the following morning[11] the Dorion family made its reappearance. Pierre came trudging in the advance, followed by his valued, though skeleton steed, on which was mounted his squaw with her[12] new-born infant in her arms, and her boy of two years old wrapped in a blanket and slung at her side. The mother looked as unconcerned as if nothing had happened to her; so easy is nature in her operations in the wilderness, when free from the enfeebling refinements of luxury, and the tamperings and appliances of art.

The next morning ushered in the new year (1812). Mr. Hunt was about to resume his march, when his men requested permission to celebrate the day. This was particularly urged by the Canadian voyageurs, with whom New-Year's day is a favorite festival; and who never willingly give up a holiday, under any circumstances. There was no resisting such an application;[13] so the day was passed in repose and revelry; the poor Canadians contrived to sing and dance in defiance of all their hardships; and there was a sumptuous New-Year's banquet of dog's meat and horse flesh.

After two days of welcome rest, the travellers addressed themselves once more to their painful journey. The Indians of the lodges pointed out a distant gap through which they must pass in traversing the ridge of mountains.[14] They assured them that they would be but little incommoded by snow, and in three days would arrive among the Sciatogas.

[11] December 31.

[12] *The* in first edition.

[13] Hunt stated his reasons in the following words: "I willingly consented because most of them were very fatigued from having, each day, only a scanty meal of horse-flesh and from carrying their packs on their shoulders across the mountains." See "Journal," 301.

[14] Blue Mountains.

Mr. Hunt, however, had been so frequently deceived by Indian accounts of routes and distances, that he gave but little faith to this information.

The travellers continued their course due west for five days, crossing the valley and entering the mountains. Here the travelling became excessively toilsome, across rough stony ridges, and amidst fallen trees. They were often knee deep in snow, and sometimes in the hollows between the ridges sank up to their waists. The weather was extremely cold; the sky covered with clouds so that for days they had not a glimpse of the sun. In traversing the highest ridge they had a wide but chilling prospect over a wilderness of snowy mountains.

On the 6th of January,[15] however, they had crossed the dividing summit of the chain, and were evidently under the influence of a milder climate. The snow began to decrease; the sun once more emerged from the thick canopy of clouds, and shone cheeringly upon them, and they caught a sight of what appeared to be a plain, stretching out in the west. They hailed it as the poor Israelites hailed the first glimpse of the promised land, for they flattered themselves that this might be the great plain of the Columbia, and that their painful pilgrimage might be drawing to a close.

It was now five days since they had left the lodges of the Shoshonies, during which they had come about sixty miles, and their guide assured them that in the course of the next day they would see the Sciatogas.

On the following morning, therefore, they pushed forward with eagerness, and soon fell upon a stream[16] which led them through a deep narrow defile, between stupendous ridges. Here among the rocks and precipices they saw gangs of that mountain-loving animal, the black-tailed deer, and came to where great tracks of horses were to be seen in all directions, made by the Indian hunters.

The snow had entirely disappeared, and the hopes of soon coming upon some Indian encampment induced Mr. Hunt to press on. Many of the men, however, were so enfeebled that they could not keep up with the main body, but, lagged at intervals behind: and some of them did not arrive at the night encampment. In the course of this day's march the recently-born child of Pierre Dorion died.

[15] The date is confirmed by Hunt's "Journal."

[16] Rolline (ed.), *Discovery of the Oregon Trail*, 325n., conjectures this may have been McKay Creek, as it is now called. The first edition reads *a small stream.*

The march was resumed early the next morning,[17] without waiting for the stragglers. The stream which they had followed throughout the preceding day was now swollen by the influx of another river;[18] the declivities of the hills were green and the valleys were clothed with grass. At length the jovial cry was given of "an Indian camp!" It was yet in the distance, in the bosom of the green valley, but they could perceive that it consisted of numerous lodges, and that hundreds of horses[19] were grazing the grassy meadows around it. The prospect of abundance of horse flesh diffused universal joy, for by this time the whole stock of travelling provisions was reduced to the skeleton steed of Pierre Dorion, and another wretched animal, equally emaciated, that had been repeatedly reprieved during the journey.

A forced march soon brought the weary and hungry travellers to the camp. It proved to be a strong party of Sciatogas[20] and Tus-che-pas.[21] There were thirty-four lodges, comfortably constructed of mats; the Indians, too, were better clothed than any of the wandering bands they had hitherto met on this side of the Rocky Mountains. Indeed they were as well clad as the generality of the wild hunter tribes. Each had a good buffalo or deer-skin robe; and a deer-skin hunting shirt and leggins. Upwards of two thousand horses were ranging the pastures around their encampment; but what delighted Mr. Hunt was, on entering the

[17] January 8, 1812.

[18] Umatilla River, which flows northwest out of the Blue Mountains into the Columbia River.

[19] Hunt says "at least two thousand."

[20] The Sciatogas were perhaps a Cayuse tribe. The name means "camass eater." See Rollins (ed.), op. cit., 354–55. The name is not listed in either Hodge, Handbook of American Indians, or Swanton, Indian Tribes. Elliott Coues says the term refers to "the Camass eaters of the N.W. The word is Paiute (Shoshonean). . . . We used to hear a good deal about the 'Sciatogas,' but the term was a loose one, indicating several different tribes of northern Paiutes (Shoshonean family), and also included the Cayuses, who are of Waiilatpuan stock. The name has, therefore, lapsed, as one having no exact classificatory sense." Henry-Thompson Journals, II, 818–19n.

[21] Hunt renders the name Toustchepas. Hodge wrote of this tribe, which he spells Tushepaw: "A term used by Lewis and Clark to designate the Indians 'residing on a N. Fork of Clark r., in the Rocky mts. in spring and summer, and on the Missouri in winter.' They have not been positively identified, but the evidence . . . makes it probable that they were Kutenai. According to Gatschet the term (Túshipa) is a Shoshoni designation for the tribes living to the N. of them and including the Nez Percés as well as the Kutenai. It is probable that the term as employed by Lewis and Clark included both the tribes named as well as bands of the Wallawalla and possibly Shahaptian divisions." Op. cit., II, 853.

lodges, to behold brass kettles, axes, copper tea-kettles, and various other articles of civilized manufacture,[22] which showed that these Indians had an indirect communication with the people of the sea-coast who traded with the whites. He made eager inquiries of the Sciatogas, and gathered from them that the great river (the Columbia) was but two days' march distant, and that several white people had recently descended it; who he hoped might prove to be M'Lellan, M'Kenzie, and their companions.

It was with the utmost joy and the most profound gratitude to heaven, that Mr. Hunt found himself and his band of weary and famishing wanderers thus safely extricated from the most perilous part of their long journey, and within the prospect of a termination of their toils.[23] All the stragglers who had lagged behind arrived, one after another, excepting the poor Canadian voyageur, Carriere. He had been seen late in the preceding afternoon, riding behind a Snake Indian,[24] near some lodges of that nation, a few miles distant from the last night's encampment; and it was expected that he would soon make his appearance.

The first object of Mr. Hunt was to obtain provisions for his men. A little venison of an indifferent quality, and some roots were all that could be procured that evening; but the next day he succeeded in purchasing a mare and colt, which were immediately killed, and the cravings of the half-starved people in some degree appeased.

For several days[25] they remained in the neighborhood of these Indians, reposing after all their hardships, and feasting upon horse flesh and roots, obtained in subsequent traffic. Many of the people ate to such excess as to render themselves sick, others were lame from their past journey; but all gradually recruited in the repose and abundance of the valley. Horses were obtained here much more readily, and at a cheaper rate, than among the Snakes. A blanket, a knife, or a half pound of blue beads would purchase a steed, and at this rate many of the men bought horses for their individual use.[26]

---

[22] Hunt mentions "some pots and kettles of copper" as well as axes, stone hammers, and wedges made of elkhorn used to split wood. "Journal," 302.

[23] Hunt wrote: "I cannot sufficiently express my gratitude to Providence for having let us reach here; because we all were extremely fatigued and enfeebled. There remained to us two horses, which were only skin and bones." *Ibid.*, 302

[24] This is the last that was ever seen of Carriere.

[25] For six days, January 9 to 16.

[26] In addition to horses bought by some of the men, Hunt bought six more plus two colts. Two horses were eaten and two were given to their Shoshoni Indian guides.

This tribe of Indians, who are represented as a proud-spirited race, and uncommonly cleanly, never eat horses or[27] dogs, nor would they permit the raw flesh of either to be brought into their huts. They had a small quantity of venison in each lodge, but set so high a price upon it that the white men, in their impoverished state, could not afford to purchase it. They hunted the deer on horseback; "ringing," or surrounding them, and running them down in a circle. They were admirable horsemen, and their weapons were bows and arrows, which they managed with great dexterity. They were altogether primitive in their habits, and seemed to cling to the usages of savage life, even when possessed of the aids of civilization. They had axes among them, yet they generally made use of a stone mallet wrought into the shape of a bottle, and wedges of elk horn, in splitting their wood. Though they might have two or three brass kettles hanging in their lodges, yet they would frequently use vessels made of willow, for carrying water, and would even boil their meat in them, by means of hot stones. Their women wore caps of willow neatly worked and figured.

As Carriere, the Canadian straggler, did not make his appearance for two or three days after the encampment in the valley, two men were sent out on horseback in search of him. They returned, however, without success. The lodges of the Snake Indians near which he had been seen were removed, and they could find no trace of him. Several days more elapsed, yet nothing was seen or heard of him, or of the Snake horseman, behind whom he had been last observed. It was feared, therefore, that he had either perished through hunger and fatigue; had been murdered by the Indians; or, being left to himself, had mistaken some hunting tracks for the trail of the party, and been led astray and lost.[28]

The river on the banks of which they were encamped, emptied into the Columbia, was called by the natives the Eu-o-tal-la, or Umatalla,[29] and abounded with beaver. In the course of their sojourn in the valley

[27] *Nor* in first edition.

[28] In explaining Carriere's disappearance, Hunt says only: "This poor fellow had perhaps taken a hunting-trail of the indians and thus lost his way." See "Journal," 302.

[29] Umatilla River. "The Sciatogas," Hunt wrote, "transferred their lodges a day's march further down the river. On the 15th we resumed travel and reached the Sciatogas' camp on the bank of the Euotalla." *Ibid.*, 303. He moved farther down the river on January 19.

which it watered, they twice shifted their camp, proceeding about thirty miles down its course, which was to the west. A heavy fall of rain caused the river to overflow its banks, dislodged them from their encampment, and drowned three of their horses, which were tethered in the low ground.

Further conversation with the Indians satisfied them that they were in the neighborhood of the Columbia. The number of the white men who they said had passed down the river, agreed with that of M'Lellan, M'Kenzie, and their companions, and increased the hope of Mr. Hunt that they might have passed through the wilderness with safety.

These Indians had a vague story that white men were coming to trade among them; and they often spoke of two great men named Ke-Koosh[30] and Jacquean, who gave them tobacco, and smoked with them. Jacquean, they said, had a house somewhere upon the great river. Some of the Canadians supposed they were speaking of one Jacquean Finlay,[31] a clerk of the Northwest Company, and inferred that the house must be some trading post on one of the tributary streams of the Columbia. The Indians were overjoyed when they found this band of white men intended to return and trade with them. They promised to use all diligence in collecting quantities of beaver skins, and no doubt proceeded to make deadly war upon that sagacious, but ill-fated animal, who, in general, lived in peaceful insignificance among his Indian neighbors, before the intrusion of the white trader. On the 20th of January,[32] Mr. Hunt took leave of these friendly Indians, and of the river on which they encamped,[33] and continued westward.[34]

[30] David Thompson? The Indians of the lower Columbia naméd him Koo-Koo-Sint, from a Salish word, *kukusem*, meaning "star," thus referring to his astronomical observations. See M. Catherine White (ed.), *David Thompson's Journals Relating to Montana and Adjacent Regions, 1808–1812*, cxlii, clvii.

[31] Jacques Raphael Finlay (d. 1828), also known as Jaco Finlay, a halfblood, who built Spokane House in 1810 or 1811. See Wallace (ed.), *Documents*, 439. See also J. A. Meyers, "Jacques Raphael Finlay," *Washington Historical Quarterly*, Vol. X (1919), 163–67.

[32] Irving correctly infers the date from Hunt's "Journal."

[33] The first edition has *were encamped*.

[34] Hunt says simply that "we left the Euotalla." The only basis upon which one can explain Irving's word *westward* is to assume that Hunt had been on the Umatilla nearer its source than its outlet, perhaps east of present-day Pendleton, Oregon, and in the area now forming the Umatilla Indian Reservation. Because the river flows in a long arc bending towards the south, it was possible for Hunt to move west from it and still be

At length, on the following day, the wayworn travellers lifted up their eyes and beheld before them the long-sought waters of the Columbia. The sight was hailed with as much transport as if they had already reached the end of their pilgrimage; nor can we wonder at their joy. Two hundred and forty miles had they marched, through wintry wastes and rugged mountains, since leaving Snake River; and six months of perilous wayfaring had they experienced since their departure from the Arickara village on the Missouri. Their whole route by land and water from that point had been, according to their computation, seventeen hundred and fifty-one miles, in the course of which they had endured all kinds of hardships. In fact, the necessity of avoiding the dangerous country of the Blackfeet had obliged them to make a bend to the south and traverse a great additional extent of unknown wilderness.

The place where they struck the Columbia was some distance below the junction of its two great branches, Lewis and Clarke rivers,[35] and not far from the influx of the Wallah-Wallah.[36] It was a beautiful stream, three-quarters of a mile wide,[37] totally free from trees; bordered in some places with steep rocks, in others with pebbled shores.

On the banks of the Columbia they found a miserable horde of Indians, called Akai-chies,[38] with no clothing but a scant mantle of the skins of animals, and sometimes a pair of sleeves of wolf's skin. Their lodges were shaped like a tent, and very light and warm, being covered with

---

on the north side. The word *westward*, however, should more properly be *northwestward* because, as Irving shows below, Hunt was moving towards the outlet of the Walla Walla River, which is north of the Umatilla. He went in this direction instead of following the Umatilla to its outlet in the Columbia on the advice of the Indians, who, he said, "told us of a river situated higher up which they called Oualla-Oualla." See "Journal," 303.

[35] See the *Astoria* map. Here the Columbia above the confluence of the Snake is labeled Clark's River. The Snake is named Lewis River.

[36] The Walla Walla River flows from the east into the Columbia about sixteen miles below the Snake and a short distance above the present-day boundary between Oregon and Washington. The *Astoria* map shows Hunt's trail leading approximately to the mouth of the Walla Walla. On the north side of the river, the Hudson's Bay Company would eventually build Fort Walla Walla.

[37] Like nearly all western rivers, it is very much narrower today. Near its outlet now is an unsightly railroad yard.

[38] *Akaitchi* in Hunt's "Journal." Hodge states: "A tribe said to have resided on Columbia r. not far from the mouth of the Umatilla, in Oregon. . . . Their location would indicate a Shahaptian division, but they can not be identified." *Op. cit.*, I, 32.

mats of rushes; besides which they had excavations in the ground, lined with mats, and occupied by the women, who were even more slightly clad than the men.[39] These people subsisted chiefly by fishing; having canoes of a rude construction, being merely the trunks of pine-trees split and hollowed out by fire. Their lodges were well stored with dried salmon, and they had great quantities of fresh salmon trout of an excellent flavor, taken at the mouth of the Umatalla; of which the travellers obtained a most acceptable supply.

Finding that the road was on the north side of the river,[40] Mr. Hunt crossed, and continued five or six days[41] travelling rather slowly down along its banks, being much delayed by the straying of the horses, and the attempts made by the Indians to steal them. They frequently passed lodges, where they obtained fish and dogs. At one place the natives had just returned from hunting, and had brought back a large quantity of elk and deer meat, but asked so high a price for it as to be beyond the funds of the travellers, so they had to content themselves with dog's flesh. They had by this time, however, come to consider it very choice food, superior to horse flesh, and the minutes[42] of the expedition speak rather exultingly now and then, of their having made a famous "repast," where this viand happened to be unusually plenty.

They again learnt tidings of some of the scattered members of the expedition, supposed to be M'Kenzie, M'Lellan, and their men, who had preceded them down the river, and had overturned one of their canoes, by which they lost many articles. All these floating pieces of intelligence of their fellow-adventurers, who had separated from them in the heart of the wilderness, they received with eager interest.

The weather continued to be temperate, marking the superior softness of the climate on this side of the mountains. For a great part of the time, the days were delightfully mild and clear, like the serene days of

[39] "They usually are naked; some few have a scrap of robe which covers their shoulders, but all have around the waist a leathern belt which passes between their thighs and proves that they aspire to be decent." Hunt, "Journal," 304. From these people Hunt bought nine dogs besides fish.

[40] The Columbia. Hunt left the Akaitchis on January 23.

[41] Until January 28. No "Journal" entries appear for January 24 to 27.

[42] Hunt's "Journal." Hunt makes an interesting comment about the lack of nourishment in horse meat, which, "however well cooked, did not nourish, no matter how much one ate of it." *Ibid.*, 304.

October on the Atlantic borders. The country in general, in the neighborhood of the river, was a continual plain, low near the water, but rising gradually; destitute of trees, and almost without shrubs or plants of any kind, excepting a few willow bushes. After travelling about sixty miles, they came[43] to where the country became very hilly and the river made its way between rocky banks, and down numerous rapids. The Indians in this vicinity were better clad and altogether in more prosperous condition than those above, and, as Mr. Hunt thought, showed their consciousness of ease by something like sauciness of manner. Thus prosperity is apt to produce arrogance in savage as well as in civilized life. In both conditions, man is an animal that will not bear pampering.

From these people Mr. Hunt for the first time received vague, but deeply interesting intelligence of that part of the enterprise which had proceeded by sea to the mouth of the Columbia. The Indians spoke of a number of white men who had built a large house at the mouth of the great river, and surrounded it with palisades. None of them had been down to Astoria themselves; but rumors spread widely and rapidly from mouth to mouth among the Indian tribes, and are carried to the heart of the interior by hunting parties and migratory hordes.

The establishment of a trading emporium at such a point, also, was calculated to cause a sensation to the most remote parts of the vast wilderness beyond the mountains. It in a manner struck the pulse of the great vital river, and vibrated up all its tributary streams.

It is surprising to notice how well this remote tribe of savages had learnt through intermediate gossips, the private feelings of the colonists at Astoria: it shows that Indians are not the incurious and indifferent observers that they have been represented. They told Mr. Hunt that the white people at the large house had been looking anxiously for many of their friends, whom they had expected to descend the great river; and had been in much affliction, fearing that they were lost. Now, however, the arrival of him and his party would wipe away all their tears, and they would dance and sing for joy.

On the 31st of January, Mr. Hunt arrived at the falls[44] of the Colum-

---

[43] On January 28.

[44] Celilo Falls, which Lewis and Clark called the Great Falls of the Columbia, east of The Dalles. Dammed-up waters of the river now regrettably cover this historic place, which, until recently, was still a salmon-fishing spot for the Indians. The date given by Irving appears in Hunt's "Journal."

bia, and encamped at the village of the Wish-ram,[45] situated at the head of that dangerous pass of the river called "the Long Narrows."[46]

[45] *Ouichram* in Hunt's "Journal." This village was below Celilo Falls. See Chapter X, note 28, above. The first edition reads *village of Wish-ram*.

[46] A turbulent, five-mile stretch of water, beginning at The Dalles. Frémont, seeing it in November, 1843, described it in the following words: "The whole volume of the river at this place passed between the walls of a chasm, which has the appearance of having been rent through the basaltic strata which form the valley rock of the region. At the narrowest place we found the breadth, by measurement, 58 yards, and the average height of the walls above the water 25 feet; forming a trough between the rocks— whence the name [Dalles], probably applied by a Canadian voyageur. The mass of water, in the present low state of the river, passed swiftly between, deep and black, and curled into many whirlpools and counter currents, but unbroken by foam, and so still that scarcely the sound of a ripple was heard. The rock, for a considerable distance from the river, was worn over a large portion of its surface into circular holes and well-like cavities, by the abrasion of the river. . . . For about five miles below the Dalles, the river is narrow, and probably very deep; but during this distance is somewhat open, with grassy bottoms on the left." *Report of the Exploring Expedition,* 187–88. Cf. Chapter X, note 25, above.

In the present chapter, Irving follows Hunt's "Journal," December 24 to January 31, 300–305.

CHAPTER XXXVIII

The Village of Wish-ram — Roguery of the Inhabitants
Their Habitations — Tidings of Astoria — Of the Tonquin Massacre
Thieves About the Camp — A Band of Braggarts
Embarkation — Arrival at Astoria — A Joyful Reception — Old Comrades
Adventures of Reed, M'Lellan, and M'Kenzie Among the Snake River Mountains
Rejoicing at Astoria

OF the village of Wish-ram, the aborigines' fishing mart of the Columbia, we have given some account in an early chapter of this work.[1] The inhabitants held a traffic in the productions of the fisheries of the falls, and their village was the trading resort of the tribes from the coast and from the mountains. Mr. Hunt found the inhabitants shrewder and more intelligent than any Indians he had met with. Trade had sharpened their wits, though it had not improved their honesty; for they were a community of arrant rogues and freebooters. Their habitations comported with their circumstances, and were superior to any the travellers had yet seen west of the Rocky Mountains. In general, the dwellings of the savages on the Pacific side of that great barrier were mere tents and cabins of mats, or skins, or straw, the country being destitute of timber. In Wish-ram, on the contrary, the houses were built of wood, with long sloping roofs. The floor was sunk about six feet below the surface of the ground, with a low door at the gable end, extremely narrow, and partly sunk. Through this it was necessary to crawl and then to descend a short ladder. This inconvenient entrance was probably for the purpose of defense; there were loop-holes also under the eaves, apparently for the discharge of arrows. The houses were large, generally containing two or three families. Immediately within the door were sleeping places, ranged along the walls, like berths in a ship; and furnished with pallets of matting. These extended along one half of the building; the remaining half was appropriated to the storing of dried fish.[2]

[1] See Chapter X, pp. 103–104.

[2] Hunt does not describe this type of dwelling. Irving obtained his information from Lewis and Clark, *History of the Expedition*, II, 219–20, under date of October 24, 1805.

The trading operations of the inhabitants of Wish-ram had given them a wider scope of information, and rendered their village a kind of head-quarters of intelligence. Mr. Hunt was able, therefore, to collect more distinct tidings concerning the settlement of Astoria and its affairs. One of the inhabitants had been at the trading post established by David Stuart on the Oakinagan, and had picked up a few words of English there. From him, Mr. Hunt gleaned various particulars about that establishment, as well as about the general concerns of the enterprise. Others repeated the name of Mr. M'Kay, the partner who perished in the massacre on board of the Tonquin, and gave some account of that melancholy affair. They said Mr. M'Kay was a chief among the white men, and had built a great house at the mouth of the river, but had left it and sailed away in a large ship to the northward where he had been attacked by bad Indians in canoes. Mr. Hunt was startled by this intelligence, and made further inquiries. They informed him that the Indians had lashed their canoes to the ship, and fought until they killed him and all his people. This is another instance of the clearness with which intelligence is transmitted from mouth to mouth among the Indian tribes. These tidings, though but partially credited by Mr. Hunt, filled his mind with anxious forebodings. He now endeavored to procure canoes, in which to descend the Columbia, but none suitable for the purpose were to be obtained above the Narrows; he continued on, therefore, the distance of twelves miles, and encamped on the bank of the river. The camp was soon surrounded by loitering savages, who went prowling about seeking what they might pilfer. Being baffled by the vigilance of the guard, they endeavored to compass their ends by other means. Towards evening, a number of warriors entered the camp in ruffling style; painted and dressed out as if for battle, and armed with lances, bows and arrows, and scalping knives. They informed Mr. Hunt that a party of thirty or forty braves were coming up from a village below to attack the camp and carry off the horses, but that they were determined to stay with him and defend him. Mr. Hunt received them with great coldness, and, when they had finished their story, gave them a pipe to smoke. He then called up all hands, stationed sentinels in different quarters, but told them to keep as vigilant an eye within the camp as without.

The warriors were evidently baffled by these precautions, and, having smoked their pipe, and vapored off their valor, took their departure.

The farce, however, did not end here. After a little while the warriors returned, ushering in another savage, still more heroically arrayed. This they announced as the chief of the belligerent village, but as a great pacificator. His people had been furiously bent upon the attack, and would have doubtless carried it into effect, but this gallant chief had stood forth as the friend of white men, and had dispersed the throng by his own authority and prowess. Having vaunted this signal piece of service, there was a significant pause; all evidently expecting some adequate reward. Mr. Hunt again produced the pipe, smoked with the chieftain and his worthy compeers; but made no further demonstrations of gratitude. They remained about the camp all night, but at daylight returned, baffled and crestfallen, to their homes, with nothing but smoke for their pains.[3]

Mr. Hunt now endeavored to procure canoes, of which he saw several about the neighborhood, extremely well made, with elevated stems and sterns, some of them capable of carrying three thousand pounds weight. He found it extremely difficult, however, to deal with these slippery people, who seemed much more inclined to pilfer. Notwithstanding a strict guard maintained round the camp, various implements were stolen,[4] and several horses carried off. Among the latter, we have to include the long-cherished steed of Pierre Dorion. From some willful caprice that worthy pitched his tent at some distance from the main body, and tethered his invaluable steed beside it, from whence it was abstracted in the night, to the infinite chagrin and mortification of the hybrid interpreter.

Having, after several days' negotiation, procured the requisite number of canoes,[5] Mr. Hunt would gladly have left this thievish neighborhood, but was detained until the 5th of February[6] by violent headwinds, accompanied by snow and rain. Even after he was enabled to get under way, he had still to struggle against contrary winds and tempestuous weather. The current of the river, however, was in his favor; having made a portage at the grand rapid, the canoes met with no further obstruction, and, on the afternoon of the 15th of February, swept round an

[3] Hunt, under date of February 1, narrates this experience with the Indians in much detail. "Journal," 306.

[4] Two axes, a hatchet, and two guns. *Ibid.*

[5] He obtained seven canoes in exchange for horses.

[6] Irving's date agrees with Hunt's "Journal."

intervening cape, and came in sight of the infant settlement of Astoria.[7] After eleven months wandering in the wilderness, a great part of the time over trackless wastes, where the sight of a savage wigwam was a rarity, we may imagine the delight of the poor weather-beaten travellers, at beholding the embryo establishment, with its magazines, habitations, and picketed bulwarks, seated on a high point of land, dominating a beautiful little bay, in which was a trim-built shallop riding quietly at anchor. A shout of joy burst from each canoe at the long-wished-for sight. They urged their canoes across the bay, and pulled with eagerness for shore, where all hands poured down from the settlement to receive and welcome them. Among the first to greet them on their landing, were some of their old comrades and fellow-sufferers, who, under the conduct of Reed, M'Lellan, and M'Kenzie, had parted from them at the Caldron Linn. These had reached Astoria nearly a month previously, and judging from their own narrow escape from starvation, had given up Mr. Hunt and his followers as lost. Their greeting was the more warm and cordial. As to the Canadian voyageurs, their mutual felicitations, as usual, were loud and vociferous, and it was almost ludicrous to behold these ancient "comrades" and "confreres," hugging and kissing each other on the river bank.[8]

[7] In the previous part of this paragraph, Irving compressed Hunt's fairly detailed entries for February 4 through February 16. Under the latter date, which Hunt found on arrival at Astoria was there "reckoned only the 15th," he entered laconically his first sight of the fort: "I found that we were navigating along a large bay, and shortly afterward I saw the fort of Astoria on the southerly bank." *Ibid.*, 308.

[8] The emotional welcome which Irving here describes is only slightly suggested in Hunt's "Journal," where all we read is: "I had the pleasure there of again meeting Messrs. Mackenzie and McClellan, who had arrived more than a month before. . . . It was a very real pleasure for travellers harassed by fatigue to rest in quiet and be surrounded by friends after so long a journey in the midst of savages of whom it is always prudent to be wary. We had covered 2073 miles since leaving the Aricaras' village." *Ibid.*, 308. At this point, which marks the end of Hunt's "Journal," Irving had to turn to other sources.

Franchère, who was at the fort when Hunt arrived, records matter-of-factly that "Mr. Hunt arrived on the 15th February, with thirty men, one woman, and two children." *Narrative*, 271–72.

The only other eye witness who left a record is Alexander Ross. He noted the event by writing: "At last, on the 15th of February, the joyful cry of white men approaching, announced at Astoria the glad tidings of Mr. Hunt's arrival.

"The emaciated, downcast looks and tattered garments of our friends, all bespoke their extreme sufferings during a long and severe winter." *Adventures*, 185.

When the first greetings were over, the different bands interchanged accounts of their several wanderings, after separating at Snake River; we shall briefly notice a few of the leading particulars. It will be recollected by the reader, that a small exploring detachment had proceeded down the river, under the conduct of Mr. John Reed, a clerk of the company; that another had set off under M'Lellan, and a third in a different direction, under M'Kenzie. After wandering for several days without meeting with Indians, or obtaining any supplies, they came together fortuitously among the Snake River Mountains, some distance below that disasterous pass or strait which had received the appellation of the Devil's Scuttle Hole.

When thus united, their party consisted of M'Kenzie, M'Lellan, Reed, and eight men, chiefly Canadians. Being all in the same predicament, without horses, provisions, or information of any kind, they all agreed that it would be worse than useless to return to Mr. Hunt and encumber him with so many starving men, and that their only course was to extricate themselves as soon as possible from this land of famine and misery and make the best of their way for the Columbia. They accordingly continued to follow the downward course of Snake River; clambering rocks and mountains, and defying all the difficulties and dangers of that rugged defile, which subsequently, when the snows had fallen, was found impassable by Messrs. Hunt and Crooks.

Though constantly near to the borders of the river, and for a great part of the time within sight of its current, one of their greatest sufferings was thirst. The river had worn its way in a deep channel[9] through rocky mountains, destitute of brooks or springs. Its banks were so high and precipitous, that there was rarely any place where the travellers could get down to drink of its waters. Frequently they suffered for miles the torments of Tantalus; water continually within sight, yet fevered with the most parching thirst. Here and there they met with rain-water collected in the hollows of the rocks, but more than once they were reduced to the utmost extremity; and some of the men had recourse to the last expedient to avoid perishing.

Their sufferings from hunger were equally severe. They could meet with no game, and subsisted for a time on strips of beaver skin, broiled

[9] The Grand Canyon of Snake River, also known as Hell's Canyon. It is 5,500 feet deep and is bordered on the west by the Wallowa Mountains of Oregon and on the east by the Seven Devils Mountains of Idaho.

on the coals. These were doled out in scanty allowances, barely sufficient to keep up existence, and at length failed them altogether. Still they crept feebly on, scarce dragging one limb after another, until a severe snow-storm brought them to a pause. To struggle against it, in their exhausted condition, was impossible, so cowering under an impending rock at the foot of a steep mountain, they prepared themselves for that wretched fate which seemed inevitable.

At this critical juncture, when famine stared them in the face, M'Lellan casting up his eyes, beheld an ahsahta, or bighorn, sheltering itself under a shelving rock on the side of the hill above them. Being in a more active plight than any of his comrades, and an excellent marksman, he set off to get within shot of the animal. His companions watched his movements with breathless anxiety, for their lives depended upon his success. He made a cautious circuit; scrambled up the hill with the utmost silence, and at length arrived, unperceived, within a proper distance. Here leveling his rifle he took so sure an aim, that the bighorn fell dead on the spot; a fortunate circumstance, for, to pursue it, if merely wounded, would have been impossible in his emaciated state. The declivity of the hill enabled him to roll the carcass down to his companions, who were too feeble to climb the rocks. They fell to work to cut it up; yet exerted a remarkable self-denial for men in their starving condition, for they contented themselves for the present with a soup made from the bones, reserving the flesh for future repasts. This providential relief gave them strength to pursue their journey, but they were frequently reduced to almost equal straits, and it was only the smallness of their party, requiring a small supply of provisions, that enabled them to get through this desolate region with their lives.

At length, after twenty-one days of toil and suffering, they got through these mountains, and arrived at a tributary stream of that branch of the Columbia called Lewis River, of which Snake River forms the southern fork. In this neighborhood they met with wild horses, the first they had seen west of the Rocky Mountains. From hence they made their way to Lewis River, where they fell in with a friendly tribe of Indians, who freely administered to their necessities. On this river they procured two canoes, in which they dropped down the stream to its confluence with the Columbia, and then down that river to Astoria, where they arrived haggard and emaciated, and perfectly in rags.[10]

[10] Irving's account of McKenzie, McClellan, and Reed is based, with the exception

Thus, all the leading persons of Mr. Hunt's expedition were once more gathered together, excepting Mr. Crooks, of whose safety they entertained but little hope, considering the feeble condition in which they had been compelled to leave him in the heart of the wilderness.

A day was now given up to jubilee, to celebrate the arrival of Mr. Hunt and his companions, and the joyful meeting of the various scattered bands of adventurers at Astoria. The colors were hoisted; the guns, great and small, were fired; there was a feast of fish, of beaver, and venison, which relished well with men who had so long been glad to revel on horse flesh and dogs' meat; a genial allowance of grog was issued, to increase the general animation, and the festivities wound up, as usual, with a grand dance at night, by the Canadian voyageurs.[11]

of McClellan's shooting the bighorn, upon Franchère's *Narrative*, 269–71. Omitted by Irving is Franchère's recital of their meeting with a deranged young man named Archibald Pelton; *ibid.*, 271. He is referred to also in this connection by Ross Cox, who calls him Archibald Petton; see *Columbia River*, 60–61.

[11] The distance from St. Louis to Astoria, by the route travelled by Hunt and M'Kenzie, was upwards of thirty-five hundred miles, though in a direct line it does not exceed eighteen hundred. (Irving's note)

THE winter passed[1] away tranquilly at Astoria. The apprehensions of hostility from the natives had subsided; indeed, as the season advanced, the Indians for the most part had disappeared from the neighborhood, and abandoned the sea-coast, so that, for want of their aid, the colonists had at times suffered considerably for want of provisions. The hunters belonging to the establishment made frequent and wide excursions, but with very moderate success. There were[2] some deer and a few bears to be found in the vicinity, and elk in great numbers; the country, however, was so rough, and the woods so close and entangled that it was almost impossible to beat up the game. The prevalent rains of winter, also, rendered it difficult for the hunter to keep his arms in order.[3] The quantity of game, therefore, brought in by the hunters was extremely scanty, and it was frequently necessary to put all hands on very moderate allowance. Towards spring, however, the fishing season commenced—the

[1] The first edition reads *had passed.*

[2] Erroneously *was* in Author's Revised Edition. The first edition correctly has *were.*

[3] Here and elsewhere in this chapter, Irving's main source was Robert Stuart's "Travelling Memoranda." Compare what Irving wrote, for example, with the following passage by Stuart: "The country is . . . so remarkably broken, and heavily timbered, that it is seldom possible to distinguish an object more than 100 yards, which when added to an impenetrable undergrowth affords such a secure retreat that the utmost efforts of the hunter are seldom crowned with success, besides from the middle of October to that of March, no man in the woods can possibly keep his Arms in order, in consequence of the unceasing rains which fall during these five months." Because the "Travelling Memoranda" is published in both Rollins (ed.), *Discovery of the Oregon Trail,* and in Spaulding (ed.), *On the Oregon Trail,* for convenience both editions will be cited hereafter, identified respectively by the names of the editors. The passage quoted above is found in Rollins, 5; Spaulding, 29.

season of plenty on the Columbia. About the beginning of February, a small kind of fish, about six inches long, called by the natives the uthle-can, and resembling the smelt, made its appearance at the mouth of the river. It is said to be of delicious flavor, and so fat as to burn like a candle, for which it is often used by the natives.[4] It enters the river in immense shoals, like solid columns, often extending to the depth of five or more feet, and is scooped up by the natives with small nets at the end of poles. In this way they will soon fill a canoe, or form a great heap upon the river banks. These fish constitute a principal article of their food: the women drying them and stringing them on cords. As the uthlecan is only found in the lower part of the river, the arrival of it soon brought back the natives to the coast; who again resorted to the factory to trade, and from that time furnished plentiful supplies of fish.

The sturgeon makes its appearance in the river shortly after the uthle-can, and is taken in different ways by the natives: sometimes they spear it; but oftener they use the hook and line, and the net.[5] Occasionally, they sink a cord in the river by a heavy weight, with a buoy at the upper end, to keep it floating. To this cord several hooks are attached by short lines, a few feet distant from each other, and baited with small fish. This apparatus is often set towards night, and by the next morning several sturgeon will be found hooked by it; for though a large and strong fish, it makes but little resistance when ensnared.

The salmon, which are the prime fish of the Columbia, and as impor-tant to the piscatory tribes as are the buffaloes to the hunters of the prairies, do not enter the river until towards the latter part of May, from which time, until the middle of August, they abound and are taken in vast quantities, either with the spear or seine, and mostly in shallow water. An inferior species succeeds, and continues from August to De-cember. It is remarkable for having a double row of teeth, half an inch long and extremely sharp, from whence it has received the name of the dog-toothed salmon. It is generally killed with the spear in small rivu-lets, and smoked for winter provision.[6] We have noticed in a former chapter the mode in which the salmon are taken and cured at the falls of the Columbia; and put up in parcels for exportation. From these dif-

[4] Rollins, 8, 30; Spaulding, 33, 45. Cf. Franchère, *Narrative*, 323.

[5] Rollins, 8, 30; Spaulding, 33, 45.

[6] To this point, this paragraph closely follows Stuart. See Rollins, 8; Spaulding, 32–33.

ferent fisheries of the river tribes, the establishment at Astoria had to derive much of its precarious supplies of provisions.

A year's residence at the mouth of the Columbia, and various expeditions in the interior, had now given the Astorians some idea of the country. The whole coast is described as remarkably rugged and mountainous; with dense forests of hemlock, spruce, white and red cedar, cottonwood, white oak, and white and swamp ash, willow, and a few walnut. There is likewise an undergrowth of aromatic shrubs, creepers, and clambering vines, that render the forests almost impenetrable; together with berries of various kinds, such as gooseberries, strawberries, raspberries, both red and yellow, very large and finely flavored whortleberries, cranberries, service-berries, blackberries, currants, sloes, and wild and choke cherries.

Among the flowering vines is one deserving of particular notice. Each flower is composed of six leaves or petals, about three inches in length, of a beautiful crimson, the inside spotted with white. Its leaves, of a fine green, are oval, and disposed by threes. This plant climbs upon the trees without attaching itself to them: when it has reached the topmost branches, it descends perpendicularly, and as it continues to grow, extends from tree to tree, until its various stalks interlace the grove like the rigging of a ship. The stems or trunks of this vine are tougher and more flexible than willow, and are from fifty to one hundred fathoms in length. From the fibres, the Indians manufacture baskets of such close texture as to hold water.[7]

The principal quadrupeds that had been seen by the colonists in their various expeditions were the stag, fallow deer, hart, black and grizzly bear, antelope, ahsahta or bighorn, beaver, sea and river otter, muskrat, fox, wolf, and panther, the latter extremely rare. The only domestic animals among the natives were horses and dogs.[8]

The country abounded with aquatic and land birds, such as swans,

[7] The previous two paragraphs describing the flora of the region are a very close paraphrase of Stuart, some of the wording being verbatim. Rollins, 6–7; Spaulding, 30–31.

[8] How closely Irving relies on Stuart may be seen by comparing what Irving wrote with the following passage from the "Travelling Memoranda": "The principal quadrupeds I have seen, are the Moose Deer, or Elk, the Stag, the fallow Deer, Hart, black and grizzly Bear, Antelope, Ibex [which Irving changes to "ahsahta or bighorn"], Beaver, Sea and River Otter, Muskrats, Foxes, Wolves, a few Panthere &ct.—Horses and Dogs are the only domestic animals in possession of the natives." Rollins, 7; Spaulding, 31.

wild geese, brant, ducks of almost every description, pelicans, herons, gulls, snipes, curlews, eagles, vultures, crows, ravens, magpies, woodpeckers, pigeons, partridges, pheasants, grouse, and a great variety of singing birds.[9]

There were few reptiles; the only dangerous kinds were the rattlesnake, and one striped with black, yellow, and white, about four feet long. Among the lizard kind was one about nine or ten inches in length, exclusive of the tail, and three inches in circumference. The tail was round, and of the same length as the body. The head was triangular, covered with small square scales. The upper part of the body was likewise covered with small scales, green, yellow, black, and blue. Each foot had five toes, furnished with strong nails, probably to aid it in burrowing, as it usually lived under ground on the plains.[10]

A remarkable fact, characteristic of the country west of the Rocky Mountains, is the mildness and equability of the climate. The[11] great mountain barrier[12] seems to divide the continent into different climates, even in the same degrees of latitude. The rigorous winters and sultry summers, and all the capricious inequalities of temperature prevalent on the Atlantic side of the mountains, are but little felt on their western declivities. The countries between them and the Pacific are blessed with milder and steadier temperature, resembling the climates of parallel latitudes in Europe. In the plains and valleys but little snow falls throughout the winter, and usually melts while falling. It rarely lies on the ground more than two days at a time, except on the summits of the mountains. The winters are rainy rather than cold. The rains for five months, from the middle of October to the middle of March, are almost incessant, and often accompanied by tremendous thunder and lightning. The winds prevalent at this season are from the south and southeast, which usually bring rain. Those from the north to the southwest are the harbingers of fair weather and a clear sky. The residue of the year, from the middle of March to the middle of October, an interval of seven months, is serene and delightful. There is scarcely any rain throughout this time, yet the face of the country is kept fresh and verdant by nightly dews, and occasionally by humid fogs in the mornings.

[9] This paragraph is almost verbatim from Stuart. See Rollins, 7; Spaulding, 32.

[10] Parts of this paragraph are verbatim from Stuart. *Ibid.*

[11] *That* in first edition.

[12] Cascade Range.

These are not considered prejudicial to health, since both the natives and the whites sleep in the open air with perfect impunity. While this equable and bland temperature prevails throughout the lower country, the peaks and ridges of the vast mountains by which it is dominated, are covered with perpetual snow. This renders them discernible at a great distance, shining at times like bright summer clouds, at other times assuming the most aerial tints, and always forming brilliant and striking features in the vast landscape. The mild temperature prevalent throughout the country is attributed by some to the succession of winds from the Pacific Ocean, extending from latitude twenty degrees to at least fifty degrees north. These temper the heat of summer, so that in the shade no one is incommoded by perspiration; they also soften the rigors of winter, and produce such a moderation in the climate, that the inhabitants can wear the same dress throughout the year.

The soil in the neighborhood of the sea-coast is of a brown color, inclining to red, and generally poor; being a mixture of clay and gravel. In the interior, and especially in the valleys of the Rocky Mountains, the soil is generally blackish, though sometimes yellow. It is frequently mixed with marl, and with marine substances in a state of decomposition. This kind of soil extends to a considerable depth, as may be perceived in the deep cuts made by ravines, and by the beds of rivers. The vegetation in these valleys is much more abundant than near the coast; in fact, it is in these fertile intervals, locked up between rocky sierras, or scooped out from barren wastes, that population must extend itself, as it were, in veins and ramifications, if ever the regions beyond the mountains should become civilized.[13]

[13] The previous two paragraphs are also from Stuart. Rollins, 5–6; Spaulding, 29–30.

A BRIEF mention has already been made of the tribes or hordes existing about the lower part of the Columbia at the time of the settlement; a few more particulars concerning them may be acceptable. The four tribes nearest to Astoria, and with whom the traders had most intercourse, were, as has heretofore been observed, the Chinooks, the Clatsops, the Wahkiacums, and the Cathlamets.[1] The Chinooks resided chiefly along the banks of a river of the same name, running parallel to the sea-coast, through a low country studded with stagnant pools, and emptying itself into Baker's Bay, a few miles from Cape Disappointment. This was the tribe over which Comcomly, the one-eyed chieftain, held sway; it boasted two hundred and fourteen fighting men. Their chief subsistence was on fish, with an occasional regale of the flesh of elk and deer, and of wild-fowl from the neighboring ponds.

The Clatsops resided on both sides of Point Adams;[2] they were the mere relics of a tribe which had been nearly swept off by the small-pox, and did not number more than one hundred and eighty fighting men.[3]

---

[1] Lewis and Clark mention these four tribes as well as others.

[2] See Chapter VIII, p. 83.

[3] For his information in this chapter, Irving relied mainly on Lewis and Clark. Here, under date of January 14, 1806, he read: "The first nation on the south are the Clatsops, who reside on the southern side of the bay, and along the sea coast, on both sides of Point Adams. They are represented as the remains of a much larger nation; but about four years ago, a disorder . . . which seems . . . to have been the small-pox, destroyed four chiefs, and several hundreds of the nation." *History of the Expedition,* II, 310.

The Wahkiacums, or Waak-i-cums, inhabited the north side of the Columbia, and numbered sixty-six warriors. They and the Chinooks were originally the same; but a dispute arising about two generations previous to the time of the settlement, between the ruling chief and his brother Wahkiacum, the latter seceded, and with his adherents formed the present horde which continues to go by his name. In this way new tribes or clans are formed, and lurking causes of hostility engendered.

The Cathlamets lived opposite to the lower village of the Wahkiacums, and numbered ninety-four warriors.

These four tribes, or rather clans, have every appearance of springing from the same origin, resembling each other in person, dress, language, and manners. They are rather a diminutive race, generally below five feet five inches, with crooked legs and thick ankles—a deformity caused by their passing so much of their time sitting or squatting upon the calves of their legs and their heels, in the bottom of their canoes—a favorite position, which they retain, even when on shore. The women increase the deformity by wearing tight bandages round the ankles, which prevent the circulation of the blood, and cause a swelling of the muscles of the leg.[4]

Neither sex can boast of personal beauty. Their faces are round, with small but animated eyes. Their noses are broad and flat at top, and fleshy at the end, with large nostrils. They have wide mouths, thick lips, and short, irregular and dirty teeth. Indeed good teeth are seldom to be seen among the tribes west of the Rocky Mountains, who live simply on fish.[5]

In the early stages of their intercourse with white men, these savages were but scantily clad. In summer time the men went entirely naked; in the winter and in bad weather the men wore a small robe, reaching to the middle of the thigh, made of the skins of animals, or of the wool of the mountain sheep. Occasionally, they wore a kind of mantle of

[4] This paragraph also is derived from Lewis and Clark, under date of January 21. Here Irving read: "The Killamucks, Clatsops, Chinnooks, and Cathlamahs . . . preserve a general resemblance in person, dress, and manners. They are commonly of a diminutive stature, badly shaped, and their appearance by no means prepossessing. They have broad thick flat feet, thick ankles, and crooked legs: the last of which deformities is to be ascribed, in part, to the universal practice of squatting, or sitting on the calves of their legs and heels, and also to the tight bandages of beads and strings worn round the ankles, by the women, which prevent the circulation of the blood, and render the legs, of the females, particularly, ill shaped and swollen." *Ibid.*, 326.

[5] From *ibid.*, 327.

matting, to keep off the rain; but, having thus protected the back and shoulders, they left the rest of the body naked.[6]

The women wore similar robes, though shorter, not reaching below the waist; beside[s] which, they had a kind of petticoat, or fringe, reaching from the waist to the knee, formed of the fibres of cedar bark, broken into strands, or a tissue of silk grass twisted and knotted at the ends. This was the usual dress of the women in summer; should the weather be inclement, they added a vest of skins, similar to the robe.[7]

The men carefully eradicated every vestige of a beard, considering it a great deformity. They looked with disgust at the whiskers and well-furnished chins of the white men, and in derision called them Long-beards. Both sexes, on the other hand, cherished the hair of the head, which with them is generally black and rather coarse. They allowed it to grow to a great length and were very proud and careful of it, sometimes wearing it plaited, sometimes wound round the head in fanciful tresses. No greater affront could be offered to them than to cut off their treasured locks.[8]

They had conical hats with narrow rims, neatly woven of bear-grass or of the fibres of cedar bark, interwoven with designs of various shapes and colors; sometimes merely squares and triangles, at other times rude representations of canoes, with men fishing and harpooning. These hats were nearly waterproof, and extremely durable.[9]

The favorite ornaments of the men were collars of bears' claws, the proud trophies of hunting exploits; while the women and children wore similar decorations of elks' tusks. An intercourse with the white traders,

[6] From Lewis and Clark: "The dress of the men consists in a small robe, reaching to the middle of the thigh, tied by a string across the breast . . . composed of the skins of a small animal. . . . Sometimes they have a blanket woven with the fingers, from the wool of their native sheep; occasionally a mat is thrown over them to keep off rain; but except this robe, they have no other article of clothing during winter or summer, so that every part of the body, but the back and shoulders, is exposed to view." *Ibid.*, 328–29. Cf. Franchère, *Narrative*, 325.

[7] From Lewis and Clark: "The robe of the women is like that worn by the men, except that it does not reach below the waist. . . . The garment which covers the body from the waist as low as the knee . . . is made either of the bruised bark of white cedar, the twisted cords of silk-grass, or of flags and rushes. . . . If the weather is unusually severe, they add a vest formed of skins like the robe." *History of the Expedition*, II, 329–30. Cf. Franchère, 325.

[8] From Robert Stuart, "Travelling Memoranda"; see Rollins, 12–13; Spaulding, 38.

[9] Here Irving combines two brief passages from Lewis and Clark. One of them reads: "These [hats] are made of cedar bark and bear-grass, interwoven together . . . with

however, soon effected a change in the toilets of both sexes. They became fond of arraying themselves in any article of civilized dress which they could procure, and often made a most grotesque appearance. They adapted many articles of finery, also, to their own previous tastes. Both sexes were fond of adorning themselves with bracelets of iron, brass, or copper. They were delighted, also, with blue and white beads, particularly the former, and wore broad tight bands of them round the waist and ankles, large rolls of them round the neck, and pendants of them in the ears. The men, especially, who in savage life carry a passion for personal decoration further than the females, did not think their gala equipments complete unless they had a jewel of haiqua, or wampum, dangling at the nose. Thus arrayed, their hair besmeared with fish oil, and their bodies bedaubed with red clay, they considered themselves irresistible.[10]

When on warlike expeditions, they painted their faces and bodies in the most hideous and grotesque manner, according to the universal practice of American savages. Their arms were bows and arrows, spears, and war-clubs. Some wore a corselet, formed of pieces of hard wood laced together with bear-grass, so as to form a light coat of mail, pliant to the body; and a kind of casque of cedar bark, leather, and bear-grass, sufficient to protect the head from an arrow or war-club. A more complete article of defensive armor was a buff jerkin or shirt of great

a small brim of about two inches, and a high crown, widening upwards. They are light, ornamented with various colours and figures, and being nearly water-proof, are much more durable than either chip or straw hats." *History of the Expedition,* II, 320. A later passage mentions the same materials but states that they are "interwoven in a conic form" and are decorated with "squares, triangles, and sometimes rude figures of canoes and seamen harpooning whales." *Ibid.,* 329.

[10] This paragraph is derived from Lewis and Clark under date of January 21, 1806. It is too long to be quoted here. An examination of this source shows that the word *waist* used by Irving in the phrase "round the waist and ankles," which also appears in the first edition of *Astoria,* is an error for *wrist.* Referring to the beads, Lewis and Clark wrote that they "are folded very tightly round their wrists and ankles." *History of the Expedition,* II, 330. Cf. Franchère, *Narrative,* 326. Lewis and Clark also call attention to the wampum as a "favourite decoration of the noses of the men." They do not, however, use the word *haiqua.* This expression Irving presumably found in Cox's *Columbia River,* 178. Here Cox defines the word to mean "a white round shell of extreme hardness, varying from one to four inches in length, and from three eights to half an inch in circumference. It is hollow, slightly curved, and tapers a little towards the ends. These shells are highly esteemed, the longest being the most valuable. They are found in the neighborhood of Nootka, and form an important article of local traffic."

thickness, made of doublings of elk skin, and reaching to the feet, holes being left for the head and arms. This was perfectly arrowproof; add to which, it was often endowed with charmed virtues, by the spells and mystic ceremonials of the medicine man, or conjurer.[11]

Of the peculiar custom, prevalent among these people, of flattening the head, we have already spoken. It is one of those instances of human caprice, like the crippling of the feet of females in China, which are quite incomprehensible. This custom prevails principally among the tribes on the sea-coast, and about the lower parts of the rivers. How far it extends along the coast we are not able to ascertain. Some of the tribes, both north and south of the Columbia, practice it; but they all speak the Chinook language, and probably originated from the same stock. As far as we can learn, the remoter tribes, which speak an entirely different language, do not flatten the head. This absurd custom declines, also, in receding from the shores of the Pacific; few traces of it are to be found among the tribes of the Rocky Mountains, and after crossing the mountains it disappears altogether. Those Indians, therefore, about the head waters of the Columbia, and in the solitary mountain regions, who are often called Flatheads, must not be supposed to be characterized by this deformity. It is an appellation often given by the hunters east of the mountain chain, to all the western Indians, excepting the Snakes.[12]

The religious belief of these people was extremely limited and confined; or rather, in all probability, their explanations were but little understood by their visitors. They had an idea of a benevolent and omnipotent spirit, the creator of all things. They represent him as assuming various shapes at pleasure, but generally that of an immense bird. He usually inhabits the sun, but occasionally wings his way through the aerial regions, and sees all that is doing upon earth. Should anything displease him, he vents his wrath in terrific storms and tempests, the lightning being the flashes of his eyes, and the thunder the clapping of his wings. To propitiate his favor they offer to him annual sacrifices of salmon and venison, the first fruits of their fishing and hunting.

Beside[s] this aerial spirit they believe in an inferior one, who inhabits the fire, and of whom they are in perpetual dread, as, though he possesses equally the power of good and evil, the evil is apt to predominate.

[11] Most of the details of this paragraph are found in Franchère, *Narrative*, 331.

[12] Lewis and Clark discuss head flattening and the geographical extent of its practice; *History of the Expedition*, II, 327. Irving used this passage.

Shoshone Falls (210 feet high) on the Snake River. Wilson P. Hunt explored 35 miles of this section of the river on October 29, 1811, to see whether canoes could be passed down. A grave crisis confronted the Overland Astorians when the Snake proved unnavigable. Photograph by W. H. Jackson, 1871.

Courtesy Idaho Historical Society

Twin Falls (*circa* 1900) on the Snake River; viewed by Wilson P. Hunt on October 29, 1811. Such obstacles threatened the Overland Astorians with disaster.

Courtesy Idaho Historical Society

They endeavor, therefore, to keep him in good humor by frequent offerings. He is supposed also to have great influence with the winged spirit, their sovereign protector and benefactor. They implore him, therefore, to act as their interpreter, and procure them all desirable[13] things, such as success in fishing and hunting, abundance of game, fleet horses, obedient wives, and male children.

These Indians have likewise their priests, or conjurers, or medicine men, who pretend to be in the confidence of the deities, and the expounders and enforcers of their will. Each of these medicine men has his idols carved in wood, representing the spirits of the air and of the fire, under some rude grotesque form of a horse, a bear, a beaver, or other quadruped, or that of bird or fish.[14] These idols are hung round with amulets and votive offerings, such as beavers' teeth, and bears' and eagles' claws.

When any chief personage is on his death-bed, or dangerously ill, the medicine men are sent for. Each brings with him his idols, with which he retires into a canoe to hold a consultation. As doctors are prone to disagree, so these medicine men have now and then a violent altercation as to the malady of the patient, or the treatment of it. To settle this they beat their idols soundly against each other; whichever first loses a tooth or a claw is considered as confuted, and his votary retires from the field.

Polygamy is not only allowed, but considered honorable, and the greater number of wives a man can maintain, the more important is he in the eyes of the tribe. The first wife, however, takes rank of all the others, and is considered mistress of the house. Still the domestic establishment is liable to jealousies and cabals, and the lord and master has much difficulty in maintaining harmony in his jangling household.

In the manuscript[15] from which we draw many of these particulars, it is stated that he who exceeds his neighbors in the number of his wives, male children, and slaves, is elected chief of the village; a title to office which we do not recollect ever before to have met with.

Feuds are frequent among these tribes, but are not very deadly. They have occasionally pitched battles, fought on appointed days, and at specific[16] places, which are generally the banks of a rivulet. The adverse parties post themselves on the opposite sides of the stream, and at such

[13] *Describable* in first edition.   [14] The first edition has *a bird or fish.*
[15] Robert Stuart's "Travelling Memoranda."   [16] *Specified* in first edition.

distances that the battles often last a long while before any blood is shed. The number of killed and wounded seldom exceed[s] half a dozen. Should the damage be equal on each side, the war is considered as honorably concluded; should one party lose more than the other, it is entitled to a compensation in slaves or other property, otherwise hostilities are liable to be renewed at a future day. They are much given also to predatory inroads into the territories of their enemies, and sometimes of their friendly neighbors. Should they fall upon a band of inferior force, or upon a village, weakly defended, they act with the ferocity of true poltroons, slaying all the men, and carrying off the women and children as slaves. As to the property, it is packed upon horses which they bring with them for the purpose. They are mean and paltry as warriors, and altogether inferior in heroic qualities to the savages of the buffalo plains on the east side of the mountains.

A great portion of their time is passed in revelry, music, dancing, and gambling. Their music scarcely deserves the name; the instruments being of the rudest kind. Their singing is harsh and discordant; the songs are chiefly extempore, relating to passing circumstances, the persons present, or any trifling object that strikes the attention of the singer. They have several kinds of dances, some of them lively and pleasing. The women are rarely permitted to dance with the men, but form groups apart, dancing to the same instrument and song.

They have a great passion for play, and a variety of games. To such a pitch of excitement are they sometimes roused, that they gamble away everything they possess, even to their wives and children. They are notorious thieves, also, and proud of their dexterity. He who is frequently successful, gains much applause and popularity; but the clumsy thief, who is detected in some bungling attempt, is scoffed at and despised, and sometimes severely punished.[17]

Such are a few leading characteristics of the natives in the neighborhood of Astoria. They appear to us inferior in many respects to the tribes east of the mountains, the bold rovers of the prairies; and to partake much of the Esquimaux character; elevated in some degree by a more genial climate, and more varied style of living.

The habits of traffic engendered at the cataracts of the Columbia, have had their influence along the coast. The Chinooks and other Indians at

[17] For the preceding nine paragraphs, Irving draws from the "Travelling Memoranda." Rollins, 8–12; Spaulding, 33–37.

the mouth of the river, soon proved themselves keen traders, and in their early dealings with the Astorians never hesitated to ask three times what they considered the real value of an article.[18] They were inquisitive, also, in the extreme, and impertinently intrusive; and were prone to indulge in scoffing and ridicule at the expense of the strangers.

In one thing, however, they showed superior judgment and self-command to most of their race; this was, in their abstinence from ardent spirits, and the abhorrence and disgust with which they regarded a drunkard. On one occasion, a son of Comcomly had been induced to drink freely at the factory, and went home in a state of intoxication, playing all kinds of mad pranks, until he sank into a stupor, in which he remained for two days. The old chieftain repaired to his friend, M'Dougal, with indignation flaming in his countenance, and bitterly reproached him for having permitted his son to degrade himself into a beast, and to render himself an object of scorn and laughter to his slave.[19]

[18] Lewis and Clark also mention this form of inflation: "They begin by asking double or treble the value of their merchandise." *History of the Expedition*, II, 339. They also discuss Indian trading practices; *ibid.*, 338–44.

[19] Both Franchère, *Narrative*, 325, and Cox, *op. cit.*, 173, mention this incident. Lewis and Clark affirm the abstention from alcohol by the Indians of this area; *History of the Expedition*, II, 337.

Spring Arrangements at Astoria — Various Expeditions Set Out
The Long Narrows — Pilfering Indians
Thievish Tribe at Wish-ram — Portage at the Falls
Portage by Moonlight — An Attack, a Rout, and a Robbery
Indian Cure for Cowardice — A Parley and Compromise
The Despatch Party Turn Back — Meet Crooks and John Day
Their Sufferings — Indian Perfidy — Arrival at Astoria

AS the spring opened, the little settlement of Astoria was in agitation, and prepared to send forth various expeditions. Several important things were to be done. It was necessary to send a supply of goods to the trading post of Mr. David Stuart, established in the preceding autumn on the Oakinagan. The cache, or secret deposit, made by Mr. Hunt at the Caldron Linn,[1] was likewise to be visited, and the merchandise and other effects left there, to be brought to Astoria. A third object of moment was to send despatches overland to Mr. Astor at New York, informing him of the state of affairs at the settlement, and the fortunes of the several expeditions.[2]

The task of carrying supplies to Oakinagan was assigned to Mr. Robert Stuart, a spirited and enterprising young man, nephew to the one who had established the post. The cache was to be sought out by two of the clerks, named Russell Farnham[3] and Donald M'Gilles,[4] con-

---

[1] Franchère says "near old Fort Henry." *Narrative*, 273. According to Hunt's "Journal," they had cached their saddles at Fort Henry, although it is possible, since they also left seventy-seven horses there, that goods were cached also. It might be doubted whether the fifteen canoes that Irving says were made there would have been adequate to transport all the goods carried by horses thus far.

[2] "Until the 30th of March, we were occupied in preparing triplicates of letters and other necessary papers." Franchère, *Narrative*, 272.

[3] Farnham, who was from Massachusetts, came out on the *Tonquin*. He later left Astoria on the *Pedler* with W. P. Hunt and was taken to Kamchatka, where he commenced to walk across Siberia to St. Petersburg. From there he crossed Europe and shipped from Copenhagen for the United States with documents and perhaps drafts for Astor in New York. Later he was employed by the American Fur Company on the Missouri River. An oil portrait is at the Missouri Historical Society. See Drumm, "More About Astorians," *Oregon Historical Quarterly*, Vol. XXIV (1923), 338-44.

[4] Franchère, in his list of the passengers aboard the *Tonquin*, gives his name as

ducted by a guide, and accompanied by eight men, to assist in bringing home the goods.

As to the despatches, they were confided to Mr. John Reed, the clerk, the same who had conducted one of the exploring detachments of Snake River. He was now to trace back his way across the mountains by the same route by which he had come, with no other companions or escort than Ben Jones, the Kentucky hunter, and two Canadians. As it was still hoped that Mr. Crooks might be in existence, and that Mr. Reed and his party might meet with him in the course of their route, they were charged with a small supply of goods and provisions, to aid that gentleman on his way to Astoria.

When the expedition of Reed was made known, Mr. M'Lellan announced his determination to accompany it. He had long been dissatisfied with the smallness of his interest in the copartnership, and had requested an additional number of shares; his request not being complied with, he resolved to abandon the company.[5] M'Lellan was a man of a singularly self-willed and decided character, with whom persuasion was useless; he was permitted, therefore, to take his own course without opposition.

As to Reed, he set about preparing for his hazardous journey with the zeal of a true Irishman. He had a tin case made, in which the letters and papers addressed to Mr. Astor were carefully soldered up. This case he intended to strap upon his shoulders, so as to bear it about with him, sleeping and waking, in all changes and chances, by land or by water, and never to part with it but with his life!

Donald M'Gillis. He went over to the North West Company with the transfer of Astoria, but by 1817 and perhaps sooner he had left the fur trade, for in that year Ross Cox (*Columbia River*, 349) visited him where he was living on the Ottawa River. See Wallace (ed.), *Documents*, 469.

[5] McClellan owned two and one-half shares. On March 1, 1812, the partners took the following action: "Resolved that Robert McClellan having expressed his intention of withdrawing from the concern should he not have an augmentation of his shares be permitted so to withdraw and that he be no longer considered a partner of the Pacific Fur Company, nor in any way entitled to any right, privilege or emolument arising from his having been a Partner." On the same day, McClellan signed the following document: "I Robert McClelan do hereby relinquish all right title and claim to all the shares or interest in the Pacific Fur Company towit—two and an [*sic*] half shares—and do also relinquish all profit emolument or privileges arising from my having been a partner thereof." Pacific Fur Company Minute Book, Missouri Historical Society, printed in Flandrau, *Astor and the Oregon Country*, 34–35. The resolution of the partners also appears in Drumm, "More About Astorians, *loc. cit.*, 335–36n.

As the route of these several parties would be the same for nearly four hundred miles up the Columbia, and within that distance would lie through the piratical pass of the rapids, and among the freebooting tribes of the river, it was thought advisable to start about the same time, and to keep together. Accordingly, on the 22d of March,[6] they all set off, to the number of seventeen men, in two canoes—and here we cannot but pause to notice the hardihood of these several expeditions, so insignificant in point of force, and severally destined to traverse immense wildernesses, where larger parties had experienced so much danger and distress. When recruits were sought in the preceding year among experienced hunters and voyageurs at Montreal and St. Louis, it was considered dangerous to attempt to cross the Rocky Mountains with less than sixty men; and yet here we find Reed ready to push his way across those barriers with merely three companions. Such is the fearlessness, the insensibility to danger, which men acquire by the habitude of constant risk. The mind, like the body, becomes callous by exposure.

The little associated band proceeded up the river, under the command of Mr. Robert Stuart, and arrived early in the month of April at the Long Narrows, that notorious plundering place. Here it was necessary to unload the canoes, and to transport both them and their cargoes to the head of the Narrows by land. Their party was too few in number for the purpose. They were obliged, therefore, to seek the assistance of the Cathlasco Indians, who undertook to carry the goods on their horses. Forward then they set, the Indians with their horses well freighted, and the first load convoyed by Reed and five men, well armed; the gallant Irishman striding along at the head, with his tin case of despatches glittering on his back. In passing, however, through a rocky and intricate defile, some of the freebooting vagrants[7] turned their horses up a narrow path and galloped off, carrying with them two bales of goods, and a number of smaller articles. To follow them was useless; indeed, it was with much ado that the convoy got into port with the residue of the cargoes; for some of the guards were pillaged of their knives and pocket handkerchiefs, and the lustrous tin case of Mr. John Reed was in imminent jeopardy.

[6] Franchère may be in error in saying they were still copying letters until March 30 (see note 2 above), for Cox, *op. cit.*, 62, says they left the fort on that date. Irving's date appears to be nine days too early.

[7] *Vagabonds* in first edition.

Mr. Stuart heard of these depredations, and hastened forward to the relief of the convoy, but could not reach them before dusk, by which time they had arrived at the village of Wish-ram, already noted for its great fishery, and the knavish propensities of its inhabitants. Here they found themselves benighted in a strange place, and surrounded by savages bent on pilfering, if not upon open robbery. Not knowing what active course to take, they remained under arms all night, without closing an eye, and at the very first peep of dawn, when objects were yet scarce visible, everything was hastily embarked, and, without seeking to recover the stolen effects, they pushed off from shore, "glad to bid adieu," as they said, "to this abominable nest of miscreants."[8]

The worthies of Wish-ram, however, were not disposed to part so easily with their visitors. Their cupidity had been quickened by the plunder which they had already taken, and their confidence increased by the impunity with which their outrage had passed. They resolved, therefore, to take further toll of the travellers, and, if possible, to capture the tin case of despatches; which shining conspicuously from afar, and being guarded by John Reed with such especial care, must, as they supposed, be "a great medicine."

Accordingly, Mr. Stuart and his comrades had not proceeded far in the canoes, when they beheld the whole rabble of Wish-ram stringing in groups along the bank, whooping and yelling, and gibbering in their wild jargon, and when they landed below the falls, they were surrounded by upwards of four hundred of these river ruffians, armed with bows and arrows, war-clubs, and other savage weapons. These now pressed forward, with offers to carry the canoes and effects up the portage. Mr. Stuart declined forwarding the goods, alleging the lateness of the hour; but, to keep them in good humor, informed them, that, if they conducted themselves well, their offered services might probably be accepted in the morning; in the meanwhile, he suggested that they might carry up the canoes. They accordingly set off with the two canoes on their shoulders, accompanied by a guard of eight men well armed.

When arrived at the head of the falls, the mischievous spirit of the savages broke out, and they were on the point of destroying the canoes, doubtless with a view to impede the white men from carrying forward their goods, and laying them open to further pilfering. They were with

[8] A direct quotation from Robert Stuart's "Travelling Memoranda." Rollins, 55; Spaulding, 59.

some difficulty prevented from committing this outrage by the interference of an old man, who appeared to have authority among them; and, in consequence of his harangue, the whole of the hostile band, with the exception of about fifty, crossed to the north side of the river, where they lay in wait, ready for further mischief.

In the meantime, Mr. Stuart, who had remained at the foot of the falls with the goods, and who knew that the proffered assistance of the savages was only for the purpose of having an opportunity to plunder, determined, if possible, to steal a march upon them, and defeat their machinations. In the dead of the night, therefore, about one o'clock, the moon shining brightly, he roused his party, and proposed that they should endeavor to transport the goods themselves, above the falls, before the sleeping savages could be aware of their operations. All hands sprang to the work with zeal, and hurried it on in the hope of getting all over before daylight. Mr. Stuart went forward with the first loads, and took his station at the head of the portage, while Mr. Reed and Mr. M'Lellan remained at the foot to forward the remainder.

The day dawned before the transportation was completed. Some of the fifty Indians who had remained on the south side of the river, perceived what was going on, and, feeling themselves too weak for an attack, gave the alarm to those on the opposite side, upwards of a hundred of whom embarked in several large canoes. Two loads of goods yet remained to be brought up. Mr. Stuart despatched some of the people for one of the loads, with a request to Mr. Reed to retain with him as many of the men[9] as he thought necessary to guard the remaining load, as he suspected hostile intentions on the part of the Indians. Mr. Reed, however, refused to retain any of them, saying that M'Lellan and himself were sufficient to protect the small quantity that remained. The men accordingly departed with the load, while Mr.[10] Reed and M'Lellan continued to mount guard over the residue. By this time, a number of the canoes had arrived from the opposite side. As they approached the shore, the unlucky tin box of John Reed, shining afar like the brilliant helmet of Euryalus,[11] caught their eyes. No sooner did the canoes

[9] The first edition reads *many men*.

[10] *Mr.* does not appear in the first edition.

[11] In Virgil's *Aeneid*, Euryalus was a young Trojan who, with his friend Nisus, attempted to pass through enemy lines to reach Aeneas. Near dawn, his shining helmet attracted the attention of the enemy. He was surrounded in a woods, captured, and slain.

touch the shore, than they leaped forward on the rocks, set up a war-whoop, and sprang forward to secure the glittering prize. Mr. M'Lellan, who was at the river bank, advanced to guard the goods, when one of the savages attempted to hoodwink him with his buffalo robe with one hand, and to stab him with the other. M'Lellan sprang back just far enough to avoid the blow, and raising his rifle, shot the ruffian through the heart.

In the meantime, Reed, who with the want of forethought of an Irishman, had neglected to remove the leathern cover from the lock of his rifle, was fumbling at the fastenings, when he received a blow on the head with a war-club that laid him senseless on the ground. In a twinkling he was stripped of his rifle and pistols, and the tin box, the cause of all this onslaught, was borne off in triumph.

At this critical juncture, Mr. Stuart, who had heard the war-whoop, hastened to the scene of action with Ben Jones, and seven others of the men. When he arrived, Reed was weltering in his blood, and an Indian standing over him and about to despatch him with a tomahawk. Stuart gave the word, when Ben Jones leveled his rifle, and shot the miscreant on the spot. The men then gave a cheer, and charged upon the main body of the savages, who took to instant flight. Reed was now raised from the ground, and borne senseless and bleeding to the upper end of the portage. Preparations were made to launch the canoes and embark in all haste, when it was found that they were too leaky to be put in the water, and that the oars had been left at the foot of the falls. A scene of confusion now ensued. The Indians were whooping and yelling, and running about like fiends. A panic seized upon the men, at being thus suddenly checked, the hearts of some of the Canadians died within them, and two young men actually fainted away. The moment they recovered their senses, Mr. Stuart ordered that they should be deprived of their arms, their under garments taken off, and that a piece of cloth should be tied round their waists, in imitation of a squaw; an Indian punishment for cowardice. Thus equipped, they were stowed away among the goods in one of the canoes. This ludicrous affair excited the mirth of the bolder spirits, even in the midst of their perils, and roused the pride of the wavering. The Indians having crossed back again to the north side, order was restored, some of the hands were sent back for oars, others set to work to calk and launch the canoes, and in a little while all were embarked and were continuing their voyage along the southern shore.

No sooner had they departed, than the Indians returned to the scene of action, bore off their two comrades who had been shot, one of whom was still living, and returned to their village. Here they killed two horses; and drank the hot blood to give fierceness to their courage. They painted and arrayed themselves hideously for battle; performed the dead dance round the slain, and raised the war song of vengeance. Then mounting their horses, to the number of four hundred and fifty men, and brandishing their weapons, they set off along the northern bank of the river, to get ahead of the canoes, lie in wait for them, and take a terrible revenge on the white men.

They succeeded in getting some distance above the canoes without being discovered, and were crossing the river to post themselves on the side along which the white men were coasting, when they were fortunately descried. Mr. Stuart and his companions were immediately on the alert. As they drew near to the place where the savages had crossed, they observed them posted among steep and overhanging rocks, close along which, the canoes would have to pass. Finding that the enemy had the advantage of the ground, the whites stopped short when within five hundred yards of them, and discharged and reloaded their pieces. They then made a fire, and dressed the wounds of Mr. Reed, who had received five severe gashes in the head. This being done, they lashed the canoes together, fastened them to a rock at a small distance from the shore, and there awaited the menaced attack.

They had not been long posted in this manner, when they saw a canoe approaching. It contained the war chief of the tribe, and three of his principal warriors. He drew near, and made a long harangue, in which he informed them that they had killed one and wounded another of his nation; that the relations of the slain cried out for vengeance, and he had been compelled to lead them to fight.[12] Still he wished to spare unnecessary bloodshed; he proposed, therefore, that Mr. Reed, who, he observed, was little better than a dead man, might be given up to be sacrificed[13] to the manes of the deceased warrior. This would appease the fury of his friends; the hatchet would then be buried, and all thenceforward would be friends. The answer was a stern refusal and a defiance,

[12] The first edition reads *to the fight*.
[13] As Stuart expressed it, "to be by them cut in pieces."

and the war chief saw that the canoes were well prepared for a vigorous defense. He withdrew, therefore, and returning to his warriors among the rocks held long deliberations. Blood for blood is a principle in Indian equity and Indian honor; but though the inhabitants of Wish-ram were men of war, they were likewise men of traffic, and it was suggested that honor for once might give way to profit. A negotiation was accordingly opened with the white men, and after some diplomacy, the matter was compromised for a blanket to cover the dead, and some tobacco to be smoked by the living. This being granted, the heroes of Wish-ram crossed the river once more, returned to their village to feast upon the horses whose blood they had so vaingloriously drunk, and the travellers pursued their voyage without further molestation.[14]

The tin case, however, containing the important despatches for New York, was irretrievably lost; the very precaution taken by the worthy Hibernian to secure his missives, had, by rendering them conspicuous, produced their robbery. The object of his overland journey, therefore, being defeated, he gave up the expedition. The whole party repaired with Mr. Robert Stuart to the establishment of Mr. David Stuart, on the Oakinagan River. After remaining here two or three days, they all set out on their return to Astoria, accompanied by Mr. David Stuart. This gentleman had a large quantity of beaver skins at his establishment, but did not think it prudent to take them with him fearing the levy of "black mail" at the falls.

On their way down, when below the forks of the Columbia, they were hailed one day from the shore in English. Looking around, they descried two wretched men, entirely naked. They pulled to shore; the men came up and made themselves known. They proved to be Mr. Crooks and his faithful follower, John Day.[15]

The reader will recollect that Mr. Crooks, with Day and four Canadians, had been so reduced by famine and fatigue, that Mr. Hunt was obliged to leave them, in the month of December, on the banks of the Snake River. Their situation was the more critical, as they were in the neighborhood of a band of Shoshonies, whose horses had been forcibly seized by Mr. Hunt's party for provisions. Mr. Crooks remained here

---

[14] The principal source for Irving's narrative of these conflicts is Stuart's "Travelling Memoranda"; see Rollins, 55–59; Spaulding, 59–63. The events are given in briefer form by Cox, *op. cit.*, 68.

[15] For this meeting, see Cox, *op. cit.*, 69.

twenty days, detained by the extremely reduced state of John Day, who was utterly unable to travel, and whom he would not abandon, as Day had been in his employ on the Missouri, and had always proved himself most faithful. Fortunately the Shoshonies did not offer to molest them. They had never before seen white men, and seemed to entertain some superstitions with regard to them, for though they would encamp near them in the daytime, they would move off with their tents in the night; and finally disappeared, without taking leave.

When Day was sufficiently recovered to travel, they kept feebly on, sustaining themselves as well as they could, until in the month of February, when three of the Canadians, fearful of perishing with want, left Mr. Crooks on a small river, on the road by which Mr. Hunt had passed in quest of Indians. Mr. Crooks followed Mr. Hunt's track in the snow for several days, sleeping as usual in the open air, and suffering all kinds of hardships. At length, coming to a low prairie, he lost every appearance of the "trail," and wandered during the remainder of the winter in the mountains, subsisting sometimes on horse meat, sometimes on beavers and their skins, and a part of the time on roots.

About the last of March, the other Canadian[16] gave out and was left with a lodge of Shoshonies; but Mr. Crooks and John Day still kept on, and finding the snow sufficiently diminished, undertook, from Indian information, to cross the last mountain ridge.[17] They happily succeeded, and afterwards fell in with the Wallah-Wallahs, a tribe of Indians inhabiting the banks of a river of the same name, and reputed as being frank, hospitable, and sincere. They proved worthy of the character, for they received the poor wanderers kindly, killed a horse for them to eat, and directed them on their way to the Columbia. They struck the river about the middle of April, and advanced down it one hundred miles, until they came within about twenty miles of the falls.

Here they met with some of the "chivalry" of that noted pass, who received them in a friendly way, and set food before them; but, while they were satisfying their hunger, perfidiously seized their rifles. They

[16] Jean Baptiste Dubreuil. See above, p. 302, and below, p. 439.

[17] For the preceding paragraph and down to this point, Irving follows a narrative of Crooks's experiences forming part of a longer article that includes Robert Stuart's crossing of the continent to St. Louis. Originally published in the *Missouri Gazette*, May 15, 1813, under the title "American Enterprise," it was reprinted in *Niles Register* on June 26, 1813. It was subsequently republished in Bradbury's *Travels*, where Irving found it; see *Travels*, 234. Irving reproduces parts of this passage verbatim.

then stripped them naked, and drove them off, refusing the entreaties of Mr. Crooks for a flint and steel of which they had robbed him; and threatening his life if he did not instantly depart.

In this forlorn plight, still worse off than before, they renewed their wanderings. They now sought to find their way back to the hospitable Wallah-Wallahs, and had advanced eighty miles along the river, when fortunately, on the very morning that they were going to leave the Columbia and strike inland, the canoes of Mr. Stuart hove in sight.

It is needless to describe the joy of these poor men at once more finding themselves among countrymen and friends, or of the honest and hearty welcome with which they were received by their fellow-adventurers. The whole party now continued down the river, passed all the dangerous places without interruption, and arrived safely at Astoria on the 11th of May.[18]

[18] This date agrees with Franchère. In preparing this chapter, Irving had two published versions to draw upon, one by Franchère, *Narrative*, 272–76, and the other by Cox, *op. cit.*, 67–69. The same events are related by Ross, *Adventures*, 186–93, but as this was published after *Astoria*, Irving could make no use of it. It is valuable, however, for providing a longer account than those in Irving or Franchère of Crooks's and Day's experiences.

◈ C H A P T E R   X L I I ◈

Comprehensive Views — To Supply the Russian Fur Establishment
An Agent Sent to Russia — Project of an Annual Ship
The Beaver Fitted Out — Her Equipment and Crew
Instructions to the Captain — The Sandwich Islands
Rumors of the Fate of the Tonquin — Precautions on
Reaching the Mouth of the Columbia

HAVING traced the fortunes of the two expeditions by sea and land to the mouth of the Columbia, and presented a view of affairs at Astoria, we will return for a moment to the master spirit of the enterprise, who regulated the springs of Astoria, at his residence in New York.

It will be remembered, that a part of the plan of Mr. Astor was to furnish the Russian fur establishment on the northwest coast with regular supplies, so as to render it independent of those casual vessels which cut up the trade and supplied the natives with arms. This plan had been countenanced by our own government, and likewise by Count Pahlen,[1] the Russian minister at Washington. As its views, however, were important and extensive, and might eventually affect a wide course of commerce, Mr. Astor was desirous of establishing a complete arrangement on the subject with the Russian American Fur Company, under the sanction of the Russian government. For this purpose, in March, 1811, he despatched a confidential agent[2] to St. Petersburg, fully empowered

[1] Count Frederick Petrovich Pahlen, son of Count Peter Ludwig van der Pahlen, leader of the conspiracy that led to the murder of Emperor Paul I in March, 1801. For his role in Astor's plan, which was made in the summer of 1810 as Astor was involved in preparations for the sailing of the *Tonquin*, see Porter, *John Jacob Astor*, I, 192–93, 439–42. Astor, in a letter to President Jefferson, summarized Count Pahlen's role in the following words: "When Count Pahlen came to this country, he . . . was charged to speak to our government on this subject. I communicated the plan to him, who was so pleased with it that he transmitted it to his Court. I sent a gentleman for this purpose to St. Petersburg, who presented it to Count Romanskoff [Rumiantsev], who also is much pleased with it." John Jacob Astor, New York, March 14, 1812, to Thomas Jefferson, *ibid.*, 510. One difficulty was the reluctance of the Russian government to grant Astor the privilege of transporting furs to Russia free of duty or with only a small duty.

[2] This was Adrian Benjamin Bentzon, Astor's son-in-law, who sailed with his wife. *Ibid.*, 194–96. Bentzon's instructions are summarized by Porter on p. 194.

to enter into the requisite negotiations. A passage was given to this gentleman by the government of the United States, in the John Adams, one of its armed vessels, bound to a European port.[3]

The next step of Mr. Astor was, to despatch the annual ship contemplated on his general plan. He had as yet heard nothing of the success of the previous expeditions, and had to proceed upon the presumption that everything had been effected according to his instructions. He accordingly fitted out a fine ship of four hundred and ninety tons, called the Beaver,[4] and freighted her with a valuable cargo destined for the factory at the mouth of the Columbia, the trade along the coast, and the supply of the Russian establishment. In this ship embarked a reinforcement, consisting of a partner, five clerks, fifteen American laborers, and six Canadian voyageurs.[5] In choosing his agents for his first expedition, Mr. Astor had been obliged to have recourse to British subjects experienced in the Canadian fur trade; henceforth it was his intention, as much as possible, to select Americans, so as to secure an ascendency of American influence in the management of the company, and to make it decidedly national.

[3] The official mission of the ship was to carry George Erving to Denmark as special minister charged with settling differences between the two countries. Erving never recovered from his indignation at having to relinquish his comfortable quarters on the ship to the Bentzons, whose sole reason for being there was the business interests of a private individual. See *ibid.*, 196.

[4] The *Beaver* had been built in New York in 1804–1805 especially for Astor's China trade. It had a capacity of 1,100 tons. On this voyage its merchandise was insured by the Boston Marine Insurance Company for $22,342.38. *Ibid.*, 138, 200. For the invoice of merchandise, see *ibid.*, 479–507. Part of the cargo was a fair-sized library, which included a *Life of Bonaparte;* books on Scotland, Ireland, Spain, and Chile; Pindar's *Works; two* volumes of Robert Burns's poems; Scott's *Works;* a *Life of Pitt;* various reviews; Crabbe's *Poems;* Campbell's *Works;* Muller's *Elements of Fortification;* a French grammar; an English dictionary; and others.

[5] The unofficial historian of this voyage was Ross Cox. See his *Columbia River,* 13–49.

The articles of agreement, dated October 8, 1811, between Astor and the men sent out on the *Beaver* is printed in Porter, *op. cit.,* I, 475–78. This gives the following list of men: Charles A. Nicoll, Benjamin Clapp, Moses Flanagan, Micajah Baker, John C. Halsey, James Travers, John Patterson, Richard Millagen, Alfred Seton, John Reveau, Henry Spicer, Ross Cox, Daniel Perry, Henry Willetts, and John Little. Cox states that Clapp, Halsey, Nicoll, Seton, and himself were clerks, but he also names George Ehninger as a clerk, making six instead of Irving's five. Ehninger, whose name does not appear on the articles of agreement, was a nephew of Astor. Alfred Seton, who subsequently returned to New York City, became in 1832 one of the financial supporters of Bonneville's fur-trading expedition.

Accordingly, Mr. John Clarke,[6] the partner who took the lead in the present expedition, was a native of the United States, though he had passed much of his life in the northwest, having been employed in the trade since the age of sixteen. Most of the clerks were young gentlemen of good connections in the American cities, some of whom embarked in the hope of gain, others through the mere spirit of adventure incident to youth.

The instructions given by Mr. Astor to Captain Sowle,[7] the commander of the Beaver, were, in some respects, hypothetical, in consequence of the uncertainty resting upon the previous steps of the enterprise.

He was to touch at the Sandwich Islands, inquire about the fortunes of the Tonquin, and whether an establishment had been formed at the mouth of the Columbia. If so, he was to take as many Sandwich Islanders as his ship could accommodate, and proceed thither. On arriving at the river, he was to observe great caution, for even if an establishment should have been formed, it might have fallen into hostile hands. He was, therefore, to put in as if by casualty or distress, to give himself out as a coasting trader, and to say nothing about his ship being owned by Mr. Astor, until he had ascertained that everything was right. In that case, he was to land such part of his cargo as was intended for the establishment, and to proceed to New Archangel[8] with the supplies intended for the Russian post at that place, where he could receive peltries in payment. With these he was to return to Astoria; take in the furs collected there, and, having completed his cargo by trading along the coast, was to

[6] Irving is in error about Clarke's nationality. He was born in Montreal in 1781, and in 1800 at the age of nineteen, he became a clerk in the North West Company, serving on both the Mackenzie and Peace rivers. There was a family connection with Astor, whom Clarke joined in 1810. He was at Astoria when his former employees gained possession. Upon returning to Canada in 1814, he joined the Hudson's Bay Company. When it merged with the North West Company in 1821, Clarke was appointed chief factor. He continued in the fur trade for another nine years and died in Montreal in 1852, aged seventy-one. Wallace (ed.), *Documents*, 432–33. Clarke's agreement to become a partner with three shares is in the Missouri Historical Society and is reproduced in Flandrau, *Astor and the Oregon Country*, 34.

[7] His full name was Cornelius Sowle (or Sowles). Born in Rhode Island in 1769, he was an experienced trader when Astor engaged him, for he had sailed the Pacific and had been to the Far East; see Porter, *op. cit.*, I, 199–200. Cox, *op. cit.*, 14, gives the names of Rhodes, Champenois, and Dean as other officers. Dean later left the ship at Honolulu.

[8] Now Sitka, Alaska.

proceed to Canton. The captain received the same injunctions that had been given to Captain Thorn of the Tonquin, of great caution and circumspection in his intercourse with the natives, and that he should not permit more than one or two to be on board at a time.

The Beaver sailed from New York on the 10th of October,[9] 1811, and reached the Sandwich Islands without any occurrence of moment.[10] Here a rumor was heard of the disastrous fate of the Tonquin. Deep solicitude was felt by every one on board for the fate of both expeditions, by sea and land. Doubts were entertained whether any establishment had been formed at the mouth of the Columbia, or whether any of the company would be found there. After much deliberation, the captain took twelve Sandwich Islanders on board, for the service of the factory, should there be one in existence, and proceeded on his voyage.[11]

On the 6th of May,[12] he arrived off the mouth of the Columbia, and running as near as possible, fired two signal-guns. No answer was returned, nor was there any signal to be descried. Night coming on, the ship stood out to sea, and every heart drooped as the land faded away. On the following morning they again ran in within four miles of the shore, and fired other signal-guns, but still without reply. A boat was

[9] Cox gives the date as October 11. Porter, *op. cit.*, I, 200, says it was the thirteenth and adds that adverse winds delayed the ship until October 17.

[10] They reached the Cape Verde Islands on November 8 and crossed the equator on the seventeenth. On December 10 they met an American whaler and sent letters to the United States with its captain. They sighted the Falkland Islands eleven days later, and presumably stopped here for water until December 24. On the day they departed, two sailors were carried away in a storm, and Cox felt it was the gloomiest Christmas he had ever known. On the first day of the new year (1812), they rounded the Horn and on the nineteenth were struck by a heavy gale that severely damaged the ship and might have wrecked it on the coast of Tierra del Fuego had the hurricane continued a few more hours. Most of their livestock was swept away. A week later one of the sailors died of what Cox calls black scurvy. They stopped on February 4 for water and wood at Más Afuera Island, made well known by Defoe's *Robinson Crusoe*, and on March 4 again crossed the equator. Three weeks later they reached the Sandwich Islands and on March 26 came to anchor at Whytetee (Waikiki) Bay, Oahu. Cox, *op. cit.*, 13–24.

[11] Cox reports that twenty-six islanders were engaged for ten dollars a month each plus a new suit of clothes every year. Ten of these men were for the ship and sixteen for the company. An American named Wadsworth, with his wife, was also "engaged for the company's service." In addition, the ship took on sixty hogs plus "two boats full of sugar-cane to feed them," about a thousand coconuts, and as many "bananas, plantains, taro, melons, &c." as there was room for. The *Beaver* left on April 5. *Ibid.*, 45.

[12] Cox gives May 5. "Light winds," he says, "joined to the captain's timidity, obliged us to stand off and on until the 8th." *Ibid.*, 47.

then despatched, to sound the channel, and attempt an entrance; but returned without success, there being a tremendous swell, and breakers. Signal-guns were fired again in the evening, but equally in vain, and once more the ship stood off to sea for the night. The captain now gave up all hope of finding any establishment at the place, and indulged in the most gloomy apprehensions. He feared his predecessors had been massacred before they had reached their place of destination; or if they should have erected a factory, that it had been surprised and destroyed by the natives.

In this moment of doubt and uncertainty, Mr. Clarke announced his determination, in case of the worst, to found an establishment with the present party, and all hands bravely engaged to stand by him in the undertaking. The next morning the ship stood in for the third time, and fired three signal-guns, but with little hope of reply. To the great joy of the crew, three distinct guns were heard in answer. The apprehensions of all but Captain Sowle were now at rest. That cautious commander recollected the instructions given him by Mr. Astor, and determined to proceed with great circumspection. He was well aware of Indian treachery and cunning. It was not impossible, he observed, that these cannon might have been fired by the savages themselves. They might have surprised the fort, massacred its inmates; and these signal-guns might only be decoys to lure him across the bar, that they might have a chance of cutting him off, and seizing his vessel.

At length a white flag was descried hoisted as a signal on Cape Disappointment. The passengers pointed to it in triumph, but the captain did not yet dismiss his doubts. A beacon fire blazed through the night on the same place, but the captain observed that all these signals might be treacherous.

On the following morning, May 9th, the vessel came to anchor off Cape Disappointment, outside of the bar. Towards noon an Indian canoe was seen making for the ship and all hands were ordered to be on the alert. A few moments afterwards, a barge was perceived following the canoe. The hopes and fears of those on board of the ship were in tumultuous agitation, as the boat drew nigh that was to let them know the fortunes of the enterprise, and the fate of their predecessors. The captain, who was haunted with the idea of possible treachery, did not suffer his curiosity to get the better of his caution, but ordered a party of his men under arms, to receive the visitors. The canoe came first alongside, in which were Comcomly and six Indians; in the barge were M'Dougal, M'Lellan, and eight Canadians. A little conversation with these gentlemen dispelled all the captain's fears, and the Beaver crossing the bar under their pilotage, anchored safely in Baker's Bay.[13]

[13] Irving closely follows Cox; cf. *ibid.*, 47–48. Franchère also reports the arrival of the *Beaver*; see *Narrative*, 273.

CHAPTER XLIII

Active Operations at Astoria — Various Expeditions Fitted Out
Robert Stuart and a Party Destined for New York
Singular Conduct of John Day — His Fate
Piratical Pass and Hazardous Portage — Rattlesnakes
Their Abhorrence of Tobacco — Arrival Among the Wallah-Wallahs
Purchase of Horses — Departure of Stuart and
His Band for the Mountains

THE arrival of the Beaver with a reinforcement and supplies, gave new life and vigor to affairs at Astoria. These were means for extending the operations of the establishment, and founding interior trading posts. Two parties were immediately set on foot to proceed severally under the command of Messrs. M'Kenzie and Clarke, and establish posts above the forks of the Columbia, at points where most rivalry and opposition were apprehended from the Northwest Company.[1]

A third party, headed by Mr. David Stuart, was to repair with supplies to the post of that gentleman on the Oakinagan. In addition to these expeditions, a fourth was necessary to convey despatches to Mr. Astor, at New York, in place of those unfortunately lost by John Reed. The safe conveyance of these despatches was highly important, as by them Mr. Astor would receive an account of the state of the factory, and regulate his reinforcements and supplies accordingly. The mission was one of peril and hardship and required a man of nerve and vigor.

[1] Alexander Ross, who apparently had access to the minutes, reports the resolution of the partners, now all assembled for the first time at Astoria: " 'That Mr. David Stuart proceed to his post at Oakinacken, explore the country northward, and establish another post between that and New Caledonia: That Mr. M'Kenzie winter on the Snake country; recover the goods left in *cache* there by Mr. Hunt; and report on the state of the country: That Mr. Clarke winter at Spokane, as an intermediate post, between Mr. Stuart on the north and Mr. M'Kenzie on the south, in order to oppose and keep in check the North-West Company established there: That Mr. Robert Stuart proceed to St. Louis across land, with despatches for Mr. Astor: That all these several parties, for mutual safety, advance together as far as the forks, or entrance of the great south branch [Snake River].' " *Adventures*, 194–95; cf. Franchère, *Narrative*, 277. Only Ross tells that Pillot, Donald McClellan, Farnham, and Cox were to go to Spokane with Clarke and that Matthews and McGillis were to go with David Stuart.

It was confided to Robert Stuart, who, though he had never been across the mountains, and a very young man, had given proofs of his competency to the task.[2] Four trusty and well-tried men, who had come overland in Mr. Hunt's expedition, were given as his guides and hunters. These were Ben Jones and John Day, the Kentuckians, and Andri Vallar[3] and Francis Le Clerc,[4] Canadians. Mr. M'Lellan again expressed his determination to take this opportunity of returning to the Atlantic States. In this he was joined by Mr. Crooks, who, notwithstanding all that he had suffered in the dismal journey of the preceding winter, was ready to retrace his steps and brave every danger and hardship, rather than remain at Astoria.[5] This little handful of adventurous men we propose to accompany in its long and perilous peregrinations. The several parties we have mentioned all set off in company on the 29th of June, under a salute of cannon from the fort.[6] They were to keep

[2] The resolution of the partners dated June 27, 1812, to send Robert Stuart to New York follows: "Resolved, that it being necessary to send an Express to New York, and all the papers and other things being prepared Mr. Robert Stuart is hereby instructed to have and to take charge of them, with which he is to go as directly to New York as circumstances will admit—and there to be governed by the directions of Mr. Astor as to the time of his returning to the N.W. Coast. It is also resolved that John Day, Benjamin Jones, Francis LeClerc, Andre Valle accompany Mr. Stuart as far as St. Louis where he is to pay them the balances due each by means of Drafts drawn by our W. P. Hunt on John Jacob Astor on account of the Pacific Fur Company." Pacific Fur Company Minute Book, Missouri Historical Society, printed in Flandrau, *Astor and the Oregon Country*, 37; also quoted in Drumm, "More About Astorians," *Oregon Historical Quarterly*, Vol. XXIV (1923), 335n.

[3] Andre Valle, one of Hunt's Overland Astorians. See Porter, "Roll of Overland Astorians," *Oregon Historical Quarterly*, Vol. XXXIV (1933), 112.

[4] Francis LeClerc. See *ibid.*, 109.

[5] Crooks had resigned his partnership in the company. The partners took the following action on May 14, 1812: "Ramsay Crooks relinquished all right to the interest he held in the Pacific Fur Co.—to-wit five shares. Also relinquishing all profits and emoluments or privileges arising from having been a partner thereof. Binds himself not to engage or be concerned in the Indian trade or in any business whatever which may effect [*sic*] the interest of said Company." Pacific Fur Company Minute Book, Missouri Historical Society, quoted in Drumm, "More About Astorians," *loc. cit.*, 335–36n. See also these three items in Flandrau, *op. cit.*, 35–36: Crooks's signed agreement, May 14, 1812; a resolution permitting Crooks to resign, dated May 14, 1812; a letter to Crooks, dated June 29, 1812, exempting him "from any losses, charges or responsibility which might arise in consequence of your having been a Partner."

[6] In relating the journey from Astoria to the Walla Walla River, Irving had the narratives of two participants. One was Cox's *Columbia River*. The other was Robert Stuart's "Travelling Memoranda," which is the more dependable of the two. The date of June 29 is given by both Stuart and Cox.

Pacific Northwest, with route of Returning Astorians,
June 29–October 30, 1812

together for mutual protection through the piratical passes of the river,
and to separate, on their different destinations, at the forks of the Columbia. Their number, collectively, was nearly sixty, consisting of partners
and clerks, Canadian voyageurs, Sandwich Islanders, and American
hunters;[7] and they embarked in two barges and ten canoes.[8]

They had scarcely got under way, when John Day, the Kentucky
hunter, became restless and uneasy, and extremely wayward in his deportment. This caused surprise, for in general he was remarkable for his
cheerful, manly deportment. It was supposed that the recollection of
past sufferings might harass his mind in undertaking to retrace the

[7] There is a discrepancy of thirty-seven in the number of men given by Stuart and by
Cox. On the basis of what Stuart says, there were sixty-one, but according to Cox, ninety-
eight. Following Stuart, Irving learned that there were three partners (McKenzie,
David Stuart, and John Clarke) in addition to Robert Stuart; seven clerks, one of whom
was Cox; thirty-two Canadian *voyageurs;* twelve Sandwich Islanders; plus Crooks,
McClellan, Ben Jones, John Day, Valle, and LeClerc. See Rollins, 3; Spaulding, 27.
Cox states that there were nine clerks, fifty-five Canadians, and twenty Sandwich Islanders, plus eight men with Robert Stuart. Cox, *op. cit.*, 74.

[8] "Our lading," wrote Cox, "consisted of guns and ammunition, spears, hatchets,
knives, beaver traps, copper and brass kettles, blue, green and red cloths, calicoes, beads,
rings, thimbles, hawk-bells, &c.; and our provisions of beef, pork, flour, rice, biscuits,
tea, sugar, with a moderate quantity of rum, wine, &c." *Op. cit.*, 75.

scenes where they had been experienced. As the expedition advanced, however, his agitation increased. He began to talk wildly and incoherently, and to show manifest symptoms of derangement.

Mr. Crooks now informed his companions that in his desolate wanderings through the Snake River country during the preceding winter, in which he had been accompanied by John Day, the poor fellow's wits had been partially unsettled by the sufferings and horrors through which they had passed, and he doubted whether they had ever been restored to perfect sanity. It was still hoped that this agitation of spirit might pass away as they proceeded; but, on the contrary, it grew more and more violent. His comrades endeavored to divert his mind and to draw him into rational conversation, but he only became the more exasperated, uttering wild and incoherent ravings. The sight of any of the natives put him in an absolute fury, and he would heap on them the most opprobrious epithets; recollecting, no doubt, what he had suffered from Indian robbers.

On the evening of the 2d of July[9] he became absolutely frantic, and attempted to destroy himself. Being disarmed, he sank into quietude, and professed the greatest remorse for the crime he had meditated. He then pretended to sleep, and having thus lulled suspicion, suddenly sprang up, just before daylight, seized a pair of loaded pistols, and endeavored to blow out his brains. In his hurry he fired too high, and the balls passed over his head. He was instantly secured and placed under a guard in one of the boats. How to dispose of him was now the question, as it was impossible to keep him with the expedition. Fortunately Mr. Stuart met with some Indians accustomed to trade with Astoria. These undertook to conduct John Day back to the factory, and deliver him there in safety. It was with the utmost concern that his comrades saw the poor fellow depart; for, independent of his invaluable services as a first-rate hunter, his frank and loyal qualities had made him a universal favorite. It may be as well to add that the Indians executed their task faithfully, and landed John Day among his friends at Astoria; but his constitution was completely broken by the hardships he had undergone, and he died within a year.[10]

[9] The date is Stuart's.

[10] For the account of John Day's derangement, Irving follows Stuart's "Travelling Memoranda"; see Rollins, 29–31, and Spaulding, 45–47. Strangely, Cox makes no mention of Day's trouble. Irving is in error about Day's death taking place within a year; see Chapter XIV, note 14.

On the evening of the 6th of July[11] the party arrived at the piratical pass of the river, and encamped at the foot of the first rapid. The next day, before the commencement of the portage, the greatest precautions were taken to guard against lurking treachery, or open attack. The weapons of every man were put in order, and his cartridge-box replenished. Each one wore a kind of surcoat made of the skin of the elk, reaching from his neck to his knees, and answering the purpose of a shirt of mail, for it was arrowproof, and could even resist a musket ball at the distance of ninety yards. Thus armed and equipped, they posted their forces in military style.[12] Five of the officers took their stations at each end of the portage, which was between three and four miles in length; a number of men mounted guard at short distances along the heights immediately overlooking the river, while the residue, thus protected from surprise, employed themselves below in dragging up the barges and canoes, and carrying up the goods along the narrow margin of the rapids. With these precautions they all passed unmolested. The only accident that happened was the upsetting of one of the canoes, by which some of the goods sunk, and others floated down the stream.[13] The alertness and rapacity of the hordes which infest these rapids, were immediately apparent. They pounced upon the floating merchandise with the keenness of regular wreckers. A bale of goods which landed upon one of the islands was immediately ripped open, one half of its contents divided among the captors,[14] and the other half secreted in a lonely hut in a deep ravine. Mr. Robert Stuart, however, set out in a canoe with five men and an interpreter, ferreted out the wreckers in their retreat, and succeeded in wresting from them their booty.

Similar precautions to those already mentioned, and to a still greater extent, were observed in passing the Long Narrows,[15] and the falls,

[11] The date is given by Stuart.

[12] Irving found the description of the leather armor in Cox, *op. cit.*, 77.

[13] The canoe was David Stuart's. Robert Stuart wrote that "in passing between two large rocks, [it] unfortunately touched the outer one, wheeled around, and before sufficient assistance could reach her, filled and upset." Rollins, 35; Spaulding, 51. Stuart gives an excellent description of the construction of this type of canoe in his entry for July 8. Because it was built of cedar boards only a quarter of an inch thick, it was inferior to the birchbark canoe, which would yield to pressure without breaking.

[14] Erroneously *captives* in first edition.

[15] They reached this point on July 14. Stuart says they expected an attack here. Guards were posted all night, which was divided into three watches, with nineteen men in each group. Nothing happened that night, but the same system of guards was continued on the following nights.

where they would be exposed to the depredations of the chivalry of Wish-ram, and its freebooting neighborhood. In fact, they had scarcely set their first watch one night, when an alarm of "Indians!" was given.[16] "To arms" was the cry, and every man was at his post in an instant. The alarm was explained; a war party of Shoshonies had surprised a canoe of the natives just below the encampment, had murdered four men and two women, and it was apprehended they would attack the camp. The boats and canoes were immediately hauled up, a breastwork was made of them and the packages, forming three sides of a square, with the river in the rear, and thus the party remained fortified throughout the night.

The dawn, however, dispelled the alarm; the portage was conducted in peace; the vagabond warriors of the vicinity hovered about them while at work, but were kept at a wary distance. They regarded the loads of merchandise with wistful eyes, but seeing the "long-beards" so formidable in number, and so well prepared for action, they made no attempt either by open force or sly pilfering to collect their usual toll, but maintained a peaceful demeanor, and were afterwards rewarded for their good conduct with presents of tobacco.

Fifteen days[17] were consumed in ascending from the foot of the first rapid to the head of the falls, a distance of about eighty miles, but full of all kinds of obstructions. Having happily accomplished these difficult portages, the party, on the 19th of July,[18] arrived at a smoother part of the river, and pursued their way up the stream with greater speed and facility.

They were now in the neighborhood where Mr. Crooks and John Day had been so perfidiously robbed and stripped a few months previously, when confiding in the proffered hospitality of a ruffian band. On landing at night, therefore, a vigilant guard was maintained about the camp. On the following morning a number of Indians made their appearance, and came prowling round the party while at breakfast. To his great delight, Mr. Crooks recognized among them two of the miscreants by whom he had been robbed. They were instantly seized, bound hand

[16] This occurred on July 17. See "Travelling Memoranda" in Rollins, 53, and Spaulding, 57.

[17] From July 6 to July 20.

[18] Irving should have written July 20, for on the nineteenth they were held back by strong winds, so that they went only to within a half-mile of the falls. A leaky boat also stopped them.

and foot, and thrown into one of the canoes. Here they lay in doleful fright, expecting summary execution. Mr. Crooks, however, was not of a revengeful disposition, and agreed to release the culprits as soon as the pillaged property should be restored. Several savages immediately started off in different directions, and before night the rifles of Crooks and Day were produced; several of the smaller articles pilfered from them, however, could not be recovered.

The bands of the culprits were then removed, and they lost no time in taking their departure, still under the influence of abject terror, and scarcely crediting their senses that they had escaped the merited punishment of their offenses.[19]

The country on each side of the river now began to assume a different character. The hills, and cliffs, and forests disappeared; vast sandy plains, scantily clothed here and there with short tufts of grass, parched by the summer sun, stretched far away to the north and south. The river was occasionally obstructed with rocks and rapids, but often there were smooth, placid intervals, where the current was gentle, and the boatmen were enabled to lighten their labors with the assistance of the sail.

The natives in this part of the river resided entirely on the northern side. They were hunters, as well as fishermen, and had horses in plenty. Some of these were purchased by the party,[20] as provisions, and killed on the spot, though they occasionally found a difficulty in procuring fuel wherewith to cook them. One of the greatest dangers that beset the travellers in this part of their expedition, was the vast number of rattlesnakes which infested the rocks about the rapids and portages, and on which the men were in danger of treading. They were often found, too, in quantities about the encampments. In one place, a nest of them lay coiled together, basking in the sun. Several guns loaded with shot were discharged at them, and thirty-seven killed and wounded. To prevent

[19] See "Travelling Memoranda," July 21. Rollins, 60; Spaulding, 64. Alexander Ross, according to whom only one Indian was involved, stated that "some [of the men] were for hanging the offender, others were for cutting his ears off." *Adventures*, 198. Before the Indian was released, Ross tells us, "M'Lellan, to show him the effect of firearms in the hands of whites, set up a piece of board, with a white spot on it, only two inches in diameter, and in three successive shots, at a hundred yards distance, with his rifle he pierced the bull's eye; then stopping up the holes of two of the shots, put a hazel-nut in the third, and broke it with two successive shots at the same distance."

[20] On July 25 they bought nine horses plus some "Lamper-eels," as Stuart calls them. The next day they succeeded in obtaining two additional horses. Stuart says nothing about butchering the horse. Irving got this detail from Cox, *op. cit.*, 84.

any unwelcome visits from them in the night, tobacco was occasionally strewed around the tents, a weed for which they have a very proper abhorrence.[21]

On the 28th of July[22] the travellers arrived at the mouth of the Wallah-Wallah, a bright, clear stream, about six feet deep, and fifty-five yards wide,[23] which flows rapidly over a bed of sand and gravel, and throws itself into the Columbia, a few miles below Lewis River. Here the combined parties that had thus far voyaged together, were to separate, each for its particular destination.

On the banks of the Wallah-Wallah, lived the hospitable tribe of the same name who had succored Mr. Crooks and John Day in the time of their extremity. No sooner did they hear of the arrival of the party, than they hastened to greet them. They built a great bonfire on the bank of the river, before the camp, and men and women danced round it to the cadence of their songs, in which they sang the praises of the white men, and welcomed them to their country.[24]

On the following day a traffic was commenced, to procure horses for such of the party as intended to proceed by land. The Wallah-Wallahs are an equestrain tribe. The equipments of their horses were rude and inconvenient. High saddles, roughly made of deer-skin, stuffed with hair, which chafe the horse's back and leave it raw; wooden stirrups, with a thong of raw hide wrapped round them; and for bridles they have cords of twisted horse-hair, which they tie round the under jaw. They are, like most Indians, bold but hard riders, and when on horseback gallop about the most dangerous places, without fear for themselves, or pity for their steeds.

From these people Mr. Stuart purchased twenty horses[25] for his

[21] Irving learned about the rattlesnakes from Cox, *op. cit.*, 84–85, 86.

[22] An error for July 27, which is in Stuart's "Travelling Memoranda." Irving's date comes from Cox.

[23] Cox, *op. cit.*, 87. Stuart gives the width of the Walla Walla as sixty yards. Stuart and his party were on the right bank—that is, west side—of the Columbia, and camped about two miles north of the Walla Walla. For Stuart's description of the Indians here, see "Travelling Memoranda" in Rollins, 62 and Spaulding, 66.

[24] This celebration was on July 27.

[25] An arbitrary number, apparently. Stuart wrote: "From this band I procured 4 more horses, which completes the 15 necessary for our voyage." Spaulding, 66. In his "Journal," however, Stuart said only that he obtained "what was wanting to complete the 12 Horses necessary for my voyage." Rollins, 62. Actually, according to his own record, until meeting the Walla Walla Indians, Stuart had bought only eleven horses— nine on July 25 and two more the next day. Irving, however, here follows Cox, not

party; some for the saddle, and others to transport the baggage. He was fortunate in procuring a noble animal for his own use, which was praised by the Indians for its great speed and bottom, and a high price set upon it. No people understand better the value of a horse, than these equestrain tribes; and nowhere is speed a greater requisite, as they frequently engage in the chase of the antelope, one of the fleetest of animals. Even after the Indian who sold this boasted horse to Mr. Stuart had concluded his bargain, he lingered about the animal, seeming loth to part from him, and to be sorry for what he had done.[26]

A day or two were employed by Mr. Stuart in arranging packages and pack-saddles, and making other preparations for his long and arduous journey. His party, by the loss of John Day, was now reduced to six, a small number for such an expedition. They were young men, however, full of courage, health, and good spirits, and stimulated rather than appalled by danger.

On the morning of the 31st of July,[27] all preparations being concluded, Mr. Stuart and his little band mounted their steeds and took a farewell of their fellow-travellers, who gave them three hearty cheers as they set out on their dangerous journey. The course they took was to the southeast, towards the fated region of the Snake River. At an immense distance rose a chain of craggy mountains, which they would have to traverse; they were the same among which the travellers had experienced such sufferings from cold during the preceding winter, and from their azure tints, when seen at a distance, had received the name of the Blue Mountains.[28]

Stuart, for Cox stated: "On the 29th we purchased twenty horses for Mr. Robert Stuart's party." Everybody had his own idea of how many horses traded hands, for Alexander Ross, who was also there, said Stuart bought ten horses. *Adventures*, 198.

[26] Irving appears to be the only authority for this incident. Stuart says nothing about such a horse. There is a strong possibility, however, that here and later, where published sources are silent about matters that Irving relates concerning Stuart's expedition, he had his information orally from one of the members, possibly Ramsay Crooks.

[27] The date is Stuart's.

[28] Seen from the Columbia, these mountains in the distance appeared blue with haze. "From their colour," Cox states, "the Canadians call this chain *Les Montagnes Bleues*." *Op. cit.*, 87. Presumably the name originated at this time.

IN tracing the route which had proved so disastrous to Mr. Hunt's party during the preceding winter, Mr. Stuart had trusted, in the present more favorable season, to find easy travelling and abundant supplies. On these great wastes and wilds, however, each season has its peculiar hardships. The travellers had not proceeded far, before they found themselves among naked and arid hills, with a soil composed of sand and clay, baked and brittle, that to all appearance had never been visited by the dews of heaven.

Not a spring, or pool, or running stream was to be seen; the sun-burnt country was seamed and cut up by dry ravines, the beds of winter torrents, serving only to balk the hopes of man and beast with the sight of dusty channels, where water had once poured along in floods.

For a long summer day they continued onward without halting, a burning sky above their heads, a parched desert beneath their feet, with just wind enough to raise the light sand from the knolls, and envelop them in stifling clouds. The sufferings from thirst became intense; a fine young dog, their only companion of the kind, gave out, and expired. Evening drew on without any prospect of relief, and they were almost reduced to despair, when they descried something that looked like a fringe of forest, along the horizon. All were inspired with new hope, for they knew that on these arid wastes, in the neighborhood of trees, there is always water.

They now quickened their pace; the horses seemed to understand their motives, and to partake of their anticipations; for, though before almost ready to give out, they now required neither whip nor spur. With all their exertions, it was late in the night before they drew near to the trees. As they approached, they heard, with transport, the rippling of a shallow stream.[1] No sooner did the refreshing sound reach the ears of the horses, than the poor animals snuffed the air, rushed forward with ungovernable eagerness, and plunging their muzzles into the water, drank until they seemed in danger of bursting. Their riders had but little more discretion, and required repeated draughts to quench their excessive thirst. Their weary march that day had been forty-five miles, over a tract that might rival the deserts of Africa for aridity. Indeed, the sufferings of the traveller on these American deserts is frequently more severe than in the wastes of Africa or Asia, from being less habituated and prepared to cope with them.

On the banks of this blessed stream the travellers encamped for the night; and so great had been their fatigue, and so sound and sweet was their sleep, that it was a late hour the next morning before they awoke. They now recognized the little river to be the Umatalla,[2] the same on the banks of which Mr. Hunt and his followers had arrived after their painful struggle through the Blue Mountains, and experienced such a kind relief in the friendly camp of the Sciatogas.

That range of Blue Mountains now extended in the distance before them; they were the same among which poor Michael Carriere had perished. They form the southeast boundary of the great plains along the Columbia, dividing the waters of its main stream from those of Lewis River. They are, in fact, a part of a long chain, which stretches over a great extent of country, and includes in its links the Snake River Mountains.

The day was somewhat advanced before the travellers left the shady banks of the Umatalla. Their route gradually took them along the Blue Mountains, which assumed the most rugged aspect on a near approach. They were shagged with dense and gloomy forests, and cut up by deep and precipitous ravines, extremely toilsome to the horses. Sometimes the travellers had to follow the course of some brawling stream, with

[1] Stuart identifies this as the Umatilla. Irving follows the "Travelling Memoranda" for the first day's march, July 31. Rollins, 88n., avers that Stuart followed an Indian trail that led to the Umatilla near the present-day city of Pendleton, Oregon.

[2] It was 180 feet wide but very shallow, according to Stuart. They followed it for three miles on August 1, and after another twenty miles camped on a fork, which Rollins, 89n., identifies as McKay Creek.

a broken, rocky bed, which the shouldering cliffs and promontories on either side obliged them frequently to cross and recross. For some miles they struggled forward through these savage and darkly wooded defiles, when all at once the whole landscape changed, as if by magic. The rude mountains and rugged ravines softened into beautiful hills, and intervening meadows, with rivulets winding through fresh herbage, and sparkling and murmuring over gravelly beds, the whole forming a verdant and pastoral scene, which derived additional charms from being locked up in the bosom of such a hard-hearted region.

Emerging from the chain of Blue Mountains, they descended upon a vast plain,[3] almost a dead level, sixty miles in circumference, of excellent soil, with fine streams meandering through it in every direction, their courses marked out in the wide landscape by serpentine lines of cotton-wood trees, and willows, which fringed their banks, and afforded sustenance to great numbers of beavers and otters.

In traversing this plain, they passed, close to the skirts of the hills, a great pool of water, three hundred yards in circumference, fed by a sulphur spring, about ten feet in diameter, boiling up in one corner. The vapor from this pool was extremely noisome, and tainted the air for a considerable distance. The place was much frequented by elk, which were found in considerable numbers in the adjacent mountains,[4] and their horns, shed in the springtime, were strewed in every direction around the pond.[5]

On the 10th of August,[6] they reached the main body of Woodpile Creek,[7] the same stream which Mr. Hunt had ascended in the preceding year, shortly after his separation from Mr. Crooks.

On the banks of this stream they saw a herd of nineteen antelopes; a sight so unusual in that part of the country, that at first they doubted the evidence of their senses. They tried by every means to get within shot of them, but they were too shy and fleet, and after alternately

[3] Grande Ronde Valley. Irving has generalized the entries of the "Travelling Memoranda" for August 2 to 5. Stuart's party camped on the Grande Ronde River, which Stuart called "Glaize River."

[4] The Blue Mountains to the west and north, the Wallowa Mountains to the east.

[5] Cf. "Travelling Memoranda" for August 7. Rollins, 78; Spaulding, 71–72. The pool is today known as Hot Lake and is located on Oregon State Highway 203.

[6] Erroneously *August 20* in the first edition. August 10 is given by Stuart.

[7] Burnt River, although Stuart says they were on a fork. The Author's Revised Edition erroneously has *Woodvile Creek*. Wood Pile Creek is given by Stuart.

bounding to a distance, and then stopping to gaze with capricious curiosity at the hunter, they at length scampered out of sight.[8]

On the 12th of August, the travellers arrived on the banks of Snake River, the scene of so many trials and mishaps to all of the present party excepting Mr. Stuart. They struck the river just above the place where it entered the mountains, through which Messrs. Hunt[9] and Crooks had vainly endeavored to find a passage. The river was here a rapid stream, four hundred yards in width, with high sandy banks, and here and there a scanty growth of willow. Up the southern side[10] of the river they now bent their course, intending to visit the caches made by Mr. Hunt at the Caldron Linn.

On the second evening, a solitary Snake Indian visited their camp, at a late hour, and informed them that there was a white man[11] residing at one of the cantonments[12] of his tribe, about a day's journey higher up the river. It was immediately concluded, that he must be one of the poor fellows of Mr. Hunt's party, who had given out, exhausted by hunger and fatigue, in the wretched journey of the preceding winter. All present who had borne a part in the sufferings of that journey, were eager now to press forward, and bring relief to a lost comrade.[13] Early the next morning, therefore, they pushed forward with unusual alacrity. For two days, however, did they travel without being able to find any trace of such a straggler.

On the evening of the second day, they arrived at a place where a large river[14] came in from the east, which was renowned among all the wandering hordes of the Snake nation for its salmon fishery, that fish being taken in incredible quantities in this neighborhood. Here, therefore,

---

[8] "Travelling Memoranda," Rollins, 79–80; Spaulding, 73–74.

[9] Erroneously *Stuart* in the first edition and the Author's Revised Edition. They struck the river southeast of today's Huntington, Oregon, and perhaps near Birch Creek. The date is Stuart's.

[10] Stuart says "the south side of the River." Rollins, 82; Spaulding, 76. Since the general course of the Snake here is northwest, one could also think of their being on the west side.

[11] Stuart stated: "An Indian came to our camp late in the evening with the grateful tidings of two white men living with his people, about a days march above." Rollins, 82; Spaulding, 76–77.

[12] *Encampments* in first edition.

[13] These conjectures are unsupported by the "Travelling Memoranda." Irving may have followed information given him by one of the party.

[14] Boise River.

Teton Basin (the Pierre's Hole of the mountain men) and the Teton Range. Through this valley passed Wilson P. Hunt's Overland Astorians in 1811 and the Returning Astorians, led by Robert Stuart, in 1812.

Photograph by Edgeley W. Todd

The Snake River as it flows through Hell's Canyon. This view shows graphically why the Overland Astorians had to turn back and search for an easier route.

Courtesy Idaho Historical Society

during the fishing season, the Snake Indians resort from far and near, to lay in their stock of salmon, which, with esculent roots, forms the principal food of the inhabitants of these barren regions.

On the bank of a small stream[15] emptying into Snake River at this place, Mr. Stuart found an encampment of Shoshonies. He made the usual inquiry of them concerning the white man of whom he had received intelligence. No such person was dwelling among them, but they said there were white men residing with some of their nation on the opposite side of the river. This was still more animating information. Mr. Crooks now hoped that these might be the men of his party, who, disheartened by perils and hardships, had preferred to remain among the Indians. Others thought they might be Mr. Miller and the hunters who had left the main body at Henry's Fort, to trap among the mountain streams. Mr. Stuart halted, therefore, in the neighborhood of the Shoshonie lodges, and sent an Indian across the river to seek out the white men in question, and bring them to his camp.

The travellers passed a restless, miserable night. The place swarmed with myriads of musquitoes, which, with their stings and their music, set all sleep at defiance. The morning dawn found them in a feverish, irritable mood, and their spleen was completely aroused by the return of the Indian without any intelligence of the white men. They now considered themselves the dupes of Indian falsehoods, and resolved to put no more confidence in Snakes. They soon, however, forgot this resolution. In the course of the morning, an Indian came galloping after them; Mr. Stuart waited to receive him; no sooner had he come up, than, dismounting and throwing his arms around the neck of Mr. Stuart's horse, he began to kiss and caress the animal, who, on his part, seemed by no means surprised or displeased with his salutation. Mr. Stuart, who valued his horse highly, was somewhat annoyed by these transports; the cause of them was soon explained. The Snake said the horse had belonged to him, and been the best in his possession, and that it had been stolen by the Wallah-Wallahs. Mr. Stuart was by no means pleased with this recognition of his steed, nor disposed to admit any claim on the part of its ancient owner. In fact, it was a noble animal, admirably shaped, of free and generous spirit, graceful in movement,[16] and fleet as an ante-

[15] Owyhee River, flowing into the Snake from the southwest. Stuart reached this point on August 15 and found ten lodges.

[16] The first edition reads *in every movement*.

lope. It was his intention, if possible, to take the horse to New York, and present him to Mr. Astor.[17]

In the meantime, some of the party came up, and immediately recognized in the Snake an old friend and ally. He was, in fact, one of the two guides who had conducted Mr. Hunt's party, in the preceding autumn, across Mad River Mountain[18] to Fort Henry, and who subsequently departed with Mr. Miller and his fellow trappers, to conduct them to a good trapping ground. The reader may recollect that these two trusty Snakes were engaged by Mr. Hunt to return and take charge of the horses which the party intended to leave at Fort Henry, when they should embark in canoes.

The party now crowded round the Snake, and began to question him with eagerness. His replies were somewhat vague, and but partially understood. He told a long story about the horses, from which it appeared that they had been stolen by various wandering bands, and scattered in different directions. The cache, too, had been plundered, and the saddles and other equipments carried off. His information concerning Mr. Miller and his comrades was not more satisfactory. They had trapped for some time about the upper streams, but had fallen into the hands of a marauding party of Crows, who had robbed them of horses, weapons, and everything.[19]

Further questioning brought forth further intelligence, but all of a disastrous kind. About ten days previously, he had met with three other white men, in very miserable plight, having one horse each, and but one rifle among them. They also had been plundered and maltreated by the Crows, those universal freebooters. The Snake endeavored to pronounce the names of these three men, and as far as his imperfect sounds could be understood, they were supposed to be three of the party of four hunters, namely, Carson, St. Michel, Detayé, and Delaunay,[20] who were

---

[17] The Indian's affectionate display for the horse does not appear in the "Travelling Memoranda." Stuart says only that on August 18 they discovered the horse had been stolen by this Indian during the night.

[18] Teton Pass in the Teton Range.

[19] Nothing in this paragraph appears in the "Travelling Memoranda." Irving possibly had an oral source.

[20] Irving follows Stuart's entry for August 16, but what Stuart wrote was: "Their names he said are, Alexis, Michel, and Mackaw." Rollins, 84; Spaulding, 78. Knowing whom Hunt had left on September 28, 1811, Irving has substituted Alexander for "Alexis," Louis St. Michael for "Michel," and Pierre Detayé for "Mackaw," adding the name of Pierre Delaunay. See p. 265.

detached from Mr. Hunt's party on the 28th of September, to trap beaver on the head waters of the Columbia.

In the course of conversation, the Indian informed them that the route by which Mr. Hunt had crossed the Rocky Mountains was very bad and circuitous, and that he knew one much shorter and easier.[21] Mr. Stuart urged him to accompany them as guide, promising to reward him with a pistol with powder and ball, a knife, an awl, some blue beads, a blanket, and a looking-glass. Such a catalogue of riches was too tempting to be resisted; besides the poor Snake languished after the prairies; he was tired, he said, of salmon, and longed for buffalo meat, and to have a grand buffalo hunt beyond the mountains. He departed, therefore, with all speed, to get his arms and equipments for the journey, promising to rejoin the party the next day. He kept his word, and, as he no longer said anything to Mr. Stuart on the subject of the pet horse, they journeyed very harmoniously together; though now and then, the Snake would regard his quondam steed with a wistful eye.[22]

They had not travelled many miles, when they came to a great bend in the river. Here the Snake informed them that, by cutting across the hills they would save many miles of distance. The route across, however, would be a good day's journey. He advised them, therefore, to encamp here for the night, and set off early in the morning. They took his advice, though they had come but nine miles that day.

On the following morning[23] they rose, bright and early, to ascend the hills. On mustering their little party, the guide was missing. They supposed him to be somewhere in the neighborhood, and proceeded to collect the horses. The vaunted steed of Mr. Stuart was not to be found. A suspicion flashed upon his mind. Search for the horse of the Snake! He likewise was gone—the tracks of two horses, one after the other, were found, making off from the camp. They appeared as if one horse had

[21] Stuart's entry is significant. From this Indian, he wrote, they learned "that there is a shorter trace to the south than that by which Mr. Hunt had traversed the Rocky mountains, and learning that this Indian was perfectly acquainted with the route I without loss of time offered him [various articles that Irving names] if he would guide us from this to the other side, which he immediately accepted." Rollins, 84; Spaulding, 78–79. A route south of Hunt's could only be one that would lead to South Pass.

[22] Irving apparently interpolates the last sentence. The Indian left Stuart on August 16, returned to Boise River, and rejoined Stuart on the seventeenth.

[23] August 18. "From his former good conduct, we had not the least suspicion that he would attempt committing an act of this nature," wrote Stuart. See Rollins, 84; Spaulding, 79.

been mounted, and the other led. They were traced for a few miles above the camp, until they they both crossed the river. It was plain the Snake had taken an Indian mode of recovering his horse, having quietly decamped with him in the night.

New vows were made never more to trust in Snakes, or any other Indians. It was determined, also, to maintain, hereafter, the strictest vigilance over their horses, dividing the night into three watches, and one person mounting guard at a time. They resolved, also, to keep along the river, instead of taking the short cut recommended by the fugitive Snake, whom they now set down for a thorough deceiver. The heat of the weather was oppressive, and their horses were, at times, rendered almost frantic by the stings of the prairie flies. The nights were suffocating, and it was almost impossible to sleep, from the swarms of musquitoes.[24]

On the 20th of August[25] they resumed their march, keeping along the prairie parallel to Snake River. The day was sultry, and some of the party, being parched with thirst, left the line of march, and scrambled down the bank of the river to drink. The bank was overhung with willows, beneath which, to their surprise, they beheld a man fishing. No sooner did he see them, than he uttered an exclamation of joy. It proved to be John Hoback, one of their lost comrades. They had scarcely exchanged greetings, when three other men came out from among the willows. They were Joseph Miller, Jacob Rezner, and Robinson, the scalped Kentuckian, the veteran of the Bloody Ground.

The reader will perhaps recollect the abrupt and willful manner in which Mr. Miller threw up his interest as a partner of the company, and departed from Fort Henry, in company with these three trappers, and a fourth named Cass. He may likewise recognize Robinson, Rezner, and Hoback, the trio of Kentucky hunters who had originally been in the service of Mr. Henry, and whom Mr. Hunt found floating down the Missouri, on their way homeward; and prevailed upon, once more,

[24] Stuart recorded just the opposite: "The excessive heat that has prevailed since we left wood pile Creek is very much diminished, and the suffocating, sultry nights have given place to agreeable cool ones, in consequence of which our musquitoe serenades are so irregular that it is only now and then we hear the song of a solitary warbler." Sand flies—"imps of darkness," as Stuart wrote—took their place. Rollins, 85; Spaulding, 80.

[25] The date is confirmed by Stuart.

to cross the mountains. The haggard looks and naked condition of these men proved how much they had suffered. After leaving Mr. Hunt's party, they had made their way about two hundred miles to the southward, where they trapped beaver on a river which, according to their account, discharged itself into the ocean to the south of the Columbia, but which we apprehend to be Bear River,[26] a stream emptying itself into Lake Bonneville,[27] an immense body of salt water, west of the Rocky Mountains.

Having collected a considerable quantity of beaver skins, they made them into packs, loaded their horses, and steered two hundred miles due east.[28] Here they came upon an encampment of sixty lodges of Arapahays, an outlawed band of the Arapahoes, and notorious robbers. These fell upon the poor trappers; robbed them of their peltries, most of their clothing, and several of their horses. They were glad to escape with their lives, and without being entirely stripped, and after proceeding about fifty miles further, made their halt for the winter.

Early in the spring they resumed their wayfaring, but were unluckily overtaken by the same ruffian horde, who levied still further contributions, and carried off the remainder of their horses, excepting two. With these they continued on, suffering the greatest hardships. They still retained rifles and ammunition, but were in a desert country, where neither bird nor beast was to be found. Their only chance was to keep along the rivers, and subsist by fishing; but at times no fish were to be taken,

[26] Stuart does not give the name. What he wrote here was: "They made that season's hunt on a River which must discharge itself into the Ocean to the Southward of the Columbia." Rollins, 86; Spaulding, 81. Irving's use of the correct name for the river is an example of the kind of geographical knowledge he acquired from Bonneville or from his maps. See Bonneville's "Map of the Sources of the Colorado & Big Salt Lake" in *The Adventures of Captain Bonneville*, facing p. 154.

[27] Great Salt Lake. Irving was the first to use this designation, which appears on the Astoria map in the first edition as well as on maps in the first edition of *The Adventures of Captain Bonneville*. There is no way of knowing who was responsible for this name, whether Irving or Bonneville himself. Bonneville did not discover Great Salt Lake nor did he ever visit it, although a party led by one of his lieutenants, Joseph R. Walker, visited it in the summer of 1833, having been ostensibly sent there for purposes of exploration; see *ibid.* (1961), 162. Although the lake no longer bears Bonneville's name, "Lake Bonneville" is now used to denote the ancient sea that once covered Utah and whose terraced shoreline can still be seen along the slopes of the Wasatch Mountains.

[28] Concerning their movements, see Rollins, 104–105, n. 178. They had, according to the distances given in Stuart and Irving, possibly gone as far east as the Medicine Bow Mountains in southern Wyoming.

and then their sufferings were horrible. One of their horses was stolen among the mountains by the Snake Indians; the other, they said, was carried off by Cass, who, according to their account, "villainously left them in their extremities."[29] Certain dark doubts and surmises were afterwards circulated concerning the fate of that poor fellow, which, if true, showed to what a desperate state of famine his comrades had been reduced.[30]

Being now completely unhorsed, Mr. Miller and his three companions wandered on foot for several hundred miles, enduring hunger, thirst, and fatigue, while traversing the barren wastes which abound beyond the Rocky Mountains. At the time they were discovered by Mr. Stuart's party, they were almost famished, and were fishing for a precarious meal. Had Mr. Stuart made the short cut across the hills, avoiding this bend of the river, or had not some of his party accidentally gone down to the margin of the stream to drink, these poor wanderers might have remained undiscovered, and have perished in the wilderness. Nothing could exceed their joy on thus meeting with their old comrades, or the heartiness with which they were welcomed. All hands immediately encamped; and the slender stores of the party were ransacked to furnish out a suitable regale.

The next morning[31] they all set out together; Mr. Miller and his comrades being resolved to give up the life of a trapper, and accompany Mr. Stuart back to St. Louis.

For several days they kept along the course of Snake River, occasionally making short cuts across hills and promontories, where there were bends in the stream. In their way they passed several camps of Shoshonies, from some of whom they procured salmon, but in general

[29] Stuart's actual statement contains an interesting clue regarding part of their travels. Stuart wrote: "Cass . . . having villainously left them with one of the horses while on the headwaters of the *big horn.*" Rollins, 86; Spaulding, 81. One of the headwaters of the Big Horn is the Popo Agie, which takes its source a few miles to the north and east of South Pass. Following the Popo Agie to Wind River, let us suppose, they remained in the area for the winter. With spring they were robbed a second time by Arapahos. Cass left them, then, and as the other men moved west (possibly across South Pass or Union Pass), they were robbed once more by Snake Indians "on this side [i.e., the west side] of the mountains." *Ibid.* Rollins seems not to have made the possible connection with the Popo Agie and understanding "this side" to mean that Cass also left them on "this side," assumed that Stuart's *"big horn"* had to be a tributary, which he could not identify, of Green River.

[30] See below, p. 440.   [31] August 21.

372

they were too wretchedly poor to furnish anything. It was the wish of Mr. Stuart to purchase horses for the recent recruits of his party;[32] but the Indians could not be prevailed upon to part with any, alleging that they had not enough for their own use.[33]

On the 25th of August they reached a great fishing place, to which they gave the name of Salmon Falls.[34] Here there is a perpendicular fall of twenty feet on the north side of the river, while on the south side there is a succession of rapids. The salmon are taken here in incredible quantities, as they attempt to shoot the falls. It was now a favorable season, and there were about one hundred lodges of Shoshonies busily engaged killing and drying fish. The salmon begin to leap shortly after sunrise. At this time the Indians swim to the centre of the falls, where some station themselves on rocks, and others stand to their waists in the water, all armed with spears, with which they assail the salmon as they attempt to leap, or fall back exhausted. It is an incessant slaughter, so great is the throng of the fish.

The construction of the spears thus used is peculiar. The head is a straight piece of elk horn, about seven inches long, on the point of which an artificial barb is made fast, with twine well gummed. The head is stuck on the end of the shaft, a very long pole of willow, to which it is likewise connected by a strong cord, a few inches in length. When the spearsman makes a sure blow, he often strikes the head of the spear through the body of the fish. It comes off easily, and leaves the salmon struggling with the string through its body, while the pole is still held by the spearsman. Were it not for the precaution of the string, the willow shaft would be snapped by the struggles and the weight of the fish. Mr. Miller, in the course of his wanderings, had been at these falls, and had seen several thousand salmon taken in the course of one afternoon. He declared that he had seen a salmon leap a distance of about thirty feet, from the commencement of the foam at the foot of the fall, completely to the top.[35]

[32] The first edition reads *recruits to his party*.

[33] But on August 22, Stuart managed to exchange two of his jaded horses for two that were fresh.

[34] One mile east of the confluence of Big Wood River, which Stuart calls Cascade Creek. This place came to be known also as Fishing Falls. The date is Stuart's.

[35] The above two paragraphs follow Stuart's "Travelling Memoranda" in all details. Rollins, 109–10; Spaulding, 85.

Having purchased a good supply of salmon from the fishermen, the party resumed their journey, and on the twenty-ninth,[36] arrived at the Caldron Linn, the eventful scene of the preceding autumn. Here, the first thing that met their eyes was a memento of the perplexities of that period; the wreck of a canoe, lodged between two ledges of rocks. They endeavored to get down to it, but the river banks were too high and precipitous.

They now proceeded to that part of the neighborhood where Mr. Hunt and his party had made the caches, intending to take from them such articles as belonged to Mr. Crooks, M'Lellan, and the Canadians. On reaching the spot, they found, to their astonishment, six of the caches open and rifled of their contents, excepting a few books which lay scattered about the vacinity. They had the appearance of having been plundered in the course of the summer. There were tracks of wolves in every direction, to and from the holes, from which Mr. Stuart concluded that these animals had first been attracted to the place by the smell of the skins contained in the caches, which they had probably torn up, and that their tracks had betrayed the secret to the Indians.[37]

The three remaining caches had not been molested: they contained a few dry goods, some ammunition, and a number of beaver traps. From these Mr. Stuart took whatever was requisite for his party; he then deposited within them all his superfluous baggage, and all the books and papers scattered around; the holes were then carefully closed up, and all traces of them effaced. And here we have to record another instance of the indomitable spirit of the western trappers. No sooner did the trio of Kentucky hunters, Robinson, Rezner, and Hoback, find that they could once more be fitted out for a campaign of beaver-trapping, then they forgot all that they had suffered, and determined upon another trial of their fortunes; preferring to take their chance in the wilderness, rather than return home ragged and penniless. As to Mr. Miller, he declared his curiosity and his desire of travelling through the Indian countries fully satisfied; he adhered to his determination, therefore, to keep on with the party to St. Louis, and to return to the bosom of civilized society.

The three hunters, therefore, Robinson, Rezner, and Hoback, were

---

[36] The date is confirmed by Stuart.

[37] Canoes had also been left here, but Stuart states that "three only remain, and these too much shattered to be fit for actual service." Rollins, 112; Spaulding, 87.

furnished, as far as the caches and the means of Mr. Stuart's party afforded, with the requisite munitions and equipments for a "two years' hunt;"[38] but as their fitting out was yet incomplete, they resolved to wait in this neighborhood until Mr. Reed should arrive; whose arrival might soon be expected, as he was to set out for the caches about twenty days after Mr. Stuart parted with him at the Wallah-Wallah River.[39]

Mr. Stuart gave in charge to Robinson a letter to Mr. Reed, reporting his safe journey thus far, and the state in which he had found the caches. A duplicate of this letter he elevated on a pole, and set it up near the place of deposit.

All things being thus arranged, Mr. Stuart and his little band, now seven in number, took leave of the three hardy trappers, wishing them all possible success in their lonely and perilous sojourn in the wilderness; and we, in like manner, shall leave them to their fortunes, promising to take them up again at some future page, and to close the story of their persevering and ill-fated enterprise.[40]

[38] The phrase is Stuart's, given under August 30.

[39] Reed, Stuart says, was to come here "for the express purpose of finding those Hunters and to carry down [to Astoria] whatever was put in the ground at this place last Fall." Rollins, 114; Spaulding, 90.

[40] Irving's principal source for this chapter is Stuart's "Travelling Memoranda," which he follows from July 31 to September 1. Every passage in what Irving writes, except where noted, is traceable to this source.

The Snake River Deserts — Scanty Fare
Bewildered Travellers — Prowling Indians
A Giant Crow Chief — A Bully Rebuked — Indian Signals
Smoke on the Mountains — Mad River — An Alarm
An Indian Foray — A Scamper — A Rude Indian Joke
A Sharp-Shooter Balked of His Shot

ON the 1st of September,[1] Mr. Stuart and his companions resumed their journey, bending their course eastward, along the course of Snake River. As they advanced the country opened. The hills which had hemmed in the river receded on either hand, and great sandy and dusty plains extended before them. Occasionally there were intervals of pasturage, and the banks of the river were fringed with willows and cotton-wood, so that its course might be traced from the hill tops, winding under an umbrageous covert, through a wide sunburnt landscape. The soil, however, was generally poor; there was in some places a miserable growth of wormwood,[2] and a plant called saltweed,[3] resembling pennyroyal; but the summer had parched[4] the plains, and left but little pasturage. The game, too, had disappeared. The hunter looked in vain over the lifeless landscape; now and then a few antelope might be seen, but not within reach of the rifle. We forbear to follow the travellers in a week's wandering over these barren wastes, where they suffered much from hunger, having to depend upon a few fish from the streams, and now and then a little dried salmon, or a dog, procured from some forlorn lodge of Shoshonies.[5]

---

[1] The date is confirmed by Stuart.   [2] Sagebrush.

[3] *Atriplex confertifolia.* In *The Adventures of Captain Bonneville*, 128, Irving describes it as growing "most plentiful in clayey and gravelly barrens. It resembles pennyroyal, and derives its name from a partial saltness. It is nourishing food for horses in the winter, but they reject it the moment the young grass affords sufficient pasturage." In the first edition of *Astoria* the phrase reads *and of a plant called saltweed*.

[4] The first edition reads *the summer heat had parched*.

[5] On September 3 they met five lodges of Shoshonis, and from them obtained a dog, a small amount of dried salmon, "and an excellent sort of Cake made of pulverized roots, and service Berries." See "Travelling Memoranda," Rollins, 115; Spaulding, 91. Here

Returning Astorians, September 2–October 12, 1812

Tired of these cheerless wastes, they left the banks of Snake River[6] on the 7th of September,[7] under guidance of Mr. Miller, who having acquired some knowledge of the country during his trapping campaign, undertook to conduct them across the mountains by a better route than that by Fort Henry, and one more out of the range of the Blackfeet. He proved, however, but an indifferent guide, and they soon be-

they also learned that they were going in the wrong direction. They returned to the Snake the following day. On the sixth they obtained more dried salmon and a horse from another small group of Shoshonis, but next day the Indians returned and persuaded Stuart to give back the animal.

[6] Here they followed the Portneuf River flowing from the southeast into the Snake. Apparently their immediate destination was Bear River. They took this route, Stuart states, because it was "less circuitous and more out of the walks of the Blackfoot Indians, who are very numerous and inimical to the whites, than that by Henry's Fort." Rollins, 128; Spaulding, 94. It was, furthermore, the route that would lead to South Pass, toward which Stuart, acting on information obtained from the Snake Indian on August 16, was clearly pointing.

[7] The date is Stuart's. The party had actually started up the Portneuf on the sixth, as evidenced by the "Travelling Memoranda."

377

came bewildered among rugged hills and unknown streams, and burnt and barren prairies.

At length they came to a river[8] on which Mr. Miller had trapped, and to which they gave his name; though, as before observed, we presume it to be the same called Bear River, which empties itself into Lake Bonneville. Up this river and its branches they kept for two or three days,[9] supporting themselves precariously upon fish. They soon found that they were in a dangerous neighborhood. On the 12th of September, having encamped early, they sallied forth with their rods to angle for their supper. On returning, they beheld a number of Indians prowling about their camp, whom, to their infinite disquiet, they soon perceived to be Upsarokas, or Crows.[10] Their chief came forward with a confident air. He was a dark herculean fellow, full six feet four inches in height, with a mingled air of the ruffian and the rogue. He conducted himself peaceably, however, and despatched some of his people to their camp, which was somewhere in the neighborhood, from whence they returned with a most acceptable supply of buffalo meat. He now signified to Mr. Stuart that he was going to trade with the Snakes who reside on the west base of the mountains, below Henry's Fort. Here they cultivate

[8] On September 8. Irving is probably correct in presuming the river to be Bear River. The *Astoria* map, however, shows them to have traveled north of Bear River and to have touched only a tributary. It is necessary to look at what Stuart wrote: "We steered due east, and in 18 miles struck a river running through an apparently level country, in about a south direction, which Mr. Miller at once pronounced the stream on which he had made his last falls hunt—this river is 100 yards wide." Rollins, 129; Spaulding, 95. The only stream of this size was Bear River, and the part on which Miller trapped was that portion south of the sharp bend at Sheep Rock (near Alexander, Idaho), where Bear River abruptly changes its course south toward the Great Salt Lake after flowing northerly to what is now Soda Springs, Idaho, and then for a short distance west.

[9] A puzzling omission in Stuart's "Travelling Memoranda" and thus in Irving's narrative is the absence of any reference to the remarkable boiling springs and small geysers which they could not have failed to see near Soda Springs had they followed up Bear River. Trappers later called them Beer Springs, and every traveler took special notice of this curious area. See, for example, *The Adventures of Captain Bonneville*, 211. Rollins, 143, n. 36, states that Stuart camped at this spot on September 9. The party here turned toward the south, following as their guide an Indian trail "which follows up the right bank of this stream, and shall be our only dependance untill we reach that part Mr. Miller explored," Stuart wrote. Rollins, 130; Spaulding, 96. They were on that part of Bear River which later formed a section of the Oregon-California Trail, which reached here by several routes from South Pass.

[10] This encounter was crucial, for, as will be seen, it forced Stuart to abandon his course toward South Pass by the route he was following and to veer sharply to the north toward Hunt's route over Teton Pass. The date is confirmed by Stuart.

a delicate kind of tobacco, much esteemed and sought after by the mountain tribes. There was a something sinister, however, in the look of this Indian, that inspired distrust. By degrees, the number of his people increased, until, by midnight, there were twenty-one of them about the camp, who began to be impudent and troublesome. The greatest uneasiness was now felt for the safety of the horses and effects, and every one kept vigilant watch throughout the night.

The morning dawned, however, without any unpleasant occurrence, and Mr. Stuart, having purchased all the buffalo meat that the Crows had to spare, prepared to depart. His Indian acquaintances, however, were disposed for further dealings; and above all, anxious for a supply of gunpowder, for which they offered horses in exchange. Mr. Stuart declined to furnish them with the dangerous commodity. They became more importunate in their solicitations, until they met with a flat refusal.

The gigantic chief now stepped forward, assumed a swelling air, and, slapping himself upon the breast, gave Mr. Crooks to understand that he was a chief of great power and importance. He signified, further, that it was customary for great chiefs when they met, to make each other presents. He requested, therefore, that Mr. Stuart would alight, and give him the horse upon which he was mounted. This was a noble animal, of one of the wild races of the prairies; on which Mr. Stuart set great value; he, of course, shook his head at the request of the Crow dignitary. Upon this the latter strode up to him, and taking hold of him, moved him backwards and forwards in his saddle, as if to make him feel that he was a mere child within his grasp. Mr. Stuart preserved his calmness, and still shook his head. The chief then seized the bridle, and gave it a jerk that startled the horse, and nearly brought the rider to the ground. Mr. Stuart instantly drew forth a pistol, and presented it at the head of the bully-ruffian. In a twinkling his swaggering was at an end, and he dodged behind his horse to escape the expected shot. As his subject Crows gazed on the affray from a little distance, Mr. Stuart ordered his men to level their rifles at them, but not to fire. The whole crew scampered among the bushes, and throwing themselves upon the ground, vanished from sight.

The chieftain thus left alone, was confounded for an instant; but, recovering himself with true Indian shrewdness, burst into a loud laugh, and affected to turn off the whole matter as a piece of pleasantry. Mr. Stuart by no means relished such equivocal joking, but it was not his policy to get into a quarrel; so he joined with the best grace he could assume in the merriment of the jocular giant; and, to console the latter for the refusal of the horse, made him a present of twenty charges of powder. They parted, according to all outward professions, the best friends in the world; it was evident, however, that nothing but the smallness of his own force, and the martial array and alertness of the white men, had prevented the Crow chief from proceeding to open outrage. As it was, his worthy followers, in the course of their brief interview, had contrived to purloin a bag containing almost all the culinary utensils of the party.[11]

The travellers kept on their way due east, over a chain of hills.[12] The recent rencontre showed them that they were now in a land of danger, subject to the wide roamings of a predacious tribe; nor, in fact, had they gone many miles, before they beheld sights calculated to inspire anxiety and alarm. From the summits of some of the loftiest mountains, in different directions, columns of smoke began to rise. These they concluded to be signals made by the runners of the Crow chieftain, to summon the stragglers of his band, so as to pursue them with greater force. Signals of this kind, made by out-runners from one central point, will rouse a wide circuit of the mountains in a wonderfully short space of time; and bring the straggling hunters and warriors to the standard of their chieftain.

To keep as much as possible out of the way of these freebooters, Mr. Stuart altered his course to the north, and, quitting the main stream of Miller's River, kept up a large branch that came in from the mountains.[13] Here they encamped, after a fatiguing march of twenty-five

[11] To show how Irving elaborated this whole incident, it is necessary to read what Stuart wrote: "They insisted on selling us horses and demanded gun powder in return.—This I refused, but they would absolutely exchange some, and at length I acceded in one instance—Their behavior was insolent in the extreme, and indicated an evident intention to steal, if not to rob—we kept close possession of our Arms, but notwithstanding our vigilance, they stole a Bag containing the greater part of our kitchen furniture.—to prevent an open rupture, we gave them about twenty loads of Power & departed, happy at getting off on no worse terms." Rollins, 131; Spaulding, 97.

[12] "Going 10 miles East, over hills, to where a large fork came in from the North," wrote Stuart, "we perceived smokes on several of the highest mountains." Rollins, 131; Spaulding, 97–98. The fork was Thomas Fork, which rises in western Wyoming.

[13] Part of Stuart's entry for September 13 reads: "This morning we thought it best to vary our former course not only the better to keep out of their way, but from the information of Mr. Miller would much sooner reach the part of the country with which he was acquainted, we left the main stream [Bear River], and after following up the

miles. As the night drew on the horses were hobbled or fettered, and tethered close to the camp; a vigilant watch was maintained until morning, and every one slept with his rifle on his arm.

At sunrise,[14] they were again on the march, still keeping to the north. They soon began to ascend the mountains, and occasionally had wide prospects over the surrounding country. Not a sign of a Crow was to be seen; but this did not assure them of their security, well knowing the perseverance of these savages in dogging any party they intend to rob, and the stealthy way in which they can conceal their movements, keeping along ravines and defiles. After a mountain scramble of twenty-one miles, they encamped on the margin of a stream[15] running to the north.

In the evening there was an alarm of Indians, and every one was instantly on the alert. They proved to be three miserable Snakes, who were no sooner informed that a band of Crows was prowling in the neighborhood, than they made off with great signs of consternation.

A couple more of weary days and watchful nights brought them[16] to a strong and rapid stream, running due north, which they concluded to be one of the upper branches of Snake River. It was probably the same since called Salt River.[17]

right bank of the [Thomas] Fork for 15 miles due north, encamped on a small branch, having come this day 25 miles—[.]" Rollins, 131–32; Spaulding, 98. Irving's Miller River, of course, is Bear River.

[14] September 14.

[15] One of the tributaries of Salt River, which drains the western watershed of the Salt River Range in Wyoming and flows north into the Snake.

[16] On September 16.

[17] Not Salt River but Greys River farther east, which drains the eastern watershed of Salt River Range and flows northward, roughly parallel to Salt River, into the Snake. See Rollins, 146–47, n. 73. At this point, Stuart's entry for September 16 becomes especially relevant: "On striking this water-course, we easily perceived how far we had failed in attaining the object in view, for from all we had learned concerning Miller's River [Bear River], we ought to have struck it hereabouts, whereas the one we are on runs quite a contrary course [i.e., north] and must be a branch of the Snake River—[.]" This puzzling statement becomes clear only if one understands that "the object in view" was to strike, by going east, Smiths Fork (flowing south) of Bear River. They had simply traveled a few miles too far north and had come to Greys River, not Smiths. It was an easy mistake to make because both rivers take their rise in the same area only a few miles from each other. Thus they were lost, and their intention of pressing east toward the goal of South Pass was thwarted. Stuart goes on: "Having thus lost the intended tract by which we proposed crossing the rocky mountains, knowing it must be to the south, and the great probability of falling in again with the Crows . . . we at once concluded that our best, safest, and most certain way would be to follow this river [Greys] down, and pass the first spur of mountains [Teton Range]

They determined to bend their course down this river,[18] as it would take them still further out of the dangerous neighborhood of the Crows. They then would strike upon Mr. Hunt's track of the preceding autumn, and retrace it across the mountains. The attempt to find a better route under guidance of Mr. Miller had cost them a large bend to the south; in resuming Mr. Hunt's track, they would at least be sure of their road. They accordingly turned down along the course of this stream, and at the end of three days' journey came to where it was joined by a larger river, and assumed a more impetuous character, raging and roaring among rocks and precipices. It proved, in fact, to be Mad River,[19] already noted in the expedition of Mr. Hunt. On the banks of this river, they encamped on the 18th of September,[20] at an early hour.

Six days had now elapsed since their interview with the Crows; during that time they had come nearly a hundred and fifty miles to the north and west,[21] without seeing any signs of those marauders. They considered themselves, therefore, beyond the reach of molestation, and began to relax in their vigilance, lingering occasionally for part of a day, where there was good pasturage. The poor horses needed repose.

They had been urged on, by forced marches, over rugged heights, among rocks and fallen timber, or over low swampy valleys, inundated by the labors of the beaver. These industrious animals abounded in all the mountain streams and water-courses, wherever there were willows for their subsistence. Many of them they had so completely damned up as to inundate the low grounds, making shallow pools or lakes,

by the route of the party [Hunt's] who came across the continent last year." Rollins, 132; Spaulding, 99. But for their fear of the Crows, they might have overcome their error by moving south and finding the correct route. Had they been able to do this, traveling due east about ninety miles would have brought them to the great natural opening south of the Wind River Mountains, namely South Pass.

[18] Greys River.

[19] Snake River. Stuart's "Travelling Memoranda" at this point shows that Ben Jones was sent east to reconnoiter the Snake and if possible to find a passage which, had they followed it, would have brought them, within about twenty-five miles, to Hoback River, following which they would have been led south to Green River. But Jones reported back and "brought accounts of the impossibility of passing where he went." Rollins, 133; Spaulding, 100. It may be recalled that Hunt had sent out Reed and two men, who had attempted to penetrate from the east the year before but had also found it impossible. Today the route is a spectacular drive on a modern highway.

[20] The date is Stuart's.　　　　　[21] An error for "north and east."

and extensive quagmires; by which the route of the travellers was often impeded.

On the 19th of September, they rose at early dawn; some began to prepare breakfast, and others to arrange the packs preparatory to a march. The horses had been hobbled, but left at large to graze upon[22] the adjacent pasture. Mr. Stuart was on the bank of the river,[23] at a short distance from the camp, when he heard the alarm cry—"Indians! Indians!—to arms! to arms!"

A mounted Crow galloped past the camp, bearing a red flag. He reined his steed on the summit of a neighboring knoll, and waved his flaring banner. A diabolical yell now broke forth on the opposite side of the camp, beyond where the horses were grazing, and a small troop of savages came galloping up, whooping and making a terrific clamor. The horses took fright, and dashed across the camp in the direction of the standard-bearer, attracted by his waving flag. He instantly put spurs to his steed, and scoured off followed by the panic-stricken herd, their fright being increased by the yells of the savages in their rear.

At the first alarm, Mr. Stuart and his comrades had seized their rifles, and attempted to cut off the Indians who were pursuing the horses. Their attention was instantly distracted by whoops and yells in an opposite direction.

They now apprehended that a reserve party was about to carry off their baggage. They ran to secure it. The reserve party, however, galloped by, whooping and yelling in triumph and derision. The last of them proved to be their commander, the identical giant joker already mentioned. He was not cast in the stern poetical mould of fashionable Indian heroism, but on the contrary, was grievously given to vulgar jocularity. As he passed Mr. Stuart and his companions, he checked his horse, raised himself in his saddle, and clapping his hands on the most insulting part of his body, uttered some jeering words, which, fortunately for their delicacy, they could not understand. The rifle of Ben Jones was leveled in an instant, and he was on the point of whizzing a bullet into the target so tauntingly displayed. "Not for your life! not for your life!" exclaimed Mr. Stuart, "you will bring destruction on us all!"

[22] *About* in first edition.

[23] The Author's Revised Edition erroneously has *a river. The river* appears in the first edition.

It was hard to restrain honest Ben, when the mark was so fair and the insult so foul. "O, Mr. Stuart," exclaimed he, "only let me have one crack at the infernal rascal, and you may keep all the pay that is due to me."

"By heaven, if you fire," cried Mr. Stuart, "I'll blow your brains out."

By this time the Indian was far out of reach, and had rejoined his men, and the whole dare-devil band, with the captured horses, scuttled off along the defiles, their red flag flaunting over head, and the rocks echoing to their whoops and yells, and demoniac laughter.

The unhorsed travellers gazed after them in silent mortification and despair; yet Mr. Stuart could not but admire the style and spirit with which the whole exploit had been managed, and pronounced it one of the most daring and intrepid actions he had ever heard of among Indians. The whole number of the Crows did not exceed twenty. In this way a small gang of lurkers will hurry off the cavalry of a large war party, for when once a drove of horses are seized with panic,[24] they become frantic, and nothing short of broken necks can stop them.[25]

No one was more annoyed by this unfortunate occurrence than Ben Jones. He declared he would actually have given his whole arrears of pay, amounting to upwards of a year's wages, rather than be balked of such a capital shot. Mr. Stuart, however, represented what might have been the consequence of so rash an act.[26] Life for life is the Indian maxim. The whole tribe would have made common cause in avenging the death of a warrior. The party were but seven dismounted men, with a wide mountain region to traverse, infested by these people, and which might all be roused by signal-fires. In fact, the conduct of the band of marauders in question, showed the perseverance of savages when once they have fixed their minds upon a project. These fellows had evidently been silently and secretly dogging the party for a week past, and a distance of a hundred and fifty miles, keeping out of sight by day, lurking about the encampment at night, watching all their movements, and

[24] The first edition reads *with a panic.*

[25] Irving reports the facts as Stuart gives them, but adds a good deal more. Stuart, for example, says nothing about an Indian's waving a red flag, nothing about another Indian's making lewd gestures, nothing about Ben Jones's threatening to shoot, nothing about any dialogue's occurring, and nothing about Jones's willingness to sacrifice a year's pay. Before concluding that Irving is fictionalizing, however, one should consider whether this may not be another instance of his use of an oral source.

[26] Nothing to this effect appears in the "Travelling Memoranda."

waiting for a favorable moment when they should be off their guard. The menace of Mr. Stuart, in their first interview, to shoot the giant chief with his pistol, and the fright caused among the warriors by presenting the rifles, had probably added the stimulus of pique to their usual horse-stealing propensites. And in this mood of mind they would doubtless have followed the party throughout their whole course over the Rocky Mountains, rather than be disappointed in their scheme.[27]

[27] Except as noted, Irving's source for this chapter is Stuart's "Travelling Memoranda," September 1 to 19. Rollins, 114–35; Spaulding, 90–102.

Travellers Unhorsed — Pedestrian Preparations
Prying Spies — Bonfire of Baggage — A March on Foot
Rafting a River — The Wounded Elk — Indian Trails
Willful Conduct of Mr. M'Lellan — Grand Prospect from a Mountain
Distant Craters of Volcanoes — Illness of Mr. Crooks

FEW reverses in this changeful world are more complete and disheartening than that of a traveller, suddenly unhorsed, in the midst of the wilderness. Our unfortunate travellers contemplated their situation, for a time, in perfect dismay. A long journey over rugged mountains and immeasurable plains lay before them, which they must painfully perform on foot, and everything necessary for subsistence or defense must be carried on their shoulders. Their dismay, however, was but transient, and they immediately set to work, with that prompt expediency produced by the exigencies of the wilderness, to fit themselves for the change in their condition.

Their first attention was to select from their baggage such articles as were indispensable to their journey; to make them up into convenient packs, and to deposit the residue in caches. The whole day was consumed in these occupations; at night, they made a scanty meal of their remaining provisions,[1] and lay down to sleep with heavy hearts. In the morning, they were up and about at an early hour, and began to prepare their knapsacks for a march, while Ben Jones repaired to an old beaver trap which he had set in the river bank at some little distance from the camp. He was rejoiced to find a middle-sized beaver there, sufficient for a morning's meal to his hungry comrades. On his way back with his prize, he observed two heads peering over the edge of an impending cliff, several hundred feet high, which he supposed to be a couple of wolves. As he continued on, he now and then cast his eye up; the heads were still there, looking down with fixed and watchful gaze. A suspicion

---

[1] The last statement in Stuart's entry for September 19 reads: "We have just food enough for one meal and rely with confidence on the inscrutable ways of providence to send in our road wherewith to subsist on from day to day." Rollins, 135; Spaulding, 102–103.

now flashed across his mind that they might be Indian scouts; and, had they not been far above the reach of his rifle, he would undoubtedly have regaled them with a shot.

On arriving at the camp, he directed the attention of his comrades to these aerial observers. The same idea was at first entertained, that they were wolves; but their immovable watchfulness soon satisfied every one that they were Indians. It was concluded that they were watching the movements of the party, to discover their place of concealment of such articles as they would be compelled to leave behind. There was no likelihood that the caches would escape the search of such keen eyes and experienced rummagers, and the idea was intolerable, that any more booty should fall into their hands. To disappoint them therefore, the travellers stripped the caches of the articles deposited there, and collecting together everything that they could not carry away with them, made a bonfire of all that would burn, and threw the rest into the river. There was a forlorn satisfaction in thus balking the Crows, by the destruction of their own property; and, having thus gratified their pique, they shouldered their packs, about ten o'clock in the morning, and set out on their pedestrian wayfaring.[2]

The route they took was down along the banks of Mad River. This stream makes its way through the defiles of the mountains, into the plain below Fort Henry, where it terminates in the Snake River.[3] Mr. Stuart was in hopes of meeting with Snake encampments in the plain, where he might procure a couple of horses to transport the baggage. In such case, he intended to resume his eastern course across the mountains, and endeavor to reach the Cheyenne River[4] before winter. Should he fail, however, of obtaining horses, he would probably be compelled

[2] Irving enlarges upon Stuart's statement that they destroyed everything they could not carry. "Resolved," Stuart wrote, "to prevent the villans [sic] benefiting more by us—for two of the same band were (by Jones) seen this morning, skulking near our camp, in order, no doubt, to observe where we should deposit what part of our effects we could not carry—[.]" Rollins, 135–36; Spaulding, 103. There is nothing in Stuart about heads of supposed wolves high on a cliff, nothing about Jones's calling his companions' attention to these same wolves, nor anything about a wish that he might fire upon them. Irving either drew upon an oral source or he was fictionalizing.

[3] It should be observed that in Irving's nomenclature, the Snake commenced at the confluence of Henry's Fork and so-called "Mad River," which name designated that portion of the river extending above Henry's Fork.

[4] This river rises in eastern Wyoming and flows east through South Dakota, joining the Missouri in the central part of that state.

to winter on the Pacific side of the mountains, somewhere on the head waters of the Spanish or Colorado River.[5]

With all the care that had been observed in taking nothing with them that was not absolutely necessary, the poor pedestrians were heavily laden, and their burdens added to the fatigues of their rugged road. They suffered much, too, from hunger. The trout they caught were too poor to yield much nourishment;[6] their main dependence, therefore, was upon an old beaver trap, which they had providentially retained. Whenever they were fortunate enough to entrap a beaver, it was cut up immediately and distributed, that each man might carry his share.

After two days of toilsome travel, during which they made but eighteen miles, they stopped on the 21st,[7] to build two rafts on which to cross to the north side of the river. On these they embarked, on the following morning, four on one raft, and three on the other, and pushed boldly from shore. Finding the rafts sufficiently firm and steady to withstand the rough and rapid water, they changed their minds, and instead of crossing, ventured to float down with the current.[8] The river was, in general, very rapid, and from one to two hundred yards in width, winding in every direction through mountains of hard black rock, covered with pines and cedars. The mountains to the east of the river were spurs of the Rocky range, and of great magnitude; those on the west were little better than hills, bleak and barren, or scantily clothed with stunted grass.

Mad River, though deserving its name from the impetuosity of its current, was free from rapids and cascades, and flowed on in a single channel between gravel banks, often fringed with cotton-wood and dwarf willows in abundance. These gave sustenance to immense quantites of beaver, so that the voyagers found no difficulty in procuring food. Ben Jones, also, killed a fallow deer and a wolverine, and as they were enabled to carry the carcasses on their rafts, their larder was well

[5] Now Green River. For Stuart's fall and winter plans, Irving follows Stuart's entry for September 19.

[6] On September 21, Stuart and Miller caught forty-five trout, but, Stuart said, "they are poor and very indifferent food; and were it not for the little meat we occasionally fall in with, I really think they would not even support life—[.]" Rollins, 136; Spaulding, 103.

[7] The date is Stuart's.

[8] The Snake flows here in a northwest direction for about seventy miles as measured on an air line but actually farther because of the numerous twistings of its course. Before turning abruptly south, it receives the waters of Henry's Fork.

supplied. Indeed, they might have occasionally shot beavers that were swimming in the river as they floated by, but they humanely spared their lives, being in no want of meat at the time. In this way, they kept down the river for three days, drifting with the current and encamping on land at night, when they drew up their rafts on shore. Towards the evening of the third day,[9] they came to a little island on which they descried a gang of elk. Ben Jones landed, and was fortunate enough to wound one, which immediately took to the water, but, being unable to stem the current, drifted above a mile, when it was overtaken and drawn to shore. As a storm was gathering, they now encamped on the margin of the river, where they remained all the next day, sheltering themselves as well as they could from the rain and snow[10]—a sharp foretaste of the impending winter. During their encampment, they employed themselves in jerking a part of the elk for future supply. In cutting up the carcass, they found that the animal had been wounded by hunters, about a week previously, an arrow head and a musket ball remaining in the wounds. In the wilderness, every trivial circumstance is a matter of anxious speculation. The Snake Indians have no guns; the elk, therefore, could not have been wounded by one of them. They were on the borders of the country infested by the Blackfeet, who carry fire-arms. It was concluded, therefore, that the elk had been hunted by some of that wondering and hostile tribe, who, of course, must be in the neighborhood. The idea put an end to the transient solace they had enjoyed in the comparative repose and abundance of the river.[11]

For three days longer they continued to navigate with their rafts. The recent storm had rendered the weather extremely cold. They had now floated down the river about ninety-one miles, when, finding the mountains on the right diminished to moderate sized hills, they landed, and prepared to resume their journey on foot. Accordingly, having spent a day in preparations, making moccasins, and parceling out their jerked meat in packs of twenty pounds to each man, they turned their backs upon the river[12] on the 29th of September and struck off to the north-

[9] September 24.

[10] The first edition reads *from rain, and hail, and snow, a sharp foretaste of the impending winter*.

[11] This last statement is Irving's conjecture and is not unreasonable, but nothing in Stuart's "Travelling Memoranda" hints at it.

[12] Rollins, 149, n. 118, believes they left the river near where today's Heise, Idaho, is now located. Irving's date for their leaving the river follows Stuart.

east, keeping along the southern skirt of the mountain on which Henry's Fort[13] was situated.

Their march was slow and toilsome; part of the time through an alluvial bottom, thickly grown with cotton-wood, hawthorn, and willows, and part of the time over rough hills. Three antelopes came within shot, but they dared not fire at them, lest the report of their rifles should betray them to the Blackfeet. In the course of the day, they came upon a large horse-track apparently about three weeks old, and in the evening encamped on the banks of a small stream, on a spot which had been the camping place of this same band.

On the following morning they still observed the Indian track, but after a time they came to where it separated in every direction, and was lost. This showed that the band had dispersed in various hunting parties, and was, in all probability, still in the neighborhood; it was necessary, therefore, to proceed with the utmost caution. They kept a vigilant eye as they marched, upon every height where a scout might be posted, and scanned the solitary landscape and the distant ravines, to observe any column of smoke; but nothing of the kind was to be seen; all was indescribably stern and lifeless.

Towards evening they came to where there were several hot springs,[14] strongly impregnated with iron and sulphur, and sending up a volume of vapor that tainted the surrounding atmosphere, and might be seen at the distance of a couple of miles.

Near to these they encamped, in a deep gully, which afforded some concealment. To their great concern, Mr. Crooks, who had been indisposed for the two preceding days, had a violent fever in the night.

Shortly after daybreak[15] they resumed their march. On emerging from the glen, a consultation was held as to their course. Should they continue round the skirt of the mountain, they would be in danger of falling in with the scattered parties of Blackfeet, who were probably hunting in the plain. It was thought most advisable, therefore, to strike directly across the mountain, since the route, though rugged and difficult, would be most secure. This counsel was indignantly derided by

[13] Henry's Fort was not their immediate goal, however, for there was no reason for them to visit it. Their course, which continued northeast, was intended to take them to Teton Pass.

[14] Now known as Pincock Springs. See Stuart's description in Rollins, 150–51, and Spaulding, 107.

[15] October 1.

M'Lellan as pusillanimous. Hot-headed and impatient at all times, he had been rendered irascible by the fatigues of the journey, and the condition of his feet, which were chafed and sore. He could not endure the idea of encountering the difficulties of the mountain, and swore he would rather face all the Blackfeet in the country. He was overruled, however, and the party began to ascend the mountain, striving, with the ardor and emulation of young men, who should be first up. M'Lellan, who was double the age of some of his companions, soon began to lose breath, and fall in the rear. In the distribution of burdens, it was his turn to carry the old beaver trap. Piqued and irritated, he suddenly came to a halt, swore he would carry it no further, and jerked it half way down the hill. He was offered in place of it a package of dried meat, but this he scornfully threw upon the ground. They might carry it, he said, who needed it; for his part, he could provide his daily bread[16] with his rifle. He concluded by flinging off from the party, and keeping along the skirts of the mountain, leaving those, he said, to climb rocks, who were afraid to face Indians. It was in vain that Mr. Stuart represented to him the rashness of his conduct, and the dangers to which he exposed himself: he rejected such counsel as craven. It was equally useless to represent the dangers to which he subjected his companions; as he could be discovered at a great distance on those naked plains, and the Indians, seeing him, would know that there must be other white men within reach. M'Lellan turned a deaf ear to every remonstrance, and kept on his willful way.

It seems a strange instance of perverseness in this man thus to fling himself off alone, in a savage region, where solitude itself was dismal, and[17] every encounter with his fellow-man full of peril. Such, however, is the hardness of spirit, and the insensibility to danger, that grow upon men in the wilderness. M'Lellan, moreover, was a man of peculiar temperament, ungovernable in his will, of a courage that absolutely knew no fear,[18] and somewhat of a braggart spirit, that took pride in doing desperate and hair-brained [sic] things.[19]

[16] *Food* in first edition.   [17] *But* in first edition.   [18] *Not* in first edition.

[19] Irving enlarges upon Stuart's information, adding details that do not appear in the "Travelling Memoranda." Stuart wrote: "Mr. McClellan, to whose lot it had fallen to carry the Trap, refused to be its bearer any longer, neither would he pack an equivalent in dried meat, but, leaving us, said he could kill enough for his daily subsistence, and when informed we would cross the mountain to the right, the better to avoid the Blackfeet in whose walks we now were, his answer was that he must consult the case of his sore feet, and went on around the base." Rollins, 151; Spaulding, 108.

Mr. Stuart and his party found the passages of the mountain some-what difficult, on account of the snow, which in many places was of con-siderable depth, though it was now but the 1st of October.[20] They crossed the summit early in the afternoon, and beheld below them a plain about twenty miles wide, bounded on the opposite side by their old acquaint-ances, the Pilot Knobs,[21] those towering mountains which had served Mr. Hunt as landmarks in part of his route of the preceding year. Through the intermediate plain wandered a river[22] about fifty yards wide, sometimes gleaming in open day, but oftener running through willowed banks, which marked its serpentine course.

Those of the party who had been across these mountains, pointed out much of the bearings of the country to Mr. Stuart. They showed him in what direction[23] must lie the deserted post called Henry's Fort, where they had abandoned their horses and embarked in canoes, and they in-formed him that the stream which wandered through the plain below them, fell into Henry River, half way between the fort and the mouth of Mad or Snake River. The character of all this mountain region was de-cidedly volcanic; and to the northwest, between Henry's Fort and the source of the Missouri, Mr. Stuart observed several very high peaks covered with snow, from two of which smoke ascended in considerable volumes, apparently from craters in the state of eruption.[24]

On their way down the mountain, when they had reached the skirts, they decried M'Lellan at a distance, in the advance, traversing the plain. Whether he saw them or not, he showed no disposition to rejoin them, but pursued his sullen and solitary way.[25]

After descending into the plain, they kept on about six miles, until they reached the little river, which was here about knee deep, and richly fringed with willow. Here they encamped for the night. At this en-campment the fever of Mr. Crooks increased to such a degree that it

[20] The date is Stuart's.

[21] Three Tetons.

[22] Teton River, which here flows north along the western base of the Teton Range through what trappers formerly called Pierre's Hole (now Teton Basin). Here in 1832 occurred the Battle of Pierre's Hole, of which Irving wrote a graphic account in *The Adventures of Captain Bonneville*, 57–64.

[23] Northwest about thirty miles. Irving's statement is supposition.

[24] The high peaks were part of the Bitterroot Range. Again Irving is adding sup-position to his narrative, for there are no volcanoes in this area, and Stuart's "Travelling Memoranda" offers nothing to suggest the fact to Irving.

[25] Stuart bears this out.

was impossible for him to travel. Some of the men were strenuous for Mr. Stuart to proceed without him, urging the imminent danger they were exposed to by delay in that unknown and barren region, infested by the most treacherous and inveterate foes. They represented that the season was rapidly advancing; the weather for some days had been extremely cold; the mountains were already almost impassable from snow, and would soon present effectual barriers. Their provisions were exhausted; there was no game to be seen, and they did not dare to use their rifles, through fear of drawing upon them the Blackfeet.

The picture thus presented, was too true to be contradicted, and made a deep impression on the mind of Mr. Stuart; but the idea of abandoning a fellow being, and a comrade, in such a forlorn situation, was too repugnant to his feelings to be admitted for an instant. He represented to the men that the malady of Mr. Crooks could not be of long duration, and that, in all probability, he would be able to travel in the course of a few days. It was with great difficulty, however, that he prevailed upon them to abide the event.[26]

[26] Stuart was sufficiently moved by their circumstances to record his feelings at length, affording the reader an insight into the mind of a sensitive person facing a hostile wilderness at a crucial hour: "The sensations excited on this occasion and by the view of an unknown & untravelled wilderness are not such as arise in the artificial solitude of parks and gardens, for there one is apt to indulge a flattering notion of self sufficiency, as well as a placid indulgence of voluntary delusions; whereas the phantoms which haunt a desert are want, misery, and danger, the evils of dereliction rush upon the mind; man is made unwillingly acquainted with his own weakness, and meditation shows him only how little he can sustain and how little he can perform—[.]" Rollins, 152; Spaulding, 109.

For this chapter, Irving closely follows the "Travelling Memoranda" from September 19 to October 19. Rollins, 135–52; Spaulding, 102–109.

CHAPTER XLVII

Ben Jones and a Grizzly Bear — Rocky Heights
Mountain Torrents — Traces of M'Lellan — Volcanic Remains — Mineral Earths
Peculiar Clay for Pottery — Dismal Plight of M'Lellan
Starvation — Shocking Proposition of a Desperate Man
A Broken-Down Bull — A Ravenous Meal — Indian Graves
Hospitable Snakes — A Forlorn Alliance

AS the travellers were now in a dangerous neighborhood, where the report of a rifle might bring the savages upon them, they had to depend upon their old beaver trap for subsistence. The little river on which they were encamped gave many "beaver signs," and Ben Jones set off at daybreak, along the willowed banks, to find a proper trapping-place. As he was making his way among the thickets, with his trap on his shoulder and his rifle in his hand, he heard a crashing[1] sound, and turning, beheld a huge grizzly bear advancing upon him, with terrific growl. The sturdy Kentuckian was not to be intimidated by man or monster. Leveling his rifle, he pulled the trigger. The bear was wounded, but not mortally: instead, however, of rushing upon his assailant, as is generally the case with this kind of bear, he retreated into the bushes. Jones followed him for some distance, but with suitable caution, and Bruin effected his escape.

As there was every prospect of a detention of some days in this place, as the supplies of the beaver trap were too precarious to be depended upon, it became absolutely necessary to run some risk of discovery by hunting in the neighborhood. Ben Jones, therefore, obtained permission to range with his rifle some distance from the camp, and set off to beat up the river banks, in defiance of bear or Blackfeet.

He returned in great spirits in the course of a few hours, having come upon a gang of elk about six miles off, and killed five. This was joyful news, and the party immediately moved forward to the place where he had left the carcasses. They were obliged to support Mr. Crooks the

[1] Erroneously *crushing* in Author's Revised Edition. The first edition has *crashing*.

whole distance, for he was unable to walk. Here they remained for two or three days, feasting heartily on elk meat, and drying as much as they would be able to carry away with them.

By the 5th of October,[2] some simple prescriptions, together with an "Indian sweat," had so far benefited Mr. Crooks, that he was enabled to move about; they therefore, set forward slowly, dividing his pack and accoutrements among them, and made a creeping day's progress of eight miles south. Their route for the most part lay through swamps caused by the industrious labors of the beaver; for this little animal had dammed up numerous small streams, issuing from the Pilot Knob Mountains, so that the low grounds on their borders were completely inundated. In the course of their march they killed a grizzly bear, with fat on its flanks upwards of three inches in thickness. This was an acceptable addition to their stock of elk meat. The next day Mr. Crooks was sufficiently recruited in strength to be able to carry his rifle and pistols, and they made a march of seventeen miles along the borders of the plain.

Their journey daily became more toilsome, and their sufferings more severe, as they advanced. Keeping up the channel of a river, they traversed the rugged summit[3] of the Pilot Knob Mountain,[4] covered with snow nine inches deep. For several days they continued, bending their course as much as possible to the east, over a succession of rocky heights, deep valleys, and rapid streams. Sometimes their dizzy path lay along the margin of perpendicular precipices,[5] several hundred feet in height, where a single false step might precipitate them into the rocky bed of a torrent which roared below. Not the least part of their weary task was the fording of the numerous windings and branches of the mountain rivers, all boisterous in their currents, and icy cold.

Hunger was added to their other sufferings, and soon became the keenest. The small supply of bear and elk meat which they had been able to carry, in addition to their previous burdens, served but for a short time.[6] In their anxiety to struggle forward, they had but little time to

---

[2] The date is confirmed by Stuart.

[3] Teton Pass (elevation 8,431 feet), which they crossed on October 7.

[4] Teton Range, crossing which they descended into the south end of Jackson Hole and to the Snake River, which they followed down for some distance, then left it to cross low mountains bordering the river on the east, and on October 9 came to Hoback River a few miles above its confluence with the Snake.

[5] Of Hoback Canyon.   [6] The first edition reads *for a very short time.*

hunt, and scarce any game came[7] in their path. For three days they had nothing to eat but a small duck, and a few poor trout.[8] They occasionally saw numbers of antelopes,[9] and tried every art to get within shot; but the timid animals were more than commonly wild, and after tantalizing the hungry hunters for a time, bounded away beyond all chance of pursuit. At length they were fortunate enough to kill one: it was extremely meagre, and yielded but a scanty supply; but on this they subsisted for several days.

On the 11th, they encamped on a small stream, near the foot of the Spanish River Mountain.[10] Here they met with traces of that wayward and solitary being, M'Lellan, who was still keeping on ahead of them through these lonely mountains. He had encamped the night before on this stream; they found the embers of the fire by which he had slept, and the remains of a miserable wolf on which he had supped. It was evident he had suffered, like themselves, the pangs of hunger, though he had fared better at this encampment; for they had not a mouthful to eat.

The next day, they rose hungry and alert, and set out with the dawn to climb the mountain, which was steep and difficult. Traces of volcanic eruptions[11] were to be seen in various directions. There was a species of clay also to be met with, out of which the Indians manufacture pots and jars, and dishes. It is very fine and light, of an agreeable smell, and of a brown color spotted with yellow, and dissolves readily in the mouth. Vessels manufactured of it are said to impart a pleasant smell and flavor to any liquids. These mountains abound also with mineral earths, or chalks of various colors; especially two kinds of ochre, one a pale, the other a bright red, like vermilion; much used by the Indians, in painting their bodies.[12]

[7] *Came* correctly appears in the first edition but was omitted from the Author's Revised Edition.

[8] The "Travelling Memoranda" shows that they had consumed these on the morning of October 8, the day before they reached Hoback River. The antelope to which Irving refers later in this paragraph they secured on October 9, and on this same day they killed a beaver. These provided their first food since breakfast the day before.

[9] Erroneously *the antelopes* in the Author's Revised Edition but *of antelopes* in the first edition.

[10] Not the Wind River Mountains but presumably the southern extension of the Gros Ventre Range separating the drainage of Hoback River and its tributaries from that of Green River and its affluents. The date is Stuart's.

[11] Erroneously *operations* in first edition.

[12] The first sentence comes from Stuart's entry for October 12: "At the dawn we re-

About noon, the travellers reached the "drains" and brooks that formed the head waters of the river,[13] and later in the day descended to where the main body, a shallow stream, about a hundred and sixty yards wide, poured through its mountain valley.

Here the poor famishing wanderers had expected to find buffalo in abundance, and had fed their hungry hopes during their scrambling toil, with the thoughts of roasted ribs, juicy humps, and broiled marrow bones. To their great disappointment, the river banks were deserted; a few old tracks, showed where a herd of bulls had some time before passed along, but not a horn nor hump was to be seen in the sterile land-scape. A few antelopes looked down upon them from the brow of a crag, but flitted away out of sight at the least approach of the hunter.

In the most starving mood they kept for several miles further, along the bank of the river, seeking for "beaver signs." Finding some, they encamped in the vicinity, and Ben Jones immediately proceeded to set the trap. They had scarce come to a halt, when they perceived a large smoke at some distance to the southwest. The sight was hailed with joy, for they trusted it might rise from some Indian camp, where they could procure something to eat, and the dread of starvation had now overcome even the terror of the Blackfeet. Le Clerc, one of the Canadians, was in-stantly despatched by Mr. Stuart, to reconnoitre; and the travellers sat up till a late hour,[14] watching and listening for his return, hoping he might bring them food. Midnight arrived, but Le Clerc did not make his appearance, and they laid [sic] down once more supperless to sleep, comforting themselves with the hopes that their old beaver trap might furnish them with a breakfast.

At daybreak they hastened with famished eagerness to the trap. They found in it the forepaw of a beaver, the sight of which tantalized their hunger, and added to their dejection. They resumed their journey with flagging spirits, but had not gone far when they perceived Le Clerc ap-proaching at a distance. They hastened to meet him, in hopes of tidings

sumed our journey, and continued on for 2 miles to the base of the mountain, the ascent of which is steep and difficult." Rollins, 155; Spaulding, 113. For the remainder of his paragraph, Irving jumps ahead to the last paragraph of Stuart's entry for October 18, which he paraphrases very closely, often verbatim, for details concerning the clays, vessels, etc., herein mentioned. Cf. Rollins, 161–62; Spaulding, 119–20.

[13] Green River, which Stuart refers to by its earlier name, Spanish River. Stuart came to it some miles north of modern Daniel, Wyoming, in a lovely open valley.

[14] Until about midnight, says Stuart.

of good cheer. He had none to give them;[15] but news of that strange wanderer, M'Lellan. The smoke had risen from his encampment, which took fire while he was at a little distance from it fishing. Le Clerc found him in forlorn condition. His fishing had been unsuccessful. During twelve days that he had been wandering alone through these savage mountains, he had found scarce anything to eat. He had been ill, way-worn, sick at heart, still he hád kept forward; but now his strength and his stubbornness were exhausted. He expressed his satisfaction at hear-ing that Mr. Stuart and his party were near, and said he would wait at his camp for their arrival, in hopes they would give him something to eat, for without food he declared he should not be able to proceed much further.

When the party reached the place, they found the poor fellow lying on a parcel of withered grass, wasted to a perfect skeleton, and so feeble that he could scarce raise his head or speak. The presence of his old com-rades seemed to revive him; but they had no food to give him, for they themselves were almost starving. They urged him to rise and accom-pany them, but he shook his head. It was all in vain, he said; there was no prospect of their getting speedy relief, and without it he should perish by the way; he might as well, therefore, stay and die where he was. At length, after much persuasion, they got him upon his legs; his rifle and other effects were shared among them, and he was cheered and aided forward. In this way they proceeded for seventeen miles, over a level plain of sand, until seeing a few antelopes in the distance, they encamped on the margin of a small stream. All now that were capable of exertion, turned out to hunt for a meal. Their efforts were fruitless, and after dark they returned to their camp, famished almost to desperation.

As they were preparing for the third time to lay [*sic*] down to sleep without a mouthful to eat, Le Clerc, one of the Canadians, gaunt and wild with hunger, approached Mr. Stuart with his gun in his hand. "It was all in vain," he said, "to attempt to proceed any further without food. They had a barren plain before them, three or four days' journey in extent, on which nothing was to be procured. They must all perish before they could get to the end of it. It was better, therefore, that one should die to save the rest."[16] He proposed, therefore, that they should

---

[15] The first edition reads *none such to give them*.

[16] The substance of what Irving placed within quotation marks appears in Stuart's

The Dalles, by John Mix Stanley. From Isaac I. Stevens, *Narrative and Final Report . . . Reports of Explorations and Surveys to Ascertain the Most Practicable and Economical Route for a Railroad from the Mississippi River to the Pacific Ocean* (1860).

Celilo Falls on the Columbia River. The view is from the south bank
to the north bank.

Courtesy Oregon Historical Society

cast lots; adding, as an inducement for Mr. Stuart to assent to the proposition, that he, as leader of the party, should be exempted.

Mr. Stuart shuddered at the horrible proposition, and endeavored to reason with the man, but his words were unavailing. At length, snatching up his rifle, he threatened to shoot him on the spot if he persisted. The famished wretch dropped on his knees, begged pardon in the most abject terms, and promised never again to offend him with such a suggestion.[17]

Quiet being restored to the forlorn encampment, each one sought repose. Mr. Stuart, however, was so exhausted by the agitation of the past scene, acting upon his emaciated frame, that he could scarce crawl to his miserable couch; where, notwithstanding his fatigues, he passed a sleepless night, revolving upon their dreary situation, and the desperate prospect before them.[18]

Before daylight the next morning, they were up and on their way; they had nothing to detain them; no breakfast to prepare, and to linger was to perish. They proceeded, however, but slowly, for all were faint and weak. Here and there they passed the skulls and bones of buffaloes, which showed that these animals[19] must have been hunted here during the past season; the sight of these bones served only to mock their misery. After travelling about nine miles along the plain, they ascended a

"Travelling Memoranda," but Irving has taken the liberty of rephrasing it and presenting it as a quotation.

[17] Irving accurately restates what Stuart wrote for October 13.

[18] Irving might have quoted Stuart's actual words, which convey better than Irving does his feeling of despair in the face of desperate circumstances: "My thoughts began to ruminate on our hapless & forlorn situation with the prospects before us: untill I at length became so agitated and weak that it was with difficulty I crawled to bed, and after being there, I (for the first time in my life) could not enjoy that repose my exhausted frame so much wanted; this naturally led my revery to a retrospective view of former happy days, when troubles, difficulties, and distress were to me only things imaginary, which now convinces one how little a man who rolls in affluence, and knows neither cares nor sorrows, can feel for those of others, and he undoubtedly of all people in the world is least qualified for pious deeds—

"Let him visit these regions of want and misery; his riches will soon prove an eye sore, and he will be taught the pleasure and advantage of prayer—If the advocates for the rights of man come here, they can enjoy them, for this is the land of *liberty and equality*, where a man sees, and feels, that he is a man merely, and that he can no longer exist than while he can himself procure the means of support." Rollins, 157–58; Spaulding, 115.

[19] The first edition reads *those animals*.

range of hills, and had scarcely gone two miles further, when, to their great joy, they discovered "an old run-down buffalo bull;"[20] the laggard probably of some herd that had been hunted and harassed through the mountains. They now all stretched themselves out to encompass and make sure of this solitary animal, for their lives depended upon their success. After considerable trouble and infinite anxiety, they at length succeeded in killing him. He was instantly flayed and cut up, and so ravenous was their hunger, that they devoured some of the flesh raw. The residue they carried to a brook near by, where they encamped, lit a fire, and began to cook.

Mr. Stuart was fearful that in their famished state they would eat to excess and injure themselves. He caused a soup to be made of some of the meat, and that each should take a quantity of it as a prelude to his supper. This may have had a beneficial effect, for though they set up the greater part of the night, cooking and cramming, no one suffered any inconvenience.

The next morning[21] the feasting was resumed, and about midday, feeling somewhat recruited and refreshed, they set out on their journey with renovated spirits, shaping their course towards a mountain,[22] the summit of which they saw towering in the east, and near to which they expected to find the head waters of the Missouri.[23]

As they proceeded, they continued to see the skeletons of buffaloes scattered about the plain in every direction, which showed that there had been much hunting here by the Indians in the recent season. Further on they crossed a large Indian trail forming a deep path, about fifteen days old, which went in a north direction. They concluded it to have been made by some numerous band of Crows, who had hunted in this country for the greater part of the summer.

On the following day they forded a stream of considerable magnitude,[24] with banks clothed with pine-trees. Among these they found the traces of a large Indian camp, which had evidently been the head-quar-

[20] A direct quotation from the "Travelling Memoranda" for October 14.
[21] October 15.
[22] The Wind River Mountains, which lie in a southeast direction and point directly to South Pass.
[23] The Popo Agie, flowing to the northeast, joins Wind River to form the Big Horn, a tributary of the Yellowstone, which empties into the Missouri. The Sweetwater, flowing east, empties into the North Platte. Its junction with the South Platte forms the Platte River, which flows across the plains into the Missouri far to the east.
[24] New Fork River, a tributary of Green River, drains New Fork Lakes, Willow

ters of a hunting expedition, from the great quantities of buffalo bones strewed about the neighborhood. The camp had apparently been abandoned about a month.

In the centre was a singular lodge one hundred and fifty feet in circumference, supported by the trunks of twenty trees, about twelve inches in diameter and forty-four feet long. Across these were laid branches of pine and willow trees, so as to yield a tolerable shade. At the west end, immediately opposite to the door, three bodies lay interred with their feet towards the east. At the head of each grave was a branch of red cedar firmly planted in the ground. At the foot was a large buffalo's skull, painted black. Savage ornaments were suspended in various parts of the edifice, and a great number of children's moccasins. From the magnitude of this building, and the time and labor that must have been expended in erecting it, the bodies which it contained were probably those of noted warriors and hunters.[25]

The next day, October 17th, they passed two large tributary streams[26] of the Spanish River. They took their rise in the Wind River Mountains, which ranged along the east, stupendously high and rugged, composed of vast masses of black rock, almost destitute of wood, and covered in many places with snow. This day they saw a few buffalo bulls, and some antelopes, but could not kill any; and their stock of provisions began to grow scanty as well as poor.[27]

On the 18th,[28] after crossing a mountain ridge, and traversing a plain, they waded one of the branches[29] of Spanish River, and on ascending its bank, met with about a hundred and thirty Snake Indians. They were friendly in their demeanor, and conducted them to their encampment, which was about three miles distant. It consisted of about forty wig-

Lake, and Fremont Lake lying north of modern Pinedale, Wyoming, and other lakes to the south.

[25] This paragraph is a close paraphrase, some of it verbatim, of Stuart's entry for October 16.

[26] Probably Boulder Creek, which drains Boulder Lake, and East Fork, formed by many small tributaries coming out of the mountains. The date is confirmed by Stuart.

[27] "Our living is of the meanest kind," Stuart recorded, "being poor Bull meat and Buck antelope, both too bad to be eat, except in cases of starvation—[.]" Rollins, 160; Spaulding, 118.

[28] The date is Stuart's.

[29] East Fork. Where Stuart first encountered it the day before, the stream flowed southwest, but only after making a sharp bend after flowing from the southeast. Stuart's statement reads: "Soon after crossing the ridge which lay before us, we found the stream we encamped on last night, coming from the S.E." Rollins, 160; Spaulding, 118.

wams, constructed principally of pine branches. The Snakes, like most of their nation, were very poor; the marauding Crows, in their late excursion through the country, had picked this unlucky band to the very bone, carrying off their horses, several of their squaws, and most of their effects. In spite of their poverty, they were hospitable in the extreme, and made the hungry strangers welcome to their cabins. A few trinkets procured from them a supply of buffalo meat, and of leather for moccasins, of which the party were greatly in need. The most valuable prize obtained from them, however, was a horse; it was a sorry old animal in truth, but it was the only one that remained to the poor fellows, after the fell swoop of the Crows; yet this they were prevailed upon to part with to their guests for a pistol, an axe, a knife, and a few other trifling articles.[30]

They had doleful stories to tell of the Crows, who were encamped on a river at no great distance to the east, and were in such force that they dared not venture to seek any satisfaction for their outrages, or to get back a horse or squaw. They endeavored to excite the indignation of their visitors by accounts of robberies and murders committed on lonely white hunters and trappers by Crows and Blackfeet. Some of these were exaggerations of the outrages already mentioned, sustained by some of the scattered members of Mr. Hunt's expedition; others were in all probability sheer fabrications, to which the Snakes seem to have been a little prone.[31] Mr. Stuart assured them that the day was not far distant when the whites would make their power to be felt throughout that country, and take signal vengeance on the perpetrators of these misdeeds. The Snakes expressed great joy at the intelligence, and offered their services to aid the righteous cause, brightening at the thoughts of taking the field with such potent allies, and doubtless anticipating their turn at stealing horses and abducting squaws. Their offers, of course, were accepted; the calumet of peace was produced, and the two forlorn powers smoked eternal friendship between themselves, and vengeance upon their common spoilers, the Crows.[32]

[30] Stuart enumerated "a Pistol, a Breech cloth, an axe, a knife, a Tin Cup, two Awls, and a few Beads." Rollins, 161; Spaulding, 118.

[31] For the basis of these rumors, see below, pp. 437–40. Cf. "Travelling Memoranda," Rollins, 161 and 178–79, n. 123; Spaulding, 118–19.

[32] In this chapter Irving paraphrases Stuart's "Travelling Memoranda" for October 2 to October 18. Rollins, 152–61; Spaulding, 110–19.

BY sunrise on the following morning (October 19th),[1] the travellers had loaded their old horse with buffalo meat, sufficient for five days' provisions, and, taking leave of their new allies, the poor, but hospitable Snakes, set forth in somewhat better spirits, though the increasing cold of the weather, and the sight of the snowy mountains which they had yet to traverse, were enough to chill their very hearts. The country along this branch of the Spanish River, as far as they could see, was perfectly level, bounded by ranges of lofty mountains, both to the east and west.[2] They proceeded about three miles to the south, where they came again upon the large trail of Crow Indians, which they had crossed four days previously, made, no doubt, by the same marauding band that had plundered the Snakes; and which, according to the account of the latter, was now encamped on a stream to the eastward. The trail kept on to the southeast and was so well beaten by horse and foot, that they supposed at least a hundred lodges had passed along it. As it formed, therefore, a convenient highway, and ran in a proper direction, they turned into it, and determined to keep along it as far as safety would permit: as the Crow encampment must be some distance off, and it was not likely those savages would return upon their steps. They travelled forward, therefore, all that day, in the track of their dangerous predecessors, which led them across mountain streams, and along[3] ridges, and through nar-

---

[1] The date is confirmed by Stuart.

[2] To the east towered the Wind River Mountains. Fifty miles to the west, across the broad Green River Valley, lay the Salt River Range, along which on Greys River they had traveled northward toward the Snake River over a month before.

[3] Erroneously *long* in the Author's Revised Edition. *Along* appears in the first edition.

Returning Astorians through area of South Pass,
October 19–November 2, 1812

row valleys, all tending generally towards the southeast. The wind blew
coldly from the northeast, with occasional flurries of snow, which made
them encamp early, on the sheltered banks of a brook.[4] The two Canadians, Vallée and Le Clerc, killed a young buffalo bull in the evening,
which was in good condition, and afforded them a plentiful supply of
fresh beef. They loaded their spits, therefore, and crammed their camp-
kettle with meat, and while the wind whistled, and the snow whirled
around them, huddled round a rousing fire, basked in its warmth, and
comforted both soul and body with a hearty and invigorating meal. No
enjoyments have greater zest than these, snatched in the very midst of
difficulty and danger; and it is probable the poor wayworn and weather-
beaten travellers relished these creature comforts the more highly from
the surrounding desolation, and the dangerous proximity of the Crows.[5]

The snow which had fallen in the night made it late in the morning
before the party loaded their solitary pack-horse, and resumed their
march. They had not gone far before the Crow trace which they were
following changed its direction, and bore to the north of east. They had
already begun to feel themselves on dangerous ground in keeping along
it, as they might be descried by some scouts and spies of that race of
Ishmaelites, whose predatory life required them to be constantly on the

[4] Big Sandy Creek, which flows generally southwest and empties into Green River.
[5] The last two sentences are Irving's interpolation.

404

alert. On seeing the trace turn so much to the north, therefore, they abandoned it, and kept on their course to the southeast for eighteen miles, through a beautifully undulating country, having the main chain of mountains on the left, and a considerably elevated ridge on the right. Here the mountain ridge which divides Wind River from the head waters of the Columbia and Spanish rivers,[6] ends abruptly, and winding to the north of east, becomes the dividing barrier between a branch of the Big Horn and Cheyenne rivers, and those head waters which flow into the Missouri below the Sioux country.

The ridge which lay on the right of the travellers having now become very low, they passed over it, and came into a level plain, about ten miles in circumference, and incrusted to the depth of a foot or eighteen inches with salt[7] as white as snow. This is furnished by numerous salt springs of limpid water, which are continually welling up, overflowing their borders, and forming beautiful crystallizations. The Indian tribes of the interior are excessively fond of this salt, and repair to the valley to collect it, but it is held in distaste by the tribes of the sea-coast, who will eat nothing that has been cured or seasoned by it.

This evening they encamped on the banks of a small stream,[8] in the open prairie. The northeast wind was keen and cutting; they had nothing wherewith to make a fire, but a scanty growth of sage, or wormwood, and were fain to wrap themselves up in their blankets, and huddle themselves in their "nests," at an early hour. In the course of the evening, Mr. M'Lellan, who had now regained his strength, killed a buffalo, but it was some distance from the camp, and they postponed supplying themselves from the carcass until the following morning.

The next day (October 21st),[9] the cold continued, accompanied by

[6] The Wind River Mountains divide Wind River and its tributaries from the Green River (Spanish River) and its tributaries. But they cannot be said to have any bearing on the headwaters of the Columbia, which in the context can mean only Snake River and its affluents. Exactly what the words *Wind River Mountains* meant to Irving we cannot say. If by them he meant also the flanking Gros Ventre Range to the northwest, which supplies part of the watershed of the Snake, the statement can be accepted. Irving, in any case, was only following what Stuart stated for October 20: "The ridge of mountains, which divides Wind river [which he had not seen, his information coming from some of the men with him] from the columbia and spanish waters, ends here abruptly." Rollins, 162; Spaulding, 120.

[7] Not sodium chloride, the common table salt, but more likely alkali, a characteristic of certain soils in the arid parts of the West.

[8] Probably Little Sandy Creek.   [9] The date is Stuart's.

snow. They set forward on their bleak and toilsome way, keeping to the east-northeast, towards the lofty summit of a mountain, which it was necessary for them to cross. Before they reached its base they passed another large trail, steering a little to the right of the point of the mountain. This they presumed to have been made by another band of Crows, who had probably been hunting lower down on the Spanish River.

The severity of the weather compelled them to encamp at the end of fifteen miles, on the skirts of the mountain,[10] where they found sufficient dry aspen trees to supply them with fire, but they sought in vain about the neighborhood for a spring or rill of water.[11]

At daybreak they were up and on the march, scrambling up the mountain side for the distance of eight painful miles.[12] From the casual hints given in the travelling memoranda of Mr. Stuart, this mountain would seem to offer a rich field of speculation for the geologist. Here was a plain three miles in diameter, strewed with pumice stones and other volcanic reliques, with a lake[13] in the centre, occupying what had probably been the crater. Here were also, in some places, deposits of marine

[10] Stuart's entry for this date includes the phrase "on the side of a lofty mountain." In contrast to the "Travelling Memoranda," his original "Journal" has the phrase "on the side of a hill." They were now at the western approach to South Pass, which looks more like a long, sloping hill than like a lofty mountain, in spite of its elevation of 7,550 feet at the summit. The broad recess forming South Pass is bounded on the north by the tapering-off remnants of the southern extremity of the Wind River Mountains, and on the south by the comparatively much lower Antelope Hills. It was toward the Antelope Hills that Stuart was now heading.

[11] This means that they had not yet come to Pacific Spring or Pacific Creek, which flows down the west slope of South Pass. The next morning, October 22, Stuart wrote: "We set out at day light, and ascended about three miles, when we found a spring of excellent water, and breakfasted." Rollins, 164; Spaulding, 122. This was Pacific Spring, later a famous campsite on the Oregon-California Trail.

[12] According to Stuart, they scrambled, but not painfully. In any case, the sentence can only mean that they ascended the north slope of Antelope Hills. By no stretch of the imagination would one have to "scramble" to the summit of South Pass, so gradual is the grade. The logic of the topography should have taken Stuart directly over the summit of South Pass, which would have led him, within a short distance, to the Sweetwater River. The most likely explanation as to why he did not follow this route is that by moving to the south slope of Antelope Hills he would be out of danger of meeting the Crows, whose traces led through South Pass.

[13] Stuart mentions "a considerable lake." The only permanent lake now appearing on maps is Picket Lake, although this may be too far east. See Map of the State of Wyoming, U.S. Department of the Interior, Geological Survey, 1927. Rollins suggests, p. 183, note 151, subnote 4, that it was possibly "a shallow ephemeral product of torren-

shells, indicating that this mountain crest had at some remote period been below the waves.

After pausing to repose, and to enjoy these grand but savage and awful scenes, they began to descend the eastern side of the mountain.[14] The descent was rugged and romantic, along deep ravines and defiles, overhung with crags and cliffs, among which they beheld numbers of the ahsahta or bighorn, skipping fearlessly from rock to rock. Two of them they succeeded in bringing down with their rifles, as they peered fearlessly from the brow of their airy precipices.

Arrived at the foot of the mountain, the travellers found a rill of water oozing out of the earth, and resembling in look and taste, the water of the Missouri. Here they encamped for the night, and supped sumptuously upon their mountain mutton, which they found in good condition, and extremely well tasted.

The morning[15] was bright, and intensely cold. Early in the day they came upon a stream running to the east, between low hills of bluish earth, strongly impregnated with copperas.[16] Mr. Stuart supposed this to be one of the head waters of the Missouri, and determined to follow its banks. After a march of twenty-six miles, however, he arrived at the summit of a hill,[17] the prospect of which induced him to alter his intention. He beheld, in every direction south of east, a vast plain,[18] bounded only by the horizon, through which wandered the stream in question, in a south-southeast direction. It could not, therefore, be a branch of the Missouri. He now gave up all idea of taking the stream for his guide,

tial rain or snow." If this were actually the case, it seems doubtful that Stuart could have referred to it as he did. Picket Lake, near the southern boundary of Fremont County, best answers the description.

[14] The Antelope Hills extend in a northeasterly direction. One could, therefore, speak of descending the eastern side. The phrase, however, is Irving's. Stuart says only that they descended "to the base of the mountain."

[15] October 23.

[16] Part of this sentence—"between low hills of bluish earth, strongly impregnated with copperas"—follows a statement in the "Travelling Memoranda" for October 23 that was incorrectly interpolated from the original "Journal" entry for October 22. Cf. Rollins, 164, 165, and 184, n. 165.

The stream to which Irving refers may have been Sand Creek, which is Rollins' identification. If correct, this would rule out Picket Lake (see note 13 above). Numerous intermittent creeks are in the area, however, and positive identification is difficult.

[17] "This hill we called discovery knob," wrote Stuart for October 23.

[18] Great Divide Basin. Stuart saw the monotonous desert waste lying north and south of what is now U.S. 30 between Rawlins and Rock Springs, Wyoming.

and shaped his course towards a range of mountains[19] in the east, about sixty miles distant, near which he hoped to find another stream.

The weather was now so severe, and the hardships of travelling so great, that he resolved to halt for the winter, at the first eligible place. That night they had to encamp on the open prairie, near a scanty pool of water, and without any wood to make a fire. The northeast wind blew keenly across the naked waste, and they were fain to decamp from their inhospitable bivouac before the dawn.

For two days they kept on in an eastward direction, against wintry blasts and occasional snow-storms. They suffered, also, from scarcity of water, having occasionally to use melted snow; this, with the want of pasturage, reduced their old pack-horse sadly. They saw many tracks of buffalo, and some few bulls, which, however, got the wind of them, and scampered off.[20]

On the 26th of October,[21] they steered east-northeast, for a wooded ravine in a mountain, at a small distance from the base of which, to their great joy, they discovered an abundant stream, running between willowed banks.[22] Here they halted for the night, and Ben Jones having luckily trapped a beaver, and killed two buffalo bulls, they remained all the next day encamped, feasting and reposing, and allowing their jaded horse to rest from his labors.

The little stream on which they were encamped, was one of the head waters[23] of the Platte River, which flows into the Missouri; it was, in fact, the northern fork,[24] or branch of that river, though this the trav-

---

[19] Green Mountains.

[20] This paragraph condenses Stuart's entries for October 24 and 25. On the twenty-fourth they traveled east by north twenty-seven miles over level ground but in high wind and severe snow. Their only fuel was buffalo chips. The next day "on the whole was mild and pleasant." They breakfasted on a small creek, traveled thirty-two miles east, and camped that night without fuel or water. This would put them a short distance west of what is now U.S. 287 and just below Green Mountain.

[21] The date is confirmed by Stuart.

[22] Stuart's entry for October 26, "a Creek (with muddy banks, and a great abundance of Willow) running N.N.W.," identifies their location as Muddy Creek directly east of present-day Bairoil, Wyoming, ten miles southeast of Muddy Gap. Where they camped, the creek runs northwest before turning north through Muddy Gap and then northeast to flow into the Sweetwater.

[23] Muddy Creek is a tributary of the Sweetwater River, which in turn is a tributary of North Platte River. They remained here until early on October 28.

[24] Northern fork only in the sense that Muddy Creek and the Sweetwater were affluents of the North Platte.

ellers did not discover until long afterwards. Pursuing the course of this stream for about twenty miles,[25] they came to where it forced a passage[26] through a range of high hills, covered with cedars, into an extensive low country,[27] affording excellent pasture to numerous herds of buffalo. Here they killed three cows, which were the first they had been able to get, having hitherto had to content themselves with bull beef, which at this season of the year is very poor. The hump meat afforded them a repast fit for an epicure.[28]

Late on the afternoon of the 30th, they came to where the stream,

[25] Irving's error for ten miles, which Stuart specifically states for October 28.

[26] Muddy Gap. U.S. 287 now passes through this opening.

[27] The valley of the Sweetwater, which Stuart truly described as "a handsome plain." They now moved ahead to the Sweetwater proper. Here they were on ground later to be traversed by the Oregon-California Trail, from which route they had departed on the western approach to South Pass. They could not at the time have possibly foreseen the great importance of the area in which they now stood or the momentous nature of the pass which they had circumvented. The fact of their having bypassed its summit meant that it had to be discovered at a later time. For twelve years no white men are known to have walked over that natural corridor until February, 1824, when a band of Ashley's trappers led by Jedediah Smith made their way over from the east. The record is in the words of James Clyman, one of the party. See *James Clyman, Frontiersman* (ed. by Charles L. Camp), 24–25. Cf. Dale L. Morgan, *Jedediah Smith and the Opening of the West*, 90–93.

Later, in 1856, when Frémont's backers were pushing him for the presidency and claiming that he discovered South Pass, Ramsay Crooks countered their claim by writing to the Detroit *Free Press* on June 28 of that year and asserting that the Stuart party were first to accomplish this feat. See Harrison C. Dale, "Did the Returning Astorians Use the South Pass? A Letter of Ramsay Crooks," *Oregon Historical Quarterly*, Vol. XVII (1916), 47–51.

[28] Irving ignores all of Stuart's entry for October 29 except the part about their killing the buffalo. It is worthy of being introduced here: "The river [Sweetwater], after running 3 miles nearly south, forced a passage [Devil's Gate, now on the Tom Sun ranch] through a high range of hills, covered with cedars, into an immense low country [south of Rattle Snake Range and north of what is today Wyoming 220], affording excellent pasture for the numerous herds of Buffalo with which it abounded. . . . after following the river 17 miles [*10 miles* in "Journal"] E.N.E. we camped among a few large white willows—To the North the plain is bounded by low bare ridges, but towards the south they are much higher, very rugged, and covered with a few Cedars—[.]" Rollins, 187; Spaulding, 126.

The most prominent feature of this plain is Independence Rock, lying on the north side of the river and in the years after Stuart's journey a favorite campsite and landmark for trappers and emigrants, whose inscriptions in the granite can in some places still be seen. In view of what Stuart says about his mileage, he camped somewhere east of here. Numerous willow groves are still to be seen today along the meandering course of the Sweetwater in this area. For a parallel description, see Frémont, *Report of the Exploring Expedition to the Rocky Mountains*, 56–57, 71–72.

now increased to a considerable size, poured along in a ravine between precipices of red stone, two hundred feet in height.[29] For some distance it dashed along, over huge masses of rock, with foaming violence, as if exasperated by being compressed into so narrow a channel, and at length leaped down a chasm that looked dark and frightful in the gathering twilight.

For a part of the next day, the wild river, in its capricious wanderings, led them through a variety of striking scenes. At one time they were upon high plains, like platforms among the mountains, with herds of buffaloes roaming about them; at another, among rude rocky defiles, broken into cliffs and precipices, where the black-tailed deer bounded off among the crags, and the bighorn basked in the sunny brow of the precipice.

In the after part of the day, they came to another scene, surpassing in savage grandeur those already described. They had been travelling for some distance through a pass of the mountains, keeping parallel with the river, as it roared along, out of sight, through a deep ravine. Sometimes their devious path approached the margin of cliffs below which the river foamed, and boiled, and whirled among the masses of rock that had fallen into its channel. As they crept cautiously on, leading their solitary pack-horse along these giddy heights, they all at once came to where the river thundered down a succession of precipices, throwing up clouds of spray, and making a prodigious din and uproar. The travellers remained, for a time, gazing with mingled awe and delight, at this furious cataract, to which Mr. Stuart gave, from the color of the impending rocks, the name of "the Fiery Narrows."[30]

[29] Stuart's "Travelling Memoranda" incorrectly gives five hundred feet instead of three hundred, which appears in his "Journal." Irving reduces the height still further. The date is Stuart's.

[30] The Fiery Narrows lies to the west of Alcova Dam. The upper end of the chasm that Stuart describes forms part of Pathfinder Reservoir. For an excellent description and an account of shooting these rapids in a rubber boat, see Frémont, *op. cit.*, 72–77.

For this chapter, Irving paraphrases Stuart's "Travelling Memoranda" for October 19 to 31. Rollins, 162–88; Spaulding, 120–27.

Wintry Storms — A Halt and Council
Cantonment for the Winter — Fine Hunting Country
Game of the Mountains and Plains — Successful Hunting
Mr. Crooks and a Grizzly Bear — The Wigwam — Bighorn and Black-Tails
Beef and Venison — Good Quarters and Good Cheer — An Alarm
An Intrusion — Unwelcome Guests — Desolation of the Larder
Gormandizing Exploits of Hungry Savages
Good Quarters Abandoned

THE travellers encamped for the night on the banks of the river[1] below the cataract. The night was cold, with partial showers of rain and sleet. The morning[2] dawned gloomily, the skies were sullen and overcast, and threatened further storms; but the little band resumed their journey, in defiance of the weather. The increasing rigor of the season, however, which makes itself felt early in these mountainous regions, and on these naked and elevated plains, brought them to a pause, and a serious deliberation, after they had descended about thirty miles further along the course of the river.

All were convinced that it was in vain to attempt to accomplish their journey on foot at this inclement season. They had still many hundred miles to traverse before they should reach the main course of the Missouri, and their route would lay [*sic*] over immense prairies, naked and bleak, and destitute of fuel. The question then was, where to choose their wintering place, and whether or not to proceed further down the river. They had at first imagined it to be one of the head waters, or tributary streams, of the Missouri. Afterwards they had believed it to be the Rapid, or Quicourt River,[3] in which opinion they had not come nearer to the truth; they now, however, were persuaded, with equal fallacy, by its inclining somewhat to the north of east, that it was the Cheyenne. If so, by continuing down it much further they must arrive among the Indians, from whom the river takes its name. Among these they would be sure to meet some of the Sioux tribe. These would apprise their rela-

[1] North Platte River.   [2] November 1.
[3] Niobrara River. *The* is lacking in the first edition.

tives, the piratical Sioux of the Missouri, of the approach of a band of white traders; so that, in the spring time, they would be likely to be waylaid and robbed on their way down the river, by some party in ambush upon its banks.

Even should this prove to be the Quicourt or Rapid River, it would not be prudent to winter much further down upon its banks, as, though they might be out of the range of the Sioux, they would be in the neighborhood of the Poncas, a tribe nearly as dangerous. It was resolved, therefore, since they must winter somewhere on this side of the Missouri, to descend no lower, but to keep up in these solitary regions, where they would be in no danger of molestation.

They were brought the more promptly and unanimously to this decision, by coming upon an excellent wintering place, that promised everything requisite for their comfort. It was on a fine bend[4] of the river, just below where it issued out from among a ridge of mountains, and bent towards the northeast. Here was a beautiful low point of land, covered by cotton-wood, and surrounded by a thick growth of willow, so as to yield both shelter and fuel, as well as materials for building. The river swept by in a strong current, about a hundred and fifty yards wide. To the southeast were mountains of moderate height, the nearest about two miles off, but the whole chain ranging to the east, south, and southwest, as far as the eye could reach. Their summits were crowned with extensive tracts of pitch pine, checkered with small patches of the quivering aspen. Lower down were thick forests of firs and red cedars, growing out in many places from the very fissures of the rocks. The mountains were broken and precipitous, with huge bluffs protruding from among the forests. Their rock recesses, and beetling cliffs, afforded retreats to innumerable flocks of the bighorn, while their woody summits and ravines abounded with bears and black-tailed deer. These, with the numerous herds of buffalo that ranged the lower grounds along the river, promised the travellers abundant cheer in their winter quarters.

On the 2d of November,[5] therefore, they pitched their camp for the winter, on the woody point, and their first thought was to obtain a supply of provisions. Ben Jones and the two Canadians accordingly

[4] Bessemer Bend. They were about eleven miles southwest of modern Casper, Wyoming. Four miles south of the campsite, on Wyoming 220, a granite marker commemorates their stay. It reads: "On bend of North Platte visible to the north Robert Stuart in 1812 erected the first white man's cabin in Wyoming."

[5] The date is confirmed by Stuart.

sallied forth, accompanied by two others of the party, leaving but one to watch the camp. Their hunting was uncommonly successful. In the course of two days, they killed thirty-two buffaloes, and collected their meat on the margin of a small brook, about a mile distant. Fortunately, a severe frost froze the river, so that the meat was easily transported to the encampment. On a succeeding day, a herd of buffalo came trampling through the woody bottom on the river banks, and fifteen more were killed.

It was soon discovered, however, that there was game of a more dangerous nature in the neighborhood. On one occasion, Mr. Crooks had wandered about a mile from the camp, and had ascended a small hill commanding a view of the river. He was without his rifle, a rare circumstance, for in these wild regions, where one may put up a wild animal, or a wild Indian, at every turn, it is customary never to stir from the camp-fire unarmed. The hill where he stood overlooked the place where the massacre of the buffalo had taken place. As he was looking around on the prospect, his eye was caught by an object below, moving directly towards him. To his dismay, he discovered it to be a grizzly bear, with two cubs. There was no tree at hand into which he could climb; to run, would only be to provoke pursuit, and he should soon be overtaken. He threw himself on the ground, therefore, and lay motionless, watching the movements of the animal with intense anxiety. It continued to advance until at the foot of the hill, when it turned, and made into the woods, having probably gorged itself with buffalo flesh. Mr. Crooks made all haste back to the camp, rejoicing at his escape, and determining never to stir out again without his rifle. A few days after this circumstance, a grizzly bear was shot in the neighborhood, by Mr. Miller.[6]

As the slaughter of so many buffalos had provided the party with beef for the winter, in case they met with no further supply, they now set to work, heart and hand, to build a comfortable wigwam.[7] In a little while the woody promontory rang with the unwonted sound of the axe. Some of its lofty trees were laid low, and by the second evening the cabin was complete. It was eight feet wide, and eighteen feet long. The walls were six feet high, and the whole was covered with buffalo skins.

[6] For a discussion of Crooks and the grizzly bear, an incident not recorded in the "Travelling Memoranda," see Editor's Introduction, xxxiv–xxxv.

[7] On November 8, Stuart wrote: "Commenced building our hut—the weather disagreeably cold—[.]" Rollins, 191; Spaulding, 130.

The fireplace was in the centre, and the smoke found its way out by a hole in the roof.[8]

The hunters were next sent out to procure deer-skins for garments, moccasins, and other purposes. They made the mountains echo with their rifles, and, in the course of two days' hunting,[9] killed twenty-eight bighorns and black-tailed deer.

The party now reveled in abundance. After all that they had suffered from hunger, cold, fatigue and watchfulness; after all their perils from treacherous and savage men, they exulted in the snugness and security of their isolated cabin, hidden, as they thought, even from the prying eyes of Indian scouts, and stored with creature comforts; and they looked forward to a winter of peace and quietness; of roasting, and boiling, and broiling, and feasting upon venison, and mountain mutton, and bear's meat, and marrow bones, and buffalo humps, and other hunter's dainties, and of dozing and reposing round their fire, and gossiping over past dangers and adventures, and telling long hunting stories, until spring should return; when they would make canoes of buffalo skins and float themselves down the river.[10]

From such halcyon dreams, they were startled one morning,[11] at day-break, by a savage yell. They started up and seized their rifles. The yell[12] was repeated by two or three voices. Cautiously peeping out, they beheld, to their dismay, several Indian warriors among the trees, all armed and painted in warlike style; being evidently bent on some hostile purpose.

Miller changed countenance as he regarded them. "We are in trouble," said he, "these are some of the rascally Arapahays[13] that robbed me last year." Not a word was uttered by the rest of the party, but they

[8] This description of the cabin conforms to details recorded by Stuart under the date of November 10.

[9] On November 11 and 12.

[10] In deciding to make this their winter quarters, Stuart wrote on November 2 that they would "leave it on the opening of navigation, in one or perhaps two Buffalo hide Canoes, till which time we are in hopes of living in peace and quiet, without being honoured with the intrusive visits of our savage neighbors—[.]" Rollins, 190; Spaulding, 129. Such hide boats were known as "bull boats." Irving himself crossed the Arkansas River in one; see *A Tour on the Prairies*, chap. XII. Irving's description in the above paragraph is perhaps justifiable license, although nothing of the sort was recorded by Stuart.

[11] December 10.   [12] *Yelp* here and above in the first edition.

[13] Arapahos.

414

silently slung their powder horns and ball pouches, and prepared for battle. M'Lellan, who had taken his gun to pieces the evening before, put it together in all haste. He proposed that they should break out the clay from between the logs, so as to be able to fire upon the enemy.

"Not yet," replied Stuart; "it will not do to show fear or distrust; we must first hold a parley. Some one must go out and meet them as a friend."

Who was to undertake the task! It was full of peril, as the envoy might be shot down at the threshold.

"The leader of a party," said Miller, "always takes the advance."

"Good!" replied Stuart; "I am ready." He immediately went forth; one of the Canadians followed him; the rest of the party remained in the garrison, to keep the savages in check.[14]

Stuart advanced holding his rifle in one hand, and extending the other to the savage that appeared to be the chief. The latter stepped forward and took it; his men followed his example, and all shook hands with Stuart, in token of friendship. They now explained their errand. They were a war party of Arapahay braves. Their village lay on a stream[15] several days' journey to the eastward. It had been attacked and ravaged during their absence, by a band of Crows, who had carried off several of their women, and most of their horses. They were in quest of vengeance. For sixteen days they had been tracking the Crows about the mountains, but had not yet come upon them. In the meantime, they had met with scarcely any game, and were half famished. About two days previously, they had heard the report of fire-arms among the mountains, and on searching in the direction of the sound, had come to a place where a deer had been killed. They had immediately put themselves upon the track of the hunters, and by following it up, had arrived at the cabin.

Mr. Stuart now invited the chief and another, who appeared to be his lieutenant, into the hut, but made signs that no one else was to enter. The rest halted at the door; others came straggling up, until the whole party, to the number of twenty-three, were gathered before the hut. They were armed with bows and arrows, tomahawks and scalping-

[14] Irving supplies all the dialogue plus the decision that Stuart should go out to meet the Indians. What really occurred is shown in what Stuart wrote: "Seizing our arms we rushed out." Rollins, 192; Spaulding, 132.

[15] From what Stuart wrote, it is evident the stream was the South Platte.

knives, and some few with guns.[16] All were painted and dressed for war, and had a wild and fierce appearance. Mr. Miller recognized among them some of the very fellows who had robbed him in the preceding year; and put his comrades upon their guard. Every man stood ready to resist the first act of hostility; the savages, however, conducted themselves peaceably, and showed none of that swaggering arrogance which a war party is apt to assume.

On entering the hut the chief and his lieutenant cast a wistful look at the rafters, laden with venison and buffalo meat.[17] Mr. Stuart made a merit of necessity, and invited them to help themselves. They did not wait to be pressed. The rafters were soon eased of their burden; venison and beef were passed out to the crew before the door, and a scene of gormandizing commenced, of which few can have an idea, who have not witnessed the gastronomic powers of an Indian, after an interval of fasting. This was kept up throughout the day; they paused now and then, it is true, for a brief interval, but only to return to the charge with renewed ardor. The chief and the lieutenant surpassed all the rest in the vigor and perseverance of their attacks; as if from their station they were bound to signalize themselves in all onslaughts. Mr. Stuart kept them well supplied with choice bits, for it was his policy to overfeed them, and keep them from leaving the hut, where they served as hostages for the good conduct of their followers. Once, only, in the course of the day, did the chief sally forth.[18] Mr. Stuart and one of his men[19] accompanied him, armed with their rifles, but without betraying any distrust. The chieftain soon returned, and renewed his attack upon the larder. In a word, he and his worthy coadjutor, the lieutenant, ate until they were both stupefied.

Towards evening the Indians made their preparations for the night according to the practice of war parties. Those outside of the hut threw up two breastworks, into which they retired at a tolerably early hour, and slept like overfed hounds. As to the chief and his lieutenants, they passed the night in the hut, in the course of which, they, two or three times, got up to eat. The travellers took turns, one at a time, to mount guard until the morning.

[16] Stuart makes no mention of their weapons.

[17] The sentence is a reasonable inference, but there is no support for it in Stuart's account. The first edition erroneously has *willful* for *wistful*.

[18] This detail is absent in Stuart's account.

[19] *The men* in first edition.

Scarce had the day dawned, when the gormandizing[20] was renewed by the whole band, and carried on with surprising vigor until ten o'clock, when all prepared to depart. They had six days' journey to make, they said, before they should come up with the Crows, who, they understood, were encamped on a river to the northward. Their way lay through a hungry country where there was no game; they would, moreover, have but little time to hunt; they, therefore, craved a small supply of provisions for their journey. Mr. Stuart again invited them to help themselves. They did so with keen forethought, loading themselves with the choicest parts of the meat, and leaving the late plenteous larder far gone in a consumption. Their next request was for a supply of ammunition, having guns, but no powder and ball. They promised to pay magnificently out of the spoils of their foray. "We are poor now," said they, "and are obliged to go on foot, but we shall soon come back laden with booty, and all mounted on horseback, with scalps hanging at our bridles. We will then give each of you a horse to keep you from being tired on your journey."

"Well," said Mr. Stuart, "when you bring the horses, you shall have the ammunition, but not before."[21] The Indians saw by his determined tone, that all further entreaty would be unavailing, so they desisted, with a good-humored laugh, and went off exceedingly well freighted, both within and without, promising to be back again in the course of a fortnight.[22]

No sooner were they out of hearing, than the luckless travellers held another council. The security of their cabin was at an end, and with it all their dreams of a quiet and cozey winter. They were between two fires. On one side were their old enemies, the Crows; on the other side, the Arapahays, no less dangerous freebooters. As to the moderation of this war party, they considered it assumed, to put them off their guard against some more favorable opportunity for a surprisal. It was determined, therefore, not to await their return, but to abandon, with all speed, this dangerous neighborhood.[23] From the accounts[24] of their re-

---

[20] All the gormandizing is supported by only one brief statement in Stuart: "They all ate voraciously."

[21] The dialogue is supplied by Irving.

[22] Stuart expected them to return, but he said nothing about a fortnight. Except as noted, Irving presents the details of the visit of the Arapahos as reported by Stuart.

[23] "We determined," Stuart wrote on December 11, "to abandon our Chateau of indolence as soon as we can finish the dressing of a sufficiency of leather for Mogasins

cent visitors, they were led to believe, though erroneously, that they were upon the Quicourt, or Rapid River. They proposed now to keep along it to its confluence with the Missouri; but, should they be prevented by the rigors of the season from proceeding so far, at least to reach a part of the river where they might be able to construct canoes of greater strength and durability than those of buffalo skins.

Accordingly, on the 13th of December,[25] they bade adieu, with many a regret, to their comfortable quarters where for five weeks they had been indulging the sweets of repose, of plenty, and of fancied security. They were still accompanied by their veteran pack-horse, which the Arapahays had omitted to steal, either because they intended to steal him on their return, or because they thought him not worth stealing.[26]

&ct., that we may be the better able to withstand the severity of the winter—[.]" Rollins, 193; Spaulding, 133. They finished dressing their leather by the next evening.

[24] Stuart relates that the Indians gave them a map.

[25] The date is confirmed by Stuart.

[26] This chapter paraphrases Stuart's "Travelling Memoranda" for October 31 through December 13. Rollins, 188–93; Spaulding, 127–34. There is a hiatus in the record from November 13 to December 9.

Rough Wintry Travelling — Hills and Plains
Snow and Ice — Disappearance of Game
A Vast Dreary Plain — A Second Halt for the Winter — Another Wigwam
New-Year's Feast — Buffalo Humps, Tongues, and Marrow Bones
Return of Spring — Launch of Canoes — Bad Navigation
Pedestrian March — Vast Prairies — Deserted Camps
Pawnee Squaws — An Otto Indian — News of War
Voyage down the Platte and the Missouri
Reception at Fort Osage — Arrival at St. Louis

THE interval of comfort and repose which the party had enjoyed in their wigwam, rendered the renewal of their fatigues intolerable for the first two or three days. The snow lay deep, and was slightly frozen on the surface, but not sufficiently to bear their weight. Their feet became sore by breaking through the crust, and their limbs weary by floundering on without firm foothold. So exhausted and dispirited were they, that they began to think it would be better to remain and run the risk of being killed by the Indians, than to drag on thus painfully, with the probability of perishing by the way.[1] Their miserable horse fared no better than themselves, having for the first day or two no other fodder than the ends of willow twigs, and the bark of the cotton-wood tree.

They all, however, appeared to gain patience and hardihood as they proceeded, and for fourteen days kept steadily on, making a distance of about three hundred and thirty miles. For some days, the range of mountains[2] which had been near to their wigwam kept parallel to the river at no great distance, but at length subsided into hills.[3] Sometimes they found the river bordered with alluvial bottoms, and groves with cotton-wood and willows; sometimes the adjacent country was naked and barren. In one place it ran for a considerable distance between rocky hills and promontories covered with cedar and pitch pines, and peopled with

---

[1] Details are from the "Travelling Memoranda," December 14.

[2] Haystack Range and Deer Creek Range, the northern extremity of the Laramie Mountains.

[3] "Travelling Memoranda," December 16.

Returning Astorians, December 13, 1812–April 30, 1813

the bighorn and the mountain deer; at other places it wandered through
prairies well stocked with buffaloes and antelopes. As they descended
the course of the river, they began to perceive the ash and white oak[4]
here and there among the cotton-wood and willow; and at length caught
a sight of some wild horses on the distant prairies.

The weather was various; at one time the snow lay deep; then they
had a genial day or two, with the mildness and serenity of autumn; then,
again, the frost was so severe that the river was sufficiently frozen to
bear them upon the ice.

During the last three days of their fortnight's travel, however, the
face of the country changed. The timber gradually diminished, until
they could scarcely find fuel sufficient for culinary purposes.[5] The game
grew more and more scanty, and, finally, none were to be seen but a few
miserable broken-down buffalo bulls, not worth killing. The snow lay
fifteen inches deep, and made the travelling grievously painful and toilsome. At length they came to an immense plain, where no vestige of
timber was to be seen; nor a single quadruped to enliven the desolate
landscape.[6] Here, then, their hearts failed them, and they held another
consultation. The width of the river, which was upwards of a mile, its
extreme shallowness, the frequency of quicksands, and various other

[4] *Ibid.*, December 20.

[5] *Ibid.*, December 25. What Stuart wrote was: "[We] were so fortunate as to find
drift wood enough for culinary purposes." Rollins, 196; Spaulding, 138.

[6] "Travelling Memoranda," December 26.

characteristics, had at length made them sensible of their errors with respect to it, and they now came to the correct conclusion, that they were on the banks of the Platte or Shallow River. What were they to do? Pursue its course to the Missouri? To go on at this season of the year seemed dangerous in the extreme. There was no prospect of obtaining either food or firing. The country was destitute of trees, and though there might be drift-wood along the river, it lay too deep beneath the snow for them to find it.

The weather was threatening a change, and a snow-storm on these boundless wastes might prove as fatal as a whirlwind of sand on an Arabian desert. After much dreary deliberation, it was at length determined to retrace their three last days' journey, of seventy-seven miles, to a place which they had remarked where there was a sheltering growth of forest trees, and a country abundant in game.[7] Here they would once more set up their winter quarters, and await the opening of the navigation to launch themselves in canoes.

Accordingly, on the 27th of December,[8] they faced about, retraced their steps, and on the 30th, regained the part of the river in question. Here the alluvial bottom was from one to two miles wide, and thickly covered with a forest of cotton-wood trees; while herds of buffalo were scattered about the neighboring prairie, several of which soon fell beneath their rifles.

They encamped[9] on the margin of the river, in a grove where there were trees large enough for canoes. Here they put up a shed for immediate shelter, and immediately proceeded to erect a hut.[10] New-Year's day[11] dawned when, as yet, but one wall of their cabin was completed; the genial and jovial day, however, was not permitted to pass uncelebrated, even by this weather-beaten crew of wanderers. All work was suspended, except that of roasting and boiling. The choicest [parts] of the buffalo meat, with tongues, and humps, and marrow bones, were

[7] This decision was reached on December 27. In the meantime they had passed the Laramie River and had proceeded into what is now western Nebraska.

[8] On this date, according to Stuart, they went back twenty-six miles.

[9] On the basis of Stuart's mileage and statements, they camped on the north side of the North Platte near modern Torrington, Wyoming, on December 30.

[10] Stuart wrote on December 31: "[We] took up our residence close to the bank, and by the middle of the day we had a shelter made and our meat scaffolded—Began building our hut, one side of which we raised before dusk." Rollins, 198; Spaulding, 140.

[11] January 1, 1813.

devoured in quantities that would astonish any one that has not lived among hunters or Indians; and as an extra regale, having no tobacco left, they cut up an old tobacco pouch,[12] still redolent with the potent herb, and smoked it in honor of the day. Thus for a time, in present revelry, however uncouth, they forgot all past troubles and all anxieties about the future, and their forlorn wigwam echoed to the sound of gayety.

The next day they resumed their labors, and by the 6th of the month it was complete. They soon killed abundance of buffalo,[13] and again laid in a stock of winter provisions.

The party were more fortunate in this their second cantonment. The winter passed away without any Indian visitors, and the game continued to be plenty in the neighborhood. They felled two large trees,[14] and shaped them into canoes; and, as the spring opened, and a thaw of several days' continuance melted the ice in the river, they made every preparation for embarking. On the 8th of March[15] they launched forth in their canoes, but soon found that the river had not depth sufficient even for such slender barks. It expanded into a wide but extremely shallow stream, with many sand-bars, and occasionally various channels. They got one of their canoes a few miles[16] down it, with extreme difficulty, sometimes wading, and dragging it over the shoals; at length they had to abandon the attempt,[17] and to resume their journey on foot, aided by their faithful old pack-horse, who had recruited strength during the repose of the winter.

The weather delayed them for a few days, having suddenly become more rigorous than it had been at any time during the winter; but on the 20th of March[18] they were again on their journey.

In two days they arrived at the vast naked prairie, the wintry aspect of which had caused them, in December, to pause and turn back. It was now clothed in the early verdure of spring, and plentifully stocked with

[12] McClellan's pouch was sacrificed.

[13] Seventeen on January 7.

[14] On January 9. Stuart says that all were hollow and that they selected the two best.

[15] A hiatus occurs in Stuart's "Travelling Memoranda" from January 10 to March 6. He resumed writing on March 7 and recorded their departure on the eighth.

[16] Only eight miles.

[17] On March 22. Their journey by land was along the left, or north, bank in what is now Nebraska.

[18] The date is confirmed by Stuart.

game. Still, when obliged to bivouac on its bare surface, without any shelter, and by a scanty fire of dry buffalo dung, they found the night blasts piercing cold. On one occasion, a herd of buffalo straying near their evening camp, they killed three of them merely for their hides, wherewith to make a shelter for the night.[19]

They continued on for upwards of a hundred miles; with vast prairies extending before them as they advanced; sometimes diversified by undulating hills, but destitute of trees. In one place they saw a gang of sixty-five wild horses,[20] but as to the buffaloes, they seemed absolutely to cover the country. Wild geese abounded, and they passed extensive swamps that were alive with innumerable flocks of waterfowl, among which were a few swans, but an endless variety of ducks.[21]

The river continued a winding course to the east-northeast, nearly a mile in width, but too shallow to float even an empty canoe.[22] The country spread out into a vast level plain, bounded by the horizon alone, excepting to the north, where a line of hills seemed like a long promontory stretching into the bosom of the ocean. The dreary sameness of the prairie wastes began to grow extremely irksome. The travellers longed for the sight of a forest, or grove, or single tree, to break the level uniformity, and began to notice every object that gave reason to hope they were drawing towards the end of this weary wilderness. Thus the occurrence of a particular kind of grass was hailed as a proof that they could not be far from the bottoms of the Missouri; and they were rejoiced at putting up several prairie hens, a kind of grouse seldom found far in the interior.[23] In picking up drift-wood for fuel, also, they found on some pieces the mark of an axe, which caused much speculation as to the time when and the persons by whom the trees had been felled. Thus they went on, like sailors at sea, who perceive in every floating weed and wandering bird, harbingers of the wished-for land.[24]

[19] This was on March 25. They remained in this camp all day because Miller's feet were too blistered to permit walking, the wind was bitter cold, and everyone needed a rest.

[20] On the next day, March 26.   [21] Stuart records this on March 27.

[22] Stuart's observation on March 28.   [23] Stuart's observation on March 27.

[24] Stuart refers to the ax marks on March 29. The simile comparing the men to sailors is suggested by Stuart's remark on the same date that the surrounding country resembled the ocean. To the south at this time they became aware of the existence of a large river. This was the South Platte. They came to its confluence with the North Platte the next day, but only the hunters could see it from the hilltops.

By the close of the month the weather became very mild, and, heavily burdened as they were, they found the noontide temperature uncomfortably warm. On the 30th,[25] they came to three deserted hunting camps, either of Pawnees or Ottoes, about which were buffalo skulls in all directions; and the frames on which the hides had been stretched and cured. They had apparently been occupied the preceding autumn.

For several days they kept patiently on, watching every sign that might give them an idea as to where they were, and how near to the banks of the Missouri.

Though there were numerous traces of hunting parties and encampments, they were not of recent date. The country seemed deserted. The only human beings they met with were three Pawnee squaws, in a hut in the midst of a deserted camp. Their people had all gone to the south, in pursuit of the buffalo, and had left these poor women behind, being too sick and infirm to travel.

It is a common practice with the Pawnees, and probably with other roving tribes, when departing on a distant expedition, which will not admit of incumbrance or delay, to leave their aged and infirm with a supply of provisions sufficient for a temporary subsistence.[26] When this is exhausted, they must perish; though sometimes their sufferings are abridged by hostile prowlers who may visit the deserted camp.

The poor squaws in question expected some such fate at the hands of the white strangers, and though the latter accosted them in the kindest manner, and made them presents of dried buffalo meat, it was impossible to soothe their alarm, or get any information from them.[27]

The first landmark by which the travellers were enabled to conjecture their position with any degree of confidence, was an island about seventy miles in length, which they presumed to be Grand Isle.[28] If so, they were within one hundred and forty miles of the Missouri. They kept on, therefore, with renewed spirit, and at the end of three days met

[25] The date is Stuart's.

[26] The first edition reads *for temporary subsistence*.

[27] Stuart records meeting them on April 3; cf. entry for April 8. Irving draws upon both.

[28] Grand Island, some forty miles long, formed by the river's dividing into two channels. French-Canadian trappers referred to it as *la grande île*. Stuart reached this point on April 6. But on March 30 they had reached another island, Brady's Island, which Stuart believed at the time was Grand Island. On the sixth he realized his error. Stuart estimated its length to be seventy-two miles and its width about twenty-four.

with an Otto Indian,[29] by whom they were confirmed in their conjecture. They learnt at the same time another piece of information, of an uncomfortable nature. According to his account, there was war between the United States and England, and in fact it had existed for a whole year, during which time they had been beyond the reach of all knowledge of the affairs of the civilized world.[30]

The Otto conducted the travellers to his village, situated a short distance from the banks of the Platte. Here they were delighted to meet with two white men, Messrs. Dornin and Roi, Indian traders recently from St. Louis.[31] Of these they had a thousand inquiries to make concerning all affairs, foreign and domestic, during their year of sepulture in the wilderness; and especially about the events of the existing war.

They now prepared to abandon their weary travel by land, and to embark upon the water. A bargain was made with Mr. Dornin, who engaged to furnish them with a canoe and provisions for the voyage, in exchange for their venerable and well-tried fellow-traveller, the old Snake horse.

Accordingly, in a couple of days, the Indians employed by that gentleman constructed for them a canoe twenty feet long, four feet wide, and eighteen inches deep.[32] The frame was of poles and willow twigs, on which were stretched five elk and buffalo hides, sewed together with sinews, and the seams payed with unctuous mud. In this they embarked at an early hour on the 16th of April,[33] and drifted down ten miles with

[29] The meeting occurred on April 11. Stuart sent Ramsay Crooks and Andre Valle with the Indian to his village "for the purpose of getting news and finding out exactly where we are—[.]" Rollins, 220; Spaulding, 156. Crooks and Valle overtook the main party early the next morning.

[30] The United States had declared war on England on June 18, 1812, eleven days before Stuart left Astoria. Although Stuart does not say specifically that they learned of the War of 1812 from the Oto Indians, Irving's inference is reasonable in light of Stuart's statement on April 13 that "Here [at the Oto village] we found Mr. F. [François] Dornin and Mr. Roi, who after a voyage of 6 weeks from St. Louis reached this place three weeks ago. . . . The disagreeable news of a war between America & Great Britain was here confirmed, but in such a confused manner was it related that we could comprehend but little [.]" Rollins, 235; Spaulding, 158.

[31] See note 30 above. Rollins, 241, n. 1, gives several variations for the name *Dornin*, such as Derouen, Deroin, and Derouin.

[32] The canoe was completed by the evening of April 15. On the fourteenth, cold weather delayed its construction, and the most they could do was to soak the hides in the river. Irving's description conforms in its details to Stuart's.

[33] The date is confirmed by Stuart.

the stream, when the wind being high they encamped, and set to work to make oars,[34] which they had not been able to procure at the Indian village.

Once more afloat, they went merrily down the stream, and after making thirty-five miles, emerged into the broad turbid current of the Missouri. Here they were borne along briskly by the rapid stream; though, by the time their fragile bark had floated a couple of hundred miles, its frame began to show the effects of the voyage.[35] Luckily they came to the deserted wintering place of some hunting party, where they found two old wooden canoes.[36] Taking possession of the largest, they again committed themselves to the current, and after dropping down fifty-five miles further, arrived safely at Fort Osage.

Here they found Lieutenant Brownson still in command; the officer who had given the expedition a hospitable reception on its way up the river, eighteen months previously. He received this remnant of the party with a cordial welcome, and endeavored in every way to promote their comfort and enjoyment during their sojourn at the fort. The greatest luxury they met with on their return to the abode of civilized man, was bread, not having tasted any for nearly a year.[37]

Their stay at Fort Osage was but short. On reëmbarking they were furnished with an ample supply of provisions by the kindness of Lieutenant Brownson, and performed the rest of their voyage without adverse circumstance. On the 30th of April they arrived in perfect health and fine spirits at St. Louis, having been ten months in performing[38]

---

[34] They stopped two miles below the Elkhorn River in eastern Nebraska and camped for the remainder of April 16. Here they stayed on April 17 because of high winds, and then left on the eighteenth.

[35] On April 19 they traveled sixty-five miles; on April 20 only twenty-seven because of poor weather; on April 21 sixty-three miles. On April 22 they sailed twenty miles and then stopped at ten o'clock in the morning to make a new frame for the canoe. See Stuart's entry for April 22.

[36] On April 23 after traveling sixty-eight miles. The same day, they covered an additional fifty-five miles and arrived in the afternoon at Fort Osage.

[37] Stuart gives a brief account of Fort Osage, which was at this time less than five years old. He records the hospitality of Lieutenant Brownson but says nothing about the luxury of bread. Here, he says, "we got satisfactory information of the melancholy truth of war having been waged since June last between the United States and Great Britain—[.]" Stuart's party remained until early on April 27 and then started out on the last stage of their journey "furnished . . . very generously with a sufficiency of Pork, Flour, &ct. to carry us to St. Louis." Rollins, 238; Spaulding, 161, 162.

[38] The first edition reads *ten months performing*.

this perilous expedition from Astoria.[39] Their return caused quite a sensation[40] at the place, bringing the first intelligence of the fortune of Mr. Hunt and his party, in their adventurous route across the Rocky Mountains, and of the new establishment on the shores of the Pacific.[41]

[39] Stuart's final entry, April 30, in the "Travelling Memoranda" concludes: "This day after descending 35 miles, we a little before sun set reached the Town of St. Louis, all in the most perfect health, after a voyage of ten months from Astoria, during which time we underwent many dangers, hardships, & fatigues, in short, I may say, all the privations human nature is capable of." Rollins, 240; Spaulding, 164. Stuart estimated the distance from Astoria to be 3,768 miles.

[40] The St. Louis *Missouri Gazette*, May 8, 1813, recorded the arrival of Stuart and his party in the following article: "Arrived here a few days ago from the mouth of the Columbia river, Mr. Robert Stuart, one of the partners of the Pacific Fur Company, accompanied by messrs. R. Crooks, Jos. Miller and Rob. M'Clellan, with three hunters. We learn that Mr. Stuart is bound to N. York with despatches. Next week we shall present our readers with an account of their journey from the Pacific Ocean to this place, a short narrative, which will evince to the world that a journey to the Western Sea will not be considered (within a few years) of much greater importance, than a trip to New York." From a facsimile in Spaulding, facing p. 162. See also Bradbury, *Travels*, 224–28, for the promised narrative. Both appear also in Flandrau, *Astor and the Oregon Country*, 41–46.

Stuart, after reaching St. Louis, soon left for New York, arriving there on June 23.

[41] In this chapter Irving paraphrases Stuart's "Travelling Memoranda" for December 14, 1812, through April 30, 1813. Rollins, 193–240; Spaulding, 134–64.

-❧{ C H A P T E R   L I }❧-

Agreement Between Mr. Astor and the Russian Fur Company
War Between the United States and Great Britain
Instructions to Captain Sowle of the Beaver
Fitting Out of the Lark — News of the Arrival of Mr. Stuart

IT is now necessary, in linking together the parts of this excursive narrative, that we notice the proceedings of Mr. Astor in support of his great undertaking. His project with respect to the Russian establishments along the northwest coast had been diligently prosecuted. The agent[1] sent by him to St. Petersburg, to negotiate in his name as president of the American Fur Company, had, under sanction of the Russian government, made a provisional agreement with the Russian company.[2]

By this agreement, which was ratified by Mr. Astor in 1813, the two companies bound themselves not to interfere with each other's trading and hunting grounds, nor to furnish arms and ammunition to the Indians. They were to act in concert, also, against all interlopers, and to succor each other in case of danger. The American company was to have

[1] His son-in-law, Adrian Bentzon. See above, p. 348, and note 2, below.

[2] According to Porter, "we know scarcely any of the details of Bentzon's negotiations at St. Petersburg." *John Jacob Astor*, I, 197. Irving's account of the agreement contains all information available. To this it should be added that Bentzon conducted his negotiations with Count Nikolai Petrovich Rumiantsev, Minister of Foreign Affairs and Commerce, whose dislike of the British was counted on to favor minimizing English influence in the Northwest. However much he favored Astor's proposals, he was limited in one regard, namely Astor's provision that furs which he should import into Russia should be admitted free of duty or for only a small duty. This right had been granted to the Russian-American Fur Company as a monopoly, and Rumiantsev was powerless to counteract it. *Ibid.*, 192–93, 197. See also Astor to Jefferson, March 14, 1812, in *ibid.*, 510.

It is to his agreement with the Russians that Astor referred in a letter to William Jones, Secretary of Navy: "The Russian government have acknowledged our Right of Poss[ess]ion & our Establishment on the Columbia[.] I have Given copey of the official Document to Mr. Gallatin. . . . the original I have here[.] perhaps it would be well to be in the hands of government—and if Desird I will send it." Astor, New York, July 7, 1813, to William Jones, Secretary of Navy, in Dorothy W. Bridgwater, "John Jacob Astor Relative to His Settlement on Columbia River," *Yale University Library Gazette*, Vol. XXIV (1949), 60.

the exclusive right of supplying the Russian posts with goods and neces-saries, receiving peltries in payment at stated prices. They were, also, if so requested by the Russian governor, to convey the furs of the Russian company to Canton, sell them on commission, and bring back the pro-ceeds, at such freight as might be agreed on at the time. This agreement was to continue in operation four years, and to be renewable for a similar term, unless some unforeseen contingency should render a modification necessary.

It was calculated to be of great service to the infant establishment at Astoria; dispelling the fears of hostile rivalry on the part of the foreign companies in its neighborhood, and giving a formidable blow to the irregular trade along the coast. It was also the intention of Mr. Astor to have coasting vessels of his own, at Astoria, of small tonnage and draft of water, fitted for coasting service. These, having a place of shel-ter and deposit, could ply about the coast in short voyages, in favorable weather, and would have vast advantage over chance ships, which must make long voyages, maintain numerous crews, and could only approach the coast at certain seasons of the year. He hoped, therefore, gradually to make Astoria the great emporium of the American fur trade in the Pa-cific, and the nucleus of a powerful American state.[3] Unfortunately for these sanguine anticipations, before Mr. Astor had ratified the agree-ment, as above stated, war broke out between the United States and Great Britain. He perceived at once the peril of the case. The harbor of New York would doubtless be blockaded, and the departure of the annual supply ship in the autumn prevented; or, if she should succeed in getting out to sea, she might be captured on her voyage.

In this emergency, he wrote to Captain Sowle, commander of the Beaver. The letter, which was addressed to him at Canton, directed him to proceed to the factory at the mouth of the Columbia, with such articles as the establishment might need; and to remain there, subject to the orders of Mr. Hunt, should that gentleman be in command there.[4]

The war continued. No tidings had yet been received from Astoria; the despatches having been delayed by the misadventure of Mr. Reed at the falls of the Columbia, and the unhorsing of Mr. Stuart by the

---

[3] It may be this desire that is reflected in a letter from Thomas Jefferson expressing his hope "for the establishment of an independent nation on the Pacific Coast, bound to the United States by ties of blood, language and friendship." Jefferson, May 24, 1812, to Astor, quoted in Porter, *op. cit.*, I, 243.

[4] Irving seems to be the sole authority for this information.

Crows among the mountains. A painful uncertainty, also, prevailed about Mr. Hunt and his party. Nothing had been heard of them since their departure from the Arickara village; Lisa, who parted from them there, had predicted their destruction; and some of the traders of the Northwest Company had actually spread a rumor of their having been cut off by the Indians.

It was a hard trial of the courage and means of an individual to have to fit out another costly expedition, where so much had already been expended, so much uncertainty prevailed, and where the risk of loss was so greatly enhanced, that no insurance could be effected.

In spite of all these discouragements, Mr. Astor determined to send another ship to the relief of the settlement. He selected for this purpose a vessel called the Lark, remarkable for her fast sailing. The disordered state of the times, however, caused such a delay, that February arrived, while the vessel was yet lingering in port.

At this juncture, Mr. Astor learnt that the Northwest Company were preparing to send out an armed ship of twenty guns, called the Isaac Todd, to form an establishment at the mouth of the Columbia.[5] These tidings gave him great uneasiness. A considerable proportion of the persons in his employ were Scotchmen and Canadians, and several of them had been in the service of the Northwest Company.[6] Should

[5] Early in 1813, Astor wrote to James Monroe, Secretary of State: "I belive at present there is no establishment on the Columbia except the one here mentiond [i.e., Astoria] but I am prety Sure that the northwest Compa[n]y will endevor to fix one as I have just now a Letter from London Datd 19 Nor. which States that they were fitting the ship Isaac Todd of about 450 tons for the northwest Coast and She will I have no Doubt go to the River Columbia—[.]" Astor, New York, February [n.d.], 1813, to James Monroe, in Bridgwater, "John Jacob Astor Relative to His Settlement on Columbia River," loc. cit., 51.

In April, he wrote to the Secretary of Navy, explaining "that a number of merchant Ships Saild under convoy to Certain Latituds[.] among them was the Ship Isaac Todd beloing [sic] to the northwest Company of Canada, Caring 20 Guns & 80 Men with a Cargo & means to make an establishment at Columbia River—[.]" Astor, Philadelphia, April 6, 1813, to William Jones, Secretary of Navy; ibid., 56.

[6] Astor expressed his apprehension to Monroe: "I was obliged to engage Some [men] from Canada Say Some Canadians & a few Scotchmen[.] altho th[e]y have all becom Citzans of the united States I am more or Less feare full that these in time of war may jone [join] any force Send by the northwest compa[n]y or the British government & the more So if no protection should apeare from this Country[.] The number of these is however few & the Princple agent is a Mr. Hunt of Trenton new jersey, a *Real* American and a man of talents and honnour[.]" Astor, New York, February [n.d.], 1813, to James Monroe; ibid., 51.

Mr. Hunt have failed to arrive at Astoria, the whole establishment would be under the control of Mr. M'Dougal, of whose fidelity he had received very disparaging accounts from Captain Thorn. The British government, also, might deem it worth while to send a force against the establishment, having been urged to do so some time previously by the Northwest Company.

Under all these circumstances, Mr. Astor wrote to Mr. Monroe,[7] then secretary of state, requesting protection from the government of the United States. He represented the importance of his settlement, in a commercial point of view, and the shelter it might afford to the American vessels in those seas.[8] All he asked was that the American government would throw forty or fifty men into the fort at his establishment, which would be sufficient for its defense until he could send reinforcements overland.

He waited in vain for a reply to this letter, the government, no doubt, being engrossed at the time by an overwhelming crowd of affairs. The month of March arrived, and the Lark was ordered by Mr. Astor to put to sea. The officer who was to command her, shrunk from his engagement, and in the exigency of the moment, she was given in charge to Mr. Northrop,[9] the mate. Mr. Nicholas G. Ogden, a gentleman on whose talents and integrity the highest reliance could be placed, sailed

[7] Part of Astor's letter follows: "I know that the northwest Company have Comunicated my undertaking to the British Government and under present Circumstances I think it more than proveble that th[e]y will apply for Some aid to Defeat it. Whether they will Suceed in obtaing it I know not but I have every Reason to believe that if the Government Dos not aid them they will make an effort to Do it themselfs. . . . in time of Peace I think I could have made [a] Stand against that company[.] In the present it becoms very Doubtfull & hazardous and in case of any Interferancs of the [English] Government Imposeble—In this Situation it becoms very Interesting to Know Some what of the views of our government on this Subject & whether the united States have or will assert any Claim to or any part of that Country and whether it will be deemd expedient for government to take possison of a Country which will aford wealth & comfordt to many & to protect the Establishment which has ben made[.] I presume If 40 or 50 Men were plaisd in the fort allready build or on Some more eligible Situation if Such there be th[e]y could with the aid of the men allready There repell any force which the British might at this time Send and in the meantime means might be found to Send more men & to Strengthen ourselfs[.]" Astor, New York, February [n.d.], 1813, to Monroe; *ibid.*, 50–51. This plea became the subject of numerous other appeals to members of the government.

[8] "There are at this time about 12 American Ships upon the northwest coast[.] many of them might Seeke & find protection in the Columbia if we had even a Small force there—[.]" *Ibid.*, 51.

[9] Samuel H. Northrop.

as supercargo. The Lark put to sea in the beginning of March, 1813.[10]

By this opportunity, Mr. Astor wrote to Mr. Hunt, as head of the establishment at the mouth of the Columbia, for he would not allow himself to doubt of his welfare. "I always think you are well," said he, "and that I shall see you again, which Heaven, I hope, will grant."

He warned him to be on his guard against any attempts to surprise the post; suggesting the probability of armed hostility on the part of the Northwest Company, and expressing his indignation at the ungrateful returns made by that association for his frank and open conduct, and advantageous overtures. "Were I on the spot," said he, "and had the management of affairs, I would defy them all; but, as it is, everything depends upon you and your friends about you. *Our enterprise is grand, and deserves success, and I hope in God it will meet it.* If my object was merely gain of money, I should say, think whether it is best to save what we can, and abandon the place; *but the very idea is like a dagger to my heart.*" This extract is sufficient to show the spirit and the views which actuated Mr. Astor in this great undertaking.

Week after week and month after month elapsed, without anything to dispel the painful incertitude that hung over every part of this enterprise. Though a man of resolute spirit, and not easily cast down, the dangers impending over this darling scheme of his ambition, had a gradual effect upon the spirits of Mr. Astor. He was sitting one gloomy evening by his window, revolving over the loss of the Tonquin and the fate of her unfortunate crew, and fearing that some equally tragical calamity might have befallen the adventurers across the mountains, when the evening newspaper was brought to him. The first paragraph that caught his eye, announced the arrival of Mr. Stuart and his party at St. Louis, with intelligence that Mr. Hunt and his companions had effected their perilous expedition to the mouth of the Columbia.[11] This was a gleam of sunshine that for a time dispelled every cloud, and he now looked forward with sanguine hope to the accomplishment of all his plans.

[10] On March 6.

[11] The newspaper article was probably a copy of the *Missouri Gazette* articles for May 8 and May 12, 1813. See Chapter L, note 40.

Banks of the Wallah-Wallah
Departure of David Stuart for the Oakinagan
Mr. Clarke's Route up Lewis River — Chipunnish, or Pierced-nose Indians
Their Character, Appearance, and Habits — Thievish Habits
Laying Up of the Boats — Post at Pointed Heart and Spokan Rivers
M'Kenzie, His Route up the Camoënum — Bands of Travelling Indians
Expedition of Reed to the Caches — Adventures of
Wandering Voyageurs and Trappers

THE course of our narrative now takes us back to the regions beyond the mountains, to dispose of the parties that set out from Astoria, in company with Mr. Robert Stuart, and whom he left on the banks of the Wallah-Wallah. Those parties likewise separated from each other shortly after his departure, proceeding to their respective destinations, but agreeing to meet at the mouth of the Wallah-Wallah about the beginning of June in the following year, with such peltries as they should have collected in the interior, so as to convoy each other through the dangerous passes of the Columbia.

Mr. David Stuart, one of the partners,[1] proceeded with his men to the post already established by him at the mouth of the Oakinagan; having furnished this with goods and ammunition, he proceeded three hundred miles up that river, where he established another post in a good trading neighborhood.[2]

Mr. Clarke,[3] another partner, conducted his little band up Lewis River to the mouth of a small stream coming in from the north, to

[1] Incorrectly *parties* in first edition.

[2] On the Thompson River in British Columbia. Franchère states that "Mr. David Stuart, reinforced by Messrs. Matthews and M'Gillis, was to explore the region lying north of his post at Okenakan." *Narrative*, 277. See Ross, *Adventures*, 204–205, 206–207.

[3] Irving's source for Clarke's expedition to the Spokane River was Cox, *Columbia River*; see pp. 89–109 therein. Clarke's party included, besides himself, four clerks, one of whom was Cox; twenty-one Canadians; and six Sandwich Islanders. An Indian guide was added when they left the Snake River.

which the Canadians gave the name of the Pavion.[4] Here he found a village or encampment of forty huts or tents, covered with mats, and inhabited by *Nez Percés*, or Pierced-nose Indians, as they are called by the traders; but Chipunnish, as they are called by themselves. They are a hardy, laborious, and somewhat knavish race, who lead a precarious life, fishing and digging roots during the summer and autumn, hunting the deer on snow-shoes during the winter, and traversing the Rocky Mountains in the spring, to trade for buffalo skins with the hunting tribes of the Missouri. In these migrations they are liable to be waylaid and attacked by the Blackfeet, and other warlike and predatory tribes, and driven back across the mountains with the loss of their horses, and of many of their comrades.

A life of this unsettled and precarious kind is apt to render man[5] selfish, and such Mr. Clarke found the inhabitants of this village, who were deficient in the usual hospitality of Indians; parting with everything with extreme reluctance, and showing no sensibility to any act of kindness. At the time of his arrival, they were all occupied in catching and curing salmon. The men were stout, robust, active, and good looking, and the women handsomer than those of the tribes nearer to the coast.[6]

It was the plan of Mr. Clarke to lay up his boats here, and proceed by land to his place of destination, which was among the Spokan tribe of Indians, about a hundred and fifty miles distant. He accordingly endeavored to purchase horses for the journey, but in this he had to contend with the sordid disposition of these people. They asked high prices for their horses, and were so difficult to deal with, that Mr. Clarke was detained seven days among them, before he could procure a sufficient number. During that time he was annoyed by repeated pilferings, for which he could get no redress. The chief promised to recover the stolen articles; but failed to do so, alleging that the thieves belonged to a distant tribe, and had made off with their booty. With this excuse Mr. Clarke was fain to content himself, though he laid up in his heart a bitter

---

[4] Pavilion River, now known as Palouse River. It joins the Snake River northwest of Grange City, Washington. Clarke's party arrived here on August 8 and remained until the fifteenth. Here they bought fifty horses from the Nez Percé Indians.

[5] *Men* in first edition.

[6] Irving combines details from two passages in Cox; cf. *op. cit.*, 88, 89.

grudge against the whole Pierced-nose race, which it will be found he took occasion subsequently to gratify in a signal manner.[7]

Having made arrangements for his departure, Mr. Clarke laid up his barge and canoes in a sheltered place, on the banks of a small bay, overgrown with shrubs and willows, confiding them to the care of the Nez Percé chief, who, on being promised an ample compensation,[8] engaged to have a guardian eye upon them; then mounting his steed, and putting himself at the head of his little caravan, he shook the dust off his feet[9] as he turned his back upon this village of rogues and hard dealers. We shall not follow him minutely in his journey;[10] which lay at times over steep and rocky hills, and among crags and precipices; at other times over vast naked and sunburnt plains, abounding with rattlesnakes, in traversing which, both men and horses suffered intolerably from heat and thirst. The place on which he fixed for a trading post,[11] was a fine point of land, at the junction of the Pointed Heart[12] and Spokan rivers. His establishment was intended to compete with a trading post[13] of the Northwest Company, situated at no great distance, and

[7] *Ibid.*, 90.

[8] "We made him a present," says Cox, "of a fathom of blue cloth, an axe, and a knife; to his wife we gave a few strings of white and blue beads, and three dozen of hawk-bells for her *chemise de cuir* [leather gown]; and among the remainder we distributed a few heads of leaf-tobacco." *Ibid.*

[9] The first edition reads *off of his feet*.

[10] Irving was unable to follow Clarke's journey because he had no record of it from here on. Cox, who had been keeping a journal of the party, became separated from the brigade shortly after they left the Indian village. He wandered lost for many days and thus left no account of Clarke's trip to the Spokane.

[11] Fort Spokane.

[12] Coeur d'Alene, that is, Spokane River. What Irving (or Cox) calls the Spokan River is now called the Little Spokane River. Their confluence is northwest of modern Spokane, Washington, about eleven miles on an air line from the center of the city. See Cox, *op. cit.*, 109, for Irving's source.

[13] Spokane House, built in 1811 by Finan McDonald (1782–1851; see Wallace [ed.], *Documents*, 462) and Jaco Finlay (d. 1828; see *ibid.*, 439). Cf. Phillips, *The Fur Trade*, II, 289. At this time James McMillan (d. 1858; see Wallace [ed.], *Documents*, 482–83), a clerk, was in charge of the post, to which ten other men were attached. Cf. Cox, *op. cit.*, 109. Alexander Ross, who came from Fort Okanogan on a visit to Clarke in December, 1812, left a brief but vivid account of the rivalry that developed. "During the three days I remained with him," he wrote, "I had frequent opportunities of observing the sly and underhand dealings of the competing parties, for the opposition posts of the North-West Company and Mr. Clarke were built contiguous to each other. When the two parties happened to meet, they made the amplest protestations of friendship, and kindness, and a stranger, unacquainted with the politics of Indian

to rival it in the trade with the Spokan Indians; as well as with the Cootonais and Flatheads.[14] In this neighborhood we shall leave him for the present.

Mr. M'Kenzie, who conducted the third party from the Wallah-Wallah, navigated for several days up the south branch[15] of the Columbia, named the Camoënum[16] by the natives, but commonly called Lewis River, in honor of the first explorer. Wandering bands of various tribes were seen along this river, travelling in various directions; for the Indians generally are restless, roving beings, continually intent on enterprises of war, traffic, and hunting. Some of these people were driving large gangs of horses, as if to a distant market. Having arrived at the mouth of the Shahaptan,[17] he ascended some distance up that river,

---

trade, would have pronounced them sincere; but the moment their backs were turned, they tore each other to pieces. Each party had its manœuvreing scouts out in all directions, watching the motions of the Indians, and laying plots and plans to entrap or foil each other. He that got most skins, never minding the cost of the crime, was the cleverest fellow; and under such tutors the Indians were apt disciples. They played their tricks also, and turned the foibles and wiles of their teachers to their own advantage." *Adventures*, 201.

[14] Cox wrote: "He [McMillan] had two other posts detached from this: one about 240 miles from it, in a north-easterly direction, among a tribe called the Flat-heads, whose lands lie at the feet of the Rocky Mountains, and are well stocked with buffaloes; the other about 200 miles, nearly due north, among a tribe called the Cootonais [Kootenais, Kootenays], in whose country there are plenty of beavers, deer, mountain sheep, and, at times, buffaloes. Mr. Finan M'Donald [see note 13 above] of the North-West Company had charge of the post among the Flatheads; and a Mr. [Nicolas] Montour [a halfblood son of Nicolas Montour (d. 1808); see Wallace (ed.), *Documents*, 487] was stationed among the Cootonais." Cox, *op. cit.*, 109–10.

Francis B. Pillot (or Pillet), a clerk who had come out on the *Tonquin*, was sent with six men to compete against Montour for the trade of the Kootenais, and Cox, with Russel Farnham, another *Tonquin* passenger, plus twelve additional men, was sent to the Flatheads to compete against McDonald. The Flathead post was located near modern Jennings, Montana. Here the rivalry of Pillot and Montour brought on a duel with pistols at six paces. Result: one coat collar and one pant leg pierced. "The tailor," Cox remarked wryly, "speedily healed their wounds." *Op. cit.*, 110, 116.

[15] Snake River.   [16] Sometimes *Ky-eye-nem*.

[17] Ross, in his account of McKenzie's journey, says he went to "the very center of the Great Shahaptain or Nez Percé nation, where he established himself for the winter. By way of clearing up some points not very intelligible to many," he goes on, "we may here mention that the Great Snake River, Louis [Lewis] River, South-branch, Shahaptain, and Nez Percé River, are all one and the same stream, with different denominations." *Adventures*, 214. Irving's phrase "mouth of the Shahaptan," in light of what Ross says, becomes unintelligible. But it seems likely that by Shahaptan, Irving means another river, possibly what is now denoted as Clearwater River in western Idaho. It joins the Snake near Clarkston, Washington. See F. D. Haines, "McKenzie's Winter

and established his trading post upon its banks. This appeared to be a great thoroughfare for the tribes from the neighborhood of the falls of the Columbia, in their expeditions to make war upon the tribes of the Rocky Mountains; to hunt buffalo on the plains beyond, or to traffic for roots and buffalo robes. It was the season of migration, and the Indians from various distant parts were passing and repassing in great numbers.

Mr. M'Kenzie now detached a small band, under the conduct of Mr. John Reed, to visit the caches made by Mr. Hunt at the Caldron Linn, and to bring the contents to his post;[18] as he depended, in some measure, on them for his supplies of goods and ammunition. They had not been gone a week, when two Indians arrived of the Pallatapalla[19] tribe, who live upon a river[20] of the same name. These communicated the unwelcome intelligence that the caches had been robbed. They said that some of their tribe had, in the course of the preceding spring, been across the mountains, which separated them from Snake River, and had traded horses with the Snakes in exchange for blankets, robes, and goods of various descriptions. These articles the Snakes had procured from caches to which they were guided by some white men who resided among them, and who afterwards accompanied them across the Rocky Mountains. This intelligence was extremely perplexing to Mr. M'Kenzie, but the truth of part of it was confirmed by the two Indians, who brought them an English saddle and bridle, which was recognized as having belonged to Mr. Crooks. The perfidy of the white men who revealed the secret of the caches, was, however, perfectly inexplicable. We shall presently account for it in narrating the expedition of Mr. Reed.

That worthy Hibernian proceeded on his mission with his usual alacrity. His forlorn travels of the preceding winter had made him acquainted with the topography of the country, and he reached Snake River without any material difficulty. Here, in an encampment of the natives, he met with six white men, wanderers from the main expedition of Mr. Hunt, who, after having had their respective shares of adventures and mishaps, had fortunately come together at this place.

Camp, 1812–13," *Oregon Historical Quarterly*, Vol. XXXVII (1936), 329–33. McKenzie's camp was possibly on the north side of the Clearwater.

[18] See above, p. 375 and note 39.

[19] Pallotepellows, so called by Lewis and Clark. More commonly known as the Palouse. See Swanton, *Indian Tribes*, 433–34.

[20] Palouse River.

Three of these men were Turcotte, La Chapelle, and Francis Landry; the three Canadian voyageurs who, it may be recollected, had left Mr. Crooks in February, in the neighborhood of Snake River, being dismayed by the increasing hardships of the journey, and fearful of perishing of hunger.[21] They had returned to a Snake encampment, where they passed the residue of the winter.

Early in the spring, being utterly destitute, and in great extremity, and having worn out the hospitality of the Snakes, they determined to avail themselves of the buried treasures within their knowledge. They accordingly informed the Snake chieftains that they knew where a great quantity of goods had been left in caches, enough to enrich the whole tribe; and offered to conduct them to the place, on condition of being rewarded with horses and provisions. The chieftains pledged their faith and honor as great men and Snakes, and the three Canadians conducted them to the place of deposit at the Caldron Linn. This is the way that the savages got knowledge of the caches, and not by following the tracks of wolves, as Mr. Stuart had supposed. Never did money diggers turn up a miser's hoard with more eager delight, than did the savages lay open the treasures of the caches. Blankets and robes, brass trinkets and blue beads were drawn forth with chuckling exultation, and long strips of scarlet cloth produced yells of ecstasy.

The rifling of the caches effected a change in the fortunes and deportment of the whole party. The Snakes were better clad and equipped than ever were Snakes before, and the three Canadians, suddenly finding themselves with horse to ride and weapon to wear, were, like beggars on horsback, ready to ride on any wild scamper. An opportunity soon presented. The Snakes determined on a hunting match on the buffalo prairies, to lay in a supply of beef, that they might live in plenty, as became men of their improved condition. The three newly mounted cavaliers must fain accompany them. They all traversed the Rocky Mountains in safety, descended to the head waters of the Missouri, and made great havoc among the buffaloes.

Their hunting camp was full of meat; they were gorging themselves, like true Indians, with present plenty, and drying and jerking great quantities for a winter's supply. In the midst of their revelry and good cheer, the camp was surprised by the Blackfeet. Several of the Snakes were slain on the spot; the residue, with their three Canadian allies, fled

[21] See p. 304.

438

to the mountains, stripped of horses, buffalo meat, everything; and made their way back to the old encampment on Snake River, poorer than ever, but esteeming themselves fortunate in having escaped with their lives. They had not been long there when the Canadians were cheered by the sight of a companion in misfortune, Dubreuil, the poor voyageur who had left Mr. Crooks in March, being too much exhausted to keep on with him.[22] Not long afterwards, three other straggling members of the main expedition made their appearance. These were Carson, St. Michel, and Pierre Delaunay, three of the trappers who, in company with Pierre Detayé, had been left among the mountains by Mr. Hunt, to trap beaver, in the preceding month of September.[23] They had departed from the main body well armed and provided, with horses to ride, and horses to carry the peltries they were to collect. They came wandering into the Snake camp as ragged and destitute as their predecessors. It appears that they had finished their trapping, and were making their way in the spring to the Missouri, when they were met and attacked by a powerful band of the all-pervading Crows. They made a desperate resistance, and killed seven of the savages, but were overpowered by numbers. Pierre Detayé was slain, the rest were robbed of horses and effects, and obliged to turn back, when they fell in with their old companions, as already mentioned.

We should observe, that at the heels of Pierre Delaunay came draggling an Indian wife, whom he had picked up in his wanderings; having grown weary of celibacy among the savages.

The whole seven of this forlorn fraternity of adventurers, thus accidentally congregated on the banks of Snake River, were making arrangements once more to cross the mountains, when some Indian scouts brought word of the approach of the little band headed by John Reed.

The latter, having heard the several stories of these wanderers, took them all into his party, and set out for the Caldron Linn, to clear out two or three of the caches which had not been revealed to the Indians.

At that place he met with Robinson, the Kentucky veteran, who, with his two comrades, Rezner and Hoback, had remained there when Mr. Stuart went on. This adventurous trio had been trapping higher up the river, but Robinson had come down in a canoe, to await the expected arrival of the party, and obtain horses and equipments. He told Reed the story of the robbery of his party by the Arapahays,[24] but it differed, in

---

[22] See above, p. 346.   [23] See above, p. 265.   [24] See above, p. 371.

some particulars, from the account given by him to Mr. Stuart. In that, he had represented Cass as having shamefully deserted his companions in their extremity, carrying off with him a horse; in the one now given, he spoke of him as having been killed in the affray with the Arapahays. This discrepancy, of which, of course Reed could have had no knowledge at the time, concurred with other circumstances, to occasion afterwards some mysterious speculations and dark surmises as to the real fate of Cass; but as no substantial grounds were ever adduced for them, we forbear to throw any deeper shades into this story of sufferings in the wilderness.

Mr. Reed, having gathered the remainder of the goods from the caches, put himself at the head of his party, now augmented by the seven men thus casually picked up, and the squaw of Pierre Delaunay, and made his way successfully to M'Kenzie's post, on the waters of the Shahaptan.[25]

[25] Irving's source for the affairs related in connection with McKenzie and Reed has not been determined. His information could possibly have come from Alfred Seton (d. 1859), a member of McKenzie's party who, in 1835, when Irving was writing *Astoria*, was a resident of New York City, where he operated a furrier's store. There is no positive evidence to support this conjecture, however. Another possibility is that Irving's information came from McKenzie himself, who, upon his retirement in 1833, took up residence in Mayville, New York, where he continued to live until his death in 1851. A hint in *Astoria*, p. 443, suggests that Irving may indeed have communicated with McKenzie.

A brief parallel account appears in Ross, *Adventures*, 214–15.

AFTER the departure of the different detachments, or *brigades,* as they are called by the fur traders, the Beaver prepared for her voyage along the coast, and her visit to the Russian establishment, at New Archangel, where she was to carry supplies.[1] It had been determined in the council of partners at Astoria, that Mr. Hunt should embark in this vessel, for the purpose of acquainting himself with the coasting trade,[2] and of making arrangements with the commander of the Russian post, and that he should be relanded in October, at Astoria, by the Beaver, on her way to the Sandwich Islands and Canton.

The Beaver put to sea in the month of August.[3] Her departure, and that of the various brigades, left the fortress[4] of Astoria but slightly

[1] The invoice of supplies intended for the Russian settlement is given in Porter, *John Jacob Astor,* I, 479–83.

[2] The partners took the following action on June 27, 1812:

"Resolved that Wilson P. Hunt is authorized and hereby instructed to accompany Cap. Soule in the Ship Beaver during the Coasting voyage of said Ship for the present season, for the purpose of transacting any business which may be in his power relative to the interest of the Concern—And that Duncan McDougall is hereby instructed to remain at Astoria and transact the business of the company until the return of W. P. Hunt." The resolution is signed by Hunt, McKenzie, McDougall, D. Stuart, R. Stuart, and John Clarke. Missouri Historical Society; printed in Flandrau, *Astoria and the Oregon Country,* 37.

[3] On August 4, 1812, according to Franchère, *Narrative,* 278. Departure was delayed a month because of unfavorable westerly winds. The ship was expected to return to Astoria by the end of October.

[4] The first edition has *little fortress.*

garrisoned. This was soon perceived by some of the Indian tribes, and the consequence was, increased insolence of deportment, and a disposition to hostility. It was now the fishing season, when the tribes from the northern coast drew into the neighborhood of the Columbia. These were warlike and perfidious in their dispositions; and noted for their attempts to surprise trading ships. Among them were numbers of the Neweetees, the ferocious tribe that massacred the crew of the Tonquin.

Great precautions, therefore, were taken at the factory, to guard against surprise while these dangerous intruders were in the vicinity. Galleries were constructed inside of the palisades; the bastions were heightened, and sentinels were posted day and night.[5] Fortunately, the Chinooks and other tribes resident in the vicinity manifested the most pacific disposition. Old Comcomly, who held sway over them, was a shrewd calculator. He was aware of the advantages of having the whites as neighbors and allies, and of the consequence derived to himself and his people from acting as intermediate traders between them and the distant tribes. He had, therefore, by this time, become a firm friend of the Astorians, and formed a kind of barrier between them and the hostile intruders from the north.

The summer of 1812 passed away without any of the hostilities that had been apprehended; the Neweetees, and other dangerous visitors to the neighborhood, finished their fishing and returned home, and the inmates of the factory once more felt secure from attack.

It now became necessary to guard against other evils. The season of scarcity arrived, which commences in October, and lasts until the end of January. To provide for the support of the garrison, the shallop was employed to forage about the shores of the river. A number of the men, also, under the command of some of the clerks, were sent to quarter themselves on the banks of the Wollamut[6] (the Multnomah of Lewis and Clark), a fine river which disembogues itself into the Columbia, about sixty miles above Astoria. The country bordering on the river is finely diversified with prairies and hills, and forests of oak, ash, maple, and cedar. It abounded, at that time, with elk and deer, and the streams were well stocked with beaver. Here the party, after supplying their

[5] Irving uses Franchère, *Narrative*, 277–78.

[6] Willamette River. The name was spelled differently earlier (*Wallamot*), as was that of William Clark (*Clarke*).

442

own wants, were enabled to pack up quantities of dried meat, and send it by canoes to Astoria.[7]

The month of October elapsed without the return of the Beaver. November, December, January, passed away, and still nothing was seen or heard of her. Gloomy apprehensions now began to be entertained: she might have been wrecked in the course of her coasting voyage, or surprised, like the Tonquin, by some of the treacherous tribes of the north.

No one indulged more in these apprehensions than M'Dougal, who had now the charge of the establishment. He no longer evinced the bustling confidence and buoyancy which once characterized him. Command seemed to have lost its charms for him, or rather, he gave way to the most abject despondency, decrying the whole enterprise, magnifying every untoward circumstance, and foreboding nothing but evil.[8]

While in this moody state, he was surprised, on the 16th of January,[9] by the sudden appearance of M'Kenzie, wayworn and weather-beaten by a long wintry journey from his post on the Shahaptan, and with a face the very frontispiece for a volume of misfortune. M'Kenzie had been heartily disgusted and disappointed at his post. It was in the midst of the Tushepaws,[10] a powerful and warlike nation, divided into many tribes, under different chiefs, who possessed innumerable horses, but, not having turned their attention to beaver trapping, had no furs to offer. According to M'Kenzie, they were but a "rascally tribe;" from which we may infer that they were prone to consult their own interests, more than comported with the interests of a greedy Indian trader.

Game being scarce, he was obliged to rely, for the most part, on horse

---

[7] This trip was headed by Franchère and Benjamin Clapp. They left Astoria on October 1 and returned October 20. A second voyage, also headed by Franchère, left not long after and returned on November 15. See *Narrative*, 278–79, which appears to be Irving's source.

[8] The above two paragraphs follow *ibid.*, 279–80. According to Franchère, McDougall was "confined to his room by sickness." Franchère and Clapp were now in sole charge of Astoria. They found each other to be agreeable company and diverted themselves with conversation, music, and reading. For what they possibly read, see p. 349, note 4. "Otherwise," Franchère said, "we should have passed our time in a state of insufferable ennui, at this rainy season, in the midst of the deep mud which surrounded us." *Ibid.*, 279.

[9] January 15, according to Franchère. *Ibid.*, 280.

[10] See Chapter XXXVII, note 21.

flesh for subsistence, and the Indians discovering his necessities, adopted a policy usual in civilized trade, and raised the price of horses to an exorbitant rate, knowing that he and his men must eat or die. In this way, the goods he had brought to trade for beaver skins, were likely to be bartered for horse flesh, and all the proceeds devoured upon the spot.

He had despatched trappers in various directions, but the country around did not offer more beaver than his own station. In this emergency he began to think of abandoning his unprofitable post, sending his goods to the posts of Clarke and David Stuart, who could make a better use of them, as they were in a good beaver country, and returning with his party to Astoria, to seek some better destination. With this view he repaired to the post of Mr. Clarke, to hold a consultation. While the two partners were in conference in Mr. Clarke's wigwam, an unexpected visitor came bustling in upon them.

This was Mr. John George M'Tavish,[11] a partner of the Northwest Company, who had charge of the rival trading posts established in that neighborhood. Mr. M'Tavish was the delighted messenger of bad news. He had been to Lake Winnipeg, where he received an express from Canada, containing the declaration of war, and President Madison's proclamation, which he handed with the most officious complaisance to Messrs. Clarke and M'Kenzie. He moreover told them that he had received a fresh supply of goods from the Northwest posts on the other side of the Rocky Mountains, and was prepared for vigorous opposition to the establishment[12] of the American company. He capped the climax of this obliging, but belligerent intelligence, by informing them that the armed ship, Isaac Todd, was to be at the mouth of the Columbia about the beginning of March, to get possession of the trade of the river, and that he was ordered to join her there at that time.

The receipt of this news determined M'Kenzie. He immediately returned to the Shahaptan, broke up his establishment, deposited his goods in *cache*, and hastened with all his people to Astoria.

The intelligence thus brought, completed the dismay of M'Dougal,

---

[11] A native of Scotland, McTavish was brought to Canada in 1798 by Simon McTavish and entered the North West Company as a clerk. He negotiated the surrender of Astoria in 1813 and in that year became a partner. Later he was appointed chief factor in the Hudson's Bay Company. From 1821 to 1828, McTavish was in charge of York Factory on Hudson Bay. He retired in 1847 and died the same year. Wallace (ed.), *Documents*, 485.

[12] *Establishments* in first edition.

and seemed to produce a complete confusion of mind. He held a council of war with M'Kenzie, at which some of the clerks were present, but of course had no votes. They gave up all hope of maintaining their post at Astoria. The Beaver had probably been lost; they could receive no aid from the United States, as all the ports would be blockaded. From England nothing could be expected but hostility. It was determined therefore, to abandon the establishment in the course of the following spring, and return across the Rocky Mountains.[13]

In pursuance of this resolution,[14] they suspended all trade with the natives, except for provisions, having already more peltries than they could carry away, and having need of all the goods for the clothing and subsistence of their people, during the remainder of their sojourn, and on their journey across the mountains. This intention of abandoning Astoria was, however, kept secret from the men, lest they should at once give up all labor, and become restless and insubordinate.[15]

In the meantime, M'Kenzie set off[16] for his post at the Shahaptan, to get his goods from the caches, and buy horses and provisions with them for the caravan across the mountains. He was charged with despatches from M'Dougal to Messrs. Stuart and Clarke, apprising them of the intended migration, that they might make timely preparations.

M'Kenzie was accompanied by two of the clerks, Mr. John Reed, the Irishman, and Mr. Alfred Seton, of New York. They embarked in two canoes, manned by seventeen men, and ascended the river without any incident of importance, until they arrived in the eventful neighborhood of the rapids. They made the portage of the narrows and the falls early in the afternoon, and, having partaken of a scanty meal, had now a long evening on their hands.

On the opposite side of the river lay the village of Wish-ram, of freebooting renown. Here lived the savages who had robbed and maltreated Reed, when bearing his tin box of despatches. It was known that the rifle of which he was despoiled was retained as a trophy at the village. M'Kenzie offered to cross the river, and demand the rifle, if any one would accompany him. It was a hare-brained project, for these villages were noted for the ruffian character of their inhabitants; yet two volun-

---

[13] See Franchère, *Narrative*, 280, 282–83. Cf. Ross, *Adventures*, 215–17.

[14] The first edition has *the resolution*.

[15] The above two paragraphs are derived from Franchère, *Narrative*, 280–81.

[16] On May 31, 1813. *Ibid.*, 282.

teers promptly stepped forward; Alfred Seton, the clerk, and Joe de la Pierre, the cook. The trio soon reached the opposite side of the river. On landing, they freshly primed their rifles and pistols. A path winding for about a hundred yards among rocks and crags, led to the village. No notice seemed to be taken of their approach. Not a solitary being, man, woman, or child, greeted them. The very dogs, those noisy pests of an Indian town, kept silence. On entering the village, a boy made his appearance, and pointed to a house of larger dimensions than the rest. They had to stoop to enter it; as soon as they had passed the threshold, the narrow passage behind them was filled up by a sudden rush of Indians, who had before kept out of sight.

M'Kenzie and his companions found themselves in a rude chamber of about twenty-five feet long and twenty wide. A bright fire was blazing at one end, near which sat the chief, about sixty years old. A large number of Indians, wrapped in buffalo robes, were squatted in rows, three deep, forming a semicircle round three sides of the room. A single glance around sufficed to show them the grim and dangerous assembly[17] into which they had intruded, and that all retreat was cut off by the mass which blocked up the entrance.

The chief pointed to the vacant side of the room opposite to the door, and motioned for them to take their seats. They complied. A dead pause ensued. The grim warriors around sat like statues; each muffled in his robe, with his fierce eyes bent on the intruders. The latter felt they were in a perilous predicament.

"Keep your eyes on the chief while I am addressing him," said M'Kenzie to his companions. "Should he give any sign to his band, shoot him, and make for the door."

M'Kenzie advanced, and offered the pipe of peace to the chief, but it was refused. He then made a regular speech, explaining the object of their visit, and proposing to give in exchange for the rifle two blankets, an axe, some beads and tobacco.

When he had done, the chief arose, began to address him in a low voice, but soon became loud and violent, and ended by working himself up into a furious passion. He upbraided the white men for their sordid conduct in passing and repassing through their neighborhood, without giving them a blanket or any other article of goods, merely because they had no furs to barter in exchange, and he alluded, with menaces of

17 *Assemblage* in the first edition.

vengeance, to the death of the Indian killed by the whites in the skirmish at the falls.

Matters were verging to a crisis. It was evident the surrounding savages were only waiting a signal from the chief to spring upon their prey.
M'Kenzie and his companions had gradually risen on their feet during
the speech, and had brought their rifles to a horizontal position, the
barrels resting in their left hands; the muzzle of M'Kenzie's piece was
within three feet of the speaker's heart. They cocked their rifles; the
click of the locks for a moment suffused the dark cheek of the savage,
and there was a pause. They coolly, but promptly, advanced to the door;
the Indians fell back in awe, and suffered them to pass. The sun was
just setting, as they emerged from this dangerous den. They took the
precaution to keep along the tops of the rocks as much as possible on
their way back to the canoe, and reached their camp in safety, congratu-
lating themselves on their escape, and feeling no desire to make a second
visit to the grim warriors of Wish-ram.[18]

M'Kenzie and his party resumed their journey the next morning. At
some distance above the falls of the Columbia, they observed two bark
canoes, filled with white men, coming down the river, to the full chant
of a set of Canadian voyageurs. A parley ensued. It was a detachment
of Northwesters, under the command of Mr. John George M'Tavish,
bound, full of song and spirit, to the mouth of the Columbia, to await
the arrival of the Isaac Todd.

Mr. M'Kenzie and M'Tavish came to a halt, and landing, encamped
together for the night. The voyageurs of either party hailed each other
as brothers, and old "comrades," and they mingled together as if united
by one common interest, instead of belonging to rival companies, and
trading under hostile flags.

In the morning they proceeded on their different ways, in style corresponding to their different fortunes: the one toiling painfully against
the stream, the other sweeping down gayly with the current.

---

[18] The source of this incident is a personal narrative, entitled "Life on the Oregon,"
written by Alfred Seton. It was published in the *American Monthly Magazine* in May
and June, 1835. It has since been edited by Fred. S. Perrine and republished in the
Oregon Historical Quarterly, Vol. XXXVI (1935), 185–204. Irving closely paraphrases Seton's account and frequently uses his words verbatim; see *ibid.*, 192–95. For
example, the direct quotation assigned to McKenzie in the Indian house originated in
Seton's recollection of McKenzie's words: "Keep your eyes on the chief while I am
speaking, and should he give any sign to his band, shoot him, and make for the door."

M'Kenzie arrived safely at his deserted post on the Shahaptan, but found, to his chagrin, that his caches had been discovered and rifled by the Indians.[19] Here was a dilemma, for on the stolen goods he had depended to purchase horses of the Indians. He sent out men in all directions to endeavor to discover the thieves, and despatched Mr. Reed to the posts of Messrs. Clarke and David Stuart, with the letters of Mr. M'Dougal.

The resolution announced in these letters, to break up and depart from Astoria, was condemned by both Clarke and Stuart. These two gentlemen had been very successful at their posts, and considered it rash and pusillanimous to abandon, on the first difficulty, an enterprise of such great cost and ample promise. They made no arrangements, therefore, for leaving the country, but acted with a view to the maintenance of their new and prosperous establishments.[20]

The regular time approached, when the partners of the interior posts were to rendezvous at the mouth of the Wallah-Wallah, on their way to Astoria, with the peltries they had collected. Mr. Clark accordingly packed all his furs on twenty-eight horses, and, leaving a clerk and four men to take charge of the post, departed on the 25th of May with the residue of his force.[21]

On the 30th, he arrived at the confluence of the Pavion and Lewis rivers,[22] where he had left his barge and canoes, in the guardianship of the old Pierced-nose chieftain. That dignitary had acquitted himself more faithfully of[23] his charge than Mr. Clarke had expected, and the canoes were found in very tolerable order. Some repairs were necessary, and, while they were making [them], the party encamped close by the village. Having had repeated and vexatious proofs of the pilfering propensities of this tribe during his former visit, Mr. Clarke ordered that a wary eye should be kept upon them.

---

[19] According to Franchère, *Narrative*, 283, Indians on the Snake River had shown McTavish "fowling-pieces, gun-flints, lead, and powder; and that they had communicated this news to Mr. M'Kenzie, presuming that the Indians had discovered and plundered his *cache;* which turned out afterwards to be the case."

[20] Cf. *ibid.*, 283, and Ross, *Adventures*, 217.

[21] Francis B. Pillot was the clerk left in charge. Irving's source is Cox, *Columbia River*, 117. The date is confirmed by Cox.

[22] The Palouse and Snake rivers. Cox says they arrived here on May 30.

[23] *Of* is supplied from the first edition. Less correctly *to* in the Author's Revised Edition.

He was a tall, good-looking man, and somewhat given to pomp and circumstance, which made him an object of note in the eyes of the wondering savages. He was stately, too, in his appointments, and had a silver goblet or drinking cup, out of which he would drink with a magnificent air, and then lock it up in a large *garde vin*, which accompanied him in his travels, and stood in his tent. This goblet had originally been sent as a present from Mr. Astor to Mr. M'Kay, the partner who had unfortunately been blown up in the Tonquin. As it reached Astoria after the departure of that gentleman, it had remained in the possession of Mr. Clarke.

A silver goblet was too glittering a prize not to catch the eye of a Pierced-nose. It was like the shining tin case of John Reed. Such a wonder had never been seen in the land before. The Indians talked about it to one another. They marked the care with which it was deposited in the *garde vin*, like a relic in its shrine, and concluded that it must be a "great medicine." That night Mr. Clarke neglected to lock up his treasure; in the morning the sacred casket was open—the precious relic gone!

Clarke was now outrageous. All the past vexations that he had suffered from this pilfering community rose to mind, and he threatened that, unless the goblet was[24] promptly returned, he would hang the thief, should he eventually discover him. The day passed away, however, without the restoration of the cup. At night sentinels were secretly posted about the camp. With all their vigilance, a Pierced-nose contrived to get into the camp unperceived, and to load himself with booty; it was only on his retreat that he was discovered and taken.

At daybreak the culprit was brought to trial, and promptly convicted. He stood responsible for all the spoliations of the camp, the precious goblet among the number, and Mr. Clarke passed sentence of death upon him.

A gibbet was accordingly constructed of oars: the chief of the village and his people were assembled, and the culprit was produced, with his legs and arms pinioned. Clarke then made a harangue. He reminded the tribe of the benefits he had bestowed upon them during his former visit,[25] and the many thefts and other misdeeds which he had over-

[24] *Were* in first edition.
[25] Erroneously *visits* in the Author's Revised Edition. The first edition has *visit.*

looked. The prisoner, especially, had always been peculiarly well treated by the white men, but had repeatedly been guilty of pilfering. He was to be punished for his own misdeeds, and as a warning to his tribe.

The Indians now gathered round Mr. Clarke, and interceded for the culprit. They were willing he should be punished severely, but implored that his life might be spared.[26] The companions, too, of Mr. Clarke, considered the sentence too severe, and advised him to mitigate it; but he was inexorable. He was not naturally a stern or cruel man; but from his boyhood he had lived in the Indian country among Indian traders, and held the life of a savage extremely cheap. He was, moreover, a firm believer in the doctrine of intimidation.

Farnham, a clerk, a tall "Green Mountain boy" from Vermont, who had been robbed of a pistol, acted as executioner. The signal was given, and the poor Pierced-nose resisting, struggling, and screaming, in the most frightful manner, was launched into eternity. The Indians stood round gazing in silence and mute awe, but made no attempt to oppose the execution, nor testified any emotion when it was over. They locked up their feelings within their bosoms until the opportunity should arrive to gratify them with a bloody act of vengeance.[27]

To say nothing of the needless severity of this act, its impolicy was glaringly obvious. Mr. M'Lennan and three men were to return to the post[28] with the horses, their loads having been transferred to the canoes. They would have to pass through a tract of country infested by this tribe, who were all horsemen and hard riders, and might pursue them to take vengeance for the death of their comrade. M'Lennan, however, was a resolute fellow, and made light of all dangers. He and his three men were present at the execution, and set off as soon as life was extinct in the victim; but, to use the words of one of their comrades, "they did not let the grass grow under the heels of their horses, as they clattered out of the Pierced-nose country," and were glad to find themselves in safety at the post.[29]

[26] According to Cox, "the Indians acquiesced in this decision; and the chief declared that the prisoner did not belong to their tribe, but was a kind of outlaw, of whom they were all afraid." *Op. cit.*, 118.

[27] Irving's source for this affair was Cox, an eyewitness. See *ibid.*, 117–19. For a somewhat different version, see Ross, *Adventures*, 212–14, 221–22, who repeats hearsay evidence.

[28] Fort Spokane.

[29] All that Cox says is that "by the time it was supposed life was extinct, Mr. M'Len-

Mr. Clarke and his party embarked about the same time in their canoes, and early on the following day reached the mouth of the Wallah-Wallah, where they found Messrs. Stuart and M'Kenzie awaiting them;[30] the latter having recovered part of the goods stolen from his cache.[31] Clarke informed them of the signal punishment he had inflicted on the Pierced-nose, evidently expecting to excite their admiration by such a hardy act of justice, performed in the very midst of the Indian country, but was mortified at finding it strongly censured as inhuman, unnecessary, and likely to provoke hostilities.

The parties thus united formed a squadron of two boats and six canoes, with which they performed their voyage in safety down the river, and arrived at Astoria on the 12th of June,[32] bringing with them a valuable stock of peltries.

About ten days previously, the brigade which had been quartered on the banks of the Wollamut, had arrived with numerous packs of beaver, the result of a few months' sojourn on that river. These were the first fruits of the enterprise, gathered by men as yet mere strangers in the land; but they were such as to give substantial grounds for sanguine anticipations of profit, when the country should be more completely explored, and the trade established.[33]

nan with three men set off with the horses on his return to Spokan, and we embarked in the canoes." *Op. cit.*, 119.

[30] *Ibid.*

[31] See Ross, *Adventures*, 217–19.

[32] June 11, 1813, according to Cox, *op. cit.*, 119. Franchère says that they arrived "in the beginning of June, with one hundred and forty packs of fur, the fruit of two years' trade at the post on the *Okenakan*, and one year on the *Spokan*." *Narrative*, 283. Ross, *Adventures*, 222, gives the date as June 14.

[33] Irving's source is Franchère, *Narrative*, 283.

⊰{ C H A P T E R   L I V }⊱

The Partners Displeased with M'Dougal
Equivocal Conduct of That Gentleman — Partners Agree to Abandon Astoria
Sale of Goods to M'Tavish — Arrangements for the Year
Manifesto Signed by the Partners — Departure of
M'Tavish for the Interior

THE partners found Mr. M'Dougal in all the bustle of preparation; having about nine days previously announced at the factory, his intention of breaking up the establishment, and fixed upon the 1st of July for the time of departure. Messrs. Stuart and Clarke felt highly displeased at his taking so precipitate a step, without waiting for their concurrence, when he must have known that their arrival could not be far distant.

Indeed, the whole conduct of Mr. M'Dougal was such as to awaken strong doubts as to[1] his loyal devotion to the cause. His old sympathies with the Northwest Company seem[2] to have revived. He had received M'Tavish and his party with uncalled for hospitality, as though they were friends and allies, instead of being a party of observation, come to reconnoitre the state of affairs at Astoria, and to await the arrival of a hostile ship.[3] Had they been left to themselves, they would have been starved off for want of provisions, or driven away by the Chinooks, who only wanted a signal from the factory to treat them as intruders and enemies. M'Dougal, on the contrary, had supplied them from the stores of the garrison, and had gained them the favor of the Indians, by treating them as friends.

Having set his mind fixedly on the project of breaking up the establishment at Astoria, in the current year, M'Dougal was sorely disappointed at finding that Messrs. Stuart and Clarke had omitted to comply

---

[1] *Of* in first edition.   [2] *Seemed* in first edition.

[3] According to Franchère, McTavish arrived on April 11 with Joseph Laroque and nineteen Canadian *voyageurs* in two birchbark canoes. "They landed on a point of land under the guns of the fort, and formed their camp. We invited these gentlemen to our quarters and learned from them the object of their visit." *Narrative*, 282. They were to await the arrival of the *Isaac Todd*, but if it did not arrive by July, 1813, they were to leave. Joseph Laroque (1787?–1866) at this time was a clerk in the North West Company. Wallace (ed.), *Documents*, 460.

with his request to purchase horses and provisions for the caravan across the mountains. It was now too late to make the necessary preparations in time for traversing the mountains before winter, and the project had to be postponed.[4]

In the meantime, the non-arrival of the annual ship, and the apprehensions entertained of the loss of the Beaver and of Mr. Hunt, had their effect upon the minds of Messrs. Stuart and Clarke. They began to listen to the desponding representations of M'Dougal, seconded by M'Kenzie, who inveighed against their situation as desperate and forlorn; left to shift for themselves, or perish upon a barbarous coast; neglected by those who sent them there; and threatened with dangers of every kind. In this way they were brought to consent to the plan of abandoning the country in the ensuing year.[5]

About this time, M'Tavish applied at the factory to purchase a small supply of goods wherewith to trade his way back to his post on the upper waters of the Columbia, having waited in vain for the arrival of the Isaac Todd. His request brought on a consultation among the partners. M'Dougal urged that it should be complied with. He furthermore proposed, that they should give up to M'Tavish, for a proper consideration, the post on the Spokan, and all its dependencies, as they had not sufficient goods on hand to supply that post themselves,[6] and to keep up a competition with the Northwest Company in the trade with the neighboring Indians. This last representation has since been proved incorrect. By inventories,[7] it appears that their stock in hand for the supply of the

---

[4] "The wintering partners (that is to say, Messrs. Clarke and David Stuart) dissenting from the proposal to abandon the country as soon as we intended, the thing being (as they observed) impracticable, from the want of provisions for the journey and horses to transport the goods, the project was deferred, as to its execution, till the following April." Franchère, *Narrative*, 283.

[5] See Ross, *Adventures*, 236–39, where this meeting is described.

[6] See note 8 below.

[7] Inventories for Astoria and the interior posts are published in Porter, *John Jacob Astor*, I, 529–32. As Porter remarks, "this account reveals the reason for the good opinion which John Clarke and David Stuart had of the prospects for the fur trade of the Columbia as contrasted with Donald McKenzie's pessimistic attitude." *Ibid.*, 529. As of June 1, 1812, the inventory at Astoria, including Fort Okanogan, totaled $34,352.08½. Furs at Astoria between April, 1811, and May 31, 1812, which included 1,750 large and 981 small beaver skins plus other furs, amounted to $9,541.45; at Okanogan, $3,059.75. The inventory at Astoria on June 1, 1813, showed a total of $27,611.68½. On this same date, 5,030 large and small beaver pelts were on hand in the amount of $15,090.00. Other skins raised this total to $16,826.50. On June 1, 1813, the amount of inventory at McKay's River was $2,273.77, furs here totaling

453

interior posts, was superior to that of the Northwest Company; so that they had nothing to fear from competition.

Through the influence of Messrs. M'Dougal and M'Kenzie, this proposition was adopted, and was promptly accepted by M'Tavish. The merchandise sold to him amounted to eight hundred and fifty-eight dollars, to be paid for, in the following spring, in horses, or in any other manner most acceptable to the partners at that period.[8]

This agreement being concluded, the partners formed their plans for the year that they would yet have to pass in the country.[9] Their ob-

---

$2,333.75. McKenzie's inventory on Snake River was $643.62½, with furs amounting to $488.00. At Spokane, Clarke's inventory was $4,102.82¼, with furs in the amount of $5,617.60. Furs at Okanogan amounted to $11,576.65. On September 17, 1813, inventory of goods, furs, meat, and tallow totaled $1,198.23¾. These figures show a grand total for furs of all kinds as of June 1, 1813, of $36,842.50.

[8] According to Franchère, "this gentleman [McTavish] having represented to us that he was destitute of the necessary goods to procure wherewith to subsist his party on their way homeward, we supplied him from our warehouse, payment to be made us in the ensuing spring, either in furs or in bills of exchange on their house in Canada." *Narrative*, 284. Irving also drew upon the following resolution, which was signed on June 25, 1813, by McDougall, McKenzie, D. Stuart, and Clarke: "As the quality of goods now on hand are unequal to our wants; disassorted and unfit for the Trade of the Country, much less for competition it is hereby unanimously resolved as our only alternative in the present necessities of our situation, that we make proposals to our opponent [John George McTavish] to divide the Trade for the ensuing winter, to wit—That we will give them up the Post of Spokan House and the establishment of the Coutonais, and also supply them with these few articles of goods for which they have already made application; payable next spring in Horses or in any other manner which may best suit us at that period—all upon condition that they on their part will abandon to us all the remaining Parts of the Columbia and forward our dispatches to Mr. Astor by their usual winter express; since it is beyond our power to fit out an express ourselves." Pacific Fur Company Letter Book, Missouri Historical Society, in Elliott, "Sale of Astoria, 1813," *Oregon Historical Quarterly*, Vol. XXXIII (1932), 44, and Flandrau, *Astor and the Oregon Country*, 37. There are a few discrepancies in wording between the versions given by Elliott and Flandrau.

[9] These plans were written down on June 25, 1813, and signed by McDougall, McKenzie, D. Stuart, and Clarke: "It is hereby resolved and agreed that Mr. David Stuart shall go and winter as usual in the North West part of the Columbia with a party of Twenty men where he shall trade as much good Beaver and also Horses as he can procure with the goods he has.

"It is further resolved and agreed that Mr. Jno. Clarke shall go and winter in our Flat Head country with a party of twenty men where he shall trade as many furs in season, Horses and Provisions as the goods he has will purchase.

"It is also resolved and agreed that a small party consisting of Mr. Jno. Reid four Canadians and two Beaver Hunters shall go and winter in the Snake Country in order to meet with those Hunters already in that quarter; to trade all the good Beaver and Provisions the goods they take along with them can procure, and also gather as many jects were, chiefly, present subsistence, and the purchase of horses for the contemplated journey, though they were likewise to collect as much peltries as their diminished means would command. Accordingly, it was arranged, that David Stuart should return to his former post on the Oakinagan, and Mr. Clarke should make his sojourn among the Flatheads. John Reed, the sturdy Hibernian, was to undertake the Snake River country, accompanied by Pierre Dorion and Pierre Delaunay, as hunters, and Francis Landry, Jean Baptiste Turcotte, André La Chapelle, and Gilles Le Clerc, Canadian voyageurs.[10]

Astoria, however, was the post about which they felt the greatest solicitude, and on which they all more or less depended. The maintenance of this in safety throughout the coming year, was, therefore, their grand consideration. Mr. M'Dougal was to continue in command of it, with a party of forty men. They would have to depend chiefly upon the neighboring savages for their subsistence. These, at present, were friendly, but it was to be feared that, when they should discover the exigencies of the post, and its real weakness, they might proceed to hostilities; or, at any rate, might cease to furnish their usual supplies. It was important, therefore, to render the place as independent as possible, of the surrounding tribes for its support; and it was accordingly resolved that

as possible of the Company's Horses that have been in possession of the Indians since these two years.

"It is likewise resolved and agreed upon that Mr. Duncan McDougall shall continue at this place as usual with a party consisting of Forty strong to guard it against the natives of whom we have reason to suspect ill designs should no reinforcements arrive—to secure this peace on which is our chief dependence, too much precaution can not be taken. And as there is no stock of provisions for its support Mr. Donald McKenzie shall go and winter in the Wallameet or thereabout, with four hunters and eight men and pay every attention to procure a constant supply of that indispensable article.

"And whereas the concern have more clerks than is required in any proportion to the number of common men in the service. It is hereby agreed and resolved upon that if it meet their own approbation their engagement shall be delivered up to Donald McLennan, Donald McGillis, and Ross Cox with full permission to engage elsewhere provided they give their notes for any balances they may owe to the concern." Pacific Fur Company Letter Book, Elliott, "Sale of Astoria," loc. cit., 44–45; and Flandrau, op. cit., 37–38. As will be seen from a comparison of this resolution and what Irving writes, he apparently drew from it for his information as well as from other sources cited below. One important discrepancy, however, is his substitution of the name of Alexander Ross for that of Donald McGillis.

[10] The various parties left Astoria on July 7, according to Franchère. Reed's purpose, he says, was to procure as many horses as possible for use in crossing the country when Astoria was abandoned. Narrative, 283–84.

M'Kenzie, with four hunters, and eight common men, should winter in the abundant country of [the][11] Wollamut, from whence they might be enabled to furnish a constant supply of provisions to Astoria.[12]

As there was too great a proportion of clerks for the number of privates in the service, the engagements of three of them, Ross Cox,[13] Ross,[14] and M'Lennan,[15] were surrendered to them, and they immediately enrolled themselves in the service of the Northwest Company; glad, no doubt, to escape from what they considered a sinking ship.[16]

Having made all these arrangements, the four partners,[17] on the first of July, signed a formal manifesto,[18] stating the alarming state of their affairs, from the non-arrival of the annual ship, and the absence and apprehended loss of the Beaver, their want of goods, their despair of receiving any further supply, their ignorance of the coast, and their disappointment as to the interior trade, which they pronounced unequal to

[11] The first edition reads, correctly, *the Wollamut.*

[12] Again Franchère tells us that McKenzie "was occupied with the care of collecting as great a quantity as possible of dried salmon from the Indians. He made seven or eight voyages up the river for that purpose, while we at the Fort were busy in baling the beaver-skins and other furs, in suitable packs for horses to carry." *Ibid.,* 284.

[13] Cox (1793–1853) was from Dublin, Ireland. He came to America in time to enlist as a clerk in Astor's service and to travel to Astoria on the *Beaver*. He left the fur trade in 1817 and returned to Ireland. Wallace (ed.), *Documents,* 434; see also *Columbia River,* Editors' Introduction, xxx–xxxi.

[14] Alexander Ross (1783–1856), a native of Scotland, made his way to Canada in 1805, where he taught school for a number of years before joining the Pacific Fur Company in 1810. He was a passenger on the *Tonquin*. After going over to the North West Company, he remained in the fur trade until 1825. He was the author of three books, two on the fur trade and one about the settlement at Red River, where he was living at the time of his death. Wallace (ed.), *Documents,* 495.

[15] Like Ross, Donald McLennan, a clerk, had come to Astoria on the *Tonquin*, and had served at Fort Okanogan and Fort Spokane. See *Henry-Thompson Journals,* II, 899.

[16] As Cox relates, part of the agreement with McTavish was to offer "to those who should wish to join the North-West Company and remain in the country, the same terms as if they had originally been members of the Company. Messrs. Ross, M'Lennan, and I took advantage of these liberal proposals." *Op. cit.,* 120.

[17] McDougall, McKenzie, David Stuart, and Clarke.

[18] This manifesto, dated July 1, 1813, is in the Pacific Fur Company Letter Book, Missouri Historical Society, and is printed in Elliott, "Sale of Astoria," *loc. cit.,* 45–46, and Flandrau, *op. cit.,* 38–39. Irving in this paragraph digests it accurately and quotes from parts of it. The final paragraph reads: "And we hereby resolve and conclude, that we take our departure from the Forks of the Columbia the first day of June next year; and that every preparation shall be made previous to that period, to the end, that we transport our Furs and conduct our party in safety to the Territory of Louisiana." The last part of this statement appears not to have been acted upon.

the expenses incurred, and incompetent to stand against the powerful opposion of the Northwest Company. And as by the 16th article[19] of
the company's agreement, they were authorized to abandon this undertaking, and dissolve the concern, if before the period of five years it
should be found unprofitable, they now formally announced their intention to do so on the 1st day of June, of the ensuing year, unless in
the interim they should receive the necessary support and supplies from
Mr. Astor, or the stockholders, with orders to continue.

This instrument, accompanied by private letters of similar import,
was delivered to Mr. M'Tavish, who departed on the 5th of July. He
engaged to forward the despatches to Mr. Astor, by the usual winter
express sent overland by the Northwest Company.

The manifesto was signed with great reluctance by Messrs. Clarke
and D. Stuart, whose experience by no means justified the discouraging
account given in it of the internal trade, and who considered the main
difficulties of exploring an unknown and savage country, and of ascertaining the best trading and trapping grounds, in a great measure
overcome. They were overruled, however, by the urgent instances of
M'Dougal and M'Kenzie, who, having resolved upon abandoning the
enterprise, were desirous of making as strong a case as possible to excuse
their conduct to Mr. Astor and to the world.

[19] The sixteenth article reads: "It is further covenanted concluded and agreed by
and between all the parties of these Presents that the said parties shall have full power
to abandon the said undertaking and to dissolve the said company if they shall find
within the term of five years above mentioned that the same is unprofitable." Flandrau, *op. cit.*, 29.

Anxieties of Mr. Astor — Memorial of the Northwest Company
Tidings of a British Naval Expedition Against Astoria
Mr. Astor Applies to Government for Protection
The Frigate Adams Ordered to Be Fitted Out — Bright News from Astoria
Sunshine Suddenly Overclouded

WHILE difficulties and disasters had been gathering about the infant settlement of Astoria, the mind of its projector at New York was a prey to great anxiety. The ship Lark, despatched by him with supplies for the establishment, sailed on the 6th of March, 1813. Within a fortnight afterwards, he received intelligence which justified all his apprehensions of hostility on the part of the British. The Northwest Company had made a second memorial to that government, representing Astoria as an American establishment, stating the vast scope of its contemplated operations, magnifying the strength of its fortifications, and expressing their fears that, unless crushed in the bud, it would effect the downfall of their trade.

Influenced by these representations, the British government ordered the frigate Phœbe to be detached as a convoy for the armed ship, Issac Todd, which was ready to sail with men and munitions for forming a new establishment. They were to proceed together to the mouth of the Columbia, capture or destroy whatever American fortress they should find there, and plant the British flag on its ruins.

Informed of these movements, Mr. Astor lost no time in addressing a second letter to the secretary of state, communicating this intelligence, and requesting it might be laid before the President;[1] as no notice, how-

---

[1] Astor's letter follows: "Last month I had the Honnour to address a letter to you on the Subject of my buisness on the northwest coast of america particularly at Columbia River—I than [*sic*] expressed Some fears that the north west Company if not the British government would make an effort to wrest from us our possison [i.e., possession] and with it a trade which promisd to becom of great Importanes to this country[.]

"I am Sorry to Say that my fears Seem to have been too well grounted [i.e., grounded] for it is understood that the northwest company have fitted a ship at London mount-ever, had been taken of his previous letter, he contented himself with this simple communication, and made no further application for aid.

Awakened now to the danger that menaced the establishment at Astoria, and aware of the importance of protecting this foothold of American commerce and empire on the shores of the Pacific, the government determined to send the frigate Adams,[2] Captain Crane,[3] upon this service. On hearing of this determination, Mr. Astor immediately proceeded to fit out a ship called the Enterprise, to sail in company with the Adams, freighted with additional supplies and reinforcements for Astoria.

About the middle of June, while in the midst of these preparations, Mr. Astor received a letter from Mr. R. Stuart, dated St. Louis, May 1st,[4] confirming the intelligence already received through the public newspapers, of his safe return, and of the arrival of Mr. Hunt and his party at Astoria, and giving the most flattering accounts of the prosperity of the enterprise.

So deep had been the anxiety of Mr. Astor, for the success of this great object of his ambition, that this gleam of good news was almost overpowering. "I felt ready," said he, "to fall upon my knees in a transport of gratitude."

At the same time he heard that the Beaver had made good her voyage from New York to the Columbia. This was additional ground of hope for the welfare of the little colony. The post being thus relieved and strengthened, with an American at its head, and a ship of war about to sail for its protection, the prospect for the future seemed full of encouragement, and Mr. Astor proceeded with fresh vigor to fit out his merchant ship.

Unfortunately for Astoria, this brights gleam of sunshine was soon overclouded. Just as the Adams had received her complement of men, and the two vessels were ready for sea, news came from Commodore

ing 20 guns and that the goverment Send with it A Sloop of war to take possison of Columbia River & of cours our fort & our property there—alltho my former Letter to you on this subject Seems to have escapd notics or not to have merited a reply. I Still think It my Duty to mak this communication which I Request you will have the goodness to make Known to the President[.]" John Jacob Astor, New York, March 22, 1813, to James Monroe, Secretary of State. National Archives, Diplomatic, Legal, and Fiscal Branch.

[2] *John Adams.*

[3] William Montgomery Crane. Porter, *John Jacob Astor*, I, 219.

[4] Stuart wrote to Astor, therefore, the day after his arrival in St. Louis.

Chauncey,[5] commanding on Lake Ontario, that a reinforcement of seamen was wanted in that quarter. The demand was urgent, the crew of
the Adams was immediately transferred to that service, and the ship
was laid up.

This was a most ill-timed and discouraging blow, but Mr. Astor
would not yet allow himself to pause in his undertaking. He determined
to send the Enterprise[6] to sea alone, and let her take the chance of making her unprotected way across the ocean. Just at this time, however,
a British force made its appearance off the Hook;[7] and the port of New
York was effectually blockaded. To send a ship to sea under these circumstances, would be to expose her to almost certain capture. The Enterprise was, therefore, unloaded[8] and dismantled, and Mr. Astor was
obliged to comfort himself with the hope that the Lark might reach
Astoria in safety and, that, aided by her supplies, and by the good management of Mr. Hunt and his associates, the little colony might be able
to maintain itself until the return of peace.

[5] Commodore Isaac Chauncey (1772–1840). During the War of 1812, he was commander of naval forces on Lake Ontario and Lake Erie.

[6] It was to have been commanded by Daniel Greene, who was also to have acted as
supercargo; but after various delays, Greene grew impatient and transferred to another
ship. Porter, *op. cit.*, 219–20. The cargo amounted to $20,000.

[7] Sandy Hook in New York Harbor.

[8] Late in December, 1813, or in January, 1814.

CHAPTER LVI

Affairs of State at Astoria — M'Dougal Proposes for the
Hand of an Indian Princess — Matrimonial Embassy to Comcomly
Matrimonial Notions Among the Chinooks — Settlements and Pin-Money
The Bringing Home of the Bride — A Managing Father-in-Law
Arrival of Mr. Hunt at Astoria

WE have hitherto had so much to relate of a gloomy and disastrous nature, that it is with a feeling of momentary relief we turn to something of a more pleasing complexion, and record the first, and indeed only nuptials in high life that took place in the infant settlement of Astoria.

M'Dougal, who appears to have been a man of a thousand projects, and of great, though somewhat irregular ambition, suddenly conceived the idea of seeking the hand of one of the native princesses, a daughter of the one-eyed potentate Comcomly, who held sway over the fishing tribe of the Chinooks, and had long supplied the factory with smelts and sturgeons.

Some accounts give rather a romantic origin to this affair, tracing it to the stormy night when M'Dougal, in the course of an exploring expedition, was driven by stress of weather to seek shelter in the royal abode of Comcomly. Then and there he was first struck with the charms of the[1] piscatory princess, as she exerted herself to entertain her father's guest.

The "journal of Astoria," however, which was kept under his own eye, records this union as a high state alliance, and great stroke of policy. The factory had to depend, in a great measure, on the Chinooks for provisions. They were at present friendly, but it was to be feared they would prove otherwise, should they discover the weakness and the exigencies of the post, and the intention to leave the country. This alliance, therefore, would infallibly rivet Comcomly to the interests of the Astorians, and with him the powerful tribe of the Chinooks. Be this as it may, and it is hard to fathom the real policy of governors and princes, M'Dougal despatched two of the clerks as ambassadors extraordinary, to wait upon

[1] *This* in first edition.

the one-eyed chieftain, and make overtures for the hand of his daughter.

The Chinooks, though not a very refined nation, have notions of matrimonial arrangements that would not disgrace the most refined sticklers for settlements and pin-money. The suitor repairs not to the bower of his mistress, but to her father's lodge, and throws down a present at his feet. His wishes are then disclosed by some discreet friend employed by him for the purpose. If the suitor and his present find favor in the eyes of the father, he breaks the matter to his daughter, and inquires into the state of her inclinations. Should her answer be favorable, the suit is accepted and the lover has to make further presents to the father, of horses, canoes, and other valuables, according to the beauty and merits of the bride; looking forward to a return in kind whenever they shall go to housekeeping.

We have more than once had occasion to speak of the shrewdness of Comcomly; but never was it exerted more adroitly than on this occasion. He was a great friend of M'Dougal, and pleased with the idea of having so distinguished a son-in-law; but so favorable an opportunity of benefiting his own fortune was not likely to occur a second time, and he determined to make the most of it. Accordingly, the negotiation was protracted with true diplomatic skill. Conference after conference was held with the two ambassadors. Comcomly was extravagant in his terms; rating the charms of his daughter at the highest price, and indeed she is represented as having one of the flattest and most aristocratical heads in the tribe. At length the preliminaries were all happily adjusted. On the 20th of July, early in the afternoon, a squadron of canoes crossed over from the village of the Chinooks, bearing the royal family of Comcomly, and all his court.

That worthy sachem landed in princely state, arrayed in a bright blue blanket and red breech clout, with an extra quantity of paint and feathers, attended by a train of half-naked warriors and nobles. A horse was in waiting to receive the princess, who was mounted behind one of the clerks, and thus conveyed, coy but compliant, to the fortress. Here she was received with devout, though decent joy, by her expecting bridegroom.

Her bridal adornments, it is true, at first caused some little dismay, having painted and anointed herself for the occasion according to the Chinook toilet; by dint, however, of copious ablutions, she was freed from all adventitious tint and fragrance, and entered into the nuptial state, the cleanest princess that had ever been known, of the somewhat unctuous tribe of the Chinooks.[2]

From that time forward, Comcomly was a daily visitor at the fort, and was admitted into the most intimate councils of his son-in-law. He took an interest in everything that was going forward, but was particularly frequent in his visits to the blacksmith's shop; tasking the labors of the artificer in iron for every kind of weapon and implement suited to the savage state, insomuch that the necessary business of the factory was often postponed to attend to his requisitions.

The honey-moon had scarce passed away, and M'Dougal was seated with his bride in the fortress of Astoria, when, about noon of the 20th of August,[3] Gassacop, the son of Comcomly, hurried into his presence with great agitation, and announced a ship at the mouth of the river. The news produced a vast sensation. Was it a ship of peace or war? Was it American or British? Was it the Beaver or the Isaac Todd? M'Dougal hurried to the water side, threw himself into a boat, and ordered the hands to pull with all speed for the mouth of the harbor. Those in the fort remained watching the entrance of the river, anxious to know whether they were to prepare for greeting a friend or fighting an enemy. At length the ship was descried crossing the bar, and bending her course towards Astoria. Every gaze was fixed upon her in silent scrutiny, until the American flag was recognized. A general shout was the first expression of joy, and next a salutation was thundered from the cannon of the fort.

The vessel came to anchor on the opposite side of the river, and returned the salute. The boat of Mr. M'Dougal went on board, and was seen returning late in the afternoon. The Astorians watched her with straining eyes, to discover who were on board, but the sun went down, and the evening closed in, before she was sufficiently near. At length she reached the land, and Mr. Hunt stepped on shore. He was hailed as one risen from the dead, and his return was a signal for merriment

[2] None of the published sources available to Irving contains an account of this marriage. The "Journal of Astoria," to which he refers as a source, has apparently been lost.

[3] Erroneously *August 4* in Franchère, *Narrative*, 284, but given correctly in Ross, *Adventures*, 236, as August 20. Confirmation of the date appears in official records of the company since published; see T. C. Elliott, "Sale of Astoria, 1813," *Oregon Historical Quarterly*, Vol. XXXIII (1932), 46, and Flandrau, *Astor and the Oregon Country*, 39.

almost equal to that which prevailed at the nuptials of M'Dougal.

We must now explain the cause of this gentleman's long absence, which had given rise to such gloomy and dispiriting surmises.

Voyage of the Beaver to New Archangel — A Russian Governor
Roystering Rule — The Tyranny of the Table
Hard-Drinking Bargainings — Voyage to Kamtschatka
Seal-Catching Establishment at St. Paul's — Storms at Sea
Mr. Hunt Left at the Sandwich Islands — Transactions of
the Beaver at Canton — Return of Mr. Hunt to Astoria

IT will be recollected, that the destination of the Beaver, when she sailed from Astoria on the 4th of August in 1812, was to proceed northwardly along the coast to Sheetka,[1] or New Archangel, there to dispose of that part of her cargo intended for the supply of the Russian estabment at that place, and then to return to Astoria, where it was expected she would arrive in October.

New Archangel is situated in Norfolk Sound, lat. 57° 2' N., long. 135° 50' W. It was the head-quarters of the different colonies of the Russian Fur Company, and the common rendezvous of the American vessels trading along the coast.

The Beaver met with nothing worthy of particular mention in her voyage, and arrived at New Archangel on the 19th of August. The place at that time was the residence of Count Baranhoff,[2] the governor of the different colonies; a rough, rugged, hospitable, hard-drinking old Russian; somewhat of a soldier, somewhat of a trader; above all, a boon companion of the old roystering school, with a strong cross of the bear.

Mr. Hunt found this hyperborean veteran ensconced in a fort which crested the whole of a high rocky promontory. It mounted one hundred guns, large and small, and was impregnable to Indian attack, unaided by artillery. Here the old governor lorded it over sixty Russians, who formed the corps of the trading establishment, besides an indefinite number of Indian hunters of the Kodiak tribe, who were continually

---

[1] Sitka.

[2] Aleksandr Andreevich Baranov (1746–1819), resident director of the Russian company from 1790 to 1819, who founded Sitka in 1804. See C. L. Andrews, "Alaska Under the Russians—Baronof the Builder," *Washington Historical Quarterly*, Vol. VII (1916), 202–16.

coming and going, or lounging and loitering about the fort like so many
hounds round a sportsman's hunting quarters. Though a loose liver
among his guests, the governor was a strict disciplinarian among his
men; keeping them in perfect subjection, and having seven on guard
night and day.

Beside[s] those immediate serfs and dependants just mentioned, the
old Russian potentate exerted a considerable sway over a numerous and
irregular class of maritime traders, who looked to him for aid and munitions, and through whom he may be said to have, in some degree,
extended his power along the whole northwest coast. These were American captains of vessels engaged in a particular department of the trade.[3]
One of these captains would come, in a manner, empty-handed to New
Archangel. Here his ship would be furnished with about fifty canoes
and a hundred Kodiak hunters, and fitted out with provisions, and everything necessary for hunting the sea-otter on the coast of California,
where the Russians have another establishment.[4] The ship would ply
along the Californian coast from place to place, dropping parties of
otter hunters in their canoes, furnishing them only with water, and
leaving them to depend upon their own dexterity for a maintenance.
When a sufficient cargo was collected, she would gather up her canoes
and hunters, and return with them to Archangel; where the captain
would render in the returns of his voyage, and receive one half of the
skins for his share.

Over these coasting captains, as we have hinted, the veteran governor exerted some sort of sway, but it was of a peculiar and characteristic kind; it was the tyranny of the table. They were obliged to join
him in his "prosnics" or carousals, and to drink "potations pottle deep."[5]
His carousals, too, were not of the most quiet kind, nor were his potations
as mild as nectar. "He is continually," said Mr. Hunt, "giving enter-
tainments by way of parade, and if you do not drink raw rum, and boiling punch as strong as sulphur, he will insult you as soon as he gets
drunk, which is very shortly after sitting down to table."

As to any "temperance captain" who stood fast to his faith, and refused to give up his sobriety, he might go elsewhere for a market, for
he stood no chance with the governor. Rarely, however, did any cold-

---

[3] The first edition has *of trade*.

[4] Fort Ross, founded on Bodega Bay, not far north of San Francisco, in 1811.

[5] Shakespeare's *Othello*, III, ii, 56.

water caitiff of the kind darken the door of old Baranhoff; the coasting captains knew too well his humor and their own interests; they joined in his revels, they drank, and sang, and whooped, and hiccuped, until they all got "half seas over," and then affairs went on swimmingly.

An awful warning to all "flinchers" occurred shortly before Mr. Hunt's arrival. A young naval officer had recently been sent out by the emperor to take command of one of the company's vessels. The governor, as usual, had him at his "prosnics," and plied him with fiery potations. The young man stood on the defensive until the old count's ire was completely kindled; he carried his point, and made the greenhorn tipsy, willy nilly. In proportion as they grew fuddled they grew noisy, they quarrelled in their cups; the youngster paid old Baranhoff in his own coin by rating him soundly; in reward for which, when sober, he was taken the rounds of four pickets, and received seventy-nine lashes, taled out with Russian punctuality of punishment.

Such was the old grizzled bear with whom Mr. Hunt had to do his business. How he managed to cope with his humor; whether he pledged him[6] in raw rum and blazing punch, and "clinked the can" with him as they made their bargains, does not appear upon record; we must infer, however, from his general observations on the absolute sway of this hard-drinking potentate, that he had to conform to the customs of his court, and that their business transactions presented a maudlin mixture of punch and peltry.

The greatest annoyance to Mr. Hunt, however, was the delay to which he was subjected, in disposing of the cargo of the ship, and getting the requisite returns.[7] With all the governor's devotions to the bottle, he never obfuscated his faculties sufficiently to lose sight of his interest, and is represented by Mr. Hunt as keen, not to say crafty, at a bargain, as the most arrant water-drinker. A long time was expended negotiating with him, and by the time the bargain was concluded, the month of October had arrived. To add to the delay he was to be paid for his cargo in seal skins. Now it so happened that there was none of this kind of peltry at the fort of old Baranhoff. It was necessary, therefore, for Mr. Hunt to proceed to a seal-catching establishment, which the Russian

[6] Erroneously *himself* in the Author's Revised Edition. The first edition has *him*.

[7] The goods, which cost $22,342.38 in New York, were sold to Baranov for $56,465.87½, payable in seal skins. See note 12 below. Porter, *John Jacob Astor*, I, 206. See also "Account Sales of the Ship *Beaver*," *ibid.*, 514–19, and "Barter Account of the Ship *Beaver*," 521–22.

company had at the island of St. Paul,[8] in the Sea of Kamtschatka.[9] He accordingly set sail on the 4th of October, after having spent forty-five days at New Archangel boosing and bargaining with its roystering commander, and right glad was he to escape from the clutches of this "old man of the sea."[10]

The Beaver arrived at St. Paul's on the 31st of October; by which time, according to arrangement, he ought to have been back at Astoria. The island of St. Paul is in latitude 57° N., longitude 170° or 171° W. Its shores, in certain places, and at certain seasons, are covered with seals, while others are playing about in the water. Of these, the Russians take only the small ones, from seven to ten months old, and carefully select the males, giving the females their freedom, that the breed may not be diminished. The islanders, however, kill the large ones for provisions, and for skins wherewith to cover their canoes. They drive them from the shore over the rocks, until within a short distance of their habitations, where they kill them. By this means, they save themselves the trouble of carrying the skins and have the flesh at hand. This is thrown in heaps, and when the season for skinning is over, they take out the entrails and make one heap of the blubber. This, with drift-wood, serves for fuel, for the island is entirely destitute of trees. They make another heap of the flesh, which, with the eggs of sea-fowls, preserved in oil, an occasional sea-lion, a few ducks in winter, and some wild roots, compose[11] their food.

Mr. Hunt found several Russians at the island, and one hundred hunters, natives of Oonalaska,[12] with their families. They lived in cabins that looked like canoes; being, for the most part formed of the jaw-

[8] One of the Pribilof Islands, named for Gerasim Pribylov, Russian sea captain who here discovered the great fur-seal rookeries in 1786.

[9] The Bering Sea.

[10] The phrase is traceable to Homer's *Odyssey* (Book IV, l. 349), where it refers to Proteus, whom Menelaus met on his wanderings and overpowered, as well as to the fifth voyage of Sinbad the Sailor. In the latter, Sinbad (to whom Hunt is likened at the end of the present chapter) finally subdues and kills "an old man of the sea"; see Richard F. Burton (trans.), *The Arabian Nights' Entertainment*. Irving's use of the phrase is doubtless from the Arabian tale, but it is noteworthy that the stories of Sinbad are in many ways reminiscent of the legends of Odysseus, which were known to the Arabs; see N. J. Dawood (trans.), *The Thousand and One Nights*, xi.

[11] *Composes* in first edition.

[12] Unalaska, one of the Aleutian Islands, where Russian settlements for capturing seals and sea otters were located in the late eighteenth century. Here, according to Fran-

bone of a whale, put up as rafters, across which were laid pieces of drift-
wood covered over with long grass, the skins of large sea animals, and
earth; so as to be quite comfortable, in despite of the rigors of the climate; though we are told they had as ancient and fish-like an odor, "as
had the quarters of Jonah, when he lodged within the whale."

In one of these odoriferous mansions, Mr. Hunt occasionally took
up his abode, that he might be at hand to hasten the loading of the ship.
The operation, however, was somewhat slow, for it was necessary to
overhaul and inspect every pack to prevent imposition, and the peltries
had then to be conveyed in large boats, made of skins, to the ship, which
was some little distance from the shore, standing off and on.

One night, while Mr. Hunt was on shore, with some others of the
crew, there arose a terrible gale.[13] When the day broke, the ship was
not to be seen. He watched for her with anxious eyes until night, but in
vain. Day after day of boisterous storms, and howling wintry weather,
were passed in watchfulness and solicitude. Nothing was to be seen but
a dark and angry sea, and a scowling northern sky; and at night he
retired within the jaws of the whale, and nestled disconsolately among
seal skins.

At length, on the 13th of November, the Beaver made her appearance; much the worse for the stormy conflicts which she had sustained[14]
in those hyperborean seas. She had been obliged to carry a press of sail
in heavy gales to be able to hold her ground, and had consequently sustained great damage in her canvas and rigging. Mr. Hunt lost no time
in hurrying the residue of the cargo on board of her; then, bidding adieu
to his seal-fishing friends, and his whalebone habitation, he put forth
once more to sea.

He was now for making the best of his way to Astoria, and fortunate
would it have been for the interests of that place, and the interests of
Mr. Astor, had he done so; but, unluckily, a perplexing question rose
in his mind. The sails and rigging of the Beaver had been much rent
and shattered in the late storm; would she be able to stand the hard
gales to be expected in making Columbia River at this season? Was it

chère (*Narrative*, 280), Hunt obtained 80,000 seal skins, but the correct figure was
74,541. See accounts in Porter, *op. cit.*, I, 518–19.

[13] On November 5. Porter, *op. cit.*, I, 206.

[14] The first edition reads *conflicts she had sustained*.

prudent, also, at this boisterous time of the year to risk the valuable cargo which she now had on board, by crossing and recrossing the dangerous bar of that river? These doubts were probably suggested or enforced by Captain Sowle, who, it has already been seen, was an overcautious, or rather, a timid seaman, and they may have had some weight with Mr. Hunt; but there were other considerations, which more strongly swayed his mind. The lateness of the season, and the unforeseen delays the ship had encountered at New Archangel, and by being obliged to proceed to St. Paul's, had put her so much back in her calculated time, that there was a risk of her arriving so late at Canton, as to come to a bad market, both for the sale of her peltries, and the purchase of a return cargo. He considered it to the interest of the company, therefore, that he should proceed at once to the Sandwich Islands; there wait the arrival of the annual vessel from New York, take passage in her to Astoria, and suffer the Beaver to continue on to Canton.

On the other hand, he was urged to the other course by his engagements; by the plan of the voyage marked out for the Beaver, by Mr. Astor; by his inclination, and the possibility that the establishment might need his presence, and by the recollection that there must already be a large amount of peltries collected at Astoria, and waiting for the return of the Beaver, to convey them to market.

These conflicting questions perplexed and agitated his mind and gave rise to much anxious reflection, for he was a conscientious man that seems ever to have aimed at a faithful discharge of his duties, and to have had the interests of his employers earnestly at heart. His decision in the present instance was injudicious, and proved unfortunate. It was, to bear away for the Sandwich Islands. He persuaded himself that it was a matter of necessity, and that the distressed condition of the ship left him no other alternative; but we rather suspect he was so persuaded by the representations of the timid captain. They accordingly stood for the Sandwich Islands, arrived at Woahoo, where the ship underwent the necessary repairs, and again put to sea on the 1st of January, 1813; leaving Mr. Hunt on the island.

We will follow the Beaver to Canton, as her fortunes, in some measure, exemplify the evil of commanders of ships acting contrary to orders; and as they form a part of the tissue of cross-purposes that marred the great commercial enterprise we have undertaken to record.

The Beaver arrived safe at Canton, where Captain Sowle found the letter of Mr. Astor, giving him information of the war and directing him to convey the intelligence to Astoria. He wrote a reply, dictated either by timidity or obstinacy, in which he declined complying with the orders of Mr. Astor, but said he would wait for the return of peace, and then come home. The other proceedings of Captain Sowle were equally wrongheaded and unlucky. He was offered one hundred and fifty thousand dollars for the fur he had taken on board at St. Paul's. The goods for which it had been procured, cost but twenty-five thousand dollars in New York. Had he accepted this offer, and re-invested the amount in nankeens, which at that time, in consequence of the interruption to commerce by the war, were at two thirds of their usual price, the whole would have brought three hundred thousand dollars in New York. It is true, the war would have rendered it unsafe to attempt the homeward voyage, but he might have put the goods in store at Canton, until after the peace, and have sailed without risk of capture to Astoria; bringing to the partners at that place tidings of the great profits realized on the outward cargo, and the still greater to be expected from the returns. The news of such a brilliant commencement to their undertaking would have counterbalanced the gloomy tidings of the war; it would have infused new spirit into them all, and given them courage and constancy to persevere in the enterprise. Captain Sowle, however, refused the offer of one hundred and fifty thousand dollars, and stood wavering and chaffering for higher terms. The furs began to fall in value; this only increased his irresolution; they sunk so much that he feared to sell at all; he borrowed money on Mr. Astor's account at an interest of eighteen per cent, and laid up his ship to await the return of peace.

In the meanwhile, Mr. Hunt soon saw reason to repent the resolution he had adopted in altering the destination of the ship. His stay at the Sandwich Islands was prolonged far beyond all expectation. He looked in vain for the annual ship in the spring. Month after month passed by, and still she did not make her appearance. He, too, proved the danger of departing from orders. Had he returned from St. Paul's to Astoria, all the anxiety and despondency about his fate, and about the whole course of the undertaking, would have been obviated. The Beaver would have received the furs collected at the factory and taken them to Canton, and great gains, instead of great losses, would have been the result. The greatest blunder, however, was that committed by Captain Sowle.[15]

At length, about the 20th of June, the ship Albatross, Captain Smith,[16] arrived from China, and brought the first tidings of the war to the Sandwich Islands. Mr. Hunt was no longer in doubt and perplexity as to the reason of the non-appearance of the annual ship. His first thoughts were for the welfare of Astoria, and, concluding that the inhabitants would probably be in want of provisions, he chartered the Albatross for two thousand dollars, to land him, with some supplies,[17] at the mouth of the Columbia where he arrived, as we have seen, on the 20th of August, after a year's seafaring that might have furnished a chapter in the wanderings of Sinbad.[18]

[15] A review of the correspondence which passed between Astor and Sowle shows that Irving's criticism of the Captain was not fully justified. See Porter, *op. cit.*, I, 236–39.

[16] Captain William Smith.

[17] Franchère shows that Hunt brought with him "35 barrels of salt pork or beef, nine tierces of rice, a great quantity of dried *Taro*, and a good supply of salt." *Narrative*, 287.

[18] A brief parallel account of Hunt's experiences on the *Beaver* and his return to Astoria appears in Franchère, *Narrative*, 285–87. Evidence within the chapter shows that Irving's main source must have been a journal kept by Hunt which has since disappeared. Porter states that Irving, "is almost our only authority for the movements of the *Beaver* and the considerations affecting them." *Op. cit.*, I, 207. Besides Franchère and Irving, other authorities are the correspondence between Astor and Sowle plus what Ross says, with his strong bias against Astor; see his *Adventures*, 233–36.

☜{ C H A P T E R   L V I I I }☞

Arrangements Among the Partners — Mr. Hunt Sails in the Albatross
Arrives at the Marquesas — News of the Frigate Phœbe
Mr. Hunt Proceeds to the Sandwich Islands
Voyage of the Lark — Her Shipwreck
Transactions with the Natives of the Sandwich Islands
Conduct of Tamaahmaah

MR. HUNT was overwhelmed with surprise when he learnt the resolution taken by the partners to abandon Astoria.[1] He soon found, however, that matters had gone too far, and the minds of his colleagues had
become too firmly bent upon the measure, to render any opposition of
avail. He was beset, too, with the same disparaging accounts of the interior trade, and of the whole concerns and prospects of the company
that had been rendered to Mr. Astor. His own experience had been full
of perplexities and discouragements. He had a conscientious anxiety for
the interests of Mr. Astor, and, not comprehending the extended views
of that gentleman, and his habit of operating with great amounts, he
had from the first been daunted by the enormous expenses required, and
had become disheartened by the subsequent losses sustained, which appeared to him to be ruinous in their magnitude. By degrees, therefore,
he was brought to acquiesce in the step taken by his colleagues, as perhaps advisable in the exigencies of the case; his only care was to wind
up the business with as little further loss as possible to Mr. Astor.

A large stock of valuable furs was collected at the factory, which it

[1] "Mr. Hunt was surprised beyond measure," writes Franchère, "when we informed
him of the resolution we had taken of abandoning the country: he blamed us severely
for having acted with so much precipitation, pointing out that the success of the late
coasting voyage, and the arrangements we had made with the Russians, promised a
most advantageous trade, which it was a thousand pities to sacrifice, and lose the
fruits of the hardships he had endured and the dangers he had braved, at one fell swoop,
by this rash measure. Nevertheless, seeing the partners were determined to abide by
their first resolution, and not being able, by himself alone, to fulfil his engagements
to Governor Barnoff [*sic*], he consented to embark once more, in order to seek a vessel
to transport our heavy goods, and such of us as wished to return by sea." *Narrative*,
288. Cf. Ross, *Adventures*, 243.

473

was necessary to get to a market. There were twenty-five Sandwich Islanders also in the employ of the company, whom they were bound, by express agreement, to restore to their native country. For these purposes a ship was necessary.

The Albatross was bound to the Marquesas, and thence to the Sandwich Islands.[2] It was resolved that Mr. Hunt should sail in her in quest of a vessel, and should return, if possible, by the 1st of January,[3] bringing with him a supply of provisions. Should anything occur, however, to prevent his return, an arrangement was to be proposed to Mr. M'Tavish, to transfer such of the men as were so disposed, from the service of the American Fur Company into that of the Northwest, the latter becoming responsible for the wages due them, on receiving an equivalent in goods from the store-house of the factory.[4] As a means of facilitating the despatch of business, Mr. M'Dougal proposed, that in case Mr. Hunt should not return, the whole arrangement with Mr. M'Tavish should be left solely to him. This was assented to; the contingency being considered possible, but not probable.[5]

It is proper to note, that, on the first announcement by Mr. M'Dou-

[2] According to Franchère, Captain Smith had been asked to remain through the summer "in order to transport our goods and people, as soon as they could be got together, to the Sandwich islands." *Narrative*, 288. Because his ship was chartered to carry a load of sandalwood to the Marquesas Islands, he was unable to comply.

[3] January 1, 1814. The resolution of the partners, dated August 25, 1813, reads, in part, as follows: "We therefore unanimously agree that W. P. Hunt again depart from this place in the Ship [*Albatross*] now here (for fear we may not have another opportunity) and proceed to see Captains Davies & Winchip who are expected about this time in California, and to go either with them or any other opportunity to the Sandwich Islands for the purpose of chartering or of procuring in any other way in his power (should none come addressed to us) a vessel to come here and relieve us by taking up our Skins and other property some of our people and the natives of the Sandwich Islands in our employ being about 25 in numbers. That said W. P. Hunt procure . . . a quantity of provisions in proportion to our wants & his means of getting them. That he take his departure from the Sandwich Islands for his return if possible on or before the first of January next but in all cases to be guided by circumstances and act at his discretion to the end that he fulfill his mission." It was further agreed, "human life being so uncertain," that Hunt should "draw three setts of exchange on John Jacob Astor Esq. . . . to the amount of twenty thousand dollars to be left with D. MacDougall in case of being disappointed in said Hunt's return, to meet the demands of our people at St. Louis or elsewhere." Elliott, "Sale of Astoria, 1813," *Oregon Historical Quarterly*, Vol. XXXIII (1932), 46; Flandrau, *Astor and the Oregon Country*, 39-40.

[4] *Ibid.*

[5] *Ibid.* See also Porter, *John Jacob Astor*, I, 225-26, for these final arrangements.

gal of his intention to break up the establishment, three of the clerks,[6] British subjects, had, with his consent, passed into the service of the Northwest Company, and departed with Mr. M'Tavish for his post in the interior.

Having arranged all these matters during a sojourn of six days at Astoria, Mr. Hunt set sail in the Albatross on the 26th of August, and arrived without accident at the Marquesas.[7] He had not been there long, when Porter[8] arrived in the frigate Essex, bringing in a number of stout London whalers as prizes, having made a sweeping cruise in the Pacific. From Commodore Porter he received the alarming intelligence that the British frigate Phœbe,[9] with a storeship mounted with battering pieces, calculated to attack forts, had arrived at Rio Janeiro, where she had been joined by the sloops of war Cherub and Raccoon, and that they had all sailed in company on the 6th of July for the Pacific, bound, as it was supposed, to Columbia River.

Here, then, was the death-warrant of unfortunate Astoria! The anxious mind of Mr. Hunt was in greater perplexity than ever. He had been eager to extricate the property of Mr. Astor from a failing concern with as little loss as possible; there was now danger that the whole would be swallowed up. How was it to be snatched from the gulf? It was impossible to charter a ship for the purpose, now that a British

---

[6] See above, Chapter LIV, note 9.

[7] One of the clerks, Benjamin Clapp, accompanied Hunt. Upon leaving Astoria, the *Albatross* was to sail along the California coast in hopes of meeting an American ship. As to the date, Franchère says only that Hunt sailed "at the end of the month." Franchère, *Narrative*, 288.

[8] David Porter (1780–1843), American naval officer who, in command of the *Essex* in the War of 1812, raided British shipping in the Atlantic and the Pacific. The *Essex* was the first U.S. warship to enter the Pacific Ocean, where Porter captured the vessels to which Irving refers. At this time, November, 1813, he also took formal possession of the largest of the Marquesas Islands, but this claim was never asserted by the United States. Porter was court-martialed in 1825. At the time (1835) when Irving was writing *Astoria*, Porter was chargé d'affaires at Constantinople.

[9] A little less than a month before Hunt received this intelligence, Astor wrote to the Secretary of Navy: "By Letters which I Recid yesterday from London under Date 9 April it is quite Certain that the British government Did Send with great secressy the Frigate Phobe to convoy the Ship Isaac Todd beloing to the north west Compa[n]y to Columbia River—and to take possison of that River[.] both Ships Left Portsmouth [England] about the Last of March haveing on board ordanancs Stores &c." John Jacob Astor, New York, July 17, 1813, to William Jones, Secretary of Navy, in Bridgwater, "John Jacob Astor Relative to His Settlement on Columbia River," *Yale University Library Gazette*, Vol. XXIV (1949), 60–61.

squadron was on its way to the river. He applied to purchase one of the whale ships brought in by Commodore Porter. The commodore demanded twenty-five thousand dollars for her. The price appeared exorbitant, and no bargain could be made. Mr. Hunt then urged the commodore to fit out one of his prizes, and send her to Astoria, to bring off the property and part of the people, but he declined, "from want of authority." He assured Mr. Hunt, however, that he would endeavor to fall in with the enemy, or should he hear of their having certainly gone to the Columbia, he would either follow or anticipate them, should his circumstances warrant such a step.

In this tantalizing state of suspense, Mr. Hunt was detained at the Marquesas until November 23d, when he proceeded in the Albatross to the Sandwich Islands. He still cherished a faint hope that, notwithstanding the war, and all other discouraging circumstances, the annual ship might have been sent by Mr. Astor, and might have touched at the islands, and proceeded to the Columbia. He knew the pride and interest taken by that gentleman in his great enterprise, and that he would not be deterred by dangers and difficulties from prosecuting it; much less would he leave the infant establishment without succor and support in the time of trouble. In this, we have seen, he did but justice to Mr. Astor; and we must now turn to notice the cause of the non-arrival of the vessel which he had despatched with reinforcements and supplies. Her voyage forms another chapter of accidents in this eventful story.

The Lark sailed from New York on the 6th of March, 1813, and proceeded prosperously on her voyage, until within a few degrees[10] of the Sandwich Islands. Here a gale sprang up that soon blew with tremendous violence.[11] The Lark was a staunch and noble ship, and for a time buffeted bravely with the storm. Unluckily, however, she "broached to," and was struck by a heavy sea, that hove her on her beam-ends. The helm, too, was knocked to leeward, all command of the vessel was lost, and another mountain wave completely overset her. Orders were given to cut away the masts. In the hurry and confusion, the boats also were unfortunately cut adrift. The wreck then righted, but was a mere hulk, full of water, with a heavy sea washing over it, and all the hatches off.

[10] Latitude $21°$ $30'$ north, longitude $150°$ west, according to Captain Samuel H. Northrop, in command, who wrote to Astor in March from Astoria. His MS letter is in the Astor Papers, Baker Library, Harvard Graduate School of Business Administration, and is published in Porter, op. cit., I, 552–54.
[11] On August 13, 1813.

On mustering the crew, one man was missing, who was discovered below in the forecastle, drowned.

In cutting away the masts, it had been utterly impossible to observe the necessary precaution of commencing with the lee rigging, that being, from the position of the ship, completely under water. The masts and spars, therefore, being linked to the wreck by the shrouds and the rigging, remained alongside for four days. During all this time the ship lay rolling in the trough of the sea, the heavy surges breaking over her, and the spars heaving and banging to and fro, bruising the half-drowned sailors that clung to the bowsprit and the stumps of the masts. The sufferings of these poor fellows were intolerable. They stood to their waists in water, in imminent peril of being washed off by every surge. In this position they dared not sleep, lest they should let go their hold and be swept away. The only dry place on the wreck was the bowsprit. Here they took turns to be tied on, for half an hour at a time, and in this way gained short snatches of sleep.

On the 14th, the first mate died at his post, and was swept off by the surges. On the 17th, two seamen, faint and exhausted, were washed overboard. The next wave threw their bodies back upon the deck, where they remained, swashing backward and forward, ghastly objects to the almost perishing survivors. Mr. Ogden, the supercargo, who was at the bowsprit, called to the men nearest to the bodies, to fasten them to the wreck; as a last horrible resource in case of being driven to extremity by famine!

On the 17th the gale gradually subsided, and the sea became calm. The sailors now crawled feebly about the wreck, and began to relieve it from the main encumbrances. The spars were cleared away, the anchors and guns heaved overboard; the sprit-sail yard was rigged for a jury-mast, and a mizzen topsail set upon it. A sort of stage was made of a few broken spars, on which the crew were raised above the surface of the water, so as to be enabled to keep themselves dry, and to sleep comfortably. Still their sufferings from hunger and thirst were great; but there was a Sandwich Islander on board, an expert swimmer, who found his way into the cabin, and occasionally brought up a few bottles of wine and porter, and at length got into the run, and secured a quarter cask of wine. A little raw pork was likewise procured, and dealt out with a sparing hand. The horrors of their situation were increased by the sight of numerous sharks prowling about the wreck, as if waiting for their

477

prey. On the 24th, the cook, a black man, died, and was cast into the sea, when he was instantly seized on by these ravenous monsters.

They had been several days making slow headway under their scanty sail, when, on the 25th, they came in sight of land. It was about fifteen leagues distant, and they remained two or three days drifting along in sight of it. On the 28th, they descried, to their great transport, a canoe approaching, managed by natives. They came alongside, and brought a most welcome supply of potatoes. They informed them that the land they had made was one of the Sandwich Islands. The second mate and one of the seamen went on shore in the canoe for water and provisions, and to procure aid from the islanders, in towing the wreck into a harbor.

Neither of the men returned, nor was any assistance sent from shore. The next day, ten or twelve canoes came alongside, but roamed round the wreck like so many sharks, and would render no aid in towing her to land.

The sea continued to break over the vessel with such violence, that it was impossible to stand at the helm without the assistance of lashings. The crew were now so worn down by famine and thirst, that the captain saw it would be impossible for them to withstand the breaking of the sea, when the ship should ground; he deemed the only chance for their lives, therefore, was to get to land in the canoes, and stand ready to receive and protect the wreck when she should drift to shore. Accordingly, they all got safe to land, but had scarcely touched the beach when they were surrounded by the natives, who stripped them almost naked. The name of this inhospitable island was Tahoorowa.[12]

In the course of the night, the wreck came drifting to the strand, with the surf thundering around her, and shortly afterwards bilged. On the following morning, numerous casks of provisions floated on shore. The natives staved them for the sake of the iron hoops, but would not allow the crew to help themselves to the contents, or to go on board of the wreck.

As the crew were in want of everything, and as it might be a long time before any opportunity occurred for them to get away from these islands, Mr. Ogden, as soon as he could get a chance, made his way to the island of Owyhee, and endeavored to make some arrangement with the king for the relief of his companions in misfortune.

---

[12] Porter, *op. cit.*, I, identifies the island as Maui, as does Alexander Henry, *Henry-Thompson Journals*, II, 846.

The illustrious Tamaahmaah, as we have shown on a former occasion, was a shrewd bargainer, and in the present instance proved himself an experienced wrecker. His negotiations with M'Dougal, and the other "Eris of the great American Fur Company," had but little effect on present circumstances, and he proceeded to avail himself of their misfortunes. He agreed to furnish the crew with provisions during their stay in his territories, and to return to them all their clothing that could be found, but he stipulated that the wreck should be abandoned to him as a waif cast by fortune on his shores. With these conditions Mr. Ogden was fain to comply. Upon this the great Tamaahmaah deputed his favorite, John Young, the tarpaulin governor of Owyhee, to proceed with a number of the royal guards, and take possession of the wreck on behalf of the crown. This was done accordingly, and the property and crew were removed to Owyhee. The royal bounty appears to have been but scanty in its dispensations. The crew fared but meagrely; though, on reading the journal of the voyage, it is singular to find them, after all the hardships they had suffered, so sensitive about petty inconveniences, as to exclaim against the king as a "savage monster," for refusing them a "pot to cook in," and denying Mr. Ogden the use of a knife and fork which had been saved from the wreck.

Such was the unfortunate catastrophe of the Lark;[13] had she reached her destination in safety, affairs at Astoria might have taken a different course. A strange fatality seems to have attended all the expeditions by sea, nor were those by land much less disastrous.

Captain Northrop was still at the Sandwich Islands, on December 20th, when Mr. Hunt arrived.[14] The latter immediately purchased, for ten thousand dollars, a brig called the Pedler,[15] and put Captain Northrop in command of her. They set sail for Astoria on the 22d January, intending to remove the property from thence as speedily as possible to the Russian settlements on the northwest coast, to prevent it from falling

[13] From similarities in wording, it is certain that Irving's chief source for the misfortunes of the Lark was Captain Northrop's letter to Astor. See note 10 above. From what Irving says below, p. 479, he appears also to have had the log of the ship, which he refers to as "the journal of the voyage." He may also have taken a few details from Franchère, who gives a brief account of the Lark's misadventures in Narrative, 315–16. See also Cox, Columbia River, 150–51. A detailed account appears in the Henry-Thompson Journals, II, 845–47.

[14] At Oahu.

[15] The Pedler was a Boston ship, which Hunt manned with the survivors of the Lark. Porter, op. cit., I, 232. The name is spelled Pedlar in the first edition of Astoria.

into the hands of the British. Such were the orders of Mr. Astor, sent out by the Lark.

We will now leave Mr. Hunt on his voyage, and return to see what has taken place at Astoria during his absence.

Arrival of M'Tavish at Astoria — Conduct of His Followers
Negotiations of M'Dougal and M'Tavish
Bargain for the Transfer of Astoria
Doubts Entertained of the Loyalty of M'Dougal

ON the 2d of October,[1] about five weeks after Mr. Hunt had sailed in the Albatross from Astoria, Mr. M'Kenzie set off with two canoes, and twelve men, for the posts of Messrs. Stuart and Clarke, to apprise them of the new arrangements determined upon in the recent conference of the partners at the factory.

He had not ascended the river a hundred miles, when he met a squadron of ten canoes, sweeping merrily down under British colors, the Canadian oarsmen, as usual, in full song.

It was an armament fitted out by M'Tavish, who had with him Mr. J. Stuart,[2] another partner of the Northwest Company, together with some clerks,[3] and sixty-eight men—seventy-five souls in all. They had heard of the frigate Phœbe and the Isaac Todd being on the high seas, and were on their way down to await their arrival. In one of the canoes Mr. Clarke came passenger, the alarming intelligence having brought him down from his post on the Spokan.[4] Mr. M'Kenzie immediately deter-

[1] Early in September, according to Franchère, *Narrative*, 294.

[2] John Stuart (1779–1847), a native of Scotland, had been in the service of the North West Company since 1791. He became a partner in 1813. Wallace (ed.), *Documents*, 500.

[3] Franchère mentions that with McTavish was Angus Bethune (1783–1858), a native Canadian who in 1813 was a clerk in the North West Company. He became a partner the next year. Wallace (ed.), *Documents*, 426. Another whom Franchère mentions was one McMillan. This would appear to be James McMillan (d. 1858), who came from Scotland and joined the North West Company sometime before 1805 as a clerk. Ross Cox met him at Spokane House in 1813, when he was in charge of it with ten men. *Columbia River*, 109; Wallace (ed.), *Documents*, 482–83.

[4] Alexander Ross states, probably with good reason, that "with the craft peculiar to Indian traders, they [McTavish *et al.*] had crammed down Mr. Clarke's throat that nothing could be done at Astoria without him, although his accompanying them was like the third wheel to a cart; but it answered their purpose: for his leaving Spokane threw at once all the trade of the district into their hands, and Mr. Clarke found out, when it was too late, that he had been duped." *Adventures*, 244.

mined to return with him to Astoria, and, veering about, the two parties encamped together for the night. The leaders, of course, observed a due decorum, but some of the subalterns could not restrain their chuckling exultation, boasting that they would soon plant the British standard on the walls of Astoria, and drive the Americans out of the country.

In the course of the evening, Mr. M'Kenzie had a secret conference with Mr. Clarke, in which they agreed to set off privately, before daylight, and get down in time to apprise M'Dougal of the approach of these Northwesters. The latter, however, were completely on the alert; just as M'Kenzie's canoes were about to push off, they were joined by a couple from the Northwest squadron, in which was M'Tavish, with two clerks, and eleven men.[5] With these, he intended to push forward and make arrangements, leaving the rest of the convoy, in which was a large quantity of furs, to await his orders.

The two parties arrived at Astoria on the 7th of October.[6] The Northwesters encamped under the guns of the fort, and displayed the British colors. The young men in the fort, natives of the United States, were on the point of hoisting the American flag, but were forbidden by Mr. M'Dougal. They were astonished at such a prohibition, and were exceedingly galled by the tone and manner assumed by the clerks and retainers of the Northwest Company, who ruffled about in that swelling and braggart style which grows up among these heroes of the wilderness; they, in fact, considered themselves lords of the ascendant and regarded the hampered and harassed Astorians as a conquered people.

On the following day M'Dougal convened the clerks, and read to them an extract of a letter from his uncle, Mr. Angus Shaw,[7] one of the

---

[5] Franchère states that "these gentlemen were in *light* canoes (i.e., without any lading), and formed the vanguard to a flotilla of eight, loaded with furs, under the command of Messrs. John Stuart and M'Millan." *Narrative*, 295.

[6] The date is unspecified by Franchère.

[7] Born in Scotland, Shaw became a clerk in the North West Company sometime in the 1780's. He was a partner by 1799 and perhaps earlier, and in 1808 became a member of McTavish, McGillivrays, and Company. In 1810 and 1811 he served as an agent of the North West Company at Fort William, "but thereafter," states Wallace, "he took little part in the fur trade, until the struggle with Lord Selkirk reached its height, when he was one of the partners of the North West Company arrested by the Hudson's Bay men in 1819." *Documents*, 497–98. He died in New Jersey in 1832. A certified copy of an extract from his letter, dated Montreal, May 9, 1813, to John G. McTavish, is in the Astor Papers, Baker Library, Harvard Graduate School of Business Administration. See also note 8 below and Flandrau, *Astor and the Oregon Country*, 39–41. Cf. Porter, *John Jacob Astor*, I, 226–27.

principal partners of the Northwest Company, announcing the coming of the Phœbe and Isaac Todd, "to take and destroy everything American on the northwest coast."[8]

This intelligence was received without[9] dismay by such of the clerks as were natives of the United States. They had felt indignant at seeing their national flag struck by a Canadian commander, and the British flag flowed,[10] as it were, in their faces. They had been stung to the quick, also, by the vaunting airs assumed by the Northwesters. In this mood of mind, they would willingly have nailed their colors to the staff, and defied the frigate. She could not come within many miles of the fort, they observed, and any boats she might send could be destroyed by their cannon.

There were cooler and more calculating spirits, however, who had the control of affairs, and felt nothing of the patriotic pride and indignation of these youths. The extract of the letter had, apparently, been read by M'Dougal, merely to prepare the way for a preconcerted stroke of management. On the[11] same day Mr. M'Tavish proposed to purchase the whole stock of goods and furs belonging to the company, both at Astoria and in the interior, at cost and charges.[12] Mr. M'Dougal undertook to

[8] A copy of the letter from Angus Shaw, Montreal, May 9, 1813, addressed to John G. McTavish, reads: "We are in hurry & confusion preparing papers &c. for the express canoe—having waited impatiently for some time, it was at last determined upon to send it off without having received the least knowledge of what has been doing in England since December last, but fortunately the arrival of a Frigate brought us account of the Isaac Todd having on board Messrs. McTavish & McDonald being ready for sea on the 18th of March. She is accompanied by a Frigate to take and destroy every thing that is American on the N.W. Coast." Elliott, "Sale of Astoria, 1813," *Oregon Historical Quarterly*, Vol. XXXIII (1932), 47–48; Flandrau, *op. cit.*, 41.

The *Phoebe* was the frigate referred to in Shaw's letter. The *Isaac Todd* sailed with letters of marque. They had "orders from the [British] government," so Franchère writes, "to seize our establishment, which had been represented to the lords of the admiralty as an important colony founded by the American government." *Narrative*, 295.

[9] The first edition also has *without*, but the context clearly dictates *with*.

[10] Thus also in the first edition instead of *flown*.

[11] *That* in the first edition.

[12] Franchère's version of what led up to this proposal follows: "As the season advanced, and their ship did not arrive, our new neighbors found themselves in a very disagreeable situation, without food, or merchandise wherewith to procure it from the natives. . . . Weary, at length, of applying to us incessantly for food (which we furnished them with a sparing hand), unable either to retrace their steps through the wilderness or to remain in their present position, they came to the conclusion of proposing to buy of us the whole establishment.

comply; assuming the whole management of the negotiation in virtue of the power vested in him, in case of the non-arrival of Mr. Hunt. That power, however, was limited and specific, and did not extend to an operation of this nature and extent; no objection, however, was made to his assumption, and he and M'Tavish soon made a preliminary arrangement, perfectly satisfactory to the latter.

Mr. Stuart, and the reserve party of Northwesters, arrived shortly afterwards, and encamped with M'Tavish.[13] The former exclaimed loudly against the terms of the arrangement, and insisted upon a reduction of the prices. New negotiations had now to be entered into. The demands of the Northwesters were made in a peremptory tone, and they seemed disposed to dictate like conquerors. The Americans looked on with indignation and impatience. They considered M'Dougal as acting, if not a perfidious, certainly a craven part. He was continually repairing to the camp to negotiate, instead of keeping within his walls and receiving overtures in his fortress. His case, they observed, was not so desperate as to excuse such crouching. He might, in fact, hold out for his own terms. The Northwest party had lost their ammunition; they had no goods to trade with the natives for provisions; and they were so destitute that M'Dougal had absolutely to feed them, while he negotiated with them. He, on the contrary, was well lodged and victualled; had sixty men, with arms, ammunition, boats, and everything requisite either for defense or retreat. The party, beneath the guns of his fort, were at his mercy; should an enemy appear in the offing, he could pack up the most valuable part of the property and retire to some place of concealment, or make off for the interior.[14]

These considerations, however, had no weight with Mr. M'Dougal, or were overruled by other motives. The terms of the sale were low-

"Placed, as we were, in the situation of expecting, day by day, the arrival of an English ship-of-war to seize upon all we possessed, we listened to their propositions." *Narrative*, 296.

[13] "They formed," says Franchère, "a camp of about seventy-five men, at the bottom of a little bay or cove, near our factory. As they were destitute of provisions, we supplied them; but Messrs. M'Dougal and M'Kenzie affecting to dread a surprise from this British force under our guns, we kept strictly on our guard; for we were inferior in point of numbers, although our position was exceedingly advantageous." *Ibid.*

[14] "The negotiations were protracted by the hope of one party that the long-expected armed force would arrive, to render the purchase unnecessary, and were urged forward by the other in order to conclude the affair before that occurrence should intervene." *Ibid.*

ered by him to the standard fixed by Mr. Stuart, and an agreement executed on the 16th of October,[15] by which the furs and merchandise of all kinds in the country, belonging to Mr. Astor, passed into the possession of the Northwest Company at about a third of their real[16] value.[17] A safe passage through the Northwest posts was guaranteed to such as did not choose to enter into the service of that Company, and the amount of wages due to them was to be deducted from the price paid for Astoria.[18]

The conduct and motives of Mr. M'Dougal, throughout the whole of this proceeding, have been strongly questioned by the other partners.[19] He has been accused of availing himself of a wrong construction

[15] Erroneously *October 23* in Franchère. The bill of sale, which is given in Davidson, *The North West Company*, Appendix M, 293–96, and also in Elliott, "Sale of Astoria, 1813," *loc. cit.*, 48–50, specifies the date as October 16, 1813. The bill of sale was signed by Duncan McDougall, John George McTavish, and John Stuart. Witnesses were John Halsey, Gabriel Franchère, Alfred Seton, William Wallace, Angus Bethune, James McMillan, and Joseph McGillivray.

[16] *Real* is supplied from the first edition.

[17] [Irving's note follows.] Not quite $40,000 were allowed for furs worth upwards of $100,000. Beaver was valued at two dollars per skin, though worth five dollars. Land-otter at fifty cents, though worth five dollars. Sea-otter at twelve dollars, worth from forty-five to sixty dollars; and for several kinds of furs nothing was allowed. Moreover, the goods and merchandise for the Indian trade ought to have brought three times the amount for which they were sold.

The following estimate has been made of the articles on hand, and the prices:—

17,705 lbs. beaver parchment, valued at $2.00 worth			$5.00
465 old coat beaver	" " 1.66	"	3.50
907 land-otter	" " .50	"	5.00
68 sea-otter	" " 12.00	"	45 to 60.00
30 " "	" " 5.00	"	25.00

Nothing was allowed for

179 mink skins, worth each			.40
22 raccoon,	" "		.40
28 lynx,	" "	[*38 lynx* in first edition]	2.00
18 fox,	" "		1.00
106 "	" "		1.50
71 black bear	" "	[*4.00* in first edition]	4.06
16 grizzly bear	" "		10.00

[18] See bill of sale in Davidson, *op. cit.*, 294, and Elliott, "Sale of Astoria, 1813," *loc. cit.*, 49.

[19] Although not a partner, Franchère frankly gave it as his opinion that "those at the head of affairs had their own fortunes to seek, and thought it more for their interest, doubtless, to act as they did, but that will not clear them in the eyes of the world, and the charge of treason to Mr. Astor's interests will always be attached to their character." *Narrative*, 303. In the opinion of Porter, however, McDougall had

of powers vested in him at his own request, and of sacrificing the interests of Mr. Astor to the Northwest Company, under the promise or hope of advantage to himself.

He always insisted, however, that he made the best bargain for Mr. Astor that circumstances would permit; the frigate being hourly expected, in which case the whole property of that gentleman would be liable to capture. That the return of Mr. Hunt was problematical; the frigate intending to cruise along the coast for two years, and clear it of all American vessels. He moreover averred, and M'Tavish corroborated his averment by certificate, that he proposed an arrangement to that gentleman, by which the furs were to be sent to Canton, and sold there at Mr. Astor's risk, and for his account; but the proposition was not acceded to.

Notwithstanding all his representations, several of the persons present at the transaction, and acquainted with the whole course of the affair, and among the number Mr. M'Kenzie himself, his occasional coadjutor, remained firm in the belief that he had acted a hollow part. Neither did he succeed in exculpating himself to Mr. Astor; that gentleman declaring, in a letter written some time afterwards, to Mr. Hunt, that he considered the property virtually given away. "Had our place and our property," he adds, "been fairly captured, I should have preferred it; I should not feel as if I were disgraced."

All these may be unmerited suspicions; but it certainly is a circumstance strongly corroborative of them, that Mr. M'Dougal, shortly after concluding this agreement, became a member of the Northwest Company, and received a share productive of a handsome income.

---

little choice in what he did and in accepting a partnership in the North West Company, and the accusations of treachery leveled against him were not fully justified. See Porter, *op. cit.*, I, 231. But Astor, on the other hand, regarded his loss of Astoria as the result of intrigue; see *ibid.*, I, 241, quoting Astor.

As for Franchère's own position, he declared that "I lost in a moment all my hopes of fortune. I could not help remarking that we had no right to expect such treatment on the part of the British government, after the assurances we had received from Mr. Jackson, his majesty's *chargé d'affaires* previously to our departure from New York. But as I have just intimated, the agents of the Northwest Company had exaggerated the importance of the factory in the eyes of the British ministry; for if the latter had known what it really was—a mere trading-post—and nothing but the rivalry of the fur-traders of the Northwest Company was interested in its destruction, they would never have sent a maritime expedition to destroy it." *Narrative*, 297.

CHAPTER LX

Arrival of a Strange Sail — Agitation at Astoria
Warlike Offer of Comcomly — Astoria Taken Possession of by the British
Indignation of Comcomly at the Conduct of His Son-in-Law

ON the morning of the 30th of November,[1] a sail was descried doubling Cape Disappointment. It came to anchor in Baker's Bay, and proved to be a ship of war. Of what nation? was now the anxious inquiry. If English, why did it come alone? where was the merchant vessel that was to have accompanied it? If American, what was to become of the newly acquired possession of the Northwest Company?

In this dilemma, M'Tavish, in all haste, loaded two barges with all the packages of furs bearing the mark of the Northwest Company, and made off for Tongue Point, three miles up the river.[2] There he was to await a preconcerted signal from M'Dougal, on ascertaining the character of the ship. If it should prove American, M'Tavish would have a fair start, and could bear off his rich cargo to the interior. It is singular that this prompt mode of conveying valuable, but easily transportable effects beyond the reach of a hostile ship should not have suggested itself while the property belonged to Mr. Astor.

In the meantime, M'Dougal, who still remained nominal chief at the fort, launched a canoe, manned by men recently in the employ of the American Fur Company, and steered for the ship.[3] On the way, he instructed his men to pass themselves for Americans or Englishmen, according to the exigencies of the case.

The vessel proved to be the British sloop of war Raccoon, of twenty-

---

[1] The date is confirmed by Franchère, *Narrative*, 298, and by Alexander Henry, *Henry-Thompson Journals*. Henry, a North Wester, arrived at Astoria on November 15, 1813. His journal provides an excellent parallel account of affairs at Astoria and vicinity.

[2] Irving's authority for this action is Franchère, *Narrative*, 299. It is confirmed by Alexander Henry; see *Henry-Thompson Journals*, II, 760.

[3] Thus in Franchère, *Narrative*, 298-99, and in Henry, *Henry-Thompson Journals*, II, 759. The latter names McDougall and J. C. Halsey, a Pacific Fur Company clerk, and mentions that there were an additional six men.

six guns, and one hundred and twenty men, commanded by Captain Black.[4] According to the account of that officer, the frigate Phœbe, and the two sloops of war Cherub and Raccoon, had sailed in convoy of the Isaac Todd from Rio Janeiro. On board of the Phœbe, Mr. John M'Donald,[5] a partner of the Northwest Company, embarked as passenger, to profit by the anticipated catastrophe at Astoria. The convoy was separated by stress of weather off Cape Horn. The three ships of war came together again at the island of Juan Fernandez, their appointed rendezvous, but waited in vain for the Isaac Todd.

In the meantime, intelligence was received of the mischief that Commodore Porter was doing among the British whale ships. Commodore Hillyer[6] immediately set sail in quest of him, with the Phœbe and the Cherub, transferring Mr. M'Donald to the Raccoon, and ordering that vessel to proceed to the Columbia.[7]

The officers of the Raccoon were in high spirits. The agents of the Northwest Company, in instigating the expedition, had talked of immense booty to be made by the fortunate captors of Astoria. Mr. M'Donald had kept up the excitement during the voyage, so that not a midshipman but revelled in dreams of ample prize-money, nor a lieutenant that would have sold his chance for a thousand pounds.[8] Their disappointment, therefore, may easily be conceived, when they learned that

[4] Irving's source is Franchère, *Narrative*, 299. Cf. Henry, *Henry-Thompson Journals*, II, 761.

[5] John McDonald of Garth (1774?–1860), a native of Scotland, became a clerk-apprentice in the North West Company in 1791. About 1800 he became a partner. His retirement from the fur trade took place in 1815. Wallace (ed.), *Documents*, 464. He had sailed from England on the *Phoebe* but had transferred to the *Raccoon* at Juan Fernández Island. McDonald brought five *voyageurs* with him. Franchère, *Narrative*, 299–300. He now took charge of Astoria.

[6] Sir James Hillyar (1769–1843). He captured the *Essex* in 1813. In 1836 he was made a rear admiral.

[7] Irving's source for the above is Franchère, *Narrative*, 299–300.

[8] Years later, in his "Reminiscences," McDonald wrote: "Washington Irving is in some part correct, but not in one principal part. I heard of no expectation of prize money, nor disappointment in any respect. The force was sent to fulfill a duty to the North West Company; it was no government measure. They were as it were under my direction as a Partner of that Company, and acted accordingly." See L. R. Masson, *Les Bourgeois de la Compagnie du Nord-Ouest*, II, 50. Both Franchère and Ross, however, concur with what Irving here states; and McDonald, moreover, referring to his landing at Astoria, says: "To our utter disappointment, we found only a few stores and barracks surrounded by a few imperfect stockades with two or three swivels mounted near the gate. The place was not fit to resist any thing but savages." *Ibid.*

their warlike attack upon Astoria had been forestalled by a snug commercial arrangement; that their anticipated booty had become British
property in the regular course of traffic, and that all this had been effected by the very company which had been instrumental in getting
them sent on what they now stigmatized as a fool's errand. They felt
as if they had been duped and made tools of, by a set of shrewd men of
traffic, who had employed them to crack the nut, while they carried
off the kernel. In a word, M'Dougal found himself so ungraciously received by his countrymen on board of the ship, that he was glad to cut
short his visit, and return to shore. He was busy at the fort, making
preparations for the reception of the captain of the Raccoon, when his
one-eyed Indian father-in-law made his appearance, with a train of
Chinook warriors, all painted and equipped in warlike style.

Old Comcomly had beheld, with dismay, the arrival of a "big war
canoe" displaying the British flag. The shrewd old savage had become
something of a politician in the course of his daily visits at the fort. He
knew of the war existing between the nations, but knew nothing of the
arrangement between M'Dougal and M'Tavish. He trembled, therefore, for the power of his white son-in-law, and the new-fledged grandeur of his daughter, and assembled his warriors in all haste. "King
George," said he, "has sent his great canoe to destroy the fort, and make
slaves of all the inhabitants. Shall we suffer it? The Americans are the
first white men that have fixed themselves in the land. They have treated
us like brothers. Their great chief has taken my daughter to be his
squaw: we are, therefore, as one people."

His warriors all determined to stand by the Americans to the last,
and to this effect they came painted and armed for battle. Comcomly
made a spirited war-speech to his son-in-law. He offered to kill every
one of King George's men that should attempt to land. It was an easy
matter. The ship could not approach within six miles of the fort; the
crew could only land in boats. The woods reached to the water's edge;
in these, he and his warriors would conceal themselves, and shoot down
the enemy as fast as they put foot on shore.

M'Dougal, was doubtless, properly sensible of this parental devotion
on the part of his savage father-in-law, and perhaps a little rebuked by
the game spirit, so opposite to his own. He assured Comcomly, however, that his solicitude for the safety of himself and the princess was
superfluous; as, though the ship belong to King George, her crew would

489

not injure the Americans, or their Indian allies. He advised him and his warriors, therefore, to lay aside their weapons and war shirts, wash off the paint from their faces and bodies, and appear like clean and civil savages, to receive the strangers courteously.

Comcomly was sorely puzzled at this advice, which accorded so little with his Indian notions of receiving a hostile nation, and it was only after repeated and positive assurances of the amicable intentions of the strangers that he was induced to lower his fighting tone. He said something to his warriors explanatory of this singular posture of affairs, and in vindication, perhaps, of the pacific temper of his son-in-law. They all gave a shrug and an Indian grunt of acquiescence, and went off sulkily to their village, to lay aside their weapons for the present.[9]

The proper arrangements being made for the reception of Captain Black, that officer caused his ship's boats to be manned, and landed with befitting state at Astoria.[10] From the talk that had been made by the Northwest Company of the strength of the place, and the armament they had required to assist in its reduction, he expected to find a fortress of some importance. When he beheld nothing but stockades and bastions, calculated for defense against naked savages, he felt an emotion of indignant surprise, mingled with something of the ludicrous. "Is this the fort," cried he, "about which I have heard so much talking? D—n me, but I'd batter it down in two hours with a four pounder!"[11]

When he learned, however, the amount of rich furs that had been passed into the hands of the Northwesters, he was outrageous, and insisted that an inventory should be taken of all the property purchased of the Americans, "with a view to ulterior measures in England, for the recovery of the value from the Northwest Company."

As he grew cool, however, he gave over all idea of preferring such a

[9] For a different version of Comcomly's loyalty and offer to intervene, see Ross, *Adventures*, 247–49. Irving's source for Comcomly's offer of intervention is Cox, *Columbia River*, 147–48. Cox, in turn, had his information from David Stuart and John Clarke, who arrived on April 24 at Spokane House, where Cox was stationed. Nothing appears in Franchère to corroborate Comcomly's gesture.

[10] According to Franchère, Captain Black, several soldiers and sailors, plus goods from the *Raccoon*, were brought off by the schooner *Dolly* on December 12 after being detained by bad weather in Baker's Bay for what would appear to be about ten days. *Narrative*, 301. This is confirmed by the *Henry-Thompson Journals*, II, 769–70.

[11] As reported by Franchère, Captain Black exclaimed in slightly different words: "What! is this the fort which was represented to me as so formidable! Good God! I could batter it down in two hours with a four-pounder!" *Narrative*, 302.

claim, and reconciled himself, as well as he could, to the idea of having been forestalled by his bargaining coadjutors.

On the 12th of December,[12] the fate of Astoria was consummated by a regular ceremonial. Captain Black, attended by his officers, entered the fort, caused the British standard to be erected, broke a bottle of wine, and declared, in a loud voice, that he took possession of the establishment and of the country,[13] in the name of his Britannic Majesty, changing the name of Astoria to that of Fort George.[14]

[12] Thus in Franchère, *Narrative*, 301. Henry, however, gives the date as December 13. *Henry-Thompson Journals*, II, 770.

[13] Ross asked pointedly what Black's claims amounted to. "What the vague term of 'whole country' in the present case meant, I know not. Does it mean the Columbia? Does it mean all the country lying west of the Rocky Mountains? Or does it merely mean the coast of the Pacific? That part of the ceremony which referred to the 'whole country' might have been dispensed with; for the country had already been taken possession of in the name of his Britannic Majesty, and that many years ago, by Drake, by Cooke, by Vancouver, and lastly by Black." *Adventures*, 250.

For a survey of the efforts of Astor, as well as of the government, to repossess Astoria, see Porter, *John Jacob Astor*, I, 239-43. In 1817, Astor was informed that James Biddle and J. B. Prevost had been commissioned to sail to the Columbia and reassert the claim of the United States to the adjacent country. They carried out their orders in August, 1818, taking temporary possession. Captain Black's action of taking formal possession of Astoria ultimately weakened England's position in 1818 when it engaged in discussions with the United States concerning Astoria. Finally on October 6, 1818, Fort George (Astoria) was restored to the United States. The North West Company, however, retained possession of the post. Their rights were affirmed by the convention between Great Britain and the United States on October 20, 1818, in which joint occupation of the Oregon country was agreed upon west of the Rocky Mountains and north of the forty-second parallel for a period of ten years. This, the so-called "Treaty of Joint Occupation," was renewed in 1827. Eventually boundary disputes between the two countries were settled in 1846, when England relinquished all claims south of the forty-ninth parallel. But long before this, the North West Company had been taken into the Hudson's Bay Company, and Fort George was abandoned in favor of a new post, Fort Vancouver, located farther up the river.

Astor, though he continued to send ships to the Northwest Coast to trade, never regained Astoria.

[14] Captain Black's report follows.

Racoon, Columbia River
15 December, 1813

Sir:

Agreeable to order from Captain Hillyer, I succeeded in entering Columbia River, in Majesty's Sloop Racoon, Novr. 30, 1813 found party of North West Company here, who had made arrangements with the American party before my arrival.

Country and fort I have taken possession of in name and for British Majesty latter I have named Fort George and left in possession and charge North West Company.

Enemies party quite broke up they have no settlement whatever on this River or Coast.

The Indian warriors, who had offered their services to repel the
strangers, were present on this occasion. It was explained to them as
being a friendly arrangement and transfer, but they shook their heads
grimly, and considered it an act of subjugation of their ancient allies.[15]
They regretted that they had complied with M'Dougal's wishes, in
laying aside their arms, and remarked, that, however the Americans
might conceal the fact, they were undoubtedly all slaves; nor could they
be persuaded of the contrary, until they beheld the Raccoon depart[16]
without taking away any prisoners.

Enemies vessel said on Coast and about [Sandwich] Islands. While Provisions last
shall endeavor to destroy them. Weather here set in very bad.

Left Phoebe and Cherub Longitude 82° 20′ W, Latitude 40° 33′ S. well. Consort
parted from Squadron before reaching Cape Horn, not yet arrived. Natives appear well
disposed toward English.

Sir,

Your Obedt Servt
W. Black

To John Wilson Croker, Esq.,
Secretary Admiralty
London

See "Captain Black's Report on Taking of Astoria," *Oregon Historical Quarterly*, Vol.
XVII (1916), 147–48.

Alexander Henry, an eyewitness of the proceeding, left the following description:
"*Dec. 13th.* . . . At 3 p.m. we fired three guns as a signal to the Raccoon, and then
hoisted the Union Jack given us by the captain. We collected all our men, armed with
muskets; the marines were drawn up in uniform under arms, and the sailors with
Quartermaster Hill attended to the guns. The captain, in full uniform, broke a bottle
of Madeira on the flagstaff, and took possession of this country and place in the name
of His Britannic Majesty, calling this post Fort George. Three cheers were given by
us all, and three rounds of musketry were then fired by our men and the marines. One
of the latter had a narrow escape from shooting himself in the face, his gun having
flashed and then gone off on being grounded. Eleven guns were fired from our four-
pounder. We drank His Majesty's health, and a speech to Comcomly's son [was made
by Mr. Franchère]. The ceremony ended by taking a few glasses of wine." *Henry-
Thompson Journals*, II, 770–71.

McDonald recalled: "Captain Black took a bottle of wine, or perhaps something
stronger, broke it against the flag staff, hoisted the Union Jack and called it 'Fort
George,' and, after taking lunch, returned on board of his own vessel." Masson, *op.
cit.*, II, 51.

[15] Irving apparently elaborates upon what he read in Franchère: "Some few Indian
chiefs had been got together to witness this ceremony, and I explained to them in their
own language what it signified." *Narrative*, 302.

[16] On December 31. The *Raccoon* took aboard John Little, "a boat-builder from
New York," who had long been ill, and P. D. Jeremie, "as under clerk." *Ibid.*, 303.
The date is confirmed by the *Henry-Thompson Journals*, II, 780.

As to Comcomly, he no longer prided himself upon his white son-in-law, but, whenever he was asked about him, shook his head, and replied, that his daughter had made a mistake, and, instead of getting a great warrior for a husband, had married herself to a squaw.[17]

[17] Irving's main source throughout this chapter is Franchère, *Narrative*, 298–303.

CHAPTER LXI

Arrival of the Brig Pedler at Astoria — Breaking Up of the Establishment
Departure of Several of the Company — Tragical Story Told by
the Squaw of Pierre Dorion — Fate of Reed and His Companions
Attempts of Mr. Astor to Renew His Enterprise — Disappointment
Concluding Observations and Reflections

HAVING given the catastrophe at the Fort of Astoria, it remains now but to gather up a few loose ends of this widely excursive narrative and conclude. On the 28th of February the brig Pedler anchored in Columbia River.[1] It will be recollected that Mr. Hunt had purchased this vessel at the Sandwich Islands, to take off the furs collected at the factory, and to restore the Sandwich Islanders to their homes. When that gentleman learned, however, the precipitate and summary manner in which the property had been bargained away by M'Dougal, he expressed his indignation in the strongest terms, and determined to make an effort to get back the furs.[2] As soon as his wishes were known in this respect,

---

[1] Thus in Franchère, *Narrative*, 315, who gives the same date, and in *Henry-Thompson Journals*, II, 841–45, where appears a long account of the arrival of the *Pedler*. According to Alexander Henry, the *Pedler* had left the Sandwich Islands on January 26 and, because of adverse weather, had been driven as far north as Juan de Fuca Strait before being able to make for the mouth of the Columbia. *Henry-Thompson Journals*, II, 847–48. He describes her as "a handsome vessel of 225 tons burden, which sailed from Boston in January, 1811. She carried eight 30-pounders, and a crew of 12 able-bodied young seamen. She cost Mr. Hunt, at the Sandwish Islands, $10,000 as she then was. The captain [Northrop] of this brig and some of her crew are a part of those formerly of the Lark." *Ibid.*, 850.

[2] Alexander Henry describes Hunt's conduct in the following words: "Mr. Hunt called and entered upon his business, explaining his demands and making his requests; some were granted, others were refused. He pleaded hard for Joe [Joseph Ashton] and the corn mill. He wished to insure his vessel against any of ours, should any such arrive previous to his sailing; this we could not take upon ourselves to do. Several conferences and arguments took place. It was evident he wished to take away as many men as he could, and, on our part, we were as desirous of keeping them. The Sandwich Islanders wished much to see their own homes. But as this would not answer our purpose, of course we opposed it, and promised them a safe passage on our own ship. We consented to his taking with him four free Americans, who were useless to us. . . . About 6 p.m. Mr. Hunt boarded his boat, hoisted sail, and steered for his vessel." *Henry-Thompson Journals*, II, 849.

494

M'Dougal came to sound him on behalf of the Northwest Company, intimating that he had no doubt the peltries might be repurchased at an advance of fifty per cent. This overture was not calculated to soothe the angry feelings of Mr. Hunt, and his indignation was complete, when he discovered that M'Dougal had become a partner of the Northwest Company, and had actually been so since the 23d of December. He had kept his partnership a secret, however; had retained the papers of the Pacific Fur Company in his possession; and had continued to act as Mr. Astor's agent, though two of the partners of the other company, Mr. M'Kenzie and Mr. Clarke, were present. He had, moreover, divulged to his new associates all that he knew as to Mr. Astor's plans and affairs, and had made copies of his business letters for their perusal.

Mr. Hunt now considered the whole conduct of M'Dougal hollow and collusive.[3] His only thought was, therefore, to get all the papers of

[3] Ross defends McDougall, saying that he "had perhaps made the best bargain he could. . . . The circumstances, however, of [his] having joined the North-West Company, and having already become a partner in that concern, threw suspicion on his conduct . . . ; and certainly . . . M'Dougall's conduct, in this particular, was indiscreet, and might in some degree justify imputation—at least, his enemies made a handle of it; yet there is not the least proof that he had betrayed his trust. M'Dougall always bore the character of integrity; he was a man of principle, faithful to his word, and punctual to his engagements." *Adventures*, 262. Franchère, however, referred to him as "the crafty M'Dougal," *Narrative*, 317, and as we have seen, was generally less charitable to his character and role.

Irving probably reflects Astor's feelings. In a letter to James Monroe, Astor referred to McDougall as having "been bought over by the North West Company," and in the same letter he refers to the arrangements as being "fraudulent." John Jacob Astor, New York, August 17, 1815, to James Monroe, Secretary of State, in Porter, *John Jacob Astor*, I, 583-85. He expressed even stronger feelings to John Quincy Adams: "He [W. P. Hunt on his arrival at Astoria, February 28, 1814] then learnt that McDougall had transferred all my property to the Northwest Company, who were [then] in possession of it, by a sale, as he called it, for the sum of about $58,000, of which he retained $14,000, for wages said to be due to some of the men. From the price obtained for the goods, &c., and he having himself become interested in the purchase, and made a partner of the Northwest Company, some idea may be formed as to this man's correctness of dealings. It will be seen, by the agreement, of which I transmit a copy, and the inventory, that he sold to the Northwest Company, 18,170¼ lbs. of beaver, at $2, which was at about that time selling in Canton at $5 and $6; 907 otter skins, at 50 cents, or half a dollar, which were selling in Canton at $5 to $6 per skin. I estimate the whole property to be worth nearer $200,000, than $40,000, about the sum I received by bills in Montreal." John Jacob Astor, New York, January 4, 1823, to John Quincy Adams, Secretary of State, included in Message of President Monroe, January 25, 1823, to the House of Representatives; quoted in Frederick V. Holcman, "Some Important Results from the Expedition of John Jacob Astor to and from the Oregon Country," *Oregon Historical Quarterly*, Vol. XII (1911), 210-11.

the concern out of his hands, and bring the business to a close; for the interests of Mr. Astor were yet completely at stake; the drafts of the Northwest Company in his favor, for the purchase money, not having yet been obtained. With some difficulty he succeeded in getting possession of the papers.[4] The bills or drafts were delivered without hesitation. The latter he remitted to Mr. Astor by some of his associates,[5] who were about to cross the continent to New York. This done, he embarked on

[4] Alexander Henry recorded on March 8: "Business with the P. F. Co. fully entered upon by all parties, with much talk, argument, and altercation. It was finally determined that the original invoices from New York should be produced. Some of us did not know before that these invoices had been here all winter, and are now on board the brig. The documents have been a bone of contention from the beginning of settling our accounts with Mr. McDougall; he always denied having these papers, which now, it appears, have been actually in his possession, and from which he took all the prices already stated on the accounts. We agreed to give up four Sandwich Islanders to Mr. Hunt, who had been desirous of taking them all.

"*Mar. 9th.* A boat was sent to the brig for original invoices of the late P. F. Co., and soon returned with those per the Beaver, Captain Cornelius Sowle. Those per the Tonquin had been taken across the continent by Messrs. Ramsay Crooks and others, to recover the insurances; but true copies were produced, which Mr. Hunt gave his word of honor were genuine, testified by Messrs. Halsey and Franchère, and these were considered sufficient. Mr. J. Stuart and Mr. Hunt examined them; many errors were found, some articles being charged too high, and others too low—convincing proof that Mr. McDougall did not take the prices from the original invoices. Many disagreeable altercations took place between the parties concerned, both yesterday and to-day. It remained for us either to settle the account according to the first arrangement, or return things to their original state, or deliver up the fort to the P. F. Co. as received from them last fall. None of these alternatives would be convenient for us; and, for special reasons, we wished to avoid pushing matters to extremes, not being prepared for an event which undoubtedly would end in the failure of our business here." *Henry-Thompson Journals,* II, 851–52.

The business between the two firms was completed on March 12, as the following extract from Henry's entry for that date shows: "The business with Mr. Hunt is nearly closed. Mr. D. McDougall having assigned the agreement over to him, he has appointed Mr. D. McKenzie to take charge of the papers, to be delivered to Mr. Astor or his agent in Montreal. Every point being now settled to the satisfaction of Mr. Hunt, the accounts are balanced and closed, bills given him by Mr. J. McDonald for the amount as per agreement of former settlement, and our account current made out and signed on sight by our party, which Mr. Hunt holds; the other by Mr. Hunt from Mr. Astor, which we hold, made out in Mr. Astor's name, same as inventories, etc.; 12 letters of advice given him, one for each copy. This evening the business was finally closed; but when the furs were offered to him, he objected to any terms, which causes us to suspect he has some views in contemplation, as in the commencement of the business he signified his readiness to take the furs off our hands." *Ibid.,* 853.

[5] Donald McKenzie in particular, as the above note from Henry shows.

board the Pedler, on the 3d of April,⁶ accompanied by two of the clerks, Mr. Seton and Mr. Halsey, and bade a final adieu to Astoria.⁷ The next day, April 4th,⁸ Messrs. Clarke, M'Kenzie, David Stuart, and such of the Astorians as had not entered into the service of the Northwest Company, set out to cross the Rocky Mountains.⁹ It is not our intention to take the reader [on] another journey across those rugged barriers; but we will step forward with the travellers to a distance on their way, merely to relate their interview with a character already noted in this work.

As the party were proceeding up the Columbia, near the mouth of

⁶ April 2, according to Franchère, who says that the *Pedler* sailed from the mouth of the river "after several fruitless attempts, in one of which she narrowly missed being lost on the bar." *Narrative*, 316.

⁷ Two other clerks who went with Hunt were Russel Farnham and Benjamin Clapp. See *ibid.*, 316, and Ross, *Adventures*, 264. Franchère would also have been a passenger had he not come down the river from Oak Point a day too late. There were also four Sandwich Islanders.

The *Pedler* had attempted to sail on March 18, but unfavorable winds held her up, so that on April 2 she was still in Baker Bay. Leaving the next day (but on April 2, according to *Henry-Thompson Journals*, II, 863), Hunt sailed to Sitka, where he met the brig *Forester*, William J. Pigot, captain, an English ship that Astor had secured and sent out. From her Hunt obtained goods valued at $1,099.26 and $2,000.00 cash, sundries valued at $757.25, and $5,000.00 worth of seal skins for sale in Canton. From Sitka the *Pedler* took Farnham to Kamchatka, where he began his trans-Siberian walk to St. Petersburg, and then sailed down the coast of California, where she was captured by the Spanish in August, 1814, near San Luis Obispo. At San Blas, Alfred Seton, clerk, left to go by land to New York. After her release in October, the *Pedler* may have engaged in illegal coastal trading before leaving for the Sandwich Islands, although there is no proof of this. In September, 1815, she was again at Sitka, and shortly thereafter left once more for the Sandwich Islands. At Oahu on December 27, she met another of Astor's ships, the *Enterprise*. Hunt then sailed her to China in January, 1816, where he took on goods. He sailed finally for New York, where newspapers announced the *Pedler*'s arrival on October 17, 1816. See Kenneth W. Porter, "Cruise of Astor's Brig Pedler, 1813–1816," *Oregon Historical Quarterly*, Vol. XXXI (1930), 223–30, and *idem*, "More about the Brig Pedler, 1813–1816," *ibid.*, Vol. XXXIII (1932), 311–12. Concerning the *Forester*, see Porter's "The Cruise of the 'Forester,'" *Washington Historical Quarterly*, XXIII (1932), 261–85.

⁸ This date agrees with Alexander Henry; *Henry-Thompson Journals*, II, 865.

⁹ Franchère mentions in addition J. G. McTavish, Francis B. Pillet (Pillot), William Wallace, Donald McGillis, John McDonald of Garth (in command), Alexander Stuart, Thomas McKay, John Stuart, Alexander Ross (to go as far as Fort Okanogan), and Franchère himself. *Narrative*, 336 and 336n. A complete list plus those assigned to each canoe, of which there were ten in all—four bark and six wood canoes—is given by Alexander Henry, who states that there were seventy-six men in addition to wives and children; see *Henry-Thompson Journals*, II, 870–75. Their route was up the

the Wallah-Wallah River,[10] several Indian canoes put off from the shore to overtake them, and a voice called upon them in French and requested them to stop. They accordingly put to shore, and were joined by those in the canoes. To their surprise, they recognized in the person who had hailed them the Indian wife of Pierre Dorion, accompanied by her two children. She had a story to tell, involving the fate of several of our unfortunate adventurers.

Mr. John Reed, the Hibernian, it will be remembered, had been detached during the summer to the Snake River. His party consisted of four Canadians, Gilles Le Clerc, Francis Landry, Jean Baptiste Turcotte, and André La Chapelle, together with two hunters, Pierre Dorion and Pierre Delaunay; Dorion, as usual, being accompanied by his wife and children. The objects of this expedition were twofold; to trap beaver, and to search for the three hunters, Robinson, Hoback, and Rezner.

In the course of the autumn, Reed lost one man, Landry, by death; another one, Pierre Delaunay, who was of a sullen, perverse disposition, left him in a moody fit, and was never heard of afterwards. The number of his party was not, however, reduced by these losses, as the three hunters, Robinson, Hoback, and Rezner, had joined it.

Reed now built a house on the Snake River,[11] for their winter quarters; which being completed, the party set about trapping. Rezner, Le Clerc, and Pierre Dorion, went about five days' journey from the wintering house, to a part of the country well stocked with beaver. Here they put up a hut, and proceeded to trap with great success. While the men were out hunting, Pierre Dorion's wife remained at home to dress the skins and prepare the meals. She was thus employed one evening about the beginning of January, cooking the supper of the hunters, when she heard footsteps, and Le Clerc staggered, pale and bleeding, into the hut. He informed her that a party of savages had surprised them, while at their traps, and had killed Rezner and her husband. He had barely strength left to give this information, when he sank upon the ground.

Columbia and then overland through Canada. A bill of lading appears in *ibid.*, 875. For a list of those remaining at Astoria, now Fort George, plus an inventory of provisions, see *ibid.*, 868–70.

[10] According to what Franchère relates, they were stopped not near the Walla Walla River but farther north beyond the Snake. Irving's authority, however, is Ross Cox, who says "a few miles above the Wallah Wallah River, they were followed by some Indian canoes, from one of which a voice hailed them in French, and requested them to stop." *Columbia River*, 151.

[11] At the confluence of the Snake and Boise rivers. *Ibid.*, 152n.

The poor woman saw that the only chance for life was instant flight, but, in this exigency, showed that presence of mind and force of character for which she had frequently been noted. With great difficulty, she caught two of the horses belonging to the party. Then collecting her clothes and a small quantity of beaver meat and dried salmon, she packed them upon one of the horses, and helped the wounded man to mount upon it.[12] On the other horse she mounted with her two children,[13] and hurried away from this dangerous neighborhood, directing her flight to[14] Mr. Reed's establishment. On the third day, she descried a number of Indians on horseback proceeding in an easterly direction. She immediately dismounted with her children, and helped Le Clerc likewise to dismount, and all concealed themselves. Fortunately they escaped the sharp eyes of the savages, but had to proceed with the utmost caution. That night they slept without fire or water; she managed to keep her children warm in her arms; but before morning, poor Le Clerc died.[15]

With the dawn of day the resolute woman resumed her course, and, on the fourth day, reached the house of Mr. Reed. It was deserted, and all round were marks of blood and signs of a furious massacre. Not doubting that Mr. Reed and his party had all fallen victims, she turned in fresh horror from the spot. For two days she continued hurrying forward, ready to sink for want of food, but more solicitous about her children than herself. At length she reached a range of the Rocky Mountains, near the upper part of the Wallah-Wallah River. Here she chose a wild lonely ravine, as her place of winter refuge.

She had fortunately a buffalo robe and three deer-skins; of these, and of pine bark and cedar branches, she constructed a rude wigwam, which she pitched beside a mountain spring. Having no other food, she killed the two horses, and smoked their flesh. The skins aided to cover her hut. Here she dragged out the winter, with no other company than her two children. Towards the middle of March her provisions were nearly exhausted. She therefore packed up the remainder, slung it on her back, and, with her helpless little ones, set out again on her wanderings. Cross-

[12] Cox, on the other hand, says that LeClerc died after he reached the hut and told Dorion's wife what had happened. *Ibid.*, 152. In this detail, Franchère is in agreement with Cox. *Narrative*, 343.

[13] One child was three years of age, the other only four months. Cox, *op. cit.*, 152. Both were boys. Franchère, *Narrative*, 343.

[14] *For* in first edition.

[15] See note 12 above.

ing the ridge of mountains, she descended to the banks of the Wallah-Wallah, and kept along them until she arrived where that river throws itself into the Columbia. She was hospitably received and entertained by the Wallah-Wallahs, and had been nearly two weeks among them when the two canoes passed.

On being interrogated, she could assign no reason for this murderous attack of the savages; it appeared to be perfectly wanton and unprovoked. Some of the Astorians supposed it an act of butchery by a roving band of Blackfeet; others, however, and with greater probability of correctness, have ascribed it to the tribe of Pierced-nose Indians, in revenge for the death of their comrade hanged by order of Mr. Clarke. If so, it shows that these sudden and apparently wanton outbreakings of sanguinary violence on the part of the savages, have often some previous, though perhaps remote, provocation.

The narrative[16] of the Indian woman closes the checkered adventures of some of the personages of this motley story; such as the honest Hibernian Reed, and Dorion the hybrid interpreter. Turcotte and La Chapelle were two of the men who fell off from Mr. Crooks in the course of his wintry journey, and had subsequently such disastrous times among the Indians. We cannot but feel some sympathy with that persevering trio of Kentuckians, Robinson, Rezner, and Hoback; who twice turned back when on their way homeward, and lingered in the wilderness to perish by the hands of savages.

The return parties from Astoria, both by sea and land, experienced on the way as many adventures, vicissitudes, and mishaps, as the far-famed heroes of the Odyssey; they reached their destination at different times, bearing tidings to Mr. Astor of the unfortunate termination of his enterprise.

That gentleman, however, was not disposed, even yet, to give the matter up as lost. On the contrary, his spirit was roused by what he considered ungenerous and unmerited conduct on the part of the North-west Company. "After their treatment of me," said he, in a letter to Mr. Hunt, "I have no idea of remaining quiet and idle." He determined, therefore, as soon as circumstances would permit, to resume his enterprise.[17]

[16] Irving's source for this narrative is Cox, *op. cit.*, 151–54. Another account is in Ross, *Adventures*, 265–69. According to Cox, Mrs. Dorion continued with the canoes as far as Fort Okanogan.

[17] Astor also wrote to Donald McKenzie, at Montreal, on September 27, 1814,

At the return of peace, Astoria, with the adjacent country, reverted to the United States by the treaty of Ghent,[18] on the principle of *status ante bellum*, and Captain Biddle[19] was despatched in the sloop of war Ontario, to take formal possession.[20]

In the winter of 1815, a law was passed by Congress prohibiting all traffic of British traders within the territories of the United States.[21]

The favorable moment seemed now to Mr. Astor to have arrived for the revival of his favorite enterprise, but new difficulties had grown up to impede it. The Northwest Company were now in complete occupation of the Columbia River, and its chief tributary streams, holding the posts which he had established, and carrying on a trade throughout the neighboring region, in defiance of the prohibitory law of Congress,[22] which, in effect, was a dead letter beyond the mountains.

To dispossess them, would be an undertaking of almost a belligerent nature; for their agents and retainers were well armed, and skilled in the use of weapons, as is usual with Indian traders. The ferocious and bloody contests which had taken place between the rival trading parties of the Northwest and Hudson's Bay Companies, had shown what might be expected from commercial feuds in the lawless depths of the wilder-

saying that "while I breath [*sic*] & so long as I have a dollar to spend, I'll pursue a course to have our injuries repair'd & when I am no more I hope you'll act in my place; we have been sold, but I do not despond." Quoted in Porter, *op. cit.*, I, 239.

[18] December 24, 1814.

[19] See above, Chapter LX, note 13, and "Captain James Biddle's Orders to Command the U.S.S. Ontario to Go to Columbia River and Take Possession of the Post and Territory in the Name of the United States," *Oregon Historical Quarterly*, Vol. III (1902), 310–11. He took possession on August 19, 1818. See T. C. Elliott, "An Event of One Hundred Years Ago," *ibid.*, Vol. XIX (1918), 181–87, and *idem*, "The Surrender at Astoria in 1818," *ibid.*, Vol. XIX (1918), 271–82. See also Katharine B. Judson, "The British Side of the Restoration of Fort Astoria," *ibid.*, Vol. XX (1919), 243–60, 305–30.

[20] *Repossession* in first edition.

[21] This law was passed on April 29, 1816. It provided that "licenses to trade with the Indians within the territorial limits of the United States shall not be granted to any but citizens of the United States, unless by the express direction of the President of the United States, and upon such terms and conditions as the public interest may, in his opinion, require." Quoted in Phillips, *The Fur Trade*, II, 162, who suggests Astor's influence.

[22] Irving here seems to assume that the Oregon country fell within the territorial limits of the United States. But this was a matter still unsettled, in spite of a provision of the Treaty of Ghent that established a boundary committee to settle the line between the United States and Canada. The convention of October 20, 1818, established joint occupancy. Not until 1846 was the matter finally determined.

ness. Mr. Astor did not think it advisable, therefore, to attempt the matter without the protection of the American flag; under which his people might rally in case of need. He accordingly made an informal overture to the President of the United States, Mr. Madison, through Mr. Gallatin, offering to renew his enterprise, and to reëstablish Astoria, provided it would be protected by the American flag, and made a military post; stating that the whole force required would not exceed a lieutenant's command.

The application, approved and recommended by Mr. Gallatin, one of the most enlightened statesmen of our country, was favorably received, but no step was taken in consequence; the President not being disposed, in all probability, to commit himself by any direct countenance or overt act.[23] Discouraged by this supineness on the part of the government, Mr. Astor did not think fit to renew his overtures in a more formal manner, and the favorable moment for the re-occupation of Astoria was suffered to pass unimproved.

The British trading establishments were thus enabled, without molestation, to strike deep their roots, and extend their ramifications, in despite of the prohibition of Congress, until they had spread themselves over the rich field of enterprise opened by Mr. Astor. The British government soon began to perceive the importance of this region, and to desire to include it within their territorial domains. A question has consequently risen as to the right to the soil, and has become one of the most perplexing now open between the United States and Great Britain. In the first treaty relative to it, under date of October 20th, 1818,[24] the question was left unsettled, and it was agreed that the country on the northwest coast of America, westward of the Rocky Mountains, claimed by either nation, should be open to the inhabitants of both for ten years, for the purposes of trade, with the equal right of navigating all its rivers. When these ten years had expired, a subsequent treaty, in 1828, extended the arrangement to ten additional years. So the matter stands at present.

On casting back our eyes over the series of events we have recorded,

[23] See Porter, *op. cit.*, I, 240–41, for Astor's efforts. Porter, however, says that "Astor's request for military assistance was, it seems, favorably received by President Madison." *Ibid.*, 241. See also below, Appendix A, Albert Gallatin to Astor, New York, August 5, 1835, pp. 508–10.

[24] He here refers to the convention between Great Britain and the United States that proposed the Treaty of Joint Occupation.

we see no reason to attribute the failure of this great commercial undertaking to any fault in the scheme, or omission in the execution of it, on the part of the projector. It was a magnificent enterprise; well concerted and carried on, without regard to difficulties or expense. A succession of adverse circumstances and cross-purposes, however, beset it almost from the outset; some of them, in fact, arising from neglect of the orders and instructions of Mr. Astor. The first crippling blow was the loss of the Tonquin, which clearly would not have happened, had Mr. Astor's earnest injunctions with regard to the natives been attended to. Had this ship performed her voyage prosperously, and revisited Astoria in due time, the trade of the establishment would have taken its preconcerted course, and the spirits of all concerned been kept up by a confident prospect of success. Her dismal catastrophe struck a chill into every heart, and prepared the way for subsequent despondency.

Another cause of embarrassment and loss was the departure from the plan of Mr. Astor, as to the voyage of the Beaver, subsequent to her visiting Astoria. The variation from this plan produced a series of cross-purposes, disastrous to the establishment, and detained Mr. Hunt absent from his post, when his presence there was of vital importance to the enterprise; so essential is it for an agent, in any great and complicated undertaking, to execute faithfully, and to the letter, the part marked out for him by the master mind which has concerted the whole.

The breaking out of the war between the United States and Great Britain, multiplied the hazards and embarrassments of the enterprise. The disappointment as to convoy, rendered it difficult to keep up reinforcements and supplies; and the loss of the Lark added to the tissue of misadventures.

That Mr. Astor battled resolutely against every difficulty, and pursued his course in defiance of every loss, has been sufficiently shown. Had he been seconded by suitable agents, and properly protected by government, the ultimate failure of his plan might yet have been averted. It was his great misfortune, that his agents were not imbued with his own spirit. Some had not capacity sufficient to comprehend the real nature and extent of his scheme; others were alien in feeling and interest, and had been brought up in the service of a rival company. Whatever sympathies they might originally have had with him, were impaired, if not destroyed, by the war. They looked upon his cause as desperate, and only considered how they might make interest to regain a situation under their former employers. The absence of Mr. Hunt, the only real representative of Mr. Astor, at the time of the capitulation with the Northwest Company, completed the series of cross-purposes. Had that gentleman been present, the transfer, in all probability, would not have taken place.

It is painful, at all times, to see a grand and beneficial stroke of genius fail of its aim: but we regret the failure of this enterprise in a national point of view; for, had it been crowned with success, it would have redounded greatly to the advantage and extension of our commerce. The profits drawn from the country in question by the British Fur Company, though of ample amount, form no criterion by which to judge of the advantages that would have arisen had it been entirely in the hands of the citizens[25] of the United States. That company, as has been shown, is limited in the nature and scope of its operations, and can make but little use of the maritime facilities held out by an emporium and a harbor on that coast. In our hands, besides the roving bands of trappers and traders, the country would have been explored and settled by industrious husbandmen; and the fertile valleys bordering its rivers, and shut up among its mountains, would have been made to pour forth their agricultural treasures to contribute to the general wealth.

In respect to commerce, we should have had a line of trading posts from the Mississippi and the Missouri across the Rocky Mountains, forming a high road from the great regions of the west to the shores of the Pacific. We should have had a fortified post and port at the mouth of the Columbia, commanding the trade of that river and its tributaries, and of a wide extent of country and sea-coast; carrying on an active and profitable commerce with the Sandwich Islands, and a direct and frequent communication with China. In a word, Astoria might have realized the anticipations of Mr. Astor, so well understood and appreciated by Mr. Jefferson, in gradually becoming a commercial empire beyond the mountains, peopled by "free and independent Americans, and linked with us by ties of blood and interest."[26]

We repeat, therefore, our sincere regret, that our government should have neglected the overture of Mr. Astor, and suffered the moment to pass by, when full possession of this region might have been taken quietly, as a matter of course, and a military post established, without dispute,

[25] The first edition has *hands of citizens*.
[26] See Jefferson's letter to Astor, pp. 32–33.

at Astoria. Our statesmen have become sensible, when too late, of the importance of this measure. Bills have repeatedly been brought into Congress for the purpose, but without success; and our rightful possessions on that coast, as well as our trade on the Pacific, have no rallying point protected by the national flag, and by a military force.

In the meantime, the second period of ten years is fast elapsing. In 1838, the question of title will again come up, and most probably, in the present amicable state of our relations with Great Britain, will be again postponed. Every year, however, the litigated claim is growing in importance. There is no pride so jealous and irritable as the pride of territory. As one wave of emigration after another rolls into the vast regions of the west, and our settlements stretch towards the Rocky Mountains, the eager eyes of our pioneers will pry beyond, and they will become impatient of any barrier or impediment in the way of what they consider a grand outlet of our empire. Should any circumstance, therefore, unfortunately occur to disturb the present harmony of the two nations, this ill-adjusted question, which now lies dormant, may suddenly start up into one of belligerent import, and Astoria become the watchword in a contest for dominion on the shores of the Pacific.

———

Since the above was written, the question of dominion over the vast territory beyond the Rocky Mountains, which for a time threatened to disturb the peaceful relations with our transatlantic kindred, has been finally settled in a spirit of mutual concession, and the venerable projector whose early enterprise forms the subject of this work had the satisfaction of knowing, ere his eyes closed upon the world, that the flag of his country again waved over "ASTORIA."[27]

[27] The last paragraph, in which Irving alludes to the settlement in 1846 of the territorial boundary dispute, does not, of course, appear in the first edition. It was added in the Author's Revised Edition, 1860-61.

⊰{ A P P E N D I X }⊱

Draught of a Petition to Congress, sent by Mr. Astor in 1812.

TO the honorable the Senate and House of Representatives of the United States, in Congress assembled,

The petition of the American Fur Company respectfully showeth:

That the trade with the several Indian tribes of North America has, for many years past, been almost exclusively carried on by the merchants of Canada; who, having formed powerful and extensive associations for that purpose, being aided by British capital, and being encouraged by the favor and protection of the British government, could not be opposed, with any prospect of success by individuals of the United States.

That by means of the above trade, thus systematically pursued, not only the inhabitants of the United States have been deprived of commercial profits and advantages, to which they appear to have just and natural pretensions, but a great and dangerous influence has been established over the Indian tribes, difficult to be counteracted, and capable of being exerted at critical periods, to the great injury and annoyance of our frontier settlements.

That in order to obtain at least a part of the above trade, and more particularly that which is within the boundaries of the United States, your petitioners, in the year 1808, obtained an act of incorporation from the State of New York, whereby they are enabled, with a competent capital, to carry on the said trade with the Indians in such a manner[1] as may be conformable to the laws and regulations of the United States, in relation to such a commerce.[2]

That the capital mentioned in the said act, amounting to one million of dollars, having been duly formed, your petitioners entered with zeal and alacrity into those large and important arrangements, which were necessary for, or conducive to the object of their incorporation; and,

[1] The first edition reads *in such manner.*
[2] The first edition reads *to such commerce.*

among other things, purchased a great part of the stock in trade, and trading establishments, of the Michilimackinac Company of Canada.— Your petitioners also, with the expectation of great public and private advantage from the use of the said establishments, ordered, during the spring and summer of 1810, an assortment of goods from England, suitable for the Indian trade; which, in consequence of the President's proclamation of November of that year, were shipped to Canada instead of New York, and have been transported, under a very heavy expense, into the interior of the country. But as they could not legally be brought into the Indian country within the boundaries of the United States, they have been stored on the Island of St. Joseph, in Lake Huron, where they now remain.

Your petitioners, with great deference and implicit submission to the wisdom of the national legislature, beg leave to suggest for consideration, whether they have not some claim to national attention and encouragement, from the nature and importance of their undertaking; which though hazardous and uncertain as concerns[3] their private emolument, must, at any rate, redound to the public security and advantage. If their undertaking shall appear to be of the description given, they would further suggest to your honorable bodies, that unless they can procure a regular supply for the trade in which they are engaged, it may languish, and be finally abandoned by American citizens; when it will revert to its former channel, with additional, and perhaps with irresistible, power.

Under these circumstances, and upon all those considerations of public policy which will present themselves to your honorable bodies, in connection with those already mentioned, your petitioners respectfully pray that a law may be passed to enable the President, or any of the heads of departments acting under his authority, to grant permits for the introduction of goods necessary for the supply of the Indians, into the Indian country that is within the boundaries of the United States, under such regulations, and with such restrictions, as may secure the public revenue and promote the public welfare.

And your petitioners shall ever pray, &c.

In witness whereof, the common seal of the American Fur Company is hereunto affixed, the   day of March, 1812.

By order of the Corporation.

[3] The first edition reads *as it concerns.*

An act to enable the American Fur Company, and other citizens, to introduce goods necessary for the Indian trade into the territories within the boundaries of the United States.

WHEREAS, the public peace and welfare require that the native Indian tribes, residing within the boundaries of the United States, should receive their necessary supplies under the authority and from the citizens of the United States: Therefore, be it enacted by the Senate and House of Representatives of the United States, in Congress assembled, that it shall be lawful for the President of the United States, or any of the heads of departments thereunto by him duly authorized, from time to time to grant permits to the American Fur Company, their agents or factors, or any other citizens of the United States engaged in the Indian trade, to introduce into the Indian country, within the boundaries of the United States, such goods, wares, and merchandise, as may be necessary for the said trade, under such regulations and restrictions as the said President or heads of departments may judge proper; any law or regulation to the contrary, in anywise, notwithstanding.

———

Letter from Mr. Gallatin[4] to Mr. Astor, dated

NEW YORK, August 5, 1835.

DEAR SIR,—In compliance with your request, I will state such facts as I recollect touching the subjects mentioned in your letter of 28th ult. I may be mistaken respecting dates and details, and will only relate general facts, which I well remember.

In conformity with the treaty of 1794 with Great Britain, the citizens and subjects of each country were permitted to trade with the Indians residing in the territories of the other party. The reciprocity was altogether nominal. Since the conquest of Canada, the British had inherited from the French the whole fur trade, through the great lakes and their communications, with all the western Indians, whether residing in the British dominions or the United States. They kept the important western posts on those lakes till about the year 1797. And the defensive Indian war, which the United States had to sustain from 1776 to 1795, had still more alienated the Indians, and secured to the British their exclusive trade, carried through the lakes, wherever the Indians in that quar-

---

[4] Gallatin was writing as a private citizen. At this time he was president of the National Bank of New York. The letter may have been written for Irving's use.

ter lived. No American could, without imminent danger of property and life, carry on that trade, even within the United States, by the way of either Michilimackinac or St. Mary's. And independent of the loss of commerce, Great Britain was enabled to preserve a most dangerous influence over our Indians.

It was under these circumstances that you communicated to our government the prospect you had to be able, and your intention, to purchase one half of the interest of the Canadian Fur Company, engaged in trade by the way of Michilimackinac with our own Indians. You wished to know whether the plan met with the approbation of government, and how far you could rely on its protection and encouragement. This overture was received with great satisfaction by the administration, and Mr. Jefferson, then President, wrote you to that effect. I was also directed, as Secretary of the Treasury, to write to you an official letter to the same purpose. On investigating the subject, it was found that the Executive had no authority to give you any direct aid; and I believe you received nothing more than an entire approbation of your plan, and general assurances of the protection due to every citizen engaged in lawful and useful pursuits.

You did effect the contemplated purchase, but in what year I do not recollect. Immediately before the war, you represented that a large quantity of merchandise, intended for the Indian trade, and including arms and munitions of war, belonging to that concern of which you owned one half, was deposited at a post on Lake Huron, within the British dominions; that, in order to prevent their ultimately falling into the hands of Indians who might prove hostile, you were desirous to try to have them conveyed into the United States; but that you were prevented by the then existing law of non-intercourse with the British dominions.

The Executive could not annul the provisions of that law. But I was directed to instruct the collectors on the lakes, in case you and your agents should voluntarily bring in and deliver to them any part of the goods above mentioned, to receive and keep them in their guard, and not to commence prosecutions until further instructions: the intention being then to apply to Congress for an act remitting the forfeiture and penalties. I wrote accordingly, to that effect, to the collectors of Detroit and Michilimackinac.

The attempt to obtain the goods did not, however, succeed; and I cannot say how far the failure injured you. But the war proved fatal to another much more extensive and important enterprise.

Previous to that time, but I also forget the year, you had undertaken to carry on a trade on your own account, though I believe under the New York charter of the American Fur Company, with the Indians west of the Rocky Mountains. This project was also communicated to government, and met, of course, with its full approbation, and best wishes, for your success. You carried it on, on the most extensive scale, sending several ships to the mouth of the Columbia River, and a large party by land across the mountains, and finally founding the establishment of Astoria.

This unfortunately fell into the hands of the enemy during the war, from circumstances with which I am but imperfectly acquainted—being then absent on a foreign mission. I returned in September, 1815, and sailed again on a mission to France in June, 1816. During that period I visited Washington twice—in October or November, 1815, and in March, 1816. On one of these[5] occasions, and I believe on the last, you mentioned to me that you were disposed once more to renew the attempt, and to re-establish Astoria, provided you had the protection of the American flag; for which purpose, a lieutenant's command would be sufficient to you. You requested me to mention this to the President, which I did. Mr. Madison said he would consider the subject, and, although he did not commit himself, I thought that he received the proposal favorably. The message was verbal, and I do not know whether the application was ever renewed in a more formal manner. I sailed soon after for Europe, and was seven years absent. I never had the pleasure, since 1816, to see Mr. Madison, and never heard again anything concerning the subject in question.

I remain, dear sir, most respectfully,
Your obedient servant,
ALBERT GALLATIN.

JOHN JACOB ASTOR, *Esq.*, New York.

[5] The first edition has *those two*.

Notices of the Present State of the Fur Trade, chiefly extracted
from an article published in Silliman's Magazine[6] for January, 1834.

THE Northwest Company did not long enjoy the sway they had acquired over the trading regions of the Columbia. A competition, ruinous in its expenses, which had long existed between them and the Hudson's Bay Company, ended in their downfall and the ruin of most of the partners. The relic of the company became merged in the rival association, and the whole business was conducted under the name of the Hudson's Bay Company.

This coalition took place in 1821. They then abandoned Astoria, and built a large establishment sixty miles up the river, on the right bank, which they called Fort Vancouver. This was in a neighborhood where provisions could be more readily procured, and where there was less danger from molestation by any naval force. The company are said to carry on an active and prosperous trade, and to give great encouragement to settlers. They are extremely jealous, however, of any interference or participation in their trade, and monopolize it from the coast of the Pacific to the mountains, and for a considerable extent north and south. The American traders and trappers who venture across the mountains, instead of enjoying the participation in the trade of the river and its tributaries, that had been stipulated by treaty, are obliged to keep to the south, out of the track of the Hudson's Bay parties.

Mr. Astor has withdrawn entirely from the American Fur Company, as he has, in fact, from active business of every kind. That company is now headed by Mr. Ramsay Crooks; its principal establishment is at Michilimackinac, and it receives its furs from the posts depending on that station, and from those on the Mississippi, Missouri, and Yellow Stone Rivers, and the great range of country extending thence to the Rocky Mountains. This company has steamboats in its employ, with which it ascends the rivers, and penetrates to a vast distance into the bosom of those regions formerly so painfully explored in keel-boats and barges, or by weary parties on horseback and on foot. The first irruption of steamboats in the heart[7] of these vast wildernesses is said to have caused the utmost astonishment and affright among their savage inhabitants.

---

[6] *Silliman's Journal* in first edition. This was the *American Journal of Science and Arts*, founded and edited from 1818 to 1838 by Benjamin Silliman.

[7] The first edition reads *steamboats into the heart*.

In addition to the main companies already mentioned, minor associations have been formed, which push their way in the most intrepid manner to the remote parts of the far West, and beyond the mountain barriers. One of the most noted of these is Ashley's company, from St. Louis, who trap for themselves, and drive an extensive trade with the Indians. The spirit, enterprise, and hardihood of Ashley, are themes of the highest eulogy in the far West, and his adventures and exploits furnish abundance of frontier stories.[8]

Another company of one hundred and fifty persons from New York, formed in 1831, and headed by Captain Bonneville of the United States army, has pushed its enterprise into tracts before but little known, and has brought considerable quantities of furs from the region between the Rocky Mountains and the coasts of Monterey and Upper California, on the Buenaventura and Timpanogos Rivers.[9]

The fur countries, from the Pacific, east to the Rocky Mountains, are now occupied (exclusive of private combinations and individual trappers and traders) by the Russians; and on the northwest from Behring's Strait to Queen Charlotte's Island, in north latitude fifty-three degrees, and by the Hudson's Bay Company thence, south of the Columbia River; while Ashley's company, and that under Captain Bonneville, take the remainder of the region to California. Indeed, the whole compass from the Mississippi to the Pacific Ocean is traversed in every direction. The mountains and forests, from the Arctic Sea to the Gulf of Mexico, are threaded through every maze, by the hunter. Every river and tributary stream, from the Columbia to the mouth of the Rio del Norte, and from the M'Kenzie to the Colorado of the West, from their head springs to their junction, are searched and trapped for beaver. Almost all the American furs, which do not belong to the Hudson's Bay Company, find their way to New York, and are either distributed thence for home consumption, or sent to foreign markets.

The Hudson's Bay Company ship their furs from their factories of York Fort and from Moose River, on Hudson's Bay; their collection from Grand River, &c., they ship from Canada; and the collection from

[8] See Dale L. Morgan (ed.), *The West of William H. Ashley* (Denver, 1964), for a comprehensive treatment of Ashley as a trader, of the fur trade up to this point, and of documents pertaining thereto.

[9] For the full story of Bonneville's venture, see Irving's *The Adventures of Captain Bonneville* (ed. by Edgeley W. Todd).

Columbia goes to London. None of their furs come to the United States, except through the London market.

The export trade of furs from the United States is chiefly to London. Some quantities have been sent to Canton, and some few to Hamburg; and an increasing export trade in beaver, otter, nutria, and vicunia wool, prepared for the hatter's use, is carried on in Mexico. Some furs are exported from Baltimore, Philadelphia, and Boston; but the principal shipments from the United States are from New York to London, from whence they are sent to Leipsic, a well-known mart for furs, where they are disposed of during the great fair in that city, and distributed to every part of the continent.

The United States import from South America, nutria, vicunia, chinchilla, and a few deer-skins; also fur seals from the Lobos Islands, off the river Plate. A quantity of beaver, otter, &c., are brought annually from Santa Fé. Dressed furs for edgings, linings, caps, muffs, &c., such as squirrel, genet, fitch-skins, and blue rabbit, are received from the north of Europe; also cony and hare's fur; but the largest importations are from London, where is concentrated nearly the whole of the North American fur trade.

Such is the present state of the fur trade, by which it will appear that the extended sway of the Hudson's Bay Company, and the monopoly[10] of the region of which Astoria was the key, has operated to turn the main current of this opulent trade into the coffers of Great Britain, and to render London the emporium instead of New York, as Mr. Astor had intended.

We will subjoin a few observations on the animals sought after in this traffic, extracted from the same intelligent source with the preceding remarks.

Of the fur-bearing animals, "the precious ermine," so called by way of preëminence, is found, of the best quality, only in the cold regions of Europe and Asia.[11] Its fur is of the most perfect whiteness, except the tip of its tail, which is of a brilliant shining black. With these black tips tacked on the skins, they are beautifully spotted, producing an effect often imitated, but never equalled in other furs. The ermine is of the

[10] The first edition has *its monopoly*.

[11] An animal called the stoat, a kind of ermine, is said to be found in North America, but [it is] very inferior to the European and Asiatic. (Article writer's note.)

genus mustela (weasel), and resembles the common weasel in its form, [and] is from fourteen to sixteen inches from the tip of the nose to the end of the tail. The body is from ten to twelve inches long. It lives in hollow trees, river banks, and especially in beech forests; preys on small birds, is very shy, sleeping during the day, and employing the night in search of food. The fur of the older animals is preferred to the younger. It is taken by snares and traps, and sometimes shot with blunt arrows. Attempts have been made to domesticate it; but it is extremely wild and has been found untameable.

The sable can scarcely be called second to the ermine. It is a native of Northern Europe and Siberia, and is also of the genus mustela. In Samoieda, Yakutsk, Kamtschatka, and Russian Lapland, it is found of the richest quality, and darkest color. In its habits, it resembles the ermine. It preys on small squirrels and birds, sleeps by day, and prowls for food during the night. It is so like the marten in every particular except its size, and the dark shade of its color, that naturalists have not decided whether it is the richest and finest of the marten tribe, or a variety of that species.[12] It varies in dimensions from eighteen to twenty inches.

The rich dark shades of the sable, and the snowy whiteness of the ermine, the great depth, and the peculiar, almost flowing softness of their skins and fur, have combined to gain them a preference in all countries, and in all ages of the world. In this age, they maintain the same relative estimate in regard to other furs, as when they marked the rank of the proud crusader, and were emblazoned in heraldry: but in most European nations, they are now worn promiscuously by the opulent.

The martens from Northern Asia and the Mountains of Kamtschatka are much superior to the American, though in every pack of American marten skins there are a certain number which are beautifully shaded, and of a dark brown olive color, of great depth and richness.

Next these in value, for ornament and utility, are the sea-otter, the mink, and the fiery fox.

The fiery fox is the bright red of Asia; is more brilliantly colored and of finer fur than any other of the genus. It is highly valued for the splen-

---

[12] The finest fur and the darkest color are most esteemed; and whether the difference arises from the age of the animal, or from some peculiarity of location, is not known. They do not vary more from the common marten than the Arabian horse from the shaggy Canadian. (Article writer's note.)

dor of its red color and the fineness of its fur. It is the standard of value on the northeastern coast of Asia.

The sea-otter, which was first introduced into commerce in 1725, from the Aleutian and Kurile Islands, is an exceedingly fine, soft, close fur, jet black in winter, with a silken gloss. The fur of the young animal is of a beautiful brown color. It is met with in great abundance in Behring's Island, Kamtschatka, Aleutian and Fox Islands, and is also taken on the opposite coasts of North America. It is sometimes taken with nets, but more frequently with clubs and spears. Their food is principally lobster and other shell-fish.

In 1780 furs had become so scarce in Siberia, that the supply was insufficient for the demand in the Asiatic countries. It was at this time that the sea-otter was introduced into the markets for China. The skins brought such incredible prices, as to originate immediately several American and British expeditions to the northern islands of the Pacific, to Nootka Sound, and the northwest coast of America; but the Russians already had possession of the tract which they now hold, and had arranged a trade for the sea-otter with the Koudek tribes. They do not engross the trade, however; the American northwest trading ships procure them, all along the coast, from the Indians.

At one period, the fur seals formed no inconsiderable item in the trade. South Georgia, in south latitude fifty-five degrees, discovered in 1675, was explored by Captain Cook in 1771. The Americans immediately commenced carrying seal skins thence to China, where they obtained the most exorbitant prices. One million two hundred thousand skins have been taken from that island alone, and nearly an equal number from the Island of Desolation, since they were first resorted to for the purpose of commerce.

The discovery of the South Shetlands, sixty-three degrees south latitude, in 1818, added surprisingly to the trade in fur seals. The number taken from the South Shetlands in 1821 and 1822 amounted to three hundred and twenty thousand. This valuable animal is now almost extinct in all these islands, owing to the exterminating system adopted by the hunters. They are still taken on the Lobos Islands, where the provident government of Montevideo restrict the fishery, or hunting, within certain limits, which insures an annual return of the seals. At certain seasons, these amphibia, for the purpose of renewing their coat, come up on the dark frowning rocks and precipices, where there is not a trace of vegetation. In the middle of January, the islands are partially cleared of snow, where a few patches of short straggling grass spring up in favorable situations; but the seals do not resort to it for food. They remain on the rocks not less than two months, without any sustenance, when they return much emaciated to the sea.

Bears of various species and colors, many varieties of the fox, the wolf, the beaver, the otter, the marten, the raccoon, the badger, the wolverine, the mink, the lynx, the muskrat, the woodchuck, the rabbit, the hare, and the squirrel, are natives of North America.

The beaver, otter, lynx, fisher, hare, and raccoon, are used principally for hats; while the bears of several varieties furnish an excellent material for sleigh linings, for cavalry caps, and other military equipments. The fur of the black fox is the most valuable of any of the American varieties; and next to that the red, which is exported to China and Smyrna. In China, the red is employed for trimmings, linings, and robes; the latter being variegated by adding the black fur of the paws, in spots or waves. There are many other varieties of American fox, such as the gray, the white, the cross, the silver, and the dun-colored. The silver fox is a rare animal, a native of the woody country below the falls of the Columbia River. It has a long, thick, deep lead-colored fur, intermingled with long hairs, invariably white at the top, forming a bright lustrous silver gray, esteemed by some more beautiful than any other kind of fox.

The skins of the buffalo, of the Rocky Mountain sheep, of various deer, and of the antelope, are included in the fur trade with the Indians and trappers of the north and west.

Fox and seal skins are sent from Greenland to Denmark. The white fur of the arctic fox and polar bear is sometimes found in the packs brought to the traders by the most northern tribes of Indians, but is not particularly valuable. The silver-tipped rabbit is peculiar to England, and is sent thence to Russia and China.

Other furs are employed and valued according to the caprices of fashion, as well in those countries where they are needed for defenses against the severity of the seasons, as among the inhabitants of milder climates, who, being of Tartar or Sclavonian descent, are said to inherit an attachment to furred clothing. Such are the inhabitants of Poland, of Southern Russia, of China, of Persia, of Turkey, and all the nations of Gothic origin in the middle and western parts of Europe. Under the burning suns of Syria and Egypt, and the mild climes of Bucharia and Independent Tartary, there is also a constant demand, and a great consumption, where there exists no physical necessity. In our own temperate latitudes, besides their use in the arts, they are in request for ornament and warmth during the winter, and large quantities are annually consumed for both purposes in the United States.

From the foregoing statements, it appears that the fur trade must henceforward decline. The advanced state of geographical science shows that no new countries remain to be explored. In North America the animals are slowly decreasing, from the persevering efforts and the indiscriminate slaughter practised by the hunters, and by the appropriation to the uses of man of those forests and rivers which have afforded them food and protection. They recede with the aborigines, before the tide of civilization; but a diminished supply will remain in the mountains and uncultivated tracts of this and other countries, if the avidity of the hunter can be restrained within proper limitations.

―――

Height of the Rocky Mountains.

VARIOUS estimates have been made of the height of the Rocky Mountains, but it is doubtful whether any have, as yet, done justice to their real altitude, which promises to place them only second to the highest mountains of the known world. Their height has been diminished to the eye by the great elevation of the plains from which they rise. They consist, according to Long, of ridges, knobs, and peaks, variously disposed. The more elevated parts are covered with perpetual snows, which contribute to give them a luminous, and, at a great distance, even a brilliant appearance; whence they derived, among some of the first discoverers, the name of the Shining Mountains.

James's Peak has generally been cited as the highest of the chain; and its elevation above the common level has been ascertained, by a trigonometrical measurement, to be about eight thousand five hundred feet. Mr. Long, however, judged, from the position of the snow near the summits of other peaks and ridges at no great distance from it, that they were much higher. Having heard Professor Renwick,[13] of New York, express an opinion of the altitude of these mountains far beyond

―――

[13] James Renwick (1792–1863), professor of natural philosophy and experimental chemistry at Columbia University from 1820 to 1853. He was the author of several books on scientific subjects, and was a long-time friend of Irving.

what had usually been ascribed to them, we applied to him for the authority on which he grounded his observation, and here subjoin his reply:—

COLUMBIA COLLEGE, NEW YORK,
February 23, 1836.

DEAR SIR,—In compliance with your request, I have to communicate some facts in relation to the heights of the Rocky Mountains, and the sources whence I obtained the information.

In conversation with Simon M'Gillivray, Esq., a partner of the Northwest Company, he stated to me his impression, that the mountains in the vicinity of the route pursued by the traders of that company were nearly as high as the Himalayas. He had himself crossed by this route, seen the snowy summits of the peaks, and experienced a degree of cold which required a spirit thermometer to indicate it. His authority for the estimate of the heights was a gentleman who had been employed for several years as surveyor of that company. This conversation occurred about sixteen years since.

A year or two afterwards, I had the pleasure of dining, at Major Delafield's, with Mr. Thompson, the gentleman referred to by Mr. M'Gillivray. I inquired of him in relation to the circumstances mentioned by Mr. M'Gillivray, and he stated, that, by the joint means of the barometric[14] and trigonometric measurement, he had ascertained the height of one of the peaks to be about twenty-five thousand feet, and there were others of nearly the same height in the vicinity.

I am, dear sir,
Yours truly,
JAMES RENWICK

To W. IRVING, *Esq.*

---

*Suggestions with respect to the Indian tribes,
and the protection of our Trade.*

IN the course of this work, a few general remarks have been hazarded respecting the Indian tribes of the prairies, and the dangers to be apprehended from them in future times to our trade beyond the Rocky Mountains and with the Spanish frontiers. Since writing those remarks, we have met with some excellent observations and suggestions, in manuscript, on the same subject, written by Captain Bonneville, of the

[14]*Barometer* in first edition.

United States army, who has lately returned from a long residence among the tribes of the Rocky Mountains. Captain B. approves highly of the plan recently adopted by the United States government for the organization of a regiment of dragoons for the protection of our western frontier, and the trade across the prairies. "No other species of military force," he observes, "is at all competent to cope with these restless and wandering hordes, who require to be opposed with swiftness quite as much as with strength; and the consciousness that a troop, uniting these qualifications, is always on the alert to avenge their outrages upon the settlers and traders, will go very far towards restraining them from the perpetration of those thefts and murders which they have heretofore committed with impunity, whenever stratagem or superiority of force has given them the advantage. Their interest already has done something towards their pacification with our countrymen. From the traders among them, they receive their supplies in the greatest abundance, and upon very equitable terms; and when it is remembered that a very considerable amount of property is yearly distributed among them by the government, as presents, it will readily be perceived that they are greatly dependent upon us for their most valued resources. If, superadded to this inducement, a frequent display of military power be made in their territories, there can be little doubt that the desired security and peace will be speedily afforded to our own people. But the idea of establishing a permanent amity and concord amongst the various east and west tribes themselves, seems to me, if not wholly impracticable, at least infinitely more difficult than many excellent philanthropists have hoped and believed. Those nations which have so lately emigrated from the midst of our settlements to live upon our western borders, and have made some progress in agriculture and the arts of civilization, have, in the property they have acquired, and the protection and aid extended to them, too many advantages to be induced readily to take up arms against us, particularly if they can be brought to the full conviction that their new homes will be permanent and undisturbed; and there is every reason and motive, in policy as well as humanity, for our ameliorating their condition by every means in our power. But the case is far different with regard to the Osages, the Kanzas, the Pawnees, and other roving hordes beyond the frontiers of the settlements. Wild and restless in their character and habits, they are by no means so susceptible of control or civilization; and they are urged by strong, and, to them, irresistible causes in their situation and necessities, to the daily perpetration of violence and fraud. Their permanent subsistence, for example, is derived from the buffalo hunting grounds, which lie a great distance from their towns. Twice a year they are obliged to make long and dangerous expeditions, to procure the necessary provisions for themselves and their families. For this purpose horses are absolutely requisite, for their own comfort and safety, as well as for the transportation of their food, and their little stock of valuables; and without them they would be reduced, during a great portion of the year, to a state of abject misery and privation. They have no brood mares, nor any trade sufficiently valuable to supply their yearly losses, and endeavor to keep up their stock by stealing horses from the other tribes to the west and southwest. Our own people, and the tribes immediately upon our borders, may indeed be protected from their depredations; and the Kanzas, Osages, Pawnees, and others, may be induced to remain at peace among themselves, so long as they are permitted to pursue the old custom of levying upon the Camanches and other remote nations for their complement of steeds for the warriors, and pack-horses for their transportations to and from the hunting ground. But the instant they are forced to maintain a peaceful and inoffensive demeanor towards the tribes along the Mexican border, and find that every violation of their rights is followed by the avenging arm of our government, the result must be, that, reduced to a wretchedness and want which they can ill brook, and feeling the certainty of punishment for every attempt to ameliorate their condition in the only way they as yet comprehend, they will abandon their unfruitful territory and remove to the neighborhood of the Mexican lands, and there carry on a vigorous predatory warfare indiscriminately upon the Mexicans and our own people trading or travelling in that quarter.

"The Indians of the prairies are almost innumerable. Their superior horsemanship, which, in my opinion, far exceeds that of any other people on the face of the earth, their daring bravery, their cunning and skill in the warfare of the wilderness, and the astonishing rapidity and secrecy with which they are accustomed to move in their martial expeditions, will always render them most dangerous and vexatious neighbors, when their necessities or their discontents may drive them to hostility with our frontiers. Their mode and principles of warfare will always protect them from final and irretrievable defeat, and secure their fam-

ilies from participating in any blow, however severe, which our retri-
bution might deal out to them.

"The Camanches lay the Mexicans under contribution for horses
and mules, which they are always engaged in stealing from them in
incredible numbers; and from the Camanches, all the roving tribes of
the far West, by a similar exertion of skill and daring, supply themselves in turn. It seems to me, therefore, under all these circumstances,
that the apparent futility of any philanthropic schemes for the benefit of
these nations, and a regard for our own protection, concur in recom-
mending that we remain satisfied with maintaining peace upon our own
immediate borders, and leave the Mexicans and the Camanches, and
all the tribes hostile to these last, to settle their differences and difficulties in their own way.

"In order to give full security and protection to our trading parties
circulating in all directions through the great prairies, I am under the
impression, that a few judicious measures on the part of the government, involving a very limited expense, would be sufficient. And, in
attaining this end, which of itself has already become an object of public
interest and import, another, of much greater consequence, might be
brought about, namely, the securing to the States a most valuable and
increasing trade, now carried on by caravans directly to Santa Fé.

"As to the first desideratum: the Indians can only be made to respect
the lives and property of the American parties, by rendering them dependent upon us for their supplies; which can alone be done with complete effect by the establishment of a trading post, with resident traders,
at some point which will unite a sufficient number of advantages to
attract the several tribes to itself, in preference to their present places
of resort for that purpose; for it is a well-known fact, that the Indians
will always protect their trader, and those in whom he is interested, so
long as they derive benefits from him. The alternative presented to those
at the north, by the residence of the agents of the Hudson's Bay Company amongst them, renders the condition of our people in that quarter
less secure; but I think it will appear at once, upon the most cursory examination, that no such opposition further south could be maintained,
so as to weaken the benefits of such an establishment as is here suggested.

"In considering this matter, the first question which presents itself
is, where do these tribes now make their exchanges, and obtain their

necessary supplies? They resort almost exclusively to the Mexicans, who, themselves, purchase from us whatever the Indians most seek for. In this point of view, therefore, *cæteris paribus,* it would be an easy matter for us to monopolize the whole traffic. All that is wanting is some location more convenient for the natives than that offered by the Mexicans, to give us the undisputed superiority; and the selection of such a point requires but a knowledge of the single fact, that these nations invariably winter upon the head waters of the Arkansas, and there prepare all their buffalo robes for trade. These robes are heavy, and, to the Indian, very difficult of transportation. Nothing but necessity induces them to travel any great distance with such inconvenient baggage. A post,[15] therefore, established upon the head waters of the Arkansas, must infallibly secure an uncontested preference over that of the Mexicans; even at their prices and rates of barter. Then let the dragoons occasionally move about among these people in large parties, impressing them with the proper estimate of our power to protect and to punish, and at once we have complete and assured security for all citizens whose enterprise may lead them beyond the border, and an end to the outrages and depredations which now dog the footsteps of the traveller, in the prairies, and arrest and depress[16] the most advantageous commerce. Such a post need not be stronger than fifty men; twenty-five to be employed as hunters, to supply the garrison, and the residue as a defense against any hostility. Situated here upon the good lands of the Arkansas, in the midst of abundance of timber, while it might be kept up at a most inconsiderable expense, such an establishment within ninety miles of Santa Fé or Taos would be more than justified by the other and more important advantages before alluded to, leaving the protection of the traders with the Indian tribes entirely out of the question.

"This great trade, carried on by caravans to Santa Fé, annually loads one hundred wagons with merchandise, which is bartered in the northern provinces or Mexico for cash and for beaver furs. The numerous articles excluded as contraband, and the exorbitant duties laid upon all those that are admitted by the Mexican government, present so many obstacles to commerce, that I am well persuaded, that if a post, such as is here suggested, should be established on the Arkansas, it would be-

[15] Bonneville is unaware of the construction in 1833 of Bent's Fort on the Arkansas River in approximately the area he recommends.

[16] *Repress* in first edition.

come the place of deposit, not only for the present trade, but for one infinitely more extended. Here the Mexicans might purchase their supplies, and might well afford to sell them at prices which would silence all competition from any other quarter.

"These two trades, with the Mexicans and the Indians, centring at this post, would give rise to a large village of traders and laborers, and would undoubtedly be hailed, by all that section of country, as a permanent and invaluable advantage. A few pack-horses would carry all the clothing and ammunition necessary for the post during the first year, and two light field-pieces would be all the artillery required for its defense. Afterwards, all the horses required for the use of the establishment might be purchased from the Mexicans at the low price of ten dollars each; and, at the same time, whatever animals might be needed to supply the losses among the dragoons traversing the neighborhood, could be readily procured. The Upper Missouri Indians can furnish horses, at very cheap rates, to any number of the same troops who might be detailed for the defense of the northern frontier; and, in other respects, a very limited outlay of money would suffice to maintain a post in that section of the country.

"From these considerations, and my own personal observation, I am, therefore, disposed to believe, that two posts established by the government, one at the mouth of the Yellowstone River,[17] and one on the Arkansas, would completely protect all our people in every section of the great wilderness of the West; while other advantages, at least with regard to one of them, confirm and urge the suggestion. A fort at the mouth of the Yellowstone, garrisoned by fifty men, would be perfectly safe. The establishment might be constructed simply with a view to the stores, stables for the dragoons' horses, and quarters for the regular garrison; the rest being provided with sheds or lodges, erected in the vicinity, for their residence during the winter months."

17 The American Fur Company already had a post at the mouth of the Yellowstone. This was Fort Union, built in 1829.

I. MANUSCRIPTS

Astor, John Jacob. Letter to James Monroe, Secretary of State, New York, March 22, 1813. National Archives, Diplomatic, Legal, and Fiscal Branch.

Gratiot, Charles. Letter to John Jacob Astor, St. Louis, May 31, 1812. Gratiot Letterbook, Missouri Historical Society.

[Hunt, Wilson Price]. Account Books. 2 vols. Astor Papers, Baker Library, Harvard Graduate School of Business Administration.

Irving, Washington. *Astoria 1835* [Notebook No. 2]. Seligman Collection of Irvingiana, New York Public Library.

———. Letter to Major General Alexander Macomb, New York, September 20, 1835. National Archives, Appointment, Commission and Personal Branch File Relating to Benjamin L. E. Bonneville.

———. *Notes Concerning the Far West*, No. 1, 1833. Seligman Collection of Irvingiana, New York Public Library.

———. *Notes Concerning the Far West*, No. 2, 1833. Seligman Collection of Irvingiana, New York Public Library.

———. *Notes Concerning the Far West*, No. 3, 1833. Seligman Collection of Irvingiana, New York Public Library.

———. *Notes for Astoria 1835* [Notebook No. 1]. Seligman Collection of Irvingiana, New York Public Library.

II. BOOKS

Abel, Annie Heloise, ed. *Tabeau's Narrative of Loisel's Expedition to the Upper Missouri.* Translated from the French by Rose Abel Wright. Norman, University of Oklahoma Press, 1939.

Allibone, S. Austin. *A Critical Dictionary of English Literature and British and American Authors.* 5 vols. Philadelphia, J. B. Lippincott Co., 1897.

Bakeless, John Edwin. *Lewis and Clark, Partners in Discovery.* New York, W. Morrow, 1947.

Baker, Ernest A. *A Guide to Historical Fiction.* London, George Routledge & Sons, Ltd., 1914.

Bancroft, Hubert Howe. *History of the Northwest Coast.* 2 vols. In *Works* of *Hubert Howe Bancroft*, Vols. XXVII–XXVIII. San Francisco, The History Co., 1884.

Beal, M. D. *A History of Southeastern Idaho*. Caldwell, The Caxton Printers, 1942.

Blair, Walter, and Franklin J. Meine, eds. *Half Horse Half Alligator: The Growth of the Mike Fink Legend*. Chicago, University of Chicago Press, 1956.

Brackenridge, H. M. *Journal of a Voyage up the River Missouri; Performed in Eighteen Hundred and Eleven*. In *Early Western Travels*, ed. by Reuben Gold Thwaites, Vol. VI. Cleveland, The Arthur H. Clark Co., 1904.

Bradbury, John. *Travels in the Interior of America, in the Years 1809, 1810, and 1811*. In *Early Western Travels*, ed. by Reuben Gold Thwaites, Vol. V. Cleveland, The Arthur H. Clark Co., 1904.

Brooks, Van Wyck. *The World of Washington Irving*. New York, E. P. Dutton & Co., 1944.

Burton, Richard F., trans. *The Arabian Nights' Entertainment, or the Book of a Thousand Nights and a Night*. New York, Modern Library, 1932.

Chittenden, Hiram M. *History of the American Fur Trade of the Far West*. 2 vols. Stanford, Academic Reprints, 1954.

Clyman, James. *James Clyman, Frontiersman: The Adventures of a Trapper and Covered-wagon Emigrant as Told in His Own Reminiscences and Diaries*. Ed. by Charles L. Camp. Portland, Champoeg Press, 1960.

Coues, Elliott, ed. *New Light on the Early History of the Greater Northwest: The Manuscript Journals of Alexander Henry, Fur Trader of the Northwest Company, and of David Thompson, Official Geographer and Explorer of the same Company, 1799–1814*. 3 vols. New York, Francis P. Harper, 1897.

Cox, Ross. *The Columbia River*. Ed. by Edgar I. Stewart and Jane R. Stewart. Norman, University of Oklahoma Press, 1957.

Dale, Harrison Clifford, ed. *The Ashley-Smith Explorations and the Discovery of a Central Route to the Pacific, 1822–1829*. Rev. ed. Glendale, The Arthur H. Clark Co., 1941.

Davidson, Gordon Charles. *The North West Company*. Berkeley, University of California Press, 1918. University of California Publications in History, Vol. VII.

Dawood, N. J., trans. *The Thousand and One Nights*. Baltimore, Penguin Books, Inc., 1955.

De Voto, Bernard. *Across the Wide Missouri*. Boston, Houghton Mifflin Co., 1947.

———. *The Course of Empire*. Boston, Houghton Mifflin Co., 1952.

Dryden, Cecil. *By Sea on the Tonquin*. Caldwell, The Caxton Printers, 1956.

———. *Mr. Hunt and the Fabulous Plan*. Caldwell, The Caxton Printers, 1958.

Ellsworth, Henry Leavitt. *Washington Irving on the Prairie, or A Narrative of a Tour of the Southwest in the Year 1832*. Ed. by Stanley T. Williams and Barbara D. Simison. New York, American Book Co., 1937.

Emerson, Ralph Waldo. *The American Scholar*. In *Complete Essays and Other Writings of Ralph Waldo Emerson*. New York, Modern Library, 1940.

Encyclopaedia Britannica. 11th ed. 29 vols. New York, Encyclopaedia Britannica Co., 1910.

———. 24 vols. Chicago, Encyclopaedia Britannica, Inc., 1956.

Flandrau, Grace. *Astor and the Oregon Country*. St. Paul, Great Northern Railway Co., n.d.

Flint, Timothy. *The History and Geography of the Mississippi Valley*. 2 vols. in 1. Cincinnati, E. H. Flint and E. R. Lincoln, 1832.

Franchère, Gabriel. *Narrative of a Voyage to the Northwest Coast of America*. In *Early Western Travels*, ed. by Reuben Gold Thwaites, Vol. VI. Cleveland, The Arthur H. Clark Co., 1904.

———. *Relation d'un Voyage à la Côte du Nord-ouest de l'Amérique Septentrionale, dans les Années 1810, 11, 12, 13, et 14*. Montréal, Impr. de C. B. Pasteur, 1820.

Frémont, Brevet Captain J. C. *Report of the Exploring Expedition to the Rocky Mountains in the Year 1842, and to Oregon and North California in the Years 1843–44*. Washington, Gales and Seaton, Printers, 1845.

Frost, Donald McKay. *Notes on General Ashley, the Overland Trail, and South Pass*. Barre, Mass., Barre Gazette, 1960.

Fuller, George W. *A History of the Pacific Northwest*. 2nd ed., rev. New York, Alfred A. Knopf, 1946.

Gabriel, Gilbert W. *I, James Lewis*. Garden City, Doubleday, Doran & Co., Inc., 1935.

Graham, Bessie. *The Bookman's Manual: A Guide to Literature*. 3rd ed. New York, R. R. Bowker Co., 1928.

Hancock, Samuel. *The Narrative of Samuel Hancock*. New York, Robert M. McBride & Co., 1927.

Harris, Burton. *John Colter: His Years in the Rockies*. New York, Charles Scribner's Sons, 1952.

Henry, Alexander. *See* Elliott Coues, ed., *New Light on the Early History of the Greater Northwest*.

Hodge, Frederick Webb. *Handbook of American Indians*. 2 vols. Washington, Government Printing Office, 1907, 1910. Smithsonian Institution, Bureau of American Ethnology, Bulletin 30.

Hoffman, Hester R. *The Reader's Adviser and Bookman's Manual.* 9th ed. New York, R. R. Bowker Co., 1960.

Holbrook, Stewart H. *The Columbia.* New York, Rinehart and Co., Inc., 1956.

Holley, Mary Austin. *Texas: Observations, Historical, Geographical and Descriptive.* Baltimore, Armstrong & Plaskitt, 1833.

Hunt, Wilson Price. *Journey of Mr. Hunt and His Companions from St. Louis to the Mouth of the Columbia by a New Route Across the Rocky Mountains.* In Robert Stuart, *Discovery of the Oregon Trail,* ed. by Philip Ashton Rollins. New York, Charles Scribner's Sons, 1935.

Innis, Harold A. *The Fur Trade in Canada: An Introduction to Canadian Economic History.* Rev. ed. Toronto, University of Toronto Press, 1956.

Irving, Pierre Munro. *The Life and Letters of Washington Irving.* 4 vols. New York, G. P. Putnam, 1863.

Irving, Washington. *The Adventures of Captain Bonneville.* Ed. by Edgeley W. Todd. Norman, University of Oklahoma Press, 1961.

————. *Astoria, or Anecdotes of an Enterprise beyond the Rocky Mountains.* 2 vols. Philadelphia, Carey, Lea, & Blanchard, 1836.

————. *Astoria, or Anecdotes of an Enterprise beyond the Rocky Mountains.* Author's Revised Edition. New York, G. P. Putnam's Sons, 1868.

————. *Journal, 1803.* Ed. by Stanley T. Williams. London and New York, Oxford University Press, 1934.

————. *The Sketch Book of Geoffrey Crayon, Gent.* New York, G. S. Van Winkle, 1819–20.

————. *A Tour on the Prairies.* Ed. by John Francis McDermott. Norman, University of Oklahoma Press, 1956.

————. *The Western Journals of Washington Irving.* Ed. by John Francis McDermott. Norman, University of Oklahoma Press, 1944.

James, Edwin, comp. *Account of an Expedition from Pittsburgh to the Rocky Mountains, Performed in the Years 1819, 1820.* In *Early Western Travels,* ed. by Reuben Gold Thwaites, Vols. XIV–XVII. Cleveland, The Arthur H. Clark Co., 1905.

James, Thomas. *Three Years among the Indians and Mexicans.* Ed. by Walter B. Douglas. St. Louis, Missouri Historical Society, 1916.

Jones, James Athearn. *Tales of an Indian Camp.* 3 vols. London, Henry Colburn and Richard Bentley, 1829.

Lahontan, Baron Louis Armand de. *New Voyages to North-America.* Ed. by Reuben Gold Thwaites. 2 vols. Chicago, A. C. McClurg & Co., 1905.

Langer, William L., comp. *An Encyclopaedia of World History*. Boston, Houghton Mifflin Co., 1940.

Langfeld, William R. *Washington Irving: A Bibliography*. New York, New York Public Library, 1933.

Latrobe, Charles Joseph. *The Rambler in North America*. 2 vols. New York, Harper & Bros., 1835.

Lavender, David. *Land of Giants. The Drive to the Pacific Northwest, 1750–1950*. Garden City, Doubleday & Co., Inc., 1958. Mainstream of America Series.

————. *Westward Vision: The Story of the Oregon Trail*. New York, McGraw-Hill Book Co., Inc., 1963.

Lewis, Meriwether. *History of the Expedition under the Command of Captains Lewis and Clark*. Reprint of the edition of 1814. 3 vols. New York, New Amsterdam Book Co., 1902.

————. *Original Journals of the Lewis and Clark Expedition, 1804–1806*. Ed. by Reuben Gold Thwaites. 6 vols. New York, Dodd, Mead & Co., 1904.

Long, John. *Voyages and Travels of an Indian Interpreter and Trader*. In *Early Western Travels*, ed. by Reuben Gold Thwaites, Vol. II. Cleveland, The Arthur H. Clark Co., 1904.

Masson, L. R. *Les Bourgeois de la Compagnie du Nord-Ouest*. Première Série. 2 vols. New York, Antiquarian Press, Ltd., 1960.

Merk, Frederick, ed. *Fur Trade and Empire: George Simpson's Journal, 1824–1825*. Cambridge, Harvard University Press, 1931.

Morgan, Dale L. *Jedediah Smith and the Opening of the West*. Indianapolis and New York, The Bobbs-Merrill Co., Inc., 1953.

————, ed. *The West of William H. Ashley, 1822–1838*. Denver, The Old West Publishing Co., 1964.

Nasatir, A. P., ed. *Before Lewis and Clark: Documents Illustrating the History of the Missouri, 1785–1804*. 2 vols. St. Louis, St. Louis Historical Documents Foundation, 1952.

O'Connor, Harvey. *The Astors*. New York, Alfred A. Knopf, 1941.

Oglesby, Richard Edward. *Manuel Lisa and the Opening of the Missouri Fur Trade*. Norman, University of Oklahoma Press, 1963.

O'Meara, Walter. *The Savage Country*. Boston, Houghton Mifflin Co., 1960.

Peckham, Howard H. *Pontiac and the Indian Uprising*. Princeton, Princeton University Press, 1947.

Phillips, Paul Chrisler. *The Fur Trade*. 2 vols. Norman, University of Oklahoma Press, 1961.

Porter, Kenneth Wiggins. *John Jacob Astor, Business Man.* 2 vols. Cambridge, Harvard University Press, 1931.

Ross, Alexander. *Adventures of the First Settlers on the Oregon or Columbia River.* In *Early Western Travels,* ed. by Reuben Gold Thwaites, Vol. VII. Cleveland, The Arthur H. Clark Co., 1904.

————. *The Fur Hunters of the Far West.* Ed. by Kenneth A. Spaulding. Norman, University of Oklahoma Press, 1956.

Russell, Raymond. *The Harpsichord and Clavichord.* London, Faber and Faber, 1959.

Seifert, Shirley. *Those Who Go Against the Current. A Novel.* Philadelphia, J. B. Lippincott Co., 1943.

Smith, Henry Nash. *Virgin Land: The American West as Symbol and Myth.* Cambridge, Harvard University Press, 1950.

Spiller, Robert E., *et al.,* eds. *Literary History of the United States.* New York, The Macmillan Co., 1953.

Stuart, Robert. *The Discovery of the Oregon Trail: Robert Stuart's Narratives of His Overland Trip Eastward from Astoria in 1812–13.* Ed. by Philip Ashton Rollins. New York, Charles Scribner's Sons, 1935.

————. *On the Oregon Trail: Robert Stuart's Journey of Discovery.* Ed. by Kenneth A. Spaulding. Norman, University of Oklahoma Press, 1953.

Swanton, John R. *The Indian Tribes of North America.* Washington, Government Printing Office, 1952. Smithsonian Institution, Bureau of American Ethnology, Bulletin 145.

Thompson, David. *See* M. Catherine White, ed., *David Thompson's Journals.*

Thwaites, Reuben Gold, ed. *Early Western Travels.* 32 vols. Cleveland, The Arthur H. Clark Co., 1904–1907.

Twain, Mark. *Life on the Mississippi.* New York, Harper & Bros., 1950.

Victor, Frances Fuller. *The River of the West.* Hartford, Columbian Book Co., 1870.

Vinton, Stallo. *John Colter, Discoverer of Yellowstone Park.* New York, Edward Eberstadt, 1926.

Wallace, W. Stewart. *The Pedlars from Quebec and Other Papers on the Nor'Westers.* Toronto, The Ryerson Press, 1954.

————, ed. *Documents Relating to the North West Company.* Toronto, The Champlain Society, 1934.

Webb, Walter Prescott. *The Great Plains.* Boston, Ginn and Co., 1931.

Webster's Biographical Dictionary. Springfield, G. & C. Merriam Co., 1958.

Wetmore, Alphonso. *Gazetteer of the State of Missouri.* St. Louis, C. Keemle, 1837.

White, M. Catherine, ed. *David Thompson's Journals Relating to Montana and Adjacent Regions, 1808–1812.* Missoula, Montana State University Press, 1950.

Williams, Stanley T. *The Life of Washington Irving.* 2 vols. New York, Oxford University Press, 1935.

Winther, Oscar Osburn. *A Classified Bibliography of the Periodical Literature of the Trans-Mississippi West (1811–1957).* Bloomington, Indiana, University Press, 1961.

———. *The Great Northwest.* 2nd ed. New York, Alfred A. Knopf, 1956.

Withington, Mary C., comp. *A Catalogue of Manuscripts in the Collection of Western Americana Founded by William Robertson Coe, Yale University Library.* New Haven, Yale University Press, 1952.

Wright, Lyle H. *American Fiction, 1774–1850: A Contribution toward a Bibliography.* Rev. ed. San Marino, The Huntington Library, 1948.

III. PERIODICALS

Andrews, C. L. "Alaska Under the Russians—Baronof the Builder," *Washington Historical Quarterly*, Vol. VII (1916), 202–16.

Anonymous. "Astoria," *The Athenaeum.* London, October 22, 1836, pp. 745–48.

———. "Astoria," *The Knickerbocker*, Vol. IX (1837), 88–90.

———. "Astoria," *New York Mirror*, Vol. XIV (1836), 131.

———. "Authority of Irving," *The Oregonian and Indian's Advocate*, Vol. I (1839), 220–21.

———. "Edward Rose, the First White Renegade to the Crows," Bradley Manuscript, Book II, in *Contributions to the Historical Society of Montana*, Vol. VIII (1917), 156–61.

———. "Irving's *Astoria*," *The Nation*, Vol. LXV (1897), 499–501.

Barbeau, Marius. "The Ermatinger Collection of Voyageur Songs (ca. 1830)," *Journal of American Folklore*, Vol. LXVII (1954), 147–61.

Barry, J. Neilson. "Astorians Who Became Permanent Settlers," *Washington Historical Quarterly*, Vol. XXIV (1933), 221–31, 282–301.

———. "Broughton on the Columbia in 1792," *Oregon Historical Quarterly*, Vol. XXVII (1926), 397–411.

———. "Madame Dorion of the Astorians," *Oregon Historical Quarterly*, Vol. XXX (1929), 272–78.

———. "The Trail of the Astorians," *Oregon Historical Quarterly*, Vol. XIII (1912), 227–39.

———. "Washington Irving and Astoria," *Washington Historical Quarterly*, Vol. XVIII (1927), 132–39.

————. "What Became of Benjamin Clapp?" *Washington Historical Quarterly*, Vol. XXI (1930), 13–17.

Biddle, Henry J. "Wishram," *Oregon Historical Quarterly*, Vol. XXVII (1926), 113–30.

Bird, Annie Laurie. "Thomas McKay," *Oregon Historical Quarterly*, Vol. XL (1939), 1–18.

Black, Captain W. "Captain Black's Report on Taking of Astoria," *Oregon Historical Quarterly*, Vol. XVII (1916), 147–48.

Bourne, Edward G. "The Travels of Jonathan Carver," *American Historical Review*, Vol. XI (1906), 287–302.

Bowen, Francis. "Adventures on the Prairies," *North American Review*, Vol. CXLIV (1849), 175–95.

Bradley, Harold Whitman. "The Hawaiian Islands and the Pacific Fur Trade, 1785–1813," *Pacific Northwest Quarterly*, Vol. XXX (1939), 275–99.

Bridgwater, Dorothy W. "John Jacob Astor Relative to His Settlement on Columbia River," *Yale University Library Gazette*, Vol. XXIV (1949), 47–69.

Brown, Judge William C. "Old Fort Okanogan and the Okanogan Trail," *Oregon Historical Quarterly*, Vol. XV (1914), 1–38.

Burpee, Lawrence Johnstone. "A Forgotten Adventure of the Fur Trade," *Queen's Quarterly*, Vol. XXVI (1919), 363–80.

"Captain James Biddle's Orders to Command the U.S.S. Ontario to Go to Columbia River and Take Possession of the Post and Territory in the Name of the United States," *Oregon Historical Quarterly*, Vol. III (1902), 310–11.

Dale, Harrison C. "Did the Returning Astorians Use the South Pass? A Letter of Ramsay Crooks," *Oregon Historical Quarterly*, Vol. XVII (1916), 47–51.

Douglas, Jesse S., ed. "Matthews' Adventures on the Columbia: A Pacific Fur Company Document," *Oregon Historical Quarterly*, Vol. XL (1939), 105–48.

Douglas, W. B. "Manuel Lisa," Missouri Historical Society *Collections*, Vol. III (1911), 233–68, 367–406.

Drumm, Stella M. "More About Astorians," *Oregon Historical Quarterly*, Vol. XXIV (1923), 335–60.

Elliott, T. C. "An Event of One Hundred Years Ago," *Oregon Historical Quarterly*, Vol. XIX (1918), 181–87.

————. "David Thompson and Beginnings in Idaho," *Oregon Historical Quarterly*, Vol. XXI (1920), 49–61.

———. "David Thompson, Pathfinder, and the Columbia River," *Oregon Historical Quarterly*, Vol. XXVI (1925), 191–202.

———. "Discovery of the Source of the Columbia River," *Oregon Historical Quarterly*, Vol. XXVI (1925), 23–49.

———. "The Earliest Travelers on the Oregon Trail," *Oregon Historical Quarterly*, Vol. XIII (1912), 71–84.

———. "The Fur Trade in the Columbia River Basin Prior to 1811," *Oregon Historical Quarterly*, Vol. XV (1914), 241–51. Also in *Washington Historical Quarterly*, Vol. VI (1915), 3–10.

———. "Jonathan Carver's Source for the Name Oregon," *Oregon Historical Quarterly*, Vol. XXIII (1922), 53–69.

———. "The Origin of the Name Oregon," *Oregon Historical Quarterly*, Vol. XXII (1921), 91–115.

———. "Sale of Astoria, 1813," *Oregon Historical Quarterly*, Vol. XXXIII (1932), 43–50.

———. "The Strange Case of Jonathan Carver and the Name Oregon," *Oregon Historical Quarterly*, Vol. XXI (1920), 341–68.

———. "The Surrender at Astoria in 1818," *Oregon Historical Quarterly*, Vol. XIX (1918), 271–82.

———. "Wilson Price Hunt, 1783–1842," *Oregon Historical Quarterly*, Vol. XXXII (1931), 130–34.

———, ed. "Journal of David Thompson," *Oregon Historical Quarterly*, Vol. XV (1914), 39–63, 104–25.

———. "Last Will and Testament of John Day," *Oregon Historical Quarterly*, Vol. XVII (1916), 373–79.

Everett, Edward. "Astoria," *North American Review*, Vol. XLIV (1837), 200–237.

———. "A Tour on the Prairies," *North American Review*, Vol. XLI (1835), 1–28.

Fee, Chester Anders. "Oregon's Historical Esperanto—the Chinook Jargon," *Oregon Historical Quarterly*, Vol. XLII (1941), 176–85.

Haines, F. D. "McKenzie's Winter Camp, 1812–13," *Oregon Historical Quarterly*, Vol. XXXVII (1936), 329–33.

Harvey, A. G. "Chief Comcomly's Skull," *Oregon Historical Quarterly*, Vol. XL (1939), 161–67.

Hockett, Homer C. "The Literary Motive in Writing History," *Mississippi Valley Historical Review*, Vol. XII (1926), 469–82.

Holcman, Frederick V. "Some Important Results from the Expedition of John Jacob Astor to and from the Oregon Country," *Oregon Historical Quarterly*, Vol. XII (1911), 206–19.

Holmes, Captain Reuben. "The Five Scalps," Missouri Historical Society, *Glimpses of the Past*, ed. by Stella M. Drumm, Vol. V (1938), 3–54.

Howay, F. W. "The Loss of the Tonquin," *Washington Historical Quarterly*, Vol. XIII (1922), 83–92.

Judson, Katharine B. "The British Side of the Restoration of Fort Astoria," *Oregon Historical Quarterly*, Vol. XX (1919), 243–60, 305–30.

Kellogg, Louise P. "The Mission of Jonathan Carver," *Wisconsin Magazine of History*, Vol. XII (1928), 127–45.

Koch, P. "The Story of Astoria, with a Sketch of the Pacific Fur Company," *Magazine of American History*, Vol. XIII (1885), 269–76.

Lindsley, Margaret Hawkes. "Major Andrew Henry," *Scenic Idaho*, Vol. X (1955), 6–28.

Louisiana Gazette, March 14, April 11, 1811.

Lyman, H. S. "Reminiscences of Louis Labonte," *Oregon Historical Quarterly*, Vol. I (1900), 169–88.

McDermott, John Francis. "The Confines of a Wilderness," *Missouri Historical Review*, Vol. XXIX (1934), 3–12. Also in Missouri Historical Society *Collections*, Vol. VI (1931), 324–25.

Maloney, Alice B. "Alexander Carson, Wilhamot Freeman," *Oregon Historical Quarterly*, Vol. XXXIX (1938), 16–21.

Mattes, Merrill J. "Jackson Hole, Crossroads of the Western Fur Trade, 1807–1829," *Pacific Northwest Quarterly*, Vol. XXXVII (1946), 87–108.

Merk, Frederick. "The Genesis of the Oregon Question," *Mississippi Valley Historical Review*, Vol. XXXVI (1950), 583–612.

Meyers, J. A. "Jacques Raphael Finley," *Washington Historical Quarterly*, Vol. X (1919), 163–67.

Morris, Grace P. "Development of Astoria, 1811–1850," *Oregon Historical Quarterly*, Vol. XXXVIII (1937), 413–24.

Morris, William A. "Historian of the Northwest," *Oregon Historical Quarterly*," Vol. III (1902), 429–34.

Parton, James. "John Jacob Astor," *Harper's Monthly*, Vol. XXX (1865), 308–23.

Poe, Edgar Allan. "Irving's Astoria," *Southern Literary Messenger*, Vol. III (1837), 59–68.

Porter, Kenneth W. "Benjamin Clapp: Notes on His Later Life," *Washington Historical Quarterly*, Vol. XXV (1934), 108–13.

———. "Cruise of Astor's Brig Pedler, 1813–1816," *Oregon Historical Quarterly*, Vol. XXXI (1930), 223–30.

———. "The Cruise of the 'Forester,' " *Washington Historical Quarterly*, Vol. XXIII (1932), 261–85.

———. "Further Notes on Benjamin Clapp," *Washington Historical Quarterly*, Vol. XXVI (1935), 26–27.

————."Joseph Ashton, Astorian Sailor, 1812–1815," *Oregon Historical Quarterly*, Vol. XXXI (1930), 343–50.

————. "More about the Brig Pedler, 1813–1816," *Oregon Historical Quarterly*, Vol. XXXIII (1932), 311–12.

————. "Roll of Overland Astorians, 1810–12," *Oregon Historical Quarterly*, Vol. XXXIV (1933), 103–12.

Sage, Walter N. "The Appeal of the North West Company to the British Government to Forestall John Jacob Astor's Columbian Enterprise," *Canadian Historical Review*, Vol. XVII (1936), 304–11.

Sampson, F. A., comp. "Washington Irving, Travels in Missouri and the South," *Missouri Historical Review*, Vol. V (1910), 15–33.

Santee, J. F. "Comcomly and the Chinooks," *Oregon Historical Quarterly*, Vol. XXXIII (1932), 271–78.

Scheffer, Victor B. "The Sea Otter on the Washington Coast," *Pacific Northwest Quarterly*, Vol. XXXI (1940), 371–88.

Scott, H. W. "Beginnings of Oregon—Exploration and Early Settlement at the Mouth of the Columbia River," *Oregon Historical Quarterly*, Vol. V (1904), 101–19.

Seton, Alfred. "Life on the Oregon," ed. by Fred S. Perrine, *Oregon Historical Quarterly*, Vol. XXXVI (1935), 187–204.

Spaulding, Kenneth A. "A Note on *Astoria:* Irving's Use of the Robert Stuart Manuscript," *American Literature*, Vol. XXII (1950), 150–57.

Thompson, David. See T. C. Elliott, "David Thompson and Beginnings in Idaho," and "David Thompson, Pathfinder, and the Columbia River."

Todd, Edgeley W. "John Colter, Mountain Man," *Colorado Quarterly*, Vol. II (1953), 79–91.

————. "Washington Irving Discovers the Frontier," *Western Humanities Review*, Vol. XI (1957), 29–39.

True, R. H. "A Sketch of the Life of John Bradbury, Including His Unpublished Correspondence with Thomas Jefferson," *Proceedings of the American Philosophical Society*, Vol. LXVIII (1929), 133–50.

White, M. Catherine. "Saleesh House: The First Trading Post Among the Flatheads," *Pacific Northwest Quarterly*, Vol. XXXIII (1942), 251–63.

of which *Astoria* is Number 44, was started in 1939 by the University of Oklahoma Press. It follows rather logically the Press's program of regional exploration. Behind the story of the gradual and inevitable recession of the American frontier lie the accounts of explorers, traders, and travelers, which individually and in the aggregate present one of the most romantic and fascinating chapters in the development of the American domain. The following list is complete as of the date of publication of this volume.

1. Captain Randolph B. Marcy and Captain George B. McClellan. *Adventure on Red River*: Report on the Exploration of the Headwaters of the Red River. Edited by Grant Foreman. Out of print.

2. Grant Foreman. *Marcy and the Gold Seekers*: The Journal of Captain R. B. Marcy, with an Account of the Gold Rush over the Southern Route. Out of print.

3. Pierre-Antoine Tabeau. *Tabeau's Narrative of Loisel's Expedition to the Upper Missouri*. Edited by Annie Heloise Abel. Translated from the French by Rose Abel Wright. Out of print.

4. Victor Tixier. *Tixier's Travels on the Osage Prairies*. Edited by John Francis McDermott. Translated from the French by Albert J. Salvan. Out of print.

5. Teodoro de Croix. *Teodoro de Croix and the Northern Frontier of New Spain, 1776–1783*. Translated from the Spanish and edited by Alfred Barnaby Thomas. Out of print.

6. A. W. Whipple. *A Pathfinder in the Southwest*: The Itinerary of Lieutenant A. W. Whipple During His Exploration for a Railway Route from Fort Smith to Los Angeles in the Years 1853 & 1854. Edited and annotated by Grant Foreman. Out of print.

7. Josiah Gregg. *Diary & Letters*. Two volumes. Edited by Maurice Garland Fulton. Introductions by Paul Horgan.

8. Washington Irving. *The Western Journals of Washington Irving*. Edited and annotated by John Francis McDermott. Out of print.

9. Edward Dumbauld. *Thomas Jefferson, American Tourist*: Being an Account of His Journeys in the United States of America, England, France, Italy, the Low Countries, and Germany.

10. Victor Wolfgang von Hagen. *Maya Explorer*: John Lloyd Stephens and the Lost Cities of Central America and Yucatán.

11. E. Merton Coulter. *Travels in the Confederate States*: A Bibliography.
12. W. Eugene Hollon. *The Lost Pathfinder*: Zebulon Montgomery Pike.
13. George Frederick Ruxton. *Ruxton of the Rockies*. Collected by Clyde and Mae Reed Porter. Edited by LeRoy R. Hafen. Out of print.
14. George Frederick Ruxton. *Life in the Far West*. Edited by LeRoy R. Hafen. Foreword by Mae Reed Porter.
15. Edward Harris. *Up the Missouri with Audubon*: The Journal of Edward Harris. Edited by John Francis McDermott.
16. Robert Stuart. *On the Oregon Trail*: Robert Stuart's Journey of Discovery (1812–1813). Edited by Kenneth A. Spaulding.
17. Josiah Gregg. *Commerce of the Prairies*. Edited by Max L. Moorhead.
18. John Treat Irving, Jr. *Indian Sketches*, Taken During an Expedition to the Pawnee Tribes (1833). Edited and annotated by John Francis McDermott.
19. Thomas D. Clark (ed.). *Travels in the Old South, 1527–1860*: A Bibliography. Three volumes. Volumes One and Two issued as a set (1956); Volume Three (1959).
20. Alexander Ross. *The Fur Hunters of the Far West*. Edited by Kenneth A. Spaulding.
21. William Bollaert. *William Bollaert's Texas*. Edited by W. Eugene Hollon and Ruth Lapham Butler. Out of print.
22. Daniel Ellis Conner. *Joseph Reddeford Walker and the Arizona Adventure*. Edited by Donald J. Berthrong and Odessa Davenport.
23. Matthew C. Field. *Prairie and Mountain Sketches*. Collected by Clyde and Mae Reed Porter. Edited by Kate L. Gregg and John Francis McDermott.
24. Ross Cox. *The Columbia River*: Scenes and Adventures During a Residence of Six Years on the Western Side of the Rocky Mountains Among Various Tribes of Indians Hitherto Unknown; Together with a Journey Across the American Continent. Edited by Edgar I. and Jane R. Stewart.
25. Noel M. Loomis. *The Texan–Santa Fé Pioneers*.
26. Charles Preuss. *Exploring with Frémont*: The Private Diaries of

Charles Preuss, Cartographer for John C. Frémont on His First, Second, and Fourth Expeditions to the Far West. Translated and edited by Erwin G. and Elisabeth K. Gudde.

27. Jacob H. Schiel. *Journey Through the Rocky Mountains and the Humboldt Mountains to the Pacific Ocean*. Translated from the German and edited by Thomas N. Bonner.

28. Zenas Leonard. *Adventures of Zenas Leonard, Fur Trader*. Edited by John C. Ewers.

29. Matthew C. Field. *Matt Field on the Santa Fe Trail*. Collected by Clyde and Mae Reed Porter. Edited and with an introduction and notes by John E. Sunder.

30. James Knox Polk Miller. *The Road to Virginia City*: The Diary of James Knox Polk Miller. Edited by Andrew F. Rolle.

31. Benjamin Butler Harris. *The Gila Trail*: The Texas Argonauts and the California Gold Rush. Edited and annotated by Richard H. Dillon.

32. Captain James H. Bradley. *The March of the Montana Column*: A Prelude to the Custer Disaster. Edited by Edgar I. Stewart.

33. Heinrich Lienhard. *From St. Louis to Sutter's Fort, 1846*. Translated and edited by Erwin G. and Elisabeth K. Gudde.

34. Washington Irving. *The Adventures of Captain Bonneville*. Edited and with an introduction by Edgeley W. Todd.

35. Jean-Bernard Bossu. *Jean-Bernard Bossu's Travels in the Interior of North America, 1751–1762*. Translated and edited by Seymour Feiler.

36. Thomas D. Clark (ed.). *Travels in the New South, 1865–1955*: A Bibliography. Two volumes.

37. John Lloyd Stephens. *Incidents of Travel in Yucatán*. Edited and with an introduction by Victor Wolfgang von Hagen. Two volumes.

38. Richard A. Bartlett. *Great Surveys of the American West*.

39. Gloria Griffen Cline. *Exploring the Great Basin*.

40. Francisco de Miranda. *The New Democracy in America*: Travels of Francisco de Miranda in the United States, 1783–84. Translated by Judson P. Wood. Edited by John S. Ezell.

41. Colonel Joseph K. F. Mansfield. *Mansfield on the Condition of the Western Forts, 1853–54*. Edited by Robert W. Frazer.

42. Louis Antoine de Bougainville. *Adventure in the Wilderness*: The

American Journals of Louis Antoine de Bougainville, 1756–1760. Translated and edited by Edward P. Hamilton.

43. James H. Simpson. *Navaho Expedition*: Journal of a Military Reconnaissance from Santa Fe, New Mexico, to the Navaho Country Made in 1849. Edited by Frank McNitt.

44. Washington Irving. *Astoria*. Edited and with an introduction by Edgeley W. Todd.

This edition of *Astoria* has been printed on a book paper intended to have an effective life of not less than three hundred years, bearing the water-mark of the University of Oklahoma Press. The type used is Caslon Old Face, a modern machine-cast reconstruction of English foundry type widely used in America for book printing since the eighteenth century.

UNIVERSITY OF OKLAHOMA PRESS

Norman